Second Edition

THE ELT GRAMMAR BOOK

An Instructor-Friendly Guide for English Language Teachers

by Richard Firsten

The ELT Grammar Book, Second Edition
An Instructor-Friendly Guide for English Language Teachers

Copyright © 2021 by Language Arts Press – Rockville, MD USA

The first edition of this book was originally published by Alta Book Center Publishers, San Francisco, California, Copyright © 2002. This second edition has been revised and redesigned.

Printed in the United States of America.

All rights reserved. No part of this book may be reproduced or transmitted in any form or by any means without permission in writing from the publisher. This restriction includes, but is not limited to, reproduction for educational or classroom purposes.

Publisher and Executive Editor: Michael Berman

Content Editor: Eileen Cotter

Interior Design and Composition: Victoria Mell

Cover Design: Laura Guzman Aguilar

Interior Art: Andrew Lange Illustration, Joe Sutliff Illustration, and Victoria Mell

Language Arts Press
PO Box 4467
Rockville, Maryland 20852 USA

Tel: 301-424-8900

Email: info@LanguageArtsPress.com

Website: LanguageArtsPress.com

ISBN 978-0-9908745-2-2

Library of Congress Control Number: 2020934800

Preface

Welcome to the Second Edition of *The ELT Grammar Book*, a reference for teachers of English to speakers of other languages. This Second Edition that you hold in your hands includes a good deal of new material besides the solid, teacher-friendly content that has been so helpful to everyone and anyone interested in exploring and mastering common and uncommon aspects of the English language. Included in the new material you'll find a chapter dedicated to coordinating, subordinating, and correlative conjunctions; new features like "Grammar in Context," which singles out discrete items and how they're applied in real-life speech and writing; updated examples to make things relevant and clear; new Teaching Tips to help deliver a practical application of material learned; and more predictions about where certain aspects of English are heading.

Right from the start, you'll notice the relaxed, informal style of *The ELT Grammar Book*; books like this one don't have to be written in stuffy academese. The purpose of the first and second editions of this book is to make difficult but basic areas of English grammar more comprehensible to a wide range of ELT professionals as well as non-professionals and students who just want to brush up on their skills in English. If you're a teacher and already have a clear understanding of how English works, the explanations in this book will prepare you to give more effective examples for your students and communicate the grammar better. If you're an advanced student or if you simply want to understand how English grammar works more clearly, this book will go a long way toward helping you master the grammar.

The ELT Grammar Book is not a manual of every aspect of the English language. Rather, it's a carefully curated guide to core grammar topics that are typically included in ESOL and EFL curricula and often found by students and teachers alike to be troublesome. Rest assured that if you master the material provided within the following pages, you'll be very well prepared to teach grammar effectively and to use the language more effectively yourself.

Here are some of the unique features which will make you pleased that you have a copy of *The ELT Grammar Book*:

The Socratic Approach: Get ready to be challenged! You'll be encouraged to observe, think about, and make conclusions about most grammar points covered. This technique, also referred to as the Inductive Method, will allow you to explore the grammar in a way that will make the material much more meaningful to you in the long run. Instead of being spoon-fed the information, you'll work through it yourself to discover exactly what's going on.

And here's a tip to help you get the most out of this approach: Whenever you're asked to think of an answer, you'll notice a relatively big blank space placed after the lines you're given to write your answers on. This is to give you a chance to put down your own answers before seeing the answers I've supplied. You might want to cover what follows the blank space with a piece of paper or something else so that you won't accidentally "cheat" – not that you'd ever cheat, of course. You'll find that the Socratic Approach is really very effective and much more meaningful if you don't look at the answers before working things out for yourself first.

Heads Up!: These asides are very helpful insights that pop up in most chapters, focusing on those points which you can anticipate will bring challenges to the teaching and learning of English because of first-language interference or other causes.

Grammar in Context: Grammar choices are often not black-and-white, right-or-wrong propositions. We constantly select, omit or adapt structures according to our situations and audience. These *Grammar in Context* sections shed light on many of these scenarios and will help teachers do the same for their students.

In a Nutshell: At the end of sections in various chapters, you'll find tidy, efficient summaries of the material that was just covered, with extra examples to make things clearer and give you a quick review.

Teaching Tips: These suggestions found at the end of most chapters offer an array of time-honored classroom activities, exercises, and games to enhance the teaching of specific grammar points.

Online Extras: To make things more interesting, to gain a good deal more knowledge on various subjects covered in the Second Edition, and to enrich your understanding substantially, visit ELTgrammar.com for more in-depth looks at information you've covered.

Appendices: You'll find appendices at the end of this book which provide suggestions and resources to support your teaching.

I'm sure that you'll find *The ELT Grammar Book*, Second Edition an indispensable text, reference, and source book, and that you'll always consider it a friend to help you out at tough moments when your mind goes blank and you're trying to remember exactly what native speakers of English say or why they say this or why they don't say that.

– *Richard Firsten*

Acknowledgments

To my parents, Hyman and Tess, who always instilled a love of learning in me and gave me the gift of a multilingual/multicultural environment to grow up in.

To Bruce Carl Fontaine, my husband, whose constant support of me and faith in me contributed greatly to this text becoming a reality. He is the wind beneath my wings.

To Jamie Ann Cross, an author's dream of an editor, whose total dedication to the First Edition of this book made it a much better work than it would have been.

To Patricia Killian, now deceased, who was responsible in large part for the Teaching Tips and for proofreading so well. Rest in peace, Patty.

To Eileen Cotter, my editor for this, the Second Edition, whose knowledge of the field of ESOL and astuteness in dealing with the written word greatly helped me update this book.

To Michael Berman, President & Chief Education Officer of Language Arts Press, whose appreciation of and enthusiasm for the First Edition of *The ELT Grammar Book* are responsible for the creation of this Second Edition.

– Richard Firsten

Sources for the Quotes that Appear under Chapter and Section Titles

Chapter 1	Throw Momma from the Train a Kiss	Adapted from a 1987 movie title
Chapter 2	By the light of the big, bright, beautiful, silvery full moon.	Edward Madden, Richard Firsten, Eileen Cotter
Chapter 3	These are the times that try men's souls.	Thomas Paine
Chapter 4	What's done is done.	Lady Macbeth in *Macbeth*, William Shakespeare
Chapter 5	Que será, será.	English heraldic motto in Spanish, 1559
Chapter 6	There's a frog on a log in a hole at the bottom of the sea.	Traditional American folksong
Chapter 7	The best-laid plans of mice and men.	Robert Burns
Chapter 8	I would if I could, but I can't, so I won't.	Unknown
Chapter 9	There's no point thinking about what might have been.	Richard Firsten
Chapter 10	What's done is done 'cause I got it done.	Adapted from a 14th century French proverb.
Chapter 11	The Queen of Hearts' men painted all the roses red.	*Alice's Adventures in Wonderland*, Lewis Carroll
Chapter 12	We may all have come on different ships, but we are in the same boat now.	Martin Luther King, Jr.
	Nothing is softer or more flexible than water, yet nothing can resist it.	Lao Tzu
	When you reach the end of your rope, tie a knot in it and hang on.	Franklin D. Roosevelt
	Neither a borrower nor a lender be.	Pollonius in *Hamlet*, William Shakespeare
	Life is either a daring adventure or nothing at all.	Helen Keller
	Wherever you go, I will go.	Ruth in *The Book of Ruth*, Old Testament
	It was the best of times, it was the worst of times.	*A Tale of Two Cities*, Charles Dickens
Chapter 13	He said that she said that I said that . . .	Richard Firsten
Chapter 14	Read it over, think about it, and get back to me.	Richard Firsten
Chapter 15	When you wish upon a star . . .	Song by Leigh Harline & Ned Washington
Chapter 16	If music be the food of love, play on.	Orsino in *Twelfth Night*, William Shakespeare
Chapter 17	His name's Castro, but he's not one of theee Castros.	Richard Firsten
Chapter 18	It's not always what you say, but how you say it.	Richard Firsten
Chapter 19	We're poor little lambs who have lost our way . . .	"Whiffenpoof Song," Meade Minnegerode
Chapter 20	A journey of a thousand miles begins with a single step.	Lao Tzu

Contents

Preface	iii
Acknowledgments	v
Sources for the Quotes that Appear under Chapter and Section Titles	vi

1 Word Order — 1
"Throw Mama from the train a kiss."

The Basics	1
Adverbs of Frequency (How often?)	5
Basic Question Making	6
Teaching Tips: The Why's and the How's	9
Teaching Tips	9

2 Nouns, Articles, Quantifiers, and Adjectives — 11
"By the light of the big, bright, beautiful, silvery full moon"

Nouns	11
Indefinite Articles	17
The Definite Article	23
Quantifiers	27
Adjectives	28
Teaching Tips	38

3 The Presents — 45
"These are the times that try men's souls."

The Present Progressive	45
The Simple Present	50
The Present Perfect	56
The Present Perfect Progressive	60
Teaching Tips	64

4 The Pasts — 68
"What's done is done."

The Simple Past	68
The Past Progressive	70
The Past Perfect	77
The Past Perfect Progressive	80
The Expression *Used To*	81
Teaching Tips	83

5 The Futures — 86
"Que será, será..."

The Present Progressive	87
The Simple Present	87
The Future with *Be Going To*	87
The Simple Future (*Will*)	89
The Future with *Be About To*	91
The Future Perfect	91
The Future Progressive	93
Teaching Tips	97

6 Prepositions — 101
"There's a frog on a log in a hole at the bottom of the sea."

Literal (Physical) Meanings	102
Figurative/Idiomatic Meanings	112
The Prepositional Bane of Banes: *At*	114
Some Teaching Strategies	121
Post-posed Prepositions	123
Teaching Tips	127

7 Genitives — 132
"Mice's and men's best-laid plans"
"The best-laid plans of mice and men"

The *-s* Genitive	132

Group Genitives	139	**11 Direct Object Companions**	**231**
The *Of*-Genitive	140	*"The Queen of Hearts' men painted all the white roses red."*	
Appositives	143		
The Double Genitive	145	Noun Phrases	232
-'s/-s' vs. *Of*: The Gray Areas	147	Adjective Phrases	235
Teaching Tips	150	Infinitive Verb Phrase DOCs	242
		-ing Verb and Base Verb Phrases	245
8 Modal Auxiliaries in the Present or Future	**152**	Past Participle Phrases	257
		Causatives and Direct Object Companions	259
"I would if I could, but I can't, so I won't."		Teaching Tips	263
Can/Could	154		
Will/Would	162	**12 Coordination, Subordination, and Correlation**	**266**
May/Might	166		
Should/Ought To	170	*"We may all have come on different ships, but we are in the same boat now."*	
Must	173		
Semi-Auxiliaries (Periphrastic Modals)	176	Coordination	267
		Subordination	272
Teaching Tips	178	Types of Subordinate Clauses	276
		Correlation	277
9 Modal Auxiliaries in the Past	**181**	Teaching Tips	284
"There's no point thinking about what might have been."		**13 Indirect Speech**	**286**
		"He said that she said that I said that ..."	
Can/Could/Could Have	181		
May Have/Might Have	187	Lexical Transformations	287
Should Have/Ought to Have	190	A Note about *Say*	289
Must Have/Had To	192	A Note about *Tell*	289
Some Words About *Would*	195	Other Reporting Verbs	290
Would Rather Have/Would Sooner Have	196	Backshifting	291
		Time and Space	299
Teaching Tips	197	Infinitives	300
		Direct to Indirect Questions	303
10 Passives and Causatives	**199**	Exclamations	306
"What's done is done 'cause I got it done."		Teaching Tips	309
The Passive Voice	199	**14 Two- and Three-Word Verbs**	**314**
Causatives	221	*"Read it over, think about it, and get back to me."*	
Teaching Tips	225		
		Two-Word Verbs	314

Three-Word Verbs	328
A Bounty of Nouns and Adjectives	330
Teaching Tips	330

15 Subjunctives, Hopes, and Wishes — 333
"When you wish upon a star..."

The Indicative and Subjunctive Moods	333
Phrases which Force the Present and Timeless Subjunctives	343
The Mandative Subjunctive	347
A Modern Language Oddity: The Formulaic Subjunctive	350
Teaching Tips	351

16 Conditional Sentences — 353
"If music be the food of love, play on."

Real Conditional Sentences: Timeless, Present, and Future Forms	354
Real Conditional Sentences and the Imperative	363
Unreal Conditional Sentences: Timeless, Present, and Future Forms	369
Because Of Goes Subjunctive	371
Unreal Conditional Sentences: The Past	373
Mixing and Matching Unreal Conditional Clauses	375
Phrases that Create Hypothetical Situations	376
Teaching Tips	377

17 Autosegmental Features, Part 1 — 380
"His name's Castro, but he's not one of theee Castros."

Stress and Single Words	382
LEGATVM PERPLEXVM ROMANVM—or, A Confusing Legacy from Rome	384
More Examples of Stress Changes and Parts of Speech	385
Stress and Noun Phrases	388
Stress and Verb Phrases	395
Teaching Tips	400

18 Autosegmental Features, Part 2 — 402
"It's not always what you say, but how you say it."

Stress and Whole Sentences	402
Some and *Any* Revisited	408
Intonation	412
Teaching Tips	421

19 Neglected Words and Phrases — 423
"We're poor little lambs who have lost our way..."

Ellipsis	423
Relaxed Pronunciation	427
Intensifiers	429
More Neglected Words and Phrases	435
Negative Questions	444

20 Where English Is Going — 447
"A journey of a thousand miles begins with a single step."

Vocabulary Changes	448
-ly Adverbs	451
Verbs	451
Other Predictions	452

Appendix 1 Teaching Strategies and Activities that Work — 455

Your Picture File	455

Slot Substitutions	459	**Appendix 6 Games**	**496**
Cloze Exercises	461		
Incomplete Dialogues	466	Tic Tac Toe (British "Naughts & Crosses")	496
		Concentration	497
Appendix 2 Notes on Pronunciation and Rules for Doubling Final Consonants	**471**	The Clothesline	498
		Oral Matching	500
The Letter "O"	471	**Appendix 7 Helpful Charts and Lists**	**502**
The "D" in Dry; The "T" in Try	472		
The *Flapped D*	473	Useful Vocabulary Lists on the Internet	502
Juncture	474		
The Most Common Vowel Sound in English	475	Overview of the 12 Tense-Aspect Combinations	503
The Final -*ate*!	476	Commonly Used Irregular Verbs	503
Other Tips for Teaching Pronunciation	477	Some Spelling Conventions with Verbs	506
Rules for Doubling the Final Consonants	479		
		Index	509
Appendix 3 More Fun with Autosegmental Features: A Stress-Caused Metamorphosis	**480**		
Phrases	481		
Various	481		
Appendix 4 A Deeper Look at Reporting Verbs	**482**		
Patterns that Follow Reporting Verbs	482		
The Tone of Reporting Verbs	492		
Appendix 5 Rejoinders, Exclamations, Etc.	**494**		

1

Word Order

"Throw Mama from the train a kiss."

The Basics

A: We're to next the beach week going.

B: What did you say?

A: I told you just next week to the are going we beach.

B: That's what I thought you said!

In the dialogue you've just read, it's obvious that Person B is quite uncomfortable with what Person A is saying and also that she's probably not alone. I'm sure you, too, feel uncomfortable trying to understand what Person A has to say. That's because he's using a word order, or syntax, that might be one in some other language, but certainly doesn't work in English. The question is, why doesn't it work? What rules are there that you can tell students when correcting their word order that will stick so that they don't continue to make the same mistakes over and over again?

From the outset, I want to make it perfectly clear that the aim of this chapter is not to cover every aspect of English word order, but to show you fresh approaches to looking at and teaching certain aspects of word order that are common and useful for English language learners. I'll demonstrate ways of perceiving word order that may make things easier for you and for your students.

For starters, let's discover the underlying basic rules for English word order by doing the exercise that follows:

Rearrange the words in each of the following sentences to put them in the word order that you consider basic to English. Write your answers on the blank lines.

1. the paper / this morning / at home / he / read.

   ....

2. in the oven / I'm roasting / tonight / a chicken.

   ....

3. send / to Delhi / right now / this contract.

   ....

4. Marc / earlier / outside / took / the garbage.

   ....

5. a movie / last night / we / saw / on campus.

   ....

6. north / drove / today / Yoko / to Kyoto / the van.

   ....

The sentences above should have this basic word order:

1. **He read the paper at home this morning.**
2. **I'm roasting a chicken in the oven tonight.**
3. **Send this contract to Delhi right now.**
4. **Marc took the garbage outside earlier.**
5. **We saw a movie on campus last night.**
6. **Yoko drove the van north to Kyoto today.**

Now let's take a good look at how these sentences are set up. There's definitely a pattern we can discern. To begin with, they all start with a subject except for Sentence 3 (which I'll discuss further on). We've got these elements to work with as **subjects** or doers of the action:

He/I/Marc/We/Yoko

These subjects are all followed by **verbs**:

read/'m roasting/send/took/saw/drove

Next we have **direct objects**:

> *the paper/a chicken/this contract/the garbage/a movie/the van*

To continue, we find **directions** or **places**:

> at home/in the oven/to Delhi/outside/on campus/north to Kyoto

Finally, there are **time** phrases:

> this morning/tonight/right now/earlier/last night/today

English tends to follow the word order that reflects the sentences that we've just looked at. For now, let's state the general rule of basic word order based on this information:

> Subject + verb + object + direction/place + time.

 Let's discuss the placement of time phrases. Notice where they appear in those six example sentences. This is one segment (and there are others!) that can be pushed to the front of a sentence if deemed appropriate to do so. It's more or less up to the individual to determine if it's appropriate to place it there. The rule of thumb tends to be that the time phrase often precedes all other segments of the sentence if the writer or speaker is communicating in a more formal or academic context and wishes to emphasize the time:

> *For the past six years*, our company has made steady profits.

This word order "translates" very nicely into a certain group of *wh*-words that many English speakers learn in a set order when they're children: **who–what–where–when**. These four *wh-* words correspond very neatly to the order of the basic English sentence. Take a good look and see for yourself.

In the basic pattern above, five separate segments are listed, but there are only four *wh-* words, so you might think that something got left out. Not so! In fact, it's amazing how this works. Follow along and everything should become clear:

> **Who** represents the subject—whoever/whatever it is;
> **What** stands for two segments: the verb and object(s);
> **Where**, of course, is the direction and/or place;
> **When** is the time.

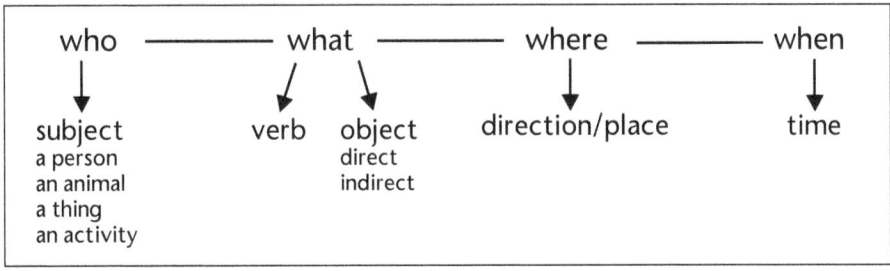

You can see that the five basic segments have been accounted for. The beauty of *what* representing both the verb and the objects is that keeping this pair of words together as a single concept reinforces one of the cardinal rules of English word order, one that many students have trouble with: **you normally don't separate a verb and its object(s) or place words in between them.** In this case, since one *wh-* word stands for both segments, there's no way to separate them. As soon as your students are able to form the most elementary English sentences, start requiring them to learn the phrase *who–what–where–when* until they've memorized the words and their order. Make sure they consciously use this pattern whenever they speak or write English. As the students progress, they can start using variations on this basic pattern, but first get them to internalize the basic word order.

Even though I've given you a nice, tidy formula for this most basic example of English word order, be aware that there are variations that do occur. For example, we can have **what** as the subject ("The fire burned out of control"), and **who** as the object ("The smoke almost asphyxiated the O'Learys"). We can also have any combination of these two: **who/who** ("The firefighters rescued the whole family") and **what/what** ("The fire destroyed everything").

Here's another important point about objects. There are direct objects and indirect objects. For example, in the sentence *Shah Jehan built the Taj Mahal for his wife*, *the Taj Mahal* is the direct object and *his wife* is the indirect object. Even when we change the order of the words (as we can sometimes do in English by dropping the preposition) and say "Shah Jehan built his wife the Taj Mahal," the segments that have been called direct and indirect object are still just that. What's interesting to note is that whether **the direct object is before the indirect object or vice versa, the two objects are still kept side by side**, and that's another aspect of word order that never varies. In fact, we can take this analysis a step further and see that these three elements (the verb, direct object, and indirect object) all stay together in this basic English word order pattern.

```
              I | gave the report to her |.
what =
              I | gave her the report |.
```

Notice that *what* will be the appropriate question word for the following questions based on the sentences above:

```
A: What did you do?
B: I gave her something.
A: What did you give her?
B: The report
```

Let's get back to Sentence 3 for a moment: "Send this contract to Delhi right now." When we utter an imperative form, a command, we're really including the subject *you* before the verb even though we don't normally say it. (*You send* sounds forceful, emphatic.) Therefore, there really is a subject in Sentence 3 as well, an understood *you*: "(You) send this contract to Delhi right now." This point can be easily demonstrated by listening to any English-speaking parent who's momentarily upset with their child and says something like, "You stop that whining this instant!" There it is! The subject *you* has surfaced. So Sentence 3 is just fine. It has a subject, albeit hidden, a verb (*send*), a direct object (*this contract*), direction (*to New Delhi*), and time (*right now*).

 Imperative forms are very common in spoken English, but they're rarely if ever used in formal written English.

In the segment we call **where**, I noted that a direction or a place might fill that spot. In Sentence 6 we can see this *where* in action: "Yoko drove the van north to Kyoto today." Here I have an example containing both the direction (*north*) and place (*to Kyoto*). Remember that when both elements are used in one phrase, **the direction word comes first**. Other direction words are the rest of the compass points and words like *home* and *away*:

Drive east on 42nd Street and make a right at Broadway.
Kenji is going home to Kobe for the summer.
Silvia went away to the mountains for the weekend.

Adverbs of Frequency (How often?)

These adverbs are words such as *always/usually/often/sometimes/seldom/rarely/never*. Figure out the rules that govern their placement by looking over this dialogue.

A: Misha's a terrific employee!

B: I know. He's rarely late for work and he's never sick.

A: Besides that, he's always had his work done on time.

B: And he seldom makes any big errors.

A: He has never argued with the boss.

B: And he's always trying to help his co-workers.

A: We could never have sold so much this year without him.

1. If the verb *be* is used, the adverbs of frequency are placed ....

....

2. If simple (one-word) verbs are used, the frequency words are placed ....

....

3. If complex (multi-word) verbs are used, these adverbs are placed ....

....

Let's check out your ideas. **These adverbs are always placed in these specific places:**

1. **after the verb *be*:**
   He's <u>always</u> on time.
2. **before other verbs in their simple forms:**
   He <u>never</u> gets to work late.
3. **after the first auxiliary in the complex verb:**
   He'll <u>rarely</u> get angry. / He's <u>never</u> been fired from a job.

For more information on word order and word inversion, please visit us at ELTgrammar.com

Basic Question Making

One area of English that's always challenging for ESOL students is question making. Sometimes English just switches some words around; other times the language introduces a verb seemingly out of nowhere that aids in the formation of certain questions. Let's briefly examine each of these ways of making questions in English.

To begin with, we need to understand that there are two kinds of questions in every language, yes/no questions and information questions. First, let's briefly discuss yes/no questions.

It's traditional to start off teaching these with the verb *be*. The rule is simply that when the verb *be* is used without auxiliaries, we exchange the position between the subject and *be*:

I am your choice for team leader. → **Am I** your choice for team leader?
She was the best player we had. → **Was she** the best player we had?

That's straightforward enough, right? And the answers to the two questions on the previous page are *Yes, you are* and *No, she wasn't*.

We do the same thing when we use modal auxiliaries or the auxiliary *have* with verbs. Take a look at these examples:

You will go to all the games. → **Will you go** to all the games?
They have seen every game. → **Have they seen** every game?

And the answers to these two questions are
Yes, I will and *No, they haven't*.

Now, what do we do with the verbs that don't have accompanying auxiliaries? We introduce that little very helpful verb *do*, which takes on the time in the sentence, and we place it at the beginning of the question, followed by the subject and the main verb:

He likes his team's uniform. → **Does he like** his team's uniform?
The team **won** all but one game. → **Did the team win** all but one game?

The answers to these two questions are
No, he doesn't and *Yes, they did*.

That takes care of yes/no question formation. But we also have information questions. These questions begin with the four *wh*-words we've already encountered plus two more: *why* and *how*. These *wh*-words always start off the question. If you have the verb *be*, that comes next:

What is his name? / **How much were** those tickets?

Notice that in these cases, the answers will supply information, not *yes* or *no*:

His name is *Michael*. / Those tickets cost *$59.00 each*.

If the *wh*-words *who* and *what* are the subjects of the question, they're the only items in the question that will be changed in the answer. The word order stays the same. For example:

Who won the game? **The Bobcats** won the game.
What flattened your tire? **A nail on the road** flattened my tire.

But what if *who* and *what* ask about the objects of the question in the simple present or simple past, not about the subjects? In this case, we use the question auxiliary *do* following these *wh*-words:

Who does your sister tutor in math?
(i.e., Your sister tutors *whom*?)

What did Eileen say to Rick?
(i.e., Eileen said *what* to Rick?)

In the two examples above, your sister and Eileen are the subjects of the questions and *who* and *what* ask about the objects.

If *be* isn't the main verb as in *Who is that guy?* or *What are their names?*, all the other *wh*-words (*where, when, why,* and *how*) also use the auxiliary question verb *do* after them in the simple present and simple past. This is because these *wh*-words ask about the object of the question rather than the subject. Take a look at these examples:

Where does your father work?
When do those flowers bloom?
Why did they leave early?
How do you make blintzes?

Similarly, if we use an auxiliary with the main verb, in other words, *have* or a modal auxiliary such as *should*, the word order is still *wh*-word + auxiliary + subject + verb:

Who have they invited? / **When should we** meet them?

So are we done with question making in English? Well, not quite. What do we do (Notice? I used *What* + *do* + subject + verb!) with two phrases that are usually lumped in with *wh*-words? I'm thinking of *how many* and *how much* when they ask about the subjects in questions. With these two phrases, the rule is to use *how many* or *how much* at the beginning of the question + the subject + *be*, a form of *do*, or an auxiliary and verb. Here's what I mean:

How many people are in that stadium?
How much do the tickets cost?
How many customers have bought those T-shirts?
How much honey will make the baklava sweet enough?

But what about when *how many* and *how much* ask about the objects of the questions, not the subjects? In this case, if *be* is used in the present or past progressive, or a form of *do*, or the auxiliary verb *have*, or a modal auxiliary is used, they come directly after our *wh-* phrases:

How much money are you going to pay him?
How many carrots do you add to your beef stew?
How much time has he allotted to the project?
How many people can we invite to the party?

And the same word order (*wh*-word + *be* or auxiliary + subject + verb) holds true for *where, when,* and *how*:

Where are they going on their honeymoon?
When does the game begin?
Why has he quit?
How might we correct that error?

Okay, that's enough about question making. It's time for you to rest your head!

Teaching Tips: The Why's and the How's

Before I begin the *Teaching Tips*, a regular feature of each chapter, I'd like to make several suggestions about them. First, you'll find that the *Teaching Tips* suggest dividing the class into pairs or small groups. The main purpose for this division is that students are much more likely to get a chance to speak and contribute when they're in small groups. It would be ideal if all teachers had small classes, but I realize that a class of eight students is a dream. Small group work is a way to increase each student's chance to speak and be heard.

Second, I'd like to suggest how to divide the class into these groups. Separate students from the same language background if you can. I know that many teachers have homogeneous classes as far as language background goes, but if you have students with several different home languages, you can mix the members in each group so that they all don't speak the same language, thereby decreasing the likelihood of students using their native languages with classmates and keeping more of the communication in English.

Third, as your students are doing the task you've set up, wander around the room and help out when you're called on or needed. Try to do so with a minimum of interference and only interrupt for a good reason. Your students need to talk more than you do! In most cases it's best to be an observer and a helper, not a participant.

Fourth, you'll notice that I often suggest putting the assignment on a handout. If that's not possible for you to do, there's always the board.

Finally, I've deliberately omitted references to proficiency levels in most of the *Teaching Tips*. It's true, for example, that nouns are taught early on in an English course and the past perfect is taught much later, but by not mentioning any particular proficiency level, I hope that each activity can be adapted for any class you may have. An activity may be too advanced for your particular needs today, but it may be appropriate for your students later on. This feature can help you to recycle teaching points: what was taught in September can be reviewed in December; what was taught in Level One can be reviewed in Level Three. And now, on to the *Teaching Tips*!

Teaching Tips

1.1 *Making Stories*

Before class, collect or write interesting phrases (choose phrases that cover different positions in a sentence: a variety of noun phrases, verbs, adverbials, prepositional phrases, etc.). They need not be on a specific topic; in fact, the activity will be more interesting if they're not all related. Distribute a set of these phrases (five to seven) to pairs or small groups of students. Have them write a coherent story using several of the phrases they've received. When the stories have been written, let the students read them aloud to the class.

1.2 *Scrambled Paragraphs*

Before class, completely scramble a paragraph, but be sure to leave the punctuation and capitalization intact (scramble the words within each sentence and rearrange the sentences within the paragraph). Dictate the scrambled sentences to your students sentence by sentence. Have the students unscramble the dictation at the sentence level first and then arrange the sentences into the correct order for the paragraph to make sense. This exercise can be done individually or by pairs or small groups.

1.3 *Acronyms*

Before class think up some well-known acronyms or invent some of your own (ASAP, LOL, BRB, AIDS). Explain what an acronym is to your students and show them how one works. Then give them a list of acronyms you've prepared and have them write phrases or sentences of their own invention by using each letter of an acronym to start each word (e.g. Allan Saw a Python; Lisa Ordered Lobster; Bill Raises Bunnies; Alice Is Dancing with Sean.) Make sure students use correct English word order in their phrases/sentences.

Variation: North American license plates are frequently combinations of letters and numbers. Have your students create license plates on cars for famous people. Here are some examples: WTC 1066 (William the Conqueror, 1066); B5S (Beethoven's 5th Symphony); BO 44 (Barack Obama 44th President). Have them create license plates for themselves, too.

1.4 *Making Questions*

Before class, prepare several questions that use adverbs of frequency (for example: How often do you read a newspaper?/Do you usually do your homework in the library?/Haven't you ever been uncooperative?) and present them to the students. Now have them brainstorm similar questions and then use the questions to interview one another (they can even interview you) and give reports to the class on what they've just found out.

2

Nouns, Articles, Quantifiers, and Adjectives

"By the light of the big, bright, beautiful, silvery full moon"

Nouns

What can we do with nouns? Can they function all by themselves? Yes, they can, sometimes. Most of the time, however, you need something to go with them, and that certain something can be either articles (**a** house; **an** angel; **the** carpet) or adjectives (**pretty** flowers) or both (**the pretty** flowers) or quantifiers (**some** guilt / **any** guilt). So let's take a good look at nouns.

We've got proper nouns and common nouns. Proper nouns are basically names and titles that we would capitalize such as when identifying people (Bruce), using titles people have (Pope Francis), or geographical places (Miami). It follows then that common nouns are words that identify things not capitalized. *Mr. Luck* is two proper nouns whereas *luck* is a common noun.

Now, if we say *luck*, can we also say *lucks*? Maybe you can do that in other languages, but not in English. The question is, why not? Check out the following examples of nouns in the plural form. Place a check mark in the boxes of those nouns that you think are wrong. After you do that, write a simple explanation for why you think the ones you've checked are wrong. And remember, we're talking only about **nouns**.

- ☐ arts
- ☐ bulbs
- ☐ datas
- ☐ shrubs
- ☐ advices
- ☐ dogs
- ☐ rices
- ☐ polices
- ☐ waxes
- ☐ offices
- ☐ evidence
- ☐ progresses
- ☐ candles
- ☐ files
- ☐ garbages
- ☐ helps
- ☐ desks
- ☐ steaks
- ☐ Spanishes
- ☐ laws

You should have placed a check mark in the boxes for the following nouns: *datas, advices, rices, polices, waxes, evidences, progresses, garbages, helps,* and *Spanishes*. So why do you think those nouns are wrong in the plural form?

....

....

....

They're wrong because they can't be counted. You can't say *three datas* or *six Spanishes*, right? Right! But you can say *five bulbs* or *two desks*. That's because there are countable and uncountable nouns, and the uncountable nouns can't be put in the plural form.

There are other kinds of nouns. Any idea about what the difference is between the following nouns in Column A compared to Column B?

Column A	Column B
pebble	thought
shoe	freedom
carrot	fear
house	humor

....

The answer is that the nouns in Column A are all **concrete nouns**, while the ones in Column B are all **abstract nouns**. You can hold a pebble in your hand and you can touch a house, but you can't hold a thought in your hand or touch a fear.

Another kind of noun to mention deals with words like *police, people, government, team, patrol, family,* and *staff*. Any idea what we call such nouns?

....

They're called **collective nouns** because they represent individual items cast together into singular units. What's interesting about all of these examples is that the verb *be* can be used in the 3rd person singular form (*is/was*) or the 3rd person plural form (*are/were*), depending on the speaker's or the writer's perspective. In fact, some of these words, such as *government*, are used commonly in the singular idea with *is* (e.g., in American English) while they're used with *are* by others (e.g., the British):

> American English: The government **is** planning to . . .
> British English: The government **are** planning to . . .

Compound Nouns

A: You know, I just bought a rubber baby buggy bumper.

B: A what?

A: A rubber baby buggy bumper.

B: What on earth is that?

A: Well, the baby buggy that I put my baby in when I go out for a walk used to have a metal bumper on it.

B: Yeah, so?

A: Well, this new bumper's made of rubber to cushion any shocks if I bump the baby buggy into something.

B: Oh, now I get it! It's a bumper made of rubber that protects your baby in the buggy from hard knocks.

A: Exactly! It's a rubber baby buggy bumper!

B: Of course.

Every language that there is has practical means of generating new vocabulary. One used commonly in English is known as *compounding*, and this is a good place to start discussing this phenomenon. In this chapter I'm going to talk first about compound nouns and later on I'll get into compound adjectives.

Examples of compound nouns are *ranch house* and *bank vault*. Consider the fact that the word *ranch* and the word *house* are two words that don't have any natural connection, but when stuck together, they create a third word. The same holds true for *bank* and *vault*. In the dialogue, the speakers talked about a baby buggy. "Baby buggy" is another good example of a compound noun. The part of the baby buggy discussed was a buggy bumper, another compound noun. What, then, would you say a compound noun is? See if you can write a simple recipe for making a compound noun on the line that follows:

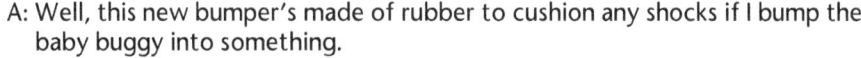

You've probably come up with something like this: **Take two nouns, put them together, and you've got a compound noun.** Okay, that's certainly the basic idea, but rarely are things that simple in language, which is so marvelous that it allows us to put two unrelated elements together in order to create a new word.

Getting back to the issue at hand, we should first ask ourselves, which noun do we place first and which one second? Is it possible to say *bumper rubber* instead of *rubber bumper*? And if it is possible, do they mean the same thing? Well, the answer to the first question is *yes*, we can say *bumper rubber*, but the answer to the second question is *no*, they don't mean the same thing at all. Let's see why.

To start, you have to understand the order that the nouns are placed in within the phrase. **The last noun is the <u>head noun</u>**, the noun being described. Therefore, **the noun before the head noun is a <u>descriptive element</u>**, one that tells us some detail about the head noun. With this information, let's see if you can interpret what it means when I say *rubber bumper* or *bumper rubber*.

A rubber bumper is ....

Bumper rubber is ....

The interpretation of ***a rubber bumper* is a bumper that's made of rubber**, and in this case, I'm using *rubber* adjectivally. This phrase is *not* a compound noun, but simply a head noun with another noun being used as an adjective. It's important to understand that it's still a bumper, whether it be a rubber bumper or a metal bumper or even a plastic bumper. Because I haven't created a new entity, but have only described what the bumper is made of, I know it's not a compound noun.

The interpretation of *bumper rubber*, on the other hand, is that it's some sort of rubber specially formulated to be made into bumpers—a totally different thing. In this case, the word *bumper* is not just being used as an adjective; rather, together with the head noun, *rubber*, it represents a totally new entity, a specific material (*bumper rubber* as compared to, say, *tire rubber*), and is indeed a compound noun.

Another example of this linguistic juggling act is *housework* vs. *workhouse*. *Housework*, of course, is all of the cleaning and washing, etc., that goes on in and around the house. This is not a compound noun because it's a phrase just describing one sort of work. We can also have *yard work*, *homework*, and *schoolwork*. A *workhouse*, on the other hand, is something totally different. It was a prison-like place in the 19th and early 20th centuries where the poorest of the poor could come to find shelter and food in return for doing menial work. *Workhouse* is a compound noun because it's a completely new entity. What a difference word order can make!

What else is important for our recipe? Here are a few more compound nouns. See if you can describe the head noun in each case with the use of paraphrasing. I've done the first one as an example.

1. A knife sharpener is *a tool or appliance that is used to sharpen knives*.
2. Candlelight is ....
3. A toy store is ....
4. A coin slot is ....

If you've followed my example, you've probably written that **candlelight is the light from candles, a *toy store* is a store where toys are sold, and a *coin slot* is a slit in a hard surface where metal money can be inserted** (like part of a vending machine). What slight but important change do you notice in the descriptive nouns as they appear in the compound form compared to their appearance in your paraphrases? Write your observation on the following line:

....

The observation is that **the descriptive nouns usually appear only in the singular when used to make compound nouns** even if they refer to more than one thing. So, even though it's the light coming from candles, it's called *candlelight*. There are exceptions to this rule, though, such as *the appropriations committee, a sports car,* and *the arms race*. These exceptions arise when words that usually appear only in the plural become the descriptive elements. The majority of descriptive elements in this kind of compound noun, however, do appear in their singular form.

Here's a question to check your general knowledge of English grammar. Can you think of a reason that the descriptive noun should stay in the singular form even when it represents a plural? Write your idea here:

....

We can answer this question about why descriptive nouns normally stay singular with a rule about adjectives. We know that **adjectives aren't pluralized in English, and since these descriptive nouns work just like adjectives, they follow that same basic rule.** That's probably why (by analogy with another common rule in English) the descriptive nouns aren't usually found in the plural.

Here's another ingredient needed in our recipe for making compound nouns.

I'm only going to treat it briefly here because I'll be dealing with it in detail later on when I delve into autosegmental features (see Chapters 17 and 18). It has to do with stress. In short, **the stress** (some people call it **the accent**) **falls on the descriptive element in a compound noun**, not on the head noun: a KNIFE sharpener; CANdlelight; a TOY store; a COIN slot.

And now there's one more thing I need to mention to you about compound nouns. I've focused only on the combination **noun + noun**, but there are two other ways to make compound nouns. One is **adjective + noun** (*hothouse, blueprint*) and the other is **verb + noun** (*checkout, walkway*).

For more information on compound nouns, please visit us at ELTgrammar.com

When Nouns are Adjectives

Why am I talking about nouns becoming adjectives? The reason is that **the first element (noun) in this compound form acts exactly as an adjective does; namely, it describes the second element, the head noun**. Let's go back to the word *house*. Of course there are all kinds of houses used for all kinds of purposes, and a very efficient way of describing them is by placing a compound element in front of *house*. In this way, we end up with such items as *schoolhouse, bathhouse, gatehouse, courthouse,* and *jailhouse*. Notice how the first element describes the following word, the head noun, just as an adjective does.

Attorneys General?

I'm going to digress a little at this point in the chapter and introduce adjectives into the mix. If you think about it, the title for this section is really strange. It seems to contradict a basic rule of English, that adjectives come <u>before</u> nouns.

So how do we explain this noun + adjective? To find the answer, we need to look at how other languages operate. In quite a few of them, the adjective normally comes after the noun (French and Arabic are examples of such languages). And that's where our answer lies. Over the centuries, English has borrowed many words and phrases from other languages, and in so doing, has sometimes anglicized the borrowed bits and pieces. There are times, however, when it's retained the original placement of the elements as they appeared in the foreign languages. Here's a case in point:

We've borrowed the French job title *notaire publique* without changing much at all. True, *notaire* has evolved into *notary*, and the spelling of *publique* has changed to the English word *public*, but we've kept the French word order in this noun phrase and call the job a *notary public* instead of a "public notary"—even though the adjective should normally be placed before the noun in English. Another phrase that has evolved like this is *proof positive*.

But what should we do about making the title *notary public* plural? Is it okay to say *notary publics*? What would be your guess? Write down your opinion and your reason for saying so. By the way, if you don't think it's okay, what should the plural form be?

In short, the answer is that it's not okay to say *notary publics* even though it probably doesn't hurt your ears to say it. So what should the correct plural form be? It should be **notaries public**. The reason goes back to that rule about adjectives: **in English, we don't put a plural marker on an adjective that accompanies its noun**. That means our only choice is to put the plural marker where it belongs, on the noun, and the noun in this case is *notary*, not *public*. Here are two more examples of this phenomenon:

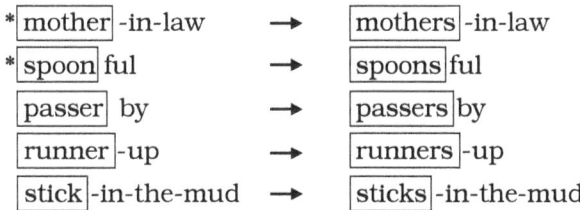

Finally, even though the following examples really don't belong here since they don't contain adjectives, I'm going to throw them in for free. They're not words that have been borrowed from other languages, but they do fit the same pattern for making plurals, and here they are:

* |mother| -in-law → |mothers| -in-law
* |spoon| ful → |spoons| ful
* |passer| by → |passers| by
* |runner| -up → |runners| -up
* |stick| -in-the-mud → |sticks| -in-the-mud

Note that, in these expressions, the plural suffix is added to the noun. Here's a special note about a number of these terms. Because so many native speakers have consistently used the more standard pluralization pattern by sticking the plural marker at the end, we now accept *attorney generals*, *court martials*, *mother-in-laws*, and *spoonfuls* as alternative plurals in *informal* speech.

Indefinite Articles

It's odd how this section wouldn't even appear in, let's say, a Russian, Chinese, or Latin grammar book, and only the second part that you're about to see, which deals with the definite article, might appear in an Arabic or Hebrew grammar book. Very curious indeed! The reason is that the articles (indefinite = *a/an*; definite = *the*) are features that simply don't exist in many languages, and the speakers of those languages get on perfectly well without them. (Other languages have other ways of indicating definite and indefinite.) This little bit of information may help you anticipate certain challenges when you teach students whose native languages have no articles or at least no indefinite article, but more about this later.

Pronunciation

Before I go on with the standard usage of the indefinite article, let's discuss its pronunciation for a moment. The usual pronunciation is like the unstressed syllable (first syllable) in the words *about* or *agree*. The symbol *schwa* /ə/ in the phonetic alphabet represents this sound. We do have an alternate pronunciation, however. It's the same sound as the name of the letter *a*, a sound represented on the next page by the phonetic symbol /e/. At one time it was used exclusively for emphasis or in slowed-down speech, but it's becoming more and more common to hear it used with no special meaning attached to it.

The Phonetic Alphabet

Here's a simplified version of the International Phonetic Alphabet (the IPA). Besides simplifying it for the purposes of this book, I've replaced some complex symbols with ones easier for English speakers to recognize.

a	(f<u>a</u>ther)	ɔɪ	(b<u>oy</u>)	r	
æ	(h<u>a</u>t)	b		s	
e	(s<u>ay</u>)	č	(<u>ch</u>ips)	š	(fi<u>sh</u>)
ɛ	(b<u>e</u>d)	d		t	
i	(s<u>ee</u>)	f		D	(butter) flapped "d"
ɪ	(s<u>i</u>t)	g		t̪	unreleased "t"
o	(n<u>o</u>)	h		θ	(wi<u>th</u>)
ɔ	(s<u>aw</u>)	j		ð	(<u>th</u>e)
u	(t<u>oo</u>)	k		v	
ʊ	(b<u>oo</u>k)	l		w	
ə	(<u>a</u>bout)	m		y	
ər	(fi<u>r</u>st)	n		z	
aɪ	(<u>eye</u>)	ŋ	(si<u>ng</u>)	ž	(plea<u>s</u>ure)
aʊ	(n<u>ow</u>)	p			

: This symbol is used to show a lengthened sound.
- A hyphen will be used to separate syllables.

"A" vs. "An"

The word *a* has a variant form, *an*. How can we know when to use *a* and when to use *an*? Here's a hint: it has to do with sound. Look at the following examples and see if you can figure out the two phonological rules that govern *a* and *an*:

a plum	an apple
a melon	an orange
a nice apple	an ugli fruit
a ripe pear	an overripe peach

As it happens, the rules seem quite clear cut: **If the noun or adjective begins with a consonant, use the noun *a*. If the noun or adjective begins with a vowel, use the word *an*.** Simple, right? Well, almost.

a harp	an hour
a happy child	an honorable man
a united faculty	an uncle
a eulogy	an ugly wart

Above are some exceptions to the rules—or are they? Figure out what's going on with the indefinite article in front of these nouns and write your conclusions below:

....

....

Come to think of it, we really haven't come across any exceptions to the rules after all; in fact, the examples just given make our case even stronger. We use *a* before *harp* and *happy* because the words after the article begin with a consonant, or rather, a **consonant sound**. We use *an* before *hour* and *honorable* because, even though the words after the article begin with a consonant letter, they don't begin with a consonant sound but with a **vowel sound** because the initial *h* is silent in both words.

One possible exception that bears mentioning is certain multi-syllabic words (e.g., *historical*, *historian*, *hysterical*, and *heroic*). Even though the traditional rule dictates that we say "a historical novel" and "a heroic deed," more and more native speakers tend to say "an 'istorical novel" and "an 'eroic deed." It seems that there's a tendency to drop the *h* in these words, which triggers people into using *an* instead of *a*. The explanation has to do with the fact that **the primary stress in these words is not on the first syllable.** Nobody says "an HIStory book," but more and more people say "an 'isTORical novel."

To continue, we say *a* before *united* and *eulogy* because the initial sound isn't a vowel (as in *onion* or *ooze*), but a glide like the sound of *y* in *youth*. After all, no native speaker would ever say "an yellow submarine." We say *an* before *uncle* and *ugly* because the words after the article in these two cases do begin with vowel sounds, but we say *a euro* because the glide sound at the beginning of *euro* is treated as a consonant.

So, our rules should be amended a bit: **Use *a* before words that begin with consonant <u>sounds</u>; use *an* before words that begin with vowel <u>sounds</u>**.

"A" vs. *"One"*

What does the word *a* mean? It represents one way that we communicate that **something is singular and countable** (*a* book, *a* flower, *a* whale). **It's also the article we use in general statements** (*An* apple is *a* fruit) and **the first time we mention something as long as it isn't something exclusive or unique** (While I was walking home, I saw *a* pretty house for sale. *The* house was in my favorite architectural style).

But the number *one* does the same thing, doesn't it? In some cases, it does, and I'll discuss them later, but right now let's look at some comparisons and see if we can find a distinction between *a* and *one*:

I bought <u>a</u> book.   I bought <u>one</u> book.
He gave her <u>a</u> flower.   He gave her <u>one</u> flower.
They have <u>a</u> parakeet.   They have <u>one</u> parakeet.

Do you sense a difference? If you do, write down the difference you find between *a* and *one* on the lines that follow:

....

....

For students whose native languages have only one word for the indefinite article and the number one, such as Spanish with *un[o]* (masculine) or *una* (feminine), there's usually some confusion as to when to use the article and when to use the number in English. As it happens, **the indefinite article means that the noun is singular, countable, and <u>just one of many</u>**. The number *one*, on the other hand, tends to be used when we respond to the question "How many . . . ?" or "How much . . . ?" or when we're stressing the singularity of something. In other words, **we normally use *one* when counting**.

Are there times when *a* and *one* can be used the same way? Let's find out. Here are some examples for you to look at. If you can substitute *one* for *a/an*, check the box after each sentence.

1. Would you like to hear <u>an</u> interesting story?   ☐
2. I found close to <u>a</u> hundred old coins in my basement!   ☐
3. I told my brother, and he said it was probably <u>a</u> treasure somebody had hidden there.   ☐

4. In fact, what I had found was only a third of the total treasure hidden in my basement! ☐

5. I looked closely at some of the coins. There was a dollar, a dubloon, a kroner, and a ruble. ☐

6. I put some of the coins in a little leather pouch. ☐

7. That tiny pouch must have weighed at least a kilo! ☐

Do you see any rules at work? In a moment we'll look into what rules there may be. The boxes I'd check go with **Sentences 2, 4, 5,** and **7.** In all of those sentences, the word *a* can be substituted perfectly well with *one*. So why is that? Why can't we do the same for the other sentences? Think about what category each of the following noun phrases belongs to. In other words, what category does each noun deal with? Write the names of those categories on the lines that follow these four noun phrases:

a/one hundred ....

a/one third ....

a/one dollar ....

a/one kilo ....

The categories I hope you've come up with are **numbers, fractions, money,** and **weights or measurements.** With words in these categories, *a* and *one* can be used interchangeably.

Here's a suggestion for you that you should consider if you happen to be teaching a class of students whose L1s vary. It will be very useful for you to do a little research on any discrete point you find your students have trouble with such as, in this case, the indefinite article. Check out how their languages deal with that discrete point so you'll be aware of what you need to stress when teaching them how English deals with it. Anticipating what language interference problems may arise actually holds true even if all your students speak just one language.

One last point I should discuss is in answer to the question, "What is the plural of the indefinite article?" The answer is simply *nothing*. When a noun that has *a* before it is pluralized, it drops the article:

> a pin   pins
> an anchor   anchors
> a grape   grapes
> an unpaid bill unpaid bills

Among many linguists, this lack of an article actually has a name of its own. It's called the "zero article."

The Zero Article

As I've just mentioned, the zero article is used when a countable noun that takes *a* in the singular is made plural. It's also used when we deal with uncountable nouns (e.g., butter/water/snow) in general terms.

There are some peculiarities in its usage, though, that I should also mention. Compare the words in bold in the following mini-dialogues and see if you can make any conclusions about when the definite or indefinite article is used as opposed to the zero article.

> A: You just bought **a car**, didn't you?
>
> B: Well, it's really **a used car**.
>
> A: Do you go everywhere **by car** or do you use the bus?
>
> B: Now I hardly ever go anywhere **by bus**.

Before you become totally perplexed, I'll make it easy for you. The simple fact is that **there's often a zero article in phrases that deal with abstract uses of concrete nouns. In other words, they don't refer to one specific item, but rather to an item in a general activity.**

For example, *a car* is a concrete item; *by car* is an abstraction that indicates a means of transportation. *Going to church* refers to an activity rather than one specific building; *the church* does that. *Staying in bed* is another example of an activity, while *the bed* refers to a concrete item.

For more information on the zero article, please visit us at
ELTgrammar.com

A Word About Change

In just about every prescriptive English grammar I've come across (the ones that tell you what you *should* say), the lesson dealing with countable and uncountable nouns is quite straightforward: here are the nouns that you can count (in which case, you can use the indefinite article or a number accompanied by a plural marker on the noun), and here are the nouns you cannot count (in which case, you can't use the indefinite article or a number and a plural marker on the noun).

In the list of uncountable nouns, we find words such as *beer, coffee, tea, water, bread,* and *lettuce*. The lesson goes on to tell us that we must use phrases such as *a glass of, two cups of, a loaf of,* and *two heads of* in order to count the uncountable items I've just mentioned. Then we go out into "the real world" and listen to what people really say. Go into any restaurant and you just may hear statements like these:

"Let's see, that'll be a vodka on the rocks and two beers, right?"

"Hey, Antoine, the chef's gotta make a little more salad, so go get a lettuce, an endive, and a can of anchovies, okay?"

So what should English teachers do? Are we to go by the book, remain staunch defenders of prescriptive grammar, and be blind to the changes that are taking place in the language? After all, if enough native speakers decide to contradict what the grammar books say, what should we do?

My advice, for the time being, is to say that you should teach the prescribed grammar, but that it's perfectly acceptable to mention the current alternatives that your students will surely hear once they're exposed to enough native speakers. Let's call these alternatives when dealing with countable and uncountable nouns "fast food English." It could have developed out of the desire for restaurant people to abbreviate their messages whenever possible in order to keep up a certain pace on the job. After enough time passed and enough customers kept hearing these fast food phrases, they caught on with the general public and have now become fairly acceptable alternatives.

The Definite Article

Pronunciation

I've already mentioned that the definite article is the word *the* and the first thing we should consider is its pronunciation. Just as when choosing to use *a* or *an*, there are pronunciation concerns that must be taken into account. Read the following examples out loud. See if you find yourself using two different pronunciations for "t-h-e."

the angel	the plant
the onion	the fruit
the elm	the birch
the ink	the pen

There are some people who would pronounce "t-h-e" the same way with all these nouns, but that's considered non-standard. Note any observations you can make about how you've pronounced "t-h-e" in the column on the left, and how you've pronounced it in the column on the right.

In the left-hand column,

....

....

In the right-hand column,

....

....

If you look back at the rules we figured out for *a* and *an*, you recall that it all depended on whether the first sound in the following word was a vowel or consonant sound. That holds true for these pronunciation rules as well. If the following word begins with a vowel sound, pronounce the vowel in "t-h-e" as the name of the letter *e*, represented by the phonetic symbol /i/. **If the following word begins with a consonant sound, pronounce the vowel in "t-h-e" the same way you pronounce the *a* in *about*,** represented by the phonetic symbol /ə/. This pronunciation rule also holds true for those deceptive words that begin with silent *h* (*honor*) or the glide *y* (*union*). When the *h* is silent, we treat those words as if they begin with vowel sounds; the *y* is a glide, so we treat those words as if they begin with consonant sounds.

One other pronunciation to keep in mind is that we often pronounce the *e* in "t-h-e" as the name of the letter when we emphasize or stress the noun it precedes:

A: Did you say that his name is Jason Kennedy?

B: Yes, I did.

A: Is he one of **theeee** Kennedys?

B: No such luck.

Meaning and Usage

I've already said that *a* is the article to use in general statements; the same can be said about *the* (*The orange is a fruit of Asian origin*). Is there a significant difference if we substitute *an* for *the* in the example in parentheses? Not really, at least, not for the purposes of this book. In fact, there are three ways that we can talk in generalities about subjects: using the indefinite article (*a*), using the definite article (*the*), or using the zero article and making the noun plural. Here's an example of the three ways we can discuss the same topic in a general statement:

1. <u>A rabbit</u> is an animal loved by children.
2. <u>The rabbit</u> is an animal loved by children.
3. <u>Rabbits</u> are animals loved by children.

Keep in mind that the use of *the* in Sentence 2 is restricted and doesn't reflect the usual meaning of this article. To discover the most typical use of *the*, let's examine another group of sentences. If the sentences sound correct to you, write the word *okay* on the lines after them; if they don't sound right, put the word *odd* on the lines.

1. Where's <u>a</u> newspaper I was reading? ....

2. A: Look at that peeling paint!

   B: Where?

   A: On <u>a</u> front door! ....

3. Want to see some card tricks? Good!

   Take <u>the</u> card out of <u>a</u> deck. ....

4. Hey, Pete, we ate at <u>the</u> great restaurant! ....

In case you were wondering about your better judgment, don't be alarmed. **You should have written *odd* on all of the lines above.** But why are they all odd? Let's examine each one and find the reason.

The question in the first example refers to a specific newspaper that the person was reading earlier, and ***the* is the article we choose when referring to a specific thing that both speaker and listener are aware of.** Example 1 should be, "Where's the newspaper I was reading?"

In **Example 2**, Person A is talking about a specific door, the one and only front door that the house would have. The door being referred to is specific; therefore, we again need to use *the* and the corrected version should be, "On the front door!"

Example 3 has two misuses. The corrected sentence should read, "Take a card out of the deck." The speaker needs to say *a* card because it's one of the fifty-two and refers to a general or vague thing (this card, that card—any card); the speaker has to say *the* deck because our magician is referring to the specific deck which the participant sees, not any deck of cards in general.

If left alone, **Sentence 4** would probably force Pete into wondering whether he'd previously recommended some outstanding restaurant to the speaker. He'd be uncomfortable because the speaker is making no reference to a previous conversation that he can pinpoint. The sentence should be, "Hey, Pete, we ate at a great restaurant!"

By now, we realize that the **all-important use of *the* is to refer to something or someone specific or known, <u>not</u> general.**

How about the following sentences? All four of them are right, but information about the direct object in each one is different. What assumptions can we make? Explain the differences between the paired direct objects (depending on which article is used with them) on the accompanying blank lines.

1a. Please pass me <u>a</u> salt shaker. ....

1b. Please pass me <u>the</u> salt shaker. ....

2a. Did you see <u>a</u> film last night? ....

2b. Did you see <u>the</u> film last night? ....

In **1a**, we can assume that **there are at least two salt** shakers on the table. The speaker is saying he doesn't care which one the other person passes to him. In **1b**, however, there can **only be one salt shaker** on the table, and the speaker needs to use *the* because it's the one and only specific item he's asking for.

In **2a**, the speaker is asking the other person if he saw just **any movie last night**; it doesn't matter which one. In **2b**, the speaker is asking if the person saw the movie that they'd previously discussed, probably at some recent point in the past. In other words, **both speaker and listener know exactly which movie** is being referred to. To sum up everything I've touched on so far, all we need to do is remember this basic difference between *a* and *the*: ***A* is for generalities about people, animals, places, things, or ideas.** The zero article works this way, too. *The*, on the other hand, is for specific people, animals, places, things, or ideas.

 Heads Up!

In many languages, e.g. Spanish and French, the definite article is more commonly used than in English. In fact, contrary to English usage, the definite article is typically used when making statements about things in general, not just specific things as in English.

Some cases in point:

→ In French, it's   C'est la vie, but in English it's
                             That's Ø life.

→ In Spanish, it's   El agua es un tesoro, which is
                             Ø Water is a treasure.

So be prepared to deal with this if your students add *the* where we wouldn't normally use it in English.

As I mentioned earlier in this chapter, there are many languages which have no articles at all—definite or indefinite. If you have students whose native languages (L1s) fit into this group (Russian and Japanese are two good examples), plan accordingly for the double challenge of getting your students to understand the concepts involved and getting them to use the articles appropriately.

For more information on the definite article, please visit us at
ELTgrammar.com

Quantifiers

I've mentioned that nouns can work alone or be accompanied by articles and adjectives. Now let's discuss other items I mentioned that can accompany nouns, namely, the two most commonly used quantifiers in English, *some* and *any*. The thing is, these two words invariably end up being difficult and even vexing points for teachers and their students. In fact, the more advanced the students are, the more troublesome *some* and *any* become. This trouble all stems from the amazing variations in meaning and usage that both words have; furthermore, as students become more and more aware of the nuances in meaning that English words can have, these sometimes subtle and sometimes not-so-subtle differences become increasingly more noticeable.

Let's begin exploring *some* and *any* by observing the most typical uses taught in lower-level classes. Here's a dialogue to start things off:

A: So how's life way out in the country?

B: It isn't really out in the country. It's just ten miles from town. By the way, have I told you what happened last weekend? Believe it or not, I saw **a** Florida panther in my back yard. I could hardly believe my eyes because they're so rare.

A: That's great! I've seen **some** panthers over the years, but usually in really remote areas.

B: Well, I was really happy to see it. I didn't think there were **any** panthers left in Florida. They're on the endangered species list, you know.

Did you notice that I have the article *a* in bold along with *some* and *any*? That's because there's a connection between the indefinite article and these quantifiers that most ELT grammar books don't touch on. Can you figure out what the connection is? If you come up with an idea, write it down on the following line:

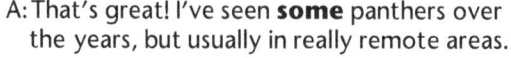

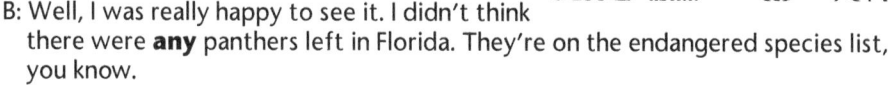

In this chapter, while discussing the uses of the indefinite article, I mentioned that we can use the zero article—in other words, nothing—when the singular noun that goes with the indefinite article is changed to the plural:

a book → books. There is, however, another way to deal with an indefinite singular becoming an indefinite plural, and that's by changing *a/an* to *some/any*: a book → some/any books. Keep in mind that **in a statement, *some/any* can be the plural of *a/an* and that it represents an unspecified number or amount.**

By analogy, we can take *some* one step further in this use as an unspecified amount and put it into the context you'll find in the following mini-dialogue. On the line below the dialogue, write down how you would interpret *some* as it appears here:

> A: So how many people finally showed up for the rally?
> B: The media figured there were some 1,500 people there.

....

This idiomatic use of *some* is an example of a meaning rarely taught, but it's a meaning we shouldn't overlook. ***Some* can be used with numbers or amounts to mean *more* or *less*, *about*, or *approximately*.**

In the same way as with numbers or amounts, ***some* can stand for an unspecified person, place, or thing** even when numbers or amounts aren't involved:

> We always like to go to <u>some</u> exotic place on our vacation.

Now let's examine the quantifier *any*. My opening dialogue shows its most typical use, the one that students learn early on. How would you explain *any* juxtaposed with *some* when Speaker B says "I didn't think there were any panthers left in Florida"?

....

Person A says that she's seen *some* panthers over the years, but Person B says that he didn't think there were *any* panthers left in Florida. Person A's idea is affirmative, and **we use *some* after affirmative verbs in statements**; Person B's idea is negative, and **we use *any* after negative verbs in statements to mean *not even one*.** These last two rules are the most typical ones that students are given for *some* and *any*. If only it were that simple!

> For more information on quantifiers, please visit us at
> ELTgrammar.com

Adjectives

Some readers may wonder why I've included a section devoted to adjectives; after all, isn't it easy to use adjectives in English? The answer is *not necessarily*, but I hope they will be easy to use by the time you've finished this chapter! What I have to offer you are helpful insights and ways to understand and teach some interesting phenomena that occur with these descriptive words. Students are often surprised to find out that adjectives are normally placed in front of the nouns they describe rather than after them. That's because it's so common in many other languages to place adjectives after the nouns. So English speakers say *a **large** portion*, whereas Spanish speakers, for example, say *una ración grande* (*a portion large*).

Another thing that surprises students is that we never pluralize adjectives in English. It's a ***large** portion* and it's ***large** portions*. In many other languages, adjectives are pluralized if the nouns they describe are in the plural. In fact, not only are adjectives pluralized in so many other languages, but they also change gender if their languages account for masculine, feminine, and possibly even neuter: *un plato rico / platos ricos / una sopa rica / sopas ricas*. In other words, adjectives are much easier in their basic use in English than in many other languages as far as these elements go. Well, I hate to tell you, but that statement isn't so true when we deal with the different forms of adjectives in English, as you'll find out as you keep reading. So hold onto your hats; it may be a bumpy ride!

Verbal Adjectives

We call two kinds of adjectives "verbal" because they grow out of verbs, the action words. Look at the following dialogue to see both kinds (verbs and adjectives made from them) in action:

A: I know you like anthropology very much What part of the subject interests you the most?

B: I'd say that paleoanthropology, the study of human origins, is the most **interesting** part for me.

A: Really? Why is that?

B: I guess it's simply that I'm very **interested** in answering that primal question: Where do we come from?

As you can see in the dialogue, the verb *interest* has two kinds of adjective forms that grow out of it, *interesting* and *interested*. The question I know that you know I'm going to ask is what the difference between these two adjective forms is.

What does the *-ing* adjective (the present participle of the verb) describe and how is that different from what's described by the *-ed* adjective (which is really the past participle of the verb)? Think about what you know about the *-ing* form of any verb (for example, which tenses does it occur in?). Consider what you know about the verb forms that end with *-ed*, for example, which tenses it occurs in and how it works in the passive voice. Think about these two points for a moment and write down any thoughts you have on the following lines:

Let's look at a basic idea that Person B supplied in the dialogue:

Paleoanthropology interests me.

Paleoanthropology is the subject, of course, but more importantly, it's responsible for creating or causing the interest in Person B. This insight gives us the answer to one part of our question: **The *-ing* adjective describes the person, thing, or situation that's the <u>cause</u> of the feeling or reaction in the direct object.**

Conversely, the direct object (Person B in this case) is receiving the reaction or feeling. **We use the past participle adjective to describe the person or thing that receives the feeling or reaction;** it describes the state or condition of the recipient. So, paleoanthropology is interest*ing* and Person B is interest*ed* (in it, by it). Remember that we said the *-ed* adjective is really the past participle, or third form of the verb; if the verb is irregular, there won't be an actual *-ed* on the end (as in the verb *to freeze*: freeze, froze, frozen). *Frozen* is still a past participle, even without the *-ed*!

At this point, I'd like to offer you a list I've compiled of 88 verbs from which the most common verbal adjectives are made, but keep in mind that there are others. You will see that some verbs are preceded by an asterisk; I'll get to the reason for that in a little while.

*absorb	challenge	deceive	hearten	mortify	stabilize
addict	charm	defeat	horrify	*move	stimulate
aggravate	*chill	demoralize	*humiliate	mystify	*strike
alarm	civilize	depress	incriminate	nauseate	*stun
amaze	clean	devastate	infuriate	overwhelm	surprise
amuse	comfort	disappoint	inspire	perplex	tempt
annoy	*compromise	exasperate	interest	pierce	terrify
appall	confuse	excite	*intoxicate	please	thrill
astonish	connect	exhaust	intrigue	*punish	tire
astound	convince	exhilirate	invigorate	puzzle	*touch
baffled	corrupt	fascinate	*invite	refresh	trust
bewilder	*crush	*freeze	jangle	relax	upset
blind	damage	frighten	love	satisfy	vex
bore	dazzle	frustrate	minimize	shock	
calm	deafen	gratify	mislead	soothe	

And now to the verbs that have asterisks. The most important reason that they've been singled out is to show that the adjectives made from these verbs have figurative meanings besides the literal ones. At the top of the next page are a few examples that demonstrate this phenomenon.

absorb:	mentally occupy completely
	It was an <u>absorbing</u> account of life in Antarctica.
	He was fully <u>absorbed</u> in his work.
chill:	make frightening, scary
	I read a <u>chilling</u> report on the increase in AIDS cases.
	(**chilled:** literal meaning only, as in *chilled water*)
compromise:	expose to danger, suspicion, or dishonor
	By asking me to disregard the corruption I've seen, you're putting me in a <u>compromising</u> situation.
	When the judge realized that he knew the defendant personally, his <u>compromised</u> position forced him to recuse himself.
crush:	devastate emotionally
	The <u>crushing</u> realization that her brother had betrayed her sent her into the depths of depression.
	When she realized what her brother had done, she was <u>crushed</u>.

For more interesting verbal adjectives, please visit us at
ELTgrammar.com

👀 Heads Up!

Three *-ed* adjectives have derived from verbs, but they're very unusual because they're pronounced in two syllables, not one. Look at what I mean:

- *aged* /e-jɪd/ as in *an aged person*, somebody who's old
  Compare with /ejd/ as in *aged cheese* that has undergone a process called "aging."
- *blessed* /blɛ-sɪd/ as in *a blessed event*, meaning an event that has good fortune attached to it
  Compare with /blɛst/ as in *a blessed church*, that is, a church that's been given a blessing.
- *learned* /lər-nɪd/ as in *a learned person*, somebody who's wise and well educated
  Compare with /lərnd/ as in *a learned behavior*, which is a behavior that didn't come naturally but was developed.

There are some adjectives that look like they're derived from the past participles of verbs, but they aren't—at least not in the same way. Here are some typical ones:

bowlegged	* peaked	wicked
jagged	ragged	wretched
naked	rugged	

Each of these words is pronounced with a separate syllable on the *-ed*. However, you'll note that there are no such related verbs as *to bowleg, to crook, to jag, to nake, to rag, to rug, to wick,* or *to wretch*. Therefore, they're only "look-alike" participial adjectives.

*Peaked is interesting for a different reason. When pronounced as two syllables, / pi-kɪd /, it means "tired," but when it's one syllable, /pikt/, it's the simple past of the verb *to peak*, which means *to bring to a high point*.

Other Uses of -ing Adjectives

There are two other important uses of this verbal adjective form that we should take a look at. See if you can figure out one use by looking over this dialogue and write your guess on the lines below.

> A: Gustav, have you seen the **watering** can? I've got to water the potted flowers in front of the house.
>
> B: Look in the tool shed out back.
>
> A: Are the **pruning** shears there, too?
>
> B: Probably. By the way, we need some more **potting** soil so I can transplant the mums into larger pots.

....
....

In these phrases, the *-ing* adjectives serve to tell us what purposes their nouns have:

- The can is used for <u>watering</u> the flowers, so it's *a watering can*.
- Those shears are used for <u>pruning</u> plants, so they're *pruning shears*.
- The soil that Gustav needs is used for <u>potting</u> plants, so it's *potting soil*.

I'll discuss more about this use of the *-ing* adjective, which is in the section on "compounding" a little later in this chapter. By the way, in the dialogue did you notice the use of *potted* in the phrase *potted flowers*? Why must we use the past participle form of the adjective to describe the flowers?

....

The past participle adjective is used here because, as our rule said, it **describes the state or condition of the flowers which received the action of being put into pots!** That is, someone potted the plants.

Now look at these sentences, which exemplify one use or more of the *-ing* adjective and figure out what they tell us in these cases. Write down your thoughts on the lines that follow.

- She's a <u>nursing</u> mother.
- Professor Fouad is <u>Acting</u> Dean this semester.
- When you scuba dive, never go near <u>feeding</u> sharks.

....
....
....

In this other use, the *-ing* adjectives explain the activities that are being carried out by the nouns they describe. For example, a **nursing** mother is a mother who's nursing her baby; an **acting** dean is a school administrator who's temporarily acting as dean until a permanent person can be found for the position; **feeding** sharks are sharks that are feeding on some prey.

Compound Adjectives

A: Darn it! It's time to get my garden ready for planting.

B: You don't seem too thrilled with the idea.

A: I'm not. It's a **backbreaking** job.

B: Maybe that's because you use **old-fashioned** methods.

A: What do you mean, old-fashioned methods?

B: You still use those **twenty-year-old** handtools of yours and nothing else, right?

A: Right. So what?

B: Go out and buy some **up-to-date** equipment like a **gas-powered** tiller and a **state-of-the-art** mulcher. They'll save you a lot of toil. And they'll save your back, too.

A: Hmm. That's a **work-saving** idea. Thanks!

Earlier in this chapter, I dealt with compound nouns. Now, as promised, I'll deal a little with compound adjectives. The most typical kind of compound adjective, and the kind that teachers need to deal with quite early on, is the **hyphenated form**. In the dialogue you've just read, all but one of the examples are hyphenated compound adjectives. Happily for us teachers, most of these adjective forms are not so wordy. Let's take a look at some common ones by doing another paraphrasing activity. Complete the following sentences by rewording what their initial parts tell you. I've done the first one as an example.

1. A note that's worth five liras is .... *a five-lira note.* ....
2. A snake that's six feet long is ....
3. Watermelons that weigh five kilos are ....
4. A wall that's two meters thick is ....
5. Children who are six years old are ....

Reworking the descriptions of these head nouns (*note, snake, watermelons, wall, children*) is really quite straightforward. The paraphrases you should have are a **six-foot-long snake / five-kilo watermelons / a two-meter-thick wall / six-year-old children**.

What's the one major internal change you had to make in order to create these hyphenated compound adjectives? Write your answer on the following line:

....

The one major internal change was that you had to make the plural items **singular** in each case: *feet* became *foot*, *kilos* became *kilo*, *meters* became *meter*, and *years* became *year*. So why is there a need for this change? By now you should have that answer down pat! Write it on the following line:

....

Even though these phrases contain plural elements when they appear after the subjects they are describing, once they've been turned into the components of compound adjectives, they're rarely pluralized in English. It's as simple as that! Let's take a moment to discuss how we can explain to students about when and why we tend to hyphenate compound adjectives. It seems to be the case that the vast majority of compound adjectives are indeed hyphenated, most assuredly ones that contain numbers (a three-year-old filly / a 100-acre farm / a 1,000-rupee check). What's very important for students to understand is that there is a reason for this convention in the written language. In short, it's to show that even though we may be using two, three, four, or even more descriptive words before the head noun, these words are being linked together as if they were one word representing one idea. The hyphens act as the links; they're a visual aid on the written page to let the reader know that these descriptive phrases are to be treated as whole units.

As I mentioned earlier, what we've gone over so far is the basic compound adjective form that's most commonly taught in classes. It's a bit tricky for students to know when to hyphenate the appropriate phrase, make any plural element singular, and then front the whole thing before the head noun. In many languages, genitive or possessive forms are used to do what we accomplish in English with compound adjectives. In Spanish, for example, it would be typical to say "a stamp of thirty cents" (una estampilla de treinta centavos) instead of "a thirty-cent stamp," so you can see how much adjusting your students may have to make when they learn this English form. As an example of how bizarre their phrases could be if they didn't use the English form, think about how your students might try to say "my mother tongue" by following the rules of their language. They'd probably end up saying the tongue of my mother!

For more information on compound adjectives, please visit us at ELTgrammar.com.

The Ordering of Adjectives

Incredible as it may seem, there are eighteen categories into which adjectives can be placed. I'll get you started with a few of these categories in this chapter, and then you can learn about the rest of them at ELTgrammar.com.

It's as if there were 18 empty slots in front of every noun into which different kinds of adjectives could fit. In other words, there are 18 kinds of adjectives and a similar number of positions in which adjectives can be put before the head noun, that is, the noun that's being described. Luckily, I've never heard anyone utter a phrase that included even close to that many adjectives, and I'm sure you haven't either!

Here's one note before we get under way. In many cases, words that are actually nouns will be referred to as adjectival forms in this section of the chapter. These nouns are actually going to be used as adjectives because they describe the nouns we're going to focus on. I'll get into all the details about these specially used nouns later on. For right now, though, we'll just concentrate on the order of real adjectives and the nouns that can function as adjectives.

Let's begin our investigation of adjective order by looking at three mixed-up phrases and seeing if we can rearrange the adjectival forms to make the phrases grammatical. (The words that are boxed in are the head nouns, the ones that get all the description.

1. coffee electric pot
2. water gas heater
3. alarm battery-operated clock

Without much trouble, we can see that the things being described are:

1. an electric coffee pot
2. a gas water heater
3. a battery-operated alarm clock

So what rule for ordering the descriptive words can we come up with? We see that the words *coffee*, *water*, and *alarm* tell us what the pot, the heater, and the clock are used for or how they're used, or what purpose they serve. These three words are examples of the nouns, not adjectives, that I've mentioned you'll be coming across in this section.

The other three words, *electric*, *gas*, and *battery-operated*, all have their own common feature: they're the power sources. Now we've discovered the order of these two categories of adjectives:

power   purpose   head noun

Let's describe these items in more detail, but before we do, I'd like to explain two things. First, that I intend to work with phrases that are longer than what people normally utter just for the sake of demonstration. Second, that I'm going to surprise you with how much figuring and interpreting and coordinating the mind goes through when ordering adjectives in English. If you're a native English speaker or a truly bilingual person with English being one of your two languages, your mind knows mostly what works and what doesn't work with adjective ordering without thinking consciously about it. However, if a student asks you why English speakers invariably say a *big, red, hydrogen-filled balloon* instead of a *red, hydrogen-filled, big balloon*, you'll be able to tell them why by the time you finish reading the material I have for you below and online!

Getting back to the items we've already discussed a little, now we want to describe what materials our items are made of. The pot is *electric* and *stainless steel*, the heater is *gas* and *aluminum*, and the clock is *battery-operated* and *plastic*. So where should we place these descriptive words? Take a moment, think about where you'd put them, and jot the phrases down on the following lines:

1. a/an .... coffee pot
2. a/an .... water heater
3. a/an .... alarm clock

The answer is that the materials should be placed before the power source words:

1. a stainless steel electric coffee pot
2. an aluminum gas water heater
3. a plastic battery-operated alarm clock

Now we have another category, material, and we can expand our ordering rule:

material   power   purpose   head noun

For more information on the ordering of adjectives and on when adverbs look like adjectives, please visit us at ELTgrammar.com

Punctuating Adjectives

The mechanics of a language (e.g., punctuation and spelling) are technically not parts of the grammar of a language. This was discussed briefly in the Preface. But when dealing with adjectives, it's quite important to understand where to punctuate with the use of commas, so let's take a look at the following phrases for a moment. See if you can determine three categories for the adjectival forms you find:

> those big, old, rusty metal garden tools
> a young, energetic Australian sheep dog
> our gorgeous, expensive, large backyard swimming pool

....

....

What we've come up with is **determiners** (demonstratives like *those* and possessives like *our*), **"real" adjectives** (big, old, rusty, young, energetic, Australian), and **nouns used as adjectives** (metal, garden, sheep, backyard). After looking over all of this information, can you make an observation about where it's necessary to punctuate with commas in phrases like the ones you've just seen?

....

The interesting point to make here is that **we only place commas between "real" adjectives**, those words listed in any English dictionary as being adjectives, the words we traditionally consider to be adjectives. **We never place a comma between a determiner and a real adjective** (e.g., *those, big ones*) **or between a "real" adjective and a noun used as an adjective** (e.g., *rusty, metal things*). This rule is neat and tidy, so you can give it to your students to help them learn where it's necessary to punctuate a phrase or sentence that contains more than one real adjective.

Teaching Tips

2.1 *Realia*

A collection of realia is very useful for teachers to have; realia can be used in many different ways (role plays, for example). In this case, bring in realia that represents occupations, sports, or actors and their roles. Examples might be a pilot's cap, stethoscope, wig, book bag, swimming goggles, mortar board, Mickey Mouse ears, etc. If you don't have any of these items, you can often get them at toy stores, second-hand shops, and yard sales. Your students may even have some they'll bring in to class. Hand out the props or let the students choose them, and say as you point to a student: "She's a rock star."/"He's a doctor."/"She's a professor." If you have duplicate props, you say: "They're pilots."/"They're Mouseketeers." Have the students repeat after you individually or as a group. Continue with questions ("Who's the doctor?"/"Is Jenna a chemist?") or by pointing to a student and saying: "Clerk." Student responses may be the following: "Who's a dentist?"/"Is Genghis a teacher?"/"I'm a swimmer."/"She's not an actor; she's a ballerina."When the students are comfortable with the articles, let them take over the questioning.

2.2 *Picture File Descriptions*

Before class, select several pictures from your Picture File (see Appendix 1). Be sure that the pictures you choose have plenty of items in them. (It's also possible for you to let your students select a picture themselves.) Ask the students to describe the various items in the pictures using articles where necessary.

2.3 *I Can Remember...*

Bring in twenty to twenty-five items that represent a variety of countable and uncountable nouns (a book, some sand, a newspaper, some paper, etc.). Spread them out on your desk before class and cover them up. When the students come in, have them gather around your desk and uncover the items. Give the students a few minutes to remember as many items as they can before you cover them up again. Have the students return to their desks and ask them to list the items, making sure they use articles in their list.

2.4 *Plans*

Divide your class into pairs or small groups and have them plan a party, barbecue, picnic, or trip. Ask them to write up a list of the equipment and items that they'll need for the event. Again, make sure that they include appropriate articles on their list. When each group has made up its list, bring the class back together and compare the lists.

2.5 I Want / I'll Change

Have your students write down (1) ten to fifteen items that they'd like to have, given unlimited money or (2) ten to fifteen things that they'd like to change about themselves, their lives, or their world. Make sure they use articles with their items. Collect the lists and redistribute them. Students need to interview one another to find out whose list they have. Students must use appropriate questions in order to discover who the lists belong to.

2.6 Menus

Before class, collect or prepare various menus. Divide the class into small groups; one student will be the "server" and the others, the "customers." Have the students role play ordering food. The server should write down the order as it's being given so that he/she can repeat the order at the end to see if it's correct. Make sure that the servers and customers use appropriate "restaurant English."

2.7 Headlines

Before class write up or collect various newspaper headlines. Have enough headlines so that each group of students has three or four to work with. Divide the class into pairs or small groups and have them reconstruct complete headlines by adding articles, helping verbs, etc.

Variations:
1. Have the students reconstruct abbreviated emails instead of newspaper headlines.
2. Ask the students to write newspaper headlines or emails using the shortened "telegraphic" style.

2.8 The Alphabet Game

This activity is commonly called The Alphabet Game because it uses the order of the alphabet in selecting items. Students build up vocabulary lists based on a pre-determined category (a supermarket, a drugstore, nouns, adjectives, etc.). One student begins the game by saying: "I went to the supermarket and bought an avocado." The first word must begin with an *a*. The next student repeats what the first student said and adds an item of his/her own, this time a *b* item. "I went to the supermarket and bought an avocado and some butter." The third student repeats what's been said by the other two, adding a *c* item, and so on through the alphabet.

Variation: Have the students write an Alphabet Poem: A is for Austria, the country of the waltz. B is for bananas, the fruit I love the most. C is for chocolate, my passion, yum, yum. D is for..., etc.

2.9 A Modified Cloze

Create a modified cloze activity (see appendix 1) that contains a good variety of the various uses of *some* and *any* in it. Have the students complete the cloze on their own or in small groups. Collect the completed cloze examples, correct them, and return them to the students. If your students are able to, let them correct their classmates' clozes.

Variation: Use that modified cloze as a dictation activity. Put the cloze on a handout making sure that the blanks aren't too close together. It's too hard for the students to complete if the blanks are too close; they can't write the word fast enough before another blank comes up. Tell the students to put their pencils and pens down as you read the entire cloze to them. Read it again, this time letting your students fill in as many of the blanks as they can. Tell them that you'll be reading it a third time so they can check what they've written and fill in any blanks that they've missed.

2.10 Sentence Combining

This Tip can be used with almost any language point. It's a sentence-combining activity that has the students put back together short dialogues that contain examples of *some* and *any* (see Appendix 6, for complete details of this activity). Before class, create or copy short dialogues with *some* and *any*. Give each dialogue a name or number. Separate the dialogues into two parts, putting each part of the dialogue on a separate slip of paper. Write "1" on the first half of the dialogue slip and "2" on the second half. Mix up the slips and distribute them to your students. Have any student who has a "1" slip read it aloud. The student who has the matching "2" slip completes the dialogue. Continue until all the dialogue slips have been rematched.

2.11 Remembering Details

This Tip can also be used with any language point that your class is working on; in this case, however, you'll be focusing on *some* and *any*. Before class begins, prepare a story containing numerous examples of *some* and *any* in it. The text needs to be sufficiently rich in details so that your students are challenged to retain the details you'll ask them to remember after they've heard the text. If you can, record the text; if not, you can read it aloud to your class. Prepare a list of details, some correct and some incorrect, about the text and put them on the board or on a handout. If you've written these facts on the board, cover them up until after you've read the text two or three times. Have the students divide a piece of paper into two columns, writing correct at the top of one column and incorrect at the top of the other. Divide the class into small groups and have them list the details under the proper column. When all the information has been put into the proper columns, read the story to them again and have them correct the facts that are wrong.

Variation: Create a dialogue with several people talking about what they have or don't have, need or don't need, etc. (Make sure the dialogue contains several examples of *some* and *any*.) Provide a handout with a list of the items discussed and some which weren't discussed in the dialogue. You can also put the items on the board. Have the students check off what they've heard and then have them divide up into groups and reconstruct the dialogue they've just worked on.

2.12 "What Do You Call...?"

An effective way to practice the *-ed* and *-ing* adjectives is to prepare situations in which you can use the phrase "What do you call _____?" The blanks are filled in with phrases that provide the noun to be described and an appropriate verb. Here are some examples: "What do you call a fluid that cleans? / lies that convince people? / information which misleads you? / events that puzzle the police? / people who exasperate you?" and the like. Note that all the answers to these questions use the *-ing* adjective (*cleaning fluid, convincing lies, misleading information, puzzling events,* and *exasperating people*).

The same question can be asked to elicit the *-ed* adjective:"What do you call a friend you trust? / an enemy that you've demoralized? / customers that you have satisfied? / sleep that was disturbed by phone calls? / pipes that the plumber disconnected?" (They are *a trusted friend, a demoralized enemy, satisfied customers, disturbed sleep,* and *disconnected pipes*.)

You can make this activity more challenging by setting up pairs of "What do you call" questions that use both verbal adjectives."What do you call fluids that clean and carpets cleaned by the fluid? ("cleaning fluid and cleaned carpets") and service that satisfies and customers that you satisfy?" ("satisfying service and satisfied customers").

2.13 "A Mixed Bag"

Before class, think up four or five nouns for each student you have and write each noun on a slip of paper. Then think up two adjectives for each of the nouns and write them in any order on a separate slip of paper. Put all the slips in a bag to mix them up and then have each student pull out eight to ten slips. The students should then go around the room to their classmates and find slips that will appropriately match the slips they have. Many different combinations are possible, not just the ones you originally thought up. Have them report their combinations to the class, making sure that they've ordered the adjectives correctly.

2.14 *Personal Preferences*

Before class prepare several grids similar to the one that follows. (You can draw them on the board if it's easier.) Fill in the boxes in the grids with appropriate vocabulary or have the students brainstorm their own vocabulary and then fill them in. Once the grids have been filled in, have students write down their preferences and collect their sheets of paper. Redistribute the responses and have the students circulate around the room to find the person whose paper they have. Ask the students to give a report on their classmates' answers.

I prefer . . .

cool	stormy
hot	sunny
bright	brisk

. . . weather

I prefer . . .

Alpine	backpacking
Canadian	ski
European	seaside

. . . vacations

I prefer . . .

quiet	romantic
noisy	secluded
peaceful	crowded

. . . places

2.15 *Another Memory Game*

(This activity is a variation of 2.3). Bring in a group of fifteen to twenty common and not-so-common items to class (dictionary, tennis ball, safety pin, hair dryer, butterfly net, can opener, table tennis paddle, etc.). Spread them out on your desk. Pick each one up and ask what it does or what it's used for. Then cover them up. Gather the students around your desk and uncover the items. Tell the students that they'll have a couple of minutes to study the items in detail. Cover the items back up and have the students return to their desks. Tell them they have five minutes to list and describe as many of the items as they can remember. After they've written down the items and their descriptions, check their responses. Give the students one point for each correctly remembered item and one point for each descriptive adjective they've used properly. Give the winning students extra points for telling what each thing does or is used for.

2.16 *Writing Ads*

Select colorful pictures of products or things from your Picture File (see Appendix 1). Divide the class into pairs or small groups. Let the groups choose one of the pictures and have them write advertising copy for the product or item they've chosen. Note that if your students aren't familiar with advertising English, it will help them if you prepare a mini-lesson on the language of advertising before they begin the project. Bring in some ads for them to examine and have them practice talking about items for sale.

2.17 *Travel Brochures*

Let the students select travel pictures from the Picture File or have them bring in pictures of places that they've been to or are interested in. Have them work in small groups to prepare a travel brochure for the tourist industry about the place they've chosen. Be sure the students use ample adjectives to entice prospective customers among their classmates to travel to these places.

2.18 *The Lost Luggage*

Help! You've lost your luggage and everything in it. Go to the Lost and Found Office of the nearest bus station/train station/airport and make a report. First divide the class into two groups: the "Lost and Found agents" and the "unfortunate travelers." The agents will brainstorm questions that they need to ask the travelers and the travelers will make up the items in their suitcases. Remind the agents that they need to ask very specific questions about the lost luggage and that the travelers must have detailed descriptions of the suitcases and their contents. When the questions and details have been worked out, pair up an agent and a traveler and have them role-play the encounter.

2.19 *"Good Lookers"*

Divide the class into small groups. Have the groups study one another carefully; they're going to need to remember as many precise details about the members of the other groups as they can. After a couple of minutes of studying the other groups, send the groups to different parts of the classroom and let them discuss what they've just observed and have them change something about themselves. One student may take off his glasses. Another may comb her hair in a different way. Two students may exchange sweaters. After a few minutes, have the groups face one another again and try to reconstruct the "original look" of the groups. Award points for correct reconstructions; the team with the most points is declared the "Best Lookers."

2.20 *The Signs of the Zodiac*

This activity gives your students a chance to discuss astrology and prepare horoscopes for themselves and their classmates. First, find out if they know their own signs of the zodiac. List them on the board; you should even include your own. Prepare a handout like the one that follows which lists the signs, dates, students' names, etc. (You can also draw one on the board.) If possible, get a copy of the actual constellations and their places in the sky and samples of real horoscopes to show the class. Have the students fill in the charts for one another and then write up horoscopes based on what they've learned.

Constellation	Sign	Dates	Traits	Student	Student's Own Traits
	Virgo	Aug. 23 to Sept. 22	Sensitive Artistic In control	Patricia	
	Libra	Sept 23 to Oct. 22	Fair Creative Outgoing	Ricardo	

2.21 *The Crime*

Before class think of an imaginary crime (you only need to provide the most general details). Divide the class into two large groups: police investigators and witnesses. Have the police investigators prepare as many questions to ask the witnesses as they can think of. At the same time, have the witnesses prepare a story of what actually happened (location of the crime, victims, sequence of events, weather conditions, etc.). When all the stories and questions have been prepared, divide the class into small groups and have them role-play the investigation of the crime.

3

The Presents

"These are the times that try men's souls."

The Present Progressive

> Auxiliary BE + Verb + ING
>
> I **am** work**ing**   we **are** work**ing**
> you **are** work**ing**   they **are** work**ing**
> he, she, it **is** work**ing**

Let's get started by asking you a question. After looking at the brain teasers given below, can you determine the time or meaning of the present progressive in these sentences? There's a blank line after each example on which you can write your descriptions. I've done the first one for you to get you started.

1. He's starring in Macbeth on Broadway. _____*real present*_____
2. Tommy's being good for a change. _____
3. What are you doing? _____

There's one basic use of the present progressive in these examples. They show the real present, that is, that the action is *at this time*, and that there's no other major focus. If you wrote something like **the real present** or **the present** on the blank lines after these examples, you're doing fine.

Present Progressive as the Real Present

Some of you may know the present progressive as the "present continuous." Whatever its name, among the important points to remember about it is that **its primary function is to communicate the <u>real</u> present**. I find that the name "progressive" is more appropriate than "continuous" because it implies that the action is "in progress," and that's a fairly accurate description. It's interesting to point out that this aspect is most frequently used in conversational rather than academic or formal writing. That's because whatever you put in writing is not going to be read in the real present, while what you actually say in conversation is heard in the real present.

I've used the term *aspect*, so I should make sure you understand what this means. Believe it or not, linguistically speaking, English only has two tenses, the (simple) present and the (simple) past. **Every other form of the verb is called an aspect.** So the present and past progressive and the present and past perfect are aspects of the verb. I'm sure this is coming as a real surprise to most of you. You've probably seen all of the verb forms I've just listed referred to as tenses—but they are not; they're aspects (see Appendix 7 for more information).

One of the most difficult things for teachers to get across to their students is that, except for a relatively small number of verbs, English normally uses the present progressive to communicate that the action is in the true present. (We'll deal with that small number of verbs at length under the heading *The Simple Present: Stative Verbs*.) Here are a couple of sample dialogues to demonstrate this focus:

A: Where are Shuwei and Min?
B: They're out in the backyard.
A: What **are** they **doing**?
B: They**'re planting** roses.

C: Is Ari at work this week?
D: No, he isn't.
C: Why not?
D: He's **moving** into his new house.

Notice how both dialogues deal with the concept of *now*, but *now* doesn't represent the same idea in both. In the first dialogue, *now* literally means "at this very moment"; in the second, *now* refers to "this week." Make it a point to explain to your students that the concept of *now* can mean this moment, this week, this month, this year, etc.

Present Progressive as a Temporary Situation

When we use a verb that can either focus on a temporary situation or a longterm (or permanent) situation, **we use the present progressive to communicate that the situation is temporary**. Look at this sample dialogue:

> A: Scientists say that the earth **is getting** warmer.
>
> B: I didn't know that. How come?
>
> A: People **are putting** too much CO_2 into the atmosphere.
>
> B: That sounds serious

In the dialogue above, Speaker A could choose to communicate that this situation is long term or permanent by using a different form for the verbs (i.e., the simple present, which we'll get to shortly). The speaker has deliberately chosen the present progressive to show not only that this situation is in the present, but also that it may not be long term.

There's one more use of the present progressive that we should consider. It's a use which is not typically covered in classes, but it's one that we can certainly hear on any day in any conversation. Take a look at the following dialogue and identify how the present progressive is being used. Also notice the use of the simple present, which we'll get to next:

> A: Happy birthday!
>
> B: Oh, you knew!
>   Well, thanks very much.
>
> A: So, any big plans for after work?
>
> B: You know, it's funny. When I got home last night, I couldn't find the kids anywhere. I look around . . . my husband **isn't puttering** in the garden as usual and the kids **are**n't **watching** TV. Noises **are coming** from the basement, so I go downstairs and there they are. They'**re making** decorations for a surprise birthday party for me. They don't see me, so I go back upstairs and say nothing the rest of the evening.
>
> A: So they'**re throwing** you a surprise birthday party, eh?
>
> B: It looks that way!
>
> A: See you this evening!

Doesn't it seem odd that Speaker B is talking about something that happened in the past but uses two forms of the present to do so? For the moment, let's concentrate on the present progressive in this dialogue. Can you think of a way to categorize it for this use? If you can, write down your idea on the following line:

....

The use of the present progressive in this dialogue is very common in conversational English as I noted a few pages back especially in what we call *colloquial speech*. We call it the **narrative style** because it's used to help narrate a story. Many people opt to use this form when they want to bring the listener into more of a sense of temporal involvement with the action of the story. Using the present progressive in this way (and the simple present, too, as we'll see momentarily) tends to make the story *come closer* to the listener in time. In other words, the narrator is deliberately trying to make the listener a party to the event.

By the way, near the end of the last dialogue, Person A says, "So they're throwing you a surprise birthday party, eh?" Here's a heads-up: In this case, the present progressive is not being used for the narrative style. It's actually a form of the future, which I'll get to in Chapter 5. If you noticed that this example of the present progressive doesn't seem to fit in this dialogue, pat yourself on the back!

Now for purposes of comparison, let's take a look at the following dialogue, which demonstrates how we can use the simple present to narrate a story:

A: I saw in the paper that Sludgeco's been fined again for polluting Silver Bay.

B: That's right, and I witnessed the pollution first hand.

A: What do you mean?

B: I go down to the bay to take some photos at sunset and I smell something awful. I realize that I'm right near Sludgeco's drain pipes. So I walk over to the pipes and tons of foul-smelling waste are pouring out of the pipes into the bay. I take some pictures—lucky I have my camera with me—and send them to the nearest Environmental Protection Agency office.

A: You mean you proved Sludgeco was polluting again?

B: Just me and my little old camera!

One curious point that we should clear up about using the simple present and present progressive in this narrative style is to determine when the speaker opts for the simple form and when she decides to use the progressive form. Can you think of any reason to choose one and then the other? Write your thoughts on the lines at the top of the next page:

There's a very interesting rule that's being put into use in the dialogue: **When the verb can be used in the past progressive, the speaker opts for the present progressive; when the verb can be used in the simple past, the speaker opts for the simple present.** In other words, there's a mirror image, so to speak, of one form with the other in the narrative style. So now you know why we say that the so-called "simple present" is not at all simple or always the true present. But I digress. Let's get back to our discussion of the present progressive.

 Heads Up!

Students tend to drop or simply forget the auxiliary *be* when making the present progressive. Be prepared for this eventuality!

Stress the use of the auxiliary and practice it as much as possible so that your students will remember it!

There's one more observation about the present progressive I'd like to bring to your attention. Check out the following short passage:

*Because of the political turmoil that **is going** on in Kush, the government **is holding** a referendum and **letting** the people determine whether or not to remain one nation or to separate into two countries.*

Now that you've read this passage, the question I have for you is this: Do you think the verbs in bold, all in the present progressive, work all right in a typical textbook? Write your answer of *yes* or *no* on the following lines and add your reason for your answer. Let's see what you come up with.

No, the verbs in bold would probably not be found in a textbook. Those with the present progressive are the ones that don't work well. The reason? If you think about it, this is in a textbook, a book that has been read, is being read, and will be read by students. It's not something that deals with the here and now, but with either the past, the general, timeless concept, or possibly the future.

> The present progressive isn't used very often in formal written English and just about never in textbooks. It's reserved mostly for conversational or spoken language, whether formal or informal.

🌰 The Present Progressive in a Nutshell

- the <u>real</u> present (for most verbs):
    She's cooking.
- temporary actions:
    We're spending this summer at the beach.

    past ———————— right now ———————— future

- the narrative form:
    "She's waiting for the bus, so I ask her if I can drop her off anywhere in my car and she says . . ."

The Simple Present

> I, you, we, they **work**
> he, she, it **works**

Here we have the one verb form in English that has the most inappropriate name. Why? Because the form is neither "simple" nor "present" in its broader usage. Here are some more brain teasers for you to consider. When you think you know how the simple present is being used, describe its time or meaning on each accompanying blank line:

1. Birds fly and fish swim.   ....*generalization*............
2. She gets up at 6:30 on weekdays.   ....
3. I work in my uncle's drugstore.   ....
4. I don't like soup   ....
5. "He takes aim. He shoots. He misses!" ....

Most of the uses of the simple present in those five examples share a common thread, but there are fine points that change the focus of the meaning. **Sentence 1** doesn't really deal with time at all; it's a **timeless** use that communicates a fact about birds and fish. It can be considered **a generalization, fact,** or **truth. Sentence 2** indicates that the activity is a **habit** or **routine. Sentence 3** communicates that this activity is **long term** or **permanent. Sentence 4** is just like **1**, a simple **fact**. Does **Sentence 5** remind you of something seen earlier in this chapter? If you said this example is another instance of the **narrative style**, you're right. In this case, it's the form commonly used by someone witnessing an event such as a sportscaster talking to his radio audience, for example.

Simple Present vs. Present Progressive
Which to Teach First?

Two great mistakes are committed in most grammar books which end up laying the foundation for student confusion that's very hard to straighten out later on. The first great mistake is teaching the simple present before teaching the present progressive. There are probably two reasons for this. First, old-style grammarians felt that the simple present was easier for students to deal with because it's just the base form of the verb with only the addition of an -*s* or -*es* on the end of the verb for third person singular. "No conjugations to speak of plus no auxiliaries to deal with in the statement form equal an easy verb form to teach." Those grammarians are wrong because of the immediate challenge of introducing the auxiliary *do/does* in the negative and question forms.

Second, those same grammarians realized that a number of high frequency verbs are among those which almost exclusively use the simple present and not the present progressive. Because they're such high frequency verbs, these grammarians figured they should be taught early on and therefore the need to teach the simple present right off. This arbitrary decision has proven to be more of a hindrance than a help. Because it's the first verb form students are typically exposed to, and since it's called the *simple present*, students naturally assume that it's indeed the present—the <u>real</u> present—in English. This is where the confusion begins. Another reason to reverse the order in which these forms are taught is that it's much easier to get across the idea of the real present to students than it is to communicate the abstract, vague concept of habitual, general, or timeless situations. To sum up, **I recommend that you teach the present progressive** (affirmative and negative statements, question forms, and short answers) **before teaching the simple present.**

Stative Verbs

Note that with some special verbs, if you change their form, you change their meaning. I've twice alluded to a relatively small group of verbs that uses the simple present almost exclusively. They're called stative verbs, which means that they deal with **states of being rather than actions**. To make these verbs more manageable for your students, you might want to teach them that these verbs can be subdivided into five basic groups: verbs of **liking, the senses, possession, mental processes,** and **states of being**. Here are the ones of higher frequency. (The asterisks preceding some verbs are there to indicate that these are the special verbs that go through a change of meaning peculiar to English if the present progressive is used instead of the simple present. These changes will be discussed in more detail later on.)

STATIVE VERBS				
Liking	Senses	Possession	Mental Processes	States of Being
adore	*hear	belong	believe	astonish
desire	perceive	*have	doubt	be
detest	resemble	lack	feel	concern
dislike	see	own	forgive	cost
hate	*seem	possess	guess	depend
like	*smell		imagine	deserve
love	sound		intend	equal
mind	*taste		know	*fit
prefer			realize	matter
want			recall	mean
*wish			recognize	need
			regard	owe
			remember	tend
			suppose	
			*think	
			understand	

Here's an overview of the special stative verbs from the box above. (SP = simple present; PP = present progressive)

feel: SP = the involuntary sense of touch anywhere on the body
Most people shiver when they <u>feel</u> cold breezes.

SP = believe
The jury <u>feels</u> that the defendant is innocent.

SP or PP = physical or mental states
I <u>feel</u> ashamed that I lied to her. / I'<u>m feeling</u> ashamed.
Jim <u>feels</u> a little ill today. / Jim'<u>s feeling</u> a little ill.

hear: SP = the involuntary use of the ears; to be told
Oh, no! I <u>hear</u> the baby crying again.
We <u>hear</u> that you've quit your job.

PP = witness what others are saying; imagine sounds

What we're hearing from the government is talk of war.
She needs psychiatric help. She's hearing voices.

see: SP = the involuntary use of the eyes; understand
Joe doesn't see well without his glasses.
I see what you mean, but I don't agree with you.

PP = witness what others are doing; have a romantic involvement with; hallucinate
What we're seeing is a slowdown in population growth.
Did you know that Boris is seeing Natasha?
I don't see anything in that field. You're seeing things!

smell: SP = the involuntary use of the nose; how the odor of something is perceived; have a bad odor
I think I smell something burning in the kitchen.
These flowers smell so good!
Throw out those old boots. They smell!

PP = the voluntary use of the nose
Mom's smelling the milk because she thinks it's spoiled.

taste: SP = how food or drink is perceived
This soup tastes wonderful!

PP = the voluntary use of the taste buds; test or check for taste
The chef's tasting the soup for seasoning.

Remember that most sensory verbs have a difference in meaning and usage depending on whether they're voluntary or involuntary actions. **Make it a point to stress to your students that the form used depends on whether these verbs are voluntary or involuntary actions.**

fit: SP = harmonize; conform
Her current project fits the company's immediate goals.
Your qualifications fit what we're looking for.

SP = able to be put into or on a certain area without difficulty
Does that carry-on bag fit in the overhead compartment?
I love this new shirt. Look how well it fits.

PP = put something into a certain area without difficulty
I won't need two boxes. I'm fitting it all into this one.

have: SP = possess, own
The Kims have a lovely house.

SP = be sick
Carla has the flu.

PP = a situation that the subject is involved in
Peter's having trouble with his car again.
We're having a party. Come over right now!

involving food or drink
Hello, Helen? We're at Robb's Grill. We're having lunch.
I'm having tea. Would you like some?

think: SP = believe
Let's postpone the picnic. I think it's going to rain.

PP = (sometimes with prepositions *of* or *about*) = use the mind; imagine; consider
Be quiet for a moment. I'm thinking.
Are you thinking of what to serve at the party?
Gus is thinking of moving to Canada.
What's he thinking about?

wish: SP = communicate unhappiness with a situation; tell people what you would like for them
Philip wishes he earned more money.
We wish you long life and happiness!

PP = (with preposition *for*) express a hope for something
Now that I've blown out the candles on my birthday cake, I'm wishing for another great year like the one I just had!

At this point, let's see if you can distinguish the differences in meaning between the following pairs of sentences:

1a. Did you know that Ken's grandparents are living with him?
1b. Did you know that Ken's grandparents live with him?
2a. Harriet's writing articles for the *New York Times*.
2b. Harriet writes articles for the *New York Times*.
3a. Faisal's being a brat.
3b. Faisal's a brat.

Here's how it goes: in **Sentence 1a**, the idea is that Ken's grandparents are with him **temporarily** and that the situation is taking place now. Perhaps they had a fire in their home or their own home is being remodeled. Whatever the case may be, it's a temporary situation. In **Sentence 1b**, however, Ken's house is their **permanent** residence because no specific time is mentioned.

The next two sentences work along similar lines. In **Sentence 2a**, Harriet is probably a freelance writer who's just writing some article for the newspaper at the present time, and it's safe to assume it's a **temporary** assignment. In **Sentence 2b**, Harriet seems to be a **regular** contributor to the paper.

The last two sentences follow suit. Some people might consider the use of *be* in **Sentence 3a** idiomatic. That doesn't change the basic meaning, which is a **temporary** situation. The speaker is communicating that Faisal isn't always a brat; he's acting this way just today or just right now. In **Sentence 3b**, however, it's clear that Faisal is a brat **all the time**; this is his personality. And that insight leads us to a rule that we can remember about the verb *be*:

we can use the verb *be* in the present progressive to describe temporary states of personality as opposed to how someone behaves all the time. Two more examples follow:

> Don't mind him. He's being petty.
> Why are you being so stubborn?

A Note About the Word "Always"

In traditional grammar books, *always* always appears with the simple present. That, of course, is reasonable since one of the key meanings of the simple present is "all the time." Language, however, isn't always reasonable or logical.

A case in point is the very common use of joining up *always* with the present progressive: "She's always making fun of my dog, Butch!" The explanation for this phenomenon is that **we use *always* with the present progressive to emphasize the habitual, unrelenting nature of an action.** In this kind of context, the speaker or writer is changing the tone rather than the essential meaning. This change in tone usually **expresses a feeling of annoyance or irritation**. By the way, *forever* and *constantly* can work the same way here as *always*:

> They're forever decorating their house.
> He's constantly doodling during our meetings.

For more information on the present progressive, please visit us at ELTgrammar.com

The Simple Present in a Nutshell

- the real present (only for a select group of verbs):
    I hear you.
- general, timeless facts:
    She cooks very well.
- habitual, routine actions:
    We spend every summer at the beach.
- narrative style:
    " . . . and runner number 3 wins the marathon!"
    "So when I tell her she's won the contest, she kisses me on the cheek and jumps up and down for joy!"

The Present Perfect

> auxiliary HAVE + Past Participle of verb
>
> I, you, we, they **have** work**ed**
>
> he, she, it **has** work**ed**

Many an English language teacher has wished that the present perfect would just disappear overnight from the language, probably because it contains many subtleties and nuances. If you take each use one by one, you can manage to do a good, clear, concise job of teaching this complex form which is **commonly found in academic writing.**

Present Perfect as a Bridge from Past to General Present

Read these sentences and answer the questions.

1. Rolf lived in Budapest for many years.
   Does Rolf live in Budapest now?   yes ☐ no ☐

2. Rolf has lived in Budapest for many years.
   Does Rolf live in Budapest now?   yes ☐ no ☐

The answer to **Sentence 1 is no.** We're clearly given to believe that Rolf either moved away from Budapest some time ago or he's now deceased. The answer to **Sentence 2 is yes.** We know for a fact (from the grammatical form) that Rolf still lives in Budapest. He moved there many years ago and he's still there.

There's one other point to mention here. The present perfect can be used for an action that's been uninterrupted since it began in the past: "Rolf has lived in Budapest for many years" is an example of an uninterrupted action. Compare it to this sentence: "Maria has visited Budapest many times." Maria has made many visits to the city and each one of them was completed in the past. You'll learn why we use the present perfect in this case as you read further.

We know the answers to these two questions because we understand the use of the simple past versus the present perfect: with the simple past, the action is completely finished in the past; with the present perfect, **the action began in the past and comes to an indefinite time in the general present.** Here's a dialogue that will demonstrate this use more fully:

> A: I haven't had a hot meal in a long time.
>
> B: That's because you've been too busy to cook one.
>
> A: And nobody's invited me to dinner either.
>
> B: You poor thing! Come over to my house tonight.

Present Perfect as a Foot in the Door to the Future

Read each of the following sentences and answer the questions.

1. My grandfather traveled from Europe to Africa many times.

   Is Grandfather alive or dead? alive ☐ dead ☐ don't know ☐

   Do you think he'll take the trip again? yes ☐ no ☐ maybe ☐

2. My grandfather has traveled from Europe to Africa many times.

   Is Grandfather alive or dead? alive ☐ dead ☐ don't know ☐

   Do you think he'll take the trip again? yes ☐ no ☐ maybe ☐

It's really amazing how a change in a verb form can create such subtle but important differences. Let's see how you did with the questions. In **Sentence 1**, which uses "traveled," most people would guess that Grandfather's **dead**, although others would be justified in saying that they don't honestly know. As for whether or not Grandfather will take the trip again, most people would check **no** because the simple past means that the action is completely finished in the past and cannot recur.

In **Sentence 2**, which uses the present perfect, most people would guess that Grandfather's still **alive**, and as for whether or not he'll take the trip again, they would check **yes** or **maybe**. Quite a difference from the answers to the first two questions! Coming up is the explanation that will make it all clear.

Why should the sets of answers be so different? The reason lies in this second important meaning of the present perfect, that **the action happened in the past and may happen again at some point in the future**. In other words, we're leaving the door open a little in case the event should happen again; we're not shutting the door forever on Grandfather's taking another trip to Africa. The simple past communicates the idea that an action is completely finished in the past and has no real connection to the present, much less the future. This is where the simple past and the present perfect differ so greatly. Let's look at another sample dialogue to see this in action.

> A: **Did** you **watch** TV last night?
>
> B: No, I **didn't**.
>
> A: Then you **haven't seen** that new show.
>
> B: No, **I haven't**, darn it!
>
> A: Don't worry. It'll be on every week.

 Heads Up!

You may have students who speak French. If that's the case, they will probably confuse the English present perfect with a form of the simple past in French known as the "passé composé," which also uses the auxiliary *have* + the past participle of the verb. They will invariably think that the present perfect means the simple past and end up using it in sentences with words like *ago*. Anticipating this problem may save you a lot of grief!

Present Perfect as a Recent Event or an Event from the Past that Affects the Present

Once again, read these sentences and answer the questions.

1. A: You know, I think my cousin Anne would be a great match for Brendan.
   B: Forget about it.
   A: Why do you say that?
   B: Because Brendan and Maureen got engaged.

   When did Maureen accept Brendan's proposal?
   some time ago ☐   recently ☐   not sure ☐

2. A: You know, I think my cousin Anne would be a great match for Brendan.
   B: Forget about it.
   A: Why do you say that?
   B: Because Brendan and Maureen have gotten engaged.

   When did Maureen accept Brendan's proposal?
   some time ago ☐   recently ☐   not sure ☐

The answer to **Sentence 1** is that **all three options can work**. We know it took place in the past, but it could have been a hundred years ago or two days ago for all we know. It's vague and leaves us guessing about the time in the past unless we have additional information. The answer to **Sentence 2**, however, is recently. We know because the present perfect was used. We still don't know the exact time in the past, but we certainly understand that the event happened recently enough that friends and family are probably still excited about the news.

This is what I mean when I say that another important use of the present perfect is **it communicates that an event happened recently and still touches on, or affects, the present**. That's why Brendan's and Maureen's relatives are probably still excited.

> A: **Have** you **heard** the news?
>
> B: What news?
>
> A: Brendan**'s** just **proposed** to Maureen!
>
> B: Well, **has** she **accepted**?
>
> A: Yes! And they**'ve** even **set** the date.

It should be mentioned that an acceptable variation in American English for this use of the present perfect is to use the simple past in situations related to the word *just*:

> A: Did you hear the news?
>
> B: What news?
>
> A: Brendan just **proposed** to Maureen!
>
> B: Well, **did** she **accept**?
>
> A: Yes! And they even **set** the date.

🌰 The Present Perfect in a Nutshell

🌰 **uninterrupted actions from the past to an indefinite time in the general present; these actions may continue into the future:**
They've raised horses ever since they bought that farm.

past ——————— general present ——————— future

🌰 **separate actions completed in the past that may occur again:**
She's received several promotions since she started working there.

past ——————— general present ——————— future

✒ recently completed actions that still affect the present:
Thanks for offering me part of your sandwich, but I've just eaten.

past ——————┼— present ———————— future

The Present Perfect Progressive

> auxiliary HAVE BEEN + Verb + ING
>
> I, you, we, they **have been** work**ing**
>
> he, she, it **has been** work**ing**

This form of the present perfect can be troublesome for students until they learn two facts. To begin with, there's a simple but effective rule that can be made about the present perfect and present perfect progressive: **Any verb that can be used in the simple present can be used in the present perfect, and any verb that can be used in the present progressive can be used in the present perfect progressive.** If we can say "Fiona lives," we can say "Fiona's lived"; if we can say "Fiona's living," we can say "Fiona's been living."

Don't forget about those stative verbs; some of them can't take the present progressive form, so that goes for the present perfect progressive as well. Since you can't say "Sean's knowing you," you can't say "Sean's been knowing you" either. It's as simple as that!

Now take a look at the following sets of sentences and see if you perceive a difference in meaning between them:

1a. Pat's worked here for three years.
1b. Pat's been working here for three years.
   ☐ a difference   ☐ no difference

2a. We've traveled in Southeast Asia.
2b. We've been traveling in Southeast Asia.
   ☐ a difference   ☐ no difference

There's really no important difference in meaning between 1a and 1b. Native speakers will use them interchangeably. **There is a difference in meaning, however, between 2a and 2b.**

These examples bring us to the second fact. In 1a and 1b, because of the nature of an action like "work," we can change the focus of our time frame and think about Pat as a permanent employee by saying "Pat works here," but we can also think about her present employment by saying "Pat's working here."

The focus of both of these forms deals with work, so we can do the same thing with the perfect forms ("Pat's worked here"/"Pat's been working here") and there's no big difference noted.

In 2a and 2b, we perceive that there's a big difference because of the kind of activity involved. In 2a, there was either one or more completed trips, so we're using present perfect to communicate that they're trips in the past and there may be a future trip as well. In 2b, we're talking about one uninterrupted trip that began at some point in the past and is still going on at this moment. In this case, the present perfect progressive is used **for an action that began in the past and is continuing up to this moment**, and not for an action that was completed in the past but may occur again.

Verbs such as *work*, *live*, and *study* usually carry equivalent meanings in the present perfect and present perfect progressive because of their long-term or permanent nature, whereas verbs like travel, consult, and share don't because of their short-term or temporary nature.

🌰 The Present Perfect Progressive in a Nutshell

🌰 uninterrupted actions from the past to an indefinite time in the general present; these actions may continue into the future:
They've been raising horses ever since they bought that farm.

past ——————— general present ——————— future

A Note about the Words "Since," "For," and "In"

When the perfect forms of the verbs are taught, the first words that always seem to accompany them are *since* and *for*, but few people ever consider *in*. First, let's look at some sentences containing *since* and *for*. Study these examples and determine what common elements can be found in each group of sentences and, therefore, what rules are in play to govern using *since* or *for*.

1. He's been a teacher for a long time.
   He's been a teacher for twenty-six years.
   He's been a teacher at this school for three terms.
   He's been a teacher here for just a couple of months.
   He's been a teacher here for only a little while.
2. He's been a teacher since he graduated from college.
   He's been a teacher since 1962.
   He's been a teacher since he moved to this city.
   He's been a teacher since the late '90's.

Have you figured it all out? Here's what's happening: phrases like *a long time*, *twenty-six years*, and *a little while* all deal with **a quantity of time. The rule is use *for* after the perfect forms of the verbs if you're going to talk about a quantity of time; use *since* to tell when an activity began.** (Note: "1962" is considered the name of a year, not a quantity.)

So what about *in*? Let's look at some sentences. Use both *in* and *for* in the blanks wherever possible.

1. I haven't heard from them .... weeks.
2. She hasn't been to work .... three days.
3. They've worked on the project .... hours and hours.
4. He hasn't seen us .... a long time.
5. We've been here .... what seems like an eternity.

Have you figured out what's going on? **In Sentences 1, 2, and 4, you should have written both *for* and *in*.** In Sentences 3 and 5, you should only have written *for*. The reason is that **if the present perfect or present perfect progressive is affirmative, you can only use *for*. If they're negative, both *for* and *in* are interchangeable.**

But what about this sentence? "Emily's gotten three promotions in the past five years." Here's a sentence that's affirmative, but we can use *in*. In fact, it would be ungrammatical to use *for*! What's going on now? We obviously have to revise our rule. How would you revise it?

....
....

The reason we use *in* in this last example is that we're dealing with separate actions completed in the past that may occur again. In our sentence, *in* really means "at some time during" or "within this time frame." In other words, Emily has gotten three promotions at some time during the past five-year period, and *in* can never mean "from five years ago to now." So our revised rule must be **if the present perfect or present perfect progressive is affirmative and an uninterrupted action, you can only use *for*. If negative or separate, completed actions, both *for* and *in* are interchangeable.** Here are a few more examples for you to look at just to make this clearer:

1. He's lived here for seven months.
    (affirmative, uninterrupted action; can only use *for*)

2. He hasn't lived here for/in seven months.
   (negative, uninterrupted action; can use *for* or *in*)
3. They've tried to quit smoking three times in two years.
   (affirmative, separate, completed actions; can only use *in*)

Note that the progressive form can't be used with *in*. Just take a look at these examples:

They've been buying a new car twice in the past five months.
The bank has been opening five new branches in six months.

Why do you think it is that the present perfect doesn't work with *in*? Write down your thoughts on the following lines:

....
....

The reason these two sentences are ungrammatical is that **the meaning of the verb form is contradicting the meaning of the sentences.** The progressive form means that the action or event is continuous, i.e., without stopping, and that goes against when we can use *in*, which can only be used in affirmative sentences with completed events.

Before we move on, there's something curious I'd like you to look at. Let's go back to one of the versions of Sentence 2 on the previous page: "He hasn't lived here for seven months." Whereas Sentences 1 and 3 only have one interpretation each, Sentence 2, using the preposition *for*, has two interpretations, depending on the context in which the sentence would normally be found in a conversation. Can you figure out the two interpretations? Write them down on the following lines:

....
....

I hope you smiled a little when you realized what the two interpretations are. On one hand, the sentence can mean simply that **he moved out seven months ago and hasn't lived here since**; on the other hand, the sentence can be a rebuttal of sorts, correcting what somebody else has just said about how long he hasn't lived here:

> A: He's lived here for seven months, I think.
> B: He hasn't lived here for seven months.

Some Other Companion Words with the Present Perfect

Traditionally, the present perfect has been the verb form to use when the following words or phrases are employed: *already, yet, lately, so far,* and *up to now*. Here are some examples:

We've already seen that movie. / We've seen that movie already.
We haven't seen that movie yet.
We've seen some very good movies lately.
We've seen two movies so far this month.
Streaming videos haven't put movie theaters out of business up to now.

It just seems to be the case that when these words or phrases are employed, the present perfect is the verb form to use. Notice, however, that we said "traditionally" the present perfect is used with all of these words. In modern, colloquial speech, it's very common to hear the simple past used with several of these expressions:

We already saw that movie. / We saw that movie already.
We didn't see that movie yet.
We saw two movies so far this month.

True, most educated speakers of English tend to feel that using the present perfect with all of these words is "better English," but this use, nonetheless, is a matter of style nowadays, not hard and fast grammar.

Teaching Tips

3.1 *Miming the Progressives*

Write up brief situations that use the present progressive on slips of paper (e.g., you're a dentist checking the teeth of one of your patients; you're frying an egg; you're waiting for a bus to come; you're trying to cross a busy road, etc.). You need at least one slip for each student in your class. The students mime their activities individually while their classmates guess what's happening.

Variation: Provide activities that are much more complicated (tying your shoes while answering the phone; feeding a baby while trying to type a term paper; putting on makeup while eating breakfast, etc.). Again, students mime the actions while their classmates figure out what's happening. Make sure your students are aware that they must prepare their pantomimes precisely in order for their classmates to be able to understand them.

3.2 *The Fashion Show*

For more advanced students and those who know the vocabulary of clothing, colors, and patterns, this is an ideal activity for practicing the present progressive. Present a fashion show, complete with walking across a mock stage, pirouetting, indicating the important features of the garments, etc., just as a real model might do. Before the show begins, divide the class into small groups. Each group will prepare commentaries that will be used to describe the clothes of the various models in their groups. The commentaries need to focus on the actual items the students are wearing and the colors and patterns of the various garments. The show begins! Students model their clothes and their group members give a running commentary on the clothes that the models are wearing.

Here's an example of what the running commentary could be: "Our first model who is sauntering down the runway is Kenji. He's wearing a stylish outfit for the fall with his checkered, flannel shirt and corduroy pants that come from L.L. Bean, not to mention a warm quilted jacket that zips up the front, which is retailing at Macy's for 25% off this week."

3.3 *Narrating Skits*

An excellent way to practice the simple present is by having students narrate skits. An added benefit of the activity is that you can recycle other grammar points. This skit recycles imperatives (commands) and possessive forms.

1. Before class, write up two or three skits using commands that, when acted out and narrated, tell a story. For this example, you have a narrator and two actors. One actor leaves the room with these commands: a) Open the door. b) Look around the room. c) Spot a friend. d) Smile at him/her. e) Enter the room. f) Take your seat.
2. Give the second actor these directions: g) Return your friend's smile. h) Wave at him/her.
3. Give the narrator all the commands in proper order and some concluding remarks:"It's 10:00 a.m. What happens then?"
4. The skit begins! While the actors are acting out their commands, the narrator describes what's going on using the simple present."Kenji opens the classroom door and looks around. He spots his friend and smiles at her. She returns his smile and waves at him. He enters the room and takes his seat. It's 10:00 a.m. The bell rings and class begins."
5. Have the students produce their own skits in small groups.

    Variations:
    1. Record bits of TV programs and play them with the sound turned down. Select programs that have action suitable for narration. But be careful; if there's too much action, students can't narrate the story fast enough. If there's too little, then there's nothing much to tell. Have them prepare the narration to be presented along with the recorded TV bits.
    2. Record a series of sound effects that have potential story lines (knocking on doors, machines running, footsteps, screams, etc.). Have students write up

narratives that describe the action as it's happening to go along with the sound effects.

3. This is the perfect opportunity for students to use the video cameras in their phones. Let your students prepare skits with accompanying narration and then record them for presentation to the entire class. Quiz the class orally about the skits after viewing them.

3.4 *Likes and Dislikes*

Put a grid on the board similar to the one that follows. Use items that your students may either like or dislike. Have students go up and check the choices that are true for them and then discuss what they've checked off. Be sure that the students use the simple present.

	Ice Cream	Poetry	Movies	Flowers	Tennis	Ballet
Rubina	✓		✓		✓	
Shaheen	✓	✓		✓		✓
Farideh	✓		✓	✓		

Variation: Students copy a blank grid on a piece of paper and go around the room filling in the information about their classmates. They then give a report about what they've found out.

3.5 *Travel Guides*

Show students symbols from travel guides or websites. Have the students write up a description of the information they've got using the simple present.

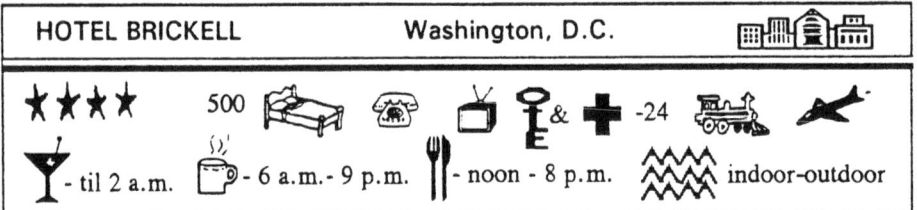

Here's a sample hotel description. I've put the symbols in parentheses to show you how they might be interpreted. Hotel Brickell is a 4-star hotel (★★★★) in downtown (🏢) Washington, D.C. The hotel has 500 beds (🛏) and a telephone (☎) and TV (📺) in each room. The hotel has a concierge (🔑) and medical personnel (✚) available 24 hours a day . . .

3.6 *What Is It?*

Before class, write up a list of animals, professions, or things for students to describe using the simple present. If your students have research skills, give them topics that they don't know much about or that they don't know at all (planets, famous people, etc.). Example: Horse: it runs fast; it has a mane; it loves apples; it often lives in a barn. Farmer: he grows crops; he plants seeds; he milks cows.

3.7 *Proverbs*

If you choose to recycle this grammar with an intermediate or advanced group, bring in some examples of proverbs: *A stitch in time saves nine*; *Familiarity breeds contempt*; *Absence makes the heart grow fonder*, etc. Discuss the meaning of those that the students aren't familiar with and then have them provide examples from their own languages. Stress the fact that you want only those proverbs that contain the simple present.

3.8 *Body Spelling*

The present perfect provides an additional problem for students—the past participles, especially those for the irregular verbs. It's fun to practice these forms by doing "Body Spelling." Prepare a list of irregular verbs before class begins. Divide the class into groups of seven to eight. You may need to make the groups larger if the verbs that you're using have more than eight letters (such as *forgotten, understood*). And if you have verbs that have fewer letters than the groups have members, two or more students can "become" one letter. Distribute several verbs to each group. The students then have to spell the past participles using their bodies as the letters and their classmates have to figure out what they're spelling. Body Spelling is an enjoyable way to practice present participles, too.

3.9 *Analyzing the News*

Because the present perfect is a difficult verb form for most students, it may be helpful for them to be able to analyze how native English speakers use the various forms in actual speech. This activity gets them thinking about these difficulties. Record bits of TV or radio news reports before class. Or, if you prefer, collect items from newspapers or magazines. Note instances of the present perfect. Present the video or clippings to the students and have them write down some examples of the present perfect forms that they hear or find. Have them analyze why present perfect was used.

Variation: After the students have done their initial analyses, have them write their own news stories, record them, and then play them for the entire class. Even if a tape recorder or video recorder isn't available, the students can still present their stories to the class.

4

The Pasts

"What's done is done."

The Simple Past

A: I call**ed** you on the phone, like a hundred times last night!

B: Sorry. I **left** my phone at home.

A: I figur**ed**.

B: So, why all the calls?

A: I **made** those calls to try out my brand new cell phone. My wife **bought** it for me.

B: You tri**ed** somebody else then, **did**n't you?

A: No. The battery **went** dead after all those calls to you.

First Meaning

The parts in bold in this dialogue show us that the time is in the past, the simple past. It's called the "simple" past because we have a verb form that's relatively uncomplicated to make and use.

There are three meanings implied by using the simple past. The first one is shown in the dialogue above with examples of regular verbs (*called/ figured/ tried*) and irregular verbs (*left/ made/ bought/ did/ went*). What simple description for this meaning can you come up with? Think about the verbs in the dialogue and then write down how you'd define the simple past on the line below:

....

What we see in the dialogue are examples of **actions that happened before now and a state of being that existed before now, and both are finished**; this is our first meaning of the simple past. Keep in mind that the verbs in the simple past in the dialogue have no connection with the present and are like a closed door. Compare this concept to the discussion we had in Chapter 3 about how verbs in the present perfect can keep that door open.

 Heads Up!

Students always have a hard time dealing with the pronunciation of the regular verbs in the simple past form with the suffix -*ed* or -*d*. Here are the three phonological rules that you can teach them:

→ If the verb ends in a voiced consonant sound* except for /d/ (b, g, j, l, m, n, ŋ, r, v, z, ð) or in a vowel sound, the -*ed* suffix is simply pronounced /d/:

/rab/ ⟶ /rabd/,   /pil/ ⟶ /pild/,   /sno/ ⟶ /snod/

→ If the verb ends in a voiceless consonant sound except for /t/ (f, k, p, š, č, s), the -*ed* suffix is simply pronounced /t/:

/pik/ ⟶ /pikt/,   /hæč/ ⟶ /hæčt/

→ If the verb ends in /d/ or /t/, the -*ed* suffix is pronounced /ɪd/ or /ɛd/:

/bred/ ⟶ /bred-ɪd/,   /ri-spɛkt/ ⟶ /ri-spɛkt-ɪd/

*Note: We're talking about sounds, not letters. Be careful that your students don't only look at the final letter of the verb; they have to think about the final sound.

Second Meaning

There's another meaning for the simple past in the opening dialogue that isn't so apparent. Maybe you can figure it out by looking at this next example. Compare the alternative responses that Person B could say at the end of the dialogue and see if you perceive a difference.

> A: I hear you **had** some excitement outside your house last night.
>
> B: I'll say! I **got** into a fight with my neighbor.
>
> A: Why? What **happened**?
>
> B: He **hit** his dog. / He **was hitting** his dog. I really hate that.

Ask yourself which one of Person B's options would make it clearer as to why he got into that fight. When you've answered that question, you'll probably have figured out what the difference between the two verb forms is. Write your conclusions on the following lines:

It turns out that Person B is saying "He was hitting his dog" seems to explain more clearly why the fight took place; with the response "He hit his dog," it just doesn't seem as much of a justification for a fight between neighbors. Why is this so? It's because Person B's response in the simple past (*hit*) leaves us with the impression that he only hit the dog *once* if no further information is supplied; the verb form *was hitting* makes us think that he did this many times—but more about that later on in this chapter.

So here we have the second meaning for the simple past that isn't so apparent: **the simple past can mean that the action happened only one time.**

Don't think I've forgotten about that third meaning for the simple past. I'm going to put it on hold for a little while.

The Simple Past in a Nutshell

- actions finished in the past (without further context, implying one time only):

  I called you like a hundred times last night!

  I sent the letter.

The Past Progressive

> auxiliary BE + VERB + ING
>
> I, he, she, it **was** work**ing**
>
> we, you, they **were** work**ing**

First Meaning

I'm going to talk about three meanings that the past progressive connotes, but to start off our investigation into this form, let's look at the following dialogue.

4 The Pasts

A: What **were** you do**ing**?

B: Doing? When?

A: Last night around 11.

B: Oh! I **was rummaging** through the trash cans outside my house.

A: I know that! But why?

B: I **was looking** for my watch. My little boy thought the trash can was a big jewelry box!

All the verbs in bold are in the past progressive. There's something very subtle, but very useful, that this form is imparting to the verbs, and there's a good reason that the speakers have chosen this form over any other.

All the actions in bold have really been caught at the moment they were happening. Let's see how you perceive this form as it appears in the dialogue. Read the following statements about the verbs from this dialogue and check the boxes in front of the statements that you agree with.

☐ 1. The verbs in bold tell us when they began.
☐ 2. The verbs don't tell us when they began.
☐ 3. The verbs tell us when they ended.
☐ 4. They don't tell us when they ended.
☐ 5. These actions are finished.
☐ 6. These actions were in progress.

Because of the way these verbs appear in the context of the dialogue, the boxes to check are **2**, **4**, and **6**, and this conclusion leads us to our first observation about this verb form: **We use the past progressive when the actions were in progress and there's no focus on any definite beginning or end.** It's the activity in progress that counts, nothing else.

Second Meaning

Now let's look at a conversation between a police officer and a motorist.

A: I **wasn't doing** anything, Officer!

B: You **were speeding**.

A: It's just that I **was hurrying** to City Hall.

B: And why **were** you **rushing** there?

A: To pay some overdue speeding tickets.

The easiest way to begin examining this verb form as it appears in this conversation is to ask the question: If we change the verbs in bold to the simple past, will the conversation work?

>"I didn't do anything, Officer!"
>"You sped."
>"It's just that I hurried to City Hall."
>"And why did you rush there?"
>"To pay some overdue speeding tickets."

It doesn't completely work, you say? You're right, it doesn't. But why not? What difference is there between using the past progressive in the dialogue and using the simple past? Take a few moments to compare each verb as it appears in both versions of the dialogue. Decide whether they're grammatical in this context and then write down any thoughts you may have about why one form works and the other doesn't, if you've found that to be the case.

(wasn't doing) ....

(didn't do) ....

(were speeding) ....

(sped) ....

(was hurrying) ....

(hurried) ....

The most important reason that the **past progressive** seems to work better for most of these verbs is that there are **implied, but unspoken, ideas** in each utterance. For example, when the motorist says "I wasn't doing anything," the unspoken idea might be ". . . when you pulled me over." Can you supply other implied ideas for the following lines from the dialogue?

1. "You were speeding ...."

2. "I was hurrying to City Hall ...."

Here are some possibilities for filling in the implied idea for **Sentence 1**: ... when I stopped you / . . . when I spotted you / . . . when I pulled you over.

Some options for **Sentence 2** are these:... when you made me stop / . . . when you caught me / . . . when you pulled me over.

Let's digress just for a moment and talk about the meaning of a couple of the sentences in this dialogue when the simple past is used. How about the lines "You sped" and ". . . I hurried to City Hall"? Why do you think we're uncomfortable with the simple past in these sentences in the context of this dialogue? Can you figure out the reason?

If you recall what I said earlier about the first meaning of the simple past, it was that *the action is completely finished*. Let's test out the two lines I've cited and add implied ideas to see if they work.

"You sped *when I spotted you*."
"It's just that I hurried to City Hall *when you saw me*."

What do these sentences really say now? Check the box that precedes the description you agree with. Both sentences mean that

☐ one action was in progress when the other happened.
☐ the first actions were the results of the second actions.

The truth is that if both verbs in each sentence are in the simple past, we get the feeling that we're dealing with cause and effect. In other words, the motorist only began to speed when the police officer spotted him, and he hurried to City Hall only when the officer saw him, so we should check the **second box**. These verbs in the simple past might work in a different context, but they're not the ideas we're trying to convey in this instance.

To compound the confusion, if the motorist says that he . . . *hurried to City Hall*, it gives us the impression that he'd already reached City Hall before he spoke to the police officer, so how could he be sitting out there on the side of the road talking to him? There's no logic in this situation.

The all-important reason for using the past progressive with these verbs is to show that the actions were *not* finished **and that they were interrupted by some other actions.** That's why these two sentences won't work in the simple past. You may have heard this verb form referred to as the "past continuous," but I prefer to call it the "past progressive" to reinforce the idea that the action was still *in progress*.

Let's go over some basic points about the past progressive before we go on to anything else. Look at the following sentences and focus on the underlined verb forms. Write **G** in the space provided if the verb is grammatical or **U** if it's ungrammatical.

1. A: What were you doing when I called you last night? ....
   B: I slept. ....

2. A: What did you do when the fire alarm went off? ....
   B: I was leading my frightened students out of the building. ....

3. A: I was hearing that you were sick last week. ....
   B: I was having a terrible cold. ....

4. A: That boy's a brat. He yanked that little girl's hair. ....
   B: It's awful that he was yanking her hair! ....

Let's check your perceptions of these verb forms in the context we've put them: **1A** is G but **1B** is U; **2A** is G but **2B** is U; **3A** and **3B** are both U; **4A** is G, but **4B** is U.

Sentence 1B is ungrammatical. Remember that the past progressive is used to show that the action was in progress and was interrupted. The simple past doesn't communicate that the speaker was already in the midst of sleeping at the moment that the phone rang. The sentence should read "I was sleeping."

Sentence 2B is ungrammatical for exactly the opposite reason. It communicates that the speaker was in the midst of leading his frightened students out of the building, but he wouldn't have been doing so before the alarm went off. The sentence should be "I led my frightened students out of the building." Using the simple past here shows cause and effect, which is logical in this case, and it also shows that the action was completed.

Sentence 3A is ungrammatical because *hear* is one of those sensory stative verbs I talked about in Chapter 3 that normally doesn't take the progressive form. The sentence should read "I heard that you were sick last week."

Sentence 3B is ungrammatical for a similar reason; when referring to illness, the verb *have* is only used in the simple form, so the sentence should be "I had a terrible cold."

Sentence 4B is ungrammatical in the context of this dialogue. "He yanked that girl's hair" suggests that he did it one time. "He was yanking that girl's hair" suggests many times and, if the second speaker is reiterating what the first speaker said, he'll be doing so inaccurately if he uses the past progressive.

Third Meaning

What's the third meaning of the past progressive, and what third meaning can we find for the simple past (remember I put off talking about this matter earlier in the chapter)?

To find the answers, let's take another look at Sentence 1A:

What were you doing when I called you last night?

We have two actions, both in the past, but there's an important difference between them. As we've previously seen, *do* (the first verb, which is in the past progressive) deals with an activity that was already happening when the other action occurred. The action *call* (the second verb, which is in the simple past) interrupts or cuts into the first action and takes but a few seconds. So, with this comparison in mind, what can we say about the length of time for the simple past and the past progressive? Check the box for the statement which best describes the verbs in our example:

☐ Both verbs lasted the same amount of time.

☐ The first verb (*do*) was of longer duration than the second verb (*call*).

☐ The first verb (*do*) was of shorter duration than the second verb (*call*).

This is the basic rule to show you if you've checked off the right box: **When two actions occur at the same time in the past, but one action is longer than the other, the longer action is put in the past progressive and the shorter action (which seems to cut into the other) is put in the simple past.** So, you should have checked off the second box.

Here are a few more examples to demonstrate this point:

1. We <u>were playing</u> soccer when it <u>started</u> to pour.
   (longer action)   (shorter action)

2. I <u>dozed off</u> while my aunt was <u>singing</u> some folk songs.
   (shorter action)   (longer action)

Here's an interesting question: Of the two actions in the past, what if one weren't significantly longer than the other? Look at the following examples and see for yourself. Only one of these four sentences is ungrammatical. Can you find which one it is and then explain why it doesn't work?

1. While I <u>was preparing</u> the salad, my son <u>was setting</u> the table.
2. While I <u>prepared</u> the salad, my son <u>set</u> the table.
3. When the car <u>backfired</u>, I <u>jumped</u> out of my seat.
4. When the car <u>was backfiring</u>, I <u>was jumping</u> out of my seat.

Sentence .... is ungrammatical because ....

....

Sentences 1 and 2 are really quite interesting. They use different verb forms and yet both seem grammatical. The reason is that **when the two actions are relatively long (i.e., not just momentary) and of more or less the same duration, they can both be placed in the same verb form**, and in the case of these two sentences, it doesn't much matter if they're both in the past progressive or simple past; they still communicate that the two people began their tasks more or less at the same time and completed those tasks also at about the same time.

Well, if those two sentences are grammatical, that only leaves us with Sentence 3 or 4 to be the ungrammatical one. The answer is that **Sentence 4 is ungrammatical**. Reason? It goes back to the concept I mentioned before about the simple past representing short actions. How long does it take for a car to backfire? How long does it take to jump out of one's seat? The answer to both questions is "no time at all," or shall we say, less than a second. If we try to use the **past progressive** for this kind of action, it **seems odd because we're using a form that normally represents long duration for two actions having almost no duration at all**. So the correct sentence should be "When the car backfired, I jumped out of my seat."

🌰 The Past Progressive in a Nutshell

- actions that are unfinished, in progress in the past, which don't focus on any beginning or end:

    Pardon me, but I wasn't talking to you.

    past ─────── right now ─────── future

- when two actions are at the same time in the past, but one action is longer than the other:

    She caught up on her correspondence while she was recuperating.

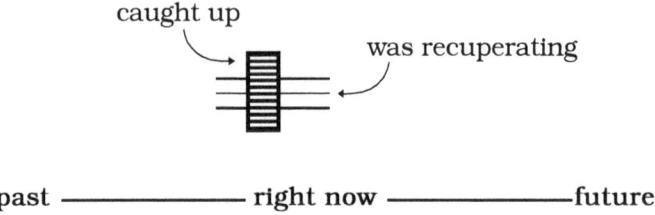

    past ─────── right now ─────── future

A Special Note About the Words "When" and "While"

In most standard grammar books, the following sort of statement is made about how to use *when* and *while*:

> Use *when* with the clause in the simple past.
> Use *while* with the clause in the past progressive.

So according to this rule, we should always say:

"When he lived in London . . . " and "While he was driving to work . . . "

That's all well and good, but it really doesn't completely reflect the way native speakers use these words. It should be mentioned here that there seems to be a great deal of overlap between the two words, and you could very likely hear people say

"While I lived in London . . . " or "When I was driving to work . . . "

What, then, accounts for this switch-over? Look at the following and check off the boxes for those sentences which you feel are *ungrammatical*. Leave the verbs alone; they're fine just the way they are. Focus on *when* and *while* and consider whether they both work in the sentences. Then see if you can figure out why some of these sentences don't work, but the others do.

☐ 1a. While he fell, he hurt his knee.
☐ 1b. When he fell, he hurt his knee.
☐ 2a. When I was watching TV, I fell asleep.
☐ 2b. While I was watching TV, I fell asleep.
☐ 3a. While she left the house, she forgot to lock the door.
☐ 3b. When she left the house, she forgot to lock the door.
☐ 4a. While the dog was napping, the cat stole his bone.
☐ 4b. When the dog was napping, the cat stole his bone.

First, let's see which boxes are ungrammatical. You should only have checked off **1a** and **3a**. Now take a moment to think about why only those two sentences don't work (considering the use of *while* and *when*) and write your conclusion on the line that follows:

....

The reason those two sentences don't work with *while* is that the verbs following are not of long enough duration to warrant the use of this word. Remember that ***while* is normally used with verbs of relatively long duration**, and we're fairly consistent about when it is or isn't appropriate to use.

So now we have to find a reason that explains why *when* works in the rest of those sentences. It's simply that *when* is more loosely rule-governed than *while*. In prescriptive grammar books, the student is led to believe that *when* should be as strictly regulated as *while*, but that's misleading. The truth is that **native English speakers don't consider it a cardinal sin to use *when* in place of *while*.**

The Past Perfect

> I, you, he, she, it, we, they **had** work**ed**

Here are some sentences for you to examine. If they're grammatical, write **G** on the line following each one; if they're ungrammatical, write **U** on the line after each one.

When I met Carlos, he lived next door for only a short time. ....

The company went bankrupt because they didn't show a profit for over two years. ....

Mintsu admitted that she didn't like cooking very much. ....

As I reached the corner, the light turned red. ....

Tom couldn't write because he broke his thumb. ....

The sentences are as follows: 1 is U; 2 is U; 3 is G; 4 is G; 5 is U. If we correct the three ungrammatical sentences, this is how they should look:

1. When I met Carlos, he <u>had lived</u> next door for only a short time.
2. The company went bankrupt because they <u>hadn't shown</u> a profit for over two years.
3. Tom couldn't write because he <u>had broken</u> his thumb.

Why should we use the past perfect in these three sentences and not the other two? What difference in time do you perceive between the two verbs used in Sentences 1, 2, and 5 and in Sentences 3 and 4? Take a moment and write down your impressions on the following lines:

In Sentences 1, 2, and 5 ....

....

However, in Sentences 3 and 4 ....

....

Notice that **Sentences 3 and 4** have both verbs in the simple past (*admitted/ didn't like; reached/turned*). That's because the two verbs in each sentence take place during the same period in the past. In Sentence 3, when Mintsu made the admission, her feelings about cooking were concurrent. In Sentence 4, both actions happened at approximately the same moment. It makes sense grammatically **that both verbs in each sentence should be placed in the same form to show that they were basically concurrent.**

On the other hand, **Sentences 1, 2, and 5** have verbs that didn't take place at the same time in the past, and that's the reason we should use the past perfect. **If two or more verbs in the past didn't happen at more or less the same time, you need the past perfect for one of them.**

But now the question arises, which verb should be in the past perfect? What would you say? Look back at those sentences and write down your answer to the question.

We should use the past perfect ....

....

In Sentence 1, Carlos moved in next door first and the speaker met him some time later. In Sentence 2, profits didn't exist for the company for two years prior to their declaring bankruptcy. In Sentence 5, Tom first did the damage to his thumb and, as a result of the mishap, he couldn't write. We can clearly see that the two verbs in each of these sentences can't be put into the same period of time. Now we can answer the question about which verb should be in the past perfect: **When two or more verbs are in the past, but they didn't happen at the same time, the verb that happened <u>first</u> is put in the past perfect.**

But does this sequence always indicate the case? Do we have a hard-and-fast rule to go by? Not necessarily. There are many cases in which the past perfect is avoidable, especially in informal or conversational speech. One example occurs when we use time words that clearly set up the chronology for us so that there's no confusion over the sequence of events. Look at the following sentences which demonstrate this:

1. <u>Before</u> he got home, he stopped at a grocery store to buy some bread.
2. I lay down on the couch to take a nap <u>after</u> I had lunch.
3. <u>As soon as</u> they reached the beach, they dived into the water.

As you can see, there's no confusion about the chronological order of the actions in these three sentences. Conservative speakers would say that the past perfect should still be used in these sentences, but in informal or conversational English, it really isn't necessary. Impress upon your students, however, that in formal usage (especially like that found on tests such as the TOEFL and the Cambridge University Test of English), they should always use the past perfect where appropriate.

 The Past Perfect in a Nutshell

🌰 **for two or more actions happening at different times in the past; use this form for the verb that happened first (further back in the past):**
I hadn't known her age until she told me.

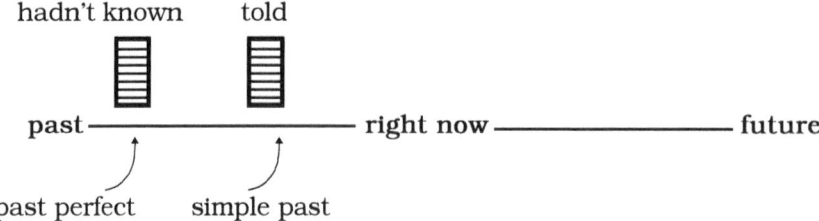

The Past Perfect Progressive

> I, you, he, she, it, we, they **had** been work**ing**

You'll recall that one of the distinctions I made in Chapter 3 between the present perfect and the present perfect progressive was that the present perfect starts in the past and continues to the *general* present rather than to one specific moment (or right now). The progressive form is more *pinpointed* since it comes up to the primary sense of "now."

This same basic principle holds true with the past perfect progressive. Let's see how this works by having you look at some pairs of sentences. Decide whether using the past perfect or past perfect progressive makes any noticeable difference.

1a. He'd worked here for twenty-five years when he retired.

1b. He'd been working here for twenty-five years when he retired.

☐ a difference   ☐ no difference

2a. She told me she'd written some letters.

2b. She told me she'd been writing some letters.

☐ a difference   ☐ no difference

There's really no perceived difference between Sentences 1a and 1b, but there certainly **is a difference between 2a and 2b.** If you recall in Chapter 3, I explained that verbs such as *work*, *live*, and *study* usually carry equivalent meanings in the present perfect and present perfect progressive because of their long-term or permanent nature. It works the same way with the past perfect and past perfect progressive!

Sentence 2a communicates that her letter-writing activities were completed by the time she talked to me. In 2b, we understand that she began the letter writing sometime before she talked to me or that she wasn't finished. It could also mean that my talking to her interrupted her letter writing.

What rule, then, can we come up with to explain the use of the past perfect progressive? Simply put, **with certain types of activities, the past perfect progressive does what its name implies: it shows that the activity was still in progress from some earlier time in the past when another past action happened.**

🌰 The Past Perfect Progressive in a Nutshell

👁 showing that one action began earlier in the past than other actions, but instead of being completely finished before the other actions happened, it overlapped onto them

They said they had been waiting for over an hour (when the train finally arrived).

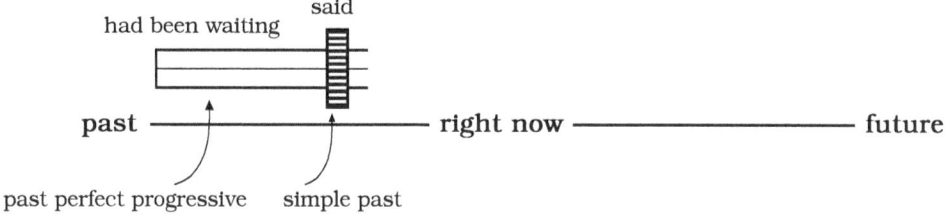

The Expression *Used To*

Read this sentence and interpret what it means to you without any further context offered. Check off the descriptions of this sentence that you agree with.

I got up at 6:00 a.m.

☐ 1. The action is in the past and finished.

☐ 2. The action is in the past, but not finished.

☐ 3. This action happened repeatedly.

☐ 4. This action happened one time only.

☐ 5. I'm not sure how many times the action happened.

What information is given to us in this sentence and how should we go about interpreting it? We know that the simple past has been used, meaning that the action is completely finished, so we should **check the first box**.

What we're uncomfortable with, lacking more context, is whether or not this happened one time or repeatedly. We might assume that it happened only once, but we just don't have enough information to be certain, so we should **check off the fifth box**.

Suppose we want to embellish our idea. How can we get more information into our sentence? The answer is that we can do so very efficiently by adding *used to*, which is often considered a semi-auxiliary or periphrastic modal, after the subject:

I <u>used to</u> get up at 6:00 a.m.

This little phrase adds important extra information to our basic idea. What further information can you interpret from this addition which has two extra pieces of information added to our basic idea? List whatever comes to mind on the following lines:

1. ....

....

2. ....

....

The first additional piece of information is that the action we're discussing **occurred repeatedly over a rather long span of time.** The second extra detail is that **we assume this action isn't so today.** We've now included an implied meaning, just as we did with the past progressive. Here's how the sentence might look if we include the implied idea:

> I used to get up at 6:00 a.m., <u>but I don't anymore</u>.

The negative form of *used to* is quite interesting. We can form the standard negative and say *didn't use to*, but many native speakers tend to use the adverb of frequency *never* and create the negative by saying *never used to*. Remember that we can often assume that the contrary is true for the present, just as it is in the affirmative:

> She never used to like spinach, <u>but now she does</u>.

 Heads Up!

Students almost invariably confuse *used to* with the expression *be used to*. Be aware that this problem will surely arise. Whenever it's appropriate to do so, point out that the grammar involved with these two expressions is quite different:

→ *be used to* needs the verb *be*, and any verb that follows the expression has -ing attached to it:
> They're used to hav*ing* dinner by 7:00 p.m.
> (It's their custom, their habit.)

→ *used to* never has *be*, and the verb after this expression is always in the base form:
> They used to have dinner by 7:00 p.m.
> (They don't anymore.)

🌰 "Used To" in a Nutshell

🖖 **state of being existed or action happened repeatedly over a relatively long span of time in the past with implied idea that the situation isn't so any longer:**
The Sahara Desert used to be a fertile, lush area.

🖖 **something didn't exist or happen before, but now it does:**
There never used to be any holes in the ozone layer.

For information on *used to* vs. *would*, visit us at
ELTgrammar.com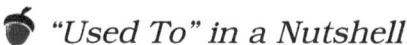

Teaching Tips

4.1 *Family Photos*

Have the students bring photos of themselves or any pictures that mean something to them to class. Bring one yourself. You can start the activity by showing your picture and explaining why the picture is important, why the picture was taken, and what other pertinent information there is about it. Urge the students to ask questions about the pictures, being sure to focus questions, answers, and discussions in the past. Then students can take turns explaining their photos and their stories. For homework, the students can write up short passages of their photos in the past.

4.2 *Who Am I?*

Write the following topic and phrases on the board: Five Years Ago/My Family/My Friends/School/Holidays/My Appearance/My Hobbies and so on. Pair up the students and have them interview one another, writing down the information that they learn about their partners. Brief statements are acceptable (*Family*: lived in Canberra; bought their first home; got a new dog. *Hobbies*: sang with a choir; went swimming almost every weekend; etc.). After the pairs have collected their information, have them give oral reports (or write up reports) based on their classmates' life experiences, using the appropriate past tense forms and *used to*.

4.3 *10,000 BC and 1500 AD*

Have the students brainstorm things that they or others use, have, or do in their daily lives (electrical appliances, transportation, entertainment, clothes). Then tell the students that they're going to consider how their ancestors lived their lives in the years 10,000 BC and 1500 AD. Have the students compare their lives today with those of their ancestors. ("I use a hair dryer to dry my hair, but in 10,000 BC, my ancestors didn't even wash their hair!"/"I wash my clothes in an automatic washing machine, but my ancestors in 1500 used to wash all of theirs by hand."/"In the year 1500, my relatives wouldn't travel more than a few miles away from home because traveling was too dangerous.")

4.4 *Family Trees*

Provide a model of a family tree (it can be an imaginary one, one for a famous person, or even your own). Tell each student to write a letter to an artist asking him/her to draw a family tree for the student's photo album. The letter should include brief details about each family member in order for the artist to draw the tree properly. ("My grandfather was born in 1908. He married my grandmother in 1931. They had six children.") Have the students exchange letters and become the artists. When the artists finish their commissions, tell them to return their work to their clients, who will check the work for accuracy.

4.5 *Intriguing Sounds*

Note: This is a variation of the second variation in 3.3. Record a variety of sounds—cars beeping, a train going by, doors slamming, interesting noises (swoosh, creak, pop, etc.). Make sure you have enough sounds; eight to ten will work well. Divide the students into small groups and have them construct a story about the events that occurred, for example,"on their way home from class," incorporating a variety of the pasts and the sounds into the story line. The students then tell their stories adding in the sound effects at the appropriate moments.

Variation: Have the students record their own sound tracks to accompany a story or skit they'll write and/or act out.

4.6 *Daily Schedules*

Prepare a daily schedule sheet similar to the one that follows. Have the students go around the room and interview several of their classmates about what they did the previous day. After they've gotten enough information, have them give a report about what they've discovered. Make sure they use the various pasts and time words. (While Nur was taking a shower, Hassan was getting up. Carla ate breakfast at 7:00 yesterday, etc.).

Time	Nur	Hassan	Carla	?	?
6:00					
6:30	shower	got up			
7:00			ate		
7:30					
8:00					
8:30					
etc.					

4.7 *Once Upon a Time*

Start out a story "Once upon a time there lived a little girl named Suzanne and her little brother, Kevin. They were very funny children, always telling jokes and doing silly things. One day while they were walking home from school, Suzanne..." Have the students add on bits to the story, letting their imaginations go where they will, but making sure they keep to the story line that's being created. Every once in a while, have a student go back and retell what's gone on up to that point. That reminds the students about what's happened and helps to keep the story line from wandering.

Variation: At the end of each student's contribution, the student suggests a verb that he/she wants incorporated into the next student's bit of story.

4.8 *The Scene of the Crime*

Invent a crime with specific details (time, place, witnesses, etc.). Call on two students to play the suspects. Have them leave the room, inventing an alibi while outside. Tell the suspects that their alibis must be as detailed and specific as possible. While the suspects are planning their alibis, have the rest of the class prepare questions to ask the suspects. Bring the suspects back into the room *one at a time*; this way neither suspect will hear what the other one has said. After the interrogations, poll the students to decide which suspect is guilty.

4.9 *I Had Never Done That Before*!

Ask the students to write down several things that they had never done before they came to North America or before they entered high school or began learning English. The students should begin their sentences with "Before I..., I had..." Collect the answers and have the class arrange their seats in a circle, or in any fashion so that they can all see one another's faces. Tell the students that you're going to read some of their responses and that they should guess who wrote them. Have them write down their guesses and be sure to tell them to keep straight faces when the responses are being read, otherwise they may give themselves away. When you've read all the statements that you've chosen and the students have made their guesses, reread them and ask the students to identify themselves. To find out who the best detective in the class is, see who guessed right the most times.

4.10 *How My Life Has Changed*

Have the students write down examples of how their lives have changed in the past ten or twenty years (brief descriptions are okay). Then have them give reports on those changes, using *used to* where appropriate.

5

The Futures

"Qué será, será..."

> A: **Are** you **taking** Jacques to the airport tomorrow?
>
> B: Yes, I **am**. His flight **leaves** at 6:15.
>
> A: **Will** you **have** enough time to get there after work?
>
> B: I'**m taking** off early so I **won't have to** rush.
>
> A: **Are** you **going to** call him so he knows what time to be ready?
>
> B: Yes. In fact, I'**m about to** call him now.
>
> A: The traffic's awful at that time of day.
>
> B: Don't worry. By the time I meet you for dinner tomorrow evening, I'**ll have dropped** Jacques off at the airport and he'**ll be flying** somewhere over the Atlantic!

How many ways are there to express the future in English? There are lots of them! Actually, you've just gone over most of them in the dialogue above. Let's see what kind of sleuth you are by having you identify as many of them as you can. Try to explain why they're being used in their particular sentences. (Here's a hint: There are seven different forms of the future that you need to come up with.)

1. ....
2. ....
3. ....
4. ....
5. ....
6. ....
7. ....

No doubt you recognized certain verb forms that we've already discussed at length in previous chapters, but there are some forms that appear here for the first time. Let's get into the forms that we've already dealt with in other contexts and then proceed to the new ones.

The Present Progressive

"<u>Are</u> you <u>taking</u> Jacques to the airport tomorrow?"

This sentence has one of the most commonly used forms **to express the future in current spoken English**, yet it's rarely introduced early on in most ELT grammar books as a way to express the future . . . and it should be!

The reason that the speaker's asking this question in the present progressive is that he's referring to **a planned event in the near future**. We can also think of it as **something in the future that is being anticipated in the present**.

While we're on the subject of planned events in the near future, I should mention an alternative form that can mean the same thing, and it's the expression *be going to*, which I'll discuss shortly.

The Simple Present

"His flight <u>leaves</u> at 6:15."

It may seem strange, when you stop to think about it, that the verb form which normally represents routines should also be used to represent the future.

The question is why the speaker would choose this verb form for something in the future. What nuance is communicated this way that isn't made if other future forms are used? The answer is that **we use the simple present to represent <u>formalized</u>, <u>scheduled</u> future events**. In this case, it's not that Jacques' flight will leave tomorrow at 6:15 and never do so again. The airlines schedule certain flights to leave at predetermined times, and even though we're referring to Jacques' flight, which is still in the future, we're also communicating that it's a scheduled flight, not just a unique event that will happen one time only in the future and never be repeated. This is the reason the speaker has chosen the simple present. Notice the neat connection to that basic concept of the simple present: routines. Note also that without the time expression (*at 6:15*), the present tense cannot have a future meaning.

The Future with *Be Going To*

"Are you going to call him . . . ?"

The expression *be going to* has two basic uses. Our dialogue features one use, namely, **future plans** or **intentions**. In this case, instead of asking "Are you taking Jacques to the airport tomorrow?" the speaker could just as easily have asked, "<u>Are</u> you <u>going to</u> take Jacques to the airport tomorrow?" Both the present progressive and *be going to* mean the same thing here, but in other situations they're not interchangeable. I'll get back to this point and discuss *be going to* more in depth a little later.

What, then, is the other use of this expression? Look at this sentence and see if you can figure it out:

A worldwide oil shortage is going to be a very big problem for future generations.

Be going to is used for ....

If you've written **a prediction**, you've got it right.

We've now covered the two basic uses of *be going to*, but we should really discuss another category which falls into the realm of both an intention and a prediction, namely, a **threat**. Just look at these lines:

> If you don't stop acting like that, you're going to be sorry!
> You'd better not come in late anymore. You're going to get fired.

A Note on Pronunciation

Many teachers fail to teach the typical pronunciation of *be going to* and inadvertently have their students practice sentences with this expression in its utterly pristine state without taking into account how native speakers normally say it.

 Although formal speech still dictates that we pronounce each word in the expression separately and clearly, "I'm going to"/ aɪm go-ɪŋ tu/, the acceptable variation in conversational English is /aɪm/ or /am gənə/ or /gɔnə/, that is, the words *going to* are pronounced as if they were written "gunnuh" or "gawnuh"—and there's nothing wrong with it!

 **Heads Up!**

Keep in mind that there's a distinct difference in the pronunciation of *going to* in the future expression *be going to* and in the case of the common verb *go* in its progressive form.

→ Most native speakers of American English tend to say /gənə/ ("gunnuh") or /gɔnə/ ("gaw-nuh") in the expression *be going to* in such sentences as *She's going to quit her job*.

→ Most native speakers tend to say /gó-ɪn-tə/ or a variation of this pronunciation when they say such sentences as *He's going to the grocery store*.

The Simple Future (*Will*)

"<u>Will</u> you have enough time to get there after work?"

Why has the speaker chosen to use *will* in this question rather than some alternative form? In this case, *will* represents what is referred to as the **pure future** or **simple future**. This doesn't mean that you couldn't hear someone say, "<u>Are</u> you <u>going to</u> have enough time to get there after work?" That's a possible form, too. We could be thinking of a planned future event or even a prediction in either case.

The "pure future" concept of *will* can also deal with future **predictions**. In our introductory dialogue, one of the speakers says, "I<u>'m taking</u> off (from work) early so I <u>won't</u> have to rush." Why do you think he switches from the present progressive in the first verb to *will* with the second?

He's using the present progressive in the first verb because ....

....

He's using will with the second verb because ....

....

The speaker has chosen the present progressive for the first verb because it communicates that this is his plan of action for the future. He's used *will* with the second verb to show that he's making a prediction.

Another example of using *will* to make a prediction can be found in a sentence like this one:

My car isn't working. When I turn the ignition key, it won't start.

Are we finished with *will*? Not by a long shot! There are more cases in which *will* has various nuances. Take a look at the following examples and see if you can categorize the way that *will* is used in each situation.

1. I'll call you tonight.   ....
2. Will you give me a hand?   ....
3. You'll be sorry you did that!   ....
4. He'll often forget the time.   ....

In the first three examples, it's clear that we're referring to things in the future even though there are differences in usage. In **Sentence 1**, the person is making **a promise**; in **Sentence 2**, someone's making **a request**; in **Sentence 3**, someone's making **a threat**.

In **Sentence 4**, however, something very different is happening. In this case, *will* doesn't carry future meaning at all; it's used here to mean what is **apt to happen** or to show **a tendency** for something to happen on a regular basis. Another example of this unusual use is in the saying "Boys will be boys," which parents might say after their sons have gotten into some sort of mischief, played too roughly, or gotten too dirty.

There's no doubt that *will* can be a very tricky word. In many ways, it's unfortunate that the word is taught exclusively as a form of the future in most ELT grammar books. What happens is that the students latch on to this word and think it can be applied to every situation in the future—and how wrong that assumption is!

Will is used less frequently in conversational language and more in academic or formal written forms to express the future.

Moreover, the simple fact is that forms like the present progressive, *be going to*, and *will* are sometimes interchangeable, but at other times, they aren't. Look at the following sets of sentences. Compare the sentences in each set and check off if you're comfortable that *all three are interchangeable* or if you're not so comfortable with that prospect.

1. They're meeting us at 3 o'clock.
   They're going to meet us at 3 o'clock.
   They'll meet us at 3 o'clock.
   ☐ comfortable   ☐ not comfortable

2. A: Any plans for today?
   B: I'm going to the beach.
      I'm going to go to the beach.
      I will go to the beach.
   ☐ comfortable   ☐ not comfortable

3. It's raining later tonight.
   It's going to rain later tonight.
   It will rain later tonight.
   ☐ comfortable   ☐ not comfortable

In the first set of sentences, we're comfortable that all three versions are interchangeable. The reason is that all three communicate variations of the same common futurity without many nuances getting in the way. The present progressive tells us that we're anticipating a near future event; *be going to* predicts that future event; *will* can also predict that future event. So all three variations share common features and seem all right to us.

With the two remaining sets, we're not comfortable with the prospect of interchanging all the variations in these three sentences. Let's look each set over and discover why we're not comfortable with it.

All three sentences in the second set are grammatical, so that's not our problem. *I'm going* and *I'm going to go* are both acceptable because they overlap in meaning: they can both represent plans for the future. *I will go*, on the other hand, is more commonly used for predictions or the pure future, so *will* just doesn't work. The sentence seems to be missing something without the idea that this is my intention or plan. Therefore, even though all three are grammatical, most native speakers would tend to use either of the first two forms, but not *will*.

For information on the modal auxiliary *shall*, please visit us at ELTgrammar.com

In the third set, the present progressive is our culprit. We're comfortable with interchanging *It's going to rain* and *It will rain* because both have something in common: they can both be used for predictions. **The present progressive isn't used for predictions; it's used for certainties**, like the real present or future planned events.

If you remember, I said a few pages back that we weren't done with *will* by a long shot—and we're still not! Because there's so much to say about this word and its counterpart, *would*, I'm going to get back to it in Chapter 8.

The Future with *Be About To*

"I'm about to call him now."

For a change, we've got something with no ambiguity and no nuances. The semi-auxiliary *be about to* has just one meaning: **the subject is on the verge of doing something**. In other words, it's the nearest that the future can be to the present.

The Future Perfect

"By the time I meet you . . . I'll have dropped Jacques off at the airport . . ."

Once again we've hit upon a verb form that leaves no ambiguity for us to wonder about. Why does the speaker use this form in our dialogue? Think about the sentence from the dialogue which I've quoted above and come up with a description of what the underlined portion means in this time frame. Write your idea on the following line:

....

The future perfect is an odd way for us to look at the past by way of the future. **We project ourselves to some point in the future, stop, turn around, and look back at what's already in the past for us at that moment.** In a way, it's a form of hindsight. There are two uses of this verb form, but in short, the future perfect tells us what will already be finished by the time we arrive at a certain point in the future.

In the sentence quoted from our dialogue, the speaker is saying that at the point in the future when he meets the other person, the action of his dropping Jacques off at the airport will already be completed. This meaning represents the first use of the future perfect.

The second use has to do with something that's happening currently. When the speaker in our dialogue says he'll drop Jacques off at the airport before the two people meet that evening, he's referring to a short-term action that has its whole beginning and end in the future. But the future perfect can also refer to another time frame.

Look at the following example and see if you can come up with an explanation of what the future perfect represents in this case. Write down your thoughts on the following line:

Midori will have been a nurse for thirty years by the year 2045.

....

We can view an action or state of being at some point in the future even though it's already happening now. Midori is a nurse now; in fact, she's been a nurse since 2015. If we want to project Midori's career status into the future from the time she first became a nurse and see what her total years in the profession will be in 2045, the future perfect is our vehicle for doing so. What we're really doing is jumping from the past into the future and bypassing the present.

We do have another aspect of this verb form, **the future perfect progressive.** Let's go back to our subject, Midori, and project something else about her professional life. Let's say that Midori began working as an operating room nurse in 2019 and she has no intention of changing her specialization. If we want to project what she'll be doing in the year 2045, we can say it like this:

> By 2045, Midori <u>will have been working</u> as an
> operating room nurse for 26 years.

Of course, we can also say that Midori *will have worked* as an operating room nurse for 26 years; in other words, we can use the simple form or the progressive form of the future perfect in this idea. Remember the discussion about these two versions for the present perfect in Chapter 3? The same basic rule we applied then holds true now, too: **If a verb can be used only in the simple present, use only the simple form of the future perfect; if the verb can be used in the present progressive form, you can opt to use the progressive form in the future perfect.**

The Future Progressive

> " . . . he'<u>ll be flying</u> somewhere over the Atlantic!"

For a while now, you've had the good fortune to deal with a future expression (*be about to*) and a verb form (future perfect) that offered simplicity of meaning and a respite from some of the more complicated topics that you've braved so far in this book. Well, the respite is over and you're back into the thick of grammar rules and exceptions!

First of all, we'll deal with the most common use of the future progressive, which reflects the basic concept of the present and past progressive forms. Let's go back to our original dialogue and take another look at the sentence we've quoted under the subtitle and compare it to the same sentence with the simple future form instead of the progressive form:

1. By the time I meet you for dinner tomorrow evening, Jacques <u>will be flying</u> somewhere over the Atlantic!
2. By the time I meet you for dinner tomorrow evening, Jacques <u>will fly</u> somewhere over the Atlantic!

One of these sentences is ungrammatical—any fluent speaker would sense it immediately. Explaining why one just doesn't work is another matter. What's your guess? Draw a circle around the number of the sentence you think is ungrammatical.

I'm sure that you didn't hesitate at all in deciding that the ungrammatical sentence is the **second one**. But why? Think of the whole idea that the sentence conveys, especially the information supplied in the first part. Then think about the basic concept of the progressive forms which we discussed in previous chapters. Now come up with a reason that makes the future progressive work in this sentence and write your conclusion on this line:

....

Just as its name implies, and just as is the case with the past and present progressive forms, the future progressive deals with an action that's in progress at a specific moment which we're pinpointing, this time an action in the future. The opening part of the sentence says "By the time I meet you for dinner," which in this case means *during that period in the future when I meet you and we are having dinner*. The opening part of the sentence sets up the idea. It means that **something else will be in progress in that same time period, so we use the future progressive to show which action will be in progress at that time.**

Here's another example which clearly shows how this verb form communicates that the underlined action will be in progress at that future time we're pinpointing:

> I know that Jacques <u>will be working</u> on that import/export deal we discussed when I get to see him in Paris next week.

Let's return to the sentence "By the time I meet you for dinner tomorrow evening, Jacques will be flying somewhere over the Atlantic." Now we need to discover why using the simple future form doesn't work in the context of this sentence. Think about what type of verb *fly* is. Then think about what meaning you get from this action in the isolated phrase "he will fly over the Atlantic." Now come up with an explanation to show why the simple future form is ungrammatical with this verb and in this context. Write your conclusion on these following lines:

....

....

Because *fly* is an action or dynamic verb, not a stative one, it conjures up a definite beginning and end. When we say "He will fly over the Atlantic," we get the impression that it's a completed future event. Perhaps in your mind's eye, you can picture him leaving New York and arriving in Paris. In other words, the idea is too complete and sabotages the very essence of what our original thought was. **We don't want to focus on a completed act; quite the contrary, we want to focus on an act *in progress***, and that's why "By the time I meet you for dinner tomorrow evening, Jacques will fly over the Atlantic" doesn't work.

Here's a sentence that does work with the simple future form because we're using a stative verb instead of a dynamic one:

> By the time I meet you for dinner tomorrow evening,
> Jacques <u>will be</u> home in Paris.

Heads Up!

In the example in the sentence on the previous page, note the part of the sentence that says *By the time I meet you . . .* In some other languages, it would be grammatical to use the equivalent of the future form of *meet*. After all, we are referring to a future form, aren't we? Many of your students will more than likely put a verb after *by the time* in the future if that's the time of the sentence. Be prepared to explain the following:

→ If we're referring to some point in the future, we don't use a future form after the following words or phrases, which are in dependent clauses:

  when/while/as soon as/just as/before/after/until/by the time

Here are some more examples:

- As soon as he *wakes* up, I'll make him breakfast.
- Before I *leave* work, she'll have the report ready.
- They won't offer more scholarships until the proper funds *are* allocated.

→ Another thing to point out to your students is that it's the *other* part of the sentence which contains the future verb form, not the one with one of the above expressions!

There are certain situations in which using the simple future form or the future progressive form can make quite a difference. Look at the following pairs of sentences. Decide if you feel there's no big difference in meaning between the sentences in each pair or if their meanings are definitely different:

1. Will you see Mr. Chang before you leave work today?
   Will you be seeing Mr. Chang before you leave work today?
   ☐ no big difference   ☐ big difference

2. The Grants won't sue their neighbors.
   The Grants won't be suing their neighbors.
   ☐ no big difference   ☐ big difference

3. Will you come to our party on Sunday?
   Will you be coming to our party on Sunday?
   ☐ no big difference   ☐ big difference

4. I'll spend next summer in the mountains.
   I'll be spending next summer in the mountains.
   ☐ no big difference   ☐ big difference

It's hard to predict whether your students will ever develop the language sensitivity needed to get a "feel" for the differences that can be found in Pairs 2 and 3, but not in Pairs 1 and 4. However, it certainly would be nice if a student asks you one day to explain the differences and you can! Let's go over each pair of sentences and find out why there are or aren't big differences in meaning.

To *see someone* can mean two basic ideas in English. It can mean to have someone in your view or it can mean to have an appointment or date with someone. In the first pair of sentences, it can even mean just to check in with someone before leaving work for the day. In this context, it seems obvious that the speaker is talking about either meeting Mr. Chang for an appointment or checking in with him before leaving work. For this reason **we don't perceive any real difference in meaning between the two forms "Will you see" and "Will you be seeing."** The key factor here is the precise context in which certain verbs are used.

In the fourth pair of sentences, the same principle applies. There are really no shifts in meaning which are carried in one form or the other, so there's really no difference perceived between saying "I'll spend" and "I'll be spending" in this context.

The second pair, however, is a different matter. The first sentence tells us that the Grants refuse to sue their neighbors. It's an idea we can even apply to a hypothetical situation that might come up in a discussion about suing. The second sentence makes us believe that a real situation has arisen in which the Grants could be considering a law suit. The sentence tells us that, at least on this occasion, the Grants aren't going to sue their neighbors, but it doesn't imply that they would never consider doing so.

The sentences in the third pair are also very different. The first sentence is an invitation in the form of a question. The second sentence is not an invitation, but a way of asking for confirmation from a person who has already been invited.

For information on two marginal future expressions (*be due* and *be to*) plus the phrases *be sure* and *make sure*, please visit us at
ELTgrammar.com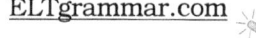

The Futures in a Nutshell

Present Progressive
- **a planned event in the near future:** I'm going to a ball game tonight.
- **present anticipation of a future event:** They're moving sometime next spring.

Simple Present
- **scheduled future events:** The next semester begins on May 28th.

Simple Future (Will)
- **a basic future idea with no nuances:** We'll see you later.
- **making predictions:** I think they'll be successful.

- **making promises:** I'll do it before I leave the office.
- **making requests:** Will you help me move this furniture?
- **making threats:** You'll regret the day you were born!
- **tendencies:** It will usually rain here every day between June and November.

Be Going To

- **showing future plans or intentions:** We're going to have a party next weekend.
- **making threats:** If you don't clean your room today, you're going to be punished!
- **making predictions:** I think she's going to have twins!

Be About To

- **on the verge of doing something:** Quiet, please! The guest speaker's about to begin.

Future Perfect

- **project ourselves to some point in the future, stop, turn around, and look back at what is already in the past for us at <u>that</u> moment:** The next time you see me, I'll have finished the last chapter of my manuscript.

Future Perfect Progressive

- **works the same way as the present perfect progressive does in relation to the present perfect, and shows something in progress:** I'll have been working on that manuscript for over six months by the time I see you again.

Future Progressive

- **can be used at times as an alternative to the simple future:** I'll be giving you this report by the end of the week.
- **can show an action in progress at some future point:** When we arrive at my folks' house, they'll be getting dinner ready.

Teaching Tips

5.1 *Making Schedules*

Before class, prepare two detailed schedules that show activities and times that are similar, but not identical. Make as many copies of the schedules as you have students. Pair up the students and give each student *one half* of a schedule. Tell the students that they need to find a time that will suit both of them to study for a big test, for example. The students must explain when they can and cannot meet by asking questions and giving responses using the present progressive form.

Note: Students aren't permitted to see one another's schedules—they have to *ask* for the information. Your two schedules might look something like these, though yours will likely have many more details:

Student A	Monday	Tuesday	Wednesday	Thursday	Friday	Saturday	Sunday
8:00 a.m.	get up		go to class	post office		shopping	rest
noon	lunch	work	lunch	work	airport		

Student B	Monday	Tuesday	Wednesday	Thursday	Friday	Saturday	Sunday
8:00 a.m.	breakfast		go to class	get up	library	breakfast	church
noon	dentist	lunch	lunch	study	lunch		party

Responses may be similar to the following: "What are you doing at 8:00 Tuesday morning?""I'm not doing anything."/"When are you having lunch on Thursday?" "I'm not eating lunch on Thursday; I'm going to the dentist instead."

5.2 *Travel Plans*

This activity focuses on the use of the simple present in scheduled future events. Feel free to prepare this activity initially as a reading exercise because it's rather involved and the students will have to refer to it to accomplish the activity. Pairs of students will set up travel plans for the president of an import/export company. They'll base the travel plans on the following information. The president, Mr. Watson, is going to Asia for his annual twelve-day buying trip and will visit the factories that he imports from in Tokyo, Singapore, Hong Kong, and Seoul. He always begins his trip in Tokyo and ends up in Singapore. As "administrative assistant" and "personal secretary" to Mr. Watson, the pairs of students must arrange the trip (arrival and departure times, meetings with factory managers, side trips) and any other details that seem appropriate for a business traveler.

Mr. Qing is the factory manager in Singapore, as is Mr. Wong in Hong Kong, Mr. Pak in Seoul, and Mr. Matsuo in Tokyo.

While in Tokyo, Mr.Watson wants to take a side trip to Mt. Fuji; in Seoul, he wants to visit the Temple of Heaven; in Hong Kong, he wants to eat at Jumbo's floating restaurant; and in Singapore, he wants to have high tea at Raffles Hotel.

1. The pairs of students are to work together to plan out the details of Mr. Watson's itinerary, and both students should write them down.
2. Once they have prepared his itinerary, rearrange the pairs of students.
3. Have one member of each new pair be the administrative assistant and the other, Mr. Watson's personal secretary. The administrative assistant needs to tell the secretary the exact details of the trip that they planned out with the *original* partner.
4. After the administrative assistant has done so and the secretary has copied it all down, the students should reverse roles and repeat this procedure.
5. When they finish, they are to read out what they wrote down while playing the role of secretary to check for accuracy.

5.3 *The Trip of a Lifetime!*

Divide the class into pairs or small groups. Have the students plan the trip of a lifetime ("The Perfect Honeymoon," a "Family Getaway," or "The Anniversary Trip"). Have the pairs/groups report their *detailed* itineraries to the class, making sure that they use *will* where appropriate. "The trip will begin at the airport where Romeo and I will board a private jet for Paris. We'll arrive there a short time later and take a limousine to the Georges V Hotel. We'll have a suite reserved for us for the three weeks that we'll be there . . . "

5.4 *What Happens Next?*

Select several pictures from your Picture File, or even have your students bring pictures that they like to class. They can be actual photos or pictures from magazines or books. Have the students brainstorm as many predictions about what "will occur" next in the various photos as they can.

Variation: After the class has brainstormed what comes next, have students develop a complete story line for their pictures. They can tell their stories as groups or individually, in writing or orally.

5.5 *A Perfect World*

Create a simple map showing unnamed streets, avenues, city blocks, a plaza. You can do this on the board for the students to copy or you can create a master blank map and make a copy for each student. Divide the class into small groups. Ask them to design their ideal city or a city of the future by naming all the streets and avenues and by indicating where the following kinds of places or buildings will be: government offices, water treatment plant, shopping centers, hospital, zoo, etc. Then have the students give a report on what they have come up with. Make sure that they use various future indicators in their reports.

5.6 *TV/Radio Predictions*

Before class, record a TV or radio program that has lots of action and a strong story line. Note points in the program where you can stop the recording and get the students to predict what's about to happen, what's apt to happen, what will happen next. Present the program to the class, stopping at each point you've noted and ask the students to use various futures to interpret the drama. Don't play them the end of the program. Have the students brainstorm various endings in small groups and then act them out for the entire class to enjoy.

5.7 *Predicting My Future*

Have your students imagine themselves ten, twenty, or thirty years from now. Ask them to predict what they think their lives will be like then. Typical answers are predictions like these: By the year 20XX, I think I'll have learned English well enough to get a good job. / By 20XX, I will have saved enough money to buy a house.

Variation: Give your students the name of a famous person and have them do some research on that person's life. Then have the students give reports on their subject. Start off the reports with the following to encourage the future perfect and future perfect progressive: "It's _____ (date) and _____ (person) has just been born. By _____, he/she will have _____."

5.8 *Predicting Events*

Find a picture of a wedding or other event which permits speculation about it. Have the students brainstorm vocabulary and questions that they want answered about the event. (Who are the people? How old are they? What are they wearing? What will they promise in their vows? What's he about to do? Where will they be spending their honeymoon? Where do people in your culture go on a honeymoon? Where will they live after the wedding? How many children are they going to have?) Write any vocabulary or information on the board that will help students with the rest of the assignment. Divide the class into small groups and have them write various versions of the picture: a newspaper report, a letter from the bride-to-be to someone who can't come to the ceremony, an invited guest, describing the event to someone over the phone, etc. Have the class share the various versions of the event with their classmates.

6

Prepositions

"There's a frog on a log in a hole at the bottom of the sea."

What are prepositions? In general, they're **words that show some sort of relationship or connection between two things.** In addition, prepositions can help to answer such questions as *where?*, *when?*, *why?*, and *how?* They can be **simple** (one word: *behind*) or **complex** (two or more words: *ahead of, in front of*).

In this chapter, I'm going to deal mostly with simple prepositions and focus on the challenging aspects of teaching them. By the way, if you want a complete list of prepositions, all you have to do is do a search online.

So what are prepositions? What they really are is the bane of all teachers!

Why is it that students always have so much trouble with prepositions? After all, don't they have them in their languages, too? Of course they do, although in some languages (like Turkish) they are *post*positions, words or word particles that show the same kind of relationship of one noun to another but come *after* the nouns they connect. In other words, learning to use prepositions isn't just a simple matter of translating a preposition from one language to another. To add to the difficulty, some languages (like English) have more prepositions than others. At any rate, English prepositions do cause a great deal of frustration and annoyance to students and their teachers.

There are three basic sections to this chapter. First, I'll deal with the meanings of some of the most commonly used prepositions. Along with this useful list, I'll give you ideas on how to demonstrate them in vivid ways so that your students start developing a "feel" for them. I'll also deal with their idiomatic uses and how choosing one preposition over another can change meaning in very important ways. In addition, I'll offer insights on how to handle the teaching of prepositions in the classroom and how to present them more meaningfully and interestingly to your students.

A look at the chapters on prepositions in most scholarly grammar books can be quite unnerving; the array of uses and meanings the reader is presented with can be intimidating, even overwhelming. I don't intend to cover every single preposition, but I'll break some of them down into their basic meanings. My main goal is to help you clarify some prepositions for yourself so that you'll be better prepared to deal with them in your classes. You can continue where I leave off and delve into the basic meanings of those I don't cover.

In many ways, the choice of which preposition to use depends on the viewpoint of the speaker or writer, especially when dealing with spatial relationships. Teaching the spatial, or literal, uses of prepositions comes early on in any curriculum, and visualizing them both on the board and with a little physical reinforcement has always proven to be an effective teaching technique.

Literal (Physical) Meanings

Let's see how astute you are at graphically visualizing the spatial meanings of some commonly used prepositions. Below, you'll find an assortment of them, each one followed by a box. Draw **an arrow** (for **movement**) or **a dot** (for **stationary location**) wherever you think it will best demonstrate the literal meaning of the preposition in relation to its accompanying box. For the sake of this exercise, let's say that the orientation of the boxes is just like this page you're reading; in other words, *the top of each box is in the same location as the top of this page.* Also, let's have all movements going *from left to right.* You'll find that it's easier to represent some prepositions graphically than others. I've done the first one to get you started. (By the way, I know you're going to cover up the section on the next page with the answers until you've finished, right?)

onto/on ☐   on ☐   off (of) ☐   into ☐   in ☐   out of ☐

over ☐   above ☐   under ☐   below ☐

towards ☐   to ☐   from/away from ☐

before ☐   after ☐   near ☐   next to/by ☐

past/by ☐   through ☐   (a)round ☐

It's interesting to visualize just what each of these prepositions looks like on paper, isn't it? Well, here are the answers I've come up with. Compare yours to mine. You may be surprised to find some answers that you didn't think of. You may also be surprised to see that it's not always very clear cut when it comes to showing a visual representation of some of these prepositions. Remember: the arrow represents movement; the dot represents stationary location.

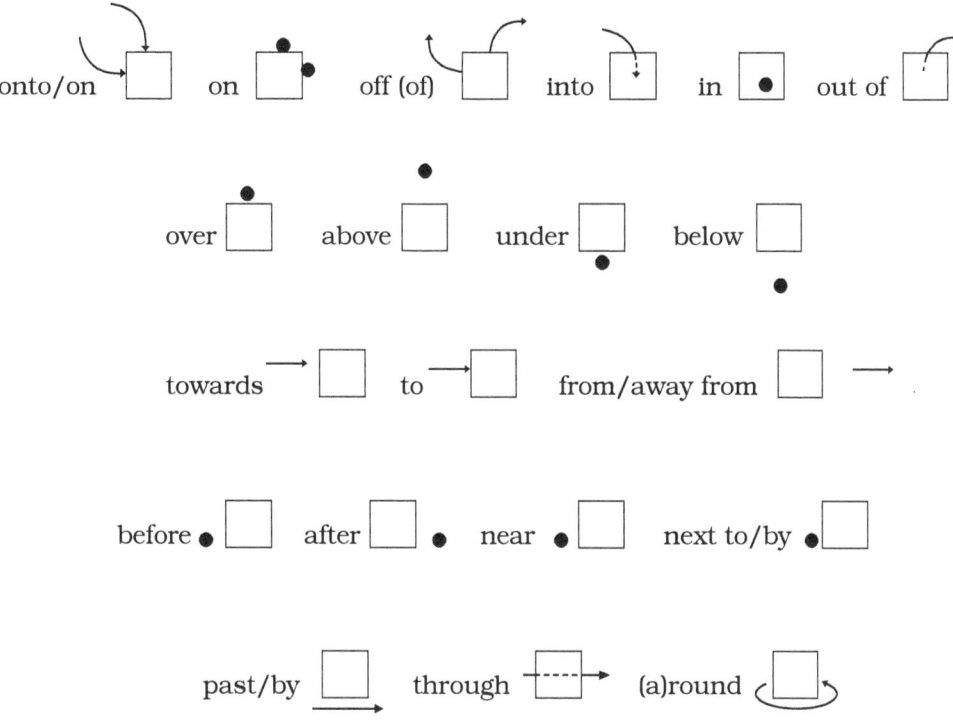

Now that you've had a chance to compare your artwork to mine, let's see if you can come up with *literal* definitions for these prepositions. If their meanings are clear in your mind, it'll be much easier to communicate them to your students. Use the visualizations I've created and the example sentences I've provided to help you. Among other things, state whether they're prepositions of location or movement or both.

onto/on: He placed the star onto/on the top of the Christmas tree.

....
....

on: His family loved all the ornaments on the Christmas tree.

....
....

off (of)[*]: During the holidays, some of the ornaments fell off (of) the tree.

into/in: As the guests arrived, they came into/in the house.

in: When the guests were seated in the living room, their host served them some refreshments.

out of: The hostess came out of the kitchen carrying a basket of bread and rolls.

out: The little dog almost fell out the window.

over: A: My legs are cold.
B: Here. Put this afghan over them.

While out in the woods on a fall day, we noticed a flock of geese flying over us on their way south for the winter.

---

[*]I'll explain why I've put the secondary preposition in parentheses later on in the chapter.

above: The helicopter hovered <u>above</u> the field for a few minutes before flying off.

During the storm, the dark clouds passed <u>above</u> us at incredible speed.

under: Our dog likes to sleep <u>under</u> the dining room table.

Did you feel all that vibration and hear the rumbling? It was the subway passing <u>under</u> this building.

below: In this part of the country, the water table is many meters <u>below</u> the surface of the land.

There are places on this planet where water travels <u>below</u> the surface in subterranean rivers.

toward(s): The explorers continued traveling west <u>towards</u> the mountains.

to: I'm sending this postcard <u>to</u> my relatives in the States.

She gave some candy <u>to</u> her assistant as a sign of her appreciation for all his hard work.

....
....

from: He comes <u>from</u> Cairo, Egypt. I just got a letter from him.

....
....

away from: He turned <u>away from</u> me because he was so embarrassed.

....
....

far from: She used to live <u>far from</u> her workplace, so she moved closer.

....
....

before: When it was time for him to be sentenced for his crime, the convicted man was made to stand <u>before</u> the judge.

....
....

If you want the all-night coffeeshop, it's the red brick building <u>before</u> the movie theater down this street.

....
....

after: Looking for the bank? It's the building <u>after</u> that gas station.

....
....

near/by: Don't you know that our house is <u>near/by</u> the stadium?

....
....

Don't go <u>near</u> the fireplace, Billy. It's very hot.

next to/by: You'll recognize our house when you see it. It's the yellow one <u>next to/by</u> the florist's shop.

close to: I thought you knew where we live. Our house is <u>close to</u> Yankee Stadium.

past/by: We drove <u>past/by</u> your house last night, but we couldn't stop to say hello.

through: Last summer, we took a car trip <u>through</u> the Canadian province of British Columbia.

(a)round: Before the tunnel was built, our trip was a lot longer because we had to drive <u>(a)round</u> the mountain.

I like that arrangement of roses all <u>(a)round</u> the wedding cake.

On Sundays they used to like driving <u>around</u> in the country and taking in the beautiful scenery.

Without any ado, let's get right to my interpretations of the literal meanings of these prepositions.

onto/on: A preposition of movement which means something lands on or is placed on something else so that it touches that object's surface. In the case of a three-dimensional object, this meaning could include the top or sides:

> He placed the star <u>onto/on</u> the top of the Christmas tree.

Note that *onto* clearly relates to movement, whereas its short form, *on*, can be ambiguous: "He jumped <u>onto</u> the desk." vs. "He jumped <u>on</u> the desk." (Did he jump from the chair and land on top of the desk, or did he jump up and down while standing on the desk?)

on: A preposition that shows that something has contact with the surface of something else. If it's a three-dimensional object, it could be the top or sides:

> His family loved all the ornaments <u>on</u> the Christmas tree.
> That dress looks just beautiful <u>on</u> you!

off (of): The opposite of *onto*, this preposition shows the movement of one object leaving a surface of another:

> During the holidays, some of the ornaments fell <u>off (of)</u> the tree.

into/in: Another preposition of movement which refers to something entering the interior of an object:

> As the guests arrived, they came <u>into/in</u> the house.

in: A preposition showing stationary location. It means that something is encompassed or enclosed by something else:

> When the guests were seated <u>in</u> the living room,
> their host served them some refreshments.

out (of): The opposite of *into* or *in*, this preposition also involves movement. It can mean one thing leaving the object that has encompassed or enclosed it. It can also mean *from*:

> The hostess came <u>out of</u> her kitchen
> carrying a basket of bread and rolls.

out: Without *of*, it means *through*:

> The little dog almost fell <u>out</u> the window.

over: In this first use, it's a preposition of stationary location. To many native speakers, *over* may mean that something is at a *slightly* higher elevation than the top of some other thing:

During the final judging of the contestants, the master of ceremonies
held his hand <u>over</u> the head of each finalist for the voting.

Over can include the idea of one thing being in proximity to or even touching or covering the other:

A: My legs are cold.
B: Here. Put this afghan <u>over</u> them.

In another use, *over* is a preposition of movement. In this use it means one thing moving horizontally at a higher elevation than the top of another thing. In the case of movement, how much distance there is between the two objects is not an issue:

While out in the woods on a fall day, we noticed a
flock of geese flying <u>over</u> us on their way south for the winter.

above: As with our first definition for *over*, this preposition means that one thing is at a higher elevation than the top of another thing. The difference between *above* and *over* is that, for many native speakers, *above* implies there's a greater distance between the two objects than *over*. In the example we've cited, the preposition is used with stationary location:

The helicopter hovered <u>above</u> the field
for a few minutes before flying off.

Above can also be used for movement:

During the storm, the dark clouds passed
<u>above</u> us at incredible speed.

under: This preposition is the opposite of *over* and is used for stationary location. It carries the same meaning as *over* in reverse:

Our dog likes to sleep <u>under</u> the dining room table.

Likewise, *under* is the opposite of *over* for movement and carries the same meaning as that preposition in reverse:

Feel that vibration and hear that rumbling?
It was the subway passing <u>under</u> this building.

below: Here we have the opposite meaning of *above*. It has the same definition as *above*, but in reverse, and can be used for stationary location:

In this part of the country, the water table is many
meters <u>below</u> the surface of the land.

Below can also be used for movement:

> There are places on this planet where water
> travels <u>below</u> the surface in subterranean rivers.

toward(s): A preposition of movement meaning that an object is going in the direction of another, but it doesn't imply that the moving object reaches any destination:

> The explorers continued traveling
> west <u>towards</u> the mountains.

to: This preposition of movement, whose opposite is *from*, means one thing going in the direction of and reaching or arriving at a destination of one kind or another:

> I'm sending this postcard <u>to</u> my relatives in the States.
> She gave some candy <u>to</u> her assistant as a sign of her
> appreciation for all his hard work.

from: This preposition, the opposite of *to*, refers to the starting point or source of something:

> He comes <u>from</u> Cairo, Egypt. I just got a letter <u>from</u> him.

away from: Here we have another preposition whose opposite meaning is *to* or *toward(s)*. Instead of reaching a destination or other object, or going in its direction, this preposition of movement means leaving a certain point or other object:

> He turned <u>away from</u> me because he was so embarrassed.

far from: This preposition of location deals with a relatively long distance between two objects.

> She used to live <u>far from</u> her workplace, so she moved closer.

before: This stationary preposition is a synonym for *in front of* (which is an example of the complex prepositions I mentioned earlier in this chapter):

> When it was time for him to be sentenced for his crime,
> the convicted man was made to stand <u>before</u> the judge.

Before can also mean something you'll come upon immediately *preceding* another thing mentioned as a reference point:

> If you want the all-night cafeteria, it's the red brick building
> <u>before</u> the movie theater down this street.

after: This stationary preposition means that the object you're looking for follows the object mentioned as a reference point:

> You're looking for the bank? It's the building <u>after</u> that gas station.

near/by: The meaning of these prepositions has to do with proximity. They mean one thing is in the general area of another thing with a relatively short distance between them. The opposite preposition is *far from*. These prepositions can both be stationary:

> Don't you know that our house is near/by the stadium?

Only *near* can also be used for movement:

> Don't go near the fireplace, Billy. It's very hot.

close to: Here we have a preposition of both location and movement. It means with very little distance between two things:

> I thought you knew where we live.
> Our house is close to the Louvre.

next to/by: A synonym for these stationary prepositions is *beside*. They carry the idea of very close proximity, that is, with just about no distance between two objects and, as their synonyms say, the reference points are the sides of two objects:

> You'll recognize our house when you see it.
> It's the yellow one next to/by the florist's shop.

past/by: These prepositions carry the idea of one thing moving in front of another thing and not stopping as it approaches. In other words, it passes the object:

> We drove past/by your house last night,
> but we couldn't stop to say hello.

through: The meaning of this preposition of movement carries with it the idea that one thing enters one end or side of another thing, traverses its interior, and comes out or reaches the opposite end or side:

> It was pitch black in our compartment as
> the train went through the tunnel.

> Last summer, we took a car trip through the
> Canadian province of British Columbia.

(a)round: This preposition can show movement meaning one thing partially or completely encircling another:

> Before the tunnel was built, our trip was a lot longer
> because we had to drive (a)round the mountain.

(A)round can also be a preposition of stationary location:

> I like that arrangement of daffodils all (a)round the wedding cake.

In its idiomatic use, in which case only *around* is used, it has the idea of movement with no specific destination:

> On Sundays they used to like driving <u>around</u> the country and taking in the beautiful scenery.

Of course, the definitions I've given you for these prepositions are ones that you might like to have for clarification, but it's probably inadvisable to give them to your students in this way. However, as I mentioned earlier, if their meanings are clear in <u>your</u> mind, it will be a much simpler job for you to demonstrate them for your classes. One further note: Remember that not all English speakers use every preposition in the same way; there's room for debate on some of these.

Figurative/Idiomatic Meanings

Notice that I've concentrated on the literal meanings of these prepositions; that is, I've focused on their physical nature. Many of them also have figurative and/or idiomatic meanings. Remember that they can appear in the following patterns:

> **preposition + (pro)noun** (*above it all/above reproach*)
> **verb + preposition** (*think over*)
> **adjective + preposition** (*angry at*)

Here are examples of figurative uses and idiomatic expressions. (Fig.= figurative use; Id. = idiomatic expression):

onto[*]: (Id.) be onto somebody (not be fooled by someone; understand a person's motives)

on: (Fig.) about; concerning
(Id.) be on (performing, as if on stage or on duty); be on something (medication or other drugs)

off: (Id.) be off (leaving/spoiled, as with food); go/be off one's rocker (crazy); be off the record (not for public knowledge)

into: (Fig.) escape into the night; get into trouble/mischief
(Id.) be into something (interested)

in: (Fig.) be in trouble/love/jeopardy/business
(Id.) be "in" (stylish/accepted); be in hock/debt

---

[*]You may have come up with something like the idiom "*Go on to* the next topic for discussion." If you did, you've confused the preposition *onto* with the preposition *on* which is allied with the verb *go*. In other words, it's really *go on*, and there's a secondary preposition needed before you can state the object, in this case, "the next topic for discussion."

out (of):	(Fig.)	be out of trouble/danger/touch
	(Id.)	be out of one's mind;
		run/be out of (have no more of something)
over:	(Fig.)	more than;
		by means of (a telephone, the Internet, an intercom, etc.);
		over the holidays/the weekend
	(Id.)	be over the hill (too old);
		be/get over an illness/bad news, etc. (recovered)
above:	(Fig.)	be above the law (not following the laws meant for everyone);
		be above someone (in social status or at work)
	(Id.)	be above it all (not bothered by mundane concerns)
under:	(Fig.)	less than/fewer than
	(Id.)	under the circumstances;
		be under arrest/the weather (feeling poorly)
below:	(Fig.)	be below one's dignity/wholesale (prices)
	(Id.)	to hit below the belt (make an unfair statement)
toward(s):	(Fig.)	toward a better tomorrow;
		be hostile/antagonistic toward(s) someone
to:	(Id.)	look to someone (for help, advice);
		do something to someone (a bad act, nasty deed)
from:	(Fig.)	from the start/very first
	(Id.)	from nowhere (appeared suddenly);
		from now on
away from:	(Fig.)	turn away from someone (abandon, reject)
before:	(Fig.)	before leaving;
		before two o'clock/the public/it gets dark
after:	(Fig.)	after dinner/six o'clock/the fact
	(Id.)	take after (resemble);
		look after (take care of)
near:	(Fig.)	be near someone's age/the end (of a story)
	(Id.)	be near the end (dying)
close to:	(Fig.)	close to $75,000 (almost)
next to:	(Fig.)	besides (Next to me, he's your best choice for the job.);
		next to nothing (very little)
past:	(Fig.)	be past one's prime (getting older);
		be past caring (apathetic)
by:	(Fig.)	by midnight (before or at midnight);
		by all means
	(Id.)	by heart (to memory; memorized);

by hook or by crook (whatever it takes);
stand by you (support);
by the way (incidentally)

through: (Fig.) through the years (spanning time)
(Id.) get through (survive/recuperate/recover; finish);
be through (be finished)

around: (Fig.) approximately
(Id.) beat around the bush (not coming to the main point of one's thought or idea);
get around someone (arrange it so that a certain person doesn't interfere)

round: (Fig.) round about (indirect)
(Id.) go round the bend (go crazy);
go round and round (not reaching a conclusion or solution)

The Prepositional Bane of Banes: *At*

There's one more preposition—a troublesome one—that we should look at in the same way we've looked at the others. It's troublesome because many people have a hard time putting their finger on just what it means. The preposition I'm thinking of is *at*. I'm giving you four boxes, so you'll have four chances to place a dot or an arrow at whatever spot you think will graphically visualize the meaning of *at*:

The truth is that you can place the dot practically anywhere outside each box (relatively close to each one, that is) and be quite accurate about how to visualize this preposition graphically. In its literal sense, **at usually means in the general area of something and, because it does refer to a general area, the dimensions of this something are really unimportant and the location isn't pinpointed.** The one notable exception to this interpretation of at is when it's used synonymously with *by* in such phrases as *at/by my side; at/by the door*.

Keep these ideas concerning the interpretation of *at* in mind as we go on exploring this troublesome preposition. As for the arrow, that can only be placed on either side of the box and pointing towards it to show direction and/or movement.

These ideas are especially useful for English speakers when they get into differences concerning location or direction that have a literal or idiomatic meaning. Using the vague word *at* or the more specific words *in* or *on* can sometimes make a great difference in meaning, but quite often that difference depends on more than just the choice of preposition. Below you'll find some sentences with this interesting twist. Check the box after each pair of sentences that you agree with:

1. They're waiting at the ship. They're waiting on the ship. ☐ a difference ☐ no difference	2. Meet us at the bookstore. Meet us in the bookstore. ☐ a difference ☐ no difference

Most native speakers would agree that there's a definite difference in meaning between the sentences in each pair above, so if you've checked **a difference** for both pairs, you're in the majority.

In the first pair of sentences, if you expect to find those people standing somewhere in the general area of the ship (at the ship), you're right; if you hear "They're waiting on the ship," you imagine them actually aboard the vessel.

As for the other two examples I've given you, "Meet me at the bookstore" probably makes you think you should be outside (perhaps in front of) the store or in the general area and wait for me there if you show up first, while "Meet me in the book store" tells you that you should be waiting inside if you get there first.

We can clearly see that there are important differences between *at* or *in/on* in the previous sentences. Now let's look at some more sentences and play the same game:

1. I work at a bank. I work in a bank. ☐ a difference ☐ no difference	2. We met them at the corner. We met them on the corner. ☐ a difference ☐ no difference

That last statement I made, that there clearly are differences between *at* and the other two prepositions, isn't always the case as the sentences you've just looked over show. If you checked **no difference** for these two pairs this time, you're once again going along with the majority opinion. Most people would say that they don't discern any real difference in these sentences between *at a bank* or *in a bank* or *at* or *on the corner*.

So now the question arises: Why do we easily perceive a difference in meaning between the two sentences in the first two pairs, but not in the second two pairs? Give it some thought and write your ideas on the following lines:

....

....

What we have here is an amazing quirk in the language. Of course it's true that *at* and *in* and *on* can have very different meanings, but since we've now seen occasions when they really don't have such different ideas, we know that something else is at work—and that something else involves the verb and the object of the preposition in the context of each sentence.

So what's the bottom line on preposition use? It's simply that their meaning comes from the context. It also sends us teachers a very good message: We can't expect our students to learn how to use prepositions based solely on simple rules which they can memorize and activate like mathematical formulas, or that they can learn prepositions in a vacuum. Language just isn't that clear cut!

And speaking of not being clear cut, there's an idiomatic use of prepositions that I need to touch on. Let's look at three pairs of sentences, one in each pair with a literal meaning, the other, idiomatic. Meanings will depend on the combination of verb and preposition used. Note that we're dealing here with *to* vs. *at* and *in* vs. *at*:

> 1a. Fatima is in the hospital.
> 1b. Fatima is at the hospital.
>
> 2a. The little girl threw the ball to the boy.
> 2b. The little girl threw the ball at the boy.
>
> 3a. The little boy shouted to the girl.
> 3b. The little boy shouted at the girl.

How would you interpret the two sentences in each pair, and how would you explain them to your students? Try it out on the following lines:

....
....
....
....
....

Sentence 1a tells us that **Fatima is a patient there**, and the sentence has an **idiomatic** meaning. **Sentence 1b** tells us **where Fatima is at the moment** and is **literal** in meaning.

Sentence 2a has a **literal** meaning. It simply tells us that **the girl tossed the ball to the boy**, intending for him to catch it. **Sentence 2b** is **idiomatic**

and means that **she didn't intend for him to catch the ball**. It could even communicate that she was angry with the boy and meant to hit him with the ball.

Sentence 3a is literal and simply tells us **the direction that his shouting was going in. Sentence 3b is idiomatic** and could mean that **he was angry with the girl** or meant to **send her a warning**. The difference in communication is amazing! Here are two more sentences. One of them makes sense, but the other doesn't.

After you've decided which is which, write an explanation showing why you think Sentence 1 or Sentence 2 is nonsensical:

1. She was so angry that she hurled a vase to the wall.

   ☐ makes sense   ☐ doesn't make sense

2. She was so angry that she hurled a vase at the wall.

   ☐ makes sense   ☐ doesn't make sense

....

....

It turns out that **Sentence 1 doesn't make sense**, and in order to understand the reason, we need to remember what the difference is between to and at in the sentences about the girl throwing that ball. With verbs like *throw* and *hurl* the preposition *to* means that the doer intends for the object of the preposition to catch something. This idea works fine if the object of the preposition happens to be a person or perhaps a chimpanzee or dog, but it won't work at all if the object of the preposition is a non-living thing—in this case, a wall! Therefore, when the object is a thing, we use the preposition *at*.

Let's turn our attention to another difference between *at* and some other preposition. How would you explain the following corrections that invariably have to be made by just about every teacher from time to time?

A: You look tired today, Ali.

B: I am tired, Mrs. Klein. I was in a party almost all night. What a party!

A: You mean, you were at a party, Ali.

B: At? Why at?

A: Uh, well, uh ... Where was the party?

B: In my friend's house.

A: That should be at your friend's house, Ali.

B: Again at? Why at?

A: Well, you see, uh ...

How would you rescue poor Mrs. Klein who's obviously stalling because she doesn't have an answer ready for Ali? What would you say to Ali? Write your explanations on the following lines:

....
....
....

If we keep in mind that *in* usually deals with one thing being *encompassed* or *enclosed* by another thing, and that *at* refers to *general location*, we should be able to deal with Ali's questions. As for why native speakers would say *at my friend's house*, it's because **we don't want to limit ourselves in this context to one specific, enclosed area or room**; we're keeping it *open* to take in the whole, general area.

For similar reasons, we say *at a party* because a party isn't any specific area that can encompass or enclose us; the kind of party that takes place at a friend's house is **an event** that takes place in one room or several rooms and even perhaps outside of the house, such as in the backyard or patio. Because of this general nature of location, *at* works much better because it simply places us in the general area of the event. Compare it with the use of *in* in this little dialogue:

A: Where's Jack? I thought he was out here weeding the flower beds as I'd asked him to.

B: Nope. He's in the house watching *Batman*.

As a side note, I want to mention that there is another kind of *party*, a group of people going somewhere together. When *party* has this meaning, we say, for example, *one person who is **in** a party of six that's reserved a table at a restaurant*. The person in that party is someone *included* in the group.

Let's get back to the idea of choosing *in* or *at*. Here are a couple of examples that will bring the point about a specific, enclosed area versus a general area in even sharper focus. Fill in these blanks with *in* or *at*:

He works .... the security office .... the annex .... the airport.

Most people will say that this person works *in* the security office *in* the annex *at* the airport. Why do we use *in* for the office and the annex? And why do we use *at* for the airport? Write your thoughts on these lines:

....
....

The person works **inside the office** (he's enclosed by it) and the office is a room **inside the annex** (the building <u>encompasses</u> the office), so he works *in* them. On the other hand, the building is located **in the general area that we call the airport**; that's why we say *at* the airport.

But I'm not through with *at*. Let's get back to some other idiomatic uses for this little demon of a preposition. Keep your mind in its "interpreting mode." Here are some prepositional phrases dealing with both literal and idiomatic aspects of *at* which I'd like you to explain as you would to your students. Be brief, but clear!

1. *at* five o'clock

....

2. *by* five o'clock

....

3. *on* Maple Street

....

4. *at* 223 Maple Street

....

5. *on* Christmas

....

6. *at* Christmas

....

These are the kinds of phrases that drive students mad—and who could blame them? Native English speakers can appreciate the exactness of these prepositions, but our students just cringe when confronted with such exactness of meaning. Let's go over them now and see how closely your interpretations match mine.

At five o'clock means exactly when that hour arrives; *by five o'clock* means that something can occur before that hour or at that hour, but not after that hour.

On Maple Street gives us only a general idea of location; something is somewhere along that street. **We use** *at*, however, **when we have the actual house/building number** to help us pinpoint the location. Does this use of *at* strike you as a contradiction of one of the first meanings I gave *at*, that it means in the general area and not a specific point? Initially, you might think so, but we have to look deeper. True, mentioning the number of the place does pinpoint the location for us, but *at* simply tells us that it's somewhere on those premises. For example, the real location of the person we're looking for could be *in* Apartment 12 *at* 223 Maple Street or *in* Suite 100 *at* 223 Maple. And even though it might border on the silly, we can take this explanation a step further and say that, if this is a private house, the person we're looking for could be *in* the kitchen *at* 223 Maple Street! So, all in all, there really isn't a big contradiction when *at* is used this way.

As for the last two phrases, **we think of** *on* **Christmas as meaning during that one specific day**, whereas **we tend to think of** *at* **Christmas as something taking place during the general time of that holiday**, not just on that one day.

Before leaving the prepositional bane of banes, let's explore other uses I have for *at* besides the ones I've covered so far. Since I've done it for the other prepositions cited in the chapter, it's only fair that I do it for this one, too. This time, though, I'm going to carry out the investigation in a different way. You'll notice that I've set up this activity as a matching exercise. Match up the examples I've given you with the uses they represent by filling in the appropriate corresponding number in front of each example.

Use 1: conditions/states
Use 2: rates/scales/ages
Use 3: in the direction of
Use 4: reactions
Use 5: abilities

............Is he going to retire at sixty-five?   ....We seem to be at odds.

............They were at a turning point.   ....I didn't shoot at the birds.

............She cried at the bad news.   ....Are you good at math?

............She's a genius at bridge.   ....We laughed at her joke.

............He aimed at the target.   ....Water boils at 212°F.

Of course you understand now that the different uses I've found for *at* depend on the context that the preposition is in. Here are the answers to this matching exercise for you to check your choices against: on the left—2, 1, 4, 5, 3; on the right—1, 3, 5, 4, 2.

Here are other examples that fit into the different uses for *at*:

Use 1: be at ease/an end/play/loggerheads/rest
Use 2: at 29,000,000 shares (stockmarket)/a fair price/age 70
Use 3: yell at/look at/glance at/grab at/lunge at/wave at
Use 4: balk at/cringe at/frown at/weep at/recoil at/sneer at
Use 5: be smart at/a whiz at/bad at/poor at/slow at

Some Teaching Strategies

Before I go on to another topic, let's discuss some basic advice I can offer you for teaching prepositions. To begin, one technique I've always found useful and efficient is to teach pairs of prepositions that are opposite in meaning. For example, don't let your students learn *up* without learning *down*; don't let them learn *over* without learning *under* at the same time. When I've asked high intermediate students to give me the opposites of certain prepositions, many of them couldn't think of the right ones—in fact, many times they came up with bizarre answers. One reason that it's important to teach prepositions in this way whenever possible is that it will come in handy as the students get into two-word and three-word verbs (what some people refer to as *phrasal verbs*). By learning at an early stage of their English that *off* is the opposite of *on*, your students will find it easier to learn converse phrasal verbs such as *put on* and *take off* or *turn on* and *turn off*.

Another bit of advice I can offer is a grammar rule that many teachers avoid until the higher levels of ELT. It's really unnecessary to put it off, as I've proven in practice, because this rule is very straightforward and has *no* exceptions: **When a verb follows a preposition, add -*ing* to it** (before leav*ing*, after eat*ing*, for mak*ing*, by heat*ing*).

Some people might want to take exception to this rule and say that it doesn't hold up if you consider examples like *used to* or *be able to*. After all, they'd say, verbs don't have the *-ing* stuck on the end if they come after these expressions that end in a preposition ("I used to like spinach."/"They aren't able to fly"). The reason I don't consider these examples exceptions to the rule is that they belong to a category called **semi-auxiliaries** or **periphrastic modals**. Since they can substitute for modal auxiliaries, the verb that follows remains untouched just as it does after a modal:

<pre>
He can go   =   He [is able to]   go
                 He [is allowed to]   go
</pre>

She <u>will</u> go	=	She [is going to]	go
		She [is about to]	go
We <u>would</u> go	=	We [used to]	go

Other expressions that fall into this category of semi-auxiliaries or periphrastic modals are *have to, have got to, be to, be about to,* and *be supposed to.* In short, the preposition *to* is an integral part of each of these semi-auxiliaries, not just a preposition on its own. Compare these expressions to something like *be used to,* which is an expression with an allied preposition that doesn't substitute for a modal auxiliary. Because this expression isn't a modal substitute, the verb that follows the preposition will have the *–ing* stuck onto it ("He's used to eat<u>ing</u> at 7 p.m.") just as any other verb would.

I'm sure you'll see that the rule for putting *-ing* on a verb that follows a preposition isn't difficult for students to master once they understand what prepositions are. An additional idea I'd like to give you is that nothing works better for teaching prepositions than physical demonstrations. If you've decided, let's say, to teach *in/out* and *on/off,* actually showing the class many different examples of these prepositions at work and then letting them go through the physical paces themselves will be your best bet for getting them to develop a feel for the concepts being taught. You should demonstrate many different examples for each preposition; if you're going to teach *on/off* in their literal uses, show them examples with a box, a desk, a board, a wall, a bulletin board, an article of clothing, etc. In order for the students to develop a feel for these words, they must be exposed to enough varied examples for the message to hit home and become real.

One last bit of advice I'd like to pass along at this point is that you're bound to come across times when your students overuse the second element in the complex forms, such as *out of* and *away from.* There are times when you may hear students say such oddities as "The dog is out of" instead of "The dog is out" or "The dog is outside." Another example is if you hear a student say "I put it into" instead of "I put it in." Why do you suppose the student sentences I've just cited are ungrammatical? Can you figure this out of . . . uh, I mean, out?

....

....

The reason is that **we only require the second element when the complex form is followed *by an object*.** It's perfectly all right to say "The dog is out of <u>the house</u>" and "I put it into <u>the drawer</u>," but when we omit the objects, we omit the secondary element as well ("The dog is out."/"I put it in.") Note that *into,* although written as one word, is really a combination of two elements. If there's no object with the preposition *into*, the *to* gets dropped just as my rule says.

While I'm on the subject of prepositions and their objects, I should mention a mistake made by many native English speakers. Unfortunately, it's quite common to hear people say such phrases as "You can go to the show *with Charlie and I*" or "Just *between you and I*, he's really not such a nice guy." Why should we say "with Charlie and me" and "between you and me?" Come up with an answer and write it on the line that follows:

....

The answer is that **you can't have a pronoun in the subject form** (*I, he, she, we, they*) **when it follows a preposition.** You must use the object form (*me, him, her, us, them*) even when there are two pronouns separated by the word *and*. Note that this mistake occurs most commonly in a phrase with the first person singular pronoun (*for so-and-so and I*). The reason for this seems to be due to what's called **overcorrection**. The speaker thinks that it sounds more educated to say *for him and I* than *for him and me*. And what really makes this a head scratcher is that the very same speaker will never accept as grammatical to say *for I*. He thinks it's all right as long as there are two people mentioned, but not just himself. Go figure!

Post-posed Prepositions

One very typical feature of English that has gone from being considered not so acceptable to acceptable is the final topic of this chapter. Its fancy name is the post-posed preposition, and many a native English speaker will remember being corrected in primary or secondary school for this infraction of old-style, traditional grammar. What was that infraction? It was ending a clause or a sentence with a preposition! Most traditional English teachers of days gone by didn't consider it "proper" to say sentences like these:

> The play (which/that) I was speaking <u>about</u> had a great plot.
> Which play were you speaking about?

Those teachers used to insist that we say these sentences as follows:

> The play <u>about which</u> I was speaking . . .
> <u>About which play</u> were you speaking?

Most native speakers consider it very formal language to place the preposition at the beginning of the clause—and they themselves would rarely speak that way. It must be said, though, that things have changed considerably in the last few decades, especially in regard to the spoken idiom. As modern teachers, we should understand our responsibility to teach the language as it's really *spoken* and written and not hold on to some idealized, traditional form that no one normally uses in everyday language. Not only would it sound odd for a native speaker to say the last two example sentences I gave and which the old-fashioned English teachers preferred, but, in some situations, it would also sound affected and out of place. On the other hand, English is an international language and therefore we have to hold with some kind of standard. Mostly, we try to strike a happy medium.

Before I go into detail about *post-posed* prepositions, I'd like to mention my viewpoint about this term. If you know some basic Latin root words, you know that *post-posed* literally means "put or place after," and I have to disagree with that term. To be "put after" gives you the idea that something is deliberately being moved and placed after something else—and that's not the case at all with this phenomenon so peculiar to English. To understand what post-posed prepositions are all about, you have to realize that the preposition isn't being moved and placed after anything; it's simply staying right where it is in the original idea/sentence. Take a look at the following diagram, which demonstrates how the preposition isn't moving anywhere—although other things are:

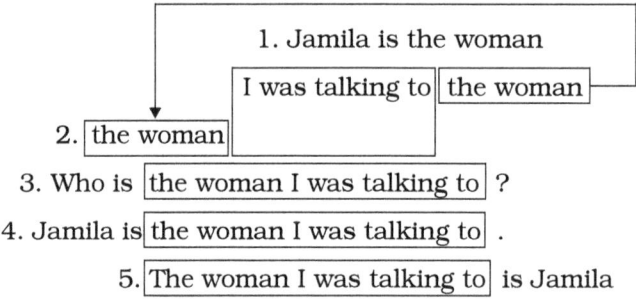

So what's happened? (1) We're looking at two basic ideas at our starting point: "Jamila is the woman."/"I was talking to the woman." (2) What I've moved to another position is *the woman* (the object of the preposition) and *not* the preposition! Note that I've moved *the woman* to the front of the sentence. Now we have the clause "the woman I was talking to," and this newly formed clause is going to serve many purposes as we can see. (3) I can add a question phrase before our new clause, or (4) some information, or (5) I can reverse the whole thing. Now I think you can see how the preposition hasn't been moved and placed anywhere new; it's actually right where it's been all along. Let's look at one more example of these changes at work:

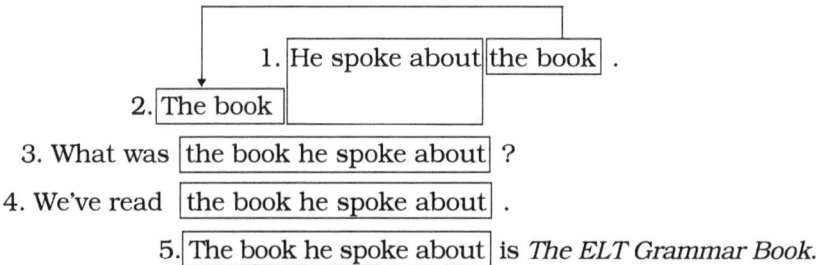

(1) Here I have my basic idea. (2) I've moved the object of the preposition (the

book) to the front of the sentence so that I now have "the book he spoke about." (3) I've chosen to add a question phrase to the front so that I have a complete question. (4) Instead, I can choose to add some information to the front of the clause so that I now have a declarative sentence. And finally, (5) I've added some information after the clause to form another declarative sentence. It's a very slick operation!

There's one more thing I need to mention when these changes are made with my basic idea: I can add the words **who/whom** or **that** after the initial noun phrase if the noun is a person:

> The woman who I was talking to . . .
> The woman whom I was talking to . . .
> The woman that I was talking to . . .

The three variations above are considered more formal by most native speakers, especially if the object form of *who* is used (*whom*). It's considered a more conversational style to omit *whom* or *that* in this construction: *The woman I was talking to . . .*

As for our sentences about the book, I can choose to use either **which** or **that** after the initial noun phrase if the noun is an animal or a thing. For some people, the effect of using *that* is to make the sentence somewhat more formal, and *which* sounds friendlier. Other people use *that* if the meaning is necessary to the sentence and *which* if the clause can be taken out without affecting the meaning much—with or without commas.

> The book <u>which</u> he spoke about . . .
> The book, which he spoke about so highly, is really excellent reading.
> The book which he spoke about so highly is really excellent reading.
>
> The book <u>that</u> he spoke about . . .
> The book that he spoke about is the one I'm reading.

Let's take a look at one more diagram that shows how we get another so-called post-posed preposition:

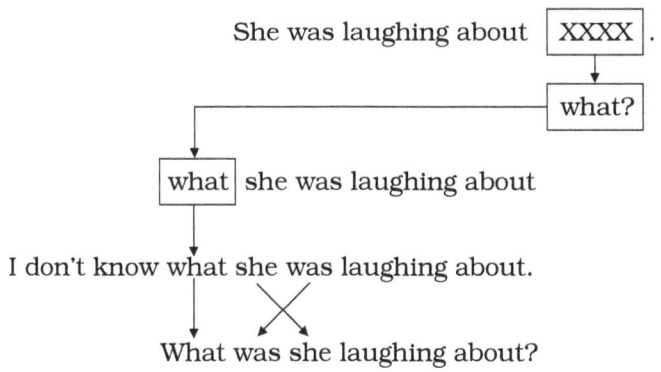

In the diagram, you can see that the operations in this case are just about the same as in the other diagrams. Here, however, there are two slight differences. The first one has to do with the fact that I have an unknown as the object of the preposition, so I use the word *what* to signify that unknown object and I move it to the front of the clause. The other difference is that in order to form the question, I need to invert *she* and *was*, which is the normal way to make a *wh-* question with the verb *be* anyway. (To refresh your memory about making *wh-* questions, see Chapter 1.) Again, notice that the preposition hasn't moved at all!

As we come towards the end of this chapter, there's a peculiar—though traditional—teaching tactic that I'd like to discuss. In many traditionally conceived English grammar books, you'll find the following order given when post-posed prepositions are dealt with:

1. The woman is my neighbor. I was talking to the woman.
2. The woman to whom I was talking is my neighbor.
3. The woman who(m)/that I was talking to is my neighbor.
4. The woman I was talking to is my neighbor.

I think this a very odd way indeed to demonstrate the changes that take place in order to arrive at a so-called post-posed preposition. Notice how the preposition in Step 1 is in its *rightful* place together with its object (to the woman). Suddenly, in Step 2, it's been thrust in front of the clause and in Step 3, it's been moved down the line again back to its original spot after the clause! Isn't this peculiar? All that these traditional grammar books need to do is leave well enough alone. The only reason the preposition has been finally **post-posed** is because it was **pre-posed** in Step 2!

For one very strange reason, these traditional grammarians felt that the pre-posed preposition was somehow a more basic construction and should therefore be Step 2. This tradition came about in the mid-17th century when the English were trying their best to fit English grammar into the way Latin grammar worked. It really doesn't work because they were trying to fit a Germanic language onto the structure of an Italic language. I feel, on the contrary, that the pre-posed construction is not so basic to the way English (i.e., Germanic) grammar works as it has been affected by influences from Latin and doesn't seem to go along with the way English constructs this kind of sentence. By the way, an interesting note about this pre-posed arrangement is that you can't use the word ***that*** any longer in place of *who* or *which* after a preposition:

1a. The woman to whom I was talking . . .
1b. The woman to that I was talking . . . (ungrammatical)

2a. The book about which he spoke . . .
2b. The book about that he spoke . . . (ungrammatical)

Before I close this chapter, I'd like to offer you a list of the clauses and sentences that you'll find post-posed prepositions in, or if you prefer, in which you'll find post-posed prepositions:

Statements:	I'd like you to look this over.
Wh- questions:	What are you thinking about?
Wh- clauses:	(Who I associate with) is none of your business.
Indirect speech:	He didn't tell me who he'd gotten the gift from.
Infinitive forms:	I can't find the right pot to cook this spaghetti in.
Relative clauses*:	"Here's another nice mess you've gotten me into!"
Exclamations:	Sit down!

Teaching Tips

6.1 *Drawing Prepositions*

Because so many prepositions are spatial, a good way for students to practice them is to draw pictures to show the meanings of these prepositions. The pictures need not be detailed or elaborate; they only need to be clear enough to represent the meanings. This activity can be done individually, in pairs, or in small groups. Once the pictures are drawn, have the class compare and contrast the ways that they chose to depict the prepositions. Then have the class choose the drawings that best visualize the prepositions or draw a class composite that synthesizes the best representations. Put these pictures on a wall chart and leave the chart up for students to look at and refer to later.

over/under   out of   through   around
above/below

6.2 *Prepositional Visualizations*

Before class, find a text that has a variety of spatial prepositions in it. Copy the text leaving blanks where the prepositions should be. Have the students fill in the blanks with pictures to represent the prepositions. Exchange papers and have students read their classmates' papers aloud, interpreting the visualizations with words. You can also do this activity in the reverse. Have the students

---

* A relative clause is a part of a sentence that acts adjectivally in that it describes something about the subject or object of that sentence. In fact, a relative clause is also referred to as an adjective clause. In the example above, "you've gotten me into" is the relative clause because it gives more information about the "mess." Another example is in this sentence: The woman **I was talking to** is my neighbor. The part in bold is a relative clause because it explains which woman I'm talking about. For more on relative clauses, see Chapter 12 (Coordination, Subordination, and Correlation) and visit ELTgrammar.com.

write stories (individually, in pairs, or in small groups) with the prepositions in them. Have them exchange their papers and let the new partners/pairs/groups visualize the prepositions. (Sami goes → _____ school _____ 8 every morning. He walks _____ the freeway and _____ a long tunnel.)

Variation: Use the same text as you used in *Teaching Tip* 6.2, only this time, leave the prepositions in. Put blanks after each preposition and have the students draw what the prepositions represent in the blanks. When all the students are finished drawing their prepositions, let them compare and contrast their visualizations.

6.3 *Back-to-Back*

Before class, find a picture that has prepositions represented in the various things and activities. Make copies for half of your students. In addition, prepare a second handout that is incomplete for the rest of the class. This handout should have one or two features from the original picture on it, which will serve as starting points or points of perspective for drawing the rest of the picture. For example, if the complete picture has one particular landmark in it, draw just that on the handout. If the picture has a building in the middle, draw that.

You decide how much needs to be put on this handout. Pair off the students and seat them back to back. Then give each student in the pair a different picture. The students who have the complete picture will describe what's in it so that their partners can draw a faithful copy of the original. Encourage the "describers" to be as accurate as possible, but the "artists" are permitted to ask as many questions as is necessary to get the drawing right, to fill in the gaps in the information.

Variation:
1. If providing photocopies is a problem, you can draw a picture or put one up on the board and have all the "describers" face the board and all the "artists" face the other way.
2. For students with very limited vocabularies, provide a handout that's ready to fill in or just a blank piece of paper for them to draw and/or color in. Give directions yourself about how you want your students to complete the pictures. For example, tell your students to draw a [brown] easy chair in the upper left corner. Put an oriental rug in front of it. Hang [blue and white] curtains in the window. Place a table next to the [brown] chair and put a table lamp on top of it, and so on.
3. Divide a sheet of paper into boxes. The boxes can be as large as half a sheet

or as small as a square inch (2½ cm.). Have the students fill in the different boxes according to directions given by you or another student. To make the exercise more interesting, don't have the students fill in the boxes in any particular order. Jump from corner to corner, from top to bottom, from center to side.

6.4 *Drawing Idioms*

In general, idioms are diffcult for students; idioms that contain prepositions are especially difficult. This *Teaching Tip* has two levels to it, a serious one and one with tongue in cheek. When it's possible to represent these idioms as drawings, do so. Before class, select a group of idioms that can be "translated" into drawings. Pair the students up or have them work in small groups. Show them how to "draw an idiom" and then let them do the artwork for several of the idioms you prepared before class. Put the finished products up around the room and compare and contrast the various ways the students chose to represent their idioms.

on top of the world   under the weather   in hot water   over the hill   in a tight spot

Variation: Pictograms: Before class, prepare a list of idioms with prepositions. Make absolutely sure that these idioms can be visually represented. Show the students what a "pictogram" is—a way to represent idioms verbatim; they show exactly what the idiom is. Once the students understand how pictograms work, let them make their own versions of the idioms that you've given them to work on in pairs or small groups. Here are some examples to show you how pictograms work.

1. ALL   AFTER   ("afterall")
2. I N B E T O   ("be into")
3. the bl^{outof}ue   ("out of the blue")
4. above
   all else   ("above all else")
5.   R   R
   D   O   D   O   ("round and round")
     N U   N U
6. thought   th^{on}ought   ("on second thought")

6.5 Obstacle Course

Before class, create an obstacle course with things that you have in your classroom. The obstacles can be as large as a desk or as small as a piece of paper on the floor. Blindfold one student and appoint another as guide. Have the guide give directions to the blindfolded student to get him/her/them through the course. It's often useful for the guide to follow along closely with the blindfolded student as he/she/they negotiates the course. This activity is particularly good for developing trust among students, precision in directions, and careful listening skills.

6.6 Hide and Seek

This activity is a version of the children's game "Hide and Seek." Before class, hide something in the classroom. Students need to find the object by asking yes/no questions that pinpoint the location of the hidden item. For example, Student: Are the keys at the front of the classroom? You: Cold. When a student asks a question, you respond "hot" if the answer to the question points to a location that is very close to where the object is hidden, "warm" if relatively close, and "cold" if far away from the hidden object. Students keep asking questions until the object is found. This activity is also excellent for practicing question formation.

6.7 Adèle's House

Before class, prepare a dialogue in which the participants discuss the layout of a room belonging to an imaginary person named Adèle. Use your mobile phone to record the dialogue. If not, you can read it to your class. Give the students a bare-bones layout of a room and tell them that they'll "furnish" it after they listen to a discussion of the layout. Read the dialogue or play the recording and have the students fix up the room.

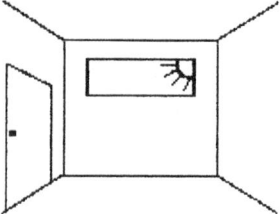

Variation: Instead of Adèle's room, you can do the same activity with a building plan, a city map, a supermarket or supermarket shelf, a library, a shopping center, a toolbox, a factory, a workshop, etc.

6.8 Legos

Bring to class a set of children's blocks or Legos (multi-colored plastic building blocks). Make sure you have enough blocks for all of your students to have several of their own. Pair the students up and have them sit back to back. Have one student in each pair create a design or pattern with his/her blocks. Limit the time to one or two minutes so that the partners don't get restless while they wait. Have the "designer" get his/her/their partner to recreate the same design or pattern by giving verbal instructions. When the students are done, have them compare their designs. Go over the differences in the patterns with the students to show them how to be more accurate in giving their instructions.

6.9 *Fractured Narrations*

Before class, find a picture or pictures with enough prepositional phrases represented for a narration. Let's say you've found a picture with the following: The sun is shining, but there are a few white, puffy clouds in the sky. A bird is in its nest. A chipmunk is arranging nuts in a tunnel, etc. Prepare a narration based on the picture that contains factual errors. (It's a beautiful day today. See? The sun is peeking out from behind the tree. A bird is next to its nest. A frisky chipmunk is taking nuts out of the tunnel, etc.)

Note: Don't change every preposition; it'll be far more challenging if some of the prepositional phrases are left correct. Tell the students that they're going to hear a narration that contains errors and that they'll be asked to write down as many of the errors as they can. Present the narration to the class several times so they can find all the errors. Go back and check to see that they've caught them all.

7

Genitives

"Mice's and men's best-laid plans?"
"The best-laid plans of mice and men?"

We're about to investigate one of the most deceptive topics of English grammar. The reason it's so deceptive is that what appears to be quite straightforward and relatively uncomplicated on the surface (after all, aren't we just talking about *-'s/-s'* and *of*?) is really somewhat perplexing when you get below the surface. As with other topics covered in this book, I'm going to focus my attention on those points that tend to be troublesome to understand and explain. Although many ELT grammar books refer to *-'s/-s'* and *of* as "possessives," I prefer to use the broader term "genitives," which includes any and all of their uses, some of which do not indicate possession. I'm sure you'll understand why I don't want to limit myself to the term "possessives" as you read on.

The -*S* Genitive

To begin with, let's examine the most typical uses of what I refer to as the *-s* **genitive** because it's found as an *-'s/-s'* on the end of a noun. Take a look at the dialogue below and note how the *-s* genitive is used.

A: **Phyllis'** daughter just joined a **girls'** football team.

B: Really? Was it the **school's** idea to create a football team for girls?

A: I think so. Anyway, she was great in **yesterday's** game. One funny thing, though. The team insists on having their mascot at every game. It's the cutest little white dog.

B: Ah, that's nice.

A: Yeah. They say the **dog's** presence brings them luck.

As already mentioned, most ELT grammar books refer to *-'s/-s'* as the possessive ending. Remember that *-'s* is attached to singular nouns (*clerk's*) and irregular plural nouns that do not end in *-s* (*children's*), but only the apostrophe is added onto singular nouns ending in *-s* (*boss'*) and regular plural nouns (*boys'*). Though often the case, it's not the only reason that *-'s/-s'* is used. In the dialogue you've just read, which examples of the *-s* genitive would you say clearly demonstrate possession or belonging? Write your observation on the following line:

....

The answer is that there are just two times when the *-s* genitive clearly shows possession or belonging in the dialogue, and that's with the name "Phyllis" and in talking about the dog. We can definitely say that Phyllis has a daughter, so she's *Phyllis' daughter*, and that the dog has presence, so it's *the dog's presence*. This way of thinking about the *-s* genitive leads us to the first use of the *-'s/-s'*: we tend to use the *-s* genitive as a marker of possession or belonging on words that represent people. We tend to use it the same way for animals (*a dog's bark; an alligator's stealth; a canary's song*). In fact, **we can make a general observation that we use the *-s* genitive for possession or belonging on words that typically represent living things (people and animals)**.

What, now, are we going to do with the rest of the cases of the *-s* genitive in our dialogue? For instance, how can we explain the *-s'* in the phrase *a girls' football team*? It's not that the team is a possession of the girls or that it belongs to the girls; similarly, we can't say that "the idea" is a possession of the school. We can say, however, that the presence does belong to the dog. Is there a simple way to paraphrase all of these phrases to see them in another light? If you were going to paraphrase them, what common way could you come up with? Write down your idea on this line:

....

I've used paraphrasing before to find the essence of a grammatical construction, and I can use it in this situation, too. Another way to say each of these phrases is "The girls have a football team." / "The school had an idea." / "The dog has presence." **The verb *have* is a common element in these sentences, and that's an easy way to explain this genitive to your students.** In fact, many teachers traditionally use *have* in a paraphrase to teach their students the meaning of *-s* genitive phrases as well as when they teach possessive adjectives (*my, your, his*, etc.). You should just keep in mind that *have* doesn't always mean the same thing, like possession; it's got lots of interpretations depending on context.

>  **Heads Up!**
>
> At times there's confusion over how to write the -s genitive when a name ends in the letter s. We can make the following observations to help you and your students on this point:
>
> → In the rules of such countries as the United Kingdom, the -'s is added to a name even if it ends in -s:
>
> Phyllis ⟶ Phyllis's
>
> → In the rules of such countries as the United States, only the apostrophe is added to a name that ends in -s:
>
> Phyllis ⟶ Phyllis'
>
> Keep in mind that there's no difference in pronunciation whether the genitive is written one way or the other.

Getting back to our dialogue, I still have to account for the -'s on the end of *yesterday*. First of all, let's take a look at some similar words and phrases and see if the -s genitive can be added to them as well. How about choices like *today/this week/Monday/next month*? Yes, the -'s works nicely with these, too: *today's newspaper/this week's stock reports/Monday's weather forecast/next month's tournament*. What observation can you make about these words and phrases?

....

If you've written that we can use the -s genitive with words and phrases that denote periods of time, you've got it right.

Let's move on by comparing the following two phrases. Decide if they're grammatical or not and check the boxes appropriately:

the school's idea ☐ grammatical ☐ ungrammatical
the school's wall ☐ grammatical ☐ ungrammatical

We already know that "the school's idea" is grammatical, but what about "the school's wall"? The answer is that it's ungrammatical although you may very well hear it said. Why is there a difference? I'm not going to answer this question just yet, but I'll get back to it very soon.

Heads Up!

Be prepared for an inevitable occurrence: Your students may tend to drop the -*s* genitive when you're not drilling them on it and produce phrases such as *my mother house* and *the teacher pen*. Don't get too exasperated over this—and don't stop correcting them either!

Another problem you'll have to deal with concerns the pronunciation of the -*s* genitive. Interestingly enough, the rules are identical for pronouncing the regular plural -*s* on nouns.

→ If the noun ends in a voiceless sound, pronounce the -s genitive as /s/:

        Jeff's /jɛfs/   Scott's /skats/

→ If the noun ends in a voiced sound, pronounce the -s genitive as /z/:

        Brenda's /brɛn-dəz/   Ann's /ænz/

→ If the noun ends in /s/, /š/, /z/, /ž/, /č/, or /ǰ/, pronounce the -s genitive as /ɪz/ or /əz/:

    Bess' /bɛs-ɪz/   fish's /fɪš-ɪz/   George's /ǰorǰ-ɪz/   Mitch's /mɪč-ɪz/

→ In some dialects of English, the /ɪz/ sound for the possessive marker is dropped on nouns that end in /z/. In other dialects, however, it's kept:

        Charles' /čarlz/ or /čarlz-ɪz/

Let's observe some other ways we use the -*s* genitive when possession is not the meaning by taking a look at another dialogue:

A: Let's have some coffee.

B: Okay. Oh! Don't use the large, white mug. That's **Mom's** mug.

A: All right. So what's happening with that lawsuit between the paper mill and us over dumping pollutants into the bay?

B: I'm happy to say the **committee's** trip to the capital was a success, and they've persuaded the government to step in.

A: That's great! Who's on our side in the government?

B: Tess Hyman. I really like her. She's a **politician's** politician.

A: Terrific! You know, I bet we used at least two hundred **dollars'** worth of stamps mailing out all of those flyers.

B: I wouldn't be surprised. Well, with Tess behind us, getting anti-pollution regulations enforced should be **child's** play.

A: I hope so. Wouldn't it be wonderful to be able to swim to your **heart's** content in that water again and not worry about pollution?

Note the words in bold print. In order to zero in on the uses of the -*s* genitive in this dialogue, I'll take each item that appears above separately and add some other examples to it. Perhaps that will help you figure out how to categorize each kind of -*s* genitive I've used. When you think you've got a category for each set of phrases, identify it on the line I've provided for you.

1. Mom's coffee mug / Dad's easy chair / John's side of the bed
   (Note: Think of a category other than possession or belonging.)

   ....

2. the committee's trip / the enemy's retreat / Tahani's promotion

   ....

3. a politician's politician / a man's man / a poet's poet

   ....

4. 100 dollars' worth / 500 pesos' worth / 6,000 liras' worth

   ....

5. child's play / everyone's dream / men's clothing / lovers' lane

   ....

6. to your heart's content / at journey's end / at death's door

   ....

Granted, this is one of the most difficult tasks I've asked you to do, but even if you've only come up with two or three of the categories, you're doing fine. Here's the way I see these categorizations of the -s genitive. You might have used different wording, but if the concepts are the same, that's all that counts:

1. **a preferred thing:**
   - That's the coffee mug that Mom is partial to. All the other coffee mugs may belong to her, too, but that one is her favorite mug and she doesn't like anybody else using it.
   - That's the easy chair that Dad likes the most.
   - That's the side of the bed that John sleeps on.
2. **actions that the head noun has done or received:**
   - The committee took that trip. (They're the "doers.")
   - The enemy retreated. (They're the "doers.")
   - Tahani got that promotion. (She's the "receiver.")
3. **the best; the epitome:**
   - a politician that other politicians would like to emulate
   - a man who other men can admire for his manly qualities
   - a poet who is held in esteem by other poets
4. **an amount of money equal to (used with " . . . worth of . . .")**

5. **things that seem appropriate (paraphrased with "for"):**
   - play that is appropriate for a child
   - a dream for everyone
   - clothing for men
   - a place that seems appropriate for lovers to meet at
6. **formulaic phrases:**
   - tend to be idiomatic and disregard rules for using -'s/-s'

Now let's get back to answer that statement I gave you about it being grammatical to say "the school's idea," but not really grammatical to say "the school's wall." **The -s genitive is normally not used with non-living things if there is a noun adjunct or compound noun commonly used.** For example, nobody will flinch if you say *the room's décor* or *my lawn's brown spots*. But nobody would normally say *the kitchen's clock*; it would be *the kitchen clock*, with *kitchen* being the noun adjunct describing the clock. Similarly, nobody would normally say *a tree's trunk*; they'd say *a tree trunk*, which is a compound noun.

So now we come back to *the school's idea* vs. *the school's wall*. In the phrase *the school's idea*, we're really talking about the administration, in other words, the people who run the school; therefore, it's proper to use -'s just like we'd say *administration's idea*. But we don't say *the school's wall* because we have a perfectly proper noun adjunct (school) to use: *the school wall*. And there you have it!

In this context, words like *school* are collective nouns representing people in one way or another. Can you think of any other collective nouns representing groups of people or geographical areas that we can add the -'s/-s' to? Here are a few examples: our *club's* next meeting/*New York's* skyscrapers/their *class'* tenth reunion/*Honduras'* coastline.

Other collective nouns represent animals, and we can use -'s on such words as *herd, pride,* and *pack*: the *herd's* migration patterns/the *pride's* adult females/a wolf *pack's* territory.

Here are other examples of things that can take the -'s/-s'. They're things that we perceive as personifications or performing some sort of actions: our *ship's* first mate/the *plane's* departure/an *ICBM's* range/the *earth's* orbit/ *Saturn's* position in the solar system.

So are we done with the -s genitive? Not quite; we still have two important areas to talk about, and one of them can be seen in this next dialogue:

A: What are you doing tomorrow?

B: Well, first I'm going to the doctor's and then I'm meeting my sister for lunch at Murphy's. I've got nothing special planned after lunch, though.

A: Well, that's not far from St. Jerome's. How about meeting me there in the afternoon to help me with my daughter's wedding arrangements?

B: Sure, I'd love to. My son's wedding there a year ago was just beautiful, and I'm sure your daughter's will be, too.

Unlike all the other forms of the -*s* genitive that we've looked at up to now, this time we have the form standing on its own without any accompanying nouns. Take a look back at the words I've boxed in and guess which nouns you could add after them through the help of context:

the doctor's	....
Murphy's	....
St. Jerome's	....
your daughter's	....

I'm sure you've filled in the blanks with **office, Restaurant (Pub/Tavern), Church,** and **wedding**. This wasn't such a hard task because the context of the dialogue helped you figure out what these words with -*'s* stood for. **We can use the -*s* genitive on its own when it's clear what it refers to.**

Now we're coming to the last point we should discuss about the -*s* genitive in this section of the chapter. Look at the following phrases and decide if they mean the same thing or different things.

Gilbert and Sullivan's works
Gilbert's and Sullivan's works

☐ same   ☐ different

Even though these phrases may seem the same at a quick glance, they're really quite different in meaning. Try to figure out what the difference is and write your thoughts on the following lines:

....

....

When we have two or more names and all the people involved are connected to the head noun (in this case, "works"), **only the final name, the one closest to the head noun, gets the -*'s/-s'*** ("Gilbert and Sullivan's works," meaning the works that Gilbert and Sullivan created together). However, **if the head noun is distinct for each person mentioned, each name gets -*'s/-s'*** ("Gilbert's and Sullivan's works"—in other words, works that they didn't create as a team).

Another example of this phenomenon is "Athena and Aristoteli'<u>s</u> children" as compared to "Athena's and Aristoteli's children." How would you interpret the difference in meaning between the two phrases?

....

....

In the **first example**, Athena and Aristoteli **have children together**; in the **second example, Athena has some children, and Aristoteli has some children, but they didn't have them together.**

Group Genitives

Another phenomenon that occurs with the -*s* genitive is called the group genitive. What happens is that the end of a compound noun or a phrase describing the head noun receives the suffixed -*'s/-s'*; in other words, the whole phrase is treated as a single unit. What follows are four examples of typical group genitives:

> a judge advocate's caseload/the notary public's office
> my sister-in-law's boss/a man-about-town's wardrobe

These next three group genitives are rather unusual but possible. They're likely to be found in colloquial speech rather than formal writing and can be a lot of fun. I'll be discussing a more formalized way of dealing with such awkward phrases later on:

> the guy who works in the mailroom's wife
> the neighbor whose wife won two Caribbean cruises' house
> the woman who I spoke to's son

🌰 *The -S Genitive in a Nutshell*

- used for people and animals:
  - **possession/belonging:**
    Myrlande's skirt/the parakeet's feathers
  - **paraphrasing with** *have*:
    Yuri's fever (Yuri has a fever.)
    the dog's fleas (The dog has fleas.)
  - **a preferred thing:**
    Iris' place at the dinner table
    my dog's spot for burying things
  - **head noun does/receives action:**
    Bill's resignation/the lion's kill (doers)
    the thief 's arrest/the zebra's capture (receivers)

- **showing esteem:**
  a surgeon's surgeon/a teacher's teacher
- **appropriateness (can be paraphrased with *for*):**
  soldiers' uniforms (uniforms for soldiers)
  a tiger's habitat (the habitat for a tiger)
- **collective nouns (groups of people or animals):**
  the committees' members/the flock's dominant ram

🌀 **used with words representing periods of time:**
this month's gas bill/tomorrow's weather/a day's wages

🌀 **amount of money equal to** (always with *worth of*):
thirty euros' worth of gasoline/100 rubles' worth of cheese

🌀 **on words representing periods of time with *worth of*:**
three weeks' worth of work done in five days

🌀 **sometimes for nonliving things that are perceived as performing actions:**
these cars' special features/the train's dining car/the sun's rays

🌀 **formulaic phrases (pat phrases):**
a stone's throw/a snowball's chance in hell/at arm's length/a dentist's appointment

🌀 **on its own when the reference is clear:**
The family reunion is going to be at my cousin's. He works at Harrod's.

🌀 **when two or more names share the head noun:**
Ben and Jerry's ice cream

🌀 **group genitives:**
The Out-of-Towners' Guide to Auckland

The *Of*-Genitive

A: Magda, did you know the brother of that boy you're dating has been arrested?

B: Anton's brother? Arrested?

A: He's been charged with stealing the car of that nice old couple who live right next door to his parents.

B: The Nagys' car? I don't believe it!

A: Believe it! I never did like him. He's nothing like Anton.

The dialogue you've just read offers us a convenient transition from the *-s* genitive to the *of*-genitive. According to what I stated in the first part of this chapter, the *-s* genitive should be the proper form when we focus on living things, but we can clearly see the *of*-genitive used for some of the people mentioned in our dialogue. Why is that? In fact, not only have I used both forms of the genitive in this dialogue, but I've even used them at different times for the same people. Isn't that strange! Or is it? After you take another look at the way -'s/-s' and of are used in this dialogue, can you come up with an explanation to defend both uses? If you can, write your ideas on the following lines:

....

....

Although the -s genitive is the more typical form we use for possession or belonging when living things are involved, **we tend to use the *of*-genitive if we're using an adjectival clause to describe the head noun:** "the brother of that boy *you're dating*"/"the car of that nice old couple *who live right next door to his parents*." True, in colloquial speech we might hear group genitives used in these two cases: "that boy you're dating's brother"/"that nice old couple who live right next door to his parents' car." Even though all group genitives are slightly bizarre, this first one seems more plausible than the second one simply because it's shorter and easier to deal with. Using the *of*-genitive in these cases certainly saves us a lot of trouble. Let's take a look at one more dialogue that demonstrates the *of*-genitive in this way:

> A: Remember that song "Scarborough Fair"?
>
> B: Yeah, sure. In fact, I remember it was on an album that was a birthday gift to me from the parents **of** a high school friend I tutored in algebra.
>
> A: So what ever happened to your friend?
>
> B: I hear he married the daughter **of** some math genius who's always winning awards!

Now that I've discussed how *of* can be used in place of -'s/-s' under certain circumstances, I should restate the most typical use for the *of*-genitive, which is that whereas the -s genitive seems to be used primarily with living things, **the *of*-genitive seems to be used primarily with non-living things (both concrete and abstract).** Here are some examples for you to look at. Note that you probably wouldn't interchange them with the -s genitive:

> the color of that <u>shirt</u>/the cost of a <u>computer</u> (concrete things)
> the taste of <u>lamb</u>/the price of <u>fish</u> (food items = non-living things)
> a line of <u>defense</u>/a standard of <u>conduct</u> (abstract things)

>  **Heads Up!**
>
> Genitive forms aren't used the same way in every language. A case in point is how the *of*-genitive is used in some languages where we use the preposition *in*:
>
> Spanish: El desierto más grande |del| mundo. (*del* = *of the*)
> English: The largest desert |in| the world.
>
> A possible explanation for this is that English focuses on *location* rather than possession in such sentences.
>
> Expect some of your students to demonstrate this bit of language interference.

Partitive Genitives

A very common use for the *of*-genitive deals with a category that I can place under the umbrella of **partitives**, concrete and abstract words that represent a part of the whole. Take a look at the following dialogue, which demonstrates this use:

> A: Have you seen that new **pair of gloves** I just bought?
>
> B: Weren't they on the **top of the dresser**?
>
> A: I thought so, but they're not there now!
>
> B: I have a **piece of advice** for you. Don't leave things lying around.
>
> A: And here I am ready to go to the store and I was going to wear them. Where can they be?
>
> B: What do we need at the store?
>
> A: Oh, let's see . . . a **can of coffee**, half a **kilo of butter**, two **loaves of bread**, and some other things as well.
>
> B: Coffee? There's a can of coffee on the kitchen counter.
>
> A: What you see is a coffee can, but it's empty. Well, gloves or no gloves, I'm on my way.

Just as you've done before, list the various highlighted phrases that appear in this dialogue and see if you can identify categories for the partitive genitives they represent. Where there aren't many examples, I've given you some more to look at. Write your categories on the blank lines.

1. a pair of gloves/a pair of scissors/a stack of dishes/a set of knives

....

2. the top of the dresser/the back of the chair/the leg of the table

....

3. a piece of advice/a time of plenty/a heap of trouble

....

4. a can of coffee/half a kilo of butter/two loaves of bread

....

So what would you call these categories under the umbrella heading of partitives? As I see it, the first category is simple—it's just anything that comes in **pairs or sets**. The next category deals with **parts of things**; the third category deals with **abstracts** that can't be counted, but which we feel the need to think of as if they could be. Finally, our fourth category deals with **measures** and, although these three examples all have to do with food, the category isn't limited to food alone: *a pound of nails/a ball of twine/a ream of paper*.

By the way, did you notice that curious twist on words at the end of the last dialogue? Person B says that she saw a can of coffee sitting on the kitchen counter, but Person A explains that what she saw was a coffee can—an empty one at that. What's going on here? How would you explain the difference between *a coffee can* and *a can of coffee*? Here are a few more examples just to help you out. When you've got an idea, write it down on the lines below:

a cup of tea/a teacup
a jar of mayonnaise/a mayonnaise jar
a barrel of oil/an oil barrel

....
....

I bet that you've been able to explain the difference in the phrases I've just given you. When describing the **specific uses for these containers**, we make compound nouns: *a coffee can/a teacup/a mayonnaise jar/an oil barrel*. But when we speak about **what's inside the containers** (amounts, in these cases), we use the partitive genitive: *a can of coffee/a cup of tea/a jar of mayonnaise/a barrel of oil*.

Appositives

Finally, I have one more use for the *of*-genitive that can seem a bit perplexing. Look at the next dialogue and see if you can figure out what the reason for this use is:

A: Why are you so excited today?

B: Because the **President of Fulania** is going to be the guest speaker at our graduation ceremony.

A: That's terrific! I hear he's a **jewel of a speaker**.

B: That's what I've heard, too. It's amazing to think that he comes from such a humble background.

A: Oh, really?

B: Yes. He comes from the little **village of Abadoo** in the desert part of the country, but he spent quite a few years in the **city of Leicester**, you know, in England.

A: Do you know what his speech is going to be on?

B: Uh-huh. "The **Art of Active Listening**," whatever that is.

What role do you think the *of-*genitive is playing in all these phrases? Here's a little hint: All of them except one deal with literal usage and the other one is idiomatic. After you've given this some thought, write your conclusions on the following lines:

....

....

In all of the phrases I've highlighted (except for "a jewel of a speaker"), there's one basic purpose for using the *of-*genitive and that is **to explain more about the preceding noun**. All these phrases answer the question *which?* or *what?* The president of what? Fulania. Which little village? Abadoo. What city? Leicester. Which art? Active listening. This quirky use for the *of-genitive* is called the **appositive use**.

As for the other phrase, "a jewel of a speaker," this is an idiomatic use of the appositive construction meaning *a very good speaker*. Other examples of this kind of usage are *a beast of a night, a prince of a man, a nightmare of a flight*.

🌰 *The Of-Genitive in a Nutshell*

🌰 **used to focus on some aspect of most non-living things (concrete and abstract):**
the texture of the snow/the roll of the waves
the heart of the matter/the depth of his anguish

- with head nouns that are followed by adjectival clauses:
  the son of the lady *I introduced you to at the party*

- used as a partitive for concrete and abstract things:
  - **pairs or sets:** a pair of glasses/a set of rollers
  - **parts of things:** the limbs of a tree/the pages of a book
  - **abstracts:** a bit of pleasure/a moment of silence
  - **measures:** 4 liters of gasoline/10 yards of cloth

- used as an appositive to explain or describe the preceding noun:
  the Book of Kells/the Cliffs of Dover

 **Heads Up!**

It's a good idea to keep in mind that there are several languages that don't have genitives such as we have in English. In those languages, the genitive is expressed simply by the syntax of the phrase, that is, where the words are placed. Let's look at some disparate languages and see how they do fine without a true genitive form. To demonstrate our point, I'll use the phrase *the boy's book*.

→ Haitian Creole:	liv the book	ptigason-an the boy	
→ Arabic:	kitab book	alwalad the boy	
→ Amharic:	yɛliǰu the boy	madzhaf book	
→ Cantonese:	nam–haɪji boy	dɛk the	sɪ book

If you find your students having a lot of trouble with the English genitive forms, it might be because their languages simply don't have the equivalents of our -'s / -s' or of.

The Double Genitive

We've covered the -s genitive and the *of*-genitive separately, but there are occasions when the two are used together—that's why this structure is called the double genitive. It's really quite an odd-looking form, especially to students, but one that's quite commonly used. Let's take a look at a couple of these:

friends of the priests'/a son of the teacher's

To the student, this construction may be very confusing. Most likely, the student would say that it's the -'s/-s' on the end of each phrase that makes it so odd. Isn't it enough to say *friends of the priests* or *a son of the teacher* and leave it at that? It might be, except for the fact that we normally use the -s genitive for living things. No, something else is going on here. The student might be more comfortable with the construction *the priests' friends* and *the teacher's son* (assuming he or she has already learned this basic genitive form), but are these accurate paraphrases of my original phrases? What's your opinion?

....

....

The answer is that **the paraphrases I've come up with *don't* accurately reflect the meaning of my original phrases.** The reason is that they inadvertently mislead us. Saying *the priests' friends* leads us to believe that the priests have only a certain number of friends or that specific friends who I've already mentioned are being cited; likewise, saying *the teacher's son* makes us think that the teacher has only one son or, once again, he's the son I've already mentioned—and that's not the case. The truth is that these people are just some friends out of several that the priests have (*friends of the priests'*) and the other person is just one of at least two sons that the teacher has (*a son of the teacher's*). There's nothing intrinsically wrong with saying *the priests' friends* and *the teacher's son* as long as it's true that the priests do only have these friends and the teacher has only one son, or that I've already mentioned these people. If, however, that isn't the case, I have to find another way to express my ideas, and this is where the double genitive helps out.

Let's focus for a moment on the indefinite articles (zero article or *a/an*) that are used in the double genitive construction. What if a student of yours says, "They're the friends of the priests'"? Is this acceptable? Think about what you'd say to your student and write it on the following lines:

....

....

It turns out that **you can't say a sentence like the one the student created because *the* indicates exclusivity.** The whole purpose of this odd construction is to communicate that these people are just *some* of their friends, so if your student uses *the*, he or she defeats this purpose. Of course, there's an easy way to circumvent this whole problem and that's by paraphrasing once again. Instead of saying *friends of the priests'*, we can say *some of the priests' friends*, and instead of saying *a son of the teacher's*, we can say *one of the teacher's sons*.

Getting back to that student for a moment, let's say he or she wasn't finished after saying, "They're the friends of the priests' . . ." but wanted to say something about these people. Could saying *the* end up being grammatical after all? See if you can figure this out:

It so happens that **your student can definitely make the phrase perfectly grammatical** by adding adjectival information that will then give exclusivity to those people. For example, he or she could say, "They're the friends of the priests' *who won that trip to Tahiti.*" If there's this kind of exclusivity, it's all right to use *the*. Note also that the clause *who won that trip to Tahiti* must go with *friends* because *priests'* —as a genitive form—cannot be the *who*.

There's one more thing to be said about the double genitive. It's quite common to use possessive pronouns (*mine, yours, his,* etc.) as the second element in this construction. Here are two examples:

friends of mine/a neighbor of theirs

This use of possessive pronouns goes hand in hand with the use of the -'s/-s' in the double genitive that I've just finished discussing. On a final note, there's one aspect of this form which is rarely taught. Here are four examples of it. Try to identify what's going on:

This nose of mine is quite aristocratic.
That cat of theirs is lovable, isn't she?
That parrot of yours woke me up again this morning!
Those kids of hers always manage to get into mischief.

If you've written that this **double genitive plus the addition of the demonstratives *this, that, these,* or *those* shows some sort of extra emotion or feeling**, you've hit on it exactly. Among other things, this special phrase can communicate **affection or disdain, approval or disapproval**.

-'S/-S' vs. Of: The Gray Areas

We've finally arrived at the last topic concerning the genitives. It's a problematic topic that perhaps deals more with style than grammar. Read the following items and choose the genitive form that seems *more appropriate to each situation* and check it off. (Here's a tip: Go by your first impressions; don't think about them too much!)

1. "My lords and ladies, ladies and gentlemen, it is my distinct honor to present to you His Royal Highness, Juan Carlos de Borbón,
    ☐ *Spain's King.*"   ☐ *the King of Spain.*"

2. "Our next story on the Evening News has to do with
    ☐ *Spain's plans* for the upcoming summer Olympics."
    ☐ *the plans of Spain* for the upcoming summer Olympics."

3. A: Are you taking any literature courses next semester?
   B: Yes. I'm going to take a course called
    ☐ *"Hemingway's Novels."*   ☐ *"The Novels of Hemingway."*

4. "Welcome to my class, ladies and gentlemen. I'm glad that you've signed up for this course, and I hope you enjoy the subject as much as I do.
    ☐ *Hemingway's novels* have greatly contributed to international literature."
    ☐ *The novels of Hemingway* have greatly contributed to international literature."

5. "Good evening. My name's Ruth and I'll be your server this evening. Besides the seafood listed on our menu,
    ☐ *the catch of the day* is sea bass. Just let me know when you're ready to order."
    ☐ *the day's catch* is sea bass. Just let me know when you're ready to order."

6. A: Hi, Joe! How did the fishing go today?
   B: Not bad at all, Frank. How about you?
   A: We did just fine, I'm glad to say. So what are you planning to do with
    ☐ *the catch of the day?*   ☐ *the day's catch?*
   B: We'll be selling it to some of those restaurants along the beach.

Style in language can be a difficult thing to pin down. There really are no hard-and-fast rules that cover every given situation concerning style and which option (-'s/-s' or *of*) to choose, but there are some conclusions I can draw from observing how a great many native speakers handle phrases like the six items you've just dealt with. I'll wait to give you my conclusions a little later; right now, let's go over the items.

First of all, here's what the majority of native speakers would choose:

1. **Juan Carlos de Borbón, the King of Spain.**
2. **Spain's plans for the upcoming summer Olympics.**
3. **a course called "The Novels of Hemingway."**
4. **Hemingway's novels have greatly contributed . . .**

5. . . . the catch of the day is sea bass.
6. So what are you planning to do with the day's catch?

Compare your choices to these. Then see if you can figure out what seems to be the underlying factor that accounts for the choices that were favored. When you've come up with an idea, write it down on the following lines:

....

....

The answer may lie in what we refer to as **formulaic phrases**, that is, certain traditional usages in a language that may or may not go along with the usual conventions. Sometimes it's quite easy for us to decide why one of these formulaic phrases is used in a given situation, but sometimes it's not so clear. We probably all agreed that saying "the King *of Spain*" in Item 1 sounded more appropriate in that situation than saying "*Spain's King*" even though *Spain's plans* seems perfectly appropriate when the newscaster says it as he refers to that country's plans for the summer Olympic games. Pretending a little, we can imagine hearing Item 1 during the formal presentation of a visiting monarch to the Court of St. James in London.

As we've said, there are no hard-and-fast rules on this subject, but there does seem to be a tendency we can discern. **It appears that the formulaic phrases that employ the *of*-genitive tend to sound more formal to us than the *-s* genitive and give the phrase an air of importance or dramatic effect.** This "feel" that native speakers have seems to govern which genitive they choose, but I want to stress that there are probably exceptions to my observation.

Now let's talk about Items 2 through 6. Because university course titles are usually presented in formal catalogs, most people would choose "The Novels *of* Hemingway" even though entitling the course "Hemingway's Novels" works just as well, grammatically speaking. Conversely, most people would feel it's appropriate for a professor to use the *-s* genitive in his introductory remarks to the class (Hemingway's novels), perhaps because there's no need for him to *sound* more formal or dramatic in his opening comments.

People are of the opinion that by saying "the catch of the day," our server seems to give the phrase that extra dramatic or important air which he or she might want to impart to the customers. The fisherman, on the other hand, is just making small talk with another fisherman, so people feel he has no need to give the phrase any special effect ("the day's catch").

There's one more troublesome issue I'd like to address concerning the gray areas of the genitives. In many scholarly, traditional works on English grammar, mention is made that the *-s* genitive is used with "higher" animals and the *of*-genitive with "lower" animals. I find this rule to be questionable; after all, where is the line to be drawn between what a "higher" animal is and what a "lower" animal is? Is it wrong to say *my turtle's food* or *a mosquito's wings*? Or is it that those two creatures are too "low" on the scale for the *-s* genitive? Many—if not most—native speakers would not flinch either way if they heard someone say *a mosquito's wings* or *the wings of a mosquito*. Likewise, would they cringe if they heard someone say *the song of a canary* instead of *a canary's song*? I doubt it. I think it best to leave well enough alone and simply say that there are certain gray areas concerning *-'s/-s'* and *of* where both forms are probably more acceptable than not, and the use of one or the other may best be left up to the individual.

Teaching Tips

7.1 *Simon Says*

Even though possessive adjectives aren't covered in this book, I wanted to include this very energetic activity here. Most students are first introduced to genitives as possessive adjectives (*my, your, his, her, its, our,* and *their*). It's fun to practice these forms with the game "Simon Says." The object of "Simon Says" is to find out who the best listener in class is. The best listener is the student who makes no mistakes carrying out what the teacher tells them to do. To play the game, the teacher asks all the students to stand up and follow directions *exactly*. This doesn't sound like such a hard thing to do, and indeed it wouldn't be but for the fact that you yourself don't have to do what you've ordered the students to do. You might say, "Put a finger on the end of your nose" as you put your finger on the end of your nose. You might just as well put your finger on your chin. But any student who's put a finger on their chin is out of the game and has to sit down. Hearing one thing and doing another is reason for expulsion. Any directions that you give should have a genitive form in them. (Touch the leg of your chair.) The game continues until there's only one student left standing.

7.2 *Descriptions: "This Is My…"*

Give each student a fairly uncomplicated picture, one that doesn't have too many details in it. Divide the class into groups of approximately ten. One by one, each student shows their picture to all the members of the group and briefly says what it contains ("There's a green sofa in my picture."/"There are two kids in mine."/"There's a beautiful queen in my picture." etc.). After all the pictures have been described, ask the students to write down as much information as they can remember about each of their group's pictures. Model example sentences, highlighting the various genitive forms. ("Charlie's sofa is green. One of the legs of the sofa is broken."/"The children in Hugo's picture have red hair. I think the tips of their shoes are dirty."/"Jean-Claude's picture had a queen in it. I think she's the Queen of Sheba.")

7.3 Family Resemblances

People in the same family often resemble one another. Have the students use genitives to describe themselves and their family members."I have my mother's disposition and my father's eyes. I've also got my grandmother's figure" and so on.

7.4 Modified Clozes

Students whose languages don't have as wide a variety of genitive forms as English does often have a difficult time trying to decide which English form to use. To help them get a better feel for the *-s* and *of-*genitives, create a group of sentences or a modified cloze exercise before class (see *Appendix 1, Cloze Exercises*). Be sure that the cloze contains a variety of the different genitive forms. Here's a brief sample, with answers below.

A (Couple/Books) .... Worth (Millions/Dollars) ....

Last month, the English-speaking world was stunned to learn that two old-looking texts discovered in (trunk/basement/one/Queen Elizabeth/castles) .... were actually written by William Shakespeare and Geoffrey Chaucer. (Shakespeare and Chaucer/works) .... were in almost perfect condition even though they'd been in the trunk for (hundreds/years) .... The texts were immediately sold, earning a (king/ransom) ....

A (Couple/Books) *Couple of Books* Worth (Millions/Dollars) *Millions of Dollars*.

Last month, the English-speaking world was stunned to learn that two old-looking texts discovered in (trunk/basement/one/Queen Elizabeth/castles) *a trunk in the basement of one of Queen Elizabeth's castles* were actually written by William Shakespeare and Geoffrey Chaucer. (Shakespeare and Chaucer/works) *Shakespeare's and Chaucer's works* were in almost perfect condition even though they'd been in the trunk for (hundreds/years) *hundreds of years*. The texts were immediately sold, earning a (king/ransom) *king's ransom*.

7.5 What's the Difference?

Before class, find or create pairs of pictures that are similar but not identical in details (like pictures from catalogs). Have two students work together and give them one of the pairs of pictures. Get them to discover the differences in their pictures by asking questions about the various items. To get the specific information that the students need, tell them to use a variety of genitives in their questions and answers. Here are some typical questions and answers: "Is there a flower on the front of the sweater?"/"No, there's nothing on the front of the sweater." "Is there anything over the back of the chair?"/"No, but there's a sweater on the seat of the chair.""What was in the dog's mouth?"/"There was nothing in the dog's mouth."

8
Modal Auxiliaries in the Present or Future

"I would if I could, but I can't, so I won't."

One of the biggest challenges to an instructor is successfully teaching the uses of the surprisingly complex little words and phrases that we call **modal auxiliaries**. Modal auxiliaries are a real challenge because

- they have several meanings,
- they can vary in usage from one part of the English-speaking world to another,
- they have many "gray areas" where they overlap in meaning, and
- they may exhibit differences in meaning and usage from one speaker to another even in the same region.

Because of all these complexities, I'd like to give you some advice for the information you're about to discover in this chapter: Pick and choose among what I have to offer; there will be points that you feel can be useful to you in your teaching, but there will be other points that you may decide aren't appropriate or necessary for your English grammar lesson or should be reserved for more advanced students. That, of course, doesn't mean *you* shouldn't become sensitized to those points—you never know when an astute person in one of your classes may throw a question at you on one of those points, and it would be nice if you could answer the student with confidence... or at least understand the question and recognize what the student is asking without surprise! I'll be referring to these grammar items either as modal auxiliaries or the short form, modals.

Just exactly which words are we talking about? Here's a list of them: *can, could, will, would, shall, should, ought to, may, might,* and *must*. Some grammarians also include *used to, would rather, had better,* and *had best,* but I'll be dealing with these four and some others under the heading "semi-auxiliaries" (also known as "periphrastic modals").

I can explain what these modals are by comparing them to ordinary verbs. (Note the asterisks [*] before most of the following examples; I'm using asterisks to mean that the phrase is ungrammatical):

- Modal auxiliaries never take the infinitive *to* (*to can/*to may).
- They never add the *-s* to 3rd person singular in the present or general time (*he mays/*it shoulds).
- They never require the *-ed* ending for the past (*we shoulded).
- They never have *-ing* attached to them (*by oughting).
- They never use forms of *do* or *be* to make negatives, yes/no questions, or tag questions (*you don't can/*he isn't mighting); instead, they use the word *not* after them for the negative (you cannot/he might not).
- Their forms don't necessarily indicate the tense of the sentence (Sure, I could do it tomorrow.).

We call them "auxiliaries" because their main function is to *help* a true verb by altering its meaning, that is, adding some extra meaning or nuance that the verb itself doesn't have alone.

There are some other general points I should mention about modals:

- In *standard* English, two modals can never be used together:

    *I think Pancho <u>might could</u> be at the office.

- All modals can refer to the present or the future using the same form—even *will* can accomplish this goal in a certain context as you'll see later on:

    We <u>can</u> take samples of the lake water *now*.
    We <u>can</u> take samples of the lake water *tomorrow*.

- What many people commonly call the past form of modals (like *could*, *would*, and *might*) isn't really the past at all the way we normally use these words:

    <u>Could</u> you give me a ride downtown tomorrow?

These forms are only truly the past when they're clarified with additional information or through context:

He <u>couldn't</u> come *yesterday.*

Because most grammar books created for students only give a superficial presentation of modals and usually don't mention semi-auxiliaries such as *would rather*, I'm going to fill in the gaps and give you a more complete picture in this chapter.

Before I get under way, I should mention that this chapter will only deal with the modal auxiliaries in their present/future use. You'll find a detailed exploration of the modals in the past in Chapter 9.

>  **Heads Up!**
>
> Be prepared for an inevitable occurrence: Many of your students will use the word *to* after each and every modal auxiliary!
>
> This may happen because they're accustomed to using *to* after so many verbs like *want*, *plan*, and *try*. It may also happen because in many languages it's quite normal to use the infinitive form (our *to* + verb) after their equivalents of modals. Therefore, they transfer the infinitive marker (*to*) from their native languages.
>
> Spanish: Puedo ayudarte. ⟶ I can to help you.
> Russian: Я должен уйти. ⟶ I must to leave.
> /ya dol-žın uy-ti./

Can/Could

I'm going to begin our exploration of the modal auxiliaries by taking a good look at the words *can* and *could*. Read this first dialogue and figure out what the exact uses of *can* are. You'll notice a number attached to the modal for each use that's being demonstrated in the dialogue. This system will help me discuss the various uses of modals in all of the dialogues that follow, too.

When you think you've figured out what each use of *can* is in this dialogue, write your idea on the following lines that numerically match them:

> A: Did you know that different species of whales **can**[1] create different kinds of "songs" to communicate with one another?
>
> B: Yes, I knew that. And I've met a famous marine biologist who **can**[1] tell one species of whale from another just by listening to their "songs."
>
> A: You **can't**[2] be serious!
>
> B: I am!
>
> A: **Can**[3] people really do that?
>
> B: Trust me. They can.

1. ....

2. ....

3. ....

Let's see how we interpret *can* in this dialogue. ***Can¹*** means **ability**. There's a slight difference, though, between the first modal labeled *1* and the second. In the first use, the modal means *innate* ability, but in the second it means *acquired* ability. Just as we don't distinguish between the two very much in real life, we don't bother differentiating these fine lines with the modal either.

Can't² has a different use. Here the modal auxiliary in the negative expresses **disbelief** or **impossibility**. Person A is saying that he's having a hard time believing that Person B is serious (not joking) about a marine biologist having that special skill. At this point, take a look at the following two sentences in which *can't* and *couldn't* represent disbelief or impossibility. See if you can perceive a difference between the two and write your idea on the following lines:

1. You've been married how many years? You can't be!
2. You've been married how many years? You couldn't be.

....

....

What many native speakers will perceive as the difference between these two sentences is that ***can't*** **is a stronger form of disbelief or impossibility than** ***couldn't***. In fact, using *couldn't* may actually soften the meaning enough so that it's used in a more tactful way communicating that something is "hard to believe" rather than "impossible." By the way, you'll be seeing another instance further on in this section when changing *can* to *could* softens its meaning.

We have yet another meaning of *can* in our dialogue. ***Can³*** expresses **hypothetical possibility**—that something is possible in theory. It doesn't mean, however, that this is a possibility likely to occur at any time soon; there's no reference to the near future as there can be with other modals as you'll soon see. I'll get back to this meaning of hypothetical possibility shortly.

I should make it clear, moreover, that *can* is limited in its use as a modal of possibility. This is probably because it's easy to confuse it with the idea of *ability* in many sentences, and I try to avoid confusion whenever I can. Just look at the following little sentence, deliberately given to you here out of context, and see what I mean:

He can be rich.

Most native speakers are likely to consider this sentence strange. They'll probably feel uncomfortable with it because they'll have trouble interpreting what *can* means. According to our definitions of *can*, however, you really have the option to interpret the idea to mean "It's possible that he's rich," or "He has the ability to get rich." You can see why we normally avoid using *can* for possibility in such ideas; it's much easier to use another modal auxiliary that unambiguously conveys the idea of possibility.

Now let's look at two more uses of *can* and *can't*:

> A: Excuse me. Can I park my car here?
> B: Sorry, you can't park here. These spaces are for tenants only.

So how would you interpret *can* and *can't* in this mini-dialogue?

Can is used here to mean ....

Can't is used here to mean ....

 **Heads Up!**

There's a point concerning pronunciation that I'd like to bring to your attention. It may not seem like a major concern at first, but because it may interfere with accurate communication, I think it's important enough to mention. It deals with an aspect of English that's quite unique for a European language and has to do with stress, or what some people refer to as accent. You'll be dealing a lot with stress and pronunciation when you get to Chapters 17 and 18, but right now, let's focus on the modal auxiliaries. (In the following examples, capitalized letters show the part of a word or a whole word that receives the primary stress.)

→ All the modal auxiliaries are unstressed in the context of a sentence when they're affirmative:

> He can GO with us on the trip.
> She can SPEAK three languages.

When the modals are negative, however, they're stressed along with their verbs:

> He CAN'T GO with us on the trip.
> She CAN'T SPEAK three languages.

→ With the modal *can* more than with the other modals, we have an important change in pronunciation between the affirmative and the negative, which truly affects communication:

- In the normal stream of speech, unstressed *can*, with its affirmative meaning, is normally pronounced /kɪn/. In fact, there's practically no vowel sound at all.
- On the other hand, stressed *can't* with its negative meaning, has a strongly pronounced vowel, /a/ in British English and /æ/ in most forms of American English.

The final /t/ in *can't* is unreleased in many dialects (/t̚/) when it comes before a verb and when it's on the stressed, negative *can't*. That means it isn't heard at all in the spoken sentence. But the fascinating thing is that even though it isn't heard and sounds like /kæn/, the listener still knows it's negative just because it receives that stress. Ah! The marvels of English!

Sensitizing your students to this change in communication brought on by these phonological shifts will go a long way to stop any misunderstandings that more than likely will arise.

These two uses of the modal are quite clear. **Can** is used here to mean **permission**. Person A wants to know if he has permission to park in that space. **Can't** is being used to mean **prohibition**. Person B is telling Person A that he doesn't have permission to park in that space.

Now let's look at another dialogue and investigate these uses of *can* and *could*:

> A: So tell me, how was your year in Rio de Janeiro?
>
> B: Just wonderful! But you know, it **can¹** get quite chilly in the hills outside of Rio in July.
>
> A: I don't care about the weather! Tell me more about that good-looking Brazilian colleague of yours.
>
> B: Well, he **can¹** be very charming. And guess what! He **could** be here in the next couple of weeks on business.
>
> A: Really? If he's as cute as you've said he is, I'd love to meet him.
>
> B: Well, that **can²** be arranged.
>
> A: Who knows. This **could** turn out to be a very interesting experience!

	Can	Could
1.		
2.		

Here we have completely different uses of *can* and we come upon *could* for the first time in a dialogue. *Can¹* represents the idea of **capability**. First, we have the idea that the temperature is capable of getting quite chilly in that area outside of Rio proper, and then we have the idea that this man is capable of being charming. Note that there's a big difference between the sentences in these pairs:

> It can get quite chilly in the hills.
> It gets quite chilly in the hills.
>
> He is very charming.
> He can be very charming.

The question is, how can you explain that important difference to your students if the subject comes up? Write your thoughts on the following lines:

The important difference is that when we use *can* in this way, we're communicating that **there's a potential for something to happen, but we're not claiming that that's always the case.** In our first example, Speaker B is saying that there's a potential for the temperature to get quite chilly in that area in July, but it doesn't necessarily mean that this weather condition is always true. In our second example, Speaker B is saying that her former colleague is the kind of person who has the potential to be quite charming, but that he isn't always like that. Actually, she might be implying that he can turn the charm on and off at will, and some listeners might even pick up a negative subtext in this case! You can see how important using or not using *can* may be to the communication.

Can² and *could* represent the idea of possibility, but there's a difference: *Can* once again expresses **hypothetical possibility**. Person B says it's possible that a meeting between her friend and the Brazilian will be arranged, implying *if things work out. Could*, on the other hand, expresses what I call **real possibility**, that is, something that may actually come to pass in the future. Person B uses *could* when talking about the future trip her Brazilian colleague is planning to take because it falls within the categories I've just mentioned: "It's possible that he'll be here in a couple of weeks." Likewise, Person A ends the dialogue by saying that there's a good chance the experience of meeting the Brazilian will be interesting, and by using *could*, she communicates this idea as a real future possibility as opposed to some idea in theory only.

Here are two sentences that demonstrate why *can* and *could* aren't always interchangeable because the focus they have on the kind of possibility being expressed is different:

1. With all the rain monsoons bring, dams can burst.
2. With all the rain we've been having, the dam could burst.

Think about the difference in meaning between these two sentences and write down your ideas on the following lines:

....

....

In **Sentence 1**, *can* represents a **hypothetical possibility**. The focus isn't so much on a possible disaster that we think is about to happen as it is on the idea that we know dams are able to hold just so much water before they burst. In **Sentence 2**, *could* represents a **real possibility**; we're saying in this case that there's a real chance the dam is going to burst. It's more appropriate for our speaker to use *could* in this context since weather conditions have created that real possibility.

Another reason that *can* isn't used too commonly to mean possibility is that we deal with real possibilities most of the time, not hypothetical ones. This difference also explains why *can* isn't usually interchangeable with *could* for this meaning.

>  **Heads Up!**
>
> Be prepared for another inevitable occurrence: Many of your students will end up using *can* to mean *possibility* in every English sentence they create containing this idea. They'll produce all sorts of sentences like, "The weatherman says it can snow tonight."
>
> This is most likely because the equivalent of the English modal auxiliary *can* is used in many languages to mean *possibility* even when it's real and not just hypothetical, unlike English, which usually uses *could* for this idea.
>
> Just keep reminding them that *could* is more common for possibility than *can*.

But I'm not done with *can* and *could* yet. What uses do you find for them in the next dialogue?

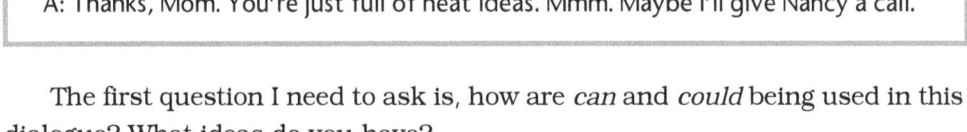

A: Here the weekend's coming and I've got absolutely no plans. I have no idea what to do.

B: Well, you **can** get together with your friend Nancy. You haven't seen her in a while.

A: That's true.

B: Or you **could** clean out your closet or finish that term paper that's due soon for your social studies class.

A: Thanks, Mom. You're just full of neat ideas. Mmm. Maybe I'll give Nancy a call.

The first question I need to ask is, how are *can* and *could* being used in this dialogue? What ideas do you have?

Can and *could* are being used ....

It seems that *can* and *could* are being used in this instance as a way of giving **advice** or **suggestions**, but it's important to mention that these two modals leave room for other options. That is, in that dialogue, Person B's suggestions are only two of the many possibilities that Person A might consider. You'll see why this alert is important later on when we explore *should* and *ought to*.

The next question I need to ask is why Speaker B chose to use *can* in her first utterance, but switched to *could* in her next sentence. Any ideas on the subject?

....

An interesting difference can be seen in the way Speaker B is thinking. When she gives her first suggestion, she's fairly confident that her daughter will react favorably to the idea of seeing her friend, Nancy. However, when she gives her next two suggestions, she knows perfectly well that there's only a slim chance her daughter will take these ideas seriously. It turns out, then, that **we tend to use *can* when we give advice that we believe has a good chance of being accepted, but we use *could* when we're not so sure our suggestions will be heeded.**

Now let's examine another two uses for *could*. Write your interpretation on the lines that follow the dialogue.

> A: Hello, Mrs. Todd. Happy birthday!
>
> B: Why, thank you, Jim. And thank you, everybody, for this lovely cake! **Could¹** you help me blow out the candles, Jim?
>
> A: I'm sure you can manage the two of them just fine!
>
> B: Well, I don't know...a woman my age. It's a good thing they didn't put one candle on the cake for each year!
>
> A: **Could²** I ask how old you are today?
>
> B: I don't mind telling you. I'm eighty-seven today.
>
> A: No way! You can't be eighty-seven!
>
> B: Well, bless your heart. However, I'm afraid I am.

1. ....

2. ....

This use of *could¹* is what most people refer to as **a polite form for making a request**. There are other ways to make requests with modals, most notably by using *can* or *would*. Most native speakers, however, perceive *could* as being more polite and more formal than *can*. In the sentence with our first example, Mrs. Todd is making a little joke by politely requesting that Jim give her some help blowing out the two candles on her cake.

The use of *could²* is a different matter; it represents **asking for permission**. In this case, Jim is **politely** and **deferentially** asking Mrs. Todd for permission to inquire about her age. Asking a person's age isn't something you normally do in many cultures, so Jim feels the need to ask for permission to pose this question and he softens it by using the polite use of *could*.

Before leaving *could*, let's read the following two mini-dialogues and decide if the lines in bold are acceptable or unacceptable:

Dialogue 1	Dialogue 2
A. Could I become a doctor? **B. Sure you could.** ☐ acceptable ☐ unacceptable	A. Could I borrow your pen? **B. Sure you could.** ☐ acceptable ☐ unacceptable

Native English speakers would say that Person B's reply in **Dialogue 1** is **acceptable**, but Person B's reply in **Dialogue 2** is probably **unacceptable**, yet they're exactly the same sentence. What's the difference, and why is it that the exact same sentence doesn't work in both cases? Here's some space for you to write down any solutions you have to solve this puzzle:

....

....

The explanations for this strange occurrence are as follows. The word *could* in Dialogue 1 expresses the idea of **possibility** and is being used by Person A as he wonders about the possibility of becoming a doctor. If we continue to develop the idea in that question, we can come up with phrases like "Could I become a doctor . . . if I wanted to/. . . if medical school weren't so hard to get into/. . . if tuition weren't so high and I weren't so poor?" In any case, *could* represents possibility both in the **question and reply**: "Of course you could [become a doctor if . . .]" which equals "Of course you'd have the possibility [of becoming a doctor if . . .]."

The word *could* in Dialogue 2 is completely different. Here Person A is using it as a polite way to ask for **permission** to use Person B's pen. Remember that *could* represents this polite form of *asking for* permission, but it doesn't represent the way we *give* permission; for that, we use *can* (among other modals). So *could* is unacceptable in the reply to Person B's question in Dialogue 2 because *could* never means "I give you permission." We say "Sure you can (borrow my pen)."

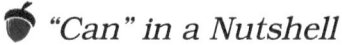
"Can" in a Nutshell

- **ability:**
  My friend Roger can speak three languages.
- **hypothetical possibility:**
  Successful surgeries can mean the start of new lives for patients.

- **permission:**
  You can park here without putting money in the meter after 6:00 p.m.
- **prohibition (when in the negative):**
  You can't smoke in a hospital.
- **capability:**
  He can be really cranky when he hasn't had enough sleep.
- **advice or suggestions (which are likely to be heeded):**
  If you're passed over for another promotion, you can always look for another job.
- **informally making a request:**
  Can you help me out for a moment?
- **informally asking for permission:**
  Can I take the car tonight, Dad?
- **disbelief/impossibility (when in the negative):**
  The ozone layer can't be disintegrating! Do you realize what that means? (disbelief)
  He can't be there already. He only left ten minutes ago and it's a good twenty-minute ride to get there. (impossibility)

🌰 "Could" in a Nutshell

- **real possibility:**
  Yes, I see your point. You could be right.
- **advice or suggestions (which aren't likely to be heeded):**
  Well, if you have nothing much to do tonight, you could take me out to dinner.
- **politely making a request:**
  Could you help me with these suitcases, please?
- **politely or deferentially asking for permission:**
  Could I take your picture?
- **"softened" form of disbelief (when in the negative); not very probable:**
  He couldn't be your brother. He looks nothing like you.

Will/Would

The next two modal auxiliaries that we'll investigate are probably just as troublesome as *can* and *could* tend to be, but before we look at the next dialogue, I want to make mention of the fact that this is a continuation of the material covered in Chapter 5. There's so much to say about *will* that it *would* be overwhelming to do so in one chapter!

Let's look at the following dialogue to see *will* in some uses not covered in Chapter 5 and some uses for its counterpart, *would*:

> A: Isn't Ahmed here yet?
>
> B: No, not yet.
>
> A: **Would¹** you call his house to make sure he's on his way?
>
> B: You **would²** ask me to do that now that I'm sitting down and comfortable. He'll be here soon enough. Just take it easy!
>
> A: I *will* take it easy, but I still think you should call him.
>
> B: **Will¹** you kindly stop nagging me?
>
> A: You know me. I **will²** go on and on when I worry. I can't help it. Please find out if he's on his way.
>
> B: All right! All right!

Let's examine the uses of *will* and *would* the same way we covered *can* and *could*. On the following lines that are numbered to correspond to the modal uses in the dialogue, write down your interpretation of what these modals mean in their contexts:

Would	Will
1.	1. ....
2.	2. ....

Would¹ and *will¹* express **polite requests**. Many native speakers, however, perceive a slight difference between the two words. They see *will* as being somewhat more direct or forceful than *would*, which sounds a little more polite, deferential, or formal.

Would² and *will²* are quite unusual. They represent **actions or behaviors characteristic of the person or thing you're talking about**. First, Person B says it's typical for Person A to insist on asking him to do something right after he's just sat down and gotten all comfortable; similarly, Person A says she knows she has the habit of going on and on about something to the point of obsessing on it, offering this thought almost as an apology. The difference between the two modals when used in this way is that **will expresses this idea about a general observation** just as the simple present can do when referring to habits, universal truths, etc. (refer to Chapter 3). **Would refers to the same characteristic behavior as *will* does, but is used by someone responding immediately to something that's just happened rather than just making a general observation.**

One more unusual point about this use of the two modals is that stress can play an important role in determining meaning. When the modals are unstressed, the usual intent is simply that this is, or was, typical behavior. When the modals are stressed, however, there's a negative implication that can be interpreted as criticism. Compare these two sentences as more examples of this usage:

> Whenever anyone's in trouble, she'll be the first one to help.
> (unstressed *'ll* carries no negative implication)
>
> A: Why is Fred always so tired in the morning?
> B: Well, he WILL stay up to watch the late night movie on TV every night. What can you expect?
> (stressed *will* carries a criticizing tone)

Go back to the dialogue for a moment and re-read the third sentence that Person A says. (The *italics* indicate stress on those words as it would be used in the spoken language by the two people.) Even though *will* appears stressed in two instances, it only changes meaning, resulting in that reproachful tone, in one instance: I *will* go on and on when I worry." In the other sentence where this stressed *will* occurs, its meaning isn't altered at all ("I *will* take it easy..."). The word is stressed in this case simply to give it an emphatic quality as a retort to what Person B has just said. Words or phrases that have their meaning changed depending on whether or not they're stressed are part of a group called "autosegmentals," which we'll take up in Chapters 17 and 18. Here's something else to note about modals and stress: **You never contract modals when you want to stress them.** That's easy to understand when you consider how impossible it would be to try to stress the *'ll* when added to a pronoun ("They*'ll* do it," for example).

Before we leave the subject of the stressed *will* that can indicate a pejorative or critical view of someone's behavior—depending on the context it's used in—I need to mention an alternative for *will* that is very typically heard in English. **Most speakers tend to use the word *do* the same way I've demonstrated *will* in this section to indicate that reproachful tone.** In other words, instead of saying "I <u>will</u> go on and on when I worry," Person A could just as easily say "I <u>do</u> go on and on when I worry."

There are four final uses for *will* that we're going to investigate now, so take a look at the following dialogue and see what you can make of the modal in these cases:

A: Let me go answer the door. Someone's knocking.

B: Oh, **that'll**[1] be Ms. Borgia. I invited her over for dinner.

A: Borgia? Oh, no! You know I can't stand her.

B: Look, she's my supervisor, and I think she's considering me for a promotion.

A: Oh, that's nice: buttering up the boss!

B: Call it what you **will**[2], I think it's just good politics and I **won't**[3] discuss it anymore. You'**ll**[4] be nice to her and you **won't**[4] do anything to sabotage my chances of getting a promotion, right? Right!

1. ....

2. ....

3. ....

4. ....

The interpretation for **will**[1] is that it represents **a deduction** or **conclusion** based on some sort of information previously known. Actually, it's just about the strongest way you can express **probability** without really knowing the facts. Person B says in this case that she's 95% sure the person knocking at the door is her supervisor.

Will[2] is a bit tricky—and it's also a linguistic throwback to many centuries ago when our modal auxiliary *will* was the Old English verb *willan* meaning *to want*. That historical information gives the answer away: in this instance, **will means want**, so Person A is saying "Call it whatever you want ... " You can often hear this use of the modal in the currently popular parenthetical expression *if you will*, a phrase that is thrown into practically any kind of sentence and seems to mean "if you want to interpret XYZ as I'm explaining it." Here's an example of how the expression is used:

> A: The steady destruction of the natural world, or the end of life as we know it, **if you will**, isn't just some bad dream anymore. It's real, and we've got to stop it.
>
> B: I just hope people all over the world wake up and realize how big the disaster will be if they don't take a stand.

Won't[3] represents **refusal** and, coincidentally, it can get stressed equally with its verb for emphasis in the spoken language.

Will[4] (both in the affirmative and negative) expresses **a command, an order**. Person B is saying in no uncertain terms that she expects Person A to be on his best behavior and expresses this idea with a strong, firm imperative form. Some native speakers take this use of *will* as the strongest imperative form we can muster up in English as it has the hidden meaning that the person saying it will accept nothing less than what's being demanded. We mentioned earlier that *will* can be used as a more forceful, polite request than *would* when used in a question ("Will you kindly stop nagging me?"). When we use *will* this way in a statement ("You will be nice to her . . ."), it's even *more* forceful.

🌰 "Will" in a Nutshell

- **used for polite requests (more forceful than *would*) and can come across as snarky:**
  Will you buckle your seat belt so I can start driving?

- **used for a typical characteristic of the person or thing being discussed (general time observation):**
  - Jack knows how to relax. He'll nap for hours under that tree.
    (unstressed *'ll* = no negative connotation)
  - Antoinette is such a stubborn woman. She <u>will</u> have to have her way.
    (stressed *will* = criticism)
  - Antoinette is such a stubborn woman. She <u>does</u> have to have her way.
    (stressed *do* as alternative for *will* = criticism)

- **used for deductions or conclusions (probability):**
  Can you get the phone? That'll be Jim. Tell him I'm leaving now.

- ***will* used to mean *want* in some formulaic expressions:**
  Do what you will with this ugly, old chair; just get it out of the living room.

- **refusal (when in the negative):**
  You can complain about my salary all you want. I won't look for a different job!

- **used for a command/order:**
  You will eat everything on your plate and you will like it!

🌰 "Would" in a Nutshell

- **used for polite requests (softer than *will*):**
  Would you answer the phone, please? My hands are wet.

- **used for a typical characteristic of the person or thing being discussed (immediate reaction to something that has just occurred):**
  I should know you by now. You <u>would</u> embarrass me like that!
  (stressed *would* = criticism)

May/Might

We'll continue our investigation into modals the same way we've discovered so many facts about those already covered. Let's look at this next dialogue to see how *may* and *might* can function:

8 Modal Auxiliaries in the Present or Future

A: Good morning, Mr. Snodgrass.

B: Good morning, Ms. Ketchum. **Might¹** I have a word?

A: Certainly. What is it?

B: You **may²** not realize it, but your dog has been going through my garbage can again and tossing the garbage all over my front lawn.

A: My Muffie? I don't believe it. I'm sure it's the work of another dog.

B: Well, it **might²** be, but I very much doubt it.

A: Well, Mr. Snodgrass, if I **may¹** say so, you **might³** consider using a garbage can with a tighter lid!

B: And if I may say so, Ms. Ketchum, **may³** you never find garbage strewn all over your front lawn as I have!

Now that you've looked over the uses of these two modal auxiliaries in the dialogue, write down your interpretation of what they mean in the different contexts on the following lines that are numbered to correspond. (The lines with an X mean there's nothing to write on them.)

Might	May
1.	1. ....
2.	2. ....
3.	3. ....X.................
4. ....X.................	4. ....

Even though not the most common use of the word, *might¹* is **the most polite, deferential, and formal way to ask for permission—therefore the least forceful.** Some native speakers even consider this use of *might* an overly solicitous way of asking for permission. ***May¹*** is the more common way we politely ask for permission to do something.

May² expresses the idea of **possibility.** "It's possible that you don't realize it . . ." is what Mr. Snodgrass is saying to Ms. Ketchum. When we see ***might²***, it expresses **possibility** just as *may* does. The question is, do you discern any difference between *may* and *might* when they both express possibility?

Many prescriptive grammar books define *might* as being a weaker version of *may* when the meaning is possibility. The way these two modals have been used for possibility in this dialogue tends to uphold that perception of *may* and *might*. Mr. Snodgrass is less certain that a dog other than Muffie is the culprit than he is about Ms. Ketchum not realizing what her dog's been up to. In other words, he's using *may* for stronger possibility and *might* for weaker possibility. I want to make it clear, though, that not all native speakers sense this difference; that's probably why so many ELT grammar books teach these two modals together to mean possibility and don't bother to clarify any subtle differences between the two.

One further point I should make about *may* and *might* when they express possibility is that they both signify **real possibility** just as *could* does (as opposed to *can*). In fact, all three modals are usually interchangeable:

> He may be late. / He might be late. / He could be late.

There's one occasion, at least, when the three modals aren't interchangeable, and that's when a rhetorical phrase is used to preface some sort of critical remark. Notice that *may* and *might* are the traditional choices for this use, but that *could* isn't:

> A: My English teacher says it's okay to say "I might could do it."
>
> B: Well, she **may (might)** be an English teacher, but she speaks a different dialect. Or maybe she doesn't know the difference between standard and nonstandard English!

As for *might³* in our dialogue, the modal expresses **an indirect way of making a suggestion**. Ms. Ketchum is gingerly suggesting to Mr. Snodgrass that he get himself a "dog-proof" garbage can. There are other ways to make suggestions with modals, and here's one you should take a look at immediately:

> A: I know you're very upset about that broken leg of yours, but you **might as well accept** it and relax.
>
> B: Relax? How can I relax? I'm so restless just sitting here day in and day out. Here it is, the middle of summer, and it **may as well be** the middle of winter since I can't go out anyway!

As you can see, we're dealing with the expression "*may/might as well* + base form verb" in this dialogue. The problem is that the expression doesn't mean the same thing in both cases. Can you paraphrase the meaning in each of these instances? Write your thoughts on the following lines:

....

....

Sometimes, finding just the right paraphrases isn't so easy, but here's what I've come up with. Compare my ideas with yours. In the first case, when Speaker A says ". . . you might as well accept it . . ." she's making a **mild suggestion** (and

I'll be discussing more about suggestions a little later on in this chapter). As for the next appearance of this expression in the dialogue, "...it may as well be the middle of winter..." isn't a suggestion at all. It means **it doesn't make any difference..**, so Speaker B is saying, "It doesn't make any difference if it's the middle of summer or the middle of winter since I can't go out anyway!"

Now, getting back to the dialogue on page 167, we come to **may³**, which signifies a very formal way of hoping that something will happen. Mr. Snodgrass is saying in his very formal tone that he hopes Ms. Ketchum will never experience the mess he's found on his front lawn. Another thing to notice is that **this use of *may* requires a word order inversion so that *may* appears before the subject. In fact, *may* always appears as the first word in this kind of sentence.** I'll be discussing more about this use of *may* later on in this book.

Now that I've discussed *may* and *might*, look at the following mini-dialogues. Check which of Person B's responses is acceptable and which is not, and then explain the reasons for your decisions:

Dialogue 1	Dialogue 2
A. Might I ask you a favor? B. **Of course you might.** ☐ acceptable ☐ unacceptable	A. Might I ask you a favor? B. **Of course you may.** ☐ acceptable ☐ unacceptable

....

....

Person B's response in **Dialogue 1** is **unacceptable**. The reason will sound quite familiar to you if you recall the discussion about *can* and *could* for asking and giving permission. We can use *might* in a super-polite request when we *ask for* permission, but we don't use it when we *give* permission since it wouldn't be appropriate to be so overly polite in this case. Person B's response in **Dialogue 2** is **acceptable** because *may* is the correct way of giving permission in the formal style.

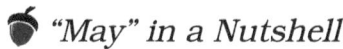
"May" in a Nutshell

- **real possibility:**
  You may not believe what I'm about to tell you, but it's true.

- **permission (in polite or formal context):**
  Ladies and gentlemen, you may now take your seats.

- **hope that something will happen (in very formal style):**
  May you be blessed all the days of your life.

🌰 "Might" in a Nutshell

- **possibility:**
  You might not believe what I'm about to tell you, but it's true.

- **an overly formal way of requesting permission:**
  Might I sit here?

- **an indirect way of making a suggestion:**
  If the regular doctors can't help, he might try a chiropractor.

- **a mild formulaic expression for making a suggestion:**
  We may/might as well leave now. What do you say?

Should/Ought To

It's time for another dialogue! Let's see how *should* and *ought to* function in the following context. I'll work with these two modals the same way I've worked with the others, so think of explanations for how they're being used and write them down on the lines whose numbers correspond to the numbered modals:

A: I hate commuting to work every day.

B: Yeah, so do I.

A: Where's the 7:20 train? It's 7:20 now, and there's no train in sight.

B: Yeah, I know. It **should¹** be here already.

A: Maybe I **ought to²** take my car to work.

B: Well, I know how you feel, but the hassles of taking your car, fighting rush hour traffic, and parking in the city **ought to¹** stop you! Just calm down, and don't let it bother you so much.

A: You're right. I **shouldn't²** let train delays and all this nonsense get to me so much.

Should	Ought to
1.	1. ....
2.	2. ....

Should¹ and *ought to¹* express **expectation**. Person B is saying that he expects the 7:20 train to be there already because the time is indeed 7:20. He then says that he expects all of those hassles to stop Person A from driving to work every day instead of taking the train.

Should² and *ought to²* have to do with **advisability**, **opinions**, or what's considered **a good idea**. Person A says that it might be a good idea for her to take her car to work. Then she says that she realizes it's not advisable for her to get so upset about such things as train delays. Both of these modals are what I call **benign advice** or **benign suggestions**; that is, when people use them to offer opinions or suggestions, they don't force their thoughts upon the listener or the person under discussion; in other words, it's up to the listener to accept or reject the advice. I'll talk about a modal that can force itself upon you when we get to *must*.

While we're on the subject of negatives like the one just used in the preceding paragraph ("I shouldn't let train delays . . . get to me."), there's a feature unique to *ought to* which doesn't happen to any other modal auxiliary. Most native speakers, especially Americans, prefer to use *should* in the negative (*shouldn't*) rather than ought to (*ought not to*); that's probably because *ought not to* and *oughtn't to* seem unwieldy to many people. The unique feature I'm talking about is that when people do use *ought to* in the negative, they sometimes drop the *to*, probably to make the phrase less unwieldy ("He oughtn't say such things!").

Going back to whether we prefer to use *should* or *ought to*, do you perceive any difference between these two modals when they both express expectation or advisability? According to prescriptive grammar books, *ought to* is perceived as being less forceful than *should* when expressing advisability, but not when expressing expectation:

> You ought to get a job. (not forceful)
> You should get a job. (somewhat more forceful)
>
> The bus ought to be here already.
> The bus should be here already. (no difference)

The difference between sentences in these pairs, however, is really quite slight, and that's why most ELT grammar books teach both of these modals at the same time when they deal with either advisability or expectation.

There are even some native speakers who claim that *should* deals with straightforward advice while *ought to* carries a moral obligation with it. Look at these two sentences and see what you think:

> You should call your poor mother more often.
> You ought to call your poor mother more often.

It's safe to say that the choice of whether to use *should* or *ought to* in the previous examples is really up to the individual. Always remember that each native speaker of a language has their own style for using the language (what linguists refer to as an *idiolect*) and that there aren't always hard-and-fast rules that I can give.

If you recall, when we were exploring *can* and *could*, I said that I was going to get back to these two modals when we got to *should* and *ought to*—and here we are. Let's bring back the suggestions that the mother gave her daughter in that dialogue that showed *can* and *could* as ways of giving advice:

> You <u>can</u> get together with your friend, Nancy.
> You <u>could</u> clean out your closet or finish that term paper.

What if we were to substitute *can* and *could* with *should* or *ought to* in these sentences? After all, they're all ways to give advice or suggestions, right? Well, let's see what happens:

> You <u>should</u> get together with your friend, Nancy.
> You <u>ought to</u> clean out your closet or finish that term paper.

Even though all four modals can be used to give advice or make suggestions, there's definitely a difference between the first two and the second two. What do you perceive the difference to be?

....

....

What it comes down to is that **when we use *can* and *could* for suggestions, there's an implied idea that there are other options. When we use *should* and *ought to*, however, we're clearly focusing in on just the one suggestion at hand with no implication that other options exist.** Quite an important difference indeed!

Heads Up!

Even though we haven't come to the modal *must* yet, this is a good time to mention a problem that you may very well encounter.

Some of your students will end up inappropriately using the modal *must* instead of using *should* or *ought to*. This is probably because in many languages the same word is used to express these quite different ideas in English.

Should and *ought to* are modals that express soft advice as opposed to *must*, which expresses a command, order, or regulation of some sort. People who have some kind of authority over others can use *must* when talking to them, e.g., parents to children, bosses to employees, teachers to students. It's probably not appropriate, though, for the employee to use *must* when talking to the boss or the student when talking to the teacher.

This can be interpreted as a linguistic problem, but it can also be a cultural problem—and we know that language should never be taught out of cultural context. Make sure you're prepared to explain why *must* is or is not appropriate to use in certain situations and why *should* and *ought to* often work better.

In fact, I'd like to make mention of the fact that English speakers are so sensitive when it comes to giving advice that they have all sorts of ways to do so in what I've called offering "soft advice." Instead of using *should* or *ought* to, they use expressions like "How about _____?" "Why not _____?" and "You might want to _____."

There's one last observation I'd like to make about *should*, and this is one time when *ought to* can't be interchanged with it. *Should* can substitute for *if* in a more formal style conditional sentence:

If he arrives before three, tell him to wait. →
Should he arrive before three, tell him to wait.

And it can even be used together with *if* as you'll see when we get to Chapter 16:

If he should arrive before three, tell him to wait.

🌰 *"Should"/"Ought To" in a Nutshell*

🌰 **expectation:**
If her work continues to be this good, she should get a raise soon.
He ought to feel much better once the medicine starts working.

🌰 **advisability/opinions/a good idea (not considering other options):**
You shouldn't eat so fast. You'll get indigestion.
You ought to slow down when you eat.

🌰 **should = if (in a conditional sentence):**
If the two companies merge, our stock will go up. →
Should the two companies merge, our stock will go up.

Must

We've now come to the only modal that I haven't dealt with yet. Let's do it just as we have the others, so get ready to write down your interpretations of *must* as you find it in this dialogue:

A: You **must¹** be Ms. Carroll, our new teacher.

B: Yes, that's right.

A: Well, I'm Hilda Pardo, your assistant principal.

B: How do you do.

A: There are just a few points I wanted to mention before classes start this morning. To begin with, you **must²** be in your room by 8:15. And while I think of it, you **mustn't²** allow students to eat or drink in the classrooms. We've had quite a problem with that.

B: Understood.

---

1. ....

2. ....

Must¹ **expresses a conclusion or deduction made from information already known.** (Recall how unstressed *will* can be used in the same way.) Ms. Pardo spots someone new at her school, knows that a new teacher is to begin working that day, and concludes that she's that new teacher, Ms. Carroll. We can paraphrase this sentence by saying "*I'm sure* you're Ms. Carroll, our new teacher." Of course, when we use *must* in this way, we wait for confirmation from the other person to be certain our conclusion is right.

Must² **expresses a requirement or necessity**, meaning that Ms. Carroll has no choice in the matter; she's obligated to comply or face the consequences. Even the negative of *must* in this use represents a requirement, although it can also be interpreted as a prohibition (***mustn't²***).

In the last "Heads-Up!" that you came upon, the discussion dealt with the cultural difference between using the modal *must* when *should* or *ought to* might be more appropriate. When you teach *should* and *ought to*, explain to your students that these are used when you give someone your advice or opinion about what to do, but that it doesn't mean the listener is obligated to take that advice. That's why I consider *should* and *ought to* as *benign* advice.

On the other hand, *must* leaves no options; when you use *must*, meaning that someone is to do something, it's a *forceful* idea—sometimes too forceful if said to a person who's in a higher social or authoritative position than the speaker is. Remember that when hearing *should* or *ought to*, the listener or subject being discussed can take the advice or not; when hearing *must*, the listener or subject of the idea supposedly has no choice in the matter. True, you'll hear native speakers at times say something like "Oh, you simply *must* see that movie! It was wonderful!" Of course, in this context, *must* isn't taken authoritatively; it simply expresses a strong suggestion that the speaker is making to a friend, for example.

Let's see how *must* can be used in other ways by looking at this next dialogue.

A: Hello, Ravi? This is Selim.

B: Hi, Selim. What's up?

A: You know, I hear the surf's really great today and we can find some big waves for our surfboards. You interested?

B: But we've got school today.

A: So what? We **don't have to** go to school every day!

B: I **mustn't** be absent today or my teacher will kill me. I've got a big test today and she hates when someone's out and she has to give a make-up.

A: That's dumb!

B: It's not dumb. What **must** the teachers think of you, Selim, with your being absent so often?

A: I never really give it any thought—nor should you!

Write your interpretations of the words in bold on the following lines:

don't have to = ...

mustn't = ...

must = ...

Don't have to is a phrase that means **it isn't necessary**. This concept is totally different from the idea of **must not** (***mustn't***), which means **prohibited** or **not to be done**. And along with this use of *mustn't*, we also find a negative imperative (command) form if it is put together with *you*:

> You mustn't blame yourself. = Don't blame yourself.

Remember to stress to your students that when we say something isn't required, we use *don't/doesn't have to*, but when we say something is not to be done or is prohibited, we say *must not* (*mustn't*).

Here are some more examples to demonstrate these points:

deductions:	He must be very happy over that news. (We're sure he's very happy over that news.)
	She mustn't be very happy over that news. (We're sure she isn't very happy over that news.)
requirements/ necessities:	You must be here by nine o'clock. (You're required to be here by nine o'clock.)
	You mustn't take this medicine without food. (Don't take this medicine without food.)
lack of requirement/ necessity:	You don't have to take this medicine with food. (You aren't required to take this medicine with food.)
	She doesn't have to see the doctor. (It isn't necessary for her to see the doctor.)

As for **must**, the word is being used in this previous dialogue in quite an unusual way. In this context, the question "What must the teachers think of you?" really means "I wonder what the teachers think of you."

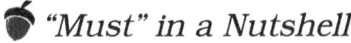 *"Must" in a Nutshell*

- **used for a conclusion or deduction:**
    Marry Arnold? You must be kidding!
- **used for requirements/necessities:**
    - You must submit a note from your doctor if you're not at work for more than three consecutive days. (requirement)

- You must eat and drink in order to stay alive. (necessity)

🖝 used for prohibition/that something <u>not</u> be done:
   An orthodox Jew or Muslim mustn't eat pork.

🖝 used in a question to mean *I wonder* . . . :
   What must it be like on Mars?

<u>Semi-Auxiliaries (Periphrastic Modals)</u>

The first thing to do is list some of the semi-auxiliaries. Although there's disagreement among some linguists as to whether certain examples of these are semi-auxiliaries or not, I'm going to include the following: *be able to, be unable to, have to, have got to, had better, had best, need, dare, used to, would rather,* and *would sooner*.

The next thing to do is explain the difference between modal auxiliaries and semi-auxiliaries. Semi-auxiliaries work the same way as modal auxiliaries do as far as altering the meanings of verbs. Unlike true modals, however, semi-auxiliaries don't always function grammatically in the same way:

- Some semi-auxiliaries don't have the same form for the present and future as true modals do (*I have to; I'm going to have to/I'll have to*).

- For questions, some semi-auxiliaries use *do/does/did* as the typical introductory question marker (*Do I have to?/Did they use to?*). Others use the inverted construction typical of modals and the verb *be* (*Is he able to?/Have I got to?/ Need we?/Dare she?/Would they rather?/Would you sooner?*). One little note: We don't normally use *had better* or *had best* in questions, preferring to use *should/must/have to/have got to* instead.

- For negatives, some semi-auxiliaries use *don't/doesn't/didn't* before them (*don't have to/didn't use to*), while others use not (*haven't got to/had better not/had best not/need not/would rather not/would sooner not*). One semi-auxiliary, *dare*, uses *not* in the present/future form (*dare not*), but *didn't* in the past (*didn't dare*)!

I'm not going to deal with every semi-auxiliary in this chapter because most of them aren't particularly troublesome; what I will do, though, is make some passing observations about those that aren't troublesome.

Be Able To (Be Unable To)

Why is it that English has this expression which is synonymous with *can/could* as long as the meaning is ability? Here are a couple of *ungrammatical* sentences for you to correct. Let's see how you correct the underlined parts:

1. For that job at the United Nations, he needs to <u>can</u> speak at least three languages fluently.

2. <u>Canning</u> speak four languages, he had no trouble getting that job at the UN.

....

Yes, I know that these are two really bizarre sentences! And that's just the point. The corrections should be "he needs to **be able to** speak..." for **Sentence 1** and "**Being able to** speak..." for **Sentence 2**. What observations can you make about why *be (un)able to* is so convenient at times?

....

....

In order for us to avoid such bizarre problems, **we use *be able to* instead of *can* after prepositions and when an *-ing* form is required.**

Along similar lines, there's a clever way we get around the problem of not being able to use two modal auxiliaries together, which was one of the general points about modals that I discussed at the start of this chapter. The way we do this in certain cases is to combine a modal with a semi-auxiliary. Look at the following examples of how this works:

We must be able to produce more food.

Nobody should have to go hungry.

Need

The meaning of *need*, when it's used as a semi-auxiliary, is the same as *must, have to,* and *have got to*, that is, **something is required or necessary**. Typically, in the affirmative and most questions, we use *need* as a regular verb with *to* after it ("I needed <u>to</u> see you."/"Does she need <u>to</u> apply right away?")

Grammar in Context

Another use of *need* can be seen in the much more formal or even antiquated "Need she apply right away?" This usage of *need* can also appear in the negative, as in the following examples:

She needn't let us know before Friday.
He needn't ever know the awful truth.
He need never know the awful truth.

In these examples, *needn't* means *doesn't have to* or *hasn't got to*, in other words, something is not required. I should mention, though, that many native speakers, particularly Americans, will probably find the sentences somewhat atypical because *need* isn't commonly used this way in most dialects of American English as a semi-auxiliary, especially in everyday speech.

Would Rather/Would Sooner

These two expressions are used to indicate **a preference**. Most native speakers consider *would rather* more formal than *would sooner* and it seems to be more commonly used than *would sooner*, but I think that's once again a matter of personal choice.

The grammar used with these semi-auxiliaries is a bit unusual. If only the subject is discussed, any verb that follows will be in its basic form ("*She*'d rather <u>have</u> a beach house than a house in town."/"*They*'d sooner <u>eat</u> chicken or fish than beef."). However, if the subject is discussing a preference for somebody, (even for him- or herself) or something else, the grammar changes radically ("I'd rather *he* <u>were</u> here than at home."/"We'd sooner *you* <u>didn't say</u> that word again.") The words I've underlined represent a grammatical form called the *present subjunctive*, a form that I'll deal with in detail in Chapter 15.

Teaching Tips

8.1 Telling Fortunes/Reading Palms

Ask the students if they know anything about fortune telling, crystal balls, or palmistry. Copy the hand you see here on the board, explaining that the lines on the palms of your hands are thought to predict your future. Students can do their own quick research about palm reading if they care to. Explain what the different lines are and what they're supposed to predict. Then ask the students to read three or four other students' palms being sure they use the various modal auxiliaries. Here are some typical answers: "You'll live a long life."/"You might work for the government when you graduate."/"You should be more careful of what you eat." Let your students read your palm, too. Students can also write up their predictions in a short composition.

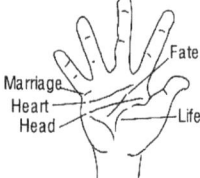

8.2 Creating Situations for Modals

Before class, create various situations about your students, other people, places, or things (a student's absence, glass on the street, a dent in your car, a bad grade, etc.). Let the students brainstorm responses to the situations using modals: "Paco might be sick."/"Someone will get a flat tire if they run over that glass."/"Jan should drive more carefully."/"Marjorie must study very hard; she always gets good grades."

8.3 Real-life Problems

Before class, create problems that contain a real-life conflict (e.g., You've just received a four-year scholarship to a very prestigious university, but you can't bring your spouse./The person you're engaged to is pressuring you to get married soon, but you want to wait./Your father is seriously ill and can no longer work./You want to study sociology, but your family wants you to be a doctor, etc.). Put the problems on the board or on a handout. Divide the class into small groups and tell the students to discuss the problems. Have them come up with solutions to the situations. Tell your students to use at least three different modals and have all the members of each group write down their group's suggestions. While the groups are discussing their responses, walk around the room and "visit" each group. When the problems have been thoroughly discussed, have each person in the group give at least one of their responses to the whole class. While the groups are sharing their ideas with the entire class, if you hear contradictory statements made between two groups, note them down and go back to them after this activity is over. You can get lots of meaty material in this way for lively conversation practice.

8.4 *Television Guides*

Do an online search and find a television programming schedule. Divide the class into pairs or small groups and give them the link (the URL) to that website. Tell them that they're going to recommend programs appropriate for various groups (children, teens, adults). After they've looked through the listings carefully, have them come up with their program schedule using modal auxiliaries whenever possible:

> "Kids shouldn't watch X, but they might enjoy Y."
> "An adult may enjoy Z, but I might not."

8.5 *Giving Advice*

Prepare a list of people that might need advice. Divide the class into pairs or small groups and have them decide what advice they'd give newlyweds, teenagers on their first date, a person entering college for the first time, the new owner of a large company, their English teacher, students just beginning to learn English, etc. Encourage your students to use modal auxiliaries.

8.6 *Inventing a New Sport*

Divide the class into pairs or small groups and tell them they're going to invent a new game or sport. Have the groups write up the rules of their game/sport using modals and semi-auxiliaries whenever possible:

> "You must face each other."
> "You can't move until the referee blows the whistle."
> "You have to/You've got to stay out of the game for two
>   minutes after a foul."

Have the different groups share their games/sports with the entire class.

8.7 *Questionnaires*

Create a questionnaire (teacher- or student-generated) about a relevant or timely topic (upcoming elections, environmental issues, exams, etc.). Have the students interview two or three of their classmates, students in other classes, their teachers, or people outside school, etc. and prepare a report on their findings. Questions should have modals in them ("Should students _____?" /"Would you rather_____?" / "Could the President_____?"/ "What might the government _____?"/ "Should we_____ exams?").

8.8 *Planning a City*

Prepare a map of a city without details. Only the streets and any relevant natural landmarks like rivers, lakes, valleys, etc. should be shown. Provide a list of buildings and institutions that the city will have.

zoo	theater	fish market	secondary school
hotel	airport	train station	municipal offices
houses	museum	supermarket	elementary school
bakery	night club	swimming pool	jail/police station
library	post office	hardware store	high rise apartments
hospital	gas station	electricity plant	water treatment plant

Students will plan out the town suggesting where the various buildings *should/would/mustn't/can't* go. Let the students draw the buildings on their outline and then put them up on the board. Have various spokespersons from each group discuss their choices.

8.9 *Dear Abby: Advice Columns*

Advice columns appear in many newspapers and magazines. The typical advice column has two elements: 1) a reader who has a problem and writes a letter asking for advice, and 2) a columnist who responds to the letter and suggests solutions. Find several examples online or write up several of your own. Divide the class into pairs or small groups and distribute the columns to your students. Have them write responses to the person who wrote the letter suggesting solutions to the problem. If students have trouble coming up with acceptable solutions, for homework, let them ask teachers, native English speakers, students in other classes, or friends for ideas about what they might do. Encourage them to use modals in their responses.

9

Modal Auxiliaries in the Past

"There's no point thinking about what might have been."

As I made clear in Chapter 8, modal auxiliaries are a very complex part of the English language. The complexities that teachers and students have to deal with stem from the amazing array of meanings and nuances that modals convey. In Chapter 8 I focused on the uses of modal auxiliaries in the present and future; now it's time to deal with them in the past. In this chapter I'll be investigating the transformations that modals go through when they're changed from the present into the past via indirect speech, also known as reported speech. For example, when "He says he *may*" is changed to the past, we end up with "He said he *might*." Such changes are basically straightforward and mechanical and are made without causing major alterations in meaning.

There's a need, however, to have another chapter in order to deal with some not-so-simple combinations in form—and some not-so-obvious changes in meaning—that modal auxiliaries undergo when they're put into the past and indirect speech isn't involved. You'll see my point as soon as you've finished looking at the first dialogue.

Can/Could/Could Have

Let's begin our investigation of modals in the past, which include what some refer to as **modal perfects**, by seeing what happens to *can* and its other forms:

> A: Did you hear what Lucia did? I **couldn't believe** my ears when Izanil told me.
>
> B: What? I didn't hear anything. Tell me.
>
> A: She turned down a one-year scholarship to the Sorbonne.
>
> B: She what? But why? What an incredible opportunity!
>
> A: I know. She **can't have been** in her right mind.
>
> B: You mean she **could have had**[1] a scholarship to the Sorbonne for a whole year?
>
> A: Uh-huh.
>
> B: Who knows . . . she **could have had**[2] a very good reason for turning it down. I'd just like to know why things like that never happen to me!
>
> A: Well, I think she **could have discussed** it with us first before saying no. After all, aren't we her best friends?

What we're confronted with in this dialogue is the fact that we have five different uses of *can*, all of which represent something in the past. How should we interpret them? Keeping in mind the context surrounding each form, think about what these phrases mean and write down your interpretations on the following lines:

I couldn't believe my ears . . . .

....

She can't have been in her right mind . . . .

....

. . . she could have had[1] . . ." ....

....

. . . she could have had[2] . . ." ....

....

. . . she could have discussed it with us . . . .

....

Now let's see how your interpretations compare to mine:

I couldn't believe my ears . . . Even though what Speaker A is saying technically means that *she wasn't able to believe what she heard*, it's being used in this context idiomatically to mean *she found it hard, if not impossible, to believe what she heard*. Whether it's idiomatic or not, however, *couldn't* does represent the past of *can't* in its meaning of **inability**. It follows, then, that the affirmative *could*, being the past of *can*, means **ability**. It seems straightforward and uncomplicated, wouldn't you say? Well, let's go on with this idea and take a look at the following. Read these two mini-dialogues and decide if the word in bold makes sense or doesn't make sense to use:

Dialogue 1

A. **Could** she hear you during the phone call yesterday?
☐ makes sense to use   ☐ doesn't make sense to use   ☐ not sure

B. Yes, she **could**. We had a good conversation.
☐ makes sense to use   ☐ doesn't makes sense to use   ☐ not sure

Dialogue 2

A. Guess what! I **could** buy that car yesterday!
☐ makes sense to use   ☐ doesn't make sense to use   ☐ not sure

B. You **could**? That's great!
☐ makes sense to use   ☐ doesn't makes sense to use   ☐ not sure

In **Dialogue 1, both** speakers' sentences **make sense to use**, but in **Dialogue 2**, neither speakers' sentences **make sense to use**. So why does *could* make sense in the first dialogue but not in the second? Can you think of a reason for this odd situation? If you've got an idea, write it down on the following lines:

....
....

The reason that *could* doesn't make sense to use in Dialogue 2 is that **we don't use the affirmative *could* in statements or questions when we talk about an action that's been <u>accomplished</u>**. Saying "I could buy that car yesterday" means the person had the money, credit line, or whatever available to buy the car, but it doesn't clearly state that the person actually bought the car. Instead of saying,"I *could buy* that car yesterday," people would just say "I *bought* that car yesterday."

The reason that *could* makes sense to use in Dialogue 1 is that **it's all right to use *could* in a question and its reply, affirmative or negative, as long as we're talking about former ability.**

Here's another example of using *could* this way:

> When I was a young girl, I could dance all night long.

She can't have been in her right mind . . . Speaker A is saying that she doesn't believe Lucia was in her right mind when she made that decision; in other words, "it's impossible that she was in her right mind" or "I'm sure she wasn't in her right mind." Obviously, this is quite a strong statement, one which leaves no room for any other opinions. I should also mention that the use of ***can't have* + past participle** tends to be more British than American, even though you'll hear it used occasionally in American speech.

Just as we did above with *couldn't*, let's see if this sentence will work for us in the affirmative:

> She can have been in her right mind . . .

Well, what do you think? Do you consider this sentence acceptable or unacceptable?

☐ acceptable   ☐ unacceptable

This sentence is **unacceptable**. We don't use ***can have* + past participle** when we're sure about what occurred in the past. There's another modal auxiliary that we use for this idea and I'll get to it in just a moment.

Before moving on to the next phrase, let's investigate if there are other ways we can express this idea of disbelief. Think about it and see if you can fill in the following line with two other phrases containing modals (modal auxiliary + have been) that basically mean the same idea as "She can't have been in her right mind":

....

We do have other phrases that will serve the same basic purpose:

> She <u>couldn't</u> have been in her right mind . . .
> and
> She <u>mustn't</u> have been in her right mind . . .

So what's the difference, if any, in using *can't*, *couldn't*, and *mustn't* in this idea? If you've got some thoughts on the matter, write them down here:

....

It turns out that there's really no big difference among the three phrases concerning the strength or force of the ideas. Some speakers feel that using *can't* or *mustn't* tends to seem stronger while others don't. Using *couldn't*, on the other hand, tends to be less forceful to some and more forceful to others. When it comes right down to it, **they all basically convey the same idea.**

. . . **she could have had**[1] **a scholarship** . . . Speaker B's communicating that Lucia had the chance to accept a scholarship, but didn't. That little underlined addition is the most important part of the idea to keep in mind, that Lucia *didn't accept* the scholarship even though it was possible for her to do so.

So how does this phrase work in the negative? Are we going to have the same problem with it that we had with the previous two? Let's see:

. . . she couldn't have had a scholarship . . .

Here we go again. Let's see what your answer is this time:

☐ acceptable   ☐ unacceptable

Well, we've finally found a negative version that's **acceptable**! But what about its meaning? Is there some sort of radical change in meaning, or has it basically stayed the same, only gone negative? What do you say?

☐ same   ☐ different   ☐ not sure

Believe it or not, the answer is that **it's the same** and yet **it's different!** What's the same is that "it was possible for her to have a scholarship," becomes "**it wasn't possible/it was impossible for her to have a scholarship**"; that's the same basic concept with the negative added. What's different, however, is that we don't have that addition tagged on to the end as we had above for *could have* (she had the opportunity, *but didn't take it*). Unlike *could have*, the meaning of *couldn't have* has no hidden extras.

. . . **she could have had**[2] **a very good reason** . . . Compared to the context of the phrase *could have had* that we've just worked on, this *could have had* has a very different meaning. In this context Speaker B means "**it's possible she had a very good reason**" for not accepting the scholarship.

And do we have additional ways to express the same idea with other modal auxiliaries? Let's see if you can come up with any on the following line:

Even though it may frustrate you, I'm going to hold off giving you my answers until we get to the next section of the chapter. Be patient with me and everything will come together nicely! In the meantime, let's look at the fifth and last phrase from our dialogue that still needs interpreting.

. . . **she could have discussed it with us first** . . . This phrase is somewhat confusing because it carries two ideas wrapped into one. As we've already seen, the basic idea is that "she had the chance to discuss it with us, but she didn't."The most important idea that Speaker A is saying, however, is that "it was wrong of her not to discuss it with us first." In other words, there's a gentle form of reproach or criticism contained within the phrase which can only be seen through the context.

"Can"/"Could"/"Could Have" in a Nutshell

- **couldn't**
  = past of *can't* meaning "wasn't/weren't able to":
  I couldn't come to your party because I was sick.
  Note 1: used in the affirmative when representing *ability* in the past:
  Years ago, my horse could run like the wind.
  Note 2: not used in the affirmative when the focus is on *an accomplished act*:
  *I could do it. (preferred version: I *did* it.)
  Note 3: *be able to* can be <u>assumed</u> to stand for an accomplished act even though this isn't strictly its meaning:
  They were able to get the shipment out by 5:00 p.m.

- **can't have + past participle**
  = **disbelief**:
  She can't have driven so many kilometers in one day if she stayed within the speed limit.
  = **impossibility (a strong statement not used in the affirmative)**:
  He's a paraplegic. He can't have gotten out of the wheelchair without assistance.

- **could have + past participle**
  = **opportunity existed, but wasn't taken or didn't occur**:
  I know she had nothing better to do that evening. She could have gone with us to the movies.
  = **mild reproach for something not done**:
  He found out about the coming lay-offs long before they happened, and I thought he was my friend. He could have warned me that I was going to be laid off. Some friend!

- **couldn't have + past participle**
  = **disbelief (perhaps weaker or more tactful than *can't have*)**:
  She's such a nice person. She couldn't have been so thoughtless.
  = **impossibility**:
  You couldn't have been there if you were with me at the time!

May Have/Might Have

For various uses in the past, *may* and *might* can be just as complicated and confusing as *can*. You'll see in Chapter 13, by the way, that *might* is used as the past of *may* in indirect (reported) speech:

> I was told that he might join us, but I bet he won't.

However, that's not what I plan to show you in this chapter.

Unlike *could*, **might can never stand on its own as a past form without indirect speech** being involved (*He might go with us./She said he might go with us). So what happens to *may* and *might* in the past when indirect speech isn't involved? Take a look at our next dialogue to see them in action:

> A: Where's Gianni? He always joins us for lunch on Mondays.
>
> B: He **may have gone** to the hospital to see his father. You know, his father's been there for a couple of days.
>
> A: Nothing serious, I hope.
>
> B: Not really. He should be out of there in another day or so.
>
> A: Well, he **might have said something**[1]. Here I've gone and ordered his usual lunch for him. I hope I can find our waitress to cancel it before they make it or I'll be stuck with two checks!
>
> B: He **might have said something**[2] to your assistant. I think I heard her talking to him on the phone this morning.

Just as we did with the first dialogue, let's see if you can come up with your own interpretations for the phrases I've marked in bold depending on their context, and then I'll compare my interpretations to yours:

He may have gone to the hospital . . . .

....

. . . he might have said something[1]. ....

....

He might have said something[2] . . . .

....

Let's get right to my interpretations and see how closely yours match mine:
He may have gone to the hospital . . . Speaker B's idea is that "it's possible that Gianni went to the hospital."

Now see if you can come up with two other phrases using different modal auxiliaries that carry the same meaning. Think about it and write your two alternate phrases on the following line:

....

The phrases I'm thinking of are

> He <u>might</u> have gone to the hospital . . .
>
> and
>
> He <u>could</u> have gone to the hospital . . .

There are native speakers who tend to think that *may have gone* is a more confident guess than *might have gone*, but you really don't have to make such fine distinctions for your students. And if you remember my discussion about *could have*, I said that there was another meaning for *could* have when found in another context—and here it is. In the previous dialogue about Lucia and that one-year scholarship, the phrase *she could have accepted it* had that additional meaning in the context, notably that she didn't accept it. In the context of this dialogue, however, "He could have gone to the hospital" simply means what was possible in the past (the speaker's guessing about what happened), and nothing more.

Now that you've seen how *may*, *might*, and *could* can be interchangeable when the meaning is possibility in the past, I can give you my answers for those two phrases I held off discussing back on page 186. "She <u>could</u> have had a very good reason. . ." can also be expressed by saying:

> . . . she <u>may</u> have had a very good reason . . .
>
> or
>
> . . . she <u>might</u> have had a very good reason . . .

It's worth mentioning that when *may/might have* is used in the negative (*may/might not have*), there's no change in meaning other than the obvious negation of the idea.

. . . **he might have said something**[1]. This phrase is quite a different matter from the use of *might have* that we've already investigated. In the context of the dialogue, this phrase doesn't deal with a past possibility at all. It actually is Speaker A's **gentle or polite way of reproaching** his friend Gianni for not having let them know that he wouldn't be joining them for lunch. Can you think of another *gentle* way of stating this idea with a different modal? If you can, write it down on the following line:

....

The other way this idea can be expressed is

> . . . he <u>could</u> have said something.

You'll recall that in the previous chapter I spoke about how *could* is used at times to soften meaning. What you've just seen is an example of that. I'll get to yet another way of expressing reproach—although in a stronger tone—later on in the chapter.

Before we move on to the next use of *might have*, we should consider what happens to the phrase ". . . he might have said something" when it's put in the negative. What do *you* think?

....

I hope you realize that you were just given a trick question! Oddly enough, the answer is that you can't use *might have* in the negative when it represents a **reproach**. When we use *might have* to reproach somebody, it's always in the affirmative. Now let's see what the last phrase means.

He might have said something[2]. . . In the context of our dialogue, Speaker B is saying that "It's possible Gianni said something" to Person A's assistant. Notice how these two identical phrases have such different meanings *in context*!

But what are two other ways this idea can be expressed with two different modals?

Write the phrases down on the following line:

....

The two phrases I'm sure you wrote are

> He <u>may</u> have said something . . .
> and
> He <u>could</u> have said something . . .

Remember that if "He could have said something . . ." is put into a different context, it can mean that gentle or polite form of criticism that we found in the sentence "He might have said something . . ." However, keep in mind that *may have* can't be used in this way no matter what the context is.

 *"May have"/"Might have" in a Nutshell*

🌰 **may have + past participle**
= **possibility (a bit more confident):**
I'm not sure, but she may have been married once before.

- might have + past participle
  = possibility (a bit less confident):
  She might have had children by her first husband, but I really don't think so.
  = mild reproach for something not done:
  I can't believe they left without me. They might have waited a little longer, you know. I was only five minutes late.

Should Have/Ought to Have

A: I'm sorry, honey. I just wanted to surprise you for your birthday.

B: Well, you've certainly done that!

A: I guess I **should have bought** you a birthday cake.

B: Did you follow the recipe carefully?

A: Well, not really. I thought I'd improvise a little. Maybe I **shouldn't have been** so daring, huh?

B: And I didn't even really want a cake. I **ought to have told** you that I wanted to start developing healthier eating habits on my birthday.

A: Nothing's gone right today! I wanted the kids here before you got home so we'd all be here to surprise you. They **should have been** here thirty minutes ago; it's only a 15-minute ride.

B: Don't worry. They'll be here soon. You know, you really **oughtn't to have gone** to so much trouble, but I think you're a sweetie for trying so hard to surprise me—and you did!

A: Happy birthday, Honey.

After all the hard work you've done with *can't have* and *could have* and *may have* and *might have*, you'll be pleased to learn that this next section, which deals with *should have* and *ought to have*, will be easier to deal with. The reason is that the meanings of these two modal auxiliaries in the past are pretty clear—just as they are in the present/future. So let's get right to work interpreting the phrases in bold from the dialogue:

. . . I should have bought you a birthday cake. ....

....

. . . I shouldn't have been so daring . . . .

....

I ought to have told you . . . .

....

They should have been here thirty minutes ago . . . .

....

You oughtn't to have gone to so much trouble . . . .

....

Now let's compare your interpretations to mine:

. . . I should have bought you a birthday cake. Speaker A is saying that he didn't buy his wife a birthday cake, and he realizes that that was a mistake. In short, he's saying "**I made a mistake by trying to bake you a birthday cake instead of buying you one.**" As you can see, the meaning of *should* in the past is not so obvious and usually ends up being somewhat of a challenge to get across to students. It can be a troublesome form because it's used in the affirmative to refer to something that *didn't* happen in the past: Speaker A didn't buy a cake, but rather baked a cake, and now realizes that it was a mistake to do that.

. . . I shouldn't have been so daring . . . Speaker A is now saying that he was too daring when he improvised on the cake recipe and he regrets it. In short, he's saying "**I made a mistake by being so daring.**" Once again, the meaning of *should* in the past can be troublesome. This time it's used in the negative to refer to something that *did* happen in the past: Speaker A was too daring in experimenting with that recipe and now realizes that it was a mistake.

I ought to have told you . . . Speaker B is saying that she didn't tell her husband her plans to get into healthier eating habits, and she realizes that it was a mistake not to tell him ahead of time. What she means is "**I made a mistake by not telling you.**" Once more, our affirmative phrase refers to something that *didn't* happen in the past. Note that we can use *should have* in this sentence just as easily as *ought to have*.

They should have been here thirty minutes ago . . . Speaker A is now using the meaning of *should* that many students tend to forget, namely, "**I expected them to be here thirty minutes ago (but they haven't arrived yet).**" This meaning of expectation can also work in the negative, that is, when you didn't expect something to happen even though it did:

We hardly studied for that exam. By all rights, we shouldn't have passed it.

There's one other modal perfect form that can express this idea of expectation. If you think you know which one I'm thinking of, write it down on the following line:

....

That other modal perfect I'm thinking of as a possibility for expectation is **ought to have**, and if I had used it in that line from the dialogue, I would have had this sentence:

> They <u>ought to have</u> been home thirty minutes ago.

You . . . oughtn't to have gone to so much trouble, . . . Speaker B is using *oughtn't to have* in a very kind, gentle way. True enough, she's saying "**You made a mistake by going to so much trouble**," but the statement comes across softly; what she really means is that "**It wasn't necessary for you to go to so much trouble.**" Note once again that we can use *shouldn't have gone* just as easily as *oughtn't to have gone* in this sentence.

By the way, some native speakers have a tendency to drop the word *to* when using this modal perfect in the negative, resulting in *ought not have* or the more typically heard *oughtn't have* ("You oughtn't have gone to so much trouble."). One last note to mention is that Americans tend to use *should* much more than *ought to* in all of these forms, present/future or past. This preference for *should* is especially noticeable in the negatives.

"Should have"/"Ought to have" in a Nutshell

- **should have/ought to have** + past participle
  = reproach for something <u>not done</u>:
  You should have called the police when that happened. You ought to have called the police when that happened.
  = expectation:
  They should have been here by now.
  They ought to have been here by now.

- **shouldn't have/oughtn't (to) have** + past participle
  = reproach for something <u>done</u>:
  Look at all these leftovers! She shouldn't have cooked so much food just for the three of us.
  Look at all these leftovers! She oughtn't (to) have cooked so much food for just the three of us.
  = expectation:
  One dose of the vaccine should have been enough.
  He shouldn't have needed another one.
  One dose of the vaccine ought to have been enough.
  He oughtn't (to) have needed another one.

<u>Must Have/Had To</u>

Even though it isn't strictly a modal auxiliary, we're going to explore the semi-auxiliary *have to* at the same time that we look at *must* in the past. The reason for this pairing of the two will become apparent to you as you read the next dialogue:

> A: Did you hear the news about Mark and Marci?
>
> B: No, what?
>
> A: I **had to sit** down when I heard it. The doctor told them that Marci is going to have quadruplets.
>
> B: What? Oh no! What **must** they **have felt** at hearing that?
>
> A: They were probably in shock. I know I would have been! But guess what?
>
> B: There's more?
>
> A: It turns out the doctor was wrong.
>
> B: I don't believe it! The doctor **didn't have to put them** through all of that. They **mustn't have** been too pleased with him.
>
> A: They were furious—and yet relieved at the same time.
>
> B: I bet. So, how did it turn out?
>
> A: Well, Marci's not having quadruplets after all—but she *is* having triplets!

Let's investigate *must have* and *have to* in the past by keeping the same format that we've been using all along. So here are the items in bold that are waiting for your interpretations:

I had to sit down . . . .

....

What must they have felt . . . .

....

The doctor didn't have to put them through all of that ....

....

They mustn't have been too pleased with him ....

....

We've got a lot of ground to cover, so let's get right to it:

I had to sit down . . . Speaker A is saying "**It was necessary for me to sit down.**"

What must they have felt . . . Speaker B is guessing about what Mark and Marci's emotions were at that time. She's really saying, "**I wonder what they felt . . .**" This use of *must* deals with asking for a logical conclusion or conjecture.

The doctor didn't have to put them through all of that . . . Speaker B is saying that "It wasn't necessary for the doctor to put them through all of that," and the idea is a form of criticism in this context. Used in a different context, *didn't have to* simply means *it wasn't necessary*.

They mustn't have been too pleased with him . . . Now Speaker B states that "I'm sure they weren't too pleased with him" (*the doctor*), which once again is making a conclusion.

You may not realize it, but something's missing. There's a very important use of *must* which we can use for a present or future idea, but not for a past idea. Can you figure out which meaning is missing from the uses in the past? Here's some help. See if you can transfer this sentence into the past:

> You mustn't park here between 7 and 9 a.m.

....

Well? Could you do it? I hope you couldn't! You'll have to pardon me, but this was another trick question. I just wanted you to discover for yourself that you can't put *mustn't* in the past for this meaning. And, of course, I'm sure you understand now that the meaning I'm talking about is **prohibition**.

So how then can we say this idea in the past? The only way to do it is by paraphrasing the idea. Let's see if you can come up with sentences that do communicate the same idea for the past. By the way, I've come up with four!

....
....
....
....

Here are the four paraphrases that I've thought of:

> You <u>couldn't</u> park there between 7 and 9 a.m.
> They <u>didn't let</u> you park there between 7 and 9 a.m.
> You <u>weren't allowed</u> to park there between 7 and 9 a.m.
> You <u>weren't permitted</u> to park there between 7 and 9 a.m.

Of course there are other variations, but these are the principal ways you'd transfer my original sentence into the past since *mustn't* has this time defect when it comes to this meaning.

 **Heads Up!**

Students have a great deal of difficulty knowing which words in a phrase or sentence should receive the main stress, an area of grammar often overlooked by their teachers.

When dealing with modal auxiliaries in the past (modal perfects), this problem needs addressing. Here are some guidelines on how modal perfects are pronounced:

→ The first auxiliary receives the stress, so *have* is unstressed
  (e.g., *He COULD have GONE.*).

→ The *h* in *have* tends to be dropped.

→ The vowel /æ/ reduces to schwa /ə/ or practically disappears altogether, so that we end up with *He COULD've GONE* in our flow of speech.

Because of these reductions, students don't seem to hear the auxiliary *have* at all when they listen to native speakers. Make sure you explain these pronunciation variations and practice them with your students.

You'll be investigating much more about these reduced sounds, like that *h* in *have*, when you get to Chapter 17.

 "Must have"/"Had to" in a Nutshell

- **had to**
  = necessity (past of *must*):
  Before they could leave the airport, they had to clear customs.

- **must have** + past participle
  = logical conclusion/certainty:
  When Carlitos saw that snake slithering toward him, he must have been petrified.
  = conclusion/conjecture:
  I can't imagine how they must have felt when they heard the dreadful news.

Some Words About *Would*

In Chapter 8 I discussed the unusual use of stressed *would* when it refers to a certain characteristic of somebody or something in a reproachful way. If you recall, I explained that it can be an immediate response to something that has just occurred:

> A: Well, everything's ready, isn't it? Let's tell everyone they can start eating now.
>
> B: Uh-oh.
>
> A: What is it?
>
> B: I don't see the dessert. Wasn't your brother supposed to bring it?
>
> A: Yes, he was. He **WOULD** forget to do that. You can never count on him to remember anything!

Now we can expand upon this use to include any time in the past:

> A: I don't know why, but I was thinking about those neighbors we used to have who drove us crazy with their stereo.
>
> B: Oh, yes, I remember them only too well. They **WOULD** always play their music too loud. Well, I, for one, am not sorry that they moved away!

Would Rather Have/Would Sooner Have

We've finally reached the last modal forms to look at in the past. Here's the final dialogue for the chapter which will show you how they're used. Write their interpretations below.

> A: Well, did you enjoy the concert?
>
> B: Not at all. I**'d rather have stayed** home.
>
> A: But I thought you liked chamber music.
>
> B: Let me put it this way: I**'d sooner have watched** the grass grow!
>
> A: Oh!

I'd rather have stayed home ....

....

I'd sooner have watched the grass grow ....

....

And now to the final comparison between your interpretations and mine:

I'd rather have stayed home. Speaker B is saying that, "If she had been given the choice, staying home was preferable to going to that concert."

I'd sooner have watched the grass grow. Speaker B reiterates her preference at the same time that she makes a sarcastic remark about doing something extremely boring. She's saying that "If she had had the choice, she would have watched the grass grow; watching the grass grow was likely to be more exciting than attending that concert."

In both cases, of course, the unspoken, but understood, second part of either idea is "I *would rather/sooner have . . . than . . .*" Well, let's see if you can finish off these sentences by adding that unspoken, but understood, second part which comes after the word *than*:

I'd rather have stayed home than . . .
or
I'd sooner have watched the grass grow than . . .

And the answer is . . . than to have gone . . . / . . . than have gone . . . / . . . than gone to that concert!

Teaching Tips

9.1 *Miming Modals*

Before class, create a list of activities for students to mime (swallow a fly; lose a checkbook or wallet; look for a lost shoe; walk on a tightrope, etc.). Have your students try to figure out the activities that volunteers have chosen to mime by using past modals in their guesses ("He shouldn't have opened his mouth!"/"She must have dropped the checkbook/wallet when she got out of the car."/"Her dog must have buried it!"/"I wouldn't have had the nerve to do that!")

9.2 *Cause and Effect*

Select pictures from your Picture File (see Appendix 1) that have a potential cause-and-effect relationship. Have students brainstorm sentences about the pictures using past modal forms. For example, if you have a picture of a man with a broken leg, some sentences that your students might come up with are, "He shouldn't have gone bungee jumping."/"He might have gotten that broken leg skiing."/"He couldn't have seen that banana peel." Note: This tip can be used for conditional practice (see Chapter 16). "If that bungee cord hadn't been so long, he wouldn't have hit the ground and broken his leg."/"He wouldn't have slipped, fallen down, and broken his leg if he'd seen that banana peel," etc.

Variation: Find a picture that's big enough for the entire class to view and that has a variety of details and action in it. Display it so that students, who have been divided into small groups, can use modal auxiliaries to brainstorm sentences about the picture. Let them work for five to ten minutes and then have them put their pencils down. Be firm about this time limit. Have each group present their "brainstorms." Give one point for each sentence that uses a modal correctly and a second point for each sentence that no other group has come up with. The group with the most points is declared the "winner."

9.3 *This Is What Might Have Been!*

Come up with the names of locally or internationally known famous and infamous people from the past or present. List them on the board. Divide the class into small groups and let them create as many sentences as they can think of about these people using past modal forms. This is what you might hear:"He must have been a better general than Napoleon."/"Marie Antoinette shouldn't have said, 'Let them eat cake!'"/"Lyndon Johnson might not have become president if Kennedy hadn't been assassinated." Note: This tip can also be used for conditional practice.

9.4 *Plan a Field Trip*

Plan a field trip with your students . . . and then take it. When you get back into the classroom, review how it went, using modal auxiliaries in your observations.

9.5 *Graphs and Charts*

Create or find a graph or chart like the following one that contains enough information to stimulate a discussion about it. Let the students think of comments about the graph or chart using modal auxiliaries. You might hear, "It must have been a hot summer; their electric bills were much higher this year than they were last year."/"They can't have had much money left over at the end of the month." Note: This activity can also be used to practice conditionals: "I would have moved to a city with lower rents if I'd had to use that much of my salary to pay my rent." Feel free to use the following example of a pie chart in your classes if you wish.

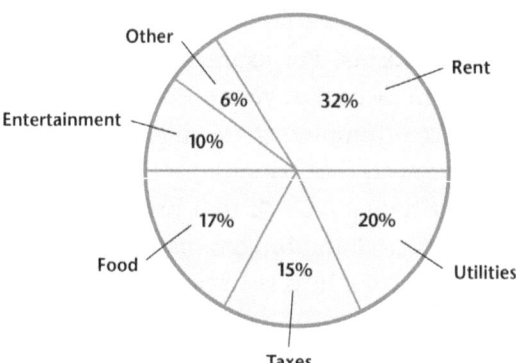

9.6 *Did You Hear What I Heard?*

Think of a controversial or lively topic for your students to discuss. Divide the class into an even number of small groups. Pair two groups together; one of the groups will discuss the topic, the other will listen and take notes. The listeners should write down comments about what they've heard that bothers them, could be restated, was incorrect, well-stated, etc. Encourage the use of past modal forms where appropriate.

10

Passives and Causatives

"What's done is done 'cause I got it done."

The Passive Voice

> auxiliary BE + PAST PARTICIPLE of verb
>
> I **am** expect**ed**.
> You **were** promot**ed**.
> She **has been told**.

Over the past several years, few areas of grammar have been discussed and debated more than the passive voice even though the heart of the matter is concerned with style rather than grammaticality. It's said that the passive voice is being overused and that it's simply a clever way to restate the active voice. The truth of the matter is—as far I see it—that passive forms aren't overdone and have practical uses that aren't simply restatements of active forms. Without doubt, the passive voice has a life, a flavor, and an importance of its own and should be taught as an essential grammatical form.

By the way, in case you haven't noticed, the opening paragraph is just chock full of passive voice constructions! Can you identify them? Let's see if you can pick them out of the first paragraph and copy them onto the following lines:

....
....
....

These are the passive voice constructions you can find in the first paragraph:

have been discussed	is concerned with
is said	is being overused
aren't overdone	should be taught

In each of these phrases, you can easily identify the auxiliary *be* (*been/is/ is being/aren't/be*) and the past participles of the targeted verbs (*discussed/ concerned/said/overused/overdone/taught*). Seeing how I've used the passive voice in the first paragraph should answer the question as to whether I feel it's overused. My answer is obviously *no*.

So what exactly is the passive voice? Read this opening dialogue, check out the parts in bold, and see if you can figure out why this verb form exists:

> A: Have those novelty items from China arrived yet?
>
> B: Yes. In fact, they **were delivered** from the port just this morning. What do you want us to do with them?
>
> A: Well, they really **should be taken** over to the Hanson Street warehouse, don't you think?
>
> B: Okay. I'll get on it right after I finish up these reports.
>
> A: Those reports **were supposed to be finished** and **sent** on to our main office a couple of days ago, right?
>
> B: Well...yes, but I **was called** out of town and didn't get back until two days ago, remember?
>
> A: Oh, yeah. I forgot. Well, let's get them out as soon as we can.

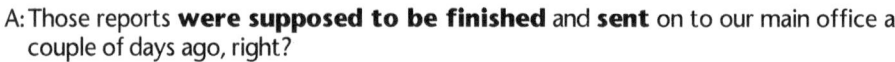

Any theory? Here's a little hint: There are subjects in sentences that actively do something, but there are other subjects that don't actively do anything. If you think you can explain why the passive voice has been used after certain subjects in this dialogue, write down your thoughts on this line:

....

In order to understand why the passive voice is needed, we have to examine the subjects in the phrases. In every case in the dialogue where we have a passive construction, **the subject isn't active**, that is, **it isn't doing the action of the verb**; someone's doing something to it, but it isn't doing the action itself. Those Chinese novelty items didn't deliver themselves; someone from the company or the port delivered them, but the delivering person is not related to the topic of the conversation. Likewise, the novelty items can't take themselves over to the warehouse; someone has to take them over there. In every sentence with a phrase in bold in the dialogue, the subject isn't the "doer." Knowing this much about passives, let's create a basic rule: **If the subject of our idea isn't the doer of the action—in other words, isn't active—the verb that follows is likely to be in the passive voice.** There are other reasons that we use the passive voice, but I'll get to those later on.

 Heads Up!

Even though every language has some form or other of the passive voice, not every language uses it the same way. English and Hawaiian tend to use the passive voice more frequently than many other languages do.

What appears as a passive voice construction in English may not be a passive form in other languages even though they communicate the same idea:

→ In French it's common to use the impersonal pronoun *on* with the active verb where the passive voice would be used in English:

> On parle français ici.
> French is spoken here.

The closest English equivalent to this would be *One speaks French here.*

→ In Russian it's often the case that the reflexive form of the verb is used where a passive voice is found in English:

> Как называется эта улица?
> /kak nazıváyɛtsa ɛta úlitsa/
> What's this street called?
> (literally: "How does this street call itself?")

Now let's see if it's really true that when the subject isn't the doer, the verb should be in the passive voice. Look at this next dialogue and pay special attention to the phrases in bold:

A: Well, Anita, today you're going to learn how to make bread.

B: Great. What's first?

A: Okay. You see that **I've already mixed together the flour, salt, and water**, right?

B: Uh-huh.

A: Now **we add the yeast that I dissolved** in some warm water. Next we mix it all up.

B: Okay. I get it.

A: Now we put the dough in a warm, dark place.

B: Why do we do that, Mommy?

A: Because **the dough has to rise**. The yeast, the warmth, and the darkness will help this process to happen.

B: What do you mean, rise?

A: **The dough will grow** and **double** in size.

B: Wow! That means we can have two loaves instead of one!

According to the rule, if the subject isn't the doer, the verb that follows is likely to be in the passive voice, and we know that we form the passive by using the auxiliary *be* plus the past participle of the targeted verb. Even though all the sentences in the dialogue are fine as they are, let's see if we can transform them into the passive voice. We'll need to go through two steps:

1. Make the object our new subject and throw out the old subject.
2. Change the targeted verb by placing the auxiliary *be* in front of it (being careful to keep the same tense or aspect as in the active form) and by using the past participle of the verb.

Here's a visual to show you what I mean:

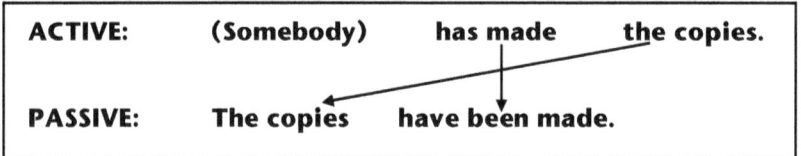

On the line below each phrase I've adapted from the dialogue, check to see whether you can write these phrases in the passive voice.

1. I've mixed together the flour, salt, and water . . .

....

2. We add the yeast that I dissolved . . .

....

3. We put the dough in a warm, dark place . . .

....

4. . . . the dough has to rise . . .

....

5. . . . the dough will grow and grow . . .

....

6. . . . the dough will double in size . . .

....

Any problems? I certainly hope so! The reason you should have had some trouble is because **Numbers 4, 5, and 6 can't be transformed into passive voice phrases.** Before I get into these three, however, let's see if your other phrases match mine:

1. The flour, salt, and water have been mixed together
2. The yeast that I dissolved/that was dissolved is added
3. The dough is put . . .

And now to those other three phrases. Why can't they be transformed into passive voice constructions? For three reasons: First, in the case of these three sentences, the subjects are the doers, and that should really be the end of it. But there are two more important reasons I'd like to bring to your attention. If you notice, there are no objects in Numbers 4, 5, and 6 to make into new subjects, and that's my second reason. Now on to the third.

To figure out what that third reason is, let's do some more linguistic sleuthing. Look at these two phrases and decide which one is grammatical and which one isn't:

1a. The sun rose.	☐ grammatical	☐ ungrammatical
1b. The sun raised.	☐ grammatical	☐ ungrammatical

And what about the next two?

2a. He rose his hand.	☐ grammatical	☐ ungrammatical
2b. He raised his hand.	☐ grammatical	☐ ungrammatical

Rose is **grammatical** in **1a**, but **ungrammatical** in **2a**. *Raised* is **ungrammatical** in **1b**, but **grammatical** in **2b**.

What could be happening to cause such a turnabout? What does *raise* need to make its phrase grammatical that *rise* doesn't need? Write down your answer on this line:

....

Perhaps you've noticed that there's no object in "The sun rose," which is the grammatical phrase, but there *is* an object in "He rose his hand," and that's ungrammatical. The same holds true with the other two phrases: "The sun raised" has no object, so it's ungrammatical, but "He raised his hand" has an object, so it *is* grammatical. So what can we interpret all this to mean? What connection is there between these verbs and the objects?

It all comes down to this simple observation: If we use the verb *raise*, there must be an object in the phrase; if we use the verb *rise*, there can be no object. This is because there are three kinds of verbs in English:

- transitive verbs, which have objects,
- intransitive verbs, which have no objects, and
- a group of interesting verbs that can either have or not have objects, in other words, which can be transitive or intransitive.

Raise is a good example of a transitive verb ("He raised his hand"); *rise* is a good example of an intransitive verb ("The sun rose"), and a verb like *weigh* is a good example of the other group of verbs that can be either transitive or intransitive:

The butcher <u>weighed</u> the turkey. (transitive)
The turkey <u>weighed</u> 20 pounds. (intransitive)

Getting back to Numbers 4, 5, and 6 on page 202, we can say that they can't be turned into passive voice constructions because they contain verbs that are acting as intransitive verbs. *Rise* is one of those verbs. What are the other two in those phrases?

....

The other two words acting as intransitive verbs in our dialogue are ***grow*** and ***double***. But are these verbs always intransitive? The answer is *no*. In other sentences, both of these verbs can have direct objects, which will make them transitive verbs ("I grow prize-winning flowers."/"By investing wisely, we doubled our income in just two years."). The important point here, however, is that they're intransitive in this dialogue and therefore can't be transformed into passive voice constructions. **No verb that is intransitive can be made into a passive voice construction.** So now you have all three reasons that Numbers 4, 5, and 6 couldn't be made into passive voice constructions.

When the Doer is Unveiled

Up to this point, I've mentioned that the passive voice is used when the subject in a transitive sentence isn't the "doer." But what if I choose to mention who or what the doer is? How can I do that? It's really quite simple; all I need to do is add the preposition *by* after the passive phrase and then fill in the doer:

>Thousands of houses were destroyed by the hurricane.
>Everyone knows that the earth is warmed by the sun.
>The suspect is being interrogated by two detectives.

That was simple enough, wasn't it? Well, maybe there's a bit more to it than that. There's another preposition that's often found in passive constructions, and you're going to find it in the next dialogue. In addition, there's an odd construction that looks like an active phrase in the simple past but really isn't, and you're going to find that in the dialogue, too. Both of these are items rarely covered in classes even though I think it's clear that they should be. Take a look to see what I'm talking about:

A: I can't get over how childish some students in this school can be.

B: I'll say. Who would have thought there'd be a food fight in the cafeteria? I still can't believe it **was started by** friends of yours.

A: And I can't believe that the assistant principal **was hit** in the face **with** all those pats of butter.

B: I only know that I was totally embarrassed when I saw the headline in the school paper today.

A: Oh? I haven't seen it. What does it say?

B: Nothing much, just "Assistant Principal **Buttered**! Two Students **Suspended**.

As I mentioned, we've got two interesting items in this dialogue and we'll examine them separately. The first one concerns the choice of preposition that follows our passive constructions. The first phrase in bold has the preposition *by* following it to introduce the doer, in this case, "friends of yours," and this is the typical preposition taught to students. But what about the next passive construction? In this phrase we don't have the word *by* introducing the doer, but rather the word *with*. Before I ask you that ever-familiar question as to why this is so, look at the following examples and think about the difference that the prepositions create.

> The instruments were sterilized <u>by the nurse</u>.
> The instruments were sterilized <u>with steam</u>.

Think you've figured out how to interpret each sentence? If you have, write your thoughts on the lines that follow:

....

....

In our first sentence, the nurse is obviously the active doer, and **the preposition *by* introduces the active doer.** So what role does *the steam* play if we use it with that alternate preposition? **Using *with* introduces what we can call the *instrument*,** in other words, what the doer used to accomplish the action. Here are a few more examples of each:

> Showing the active doer: She was bitten <u>by a squirrel</u>.
> The violinist was accompanied <u>by a pianist</u>.
> The car was checked out <u>by my mechanic</u>.
>
> Showing the instrument: He was knighted <u>with a sword</u>.
> The newlyweds were showered <u>with rice</u>.
> They were honored <u>with the Nobel Prize</u>.

Simple and clear cut, right? Well, before you get too comfortable, compare the next two sentences with the ones you've just seen:

> The windshield of his car was smashed <u>by a brick</u>.
> The windshield of his car was smashed <u>with a brick</u>.

Maybe it's not so simple after all. Most native speakers would say that both of these sentences sound all right, but they certainly wouldn't accept this interchange of *by* and *with* in those other sentences you've just seen. Would you?

> She was bitten <u>with a squirrel</u>.
> The car was checked out <u>with my mechanic</u>.
> He was knighted <u>by a sword</u>.
> The newlyweds were showered <u>by rice</u>.

So what's going on? If these four sentences are clearly strange, why don't you feel the same way over those two sentences about the car windshield? Before you answer this question, let's just look at another example where *by* and *with* seem to work equally well:

>Wilting plants can be revived <u>by warm water</u>.
>Wilting plants can be revived <u>with warm water</u>.

Can you find a reason to explain why these pairs of sentences sound equally good, but those others don't? When you think you've hit on something, write your ideas down on these lines:

....

....

This is a very tricky feature of the passive voice, as I'm sure you've discovered for yourself. The answer to the last question is that **we can use either *by* or *with* when the person or thing mentioned can act either as the doer or the instrument.** In basic terms, it's all a matter of focus. Let's go back to the sentences about the car windshield. We can look upon the brick as the thing that actually smashed the windshield and say:

>The windshield of his car was smashed <u>by</u> a brick.

In this case, the brick might have fallen from the rooftop. On the other hand, we can say that the brick was the instrument used by someone to break into the car or attack it. In that case, we can also say:

>The windshield of his car was smashed <u>with</u> a brick.

Perhaps in this expanded version, this last sentence will be clearer:

>The windshield was smashed (<u>by an irate pedestrian</u>) <u>with</u> a brick.

The same explanation holds true for the other pair of sentences where both *by* and *with* seem to work. When we say "Wilting plants can be revived <u>by</u> warm water," we're focusing on the fact that the warm water itself can actually revive those plants and is therefore the doer. When we say "Wilting plants can be revived <u>with</u> warm water," we're focusing on what can be used by someone to accomplish this result. It's amazing how troublesome two little words can be! And it is also amazing how much information they carry.

Reduced Passives

Now that we've explored *by* and *with*, let's get to that other item we found in the last dialogue. One of the speakers mentioned that the headline in the school paper read "Assistant Principal Buttered! Two Students Suspended." Many students get confused when they read headlines like this one because they think it means that the assistant principal buttered something and that two students suspended somebody. Why do you think they come up with such odd interpretations?

....

The reason is that **they're assuming the verbs *butter* and *suspend* are being used in their active sense rather than their passive sense**, and the fact that direct objects are lacking totally escapes the students. What they need to be shown is that it's a time-honored practice in newspaper headlines to save space by omitting determiners and auxiliaries. As far as the passive voice is concerned, the auxiliary *be* is omitted to save space. When the students are shown that the phrases are really "The Assistant Principal was 'Buttered!' Two Students were Suspended," they should remember that these omissions occur the next time they see such headlines.

Another occasion when we find reduced passive forms can be seen in the following dialogue:

> A: Hello, Professor Ozawa. How's your visit to the States?
>
> B: Fine, but I don't understand American holidays very well.
>
> A: Oh? Tell me about it.
>
> B: Well, the holiday just **celebrated**[1] **called**[2] "Halloween"—it's very odd. I saw children and adults **frightened**[3] by one another, but they seemed to enjoy it. I found a pumpkin **lit**[4] with a candle inside **placed**[5] near the front door of my apartment building. And there was this grotesque face **carved**[6] on it!
>
> A: Well, you see, Professor . . .
>
> B: But nothing was as strange as the apples. Nothing.
>
> A: The apples?
>
> B: Yes, the apples. When I went to a Halloween party, I could not believe how the host was serving the fruit. There were the apples, **put**[7] in a large tub of water. And I saw the guests **forced**[8] to take them out of the water with their teeth!
>
> A: Now, Professor, give me a chance to explain. You see . . .

You know that we're dealing with reduced passive forms, so what words do you think have been eliminated from the parts that appear in bold in the dialogue?

1. ....   5. ....

2. ....   6. ....

3. ....   7. ....

4. ....   8. ....

With a little bit of reconstruction work, we're sure you've realized that *which*, *that*, or *who* has been eliminated from all the parts in bold together with various forms of the auxiliary *be*. Here are the answers I have that should match yours. (Keep in mind that in *informal* English, *which* and *that* are interchangeable, as are *who* and *that*):

1. **that has [just] been/was**
2. **that is**
3. **who were (being)**
4. **that was**
5. **that had been**
6. **that had been**
7. **that had been**
8. **who were being**

And now to the reasons. There's a simple rule that you can use for all of the bold parts in the dialogue: **When you have a relative clause that begins with *who* or *that* and contains a passive voice form, the relative pronoun and the auxiliary *be* can be eliminated.** That's how we go from "... this holiday <u>that is</u> called 'Halloween' ..." to "... this holiday called 'Halloween' ..." Here are a few more examples to show you this rule in action:

Turkey (that is) <u>roasted</u> slowly comes out succulent.
Plants (that are) <u>cared</u> for well will flourish.
They adopted that child (who had been) <u>orphaned</u> during the war.

Finally, I want to mention that other occurrences of a reduced passive construction can be seen typically on signs. Sometimes, in fact, not only is the auxiliary *be* eliminated, but even the subject can be eliminated when the sign clearly shows who or what is intended:

Why Bother with the Passive Voice?

Why should we bother using the passive voice at all? Why not make things simpler and just stick to the active voice? Let's take one more look at the sentences we used to show how *by* introduced the active doer in our passive constructions and compare them to the same ideas in the active voice:

Thousands of houses were destroyed by the hurricane.
Everyone knows that the earth is warmed by the sun.
The suspect is being interrogated by two detectives.

The hurricane destroyed thousands of houses.
Everyone knows that the sun warms the earth.
Two detectives are interrogating the suspect.

Any ideas? See if you can think of a reason that, at times, we might prefer the three passive voice sentences over their active counterparts and write your thoughts on these lines:

....

....

What it all comes down to once again is a matter of focus. Are we focusing on the hurricane or on the houses? Are we discussing the sun or the earth? Is our attention on the detectives or the suspect? When we answer these questions, we also answer whether or not to use the passive voice. **If we want the focus to be on the doer, we use the active voice; if we want the focus to be on the receiver, we use the passive voice.**

Two other good reasons for using the passive voice can be found in the next dialogue, so let's examine it:

A: Did you hear that **it was announced** we can expect an increase in taxes again?

B: Not again! **Haven't taxes been raised** enough over the past few years?

A: I know. It's getting ridiculous. Well, **I've been told** that my company may just move out of the country and go to one where they won't have to pay so much corporate tax.

B: Really? Well, I can't say I'm surprised.

Why do you think that both Speaker A and Speaker B have used the passive voice in talking about possible future tax hikes? They could just as easily have chosen to use the active voice, but they didn't. Concentrate on only the first two phrases in bold and see if you can figure out why they've chosen the passive voice:

....

One reason that both speakers have chosen the passive voice is that **the doers are understood**, which is a clever way **to avoid redundancy** in the conversation. When Speaker A says ". . . it was announced . . . ," we understand immediately from the context that she means *by the government or the media*; when Speaker B says "Haven't taxes been raised enough . . ." it's clear she means *by the government*.

But what about the last statement in bold when Speaker A says ". . . I've been told . . ."? Why has she chosen to go with the passive voice in this instance?

....

The reason is that **she doesn't want to divulge her source**. Many people use the passive voice to avoid giving away their source of information or to be tactful so as not to point an accusatory finger directly at someone. Here's an example that demonstrates tact:

>A: I hear you had some bad luck with the EireCo merger.
>B: Well, because the contracts weren't delivered on time,
>   the deal fell through.
>A: Tough luck, Cormac.

Perhaps Person A knew exactly who was responsible for those contracts not reaching their destination on time, but Cormac wasn't going to be the one to point that finger or rub it in. Just imagine if the conversation had gone something like this:

>A: I hear you had some bad luck with the EireCo merger.
>B: Well, because Hayes didn't deliver the contracts on time,
>   the deal fell through.
>A: Tough luck, Cormac. Never did think much of that Hayes
>   fellow.

Whew! Quite a different "flavor" in the conversation! In this case, at any rate, there may very well be something cultural in the use of the passive voice.

Interestingly enough, many of the verbs that can be used as a way to avoid divulging the source of information or to be tactful belong to a group of verbs called "reporting verbs," which I'll be covering in Chapter 13. Besides *announce*, which you've already seen, here are some of the more typical ones you'll find that go a long way to accomplish these ends: *admit, declare, explain, mention, point out, report, say, state,* and *suggest*.

👀 **Heads Up!**

One of the toughest ideas to get across to students when they learn the passive voice is the difference between a sentence in the timeless form and one in the real present:

>   A suspect | is | interrogated.
>   A suspect | is being | interrogated.

Almost without exception, your students will tend to think that the first sentence above is in the present and never consider the second example.

Stress to them that, except for stative verbs, *am/are/is being* + past participle is the *real* present in the passive voice.

A Word About "Get"

To begin our discussion about *get*, let's first consider how it's used with adjectival forms. What's the difference between *get married* and *be married*? Write down your thoughts here:

Get means "become" when it's followed by an adjective and *become* means that there's a change in a condition or state of being; in other words, something that existed previously is now being changed. The verb *be*, on the other hand, deals only with the state of being at a certain time and has no reference to what conditions were like before.

>Examples: Antonio got angry with Sara when she embarrassed him.
>(= the moment when his mood changed)
>
>Antonio was angry with Sara for a couple of days.
>(= the period of time that his anger lasted)

Let's see if you can explain the difference between these next two sentences. Write your interpretations on the lines that follow:

>I <u>got</u> sick after eating greasy food.
>I <u>was</u> sick for a whole day after eating greasy food.

Using *get* in our first sentence shows us a change that took place in the speaker's condition. He obviously felt fine before eating that greasy food, but his condition changed and he became sick later on. (Remember that when preceding an adjective, *get* is synonymous with "become.")

As you recall, the verb *be* **deals only with the state of being at a certain time and has no reference to what conditions were like before.** It's true that we can also say "I was sick after eating greasy food," but most native speakers would tend to perceive a difference because *be* is ambiguous in this context: Is the speaker talking about his immediate reaction to the food after eating it or is he talking about a longer condition of being unwell, possibly as a result of having eaten it or possibly just coincidentally? Using *get* eliminates the potential for this kind of ambiguity.

Now let's consider how *get* is used in passive voice phrases. Some speakers consider *get* more informal than *be* with passive constructions. However, there are certain nuances we can create by using *get* that are simply not communicated with *be*, which tends to be a more *neutral* verb. It's a very tricky area, this difference between *be* and *get*, and one that's often a matter of personal preference or interpretation.

See if you find any difference between the sentences in each of the following pairs. If you do, try to put into words what that difference is on the lines that I've provided:

    1. She was transferred. / She got transferred.
       ☐ a difference   ☐ no difference

....

    2. He was arrested. / He got arrested.
       ☐ a difference   ☐ no difference

....

    3. She was chosen. / She got chosen.
       ☐ a difference   ☐ no difference

....

    4. Were you observed? / Did you get observed?
       ☐ a difference   ☐ no difference

....

I told you this matter would be tricky! I myself doubt that there's just one interpretation for any differences between *be* and *get* in sentences such as the ones I've given you. However, I'll give you an interpretation that many native speakers do make.

Some people feel that there may be a sort of psychological involvement with *get* as it appears in the first three examples that isn't felt with *be*. They tend to feel that *be* simply has no special nuance to it and that it just seems to report what happened. ***Get* may help to create a stronger sense of the subjects having helped cause the outcomes.** Using *get* in the sentences leads some people to think that the subjects may have played an active role in the outcomes; they themselves did something. In other words, they weren't just totally *passive*.

Example 4 is perhaps the most interesting of our pairs of sentences. Some people report that **using *get* in this idea connotes that the subject was scheduled for some sort of visit/evaluation** (perhaps by a supervisor at work), whereas using *be* could be interpreted simply to mean "Did anybody see/evaluate you?"

I want to stress once again that these are interpretations that many native speakers have come up with, but they certainly aren't the only ones. Some people may find no appreciable difference between *be* and *get* in my pairs of sentences, and others may say they'd never say this one or that one in their idiolects.

Of course, nuances like these aren't easy to communicate to students, and there's a good chance that these fine points won't even come up in your classes. I feel, all the same, that it's good for you to be aware that they do exist because an observant student of yours may ask you one day what *get* means in a passive construction.

Passive Oddities

The passive voice can lead us into some really strange areas which drive teachers slightly mad when trying to explain certain specific items and drive students slightly mad when trying to understand them. Let's examine three of these in the next dialogue:

A: Hello, Shahd! I'm so excited! I couldn't wait to call you up and tell you what just happened.

B: It takes a lot to get you this excited, Fawzi. What is it?

A: My daughter, Aziza—you know, the one who works for the Supreme Council for Antiquities—well, she just discovered a royal tomb that **had** never **been broken into** by tomb robbers!

B: That's wonderful, Fawzi! Where is it?

A: It's near Tell-el-Amarna. And guess what! I have permission to visit the site while the tomb contents **are** still **being emptied out**!

B: I guess Aziza **will be given** some sort of award for having made such a discovery.

A: I doubt that an award **will be given** to her. It seems that awards for such things **have been done away with** in order to create more team spirit in the Supreme Council.

The first oddity that we can see in bold is something quite peculiar to English and very troublesome for students. How did we ever arrive at such an odd-looking construction as *had been broken into*? The first thing our students probably wonder is "broken into *what*?" They find it most unusual to end a phrase with a preposition in this way (see Chapter 6), especially in a passive construction. How would you explain this construction to your students? Think about it and write your ideas on the following line:

....

To help us deal with the construction in question, first we should look at the active verb form, which in this case is *break into*. This is what some call a two-word verb and others call a phrasal verb. Still others call it an idiomatic verb (see Chapter 14 for more about two-word verbs). Actually, all three names work perfectly well. The important thing to notice about *break into* is that it must be treated as a whole unit and not looked upon as two separate words. We can see that this is important since the word "break" has a different meaning without that preposition-like particle *into*. Moreover, we can find one-word synonyms for this two-word verb such as "burglarize" or "loot."

Now, if we understand that *break into* must be treated as a single unit, we can see how it will appear in the passive construction. Just as we can say "be burglarized" or "be looted," we can also say **be broken into**. This is how we arrive at a sentence like "The tomb hadn't been broken into." Stress to your students that they should **always consider two-word verbs as single units, not as individual parts**.

The next encounter we have with a two-word verb in the dialogue works the same way. We can think of *remove* as a one-word synonym for *empty out*, and go from "They're removing the tomb contents" to "The tomb contents are being removed." It works no differently for *empty out*:

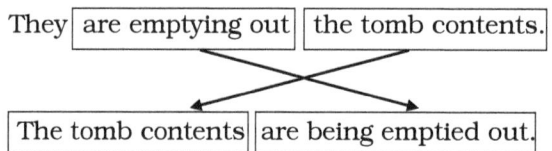

Going along with this method of changing a two-word verb from active to passive, I might as well mention the three-word verb (also known as a phrasal-prepositional verb or idiomatic verb) that's in the dialogue. "They <u>have done away with</u> awards for such things" becomes "Awards for such things <u>have been done away with</u>." Other verbs in this group are ones like *check up on*, *look in on*, and *put up with*.

The last oddity in the dialogue has to do with the verb *give*. Following are two short sentences I've derived from the longer ones in the dialogue. Let's take a look at what's happening:

> She will be given an award.
> An award will be given to her.

What strikes students as so strange about a pair of sentences like this pair is that the same verb is being used to create both ideas. If "<u>She</u> will be given...," how can we say "<u>An award</u> will be given..."? How can the two different things *be given*?

Let's see if you can figure out a way to explain this phenomenon. I'll give you a couple of hints: If you collapse the two sentences into one sentence in the active voice, you'll be on the right track and you should end up with an active verb and two objects.

The active sentence is ....

Now that you've arrived at the active sentence, how can you account for being able to use *give* to make both passive sentences? Any ideas?

The fact is that we're dealing with something unusual about the verb *give*, and that unusual quality is that it has both a direct object (an award) and an indirect object (her). What we've got here is called a **ditransitive verb**, that is, a verb that has two objects, both a direct and an indirect object. When **we have ditransitive verbs like *give*, we can form two passive voice constructions, one for each of the objects.**

If our active voice sentence is

> They will give her an award.
> or
> They will give an award to her.

we can say

> She will be given an award.
> or
> An award will be given to her.

Other common ditransitive verbs are *bring, deliver, do, mail, owe, read, send, tell,* and *write*.

Let's move on to another oddity; let's look at the next dialogue and see what's in store for us. Focus your attention on how each of the three verbs in bold is used in the active and passive voice and what that does to its meaning:

A: Aziza, your father told me all about your wonderful find. We're all very proud of you.

B: Thank you, Uncle Shahd.

A: I understand the tomb **is located** near Tell-el-Amarna.

B: That's right. I **located** the tomb not far from the southern limits of the ancient capital.

A: Tell me, Aziza, does the tomb **contain** lots of gold and precious stones?

B: Well, yes. And it's interesting that almost all of the jewelry is **contained** in just two rooms. But there's a lot of wealth in those two rooms!

A: You know, I've always wondered why Pharaoh Akhenaton wanted to build his capital in such an arid, dusty part of the country.

B: Oh, no, Uncle Shahd. It wasn't so dry and inhospitable 3,500 years ago. Papyrus always **grew** around there, and wheat and barley **were grown** there for hundreds of years

Find anything odd about the meaning of each verb when it appears in the active voice and when it appears in the passive voice? Let's come up with synonyms or interpretations for some of the words in bold. First, you give it your best effort, and then I'll give it mine:

The tomb is located . . .

....

I located the tomb . . .

....

Does the tomb contain . . .

....

. . . the jewelry is contained . . .

....

Papyrus always grew . . .

....

. . . wheat and barley were grown . . .

....

The remarkable thing about these verbs is that they undergo an amazing change in meaning when they switch from the active to the passive voice. Let's see how my interpretations compare to yours:

The tomb is located	=	the tomb is/lies
I located the tomb	=	I found/discovered the tomb
Does the tomb contain	=	Does the tomb have
the jewelry is contained	=	the jewelry is held/kept
Papyrus always grew	=	Papyrus always lived/flourished
wheat and barley were grown	=	wheat and barley were cultivated/farmed

There are a number of verbs that go through this same change or metamorphosis when they're used in the active or in the passive voice. Among them are *fly/be flown*, *turn/be turned*, *work/be worked*, and *leave/be left*. A most amazing phenomenon indeed! One more oddity involves the following verbs. If you think in terms of active and passive voice and about the steps we use to transform an active sentence into a passive one, what strange thing do you notice about sentences like the following?

She has a new fitness app.
He lacks initiative.
That car costs £10,000.

I notice that ....

What you should notice is that you can't transform those three sentences into the passive voice. The verbs in question (*have*, *lack*, and *cost*) belong to the group we call **stative verbs** (see Chapter 3), and they don't have passive counterparts even though they appear to be transitive by having objects. Most stative verbs don't have this oddness about them, but the ones that do are quite common. They include *ache, belong, contain, equal, fit, hold* (=*contain*), *hurt* (=*be painful*), *matter, mean, mind* (=*object*), *resemble, seem, sound* (intransitive use), *suit*, and *tend*.

And since I've mentioned some verbs that have no passive voice counterparts, let's give equal time to some verbs that have no active voice counterparts. "What?" you say. "Can there be such verbs?" Well, there certainly can be—in fact, there are.

> A: I know if we just persevere, we'll find King Solomon's mines.
>
> B: But the ancient map says the treasure should **be situated** right here. Do you see any sign of a fabulous treasure?
>
> A: I'm sure the mines **are located** right in this area—maybe right under our very feet. The problem is, it**'s rumored** that only those who truly believe in the legend will find the treasure!

If we take the three verbs in bold and mechanically transform them into active voice forms, we get:

. . . someone should situate the treasure right here.

. . . someone locates the mines in this area . . .

. . . someone rumors that only those who believe in the legend . . .

The problem we have with the first two lines is that they're misleading. Nobody is situating or locating anything anywhere. As we've already discovered with the verb *locate*, in the passive voice the idea is that something *is* or something *lies* someplace, and people finding it have nothing to do with the idea.

As for our third example, it's not even grammatical because, believe it or not, there's no such verb—transitive or intransitive—as *to rumor*. It turns out that the phrase *it's rumored* is very idiomatic, very strange, and very specialized, to say the least. Talk about oddities! And two more extremely common examples of such oddities are *be born* and *report*:

In a hospital, babies are born in the delivery room.

The oldest person on record is reported to have been 124 when she died.

These verbs are a passive form. *Be born* is the passive form of the active verb *bear*. Originally it was that a woman bears (i.e., carries) a child for nine months and then gives birth, so the baby is born (carried) for nine months and then delivered. Now, however, in modern usage, instead of meaning "be carried," *be born* has taken on the meaning of *to be delivered*.

To be reported is the passive form of *to report*. Somebody reports on something, so something is reported on. That's how we get the phrase *it is reported that* . . .

But I'm not through yet! Take a look at the following dialogue:

> A: Wish I could go to lunch already. I'm starving!
>
> B: Well, here's a banana.
>
> A: Thanks.
>
> B: Why are you having such a problem with it? Bananas **peel** with no trouble at all.
>
> A: I don't know why. Okay, I finally got the skin off!
>
> B: I love bananas. They **eat** easy.
>
> A: Well, let's get back to the work we're doing on my car. This owner's manual is driving me nuts. It **reads** like a mystery novel!
>
> B: By the way, how much is your car worth now?
>
> A: It **sells** for around $23,000.

See anything very odd indeed about the verbs in bold? What do you think?

What's so very strange about those verbs is that they're in the active voice, yet their subjects can't do those actions. Bananas don't peel themselves or eat anything, a book can't read, nor can a car sell anything. And yet these verbs are used in this way all the time in normal, conversational English. They belong to a small group of verbs that some linguists refer to as **pseudo-passives**. They look active in form, but they're passive in meaning. They're just another quirk of English grammar.

Other verbs that can work the same way are:

iron:	Those blouses <u>iron</u> easily.
measure:	The bedroom <u>measures</u> 8' x 12'.
test:	She <u>tested</u> negative for HIV.
wash:	Unlike most sweaters, this one <u>washes</u> well.

Before we leave the passive voice, there's just one last oddity that I'd like to bring to your attention, and here it is:

> All of us assume that we will colonize the moon one day.

The way this sentence stands now, the subject is *all of us*. But if we want to change the focus of the sentence and put it on the part of the sentence that deals with the assumption, in other words, make the assumption our subject, we can transform this into a passive voice sentence. What should the sentence end up being if we do this? You try it out first:

We know that we have to take the current object and transform it into our new subject. So what's the object of our verb *assume*? It's actually everything after the verb. Note that an object doesn't necessarily mean just one or two words; it can end up being a whole phrase or clause. To see how incredibly varied objects can really be, take a look at the first *Heads Up!* in Chapter 11. At any rate, this is how your transformed sentence should have come out:

That we will colonize the moon one day is assumed by all of us.

We can change our focus even more if we want to by concentrating our attention on the moon rather than on ourselves. If we make this change, how will our new sentence look? (Here's a hint: You should still begin your sentence with "That . . ."):

If we want to make the moon our focus in that part of the sentence, we're going to have to make it our new subject in the clause, so our revised sentence should be:

That the moon will be colonized one day is assumed by all of us.

Fine, you say. We've now done our little juggling act and created some passive voice counterparts for our original active voice sentence. All three of these sentences are perfectly usable even though our second and third versions do seem awkward. But why are they awkward? It's because English has this interesting "balancing act" between the subject of a sentence and everything that follows the head verb. In English we prefer to keep the subject relatively short and simple, but don't mind building up whatever comes after the head verb:

All of us assume <u>that the moon will be colonized one day</u>.

So when we load up the subject instead of what comes on the other side of the head verb, we find it awkward and uncomfortable:

<u>That the moon will be colonized one day</u> is assumed by all of us.

We can pick and choose among all of these versions of the same idea depending on where we want to place the focus.

Just when you might think we're done with this topic, I've got a surprise for you. There's one more version of our idea that we can come up with. It's perhaps the oddest version of them all, especially for students. Let's see if you can produce it before we give it away. (Here's another hint: You should begin the sentence with "It. . ."):

The only reason we have to begin our last version with *It* is because English requires us to begin with some sort of subject, even if it's what we call the **empty subject**, that is, one that really has no major significance except that it helps us conform to the rules of grammar. Actually, you'll see how *It* is redundant in our new version:

It's assumed by all of us that the moon will be colonized one day.

Does your version match mine? I hope so! And can you see why it is really redundant? Just imagine two people having this slightly odd chat:

> A: Yes, it's definitely assumed.
>
> B: What's assumed?
>
> A: That the moon will be colonized one day.
>
> B: Well, why didn't you say that in the first place?

This last version of mine is the most difficult for students to grasp and master on their own, even though native speakers don't think it particularly awkward, at least in very formal English. Consider the *it* subject to be a fill-in. When there is no real subject (just a verb), we often plug *it* in as subject:

It's raining.   It's snowing.   It's a shame.   It's funny.

The Passive Voice in a Nutshell

- **used when the subject isn't the doer:**
  I'm being helped, thank you.
- **used to avoid redundancy when doer is understood:**
  Don't you think midterm exams have been scheduled early this term?
- **used to avoid giving away a source of information:**
  I'm told you don't like it here.
- **used to be tactful:**
  My goodness! The bathroom floor still hasn't been washed.
- **used only with transitive verbs:**
  The pies were baked in the oven.
  Bake **is transitive here:** [They] baked the pies in the oven.
  Bake **is intransitive here; no passive voice possible:**
  She bakes well. The pies baked in the oven. They just sat in there on the rack and baked.

- *by* is used to introduce the doer:
  These pies were baked by our son.
- *with* is used to introduce the instrument:
  Those items were purchased with a credit card.
- reduced passive voice is used in headlines (to shorten the number of words used):
  More Investigations Demanded on Environmental Issues
- reduced passive voice is used in relative clauses:
  Houses painted with a primer and two coats of paint hold up better against weathering.
- commonly used on signs:
  Copies Made Here
- passive voice meaning can differ from active voice:
  She left at about 4:15. (= departed)
  He was left penniless. (= ended up)
- pseudo-passives:
  Merchandise sells for much more at retail prices than at wholesale prices.

Causatives

We'll now take a look at a small but important group of verbs that do just what their name says: **they cause something to happen**—usually. Causative verbs like *order* and *want* are very clear in meaning to students, but two others are quite difficult for them to understand. Let's see how these two verbs work in the next dialogue:

> A: Didn't you **have** your house **painted** recently?
>
> B: Yes, after a lot of grief. Would you believe I went through three painters before I **got** it **done**?
>
> A: Three? That's incredible! Why three?
>
> B: Well, the first one hurt his back and the second one **had** his truck **stolen**. I was a nervous wreck thinking that something would happen to the third one, too.
>
> A: So how did the job turn out?
>
> B: Oh, just great! First I **had** the walls **pressure-washed** and then I **had** them **covered** with one coat of primer and two coats of paint. The house looks sensational.
>
> A: Well, I've got to **get** my house **painted** too, so let me have your painter's name and phone number, okay?

You can see that the two verbs we're dealing with in this dialogue are *have* and *get*. A question like the opener in the dialogue usually confuses students because they can't understand what *have* is doing in the sentence. It's obviously not possession and it certainly isn't the present perfect auxiliary, so what is it? How would you define the verb *have* as it appears here? Before you answer this question, you should look at the grammatical pattern and context that the verb is in. In fact, you might as well look at the pattern that *get* is in, too, since it's the same one. On the line below, write down what you see as the grammatical pattern:

....

What I'm talking about is this structure:

have/get + direct object + past participle of verb

That's how we come up with sentences like "I had my house painted."/"I had the walls covered."/"We got the job done."

As an aside, I'd like to mention that there are two other patterns we have for the causatives that are used in the active sense rather than the passive sense described in this chapter:

have/get + direct object + base verb
have/get + direct object + *-ing* verb

They're used with direct objects that are animate and can do things:

I had the painter <u>apply</u> two coats of paint.
He got me <u>thinking</u> that he really didn't know his job.

We'll be coming back to these uses of *have* and *get* and other causatives in Chapter 11.

Now we can try to define *have* and *get* when they appear with this special pattern. Let's focus on *have* for the moment. How would you define the verb in this context for your students?

....

Have is really quite interesting in that it's actually **a combination of two ideas**: to ask/tell someone to do something and that something is done. It's a more exact idea than simply saying:

I asked him to paint my house.

In the sentence you've just read, we know what the request was, but we can only assume that the work was carried out. Now read this sentence:

I had my house painted.

In this sentence, we know that not only was the request made, but the work was also completed. It's a very efficient verb, this *have*. Even if we put the sentence in the future and say "I'm going to have my house painted," we still have a strong sense that the job will be done.

But why do we need the past participle in this pattern? Why not use the base verb or the simple past for that matter if the sentence is in the past? If you've got an answer, write it down on the following line:

....

What we're looking at is another example of **a reduced passive voice**—which is why this causative pattern is included in this chapter. We could interpret our causative sentence to mean that "I told someone to paint the house, and it was <u>painted</u>":

I had the house <u>painted</u>.

In one other use of *have* in the dialogue, the meaning is the same:

I had the walls <u>pressure-washed</u> . . .

Before I move on to *get*, there's still one use of *have* as a causative that's very different from what I've already discussed. Let's go back to the sentence in the dialogue which says ". . . the second one had his truck stolen." This is where things may get very troublesome. What on earth does *have* mean in this context? If we go with the meaning we've already discovered for this causative, what interpretation can you give to the sentence?

....

According to the strict definition of *have* in a causative pattern, the sentence must mean that **the painter arranged for his truck to be stolen, and it was!** Even though this is highly unlikely in this particular context, keep in mind that it *is* a plausible interpretation. For the context of the dialogue, though, there's got to be some other meaning for this sentence—but what is it? Think about it for a moment and see if you can figure it out. Then write your interpretation on the following lines:

....
....

This is a tough one. To begin with, it will help if we think about the meaning of *have* in a sentence like *I had car trouble last week*. We certainly don't mean possession in this sentence, so what does *have* stand for? In Chapter 3, I discussed the various uses of stative verbs and changes in their meanings depending on how they're used. In the sentence about the car trouble, *have* really means "this was my experience last week." **Have can mean what is happening to someone.** Another example of this use can be seen in a sentence like "I'm having a party next week at my house."

Now, if we keep this use of *have* in mind, how can we interpret ". . . the second one had his truck stolen . . ."?

....

The answer is that it means **his truck being stolen/that his truck was stolen is what happened to him**. This is an unusual use of *have*, and one that really challenges teachers to explain and students to understand and use properly.

Now we have to consider *get*, which isn't as easy an undertaking as you might think. Let's take another look at the first sentence containing *get*:

> I went through three painters before I got it done.

Why did the speaker choose to use *get* instead of *have*? What difference, if any, is there in meaning between *have* and *get*? Here's another chance for you to show your linguistic prowess, so write your idea on the following line:

....

If you remember during the discussion of *be* and *get* in the passive voice on page 211, we said that *be* seems to have a more *neutral* usage than *get* does. There are certain nuances we communicate with *get* that don't seem to come across with *be*, and their interpretations can differ depending on the context. This difference is reflected in the use of *have* and *get* as causatives. There are times when both verbs can be used the same way, but there are other times when native speakers feel that *get* communicates something more than *have* does. In the example sentence we've just seen, the speaker probably used *get* instead of *have* because what should have been a simple project turned into a difficult situation. **Get can carry with it a sense of extra effort or a greater level of difficulty or force than *have***, and because the speaker had to put more into accomplishing his goal (using three painters) than he might otherwise have had to do, he chose to use *get* to communicate this idea.

Let's try a little experiment now. Look at the following sentences and decide if you'd prefer to complete them with *have* or *get* or, if you don't feel there's any marked difference with either one:

1. After long and hard negotiations, she .... the contracts signed.
   ☐ had ☐ got ☐ either one
2. I just .... my poodle clipped. Doesn't she look beautiful?
   ☐ had ☐ got ☐ either one

3. We're thinking about .... a room added on to our house.
    ☐ having ☐ getting ☐ either one

4. How many times have I mentioned that this door still doesn't close right? .... it fixed!
    ☐ Have ☐ Get ☐ either one

5. Because of her political clout, she .... herself appointed to the Council.
    ☐ had ☐ got ☐ either one

6. It's really late. .... the baby dressed so we can leave.
    ☐ Have ☐ Get ☐ either one

7. How dare you say such things! I won't .... my wife spoken to like that!
    ☐ have ☐ get ☐ either one

Interesting little exercise, isn't it? For the most part, there really are no right or wrong answers, just tendencies that native speakers have as to which verb they'd use or whether either verb will do. Here's what many people checked off for their answers. Let's see how close your answers are to theirs:

   1. got   2. either one   3. having   4. Get   5. got   6. Get   7. have

There are two closing comments I'd like to make. The first concerns numbers 4 and 6, which are commands (imperatives). There seems to be a tendency to use *get* in a causative sentence when giving an order. This may be because *get* has a stronger feeling about it than *have* does. The other comment is about Number 7. The fact is that *have* can take on a different meaning when combined with certain direct objects and past participles. In Number 7, *have* really means "permit," "allow," or "let."

Teaching Tips

10.1 *Writing Definitions*

Before class, prepare different lists of ten to fifteen common or proper nouns. Distribute the lists to small groups of students, who'll prepare short definitions for these nouns. Have them write their definitions on separate pieces of paper without including the nouns being described. Be sure that they use passives in their definitions. Here's a sample of what you might give the students: "Television Sets," "Salt," and "Greenland." And here are some definitions that they might come up with: "machines that are created to be modern-day baby sitters," "the only rock that is eaten by people," and "the first part of North America settled by the Vikings in the 10th century." When all the nouns are defined, distribute only the definitions to different groups of students and ask them to figure out what their classmates have defined.

Variation: Prepare a list of sentence beginnings similar to the ones below. Divide the class into small groups and have them complete the sentences. Encourage the use of passives in the completions. "I know a person who . . ."/ "I dislike things which . . ."/ "I've never been to a place that . . ."/ "Teachers who . . ."/ "Books that . . ." etc.

10.2 *Transactions, Events, Activities*

Give the students a list of establishments where transactions, events, and activities take place (a restaurant, hotel, gym, laboratory, gas/petrol station, store, etc.). Have your students come up with as many examples of what happens there as they can think of by using passives. (This can be done as a contest and/or individually or in groups.) If this activity is done as a game, give each student or group a point for every passive example they come up with. Give them a bonus point for every passive example that no one else has thought up. Here are some examples they might create: "Food is served there."/ "Customers are waited on there."/ "The guest rooms are cleaned by housekeepers."/ "The guests are greeted by the front desk clerks."

10.3 *Describing Processes and Procedures*

Have students describe a procedure or process that they know about, being aware of where passives might be appropriate. Some procedures that they might describe are: how to test the pH of a liquid, how to reupholster a chair, how to make cheese, etc. Let the students share their knowledge with the entire class.

10.4 *Newspaper Headlines*

Go online and bookmark a variety of newspaper headlines containing reduced active and passive forms. Have students work in small groups to reconstruct the complete headlines, i.e., with no reductions.

10.5 *Before and After Scenes*

Find or make pairs of pictures that show "before" and "after" scenes. Have the students use passives to describe the changes that they notice. ("A beautiful skyscraper is being erected on the corner. When that's done, the roads around the construction site will be resurfaced," etc.)

Variation: Find a photo of a run-down inner city. Have small groups of students clean up the city and share their revitalization plans with the entire class. They should discuss what has/hasn't been done, what will/won't be done in the near future, what could/couldn't be done right away, etc.

10.6 *Maps*

Use the map of a country that has the country's products on it (oil, corn, rice, cattle, etc.). Have the students describe the various products shown by making up appropriate sentences: "Corn and wheat are grown in the Midwest."/ "Dairy products are produced in Wisconsin." / "Petroleum is produced in Venezuela and emeralds are mined in Colombia."

Variations:

1. Cut whatever map you've used into states, provinces, etc. and have the students piece it back together, all the while describing what information is provided.

2. Replace the map just described with one the students have invented or one you've found of their own country, state, province, etc. Describe the products using appropriate passives.

10.7 *Keeping Abreast of the News*

Here's an activity that will have your students looking at newspaper headlines, either online or, if you teach in an English-speaking country, in print. After they're able to recognize the various passive forms, reduced or otherwise, have them keep abreast of the news by posting passive forms that they find in the news on bulletin boards you've put up around the room. Label the various boards: "Local News," "National News," and "International News." The kinds of news that get posted might be items like these:

Local News	**National News**	**International News**
New School Board Elected Tuesday	President's Spouse to Be Awarded Franklin Prize by TangeloCorp	Peace Declared in...

10.8 *Conducting Surveys*

This tip is meant for teachers who have classes in English-speaking countries or in countries where there's a sufficient number of English speakers. If you have students who can do some of their classwork outside the classroom, this is a golden opportunity to get outside and talk to people and practice passives at the same time. Divide your class into groups of four or five and have them create surveys on subjects that are important to them or topical at the moment. Tell them that they'll actually conduct the surveys (surveying at least twenty-five people) and will give a formal report on their findings. To reinforce the activity, have them write up their findings.

10.9 *Creating Ads*

Bring in newspaper ads or print out ads from the Internet. Distribute the ads to small groups of students. Ask them to go through the ads to prepare a list of any passives they've found. Display the phrases from the various groups and ask the students to create an ad for a product of their choice, real or imagined. Have them use the passive phrases they've seen in the newspaper ads or they can come up with their own passive phrases.

10.10 *Reconstructing Headlines*

This activity gives your students practice using their knowledge of the world to solve a problem. Before class, cut out or print out as many newspaper headlines as you need so that when your class does this activity, each small group will have their own headline or two to work with. Put the articles they came from aside for the moment. Number each article and then number each word of the headline with the same number that you've given to its article. Cut up each headline into separate words, and, if you are using headlines from actual print newspapers, attach each of the words to a separate small piece of paper. If you can't put the individual words on *separate* slips of paper, blacken out the backsides of the headlines so that the students don't get confused as to what exactly they're supposed to be looking at. Mix up the words belonging to one headline and then hold the words together with a paper clip. Divide the class into groups and give them one or two of the headlines that have been clipped together. Tell the students to reconstruct each headline, and when they've done so, to brainstorm what they think the article that goes with it is about. Now give each group the article that its headline belongs to. Tell them to have someone read the article aloud to the group so they can compare the real article to what they guessed the article was about.

10.11 *Flow Charts and Far-reaching Consequences*

Create a situation that has far-reaching consequences (a 72-hour blackout in a large city; an epidemic; people being able to live up to 150 years of age, etc.). Divide the class into small groups and have them create a flow chart of the consequences that might occur during or after the event. Here's an example of what I mean:

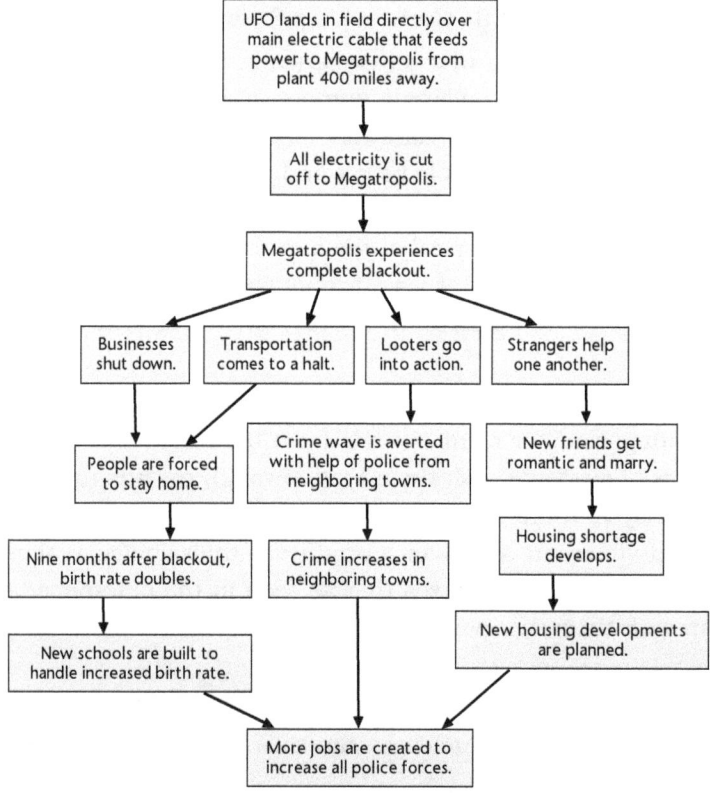

Put up the charts around class and have a discussion about their similarities and differences. Focus the students' attention on places where the passive can/should be used.

10.12 *Writing Campaign Speeches*

Divide the class into groups of three or four and have them write a campaign speech for someone running for office or someone who wishes to be principal or headmaster of a school, director of a company, etc. Encourage the use of passives in the speeches ("If I'm elected, taxes will be reduced."). Have the groups present their speeches to the entire class and then hold an election; students will vote for the candidate that presented the most convincing speech. After the winner is announced, ask the students to discuss why they voted for the candidates they did.

10.13 *Animal Escapes Zoo!*

Divide the class into small groups. Have them create a news report about an animal that has escaped from the zoo. They'll need to brainstorm details of the event so that the report will have plenty of relevant details and facts.

10.14 *Interviews*

Divide the class into groups of three to four. Have the groups think of people they'd like to interview. After five minutes, bring the class back together and list on the board four or five of the better, more interesting, more unusual interview choices. Put the groups back together and let them choose the person they'd like to interview from this list on the board. Ask them to write down questions that a reporter from a local newspaper, radio station, TV station, or online magazine might ask this person. Encourage the use of passives.

10.15 *Writing a Critique*

Let your students become art critics for a day. Find pictures in your Picture File (see Appendix 1) that have pieces of art in them (sculptures, paintings, wall hangings, etc.). In small groups, students will write critiques of the artwork using passives where appropriate. Let students share their works of art and critiques with their classmates.

10.16 *Matching Headlines and Articles*

Before class, cut out or print out several newspaper articles and number each article. Remove the headlines from the articles you've chosen. Think up less obvious headlines for the articles, making sure to use passive and causative verb forms. To make the activity more challenging, create more headlines than you have articles. In class, write these new headlines on the board and place the numbered articles on your desk. Let each student or group of students take an article and match it to one of your new headlines. Once the headlines and articles have been properly reconnected, ask the students to read the article that they have, letting them know that they'll eventually be asked to explain what they've read to the whole class or a smaller group of students.

10.17 *Creating a New Game*

Divide the class into groups and have them invent an entirely new game: the rules, the equipment needed, the name of the game, etc. Make sure students are aware how rules can use passive and causative forms ("Two dice are needed."/"The fastest runner is declared winner."/"Get the students divided into three teams."/"Have one student from each team chosen as captain," etc.). When everything has been worked out, tell the groups that they're going to "act out" their games for their classmates. The "action" is to be done silently. The rest of the class, working in groups or individually, writes down the rules as they perceive them. Have them compare the rules they've perceived with the rules as they were originally written.

10.18 *Creating a New Product*

Have the students work in groups of two or three to create a product and its logo, slogans, advertising copy, etc. They'll write up their advertising layout for the product and present the finished ad for the entire class to see. The students will then vote for the most effective ad, which will be given "The EngAd" award ("English in Advertising"). Encourage the use of passives and causatives.

10.19 *Demonstrate*

Have your students plan a street demonstration. They need to prepare all the details of the demonstration: what they're demonstrating against, how angry they are, where the demonstration will take place, etc., making sure that they incorporate passives and causatives where appropriate. Students will also prepare the picket signs, banners, and slogans for the demonstration. Stage the demonstration, but be careful. If noise is a problem, take the groups outside or to the school cafeteria, etc. If demonstrations are too touchy a subject, substitute the demonstration with a meeting in which consumers air a complaint against a certain company.

11

Direct Object Companions

"The Queen of Hearts' men painted all the white roses red."

We're about to examine what I've dubbed **direct object companions**, troublesome grammatical gems which are really quite commonplace. They're troublesome because some of them don't seem to have obvious explanations, while others don't seem to conform to some of the basic rules of English. The first thing I should do in this chapter is explain what I mean by direct object companions as far as teachers are concerned. I see them as **phrases placed right after the direct objects which have special descriptive connections to those direct objects**, and they're classified into seven distinct types:

> noun phrases
> adjective phrases
> base verb phrases
> infinitive verb phrases
>
> -*ing* verb phrases
> past participle phrases
> prepositional phrases

Besides the fact that they all share the important characteristic of describing the direct objects they follow, they also share a certain pattern which you'll soon discover. It's important for you to understand from the start that what I've labeled direct object companions (I'll call them DOCs for short from now on) come from quite diverse backgrounds and have quite different uses and meanings, which is probably why they aren't put together under one label in other grammar books as I'm doing here. I'm presenting these forms in this way because it makes sense, from a teacher's standpoint, to see all of these varied types under one umbrella, direct object companions. And because they all share the same pattern, it makes more sense for students, too. As you're going through this chapter, remember that all the DOCs are quite diverse and that you might not teach them together as a unit.

In this chapter we'll be investigating the first six types I mentioned earlier; the seventh, prepositional phrase DOCs, really needs no special investigating, although you'll see numerous examples of them anyway as we go on.

To start things off, then, we really should first consider what I mean when I say a "direct object":

>  **Heads Up!**
>
> One of the most neglected elements in ELT is the direct object. The majority of students assume that direct objects are nothing more than nouns—and nothing could be further from the truth!
> Here's a breakdown of all the various forms that can be direct objects:
>
> | | |
> |---|---|
> | noun phrase: | She bought a gorgeous necklace. |
> | pronoun: | They congratulated us. |
> | *that* clause: | I doubt that he'll get here in time. |
> | *wh-* clause: | I know when the show starts. |
> | *wh-* + infinitive clause: | I told her what to do. |
> | infinitive clause: | We'd like to stay. |
> | *if/whether* clause: | He didn't reveal if he knew my whereabouts. |
> | *-ing* clause: | They enjoy helping others. |

Noun Phrases

Let's get started by looking at our first DOC:

A: Have you heard the news?

B: What news?

A: The Board's appointed Kirby **CEO***.

B: You don't say! Well, I call that **a coup**!

A: You must be joking! I consider Kirby **a fool**!

B: What's that thing we used to say as children? Oh, yes. "It takes one to know one."

*CEO = Chief Executive Officer

If we check out the sentences in the dialogue that contain the nouns in bold, we can discover a certain pattern emerging with the kinds of words that are being used and the order they fall into. Let's pluck those sentences out of the dialogue and discover if we can see a clear picture as to what the pattern is, the one I mentioned at the beginning of the chapter:

The Board	's appointed	Kirby	CEO.
I	call	it	a coup!
I	consider	Kirby	a fool!

Obviously, there are four basic elements in the DOC pattern that fall into this special order. How would you write out what the order is?

....

The basic order that's emerged is the way all sentences with noun phrase DOCs are formed and the four elements are immovable. So what is our word order?

subject +	**verb** +	**direct object** +	**noun phrase**
The Board	has appointed	Kirby	CEO.
I	call	it	a coup!
I	consider	Kirby	a fool!

This is a good time to mention that the basic pattern is the same for every kind of DOC: **subject + verb + direct object + DOC**. In addition, I want to point out that the noun and adjective phrase DOCs are also called **object complements**. One thing these object complements do is that both of them "rename" the object. What I mean is that we can imagine an equals sign or the verb *be* between the object and the DOC. Here's an example for each object complement:

> The Board's appointed Kirby CEO. ⟶ Kirby = CEO/Kirby is CEO.
> We painted the house peach. ⟶ The house is peach.

Just to digress for a moment and probe a little deeper, it's worth pointing out that there are two ways of interpreting the nature of noun phrase DOCs depending on what the whole statement tells us. Let's look at the following two sentences and see if you can find any noticeable difference in the relationship between the noun phrase DOCs and their verbs:

> 1. They appointed Kirby CEO.
> 2. I consider Kirby a fool!

In Sentence 1 the speaker is describing the result of what the Board did and how Kirby (the direct object) was affected. The verb being used is one that's brought about change, so the nature of this kind of noun phrase DOC is that it deals with **a resulting condition**. Here are some more examples of sentences with verbs that can bring about some form of change and noun phrase DOCs that show a resulting condition:

> We <u>named</u> the kitten <u>Kukui</u>.
> They <u>elected</u> her <u>president</u>.
> Circumstances <u>made</u> him a <u>hero</u>.

Other verbs commonly found in conjunction with noun phrase DOCs that show resulting conditions include

designate: Hasn't the boss designated Robin head secretary yet?
nominate: They're going to nominate Sharif Secretary General.
select: The Dean selected Zoltan department chair.

In Sentence 2, on the other hand, the speaker is describing his perception or opinion of Kirby. The kind of verb being used doesn't bring about change, so this kind of noun phrase DOC deals with **a pre-existing condition** (in this case, Kirby's). Here are two more examples of sentences that demonstrate pre-existing conditions:

Hollie calls her boat the "Wave Dancer."
They think me a coward.

Here are other verbs that are used for pre-existing conditions:

consider: They consider her a genius.
find: We found him a boor.
imagine: I imagined myself king of Atlantis.
prove: She proved the story a hoax.

Verbs with Prepositions and Noun Phrase DOCs

One last area concerning noun phrase DOCs has to do with a small group of verbs that go hand in hand with a preposition, usually *as*. Sometimes the preposition is optional, but sometimes it isn't. Remember, though, that there is still that "renaming" of the object (object = *be* DOC). Here's an example of each type:

They chose Edison Park (as) the site for their picnic. (optional preposition)
She mistook me for her son's teacher. (mandatory preposition)

Other verbs with the optional use of the preposition include these:

appoint: The President appointed her (as) Ambassador to Fulania.
consider: They consider her (as) the hospital's top surgeon.
elect: We elected him (as) club treasurer.
make: They're going to make the spare bedroom (into) a nursery.

Other verbs with the mandatory use of the preposition include the verbs in this list:

accept: Believe it or not, our pet pig accepted a stray kitten as her own baby!
change: The wicked witch changed the prince into a frog.
define: Psychiatrists define his behavior as schizophrenic.
intend: They only intend the cottage as a summer home.
mistake: When Columbus reached the New World, he mistook it for India.
regard: I regard her as my best friend.
see: We see this epidemic as the worst health crisis of the century.
take: She took her miraculous recovery as a sign from heaven.
Do you take me for a fool?

treat:	Cinderella's step-sisters treated her as a maid.
turn:	Maeve's kiss turned the frog back into a prince.
use:	People now use the stevia plant as a sweetener.

And as for two-word verbs (phrasal verbs) that have the mandatory use of the preposition, we can cite these three:

count on:	I can't count on them as good financial advisors.
put on:	We want to put on this show as a charity event.
settle on:	They settled on that site as their future headquarters.

Adjective Phrases

Let's get right to it by looking at how adjective phrase DOCs work in the next dialogue. Remember that they're object complements, too, just as nouns were:

A: Didn't your home use to be white?

B: That's right, but we painted the house **peach** last month. Why do you ask?

A: Well, I thought I'd drop by yesterday and say hello. Only trouble was I got confused because I was looking for a white house.

B: That's a shame. We'd still love for you to come over.

A: So why peach?

B: Well, we consider the color **tropical**, and this is the Riviera after all. My wife wanted the house **hot pink**, but that color makes me **nauseated**, so I couldn't agree to that.

A: I find peach **pretty** for houses. Good choice!

B: Thanks!

As I've pointed out a few times, perhaps the most awkward situation that can happen to a teacher occurs when a student asks a question that puts the unwary instructor on the spot because he or she is at a loss to give a quick response. The questions that follow, which relate to our dialogue, will give you a taste of how that feels:

Question 1: Aren't *peach, tropical, hot pink, nauseated,* and *pretty* just adjectives in these sentences?

☐ yes ☐ no

If you've answered **yes**, that leads us to . . .

Question 2: Don't we always teach beginning students that we put adjectives before the nouns they describe (for example, *the large box* and not *the box large*)?

☐ yes ☐ no

If you've answered **yes** again, that leads us to . . .

Question 3: Then why is it that the speakers in our dialogue have gone against that basic rule by placing the adjectives *after* the nouns they describe?

If we check out the sentences in the dialogue that contain adjectives in bold, we can see the same pattern emerges as we found with noun phrase DOCs. Let's go back to the dialogue and plug those sentences into our pattern to see how it develops:

subject +	**verb** +	**direct object** +	**adjective phrase**
We	painted	the house	peach.
We	consider	the color	tropical.
My wife	wanted	the house	hot pink.
Hot pink	makes	me	nauseated.
I	find	peach	pretty.

Just as before, all of these sentences conform nicely to our pattern. As I mentioned previously, the four basic elements in the DOC pattern are immovable, but additional words can be placed between some of these elements. For example, we can use a frequency adverb between *I* and *find* and place an intensifier like *very* before *pretty* to end up with this sentence:

I <u>always</u> find the color peach <u>very</u> pretty for houses.

We should also mention that the adjective phrase DOC can appear in the comparative form:

I find peach *prett<u>ier</u>* than pink.

and the superlative form:

Of all the students in our class, the teacher considers Ed the *bright<u>est</u>*.

Is there any other similarity you can notice about adjective and noun phrase DOC sentences besides the fact that they share the same pattern? Do adjective phrase DOCs reflect pre-existing and resulting conditions?

☐ yes ☐ no

The answer to my question is **yes**. Just as with noun phrase direct object companions, there are really two conditions for the adjective phrase DOCs, depending on what the whole statement tells us. Let's examine the following two sentences to find the noticeable difference in the relationship between the verbs and the adjective phrase DOCs:

1. We painted the house peach.
2. We consider the color tropical.

In **Sentence 1** the speaker is describing the result of what he and his wife did and how the house (the direct object) was affected. The verb being used is one that's brought about change, so the adjective phrase DOC has **a resulting condition**. Here are some more examples of sentences with verbs that can bring about some form of change and adjective phrase DOCs that show resulting conditions:

We <u>made</u> the baby <u>happy</u>.

My next-door neighbor <u>got</u> me <u>upset</u>.

He <u>licked</u> the spoon <u>clean</u>.

The auctioneer <u>declared</u> the bidding <u>open</u>.

She <u>sliced</u> the bread <u>thin</u>.

Here are verbs other than those I've used that are commonly found in conjunction with adjective phrase DOCs which have resulting conditions:

pull: He pulled the rope tight.
push: I pushed the door open.
put/set: He put/set me straight.
wipe: She didn't wipe the table clean.

And then there's the idiomatic use of *drive*: That perfume drives him wild/crazy!

In **Sentence 2** ("We consider the color tropical.") the speaker is describing his perception or opinion of that color. The kind of verb being used doesn't bring about change, so the nature of this kind of adjective phrase DOC is that it's a **pre-existing condition** (in this case, of the color). Here are some more examples of sentences that demonstrate pre-existing conditions:

I <u>found</u> her <u>charming</u>.

He <u>drank</u> the tea <u>cold</u>.

They <u>left</u> the door <u>open</u>.

Did you <u>buy</u> the fish <u>fresh</u>?

There are other verbs that can produce sentences with adjective phrase DOCs which show pre-existing conditions:

call: I call him impulsive.
declare: They're about to declare themselves bankrupt.
find: We found it really hard to do.

hold:	She isn't holding the camera steady.
imagine:	I'd imagined her older than she was.
keep:	Did she keep the food warm?
prove:	They proved me wrong—again!
think:	Do you think my opinion outrageous?

And then there's the idiomatic use of these two verbs:

hold:	I hold you responsible.
run:	New babies run their parents ragged.

A Word About "It"

An odd thing can happen with the pronoun *it* in the adjective phrase DOC pattern. Take a look at what I mean:

> A: Well, Smithers, have you decided on whether or not you'll be joining our expedition?
>
> B: I've given the subject a great deal of thought, and I think **it** ludicrous **to put together yet another expedition in search of the Yeti.**
>
> A: I'm sorry to hear you say that. I find **it** disappointing **that you've taken such a conservative position.** We believe **it** very possible **that the Yeti,** that strange, hairy, half-man/half-ape creature, **does in fact exist in the Himalayas.** There certainly have been enough sightings over the years.
>
> B: Well, Pinkerton, I'm sorry to disappoint you, but I consider **it** foolish **to invest more time and money on such an absurd enterprise.**

Why on earth do we have the word *it* in the direct object position within all of these sentences containing adjective phrase DOCs? And what exactly does *it* mean in these sentences? See if you can answer these questions on the following lines:

....

....

You can look at the word *it* in these sentences as being either **anticipatory** or **redundant**. *It* is basically a device we use to introduce the following part of the sentence that explains what *it* means. In other words, *it* actually means the same thing as the part of the sentence it anticipates. That's why many call this *it* the "anticipatory *it*."

For example, in our first sentence,

> I think <u>it</u> ludicrous to put together yet another expedition . . .

the word *it* really means

> to put together yet another expedition . . .

The same is true in the next sentence that contains *it*:

> I find *it* disappointing that you've taken such a position . . .

What does *it* stand for in this sentence?

The answer is that *it* stands for **that you've taken such a conservative position.**

Notice that there are two kinds of explanatory sections, one that begins with *an infinitive* and one that begins with *that*. Both are quite commonly used in this type of adjective phrase DOC sentence. And it's worth mentioning that a certain verb is dropped in this construction, which gives the sentence a much more formal sound when it's dropped. Can you think of which verb it is?

The answer is that it's some form of the verb *be*:

> . . . and I think it <u>is</u> ludicrous to put together yet another expedition . . .

We can say that with certain verbs that exhibit the adjective phrase DOC pattern, it's not unusual to find the anticipatory *it* placed in the direct object position with an explanatory part following. We should also mention that, in some cases, this same phenomenon of the anticipatory *it* plus DOC can occur with nouns as well:

> I consider <u>it</u> a crime <u>that you're going to waste that food</u>.
> We think <u>it</u> a mistake <u>to get married at such a young age</u>.

Later on in this chapter we'll be looking at how whole sentences can be used as DOCs with just a couple of grammatical changes.

An Adjective DOC Puzzler

Just when you think you're getting comfortable with direct object companions, I'm going to ask you to contend with a peculiar phenomenon that sometimes occurs with adjective DOCs. This is another example of when your students could get very confused considering what they've already been taught about adjective word order. You'll see what I mean when you read this next dialogue:

> A: Oh, Martha! Loving you is the greatest joy of my life!
> B: Oh, George! Loving you is the greatest joy of my life, too!
> A: Oh, Martha! We have so much in common.
> B: Oh, George, I know! Our tastes are definitely compatible.
> A: I like steak **rare**, and so do you.
> B: And I like coffee **black**, and you do, too.
> A: I only eat oysters **raw**, and so do you.
> B: And I only enjoy yogurt **plain**, and you do, too.
> A: Oh, Martha!
> B: Oh, George!

We can see that the sentences with words in bold fit our pattern just as the other DOCs did:

subject	+	verb	+	direct object	+	adjective
I		like		steak		rare.
I		like		coffee		black.
I		eat		oysters		raw.
I		enjoy		yogurt		plain.

But so what? Can't we say "I like rare steak" or "I eat raw oysters?" Aren't these two sentences with the adjectives in the *right* place okay?

☐ Yes, they are. ☐ No, they aren't. ☐ Perhaps.

Of course, the answer to our question is **Yes, they are.**

And don't those sentences with the normal adjective placement mean the same thing as the sentences in our dialogue?

☐ Yes, they do. ☐ No, they don't. ☐ Perhaps.

The answer to this second question is **Perhaps**. So what exactly is going on? The answer lies in the fact that we're not just dealing with ordinary adjective phrase DOCs, but with a very special kind indeed.

What's the difference in meaning between using adjectives like *rare*, *black*, *raw*, and *plain* in their regular positions before the nouns and making them into adjective DOCs by placing them after the nouns? You can find the answer if you examine the meaning of both kinds of sentences. The truth of the matter is that in the sentences found in the dialogue, we're dealing with some verbs that create a special meaning if we use the adjective DOC pattern.

Take a closer look at these two sentences to see what I mean:

> 1. I like black coffee.   2. I like coffee black.

I can sum up the difference between them very simply: **it's a matter of focus.** In **Sentence 1** we're focusing on **an entire item** and not on any particular condition of that item; it's not just coffee and it's not just something black—it's black coffee. But in **Sentence 2** our focus has changed. We're really saying we like coffee, but only when it's black (that is, without cream or sugar). Now we're focusing on a **condition** **of the item** rather than on the whole item.

By the way, notice how the verb *to be* has been dropped from these sentences with object complements:

> I like steak (to be) rare.
> I like coffee (to be) black.

To get back to my point, compare these next two sentences:

> 1. I like raw oysters.   2. I like oysters raw.

Which statement would you say is focusing on a certain condition rather than on the item as a whole?

> ☐ Sentence 1   ☐ Sentence 2

If you've checked **Sentence 2**, you're getting the idea. In Sentence 1 the speaker says that he likes a particular type of seafood dish, "raw oysters," and there's really nothing else under discussion. In Sentence 2, however, the speaker's saying that he likes oysters, and then he quickly adds how he likes them, ". . . (when they're) raw." I'm sure you see now that there's a definite change in focus even though in many cases I admit it can be a minor one.

Another way to look at these special adjective DOC sentences is to realize that they usually answer the questions "How do you like ___?" "How do you prefer ___?" or "How do you want ___?" For example:

> A: How do you like your steak?
> B: I like it medium rare.

It's important to remember that this minor but real difference in focus is found in this adjective DOC pattern only with certain verbs. Besides the ones I've used in my examples, I can include other verbs in this list:

dislike:	Many people dislike their drinks cold.
have:	They always have their tea sweet.
keep:	Keep this ring safe for me.
like:	When they work outdoors, they like the weather cool.
love:	Patti loves her clothing bright and colorful.
need:	The surgeon needs her instruments ready at all times.
prefer:	When I go swimming, I prefer the water calm.
serve:	They serve this potato soup cold.
take:	We normally take our coffee black.
want:	She wants her vegetables crisp.

Infinitive Verb Phrases

Here we are at our third type of direct object companion. It may surprise you to find infinitive verb phrases in a chapter on DOCs. Nevertheless, they are a type of DOC, so let's get right to them. This short dialogue will show you how the infinitive verb phrase DOC works:

A: Did Marcel get everything we need from Jean Louis to make more signs for our yard sale?

B: Yes, he did.

A: Good. By the way, do you know where he is now?

B: I think he's downstairs. **Would** you **like me to get him**?

A: Yes, please. I **want him to do something** important for me.

As with the other DOCs we've explored so far, we have the same basic pattern for the infinitive verb phrase DOC:

	subject +	**verb** +	**direct object** +	**infinitive verb phrase**
Would	you	like	me	to get him?
	I	want	him	to do something.

The fact is that there's a group of verbs that prompt this particular pattern. It's interesting to note that certain causative verbs (see Chapter 10) are included in this group, as you'll see.

Besides the verbs I've already used in my examples, there are other verbs that prompt this pattern with the infinitive verb phrase DOC. (Note that the verbs with an asterisk can trigger an alternate syntax, which you saw earlier with noun phrase DOCs.) The verbs with the infinitive phrase DOC include

allow:	She allowed him to leave.
***appoint:**	The committee appointed them to lead the expedition.
***believe:**	They believe him to be a spy.
***cause:**	What caused them to get so upset?
compel:	A strong feeling of guilt compelled him to confess.
condemn:	The court condemned him to serve thirty years.
***consider:**	Don't you consider it to be a victory for our side?
***expect:**	We expect her to arrive here shortly.
***feel:**	They feel his attitude to be too pessimistic.
***find:**	Haven't you found Mr. Greenbaum to be quirky?
force:	She'll force us to resign.
***get:**	Did you get her to agree?
***hate:**	We hate for Grandpa to sit all alone in the park every day.
help:	Can you help me to tie this package?
***imagine:**	They'd imagined her to be shorter than she was.
intend:	We intend for him to fulfill his obligations.
know:	I know him to be a man of his word.
***like:**	She likes her curry to be spicier than most people do.
mean:	I meant this chapter to have only twenty pages.
***need:**	We need them to be here by 5 o'clock.
permit:	They won't permit us to stay past noon.
***report:**	She reported the town to be under quarantine.
***suppose:**	We supposed the place to be more tranquil.
***want:**	I want you to be home early tonight.
***would like:**	We would like dinner to be ready by 7.

As I said, the verbs with an asterisk have an alternative; they can drop the infinitive part of the DOC and then be left with a noun, an adjective, a prepositional phrase, or an adverb, which will then become the DOC. Take a look at what I mean and keep in mind that *to be* can be placed in the blank before the underlined words. There's one exception you should find:

    The committee appointed them _____ the leaders.

    They believe him _____ a spy.

    The arthritis causes him _____ great pain.

    Don't you consider it _____ a victory for our side?

    They had imagined her _____ a boor.

Have you figured out which sentence above contains our exception? It's "The arthritis causes him great pain." The infinitive verb which has been dropped in this instance could be *to have, to suffer, to experience,* or *to feel.*

As I said, you can also end up with an adjective phrase DOC when the infinitive phrase DOC *to be* is dropped:

> They don't believe him ____ sincere.
>
> Don't you consider our side ____ victorious?
>
> She felt them ____ untrustworthy.
>
> We find this strategy ____ risky.
>
> They'd imagined her ____ shorter than she was.
>
> He needs these copies ____ darker.
>
> We'd supposed the place ____ more pristine.
>
> The doctor wants you ____ thinner.

You can also drop *to be* and be left with a prepositional phrase DOC (and here are the examples I said that you'd see when we started this chapter off):

> Should we consider him ____ at risk?
>
> They expect us ____ on time.
>
> We felt her ____ in terrible danger.
>
> I didn't find them ____ in financial straits.
>
> Don't you hate syrup ____ on ice cream?
>
> We imagined her ____ in silks and gold.
>
> She doesn't like nuts ____ in candy bars.
>
> She reported the town ____ under attack.
>
> Mom wants the kids ____ in bed now!
>
> She would like dinner ____ by seven.

Continuing right along, we find that there are some verbs that permit you to drop *to be*, leaving you with an adverb in the DOC position:

> The director expects all of us ____ there at noon.
>
> The pharmacist says he needs you ____ here right away.
>
> The 6 o'clock news reported Godzilla ____ downtown.
>
> My parents really want me ____ home early tonight.

There's one more element that can become part of the new DOC when the verb *to be* is dropped. It's the past participle, but I'll talk about that at length later in the chapter. Until we get to it, here are two examples:

> She expects the copies ____ made by noon.
>
> They found him ____ unaffected by the news.

One extra note: The verb *help* is very strange because it can have an infinitive verb phrase DOC, as already shown in my list ("Can you help me to tie this package?"), or it can have a base verb DOC without any change in meaning ("Can you help me tie this package?"). Just as with the past participle phrase DOCs, you'll be exploring base verb phrase DOCs in this chapter. In fact, the base verb phrase DOCs are coming up right away.

-ing Verb and Base Verb Phrases

We've now arrived at the fourth and fifth types of direct object companions, and it will make matters more interesting to examine them in the same section. The next dialogue is a continuation of the conversation about Kirby becoming CEO on page 232; it will show you just how these two DOCs work, so let's take a look:

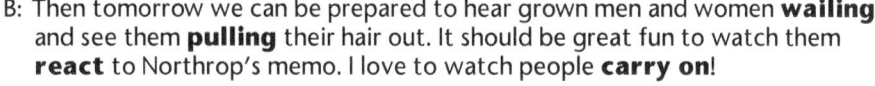

B: And just how did you happen to learn of this marvelous news?

A: I overheard Northrop **dictating** a memo to his secretary. He must have been preparing the official announcement of this ghastly news about Kirby.

B: Did you actually hear him **proclaim** that Kirby had definitely been selected?

A: Yes, unfortunately.

B: Then tomorrow we can be prepared to hear grown men and women **wailing** and see them **pulling** their hair out. It should be great fun to watch them **react** to Northrop's memo. I love to watch people **carry on**!

A: Well don't be so overjoyed, my friend. I recently heard Kirby say that he thought your department could stand some new blood in charge of it.

B: Really? Hmm. Well, early retirement does have its bright side.

We can see that there are two types of DOCs in this dialogue, the base verb phrase (and, by the way, the base verb is also known as the "bare infinitive") and the *-ing* verb phrase (and the *-ing* is also known as the present participle). Naturally, the question I have to ask right off is, what do these two DOCs represent? By discovering the answer, we'll understand how to use them.

-ing Verb Phrases

For the moment, let's deal only with *-ing* DOCs. In order to make it easier to work on them, I'll let you in on one important fact: **The sentences containing *-ing* and base verb phrase DOCs are really either combined forms of two smaller sentences or they're reduced forms from longer, single sentences.** In fact, I can come up with at least three reconstructed versions for most of these DOC sentences. In just a moment I'll give you examples of what I mean.

First off, let's take another look at the sentences that contain the *-ing* DOC. Here's the same pattern that we've seen with the other DOCs:

subject	+	verb	+	direct object	+	*-ing* verb phrase
I		overheard		Northrop		dictating a memo
We		'll hear		grown men and women		wailing
We		'll see		them		pulling their hair out

Now let's see if you can reconstruct one pair of shorter sentences and one or two versions of longer, single sentences for each of the following "finished products." Here's an example to show you what to do:

I saw some geese flying south for the winter. =

I saw some geese. They were flying south for the winter.
I saw some geese that were flying south for the winter.
I saw some geese as they were flying south for the winter.

Now you try it:

1. I overheard Northrop dictating a memo. =

....

....

....

2. We'll hear grown men and women wailing. =

....

....

....

3. We'll see them pulling their hair out. =

....

....

Let's compare your versions to mine. I can reconstruct **Sentence 1** in the following ways:

    a. I overheard Northrop. He <u>was dictating</u> a memo.
    b. I overheard Northrop, who <u>was dictating</u> a memo.

c. I overheard Northrop while/as/when he <u>was dictating</u> a memo.

For **Sentence 2** I've come up with these other versions:

a. We'll hear grown men and women. They'<u>ll be wailing</u>.
b. We'll hear grown men and women who'<u>ll be wailing</u>.
c. We'll hear grown men and women while/as/when they'<u>re wailing</u>.

And finally, for **Sentence 3** I have these alternatives:

a. We'll see them. They'<u>ll be pulling</u> their hair out.
b. We'll see them while/as/when they'<u>re pulling</u> their hair out.

So what do we get from having done all of this reconstruction work? We can now clearly see what verb form the *-ing* verb phrase DOC represents. What does it stand for?

....

You can see that we keep finding the **progressive form of the verb** in these reconstructed sentences with the *-ing* verb phrase DOC. This can be the past progressive ("He <u>was</u> dicta<u>ting</u> a memo.") or future progressive ("They'<u>ll be</u> pull<u>ing</u> their hair out.") depending on the time frame and context of the sentence. There are also times when we use the *-ing* DOC to **emphasize an action that went, goes, or will go on and on** ("We'll hear them <u>complaining</u> about the Board's decision for weeks.").

Well, if we can use the past and future progressive, we certainly should be able to use the present progressive as well, and here's an example of that:

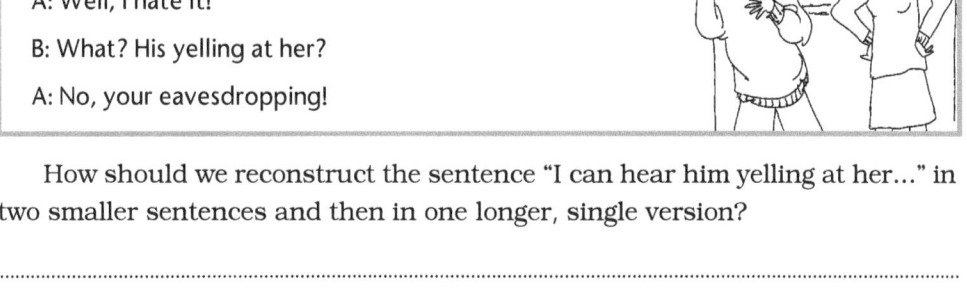

A: I can't believe you're eavesdropping on the people in the next apartment! Well... what do you hear?

B: I can hear him **yelling** at her about some bills or something.

A: Well, I hate it!

B: What? His yelling at her?

A: No, your eavesdropping!

How should we reconstruct the sentence "I can hear him yelling at her..." in two smaller sentences and then in one longer, single version?

....

....

What you come up with is probably something like these:

> a. I can hear him. He's yelling at her . . .
> b. I can hear him as he's yelling at her . . .

As you can see, the present progressive is what's produced the *-ing* verb phrase DOC in this case.

I'm about to list other verbs that are commonly used with the *-ing* DOC, but first I'd like to mention the fact that some of these verbs require the *-ing* verb phrase DOC while others use it optionally. For example, a speaker may choose to say something like this:

> I heard him play his violin last night.
>
> or
>
> I heard him playing his violin last night.

Unless you want to be a stickler, there's really very little difference in this instance between those two sentences. This is an important point to keep in mind. As you can see from my two examples, **those verbs that use the *-ing* verb phrase DOC may opt for the base verb phrase DOC in certain cases.** To help you out, I'm going to list the following verbs in two categories, one with verbs that require the *-ing* DOC and one with verbs that use it optionally:

Verbs that Require the -ing DOC

catch:	The teacher caught her daydreaming again.
discover:	He discovered a new tributary flowing into the Amazon River.
find:	Have you found many flies buzzing around?
keep:	They kept me waiting for almost an hour!
leave:	I left her napping when I went to work.
perceive:	It's almost impossible to perceive plants growing.
smell:	I definitely smell something burning.
spot:	They spotted an owl feeding her young.

Verbs with the Optional -ing DOC

feel:	I felt someone staring/stare at me.
get:	She got the car running/to run by popping the clutch.
hear:	We've heard him singing/sing in the shower.
notice:	I noticed you wearing/wear new clothes every day this week.
observe:	They observed the comet chunks smashing/smash into Jupiter.
overhear:	Did you overhear him dictating/dictate a memo?
see:	I see her leaving/leave home at the same time every morning.
watch:	I love to watch waves pounding/pound against the shore.

It's interesting to note that all of the verbs in this second category of having the optional *-ing* DOC are verbs of perception except for *get* (see *Causatives and Direct Object Companions* further on in this chapter).

An Odd Direct Object Alternative

In all of the examples just cited, we clearly see the direct objects in their proper position within the DOC pattern I revealed at the very beginning of this chapter. But as the next dialogue will show, things can change:

A: Why did you ever get Nagib those drums for his birthday? **I can't stand him practicing** day after day after day! There's no peace in this house anymore!

B: I didn't know **you couldn't stand his practicing. I rather like his beating** out those rhythms.

A: You can't mean it! How **can you** possibly **like him pounding** away incessantly on that blasted contraption!

B: Well, if it really bothers you that much, I'll tell him to go practice outside in the backyard.

A: What? And have all the neighbors complaining? Just **forget my saying** anything about it. I'll just put cotton in my ears!

B: Fine. As far as I'm concerned, **I've already forgotten you saying** a word about it!

As I'm sure you've noticed, we have three pairs of phrases in bold in this dialogue with the same verb appearing in each pair. But what strange occurrence do you see when you compare the components of each pair? On the following line, indicate what you think this oddity is:

....

Something very odd indeed has happened to the direct object in one of the phrases of each pair. What's happened is that **the direct object pronoun has been replaced by a possessive adjective, or vice versa**:

   . . . stand him practicing . . . → . . . stand his practicing . . .

   . . . like his beating . . . → . . . like him beating . . .

   . . . forget my saying . . . → . . . forget you saying . . .

By the way, these changes don't just happen with direct object pronouns, but with proper nouns and all animate nouns as well:

I hate {Nagib / Nagib's} banging away on his drums.

We dislike arguing over {our son / our son's} practicing on his drums.

At face value, this bouncing back and forth between direct objects and possessive forms certainly seems like a strange change all right, but it really isn't so strange once you understand what's going on. There's a small group of verbs that gives the speaker the option to use either the direct object or the possessive form before an *-ing* phrase because of a change in focus.

Let's go back to our first pair of phrases and take a closer look. Although some consider this difference a minor shift in focus, it seems that saying "I can't stand <u>him</u> practicing day after day" focuses the speaker's ire on Nagib. On the other hand, saying "I didn't know you couldn't stand <u>his</u> practicing . . ." seems to focus more on Nagib's activity rather than on Nagib himself. And there's the key to understanding why it isn't so odd to use the possessive form in place of the direct object. After all, the speaker's discussing Nagib's activity, in other words, <u>his</u> activity, that is, his beating the drums, and not Nagib himself.

Before I move on to another topic, I'd like to take you back for a moment to the dialogue that accompanied the section dealing with that "anticipatory *it*" in the direct object position with the explanatory phrase following the adjective DOC. As the proverb goes, "There's more than one way to skin a cat," and so it is at times with grammar, too. Here are the sentences I focused on in that previous section for you to look over again:

I think <u>it</u> ludicrous to put together yet another expedition . . .
I find <u>it</u> disappointing that you've taken such a . . . position . . .

As far as the first sentence is concerned, instead of saying "I think it ludicrous to put together...", which doesn't spell out just who exactly would do this "putting together," we can clarify things by saying "I think it ludicrous *for us* to put together..." Aha! "...for us to put together..." shows whose activity this activity would be, so we can opt for the possessive adjective to accomplish the same thing: We can use a possessive adjective (in this case, *our*) and change the explanatory phrase into an *-ing* phrase:

I think <u>(our) putting</u> together yet another expedition . . . ludicrous.

And as for the second sentence, we know that *you* is the subject of the explanatory phrase, so we can change that to the possessive adjective *your*, convert the explanatory phrase to an *-ing* phrase, and end up with

I find <u>your taking</u> such a . . . position disappointing.

We can't use this alternative for the direct object in every phrase that has an *-ing* DOC, but some typical verbs other than the ones I've already shown you that will allow this switch are in this list:

adore:	She adores her son/son's playing accordion.
afford:	We can't afford Mary/Mary's taking ballet classes.
can't stand:	Yussef can't stand Nagib/Nagib's playing his drums.
despise:	Mina despises her neighbors/neighbors' partying all night.
dislike:	Yussef dislikes Nagib/Nagib's practicing on the drums.
distrust:	They distrust their nasty neighbor/neighbor's being so nice.
enjoy:	Why don't you enjoy our daughter/our daughter's singing?
hate:	Do you hate him/his fawning over you all the time?
love:	They love their mother/mother's going back to school.
mind:	Do you mind me/my sitting here?
regret:	She regretted him/his leaving so soon.
remember:	They don't remember us/our inviting them to the party.
resent:	Pauline resents you/your blaming everything on Arthur.
risk:	Michelle can't risk Grant/Grant's finding out the truth.
stop:	I've tried to stop him/his eating all those rich foods.

Have you noticed any interesting connection that most of these verbs have? It seems that the majority of them share the common theme of being verbs of "like" or "dislike." The only exceptions are *afford, remember, risk,* and *stop*.

Another Option to the -ing Verb Phrase Direct Object Companion

Since I'm on the subject of options, there's one more I'd like to mention. A quick glance at the following two sentences will show you what that option is:

I really don't mind Nagib playing his drums in the afternoon,

but I really don't like him $\begin{Bmatrix} \text{playing} \\ \text{to play} \end{Bmatrix}$ in the evening .

So what's the difference between these two sentences? Write your observation on the following line:

....

We can substitute the *-ing* verb phrase DOC in this sentence with an infinitive verb phrase DOC. I have to point out, however, that this substitution can occur only when a very small group of "like"/"dislike" verbs is used, but I think them worth mentioning because they're such commonly used verbs. They include the verbs on the next page:

dislike:	She dislikes her son coming/to come home so late.	
hate:	I hate Grandpa being/to be left alone all day.	
like:	She likes me making/to make dinner once in a while.	
love:	Don't you love the rain tapping/to tap on your windows at night?	
prefer:	I'd prefer them arriving/to arrive a little earlier.	

Base Verb Phrases

Now we'll move on to the other sentences from the dialogue on page 245 which contain base verb phrase DOCs. As I can confirm once again, the pattern that the base verb phrase DOCs appear in is identical to the pattern for all the other DOCs:

subject +	verb +	direct object +	base verb phrase
Did you	hear	him	proclaim that ...
I	'll enjoy	watching them	react to Northrop's memo.
I	love	to watch people	carry on!
I	heard	Kirby	say that ...

Let's examine base verb phrase DOCs by repeating the activity you did for the *-ing* verb phrase DOCs. This time, reconstruct two shorter sentences and one longer sentence that reflect the ideas in the following examples:

1. Did you hear him proclaim that Kirby had been selected? =

....

....

2. It should be fun to watch them react to Northrop's memo. =

....

....

3. I love to watch people carry on! =

....

....

4. I heard Kirby say your department needs some new blood. =

....

....

Let's get right to the reconstructions and see how closely yours resemble mine. For **Sentence 1** I've come up with these two:

   a. Did you hear him? <u>Did</u> he <u>proclaim</u> that Kirby had been selected?
   b. Did you hear him when/as he <u>proclaimed</u> that Kirby had been selected?

For **Sentence 2** I have these:

   a. It should be fun to watch them. They <u>will react</u> to Northrop's memo.
   b. It should be fun to watch them when/as they <u>react</u> to Northrop's memo.

For **Sentence 3** I've got these revisions:
   a. I love to watch people. They carry on!
   b. I love to watch people when/as they carry on!

And finally, for **Sentence 4** I can substitute either of these:

   a. I heard Kirby. He <u>said</u> your department needs some new blood.
   b. I heard Kirby when/as he <u>said</u> your department needs some new blood.

Things are more complicated with the base verb phrase DOC than they were with the *-ing* verb phrase DOC. Instead of one common quality found in the reconstructed *-ing* DOC verbs (forms of the progressive aspect), we find one surface form (the base verb) representing three underlying verb forms (past, future, and timeless) exhibiting one commonality, a non-progressive aspect. I know this by looking at the time of the first verb in the sentence. Here's a diagram to show you what I mean:

```
We went to watch the birds    ┐
We'll go to watch the birds   ├ feed their young.
We go to watch the birds      ┘
```

Getting back to all of those sentences we've just looked over, I'll deal first with Sentences 1 and 4. What verb form does the base verb phrase direct object companion represent in these two sentences?

....

The answer is that the base verb phrase DOC can represent the **simple past**.

But now we have to deal with Sentence 2. Obviously the base verb DOC doesn't represent the simple past in that sentence, so what does it mean? If you have any hunches, write them down on this line:

....

First of all, let's think about what our **verb phrases** are: **they will react** and **when/as they react**. Of course, our first verb phrase is the simple future, and we can interpret it in this case to mean a future prediction (see Chapter 5). The second verb phrase also signifies the simple future, but we know that when words such as *when* precede the verb, we don't show the future form in the verb; nevertheless, it's still the simple future. (Once again, see Chapter 5)

Before we come up with the definitive answer as to what the base verb phrase DOC represents in Sentence 2, I have to ask you this question: What big difference do you perceive between an *-ing* DOC and the base verb DOC that we find in Sentence 1 ("Did you hear him proclaim that Kirby had been selected?") and Sentence 4 ("I heard Kirby say your department needs some new blood") now that we understand what their underlying reconstructed forms are? Check the boxes for the answers you agree with:

The *-ing* DOC represents that the speaker
- ☐ made it clear he witnessed the completion of the action.
- ☐ made it clear he witnessed an action in progress.

The base verb DOC represents that the speaker
- ☐ made it clear he witnessed the completion of the action.
- ☐ made it clear he witnessed an action in progress.

The answer to our first statement is that the *-ing* DOC represents that the speaker **made it clear he witnessed an action in progress**. We can figure this out because the *-ing* DOC represents the progressive verb form, so the action was *in progress* at the moment that the speaker was referring to.

The answer to our second statement is that the **base verb DOC** represents that the speaker **made it clear he witnessed the completion of the action**. We can figure this out because the base verb DOC represents the simple past, which is always used for finished actions, so the speaker knows that the action *was finished* during the time he was referring to.

Now, getting back to Sentence 2 with the use of the future ("It should be fun to watch them *react* to Northrop's memo"), do you figure that this use of the base verb DOC means the speaker thinks he will or will not witness the completed action?

☐ will ☐ will not

If you've checked off that the speaker thinks he **will** witness the completed action, you're doing just great! There's nothing inherent in the simple future that represents an unfinished or continuing action; on the contrary, it normally means that the action will be a thing done. So, even though the reconstructed forms of the DOC verb for Sentence 2 look quite different from those in Sentences 1 and 4, the base verb

DOC really does represent the same fundamental idea of a finished action after all.

Finally, we have Sentence 3 ("I love to watch people carry on!"). What verb form do you think is represented in this case?

....

It's the simple present or, as I prefer to think of it, **the timeless form** (see Chapter 3). In fact, the whole statement is timeless. The speaker is simply making a general observation about something he loves to do, and time really doesn't enter into it at all.

There's one more point to make about Sentence 3 before I move on. It would be perfectly grammatical for the speaker to say "I love to watch people <u>carrying on</u>" instead of *carry on*. Both sentences are general observations, so what nuance can you find between the two? Write any thoughts you have on the line that follows:

....

If you recall my discussion about the *-ing* DOC representing an ongoing action, the difference between using the *-ing* DOC and the base verb DOC in this sentence is that **the *-ing* DOC means** the speaker loves to **watch the process as it's happening**, whereas **the base verb DOC signifies** that the speaker loves seeing **the whole action happen from start <u>to finish</u>**.

Here's a list of the other verbs that are commonly used in conjunction with the base verb phrase:

feel:	I felt something bite me.
notice:	She noticed him take something out of her purse.
observe:	We observed the eagle catch its prey in one swoop.
overhear:	The manager overheard us complain about the food.
spot:	Did you ever spot a little bitty toad catch a big, fat horse fly?

Before we leave these revelations about the *-ing* and the base verb phrase direct object companions, let's have a little fun with the two following pairs of sentences. In the first pair, one of the sentences is grammatical, but the other one isn't. You decide which is which.

1. I saw two cars crashing.   ☐ grammatical   ☐ ungrammatical
2. I saw two cars crash.   ☐ grammatical   ☐ ungrammatical

Now let's see if you can defend why you believe each sentence to be grammatical or ungrammatical. Write down your thoughts on these lines:

....

....

Because it means that the speaker didn't witness the end of the action since the *-ing* DOC represents the progressive verb form, **Sentence 1 is ungrammatical**. The problem with the sentence is that when two cars crash, the action is so short, it's highly unlikely—if not impossible—that the speaker didn't witness the event from beginning to end. That's why **Sentence 2 is grammatical** because it uses the base verb DOC to represent the simple past to show that the speaker witnessed the completed action.

Now let's just have a little more fun by doing the same thing with this second pair of sentences, except in this case, decide which sentence means that the DOC action happened repeatedly and which sentence means that it happened only once:

1. I heard her sneezing. ☐ once ☐ repeatedly
2. I heard her sneeze. ☐ once ☐ repeatedly

Can you defend why you believe she sneezed only once or repeatedly in each sentence? Write down your thoughts on these lines:

....

....

It turns out that she sneezed **repeatedly** in **Sentence 1**, but she sneezed only **once** in **Sentence 2**, and the reasons are as follows:

In the first sentence, we have the *-ing* DOC, which represents an action *in progress*. Since an individual sneeze is of such short duration, it stands to reason that we're dealing with a series of sneezes in order for it to be in progress, not just one; therefore, the action happened repeatedly.

In the second sentence, we have the base verb DOC, which represents a *completed action*. Since we're talking about a sneeze—and it's very possible to sneeze just one time—we tend to think that she only sneezed once. Amazing how a little grammar can change things!

I don't want to beat a dead horse, but there's just one more group of sentences I'd like you to consider, so take a look at these and check off the corresponding box you agree with for each:

1. They saw a man standing in a field.
    ☐ plausible   ☐ implausible
2. They saw one lone tree standing in a field.
    ☐ plausible   ☐ implausible
3. They saw a man stand in a field.
    ☐ plausible   ☐ implausible
4. They saw one lone tree stand in a field.
    ☐ plausible   ☐ implausible

Isn't it interesting?! **Sentences 1, 2, and 3 are plausible, but 4 is implausible.** Why do you think that is? Here's your chance to solve yet another minor mystery of the language:

....

The reason that Sentence 4 is implausible while the other three are plausible goes along with everything we've said about the *-ing* DOC and the base verb phrase DOC. **Sentence 1 means that they saw a man who was already standing**, or upright, in a field, and **the same holds true in Sentence 2 for that one lone tree.** Sentence 3, on the other hand, **means that they saw a man stand**, or stand up, in a field because the base verb DOC means they witnessed a completed action—and there's the catch. **I've never** (and I'm sure you've never) **seen a tree do this sort of action.** That's why **Sentence 4 is implausible.**

It's important to remember, however, that the interpretations I've just made only hold up because I've been having fun with actions of very short duration or actions that can only apply to animate direct objects, not trees. As I mentioned previously, there are other occasions when the speaker has a perfectly grammatical choice of using the *-ing* or base verb phrase DOC almost at random without any major change in meaning or grammaticality. As you'll recall, the examples I cited on page 248 were "I heard him <u>playing</u> his violin last night" and "I heard him play his violin last night."

Past Participle Phrases

At long last, here we are at the sixth and final type of direct object companions we need to investigate. One interesting point to mention from the outset is that we can find pre-existing as well as resulting conditions with past participle phrase DOCs just as we did with nouns and adjectives.

So without further comment, let's see how they appear in context:

A: I'm so excited, I could burst!

B: Why? What's happening?

A: It's my wife. I'm going to see her **honored** as Teacher of the Year!

B: I didn't know she'd even been nominated.

A: Let me tell you, it's been a long, difficult process, and I witnessed practically everything. I saw her **interviewed** and **re-interviewed**, I saw her **tested** and **re-tested** on her subject area, and I saw her background **checked** and **re-checked**.

B: But I'm sure it was all worth it. Congratulate her for me!

Before we get into the thick of things, let's just quickly see how the DOC pattern works with past participles, too:

subject	+	verb	+	direct object	+	past participle phrase
I		'm going to see		her		honored...
I		saw		her		interviewed...
I		saw		her		tested...
I		saw		her background		checked...

Well, it's certainly obvious that the past participle verb phrase DOC fits our pattern like a glove. And speaking of obvious, the obvious question I want to ask you is why these DOCs are past participles. Why should that form of the verb be used in these instances? Any idea? Write it down on the following line if you think of a reason:

....

The answer to my question is that the past participle is used for this type of DOC because **it represents the remnants of a phrase that contains the passive voice.** To prove my point, let's see if we can expand on the first sentence in the dialogue with the past participle DOC:

I'm going to see her when she's being honored as Teacher of the Year.

Now that we have a reconstruction of what the expanded sentence can look like, we see how this phrase has been reduced with only the past participle remaining. In fact, the sentence has actually been reduced twice. The first reduction is the elimination of "... when she's ...," so that we have

I'm going to see her being honored as Teacher of the Year.

From there we can reduce it even further by eliminating the auxiliary *be* from the passive voice construction:

I'm going to see her honored as Teacher of the Year.

Yet there's another way of looking at the totally expanded sentence before it's reduced. The sentence might also be, "I'm going to see her when she is honored as Teacher of the Year." This sentence also neatly reduces by first eliminating "... when she ..." and then eliminating *is*.

Now we have the "finished product," so to speak. Of course, the part or parts that are eliminated to reduce the sentence to only the past participle phrase as a DOC can vary quite a bit. Look at the following sentences and see if you can reconstruct the parts that have been eliminated to arrive at the reduced finished products:

I saw a koala .... cuddled in a little girl's arms.

I found the boat .... tied up to the dock.

Among the variations that you could come up with for the first sentence are:

. . . when/as/while it was (being) . . . ; . . . that/which was (being) . . .

And for the second sentence we have:

. . . which/that had been . . . ; . . . which/that was . . .

Besides the verbs that I've used in my examples of past participle phrase DOCs, I can also include:

feel:	She felt her mouth numbed by the dentist's injections.
hear:	I heard the march played by two bands.
like:	Oddly enough, Samantha likes her toast burned/burnt.
need:	The doctor needs these instruments sterilized.
want:	They want their bathroom remodeled.
watch:	Have you ever watched hatchlings fed by their mother?

Once again, there's a commonality shared by most of these verbs. It's the fact that they are verbs of perception.

Causatives and Direct Object Companions

It's worth making further observations about a few of the causative verbs I included in my discussions earlier in this chapter because of their interesting relationship to certain DOCs. This next dialogue will show you what I mean:

A: Hi, Krystyna! Ooh, you look disgusted.

B: I'm trying to figure out why my car stalls almost every time I stop at a red light. It's infuriating!

A: I'll give you a hand if you'd like.

B: Great! Do me a favor. Get behind the wheel and start the engine for me, okay?

A: Sure thing. But what are you trying to do?

B: Well, I first want to **get** it **started**, then **keep** it **idling** for a few minutes, and see if it stalls again.

A: Okay. Ready when you are.

B: Fine. **Start** it **going**. That's it. Good. Now **let** it **run** for a while. I'm sure we'll **have** it **working** fine in no time at all.

You'll recall that we covered quite a lot about causative verbs back in Chapter 10. We can see another example of the forms we covered in that chapter in the first phrase in bold from this dialogue, "get it started." Now, however, we're up against something else with the remaining phrases in bold. We can see two other kinds of DOCs being used, the *-ing* verb phrase DOC, which represents an action in progress, and the base verb phrase DOC, which stands for a completed action.

The question is, why should we use the *-ing* DOC after the verbs *keep*, *start*, and *have*, but we use the base verb DOC after the verb *let*? (By the way, even though *let* isn't strictly a causative verb, it functions the same way in a sentence with a DOC, and that's why it's being included here.) Is there a reason for the choice of DOC, or is it just a random, arbitrary decision in the language?

We certainly know by now that we can create reconstructions of most sentences with DOCs by making either two shorter sentences or one longer one before anything is reduced, so before you try to answer my last two questions, see if you can make one reconstruction of each phrase, and do it in any way you find convenient:

1. I want to keep it *idling*. =

....

2. Start it going. =

....

3. Now let it run for a while. =

....

4. We'll have it working fine. =

....

Some possible reconstructions I've come up with are as follows. See how closely yours come to mine:

   1. **I want to keep it in a state in which it's <u>idling</u>.**
   2. **Start it so that it's <u>going</u>.**
   3. **Now let it alone. It <u>will run</u> for a while.**
   4. **We'll have it in a condition in which it's <u>working</u> fine.**

If we look at the reconstructions in this way, we can see why the choice of DOC after these causative verbs isn't random or arbitrary at all. In Sentence 1 the idea of *keep* is to maintain an action, so it makes sense that *idle* should appear in the progressive verb form to show an action in progress. Once this form has been reduced, it becomes the *-ing* DOC.

In Sentence 2 the idea of *start* similarly means that something is to begin its operation, so it makes sense once again to have *go* in the progressive form.

And in Sentence 4 the same idea holds true for *have*, since the meaning is that the car *will be working fine*—again, the progressive aspect. And as before, when these forms are reduced, they become the *-ing* DOC.

But why should the base verb DOC be used after *let* in Sentence 3? The answer is that *let* means to allow something to happen, and it covers from the beginning to the end of that something. Since the whole duration of the action is implied, it makes sense to use the base verb DOC to represent the idea of a completed action. Here are the other verbs that work in this way:

help:	She's helping me plan the party.
make:	He made his son apologize.
have:	I had them redo their work.

Before I end this chapter, let's take a closer look at one of our causatives. Even though it's going to be somewhat of a repetition from Chapter 10, I think causatives worth reviewing. As you look at the final dialogue for this chapter, notice that the causative in question, *have*, can carry three different DOCs depending on the action cited or the nature of its direct objects:

A: Did I tell you how much I like the new paint job on your house?

B: Why, thanks a lot. You just wouldn't believe the aggravation I had with the painter!

A: What happened?

B: To begin with, he didn't think it necessary to pressure-wash the sides before putting on the primer. He **had** me **pulling** my hair out over that. So I stayed home from work and **had** him **pressure-wash** the sides while I watched to make sure he'd do it.

A: You don't say!

B: Oh, yes. When I need repairs or maintenance around my house, I **have** it **done** right!

You've noticed that the *-ing* verb phrase DOC has been used with the causative *have* ("He had me pulling my hair out over that."). We now know that the *-ing* DOC represents the past progressive verb form in this case ("I was pulling my hair out.") to show the action caught in progress at that moment.

Next, we see that the base verb phrase DOC has been used with *have* ("I had him pressure-wash the sides"). As we know by now, the reason for this DOC is to communicate that the action was completed, that the speaker witnessed the action from beginning to end.

But now we have to wonder why the past participle verb phrase DOC has been used in the last sentence of the dialogue after the same causative ("I have it done right!"). Let's focus our attention on just the base verb DOC and the past participle phrase DOC. Why isn't the base verb phrase DOC being used in talking about doing a job right? What difference do you see between these two sentences in the dialogue that can account for this change in DOC?

....

The answer lies in our understanding of whether the direct object is **the doer, in which case we use an active voice form** (base verb or *-ing* form), **or isn't the doer, in which case we use a passive voice form** (past participle). In the sentence "I had him pressure-wash the sides," *him* means the painter, and obviously the painter was the doer:

>(I had him.) He pressure-wash<u>ed</u> the sides.

That's why we need the base verb DOC, which represents a form of the active voice. On the other hand, in the sentence "I have it done right," *it* represents the job, and the job is obviously not the doer, so we have the need for the past participle DOC to represent the reduced passive voice form:

>(I have it.) It is done right.

Here is another example of *have* with these two kinds of DOCs:

>I had the tailor <u>alter</u> my pants.
>I had my pants <u>altered</u>.

🌰 Direct Object Companions in a Nutshell

🌰 **noun phrase:**	The voters elected her Prime Minister.
🌰 **adjective phrase:**	He keeps his life simple.
🌰 **base verb phrase:**	Do they like to watch planes take off?
🌰 **infinitive verb phrase:**	She asked her neighbor to rake his leaves.
🌰 ***-ing* verb phrase:**	I felt the horsefly biting me on the arm.
🌰 **past participle phrase:**	You didn't send that letter registered, did you?
🌰 **prepositional phrase:**	We left the house in shambles.
🌰 **causative verbs:**	We had the vet spay our cat.
	We got our cat spayed.
	The comedian had the audience roaring with laughter.

Teaching Tips

11.1 *I've Got a Problem . . .*

No Tip in this book could ever be used with just one grammatical point, and this one is no exception. This one gives you a chance to recycle a second grammar point, gerunds (*-ing* nouns). Have students write down five to six things that bother them, make them crazy, nervous, sad, frustrated, etc. Here are some typical answers: "My daughter leaves her clothes all over her room." / "My husband never thanks me for fixing his meals." / "My children fight all the time."/ "My teacher always asks me the hardest questions." Once they've written down their gripes or worries, collect and redistribute them to different students. Have the students walk around the room to find out who wrote the papers that they have. Once all the students have matched papers and authors, let them choose one or two of the most interesting statements to share with the class. Make sure that they use *make*, *drive*, and *get* in all their answers. ("Her son's leaving clothes all over his room gets Shelley very upset." / "Never being thanked for fixing her husband's meals makes Vianney sad."/ "Hearing his children fight all the time drives Robin mad," etc.)

11.2 *Nationalities*

Before class, cut sheets of paper up into strips. Have enough strips for each student to have six or eight (whatever the number you give them, make sure they get an even number of strips). On half their strips of paper, have the students write one nationality per strip. Then tell them to write down a characteristic of each nationality they've chosen—one per strip—making sure they use an appropriate DOC (e.g., "Americans"/ "The Japanese"/ "The Irish"/ "Russians" on four strips, and "like their drinks cold."/ "cook their rice sticky." / "don't like the weather too warm./ "have borscht hot or cold" on the other four strips). When they've finished, collect all the strips, mix them up well, and redistribute them to the students. If they get one of their own, give them another. Let the students walk around the room to find out who has a match to whatever strips they have. If you want to ensure that the right nationalities get matched to their characteristics, thus eliminating mismatches when all is said and done, have students compare handwriting to verify a proper match before claiming one.

11.3 *Free Help!*

There are few people who would refuse to take all the free household help they could get if offered it. Divide the class into pairs or small groups and ask them to imagine that they now have this help. Their job is to prepare lists of chores for their help to do. What would they *expect/ want/ ask/ order/ get/ permit/ allow/ compel* these people to do? Share ideas once the groups have brainstormed their lists with their classmates.

11.4 *Imagine*

Divide the class into small groups. Tell them they're going to go camping, hiking, snorkeling, wandering about a big city, etc. Have them imagine what they *might/ won't see, hear, smell, watch, catch, notice, discover, observe, spot*, etc. while they're out. For example: (camping) "I might see a bear feeding her cubs" / (snorkeling) "I won't watch a shark eating a fish". Have the students share their answers with their classmates after they've discussed them.

11.5 *I Can't Stand...*

Verbs of "liking" and "disliking" are commonly used, and when they are, a DOC is likely to be used, too. Here's a chance to release pent-up frustrations and practice DOCs at the same time. All of us have pet peeves, things that we don't like. In small groups, have students write down things they can't stand. For example: *I dislike a person tapping their fingers on a table*. When they've produced their lists, ask them to share their pet peeves with their classmates, making sure that they use "can't stand" in all their answers. Are there any trends? Unusual answers? Discuss them.

Variation: Your students have practiced making complaints. Now repeat the activity and have them use a wide variety of "like" and "dislike" verbs (*adore, despise, enjoy, hate, like, love, regret, resent*, etc.). Make sure that they match a verb with an appropriate situation; it would be ludicrous for them to match despise with "see butterflies in my backyard"!

11.6 *Pantomimes*

Divide the class into groups of four to five. Ask each group to prepare a one- or two-minute pantomime. Make sure all members of each group are included in the pantomime and that there's a lot of action in it. Have one group present its pantomime while the rest of the students jot down notes about what's happening. After a pantomime is presented, have each group review their notes and create a master list of what they saw. Then lead a discussion of what actually happened. Each action that a group has correctly noted earns them a point; each action that no other group has mentioned gets them two points. Each use of a DOC or causative verb and a DOC gets three points. Tally up the scores and the "best describers" win.

11.7 *Commands and Permissions*

Before class, prepare various commands and permissions and write each on an individual slip of paper. Make sure that you create enough so that each student has a couple of slips. Here are some typical commands and permissions: "Sit on the floor."/"Hum a tune."/"Escort me to the back of the room."/"It's okay to chew gum in class."/"You can put away your books," etc. Let each student do what one of their slips says to do—without directly saying what's going on. Ask other students to explain what they see and make sure they use *have, let,* or *make* in their comments. For example: "Pierre had Jean-Claude sit on the floor." / "Our teacher lets the students chew gum in class."

11.8 *Fix It Up*

Before class, think up things that need some sort of fixing: a broken air conditioner, a floor that's sticky, a skirt that's too long, a table that's scratched, etc. Based on these things, make up a list that might look like this: "Have it fixed."/"Have it mopped."/"Get it shortened."/"Get it refinished." Make copies of these sentences or write them on the board. Tell students that they need to figure out what needs fixing or doing. Have them write down their ideas. When all the groups have finished creating their lists of guesses (e.g., "a broken appliance"/"a dirty floor"/"a skirt that's too long"/"a scratched table"), let the various groups share their ideas.

12

Coordination, Subordination, and Correlation

"We may all have come on different ships, but we are in the same boat now."

Among the most frequently used and helpful tools of a language are conjunctions, words that join two or more other words together. Before I go any further into the topic of conjunctions, I'd like to go over a few terms, so let's have at them.

Besides simple words, I'm going to be dealing with phrases. Phrases are two or more words used together that don't include a subject and verb, meaning that they don't communicate a complete idea. *Boys and girls* is an example of a phrase. Other examples of phrases are *faster than lightning*, or *on the porch*.

In addition we've got clauses, which, unlike phrases, are a string of words that do contain a subject and a verb. There are two kinds of clauses to keep in mind. We have **independent clauses**, which contain subjects and verbs, and communicate complete ideas. They're called "independent" clauses because they can stand alone; they can stand independently. Two examples are *My husband cooks.* and *Everyone participated.* By the way, I'm sure you've noticed that independent clauses are actually simple sentences.

We also have **dependent clauses**. They, too, contain subjects and verbs, but they don't give us complete ideas. They're like "cliff hangers" in the movies, when you're waiting for the rest of the scene to know what will happen, i.e., when you're waiting for the other shoe to drop, so to speak. Here's an example to show what I mean:

>When I finally got there . . .

And here's another:

>. . . until I hear from them.

So why do you think we call these dependent clauses? On the lines below, write down your thoughts about this.

....

....

In the first example, you're waiting for the rest of the idea to come out. If nothing further is said, you're thinking something like, "Well, uh, okay. So what happened next?" In that second example, you're really confused because you have no idea what was said before. You can see that in both cases, even with subjects and verbs, these utterances can't stand alone. They depend on more information (coming from independent clauses) in order to make sense—and be part of a complete sentence; that's why they're called "dependent" clauses.

Coordination

"Nothing is softer or more flexible than water, yet nothing can resist it."

So why this mini-lesson/review about phrases and clauses? It's because this first part of Chapter 12 is going to deal with coordinating conjunctions, and simply put, coordinating conjunctions connect two more-or-less equal elements (singular words, phrases, or independent clauses) so that there's a kind of balance between both parts. There are just seven of these helpful, little words: *for, and, nor, but, or, yet,* and *so*. At some point in the study of English grammar, a very clever person thought up a mnemonic device to help us remember them, resulting in the catchy acronym FANBOYS. As you can see, FANBOYS is comprised of the first letter of each of our seven coordinating conjunctions. Just as a little aside, it's interesting to note that three of our little gems are high frequency items (*and, but,* and *so*), while the other four are low frequency items (*or, nor, for,* and *yet*). Take a look at the following dialogue to see some of these coordinating conjunctions in use.

A: Here's your coffee. Now, how about a cookie? I've got chocolate chip **and**[1] oatmeal raisin.

B: Why are things that are so good so bad for you at the same time, tasty on the palate, **but** harmful on the waist?

A: Beats me! It's one of the mysteries of the Universe. Anyway, my philosopher friend, just help yourself.

B: Well, oatmeal raisin sometimes gives me heartburn, **so** I'll take a couple of chocolate chip cookies.

A: You know; we're really terrible when you think about it.

B: Why do you say that?

A: We're both supposed to be dieting, **yet** here we are, attacking this plate of cookies.

B: You're right. Shame on us! Hmm . . . I think I'll have just one more chocolate chip cookie—**and**[2] I'll go back on my diet tomorrow.

A: Sure you will. Yep, we're terrible!

You've just seen four coordinating conjunctions at work (those words in bold) with one of them repeated. Can you identify what they're connecting in the dialogue? Let's see if your answers match up with mine.

and[1] : ....

but: ....

so, yet, and[2] : ....

The first *and* is connecting **two nouns**. Then we've got *but*, which is connecting **two adjective phrases**. And finally we have *so, yet*, plus the second *and*, all of which are connecting **two independent clauses**.

For the most part, teaching coordinating conjunctions isn't a big challenge, especially if teachers and students alike keep that acronym FANBOYS in mind. One thing I'd like to discuss for a moment is the *for* represented by the *F* in FANBOYS. Check out the following sentence, which admittedly is pretty contrived, and see if you sense that *for* means or doesn't mean the same thing in both cases that it's used here. If you feel that *for* has the same meaning in both cases, check the box that says "same." If you feel, however, that there's a difference in meaning, check the box that says "different." And if you check the "different" box, on the lines below, explain what you think the differences are by identifying the parts of speech of *for* that you discern in each case and what the meaning is in each case.

She made a beautiful afghan for her mother, for the woman was cold all the time.

☐ same   ☐ different

....

....

I don't doubt that you found the sentence a bit odd; that's because of the second *for*, I'm sure. You should have checked the **different** box, by the way, and here's the information you should have furnished on those lines. Let's see if your ideas jibe with these.

- a preposition: shows the person/thing that receives or benefits from something
- a coordinating conjunction: because/the reason being that . . .

 Using the coordinating conjunction *for* to mean *because/the reason being that* is quite formal sounding or even archaic; very few people employ it with this usage in informal speech.

It is important, though, that *for* in FANBOYS is clearly understood not to have the typical definition found in its use as a preposition. A little later we'll take a rather close look at *nor*, another coordinating conjunction, which, like *for*, isn't discussed enough in most ESOL (English for Speakers of Other Languages) teacher reference books.

Right now, however, let's just have a bit of fun with five of our seven coordinating conjunctions. As I've already noted, these conjunctions are used to "glue" two words, phrases, or independent clauses together, and the phrases and clauses are normally well balanced, so to speak, having more or less some sort of equality between them in their construction and/or communication. At any rate, let's use some of this "glue" to turn independent clauses, also known as **simple sentences**, into what we call **compound sentences**.

Look at the following pairs of simple sentences, aka independent clauses. Fill in the blank between each pair of them with one of the coordinating conjunctions below. Notice that only five of the seven are listed; that's because I don't want you to use *and* or *yet*.

        for   but   nor   or   so

He lost weight, ... the jacket still didn't fit.

She wasn't feeling well, ... she went home early.

Tomorrow we can go to the state fair, ... we can stay home and just relax.

Farmers were getting very nervous, ... the drought was getting worse.

I can't ride a bike, ... can I drive a car.

And now for the answers:

He lost weight, *but* the jacket still didn't fit.

She wasn't feeling well, *so* she went home early.

Tomorrow we can go to the state fair, *or* we can stay home and just relax.

Farmers were getting very nervous, *for* the drought was getting worse.

I can't ride a bike, *nor* can I drive a car.

Speaking of *nor*, I'd like to remind you of something this coordinating conjunction can cause to happen. Have you noticed anything unusual in the sentence above that contains *nor*? Hint: It's something I discussed in the online material (ELTgrammar.com) for Chapter 1. Write your answer on the following line.

....

It's the fact that we have a case of word order inversion and the creation of a yes/no question construction triggered by *nor* being placed at the beginning of the independent clause (simple sentence):

I can't ride a bike. →..., nor can I drive a car.

In the Chapter 1 online material, I mention the rule about this phenomenon with *nor*, stating that if adverbs of frequency and other sorts of adverbs such as *barely* (that are more negative than affirmative) are placed at the beginning of a <u>sentence</u>, this inversion will take place. Now, however, I can state that **it's also at the beginning of the second independent clause that's been glued to another independent clause with *nor*.** Here's another example of this happening because of *nor*:

He doesn't smoke, nor <u>does he</u> drink.

Before I move on to another topic, there's a final observation I'd like you to make about using coordinating conjunctions. Have a look at these pairs of sentences. Think about whether one of the two clauses seems to be more important than the other, or if both clauses can be equally important, depending on your point of view or what's going on at the time this sentence is uttered:

It looks like rain, so I'll bring an umbrella.

Does *It looks like rain* seem more important to you in this sentence or does . . . *so I'll bring an umbrella* look more important, or does neither one seem more important? The way I see it, neither independent clause seems more important than the other, and that's why I'm forced to use a coordinating conjunction if I want to combine the two into one (thereby creating a compound sentence). As you can see, I've chosen to use *so* to glue the two simple sentences together.

But what if you actually do come across an utterance in which you feel that one clause is more important than the other to get across your idea? When it's a matter of choice, things may become less easy and convenient to deal with. But not to worry – I'll get to that!

So now it's your turn. Have a look at the following pairs of sentences. All I'm asking you to do is decide whether one of the two simple sentences in each pair seems more important than the other. Check the appropriate box for each.

---

1. a. Vlad set the table.
   b. Elizabeta poured the wine.

In Pair 1, . . .

☐ *a* and *b* share equal importance.
☐ *a* is more important than *b*.
☐ *b* is more important than *a*.

---

2. c. Bruce had been sick for days.
   d. He continued to go to work.

In Pair 2, . . .

☐ *c* and *d* share equal importance.
☐ *c* is more important than *d*.
☐ *d* is more important than *c*.

Not so easy? That's because you're now dealing with an opinion, not a rule. The way I see it, in Pair 1 *a* and *b* share **equal importance**. They're also of equal construction and quite balanced. To combine these two independent clauses, you'll need a coordinating conjunction that makes sense. Which conjunction will you use to glue the two clauses together, and what will your compound sentence be? Write the sentence on the following line.

....

If you run that acronym FANBOYS through your mind, you'll come to the conclusion that the only coordinating conjunction that will work in this case is *and*, so your newly created compound sentence will be . . .

Vlad set the table **and** Elizabeta poured the wine.

 Heads Up!

Typically, in a written compound sentence, we place a comma before the FANBOY, as you've seen with almost all the example sentences that I've offered so far. As you can see, however, the sentence above about Vlad and Elizabeta does not have a comma before *and*. The basic rule at work here is that **when you have a sentence containing two balanced independent clauses connected by *and*, you don't need a comma**.

But what about Pair 2? Let's say you and I had been talking about people's work ethics. Perhaps to my way of thinking, Bruce's continuing to go to work was just as important as his having been sick for days. Since I feel this way, which means both clauses are more or less equally balanced, I'll want to combine the two independent clauses into one compound sentence, and I'll need a coordinating conjunction. Can you find one that will tie these two clauses together? I'm sure you can! Write the compound sentence you've created for me on the following line.

....

I bet you came up with the sentence below, but did you consider that there are two coordinating conjunctions that can work in this sentence? This is the sentence you should have written on the line above:

Bruce had been sick for days, **but/yet** he continued to go to work.

Uh . . . but wait a moment. Maybe you disagree and have a different opinion. In your way of seeing things, maybe you think the two clauses don't share equal importance. Perhaps you feel that since we're discussing people's work ethics, Bruce's continuing to go to work under these circumstances was more important than the fact that he'd been sick for days. How can you communicate that idea then? Well, here's something you could say:

> Bruce continued to go to work even though he'd been sick for days.

Or you could say:

> Even though Bruce had been sick for days, he continued to go to work.

Well, I've certainly combined the two clauses all right, but two things have changed. First, FANBOYS aren't in the picture anymore. There's no coordinating conjunction in sight. Second, I don't have two independent clauses anymore. If you check back at the beginning of this chapter, you'll realize what I now have going on. What happened to my clauses? Note down your thoughts on the following lines:

....

....

What's happened is that I now have **one independent clause** (*Bruce continued to go to work*) and **one dependent clause** (*even though he'd been sick for days*). And what's just happened leads us into the next part of this chapter.

Subordination

"When you reach the end of your rope, tie a knot in it and hang on."

Let's do a little sleuthing. I'd like you to be an outstanding grammar detective and pick out two things in each of the following sentences. First, identify which part of each sentence is an independent clause and which part is a dependent clause. Check the box next to your choice. Second, circle the word that you feel is the subordinating conjunction, i.e., the word that introduces the dependent/subordinate clause. Have fun, Sherlock Holmes!

1. <u>She'll take the dog for a walk now</u>   <u>although she normally takes him later</u>.
                  a   *b*

   Section *a* is   ☐ a dependent clause   ☐ an independent clause
   Section *b* is   ☐ a dependent clause   ☐ an independent clause
   The subordinating conjunction is ....

2. <u>Because he'd eaten some very spicy food,</u>   <u>he got a terrible heartburn</u>.
                         a   *b*

   Section *a* is   ☐ a dependent clause   ☐ an independent clause
   Section *b* is   ☐ a dependent clause   ☐ an independent clause
   The subordinating conjunction is ....

3. <u>While I like my in-laws a lot,</u> <u>I'd never want to live next door to them.</u>
       a   b

Section a is   ☐ a dependent clause   ☐ an independent clause
Section b is   ☐ a dependent clause   ☐ an independent clause

The subordinating conjunction is ....

4. <u>I'll help you with your homework</u> <u>unless you want to do it on your own.</u>
         a   b

Section a is   ☐ a dependent clause   ☐ an independent clause
Section b is   ☐ a dependent clause   ☐ an independent clause

The subordinating conjunction is ....

So, Sherlock, was that a piece of cake? Let's find out. Here are my answers:

1a. an independent clause	1b. a dependent clause	*although*
2a. a dependent clause	2b. an independent clause	*because*
3a. a dependent clause	3b. an independent clause	*while*
4a. an independent clause	4b. a dependent clause	*unless*

Now, to review what the simplest way is to know if a clause is dependent or independent, all you need to do is ask whether or not a section of a sentence is a complete idea or not. By looking, for example, at Sentence 3 above, it's clear that saying "While I like my in-laws" is a cliff hanger; you're waiting for the rest of the idea, but it's not there. If somebody said this to you, you'd wait a moment or two, and after that silence, you'd say something like, "Yeah, so, what are you trying to say about your in-laws?" And that person might say "I'd never want to live next door to them," "Oh!" you exclaim. "Now I get it!" (It's not a cliff hanger anymore.) So the long and short of it is that the section of the sentence that's a cliff hanger, that leaves you with an incomplete idea, is the dependent clause, and the other section, which is a complete idea, is the independent clause.

So where do you stick the subordinating conjunction if you're going to create a complex sentence? Write down your observation on the following line.

....

The answer is that you always stick the subordinating conjunction **onto the beginning of the dependent clause**; that's what turns an independent clause into a dependent one:

I like my in-laws. (independent clause, complete idea)
While I like my in-laws, . . (dependent clause, incomplete idea)

Here's another pair of clauses that show this differentiation:

> She'll take the dog for a walk now. (independent clause, complete idea)
> . . . although she normally waits until after lunch.
> (dependent clause, incomplete idea)

Unlike coordinating conjunctions, of which there are a measly seven, there are lots of subordinating conjunctions to pick and choose from. In fact, they can be placed into categories to make it easier to "digest" them all, but before I get into the categories, there's something interesting about the parts of speech some of these words in question fall into.

Let's do a little more sleuthing, Sherlock. Look at the following dialogue and see if you discern which of two parts of speech these words are. You'll be looking for **prepositions** and **subordinating conjunctions**. Let's see if you can figure out which is which by the context.

> A: Hey, Mike, **before**[1] the movie starts, I need to talk to you.
>
> B: **Before**[2] the movie? Can't it wait? It's gonna start any minute. Hold it **until**[1] we have time to talk. Unfortunately, right **after**[1] the movie, I've gotta run, but I'll stop by your house tomorrow **after**[2] I pick up my kid. It can wait **until**[2] tomorrow, right?
>
> A: Well, okay. But **since**[1] this morning, something's been worrying me.
>
> B: You mean **since**[2] you heard the news about the coming layoffs at your plant.
>
> A: Yeah. How did you know about that?

before[1] ....
before[2] ....
until[1] ....
until[2] ....
after[1] ....
after[2] ....
since[1] ....
since[2] ....

It's interesting how context can change the part of speech for some of these words. Here are the answers for you to check: **Before**[1] is a subordinating conjunction; **before**[2] is a preposition./**Until**[1] is a subordinating conjunction;

until² is a preposition./After¹ is a preposition; after² is a subordinating conjunction./Since¹ is a preposition; since² is a subordinating conjunction.

But what's going on? How do you know when these words are prepositions and when they're subordinating conjunctions? By looking over all the sentences and the context these words are in, can you tell what's going on? Write your conclusion on the following line.

....

The simple explanation is that if these words are **followed by noun phrases only, they're prepositions**, and used as such. If, however, the same words are **followed by subjects and verb phrases, they're subordinating conjunctions**.

Now, remember I stated that there are lots of subordinating conjunctions, unlike coordinating conjunctions of which there are only seven? Well, let's discuss the categories that subordinating conjunctions can be placed in. Check out each of the following sentences. Pick out the subordinating conjunction in each one and then identify what category you would put it in. Here are the categories to pick from:

CONDITION   TIME   CAUSE & EFFECT   PLACE   COMPARISON   CONTRAST

1. Wherever you go in Europe, you'll find interesting things to see and do.
   subordinating conjunction:................................ category:................................

2. The doctor says she'll give him that blood test whenever he wants.
   subordinating conjunction:................................ category:................................

3. Now that I know you've ordered pizza, there's no point cooking this meat tonight.
   subordinating conjunction:................................ category:................................

4. The kids can go to the circus as long as they do all their chores every day.
   subordinating conjunction:................................ category:................................

5. Why are you acting as though there weren't a problem?
   subordinating conjunction:................................ category:................................

6. They decided to go to the beach even though there had been shark sightings.
   subordinating conjunction:................................ category:................................

And now for the answers:

subordinating conjunction	category
wherever	place
whenever	time
now that	cause and effect
as long as	condition
as though	comparison
even though	contrast

Of course each category contains more than just one subordinating conjunction, so here are the most frequently used ones in each category:

Condition: if / if only / even if / unless / as long as
Time: when / whenever / while / after / before / until / till / since / once
Cause and Effect: because / so that / in order that / now that
Place: where / wherever
Comparison: as / as if / as though
Contrast: though / although / even though / whereas

 **Heads Up!**

A big challenge for teachers is to get students to understand which clause in a complex sentence is the more important idea. It's crucial for your students to understand that the main clause of a sentence carries a higher level of importance.

The first task that you worked on in this chapter demonstrates a great way for you to get your students sensitized to recognizing main (independent) clauses and picking out subordinating conjunctions. When you feel it's time, give your students a number of exercises just like this first task you worked on to have them identify the main ideas and subordinating conjunctions. Once they get the knack of doing these two things, make sure they understand that the clause second in importance (the dependent clause) is the one that gets the subordinating conjunction attached to it. If they understand this, they should have little trouble putting these complex sentences together.

Types of Subordinate Clauses

I've talked a good deal about subordinating conjunctions, and at the beginning of that section, I mentioned how you stick a subordinating conjunction onto an independent clause to turn it into a dependent, subordinate clause. You'll always know a subordinate clause when you come across one because it's never a complete idea.

Speaking of complete and incomplete ideas, so far I've only been dealing with **adverbial** subordinate clauses. That's all well and good, but I don't want to mislead you into thinking that an adverbial subordinate clause is the only kind of subordinate clause there is—because it isn't! Besides adverbial subordinate clauses, we also have **adjectival** and **noun** subordinate clauses.

Here are explanations of the three types of these clauses accompanied by some examples.

The Adverbial Subordinate Clause

This is simply a subordinate clause that acts as an adverb. The subordinating conjunction that's stuck on to the clause will act as some kind of adverb. An adverbial subordinate clause acts as an adverb because it affects or modifies the verb in the independent clause. The underlined parts below are the adverbial subordinate clauses.

<u>Before she became a judge</u>, she'd been an assistant district attorney for many years.

They couldn't watch that video <u>until the children fell asleep</u>.

The Adjectival Subordinate Clause

We all know that an adjective describes or modifies a noun. We also know that an adjective doesn't have to be just one or two words; it can be a whole phrase or even a clause. When one of these gems becomes an adjectival subordinate clause, instead of having a conjunction stuck onto its beginning, it uses a **relative pronoun**, a word like *who*, *that*, and *which*.

My Aunt Jenny is the only woman <u>who's running for club treasurer</u>.
Most everyone loves tomatoes, <u>which are actually a fruit, not a vegetable</u>.

Notice that in the first sentence, the adjectival subordinate clause is describing the noun *woman*, while in the second sentence, the adjectival subordinate clause is describing the noun *tomatoes*.

The Noun Subordinate Clause

The complete idea of a noun in a sentence is often represented by more than one word; a noun can be comprised of a number of words acting together to create one thing. Take a look at the following examples to see how we can find noun subordinate clauses.

<u>Whoever saved the dog</u> should be rewarded.
I'm not interested in <u>how he makes a living</u>.

For more information on subordinate clauses, please visit us at ELTgrammar.com

Correlation

"Neither a borrower nor a lender be."

We've done quite a thorough job investigating coordinating conjunctions and we've done the same with subordinating conjunctions; now is the time to take a good look at a third type of conjunction, correlative conjunctions.

So what are they? You saw that coordinating conjunctions join together words, phrases, or more or less balanced independent clauses with both clauses sharing importance. You also saw that subordinating conjunctions join together unequal clauses, one dependent and the other independent, the latter having more importance since it's the main idea.

Now, however, we're going to deal with a change in focus. Correlative conjunctions are pairs of words that tie together no more than two things, and those two things should have parallel construction:

You should buy **either** Swiss cheese **or** Cheddar cheese. (two noun phrases)

Their house was **both** reroofed **and** repainted. (two past participle adjectives)

We can't decide **whether** to put siding on the house **or not**. (two infinitive verb phrases implied)

Not only will they visit the Vatican, **but** they'll **also** have an audience with the Pope. (two simple future verb phrases)

Just as with subordinating conjunctions, there are quite a few correlative conjunctions that are used to tie together words, phrases, or clauses. Let's have some fun with these very useful conjunctions. Below is a list of the more commonly used correlative conjunctions. Under the list you'll see sentences with blank lines. Choose which pairs of correlative conjunctions can be plugged into these sentences.

as . . . as . . .	not . . . but . . .
both . . . and . . .	whether . . . or . . .
either . . . or . . .	the more . . . the less . . .
*Scarcely . . . when. . .	the more . . . the more . . .
*No sooner . . . than. . .	**not only . . . but also . . .
*Hardly . . . when . . .	**neither . . . nor . . .

1. _____ Alex _____ Lisa speaks Pashtu.
2. I don't know _____ we should go to Peru _____ Brazil on vacation.
3. _____ she explains that calculus problem to him, _____ he understands.
4. Let's order _____ egg foo young _____ lo mein for the main course.
5. _____ I eat this tasty dish, _____ I like it.
6. Their new apartment is _____ brightly lit _____ cheerful looking.
7. He can speak Mandarin _____ well _____ he can speak Cantonese.
8. _____ just the rye bread was moldy, _____ the white and whole grain, too.

It's interesting to see how these pairs of correlative conjunctions work to tie things together. On the next page are the answers to the sentences above:

1. **Neither** Alex **nor** Lisa speaks Pashtu.
2. I don't know **whether** we should go to Peru **or** Brazil on vacation.
3. **The more** she explains that calculus problem to him, **the less** he understands it.
4. Let's order **either** the egg foo young **or** the lo mein for the main course.
5. **The more** I eat this tasty dish, **the more** I like it.
6. Their new apartment is **both** brightly lit **and** cheerful looking.
7. He can speak Mandarin **as** well **as** I can.
8. **Not** just the rye bread was moldy, **but** the white and whole grain, too.

Take another look at the box with the list of correlative conjunctions on the previous page. Did you happen to notice those asterisks in front of five of the pairs of correlative conjunctions? And did you notice that two of those pairs have double asterisks in front of them?

Let's get creative! Come up with five sentences using *Scarcely, No sooner, Hardly, Not only,* and *Neither* in initial position + a verb phrase.

Scarcely ....
No sooner ....
Hardly ....
Not only ....
Neither ....

Have you noticed anything interesting going on with your sentences and the correlative conjunctions? I'd hazard a guess that you have if you're up on your grammar. These correlative conjunctions in initial position have forced you to use **question inversions (question word order)** after them in your verb phrases. Here are examples of my sentences for you to compare with yours to see how this works:

Scarcely <u>was his new car</u> off the dealer's lot **than** it got rear ended.
No sooner <u>will she be hired</u> **than** she'll be offered overtime.
Hardly <u>had they arrived</u> at the theater **when** the curtain went up.
Not only <u>are they</u> great gymnasts, **but** they're **also** good ballet dancers.
                                              (**but** they're good ballet dancers **as well**).
Neither <u>did I order</u> an appetizer, **nor** <u>did I have</u> dessert. I just wasn't very hungry.

Finally, let's repeat using *not only* and *neither* to find out the reason I placed double asterisks in front of them in my list. Create another sentence for each of these correlative conjunctions, but this time (1) place them in mid-position and (2) don't follow them with verb phrases. Can you figure out what else you can write in these cases besides verb phrases? Here's the pattern I'd like you to use. Can you fill in the blanks on the next page?

.... not only .... but also ....
.... neither .... nor ....

Have you come up with what can be used after these correlative conjunctions when they're not in initial position? The answer is **nouns** or **noun phrases**. Did you get that or are you kicking yourself now for missing it? I hope you're not kicking yourself!

And now for my examples to compare with your sentences:

Her husband cleaned **not only** <u>the house</u>, **but also** <u>the garage</u>! What a guy!
Because of his food allergies, he can eat **neither** <u>peanuts</u> **nor** <u>raw almonds</u>.

Are Correlative Conjunctions Tricky? You Might Say So!

"Life is either a daring adventure or nothing at all."

Up to now nothing has really been said about how register can be affected by the use of correlative conjunctions and about how there are quite a few pitfalls that teachers face in dealing with this topic and students face in mastering this material, so let's get to that!

Using a correlative conjunction in a sentence can indeed be a tricky thing to do. Here's information that will clue you in on how to avoid some of that trickiness.

Subject-Verb Agreement with Correlative Conjunctions

Familiarizing yourself with the following strategies to deal with this issue will go a long way to prepare you to see just how English deals with subject-verb agreement.

If you use any appropriate correlative conjunctions to combine **two subjects**, **both singular**, the verb should be singular:

Neither Abby nor Carly **eats** meat.
I don't recall whether Abby or Carly **is** vegan.

If, however, the conjunction is *and*, the verb should be plural:

Both Arabic and Hebrew **are** Semitic languages.

But what about if you've got **two subjects, one singular and the other plural**? In this case, the verb should agree with the noun that's closer to it:

Neither the Stillmans nor <u>Carly</u> **eats** meat.
Neither Carly nor <u>the Stillmans</u> **eat** meat.

>  **Heads Up!**
>
> But wait a minute. Not so fast! There's another point of view about this. There are some grammar mavens who say that it doesn't matter which subject, the singular one or the plural one, is closer to the verb; the verb should be plural regardless since at least one of the subjects is plural. So that first example sentence before this "Heads Up!" box doesn't work in this way of looking at the grammar. Whether it's "the Stillmans nor Carly" or "Carly nor the Stillmans," the verb should be plural, so only *eat* will work for those grammar mavens.

Subject-Possessive Adjective Agreement with Correlative Conjunctions

Just as I explained how you deal with subject-verb agreement, I now want to explain how you deal with possessive adjectives that reflect the subjects of a sentence when employing correlative conjunctions. The following information will deal with the same kinds of issues that you saw with subject-verb agreement.

It goes without saying that **two singular subjects** require the use of a **singular possessive adjective** form.

>   I'm not sure who, but either <u>Paul or Bob</u> lost **his** wallet.

Of course, when the conjunction *and* is used instead, the **plural** form needs to be used:

>   Both <u>Nelson and his twin sister</u> need to renew **their** driver's licenses.

As for stating the obvious, if you have **two plural subjects**, of course the **possessive adjective** will be in the **plural** form to reflect this.

>   Neither the <u>Sharifs</u> nor the <u>Maloufs</u> like **their** apartment.

Now, what about when **one subject is singular** and **the other is plural**? You deal with this the same way you deal with subject-verb agreement in those two schools of thought on this topic. That means the possessive adjective can agree with the subject that it's closer to:

>   Neither <u>Paola's siblings</u> nor <u>Paola</u> received **her** inheritance.
>   Neither <u>Paola</u> nor <u>her siblings</u> received **their** inheritance.

But once again, we have that other school of thought held by some grammarians that if either subject is plural, the possessive adjective should reflect this.

>   Neither <u>Paola's siblings</u> nor Paola received **their** inheritance.

Parallelism

To end this section of the chapter, I'd like to touch on one aspect of English that's usually taught starting at the intermediate level, and that's parallelism, also referred to as **parallel structure**. It's something that needs to be given more attention to in formal or academic writing and speaking more than in informal or colloquial writing and speaking.

And guess what. I just snuck in an example of parallelism! Can you figure out the two elements that, together, demonstrate parallelism in the second sentence of the previous paragraph? If you've picked them out, write them on the following lines.

....

....

The two elements that offer an example of how parallel structure works are

> . . . **in formal or academic writing and speaking** . . .
> . . . **in informal or colloquial writing and speaking.**

So how do these two phrases demonstrate parallelism? If you break their parts down, you'll see how: they both have a preposition (*in*), they both have conjunctions (*or/and*), and adjectives (*formal/academic/informal/colloquial*), and lastly gerunds (*writing/speaking*).

As I've mentioned, parallelism, especially with correlative conjunctions, is something more important to the written language or to formal speaking situations like speech giving than in the normal use of informal writing or day-to-day speaking. And just to make sure you've got this, take a look at the following sentences, all of which have correlative conjunctions and errors in parallel structure. Underline the parts containing the errors and correct them by rewriting them on the lines provided.

1. The movie isn't just well directed and well paced, but the acting is also good.

....

2. I can't decide whether more garlic or adding some jalapeño will improve the dish.

....

3. They were supposed to bring some kind of dessert to the pot-luck dinner, either a box of cookies, two pies, or they could make sundaes or something for everybody.

....

Now that you're more sensitized to parallel structure when correlative conjunctions are involved, the incorrect part of each sentence should stick out like the clichéd sore thumb.

In **Sentence 1**, it's the third descriptive part that's the problem. You should have underlined "but the acting is also good." Correction: ***but it's also well acted***.

In **Sentence 2**, the problem section is "more garlic or adding some jalapeño," so that's what you should have underlined. Now, as I see it, there are two ways to go to correct the error in this case by stating ***adding more garlic*** or ***more garlic or some jalapeño***.

And in **Sentence 3**, the problem is that we have two noun phrases mentioned (a box of cookies/two pies) but then we suddenly have an independent clause (they could make sundaes or something for everybody). One way we can fix this is by saying something like or **the fixings for sundaes**.

Here we are at the end of this chapter. Before we finish up, let's take a look at one more dialogue. This dialogue contains all three items I've led you through, coordinating, subordinating, and correlative conjunctions. Let's see how many of them you can pick out—hopefully all of them! Write your answers in the order that you find them under the dialogue box. You won't find any blank lines to write on, just a blank space, so as not to give you any hint about how many conjunctions you'll find. And no cheating, please!

A: May I help you?

B: Oh, I hope so! No sooner had I entered your delightful shop than my eyes latched onto these two stunning dresses, but I can't decide which dress to purchase.

A: They'd both look fetching on you.

B: While I like this solid red one, the paisley has panache.

A: I see your point, although the red dress exudes authority, don't you think?

B: I do indeed, yet it also communicates passion in my opinion.

A: You can wear the red dress when you're in the mood for passion and you can wear it when you want to communicate authority. It will serve both purposes!

B: That's true. It will show not only how passionate I can be, but it will also show what an authority figure I can be. I'll take it!

A: But what about the paisley?

B: Panache is nice, but give me authority and passion any day of the week over panache!

A: Well, whether you take the solid red dress or the paisley dress, you'll look marvelous in either one.

Okay, here's the space where you should write the conjunctions you've identified and which kind of conjunction each one is.

And here are all the coordinating, subordinating, and correlative conjunctions in this dialogue:

No sooner… than	(correlative)
While	(subordinating)
although	(subordinating)
yet	(coordinating)
and	(coordinating)
not only… but also	(correlative)

but... and	(coordinating)
whether... or	(correlative)

Teaching Tips

12.1 Coordination

Write 15 sentences on a sheet of paper and give each student a copy. Each of the 15 sentences should have at least one FANBOY. Some of them should connect noun phrases, others verb phrases, others adjectives. Finally, some should connect independent clauses. Instruct the students to circle every FANBOY and underline the words that are connected by the FANBOY.

12.2 Counting Independent Clauses

Type up 20 sentences with a blank line in front of each sentence. Some sentences should be simple, but most should include coordination and/or subordination. Have the students label each sentence with the number of independent clauses.

12.3 Sentence Completion - Coordination

Divide your students into pairs. Give each pair a sheet with four simple sentences followed by blank lines. Have the pairs use four different FANBOYS to expand the original simple sentences into compound sentences. Have each pair of students trade papers with other pairs and compare their answers.

12.4 Sentence Completion – Subordination

Divide your students into pairs. Give each pair a sheet with six simple sentences followed by blank lines. Write nine subordinating conjunctions on the board. Have the pairs of students use six of the subordinating conjunctions to expand the original simple sentences into complex sentences. Have the pairs trade papers with other pairs of students and compare their answers.

12.5 Sentence Completion – Correlation

Divide your students into pairs. Write this chart on the board:

as . . . as . . .	not . . . but . . .
both . . . and . . .	whether . . . or . . .
either . . . or . . .	the more . . . the less . . .
Scarcely . . . when . . .	the more . . . the more . . .
No sooner . . . than. . .	not only . . . but also . . .
Hardly . . . when . . .	neither . . . nor . . .

Alternatively, you can give each pair a copy of the chart. You can give the students a theme to follow or just tell them to make sentences on any topic with the correlative conjunctions on the chart. Have the pairs of students trade papers with other pairs and compare their answers.

13

Indirect Speech

"He said that she said that I said that..."

One of the reasons that language teaching has always proven to be such a stimulating—and at times vexing—discipline is the never-ending array of points of contention among grammarians. One area of English teaching that has been traditionally troublesome deals with indirect speech, that is, **communicating what you or someone else has said or thought or is going to say or think.** In many cases, indirect speech is also known as **reported speech**, but I'll only use the term "indirect speech" in this chapter.

A certain degree of controversy exists over what's considered acceptable and unacceptable in this problematic area of English grammar. In this chapter I'll be exploring the more traditional forms that are commonly taught in ELT grammar books. I'll also be dealing with the conversational forms that seem to go against the rules, but which most people now consider to be just as acceptable. In addition, I'll be exploring certain grammatical patterns that aren't traditionally placed in the unit on indirect speech in most ELT grammar books even though they're definitely part of this topic. And later in this book (Chapter 20), I'll be discussing some changes that I've observed occurring with indirect speech.

Besides being troublesome for grammarians, indirect speech creates numerous headaches for teachers and their students. If you're wondering what makes this area of English such a problem, it's because changing direct into indirect speech, or vice versa, requires quite a number of transformations, and it's the complications resulting from these transformations that create all the hassles.

There's one final note I'd like to make before starting our investigation into how we go from

"Where can I buy a copy of this book?" he asked.

to

He asked me where he could buy a copy of that book.

Verbs like *say* and *ask*, which are commonly used in indirect speech, are referred to as **reporting verbs**, and in Appendix 4 you'll have a chance to take a deeper look at reporting verbs and what grammatical patterns go with them.

Lexical Transformations

Let's take a look at this dialogue to discover four transformations involved in going from direct to indirect speech:

> Hans: The lawn's a mess! Jost should help me rake the leaves up.
>
> Jost: What's Dad saying?
>
> Anna: **He says you should help him** rake all the leaves up because the lawn's a mess. (Minutes pass.)
>
> Hans: Well, is Jost going to help me or not?
>
> Anna: Jost, are you going to help your father out?
>
> Jost: Sure, in a minute. I want to hear the end of this album that my friend Julia's been talking about.
>
> Anna: Hans, **he says he wants to hear** the end of that album his friend Julia's been talking about. He'll be right out.

If we examine what the speakers say in this dialogue, we can find four transformations that have taken place. First, let's compare what Hans originally says to Anna and what Anna says when she relays the message to their son, Jost. Underline any changes that you see between the two statements:

> Hans: Jost (He) should help me rake all the leaves up.
> Anna: . . . you should help him rake all the leaves up . . .

The first transformation we can see is that there's been a change in the pronouns. If you underlined **Jost (He)**, **you**, **me**, and **him**, you're doing just fine. When Hans communicated his feelings, he said "**Jost (He)** should help **me**..." When Anna relayed that message, however, she had to change the two pronouns when talking directly to Jost about his father: "...**you** should help **him**..." Although many teachers new to ELT find this transformation to be very elemental and logical, seasoned teachers know how confusing this sort of transformation can be for students. It follows, then, that if the pronoun subjects are changed, the possessive adjectives like *my* and *your* and possessive pronouns like *mine* and *yours* will change, too. You'll see this change when you compare the following two phrases. Underline any change you notice:

> Jost: . . . this album that my friend Julia's been talking about . . .
> Anna: . . . that album that his friend Julia's been talking about . . .

You should have underlined **my** and **his** for this change. This is the second transformation we've noted for indirect speech.

The next transformation ties in with the first, when the subject changes. In this case we're dealing with verbs, which will change, too. In our first pair of example sentences, since the verb *help* is preceded by a modal auxiliary in the preceding phrases (*should*), there's no obvious change in the verb form between ". . . he should help . . ." and ". . . you should help." This change, our third transformation, is obvious in our next pair of phrases when ". . . I want . . . changes to . . . he wants . . ."

The fourth transformation takes place when we compare what Jost said and what Anna said. Underline any *new* difference you see between these two statements:

        Jost: . . . I want to hear the end of this album . . .
        Anna: . . . he wants to hear the end of that album . . .

This is a perfect time for us to discuss an interesting phenomenon of language called **deixis**, which deals with the nearness or remoteness of something to the speaker. To explain it simply, deixis has to do with our perception of what is "near" or "far" from us. At times, it can be literal, as when I say *this book* for a book that I have in my hand or *that book* for a book sitting on a table across the room. At other times, we can apply this concept of "near" and "far" to abstract things.

To continue with this point, we normally say "<u>That</u>'s too bad" because we're talking about a situation which we can separate ourselves from and *that* refers to the situation. Moreover, *That's too bad* has become a formulaic or pat sentence which we don't have other ways to express except to substitute *That's* with *It's*.

Another interesting way deixis can be noticed is in the response "That's true." When someone has made a statement that you agree with, you say "<u>That</u>'s true" because the other person said it, not you. In recent years, however, many people have started saying "This is true," and even though it isn't the standard response, people are probably using *this* instead of *that* to show even greater agreement with what the other person has said by bringing it "closer."

Getting back to identifying that fourth transformation in the conversation between Jost and Anna, if you underlined **this** and **that**, you're doing great. Because Jost was listening to an album on his phone, he referred to it as *this* CD; when Anna relayed what her son was saying to Hans, she said *that* album because she was distanced from the album. The change of *this* to *that* is another typical, but tricky, transformation that occurs with indirect speech. Such a transformation brought on by deixis is not confined only to *this/that* and *these/those*; we also find it common with words or phrases that deal with time, but I'll get to those transformations later on.

To recap what we've already discovered about indirect speech, we can state that **changes will occur with pronouns, with possessive adjectives and possessive pronouns, with verbs, and with words that deal with relative distance such as** *this/that*.

A Note about *Say*

One note I'd like to make before going on has to do with the verb *say*. When Anna relays what Hans has said about Jost and what Jost has replied, she uses the simple present *(he says)* instead of the simple past *(he said)* even though both speakers were finished talking before Anna relayed their messages. What do you think accounts for this use of the simple present which might not seem the appropriate form at first glance? Write down any thoughts you have on the following line:

....

It's so customary for native speakers to use the simple present when reporting what someone has just said that the reason for this use tends to get obscured. The answer is that it's similar to the use of the simple present called the narrative style (see Chapter 3). Even though it isn't truly the **narrative style**, Anna has chosen the simple present because she's relaying what someone has just said; in other words, she's doing so *immediately* after the other person has spoken. This immediate reporting is also evident when sportscasters use the simple present as the narrative style to bring the listeners as close as possible to the event that's happening:

He <u>gets</u> the ball! He <u>kicks</u> it past the goalie! He <u>scores</u>!

A Note about *Tell*

An interesting thing happens with the verb *tell* in one special use of indirect speech. Look over these two sentences and check the boxes for the statements you agree with:

1. They told me that you're doing a fine job.
    ☐ The speaker has heard this once.
    ☐ The speaker has heard this more than once.

2. They tell me that you're doing a fine job.
    ☐ The speaker has heard this once.
    ☐ The speaker has heard this more than once.

With the use of the **simple past** for the verb *tell* in **Sentence 1**, most native speakers would say that the speaker has heard this **only once**, but with the use of the **simple present** for that verb in **Sentence 2**, we have quite a different situation. In this case it can signify that what the speaker has heard has been said **more than once**, which neatly reflects that typical use of the simple present for events that happen repeatedly.

Other Reporting Verbs

I've now focused a bit on the reporting verbs *say* and *tell*, but as teachers, we need to keep in mind that there are lots of reporting verbs to choose from that may contain nuances which make them much more interesting than the trusty standbys *say* and *tell*. Let's have some fun trying this out.

Here are some sentences, each one containing a direct quotation. Think of a reporting verb other than *say* or *tell* to use in each sentence to create indirect speech. I've done the first one for you. Let's see if your sentences come close to or equal my own. Write your sentences on the lines under mine.

1. "You know, Pia, you should buy good running shoes if you want to go jogging."

    I advised Pia to buy a good pair of running shoes if she wanted to go jogging.

2. Sheila told me, "Remember to make an appointment with the chiropractor."

3. Claude said, "Marcel, you stole the cash I had in my desk drawer."
   Marcel said, "I didn't do it!"

4. "Hey, Cathy, would you and Phil like to go on a picnic with Tom and me?"
   "Thanks, Marge. We'd love to."

Here are the sentences in reported speech that I've come up with:

2. Sheila reminded me to make an appointment with the chiropractor.
3. Claude accused Marcel of stealing the cash he'd had in his desk drawer.
    Marcel (strongly) denied doing it.
4. Marge invited Cathy and Phil to go on a picnic with her and Tom.
    Cathy thanked Marge for inviting her and Phil (and said they'd love to go).

So how did you do? I hope you at least came close to what I thought of. As you can clearly see, using reporting verbs like *advise, remind, accuse, deny, invite,* and *thank* is much more interesting than just using *say* and *tell*. True, a number of these verbs force the use of more advanced grammatical patterns in the rest of each sentence, so you can introduce ones that your students can handle now and hold off on those that force more advanced grammar, or this might be an opportunity to teach that more advanced grammar and paraphrasing skills in meaningful context. That's up to you!

Before moving on, here's an important connection between some of the patterns presented in this chapter on indirect speech and the part of Chapter 12 that deals with subordination. I'm referring to the fact that indirect speech depends in many instances on **subordinate noun clauses**:

>He denied that he had done it.   She explained what she would do.

Backshifting

Let's move on now to other important transformations that are usually necessary for indirect speech. Read the following dialogue and note changes that occur from what the original statements are to what they become when reiterated. To help you out, I've copied the original sentences on the first, third, and fifth lines that follow the dialogue. You write the reiterated phrases on the second, fourth, and sixth lines and underline any changes you notice:

Anna: Jost, your father's still waiting for you to help him.

Jost: I'm going to help him in just a minute.

Anna: You said you were going to help him in just a minute ten minutes ago!

Jost: Okay! This album's almost over.

Anna: You said that album was almost over ten minutes ago, too! Do you remember what I told you just the other day?

Jost: Of course I do. You said, "If you want your allowance, young man, you'll have to earn it."

Anna: That's right. I told you if you wanted your allowance, you'd have to earn it. So take off those headphones and go earn it!

1a. I'm going to help him in just a minute.

1b. You said you ....

2a. This album's almost over.

2b. You said ....

3a. If you want your allowance, you'll have to earn it.

3b. I told you ....

We've now entered into the area of verbs and auxiliaries. Here are the three phrases written in indirect speech:

1b. You said you <u>were</u> going to help him in just a minute . . .
2b. You said that album <u>was</u> almost over ten minutes ago, too!
3b. I told you if you want<u>ed</u> your allowance, you<u>'d</u> have to earn it.

The new change we notice in the indirect forms of these sentences involves the tenses in the original statements:

$$\text{I'm} \longrightarrow \text{you were}$$
$$\text{this album's} \longrightarrow \text{that album was}$$
$$\text{you want} \longrightarrow \text{you wanted / you'll} \longrightarrow \text{you'd}$$

This phenomenon happens quite often. When reporting verbs are in the past, the verbs from the original statement are usually affected. Most grammarians call this **backshifting**. A general, traditional rule of thumb that we can use is that **if the reporting verb is in the past, most auxiliaries and all verbs that follow will take "one step" back into the past as well. If they're already in the past, they'll go back further into the past—to past perfect.**

Let's see if we can apply this traditional rule. What follows are phrases in indirect speech that can be put into the past. Rewrite the phrases in the past on the lines I've provided. I've done the first one for you as an example:

1. He says he is   *He said he was*
2. She admits she was   ....
3. I swear I'm going to   ....
4. We promise we will   ....
5. He denies he's been   ....
6. You claim you can   ....
7. They think they may   ....
8. He says he shall   ....
9. We admit we have to   ....
10. I tell you I must.   ....

Here are the phrases as they appear with the traditional transformations when the reporting verbs are in the past:

2. She admitted she**'d been**
3. I swore I **was** going to
4. We promised we **would**
5. He denied he**'d been**
6. You claimed you **could**

7. They thought they **might**
8. He said he **should**
9. We admitted we **had to**
10. I told you I **had to.**

There are three observations I should make at this point:

The first one is that Number 2 and Number 5 have become the same; both now have the verb in the past perfect. **When the simple past (*was*) moves "a step back" into the past, it goes into the past perfect; when the present perfect (*has been*) moves into the past, it also goes into the past perfect.**

The second observation I can make is that ***must*** has become ***had to*** for this past transformation, but only when it means **necessity**.

My third observation is quite interesting because it doesn't adhere to the rule about backshifting in this situation. With modal auxiliaries like *will*, *may*, *can*, and *shall* there's only one so-called step back into the past, and that's to say *would*, *might*, *could*, and *should*. That's why you can go from she says to she said to she had said, but you can only go from *can* to *could* when it comes to modal auxiliaries.

At this point, let's take a look at some more phrases we'll change from the present to the past. See what you can do with these:

1. He admits he could   *He admitted he could*
2. He admits he could have   _____
3. She says she would   _____
4. She says she would have   _____
5. I swear I should   _____
6. I swear I should have   _____
7. We think we ought to   _____
8. We think we ought to have   _____
9. They claim they might   _____
10. They claim they might have   _____
11. I tell you you'd better   _____
12. I'm sure it must be old.   _____

I'm sure you've noted that the only change you can make in each phrase is with the reporting verb by putting it into the past (***admitted***, ***said***, ***swore***, etc.). So, one last observation about these auxiliaries and backshifting is that **they don't change when they're put into indirect speech**. The reason is that they're past forms historically, so no changes are needed.

So that you'll have a clear picture of how the traditional rules for backshifting work, here's a chart that shows just what often happens when a direct statement is converted into indirect speech:

TENSE TRANSFORMATIONS		
Direct Speech → **Indirect Speech**		**Examples**
simple present → simple past		"I **live** here." → She said she **lived** there.
present progressive → past progressive		"I**'m** feeling fine." → He said he **was** feeling fine.
present perfect → past perfect		"We**'ve** been busy." → They said they**'d** been busy.
present perfect progressive → past perfect progressive		"She**'s** been working late." → I told you she**'d** been working late.
simple past → past perfect		"I **tried** to call you." → He said he**'d** tried to call me.
past progressive → past perfect progressive		"He **was** working too hard." → I told you he**'d been** working too hard.
past perfect → no transformation		"We **hadn't thought** of that." → I admitted we **hadn't thought** of that.
past perfect progressive → no transformation		"**He'd been telling** the truth." → I told you **he'd been telling** the truth.

And what about the auxiliaries? They, too, have formal rules to change them from direct to indirect speech. Here are two charts that show you those transformations. The first one deals with modal auxiliaries and the expression *had better* when they represent present or future time:

PRESENT/FUTURE AUXILIARIES		
Direct Speech → **Indirect Speech**		**Examples**
will → would		"I **will** (**'ll**) do it." → He said he **would** (**he'd**) do it.
would → no change		"I **wouldn't** do it." → You said you **wouldn't** do it.
can → could		"I **can** do it." → She said she **could** do it.
could → no change		"We **couldn't** do it." → They said they **couldn't** do it.
may → might		"I **may** do it." → I said I **might** do it.
might → no change		"I **might** not do it." → He said he **might** not do it.
should → no change		"I **should** do it." → He said he **should** do it.
ought to → no change		"I **ought to** do it." → She said she **ought to** do it.
must → had to		"I **must** do it." → She said she **had to** do it.
had better → no change		"I **had** (**'d**) better do it." → He said he **had** (**'d**) better do it.

The second chart deals with the modal perfects, which you'll recall are the modal auxiliaries in the past:

MODAL PERFECTS		
Direct Speech → **Indirect Speech**		**Examples**
would have → no change		"I **wouldn't have** done it." → He said he **wouldn't have** done it.
could have → no change		"I **could have** done it." → She thinks she **could have** done it.
may have → no change		"I **may have** done it." → I think I **may have** done it.
might have → no change		"I **might have** done it." → They think I **might have** done it.
should have → no change		"I **should have** done it." → You think I **should have** done it.
ought to have → no change		I **ought to have** done it." → He says I **ought to have** done it.
must have → no change		"I **must have** done it." → You told me you **must have** done it.

Now I have to pose another question: Can the verb *is* remain unchanged in the phrase "He told me he is . . ." or is it necessary to change it to "He told me he was . . ."? Before answering this question, let's examine some phrases that don't adhere to the traditional transformations. Decide if they're acceptable or unacceptable and check the appropriate box:

1. He told me he is . . .   ☐ acceptable   ☐ unacceptable
2. I said she's been . . .   ☐ acceptable   ☐ unacceptable
3. They admitted they'll be . . .   ☐ acceptable   ☐ unacceptable
4. She wrote she's going to . . .   ☐ acceptable   ☐ unacceptable
5. You denied you were . . .   ☐ acceptable   ☐ unacceptable
6. He realized he must . . .   ☐ acceptable   ☐ unacceptable

Most native speakers would say that **all six phrases are acceptable**. Well, if these six are acceptable, what does that say about all those transformations we previously made, and what does it say about those two charts which list the indirect speech transformations?

Time is a relative concept; what a short span of time is for you can seem like an eternity to someone else. This holds true for what I call the **time continuum**. As I write these words on this page, it's the present for me; when you read these words, it will be my future but your present. The same can be demonstrated for the past: The time that I'm working on this page is your past but my present. In short, time really is a constantly moving, relative dimension, and this fact of perception can impact heavily on how we create a sentence in indirect speech.

Let's take another look at the phrase "He said he'd been" and discuss some other forms we can come up with. "He <u>said</u> he'<u>d been</u>" clearly shows us two different time periods in the past, the simple past (said) and the past perfect (had been), so at the time he said this, he was referring to something at a time further in his past."He <u>said</u> he <u>was</u>" is another possibility, though. When he made this statement, he was talking about the same period of time he was in or possibly about some general observation. Both phrases, however, do refer to some concept of the past.

What about if the period discussed is *not* in the past even though the statement was made in the past? That's when we get an indirect sentence like "He <u>said</u> he <u>is</u>." **This use of the present shows us that the situation is still true for both the person who made the statement and for the listener or reader. It can also be used for universal truths or facts that are timeless** (see Chapter 3):

Isaac Newton show<u>ed</u> compelling evidence that gravity <u>is</u> a real force.

True, this statement can also be kept completely in the past so that we can say "Isaac Newton show<u>ed</u> compelling evidence that gravity <u>was</u> a real force," but it's perfectly acceptable to use the simple present in the part of the sentence about gravity since this is a universal, timeless fact.

And what about the future? As I've already demonstrated to you, one person's future will eventually end up being another person's past: "She <u>said</u> she <u>would</u> be" signifies that her future falls into what we now consider the past, but "She <u>said</u> she <u>will</u> be" shows that it's just as much our future as it is hers.

The best way to make these ideas clearer is to add some extra context to my phrases, so let's see how they seem to you with that extra context:

1. A week ago, Vitus <u>said</u> he'<u>d been</u> in the hospital for six months last year.
2. At the time he was hospitalized, the doctors <u>said</u> he <u>was</u> in need of surgery on both legs.
3. During our talk last week, Vitus <u>said</u> he'<u>s</u> still in physical therapy.
4. When Vitus started his physical rehabilitation program, he <u>said</u> he'<u>d be</u> a difficult patient for his therapist.
5. During our conversation the other day, Vitus <u>said</u> he'<u>ll be</u> in need of a rehab program for a long time to come.

In the most rigid approach at transforming these statements into indirect speech, Number 3 becomes ". . .Vitus <u>said</u> he <u>was</u> still in physical therapy" and Number 5 becomes ". . . Vitus <u>said</u> he'<u>d be</u> in need of a rehab program for a long time to come." These are traditional, clear-cut transformations, and no one can seriously dispute the fact that they're perfectly grammatical. The point is, however, that a great number of native speakers feel more comfortable with Numbers 3 and 5 as they appear on the previous page—so much so that we have to accept them as viable alternatives as long as the time reference is clear and hasn't been compromised. The reason that so many people feel more comfortable with Numbers 3 and 5 brought into the present and the future respectively is that the sentences relate better to my time, showing that I'm sharing the same time continuum with Vitus.

But what about the following two sentences?

1. Cleopatra said she loves Marc Antony.   ☐ acceptable   ☐ unacceptable
2. Cleopatra admitted she always will.   ☐ acceptable   ☐ unacceptable

The answer to these two sentences is that they're both **unacceptable**, and we're sure you agree. But why is it so easy in these two cases to say firmly that they're unacceptable when we had alternatives for the sentences we covered about Vitus? Think of an answer to this question and write your thoughts on the following line:

....

The reason these two sentences are unacceptable is that the subject of both sentences is a long-dead historical figure, and this totally eliminates any chance of something about Cleopatra being in *our* present or *our* future. Vitus, on the other hand, being someone who's still very much alive, is a person whose past can be our past, whose present can be our present, and whose future can be our future. Because of this important difference between Cleopatra and Vitus, we have more alternatives when creating indirect statements about Vitus than we do about Cleopatra.

Heads Up!

It's safe to say that most—if not all—languages have forms of indirect speech. The problem for teachers, however, is that it's not customary in many languages to use indirect speech as much as we do in English. Direct reporting of what has been said is quite common in many other languages and presented to the listener almost like lines from a script. This does occur in English, too:

> A: So he says, "I don't feel like going."
> B: And what did you say to that?
> A: Stay home and sulk if you want to!

If you find your students having trouble with all the transformations common to indirect speech (changes in pronouns, determiners, verb forms, etc.), it may simply be that they're not used to this style of recounting what someone said.

Before leaving this topic, let's take a quick look back at the phrase "We realiz<u>ed</u> we <u>must</u>" and give it some more context just as we did to those other phrases about Vitus. After you read my expanded sentence, check off the boxes that voice your opinions:

When I told him how unhappy we were with his procrastinating, he realized he must¹ complete the stock analysis reports by the end of the month or suffer the consequences and that he must² get on the ball and stop putting things off.

1. *Must¹* refers to general time.
   ☐ agree   ☐ disagree   ☐ don't know
2. *Must²* deals with a general observation, not a specific point in time.
   ☐ agree   ☐ disagree   ☐ don't know
3. I tend to think that those reports are one of his ongoing duties.
   ☐ agree   ☐ disagree   ☐ don't know

The answer to **Sentence 1 is disagree**. In this case, *must¹* is dealing only with the past because the sentence says "by the end of the month," so the time is framed in the past. *Must²* can, in fact, refer to a timeless idea and a general observation just as the simple present can, so the box to check for **Sentence 2** is **agree**. As for the last statement, because *must* reflects the simple present, which can mean routine or repeated activity, I tend to feel that those stock analysis reports are an ongoing responsibility of his, so for **Sentence 3** I'd check **agree**.

We know that we can also say "He realized he had to," so our sentence can read:

When I told him how unhappy we were with his procrastinating, he realized he had to complete the stock analysis reports by the end of the month or suffer the consequences.

What, then, is the difference? See if you can figure out a different interpretation for this sentence and check off the boxes that follow just as you did before:

1. *Had to* refers mainly to that situation in the past.
   ☐ agree   ☐ disagree   ☐ don't know
2. *Had to* refers to a general observation in this sentence.
   ☐ agree   ☐ disagree   ☐ don't know
3. I tend to think that those reports are one of his ongoing duties.
   ☐ agree   ☐ disagree   ☐ don't know

Because *had to* is in the past, I can assume that it refers mainly to that specific situation at that specific time, so I'd check **agree** for **Sentence 1**. In the strictest sense of backshifting for indirect speech, I can say it's possible that *had to* refers to a general observation, but most native speakers would tend to feel it doesn't since it *is* in the past. For that reason, I'd check **disagree** for **Sentence 2**. Finally, because *had to* is in the past, I tend to think that those reports were a one-time responsibility, or at least not an ongoing one, so I'd check **disagree** for **Sentence 3**.

 The point that I want to stress is that, although there are definite rules for backshifting, they tend to be adhered to much more in formal spoken and written English than in conversational English. There are many exceptions to those rules (if you want to think of them as exceptions), and they can easily be defended depending on where the person making the indirect statement is on the time continuum in relation to the person that he/she is referring to.

Time and Space

If you remember, near the start of this chapter I touched on the phenomenon known as deixis and showed how it influenced the transformation I made from *this* to *that*. Now let's get back to some other ways that deixis affects indirect speech. Look at the following sentences written in direct speech. You'll notice that I've rewritten them into indirect speech and underlined the part of each sentence that needs to be changed. I've inserted blanks where one word or more than one word should go to complete the transitions, and I'm going to leave it to you to decide what should go in those blanks. Write your answers on the lines:

1. "I've lived here for five years," Dot told me.
   When I visited Dot at her home the other day, she told me that she'd lived .... for five years.

2. While I was visiting Angie, she said, "It's 4:30 now, so it's time for me to go to work."
   Angie told me it was 4:30 .... and time for her to go to work.

3. At the end of our chess match last Thursday, Jules said, "I'll meet you tomorrow at 7:30 for a rematch."
   Jules told me he'd meet me .... at 7:30 for a rematch.

4. "The mail wasn't delivered yesterday," Ian said the other day.
   The other day, Ian said that the mail hadn't been delivered ....

5. Sanjay said yesterday,"We tried that new Vietnamese restaurant last night."
   Yesterday Sanjay told us that he and his wife, Gita, had tried that new Vietnamese restaurant ....

6. "If you come to my office, I'll have the report ready for you," David said when I asked him about it last week.
   Last week, David said if I .... to his office, he'd have the report ready for me.

7. "Blossom, did you take the desserts and coffees to table 12?" "Yes, I did."
   "That's odd. The customers at table 12 told me you'd forgotten to .... the desserts with their coffees."

Without any delay, let's get to the answers:
1. here/there
2. then
3. the next/following day
4. the day before
   the previous day
5. the night before
   the previous night
6. went/came
7. bring

The only answer we need to comment on is Number 1. Why can we leave *here* unchanged or change it to *there*? Can you think of two different things that *here* can refer to in the original quote which would make you decide to leave *here* alone or change it to *there*?

....

When Dot said, "I've lived here for five years," we don't really know without more context whether she means "in this house/apartment" or if she means "in this city/town/country." If Dot means her home, we should change *here* to *there* because we're somewhere else now. However, if she means "this city/town/country" and we're in one of those places, we can leave *here* unchanged since the reference is the same for us as it was for her at the time she made the statement.

The seven examples you've just worked on give you a good idea of how complicated these transformations are for students. Not only do we have the twelve changes I've focused on for this exercise, but we also have the typical changes with the pronouns, possessives, verbs, and auxiliaries that I've already discussed—and we're not done yet!

Infinitives

Let's look at the following dialogue to continue our exploration of indirect speech:

Her: **We have to make more banners** for the Independence Day parade.

Me: Okay. Do we have enough cardboard, wood, and marking pens to make them?

Her: No, as a matter of fact, but Jeremy has all that stuff. **Stop off at his place after work and pick it all up**.

Me: Fine.

Her: Oh, and **could you make sure that he and all of his friends know what time we're supposed to meet at City Hall**?

Me: Sure.

Her: By the way, **don't forget to bring the snacks and drinks for all the hungry banner makers or they may strike**!

Did you notice a difference as to who the speakers are in this dialogue? No Person A and no Person B this time! Let's pretend that one of the speakers is you and the other one is a friend of yours. You'll also notice that certain phrases have been written in bold because we're going to focus our attention on them.

Let's also pretend that you're being questioned about this conversation you had with your friend. Based on what was said during the conversation, answer the following questions that the questioner (Q) is about to put to you.

By the way, don't use *that* or *if* when you begin filling in the blanks for your second and third replies:

Q: At the start of the conversation, what did your friend tell you?
Me: She told me that ....

Q: So what did she say when she realized you didn't have the materials to make more banners?
Me: She asked me ....

Q: What else?
Me: She told me ....

Q: Is that it?
Me: Before I left, she warned me ....

Here's what I'd put in those blanks. Compare my completions to yours:

- She told me that **we had** to make more banners for the Independence Day parade.
- She asked me **to stop off** at Jeremy's place after work to pick up the stuff we'd need to make the signs.
- She asked me **to make sure** that Jeremy and all of his friends knew what time we were supposed to meet at City Hall.
- . . . she warned me **not to forget** to bring the snacks and drinks.

I'm sure that your completions match mine pretty closely. The most important parts are the ones in bold, and I hope that yours match these exactly. The first one reflects the kind of transformation I've already discussed concerning the backshifting of the semi-modal *have to*, which just as easily could have been *must* in the direct speech sentence. There's a marked difference, however, in the grammar I've used for the other three completions.

In these three cases, I've used infinitive forms (*to stop off/ to make sure/ not to forget*) after *tell*, *ask*, and *advise*, and this infinitive use has led me into a different way of creating indirect speech. There are some reporting verbs which can cause the use of a special grammatical pattern that goes as follows:

	reporting verb +	indirect object +	infinitive verb
She	told	me	to stop off
She	asked	me	to make sure
She	warned	me	*not to forget

 **Heads Up!**

Notice I have an asterisk before *not to forget*. This is to call your attention to the fact that the grammar has changed. It used to be that the only acceptable construction was to place the negative *not* before the infinitive so that you wouldn't have a so-called "split infinitive." This has changed, and now it's considered acceptable to place *not* between *to* and the base verb.

Be aware that most students get confused over how to create the negative infinitive form. It's very common for students to create forms such as *to don't say*. Make sure you point out that the negative word *not* is used, not *don't*.

I'd like you to note that imperative forms quite often take on the pattern with the infinitive verb when they're transformed into indirect speech. In the last dialogue, the person you were talking to used three imperative forms:

<u>Stop off</u> at his place and <u>pick</u> it all <u>up</u>.
. . . <u>make sure</u> he and all his friends know what time . . .
. . . <u>don't forget</u> to bring the snacks and drinks . . .

When we put these ideas into indirect speech, we used the infinitive verbs:

She told me <u>to stop off</u> and <u>(to) pick</u> it all <u>up</u>.
She asked me <u>to make sure</u> he and his friends knew what time . . .
She warned me <u>not to forget</u> to bring the snacks and drinks . . .

Even though we've now seen that some verbs can trigger a pattern with an infinitive verb, there's another pattern that we can use after such verbs to create indirect speech statements. Can you think of an alternative way to communicate the following ideas?

1. She's convinced me to see a doctor.
   She's convinced me (that) _____
2. They told us not to report the accident.
   They said (that) _____

The other way that we can create indirect speech phrases after verbs like *convince*, *tell*, and *say* is by using the modal auxiliaries **should** or **ought to** so that we end up with the following indirect statements:

1. She's convinced me (that) <u>I should/ought to see a doctor</u>.
2. They said (that) <u>we shouldn't/ought not to report the accident</u>.

Before leaving this section on infinitives, I want to mention some verbs that give us a choice in the following pattern; they can be directly followed by an infinitive verb with or without an indirect object:

> She asked (me) to be excused.
> The kids are begging (us) to go to the circus.
> I've promised (them) to help you.

Direct to Indirect Questions

For the last major area that we need to investigate in indirect speech, let's look at the following dialogue. As you read it, think about what new changes, additions, and transformations you can pick out, and then see if you can supply the information I ask you for after you've read the dialogue:

> A: Good morning, Jason. You're late again, aren't you?
>
> B: Good morning, Wendy—and yes, I am. You haven't seen the boss yet this morning, have you?
>
> A: As a matter of fact, just a little while ago he asked me **if I'd seen you this morning.**
>
> B: Oh, great! He warned me about being late again. Well, why did he ask you that?
>
> A: I think he wanted to know **whether you had the tax files in order**.
>
> B: The tax files? Oh, no! I forgot all about them!
>
> A: He even asked me **where you keep them**, but I didn't know.
>
> B: Why do I get the feeling that I should start checking out online job hiring sites?
>
> A: Hmm. You don't have to ask me **why you get the feeling**. I think we both know!

You'll notice that I put some key phrases in the dialogue in bold print. Here's what I'd like you to do:

> a. Reconstruct each phrase in bold print as you think it would appear exactly as the person asked it.
> b. List any lexical addition or deletion you find.
> c. List any new transformation you find in each phrase (a transformation that I haven't discussed already).

I've done all of Number 1 for you to show you what I mean.

1. a. *"Have you seen . . . / "Did you see Jason this morning?"*
   b. *"If" has been added.*
   c. *Word order inverted (in addition to changed pronouns and verb forms).*

2. a. ....
   b. ....
   c. ....
3. a. ....
   b. ....
   c. ....
4. a. ....
   b. ....
   c. ....

If you've found this activity challenging, you'll develop a lot more compassion for your students who have to tackle all of these additions and transformations in their new language! Well, here are the answers as I see them.

2. a. **"Does he have the tax files in order?"**
   b. ***Whether*** **has been added and question word** ***Does*** **has been dropped.**
   c. **Question word order has been changed into statement word order.**
3. a. **"Where does he keep them?"**
   b. **Question word** ***Does*** **has been dropped.**
   c. **Question word order has been changed into statement word order.**
4. a. **"Why do I get the feeling ...?"**
   b. **Question word** ***do*** **has been dropped.**
   c. **Question word order has been changed into statement word order.**

The first two questions (Have you seen Jason this morning?/Does he have the tax files in order?) belong to a certain type of question. Do you remember what we call it?

☐ yes/no question   ☐ *wh-* question

The next two questions (Where does he keep them?/Why do I get the feeling . . . ?) belong to another type of question. Can you identify what type of question those are?

☐ yes/no question   ☐ *wh-* question

Those **first two** are **yes/no questions** and the **other two** are ***wh-* questions**, also known as **information questions** (see Chapter 1).

What we now need to consider is what difference and what similarity exist between the way the yes/no questions are transformed into indirect speech and the way the *wh-* questions are transformed. What major difference and similarity do you see? Let's take a second look at two items from our dialogue to work this problem out:

Yes/No Question: The boss said, "Have you seen Jason today?"
　　　　　　　　　The boss asked me if I'd seen you today.

Wh- Question:　　The boss said, "Where does he keep the tax files?"
　　　　　　　　　The boss asked me where you keep the tax files.

Think about what difference and similarity you see between the indirect sentences based on these two question types and then write your observations on the following lines:

Difference: ....

....

Similarity: ....

....

Let's first discuss the major difference between transforming the two types of questions into indirect speech. When we deal with a yes/no question, we have to add either *if,* **whether**, or **whether or not** before the transformed question phrase. We can even add **whether** before the question phrase and place **or not** at the end of the sentence:

"Have you seen Jason this morning?"
The boss asked me if I'd seen you this morning.
The boss asked me whether I'd seen you this morning.
The boss asked me whether or not I'd seen you this morning.
The boss asked me whether I'd seen you this morning or not.

And likewise:

"Does he have the tax files in order?"
The boss asked me if you had the tax files in order.
The boss asked me whether you had the tax files in order.
The boss asked me whether or not you had the tax files in order.
The boss asked me whether you had the tax files in order or not.

However, when we deal with an information question (*wh-* question), we don't add words like *whether* or *if* when we transform the question into indirect speech. This is because the phrases *if, whether,* and *whether or not* show us that the questioner really has no idea what the answer will be; it could just as easily be *no* as *yes*. In other words, there's a fifty-fifty chance as to what the initial reply will be and the phrases I've added reflect that situation. This doesn't hold true for *wh-* questions, which seek information of a different nature.

By the way, the most common reporting verbs that can cause the addition of *if, whether, whether or not, or whether . . . or not* are **ask** and **wonder**.

Now what about the transformational similarity between the two types of questions when they end up in indirect speech? What we see is that both question forms are normally changed into statement forms by dropping the auxiliary *do/does/did* when it's used to form a question and by changing the word order from a question to a statement:

Have you seen . . . ?	→	. . . I had seen . . .
Does he have . . . ?	→	. . . you had . . .
Where does he keep . . . ?	→	. . . where you keep . . .
Why do I get the feeling . . . ?	→	. . . why you get the feeling . . .

So why do we tend to make this complex change from question to statement form? It's really quite understandable: **The speaker is <u>telling</u> you what she or someone else said, not asking you, so keeping question auxiliary words or question word order would just not be appropriate.**

Exclamations

Shirley: How cute!

Judy: Why, thank you.

Shirley: What a beautiful baby you have!

Judy: You're very kind.

Shirley: Not at all. Have you ever thought of putting her in television commercials?

Judy: What a great idea! I'll give it some thought.

In this dialogue, we've got three sentences that are considered exclamations. I've repeated them below so that you can work with them. Think about how you'd explain what these two people have said by using indirect speech. Then write your versions on the lines I've provided. Notice that I've given you two lines for each direct exclamation— see if you can come up with two versions. I've started you off on Number 1:

1. How cute!

   Shirley told Judy ....

   Shirley said (that) ....

2. What a beautiful baby you have!

   ....

   ....

3. What a great idea!

....
....

Here are the versions I've come up with. Compare yours to mine and let's see how close we all are:

1. Shirley told Judy how cute her baby is/was.
   Shirley said (that) Judy's baby is/was cute.
2. Shirley said (that) Judy has/-'s got/had a beautiful baby.
   Shirley told Judy what a beautiful baby she has/-'s got/had.
3. Judy told Shirley (that) it/that was a great idea.
   Judy said what a great idea it/that was.

Just to make sure we've got this nailed down, how would you interpret this next exclamation in indirect speech? Again, think of two possible ways to talk about this emergency situation:

....
....

We can interpret this exclamation two ways: **He shouted that there was a fire./He yelled that the place was on fire.**

 Indirect Speech in a Nutshell

Changes occur with the following elements:

- **pronouns:**
  "I'll see you later, guys."
  Fouad says (that) he'll see us later.

- **possessive adjectives and pronouns:**
  "It's my book, not yours!"
  Kim says (that) it's her book, not mine.

- **verbs (tenses/aspects):**
  "He isn't coming in."
  She told us (that) he wasn't coming in.

- **deixis:**
  "<u>This</u> child of mine is a genius!"
  He says (that) <u>that</u> child of his is a genius.
  "We'll see you <u>here</u> later."
  They said (that) they'd see us <u>there</u> later.

- **auxiliaries:**
  "My company <u>can't</u> finish the project on schedule."
  She admitted (that) her company <u>couldn't</u> finish the project on schedule.

- **time words and time phrases:**
  "I'll see you <u>tomorrow</u> evening."
  He said (that) he'd see us <u>the following</u> evening.

- **the use of the infinitive verb (to report imperatives):**
  "Please fax the contracts to St. Petersburg."
  The boss told me <u>to fax</u> the contracts to St. Petersburg.

- **additions (*if/whether/whether or not/whether...or not*):**
  "Are you planning to visit her soon?"
  He asked us <u>if</u> we were planning to visit her soon.
  He asked us <u>whether</u> we were planning to visit her soon.
  He asked us <u>whether or not</u> we were planning to visit her soon.
  He asked us <u>whether</u> we were planning to visit her soon <u>or not</u>.

- **deletion of *do/does/did* in questions:**
  "Why <u>does</u> he hold down two jobs?"
  She wonders why he holds down two jobs.

- **word order changes (from question to statement order):**
  "<u>Have they</u> handed in their reports?"
  He's asking if <u>they've</u> handed in their reports.

- **exclamations:**
  "Quick! <u>Help</u> me, Jodi!"
  He shouted to Jodi that he needed help. / He shouted for Jodi to help him.

Well, we've finally made it through all the complications of indirect speech. Before bringing this chapter to a close, though, I'd like to make one last note about reporting verbs and the grammatical patterns that follow them.

Believe it or not, there are fourteen patterns that can follow these verbs, and because this can be overwhelming, I'm going to present this deeper look in Appendix 4. Use that section as a reference whenever the need arises.

Teaching Tips

13.1 *Transforming Sample Sentences*

The most common way to practice the changes that take place when direct speech is transformed into indirect speech is to give students sentences to "transform." Make sure you include a wide variety of verb forms, pronouns, and adverbs that necessitate changes in the sentences you give your students.

13.2 *"Don't Do What I Say..."*

Find things that are good for providing directions (recipes, road maps, road signs, obstacle courses, etc.). Ask the students to prepare directions and then have individual students give directions to you. Follow some of the directions, but *don't* follow all of them. When students call your attention to your mistakes or exclusions, they should use indirect speech. For example, "No, Mamata said that you were to turn right, not left."/"Didn't Iris tell you to put in two teaspoons of sugar, not one?" etc.

13.3 *Telephone*

This is the traditional "Telephone Game." It requires basically no preparation and needs only quiet in the classroom. Before class, prepare a short message containing an example of direct speech. One student whispers this sentence to the student to the right using appropriate indirect speech. Let your students know that they're permitted to hear the details only *once*, and only then, through whispers. That student whispers what she "thinks" she's heard to the person next to her. *He* whispers what he thinks he's heard to the person on his right. *She* whispers the sentence... This continues until all the students have passed the message on. At the end of the telephone conversation chain, the final student reports out loud what's been passed on to him or her. Because it's rare to have the message reach the end of the class unadulterated, the person who started the conversation can tell the class what her or she initially said. Backtrack on the chain to find out where and how the message has gone astray.

13.4 *Giving Directions and Instructions*

Prepare several barebones instructions before class (how to repair a dripping faucet, how to steam mussels, how to get to a particular place, etc.). Give one of your students one of the instruction sheets and have her go out of the class, staying right by the door. She'll explain the instructions she has to a second student who's been chosen to stand just inside the door and relay the information his classmate has given. The classmates left inside will write down the instructions as they've been relayed. Make sure that the student relaying the instructions uses a wide variety of indirect speech. Repeat the activity several times so more than just a couple of students get a chance to explain their instructions.

13.5 *Interviews*

Have each student write a note to a classmate next to, behind, or in front of them. Questions and personal comments work very well ("Where do you live?"/"Who's your favorite actor?"/"You speak English very well," etc.) Let the students pass the messages to their classmates and have them respond in any appropriate manner to the questions or comments. Ask several volunteers to tell the class what messages or questions they've received. ("Paolo asked me where I lived."/"Nana asked me who my favorite actor is."/"I'm glad that Telly said that I spoke English very well," etc.) Collect the comments, check them, and return them during the next class. Read aloud any interesting ones that you've come across.

13.6 *Relating Stories*

Divide the students into groups of three: a "storyteller," a "secretary," and a "reporter." The storyteller's job is to relate an interesting experience to the secretary and the reporter. The secretary listens carefully and takes notes. When the storyteller is finished relating the experience, the secretary repeats it. Notes can be used to help remember the specifics. The reporter corrects any faulty details and adds omissions. Rotate roles twice and repeat the activity. This way, each student will be storyteller, secretary, and reporter.

13.7 *Discussing Comic Strips*

Collect a wide variety of comic strips. Divide the class into small groups. Make sure that you've got enough strips for each group of students to have a couple of them and that the strips contain a wide variety of speech patterns (statements, questions, commands, etc.). Hand out the comic strips and tell the students to recount what the characters are saying. Then write up a summary of their strips using indirect speech. Let the students share their summaries with their classmates.

13.8 *What Does This Picture Say?*

Select several pictures from your Picture File, ones with people or animals in them. Ask your students to tell you what's being said, asked, discussed, reported, denied, etc. by those in the pictures. This is what you might hear:"The cow told the farmer that the grass was a little dry for her taste."/"The farmer explained that the grass was dry because it hadn't rained in a long time."/"Her calf said that she preferred clover," etc.

13.9 *Back-to-Back... What Did You Say?*

Select a picture from your Picture File (see Appendix 1) for every two or three students, making sure the pictures don't have too many or too few details. Separate the students into groups of two or three and ask them to sit back-to-back. Give one of the students a picture. The student who has the picture is the "art expert," the other(s), the "artist(s)." The job of the art expert is to describe the picture to the artists, who'll reconstruct the picture as faithfully as possible without being able to see it. The art expert isn't permitted to show the picture to the artists until their drawings are complete. Stress that accuracy is the goal of the drawing, not quality. Encourage the use of indirect speech as the artists ask for clarification and the experts restate their directions. For example, one of the "artists" says, "Did you say that there's an old man leaning against the lamppost?"

13.10 *Eavesdropping*

Divide the class into an even number of groups of two or three so that two groups ("talkers" and "eavesdroppers") can work together. The talkers have a conversation about anything they want; let them talk for two or three minutes. The eavesdroppers listen intently to the talkers. When all the groups of talkers have finished, rearrange the groups, making sure that you've paired different pairs of talkers and eavesdroppers. Ask the eavesdroppers to tell the members of this new group of talkers what they overheard. Switch talkers and eavesdroppers and repeat the activity a couple of times, letting each group be talkers and eavesdroppers at least once. Wander around the class to provide assistance with accurate eavesdropping.

13.11 *Interpreting Letters*

Divide the class into groups of two or three and ask them to write a love letter, letter of complaint, business letter, etc. to an imaginary person or company. Have them include as many details as possible in their letters. Have each group exchange its completed letter with another group of students and ask one of the members of each group to "interpret" their letter aloud... in indirect speech. Let the groups exchange letters several times so each member of the group has a chance to "interpret" at least one letter.

13.12 *Application Forms*

Bring in enough application forms (any simple application form will do) for all the members of your class to have one of their own. Distribute them to your students and have them fill the forms out *except for the blank where their names go!* Collect the forms and redistribute them. Have the students go around the room trying to find out who completed the form they've been given. Encourage the use of indirect speech as the students circulate around the room. Don't let students show the application forms to their classmates; they need to ask questions to find out who wrote the application. For example: "Who claims to be 43 years old?"/"Who says that he lives on Beacon Street?" etc. At the end of the activity, collect all the application forms so that they can be used for *Tip 13.16.*

13.13 *Who Said That?*

Have students brainstorm quotes that are famous or quotes that have been made by people around them. They can even be ones linked to people they know of. Here are some examples:

"Let them eat cake!"—Marie Antoinette
"I have a dream."—Martin Luther King, Jr.

"Ask not what your country can do for you, but what you can do for your country."—John F. Kennedy
"I came, I saw, I conquered."—Julius Caesar
"I think; therefore, I am."—Descartes
"That's one small step for man, one giant step for mankind."—Neil Armstrong
"Workers of the world, unite!"—Karl Marx
"Grandma, what big teeth you have!"—The Wolf in "Little Red Riding Hood"
"Drink your milk!"—your mother

Put the quotes on the board (you or your students can do it) or write them out on small slips of paper, but don't identify who said them. Assign several quotes to small groups of students and have them write questions about the quotes: "Can you remember who said he thought, therefore, he was?" etc. Have students from the various groups ask their classmates to answer their questions and reconstruct their group's quotes.

13.14 *Enrolling in a New School*

Divide the class into two groups, "school principals" ("head masters") and the "parents of a potential student" at the principal's ("head master's") school. If your class is too large for the two halves to work together comfortably, divide the groups further into smaller groups of principals and parents. Tell the parents that you understand they're thinking about enrolling their child in this school and that they need to get information about the teachers, curriculum, students, etc. in order to decide if this is the right school for their child. How do they get this information? They need to think up questions to ask the principal or head master. Typical questions can be: "We need to know when school begins and gets out."/"How much do books cost?"/"What immunizations does our child need?" etc.

While the parents are thinking up questions, the principals will brainstorm information that they should give to all potential parents. Principals might say: "We should tell them what class their child will be in, how much the tuition is, what field trips we're planning," etc. Give the parents 10 to 15 minutes to come up with their questions and the principals the same amount of time to come up with their information. Then pair two or three parents and two or three principals together. Have them ask and answer the questions, writing down the information they get. Be sure students use appropriate indirect speech for clarifications when needed. Bring the class back together and discuss the questions and information that they've heard. Let them decide who they think the best parents and the best principals are.

Variation: Have your students brainstorm situations in which someone needs to know something. ("What do doctors need to know about their patients?"/"What should drivers know before they get a driver's license?"/"What do immigrants need to know about moving to another country?" etc.) After a number of situations have been thought up, ask students to brainstorm responses to the topics raised. Encourage the use of indirect questions and statements. For example, "Did Anwar ask you if you have any idea what doctors need to know about their patients?"

13.15 *Relaying Instructions*

Before class create situations in which one person relays instructions or information to another (a woman is under the sink trying to fix a leak; her husband is on the phone relaying directions from a plumber/a man is trying to change a baby's diaper (nappy); his friend is on the phone to his wife, who's giving instructions/a child is trying to figure out the rules to a game; a friend is talking to someone outside who knows how to play the game/a nurse in a hospital is interviewing someone who's brought an amnesia victim into the hospital/a witness at a trial is giving testimony; the judge can't hear, so the court stenographer repeats what the witness is saying, etc.). Make copies of the situations and distribute them to your students, who are divided into groups of three. Have them prepare role plays for the situations.

13.16 *Amnesia*

Use the application forms that your students previously completed (see *Tip 13.12*) and hand them out, making sure that you don't give a form to its real owner. Pair up the students; one student will be an amnesia victim, the other, someone who knows the victim. The amnesia victims ask their partners questions to help them reconstruct their pasts. The partners respond with information from the application forms that they have. Here's an example of how this should be done:

Amnesia Victim: "Do you know if I have brothers and sisters?"
Informer: "Yes, I do. The form says that you're an only child."

13.17 *Repeating Dialogues*

For those of you who are acquainted with the listening section of the TOEFL, prepare enough TOEFL-like dialogues before class so that each group of students (who are divided into groups of three) have at least one dialogue. The students will memorize their dialogues and present them to the entire class. Have students from other groups repeat the information they've heard, using indirect speech.

13.18 *Campaign Speeches*

It's election time. Divide the class into groups of two or three and have them create campaign speeches for someone running for senator, premier, president, etc. Be sure the candidates make lots of campaign promises. When the speeches are complete, have the students of each group divide their speech into halves or thirds with each member of the group giving their half or third of the speech in front of another group. Tell the students who'll be listening to the speeches that they need to take notes. After all the groups have given their speeches and notes have been reviewed and refined, hold an election to see who will become the next prime minister or whatever. In addition, tell the students to write up a news report of the winning speech for homework. Make it clear to the students that they are to use indirect speech for this homework assignment.

14

Two- and Three-Word Verbs

"Read it over, think about it, and get back to me."

Two-Word Verbs

One of the characteristic features of Germanic languages—and English is one of them—is the existence of and great dependence on what are commonly referred to as two-word verbs, phrasal verbs, or idiomatic verbs. **What is a two-word verb? It's a verb that has a very special relationship with a following preposition-like word. (I'll call it just a preposition because that's what it looks like.)** I have to tell you, though, that while I'll begin the chapter with two-word verbs, I won't end with them. In the first part of the chapter we'll be exploring two-word verbs, but later on we'll be venturing into the realm of three-word verbs.

An Overview

Let's talk a little about the nature of two-word verbs. The first thing to note is that two-word verbs share all of the common features we find in one-word verbs:

They can take tense:

> She <u>listens to</u> that radio program every Friday night.
> They <u>thought of</u> an unusual name for the baby.

They can take aspect:

> I'<u>m planning on</u> throwing a party. Want to come?
> We <u>haven't looked at</u> these old photos in many years.

They can be transitive and/or intransitive:

> He <u>gave up</u> the cause.
> He <u>gave up</u>.

Without doubt, it would be almost impossible to hold down a normal-sounding conversation in English without these words that are so typical of the language. Take a look at our first dialogue and see what I mean:

> (Knock! Knock! Knock!)
>
> A: Enter.
>
> B: Hi, Griselda! It's five o'clock, time to dress yourself in your hat and coat and remove yourself from the office. A group of us are contemplating descending to "The Blue Dragon," removing some food from the premises, returning to Maria's, then having dinner together. What do you say? Want to join us?
>
> A: I really don't have the desire to because I'm trying to recover from this terrible cold I've had for days. Oh, and could you please extinguish that cigarette? It'll cause another one of my famous coughing spells to happen.

Odd, you say? It certainly is! Yet even though there's nothing inherently wrong with the dialogue, it just doesn't sound "natural." Let's see how this dialogue appears if said in "normal-sounding," conversational English:

> (Knock! Knock! Knock!)
>
> A: **Come in**.
>
> B: Hi, Griselda! It's five o'clock, time to **put on** your hat and coat and **take off**. A group of us are **thinking about going down** to "The Blue Dragon," **picking up** some food to **take out**, **going back** to Maria's, and having dinner together. What do you say? Want to join us?
>
> A: I really don't **feel like** it because I'm trying to **get over** this terrible cold I've had for days. Oh, and could you please **put out** that cigarette? It'll **bring on** another one of my famous coughing spells.

That's more like it, you say? It certainly is! This second version is definitely the way almost all—if not all—native speakers would carry on this conversation, except for the verb *take out* which, in some dialects of English, is *take away*.

But what's happened? Why is it possible for us to come up with two versions of the same conversation, both containing perfectly acceptable vocabulary, yet one is looked upon as being "odd" and the other is considered "normal"? This isn't something you could easily do in other languages.

The reason lies in the historical development of English vocabulary, and for more insights into that, you might want to take a course in the history of the English language if you haven't already done so. I will mention, though, that English is really comprised of two major "camps" of vocabulary, the Anglo-Saxon (Old English) and Norman French (Latin-derived although Scandinavian influenced).

Although I am grossly oversimplifying, the key to it all is that the Norman French greatly influenced the language. Beginning in the late eleventh century, Norman

French was the language of the new English royalty, nobility, government officials, clerics, and academicians (when they weren't speaking Medieval Latin). Because of that, a good deal of the vocabulary which started coming into English at that time is even now associated with so-called high society or so-called intellectuals. In fact, many native English speakers even have a somewhat derisive name for a lot of the words that came into English through Norman French; they call them "two-dollar words" or "five-dollar words" or something along those lines. Because of all this, much of the vocabulary English inherited from Norman French is still the lexicon that's either preferred in print and in formal situations—or at least it sounds more formal to native speakers.

Vocabulary that's come down to us from Anglo-Saxon, which was the common language of the peasants and what had previously been the native ruling class, is still considered more "down to earth" and the language of the ordinary man and woman. This differentiation between the two vocabularies is so noticeable that, if Norman French-derived words are used in place of a great many commonly used Anglo-Saxon words in an informal conversation among friends, you can be sure that the person not using the Norman French words will take unwanted notice of the lexical choices the other speaker's making and may even make a derisive joke about it.

 **Heads Up!**

If you have students whose native language is a member of the Romance languages, which come from Latin, you should understand that they won't have the attitude about "formal" vocabulary that native English speakers do. These students are more likely to use the words on the left (Latin) than the words on the right (Anglo-Saxon):

extinguish	put out
distribute	hand out
surrender	give in
vomit	throw up

There's nothing wrong with the words on the left except they're not the common choices in many types of everyday situations. Moreover, this problem isn't only true with two-word verbs, but with English vocabulary in general.

A rule of thumb: If there's a choice between an Anglo-Saxon derivative and a Latin derivative and meaning doesn't change between the two, students should go for the Anglo-Saxon word until they've spoken English for a long time and have learned the fine points that exist between quasi-synonymous Anglo-Saxon and Latin-derived words like the following:

→ *Student*: I have to go to the airport to *receive* a friend.
Native Speaker: I have to go to the airport to *meet* a friend.

And yet we can still say *Her Majesty will receive the ambassador at two o'clock*. And we still have reception lines! Be careful of these tricky words like *recevoir/recibir/receive*, which are called "false or deceptive cognates."

→ *Student*: It's so hot in here, I'm incinerating!
Native Speaker: It's so hot in here, I'm burning up!

"I'm Stuck on You": Necessary Partnerships

Two-word verbs only mean what they mean because of the combination of verb plus preposition. Some grammarians make a difference between a verb plus a preposition ("Look at it.") and a verb plus a particle ("Look it up."). I'm not going to make that distinction here and split hairs over it since this differentiation won't be relevant to what I'm about to discuss. I'll just use the term "preposition" throughout this chapter.

A great example of how important the preposition is together with the verb to convey meaning is the verb *look*. If you simply shout "Look!" the listeners will immediately be confused. Where are they supposed to direct their vision? In another case, if you simply say "Look, Mary..." it's just a way for you to stall for time as you collect your thoughts or as a way of telling Mary that you're serious about what you're about to say and she should pay attention.

But what about when we say *look into* or *look over*? We now have two totally distinct verbs with totally distinct meanings. This happens to be another rough part of dealing with two-word verbs. *Look into* means *investigate* and *look over* means *check, examine,* or *observe*. In two-word verbs like those I've cited, there's such a close relationship between the two elements that, if viewed as individual elements, the meaning they create together disintegrates. But more on this point later.

 **Heads Up!**

Native speakers don't normally think of two-word verbs as separate elements; rather, they view them just like the expression, *two peas in a pod*.

Students, on the other hand, focus their attention on the verb element and disregard the accompanying preposition in most instances.

Here are two tips to make learning two-word verbs easier on your students:

→ Emphasize the fact that they should view each two-word verb as a **single item** and learn it that way.

→ Don't present your students with a list with one verb and a slew of prepositions. Don't give them a "killer" like *get* and confront them with *get around, get away, get by, get behind, get in, get over, get through, get up,* etc.

Let your students learn two-word verbs as they come up naturally in conversations, readings, or compositions.

Literal vs. Figurative Meaning

While we're on the subject of discussing what two-word verbs are and what they mean, let's discuss the fact that a combination like *look up* has two meanings. One of these meanings is literal:

> A: Marie! Hey, Marie!
>
> B: Where are you?
>
> A: **Look up!** Here in this apple tree. I'm picking apples!
>
> B: Oh! There you are! Please pick a couple for me.

But then we also have a figurative, or idiomatic, meaning:

> A: What are you doing?
>
> B: Using my laptop to go to Wikipedia.
>
> A: How come?
>
> B: I've got to **look up** info about the Stonewall Inn Uprising.

The problem here is that *look up* isn't a two-word verb in both of these dialogues. In our first dialogue with the literal meaning, we're really dealing with the verb *look* on its own and the directional adverb *up*. In our second dialogue, though, *look up* is a single unit with the idiomatic meaning "to gather information." **Be careful not to confuse a verb followed by an adverbial preposition and a real two-word verb!** This topic will come up again a little later, at which time I'll delve into some helpful hints on the subject about distinguishing when a verb just has an accompanying adverb or when it's really a two-word verb.

As for real two-word verbs, not all of them have both a literal and a figurative meaning, but a great many of them do. The literal meanings stem from the literal use of the preposition, so *put on* can really mean "to put something on your body" (e.g., *clothing, make-up, cologne*). This verb has its figurative meaning, too: "put (someone) on" can mean "to fool" or "play a joke on someone by telling the person something untrue." Before we leave this area of literal and figurative meanings, I'd like to mention one special figurative use that four prepositions share when they're combined with certain verbs. Check out the two-word verbs in bold in the next dialogue. What's the one meaning you can come up with for the prepositions *down, off, out,* and *up*?

> A: Oh, no! All the lights have **gone out**!
>
> B: This is ridiculous! Ours is the only house in the dark.
>
> A: Ouch! Darn it! I stubbed my toe on the couch.
>
> B: Walk slowly. It's easy to get **mixed up** about where things are in the dark.
>
> A: It's funny how, when you don't pay your electric bill, they'll **cut off** your electricity in a flash.
>
> B: So, you didn't pay the bill on time again!
>
> A: It's at moments like this that I feel like **burning down** their plant!

So what do you think our four prepositions mean when combined with those verbs and used in this context?

Down, off, out, and *up* all mean ....

The basic idea that these four prepositions share in the dialogue is **completely** or **something completed.** By the way, it turns out that *up* is the one that occurs most often in two-word verbs with this use.

To show you how these four prepositions work to give their accompanying verbs this extra meaning of "completely," I have some more examples:

add up	mix up	throw off
burn out/up/off	pack up	total up
clean up/out/off	rinse off/out	tough out
curl up	sell out/off	wear out/off/down
eat up	speak up/out	work off
ice up	size up	block up/off/out
lace up	straighten up	chop up/off/down
mess up	tear down/up/off/out	cool down/off
open up	toss out/off	dust off
rev up	trim down/off	hack up/off/down
save up	wash up/off/down	knot up
slow down/up	wipe off/up/out/down	match up
single out	beat up	nail up
stock up	chew up/off	plug up
take on/up/away/over/out	cloud up	shut up/down/off/out
tie up/down/off	dry off	stir up
trade off	grow up	stitch up
warm up	knock off	sweep up/out/off
wind up/down	mark up	tidy up
air out	mop up	round up
cheer up	pay off	touch up
clog up	roll up/down	use up
drink up	sew up	weed out
fill up/out	stamp out	wrap up
jazz up	slice up/off	zip up
lock up	sum up	

...and the list goes on and on!

To Separate or Not to Separate—That Is the Question!

We're now coming to the trickiest part of dealing with two-word verbs, but before we begin, I should mention that I'll only be dealing with transitive two-word verbs, those that require a direct object ("Pick it up, Billy."), since intransitive two-word verbs ("Listen up, Billy.") can't have direct objects and are therefore irrelevant to this discussion on separating or not separating two-word verbs when dealing with direct objects.

In the next dialogue, you'll see just how confusing the way two-word verbs are used can be for English language learners—and their teachers:

> A: Nikos! Come here this instant!
>
> B: What is it, Mom?
>
> A: **Look at** your room! Just **look at** it!
>
> B: Aw, gee, Mom.
>
> A: It's a pig sty! How can you be my son?
>
> B: I'll **clean up** my room. I will.
>
> A: You'll **clean** it **up**? When? A human life span is just so long! I'm going to **call up** your father in Athens and tell him not to bring you any gifts when he comes home next weekend!
>
> B: Oh, no, Mom! Don't **call** him **up**! Don't do that!
>
> A: Well then, **put away** all those clothes and games and books. **Put** them **away**—now!
>
> B: Okay, okay!
>
> A: You know, I was **looking for** your yellow sweater to sew on a button that had fallen off and I couldn't find it under all of this mess! I **looked for** it everywhere, but it was hidden! From now on, **listen to** your mother. **Listen to** me when I tell you to do something!

The important thing for us to observe in this dialogue is that some of the two-word verbs in bold have been kept together whenever they appear, but others are together in one spot and split apart in another. Let's make a preliminary list of those that you find kept together throughout and another list of those which have been split apart:

Always Kept Together	Sometimes Split Apart
....	....
....	....
....	....

Here's the list that I've come up with:

Always Kept Together	Sometimes Split Apart
look at	clean up
look for	call up
listen to	put away

When you examine these verbs, the two questions that must come to mind are, why can we separate *clean up*, *call up*, and *put away* but not the others, and when is it okay to separate the ones that can be separated?

When we examine the prepositions that we've seen linked to the verbs *look* and *listen*, we find that they belong to a group which has restrictions on them. These prepositions are **about, across, against, ahead (of), at, by, behind, for, from, into, of, through, to, upon,** and **with(out)**. Let's call them **Group A**. With Group A prepositions, you can make any number of two-word verbs. For example:

come across	look for	look upon
deal with	look into	mean by
look at	look to	think of

Notice how I've used *look* as much as possible? I've done this simply to make a point about how important the prepositions are for the new meanings that are created when they're linked up even with the same verb. Nevertheless, as I strongly recommended in the last *Heads-Up!*, they shouldn't be taught together in this way.

Getting back to the topic at hand, what can you say about the other prepositions that are linked to verbs in the dialogue? It happens that they belong to another group which includes **up/down, in/out, on/off,** and **aside/away/back/over**. Let's call them **Group B**. Just as with Group A, you can make any number of two-word verbs with Group B prepositions:

put away	put in	put out
put back	put off	put over
put down	put on	put up

There's an interesting observation I can make about these ten prepositions. Look back at them as they've been presented to you and see if you can figure out what my observation is. I'll give you a hint by saying that it's got to do with the relationship that each one in a set has to the other one it's paired with. When you've got an idea, write it down on the following line:

....

The observation I have in mind has to do with the fact that these ten prepositions are **opposites**. The first three pairs of them should be obvious, but even the grouping of those last four fall into this category as you can see when you contrast such two-word verbs as *go away/come back* and *turn over/turn back*. This fact may be very useful to your students as they try to get a handle on these verbs.

So why do you need to know which prepositions belong to Group A and which belong to Group B? The answer lies in the fact that **none of the two-word verbs made with Group A prepositions can be separated, but the great majority of those that belong to Group B can be separated.** That's why we saw some verbs (*look at, look for,* and *listen to*) always kept together in the dialogue, but others (*clean up, call up,* and *put away*) kept together or separated:

Inseparable Group A Prepositions:
"Look at your room! Just look at it!"
"I was looking for your yellow sweater."
"I looked for it everywhere."
"Listen to your mother. Listen to me when I tell you to do something."

Optionally Separable Group B Prepositions:
"I'll clean up my room." "You'll clean it up?"
"I'm going to call up your father." "Don't call him up!"
"Put away all those clothes and toys.
"Put them away – now!"

Focusing on these two-word verbs which have Group B prepositions, can you see when the prepositions have been separated from the verbs? First consider what's happened to the direct objects and from your observations, come up with a rule you can give your students: With two-word verbs containing Group B prepositions, we must separate the verb from its preposition when . . .

When we look over the separable two-word verbs that contain Group B prepositions, we see that **they've been split apart** because **when the direct object is a pronoun, it gets placed between the two elements.** That's why when Nikos' mother changed *room* to *it*, the verb *clean up* had to be split apart and *it*, the pronoun, was placed between the two elements:

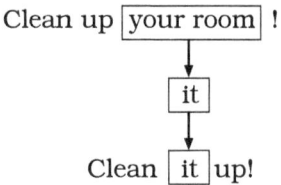

And so it goes with the rest of the two-word verbs that have Group B prepositions.

But there's one more little trick that two-word verbs with Group B prepositions can do. Let's go back to those verbs from the dialogue and see if you can split them apart without transforming the direct objects into pronouns:

I'll clean up my room.   ....
I'll call up your father.   ....
Put away those clothes.   ....

We can make the same maneuver with these two-word verbs even when the direct objects aren't changed into pronouns, so we end up with sentences like these:

> I'll clean <u>my room</u> up.
> I'll call <u>your father</u> up.
> Put <u>those clothes</u> away.

Remember that this separation with a noun phrase as direct object is optional, whereas when a pronoun is used, the separation is a *must*!

You now have all the information you need to make some general rules for two-word verbs with **Group B** prepositions:

- **We can leave the verb together with its preposition.**
- **We can choose to separate the verb from its preposition and place the direct object in between the two elements when the direct object is a noun phrase.**
- **We have to separate the two elements and place the direct object in between when it's a pronoun.**

But when we say that we can *choose* to separate the verb and Group B preposition when the direct object isn't a pronoun, how do we know when we've made the right choice? When should we leave the two elements together and when should we separate them? It would be nice to have guidelines to help us out.

Well, the only rule of thumb that I can offer you is that **when the direct object tends to be lengthy, most native speakers find it awkward to separate the verb and its Group B preposition:**

> Please look over <u>those files I left on your desk</u>. (comfortable)
> Please look <u>those files I left on your desk</u> over. (awkward)

Other than that, it's really up to the speaker to decide on how to handle the verb and preposition.

There's one final point worth noting. For the most part, the more idiomatic a two-word verb is, the greater the likelihood that the two elements (the verb and the preposition) will be separated when the direct object is a pronoun. (You'll be seeing a notable exception to this observation quite soon, though.)

By idiomatic, I mean that, as separate entities, the verb and the preposition don't give us any hint as to what their meaning will be when they're used together. For example, when we examine the two elements in *give up* (meaning *to stop using* or *doing*), we have *give*, and we have *up*, but when they're separate entities, we have no notion as to what they can mean when put together.

As for this tendency of idiomatic two-word verbs to separate the verb and preposition when the pronoun is introduced, let's see how two examples work like this. We can see that the two-word verb *look at* isn't idiomatic at all; it means exactly what it says. In this case, the verb and preposition stay together and we say "<u>Look at</u> that bird's nest."/"<u>Look at</u> it." But when we have a highly idiomatic two-word verb such as "turn down" (meaning to *reject*), the verb and preposition must separate when the pronoun is used: "I <u>turned down</u> his offer."/"I <u>turned</u> it <u>down</u>."

At any rate, take my advice and don't fret over it. Did I just say "don't fret over it" instead of saying "don't fret it over"? Wait a minute! Isn't *over* in our list of Group B prepositions and isn't *it* a pronoun? Doesn't that mean we have to separate the verb from the preposition and stick the pronoun in between? What's going on now?

Verbs with Allied Prepositional Phrases

Before you start fretting over what I realized about *fret over it*, I can give you a simple explanation. The point is that *fret* is <u>not</u> a two-word verb. Actually, *fret* is a one-word verb that can have an allied prepositional phrase. As I mentioned earlier in this chapter, don't get confused between two-word verbs and one-word verbs that have allied prepositional phrases!

So how do I know the difference between a real two-word verb and a one-word verb with one of those allied prepositional phrases? Sometimes it's easy to tell the difference, but sometimes it isn't. Let's go back to *fret* for a moment to see how easy it can be to spot the difference.

In the following example, *fret* is intransitive:

> She was fretting all day.

But let's say I want to mention what she was concerned about. I can do that, but I have to use either *over* or *about* to accomplish it:

> She was fretting <u>over her upcoming job evaluation</u>.

I've now created an allied prepositional phrase.

As you can see, *over* is simply a preposition in this context that I use before the noun phrase, so I don't have to deal with the intricacies of two-word verbs. If I want to change the object of the preposition (*her upcoming job evaluation*) into the pronoun (*it*), I keep the verb and preposition in their original positions and say:

> She was fretting <u>over it</u>.

But as I've said, it isn't always easy to know whether I'm dealing with a two-word verb or not, and here's a case in point. Even though ELT grammar books normally show *look at* as a two-word verb, no one's come up with the definitive proof of this one way or the other:

> Is it   He $\boxed{\text{looked at}}$ me ?
>
> Or is it   He looked $\boxed{\text{at me}}$?

Hmm . . . Not so simple, right? This is exactly how most grammarians feel about it, too! The point is that there are cases that show some sort of overlapping, and these cases are not worth troubling over since nothing has really been settled in the debate over whether or not they're two-word verbs. Therefore, because I don't think you have to bother about getting too deep into this topic, your students don't have to bother with the problem either.

Verbs with Allied Adverbial Phrases

This situation is different from what I've just discussed about prepositional phrases. Now I'm going to investigate how to distinguish real two-word verbs from one-word verbs with allied **adverbial** phrases. In this case, I really can see a big difference, and I have easy guidelines to help me make the distinction.

Following are some examples of verbs with allied adverbial phrases. There are two things I'd like you to do while you read these examples. First, notice how the prepositions are inside the brackets (to highlight the fact that they're part of the adverbial phrases). Second, think about which *wh-* words you would use to create questions that have the *bracketed* parts as their answers:

The teacher called. / The teacher called [on her cellphone].

He ran. / He ran [up the stairs].

The report went. / The report went [into his personnel file].

The reason I asked you to notice that the prepositions are inside the boxed-in parts of these sentences is to show you that they aren't prepositions that go with the verbs. On the contrary, their relationship to the verbs is just a momentary alliance that can be changed easily enough. Instead of saying "The teacher called on her cell phone," I might want to say "The teacher called from the top of the stairs." What I want to stress is that there is no intrinsic, locked-in relationship between the verb and the preposition that's part of an adverbial phrase.

And as far as which *wh-* words can be used to create questions for each of those bracketed parts, which ones would you come up with?

.... and ....

The ones I'd use to create questions are *how* and *where*:

    Q: How did the teacher call?
    A: On her cell phone.
    Q: Where did he run?
    A: Up the stairs.
    Q: Where did the report go?
    A: Into his personnel file.

This examination of evidence leads me to a tip that can help you figure out if you're dealing with a verb that just happens to be followed by an adverbial phrase or a real two-word verb. If *where*, *when*, *why*, or *how* can be used to ask a question about the phrase that follows the verb, the verb is <u>not</u> a two-word verb.

Just to make sure that you get the point, here are examples for the other two *wh-* words I've cited:

>She called <u>in time</u> to stop us from leaving without her.
><u>**When**</u> *did she call?*
>
>He was punished <u>for telling a lie</u>.
><u>**Why**</u> *was he punished?*

So what you've just looked at is not *call in* or *punish for*. You're simply looking at *call*, which happens to be followed by the preposition *in*, and *punish*, which is followed by the preposition *for*. These are not two-word verbs. However, what about this gem?

>She called in in time, so we didn't leave without her.

Now we've got a double-whammy! We've got the two-word verb *call in* plus an adverbial phrase, *in time*. Just imagine how your students' eyes would be popping out while looking at this sentence!

But now what about real two-word verbs? I'm about to give you three more examples of them. (Note that I'm using the three identical "openers" that I've used previously just to show you the contrast.) I'm going to ask you to do the same things you did before for those three sentences. First, note that in these examples, the prepositions are together with the verbs inside the boxes. Second, think about which one-word verbs you can use as substitutes for the boxed-in parts.

>The teacher called. / The teacher │called on│ a student to recite.
>
>He ran. / He │ran up│ a big bill at the hotel.
>
>The report went. / The report │went into│ his financial dealings.

The boxed-in parts, our two-word verbs, should be looked at as whole units. As far as my request goes, which one-word verbs would you use as synonyms for the boxed-in parts?

.... , ... , and ....

The verbs are ***selected/chose***, ***charged***, and ***investigated***. And now we have the second part of my tip for you on how to make sure you're dealing with a one-word verb with an adverbial phrase or a two-word verb: **If you can think of a one-word verb as a synonym for it, it's likely that you have a two-word verb.**

Another Two-Word Verb Headache

Up to this point in the chapter, I've told you which prepositions I've labeled as Group A and which ones I've labeled as Group B, but the sad truth of the matter is that there are times when a few prepositions cross over that fine line that could distinguish them so neatly. Sometimes Group B prepositions end up taking on Group A characteristics as the next dialogue will demonstrate. That's why I didn't say earlier that *every* Group B two-word verb can be separated:

> A: I can't **get over it**.
>
> B: What?
>
> A: Tanya. She's always been so shy.
>
> B: What happened?
>
> A: She told Robert to go jump off a bridge! Can you believe it?
>
> B: Tanya said that? I wonder what **came over her**?

Well, there you have it, an example of a so-called Group B preposition (*over*) suddenly acting like a Group A preposition. Is there an easy explanation for it? Not really; it just happens sometimes with certain two-word verbs with idiomatic meanings in which the prepositions behave like Group A prepositions. So accept the fact that there are some two-word verbs that the students will have to learn to use in special ways that differ from the norm. Here's a little hint about all of these: Group B prepositions can become A's, but A's can never become B's!

And speaking of idiomatic meanings, here are some examples of where the meaning of the phrase changes when the position of the preposition and the object changes:

> I know there's a lot of noise outside, but we can talk over it.
> ("talk over it" meaning "talk louder than the noise")
>
> I know we don't agree on the issue, so let's talk it over.
> ("talk it over" meaning "discuss the issue")
>
> Your investigation is going very well. Keep on it.
> ("Keep on it" meaning "continue the investigation.")
>
> If you're feeling cold, don't take your sweater off. Keep it on.
> ("Keep it on" meaning "Don't remove the sweater.")

Happily, most two-word verbs don't create this kind of nightmare for English language teachers and their students, but it's important to be aware that they do exist.

A Word About the Passive Voice

Let's look at this next dialogue to see how two-word verbs and the passive voice work together:

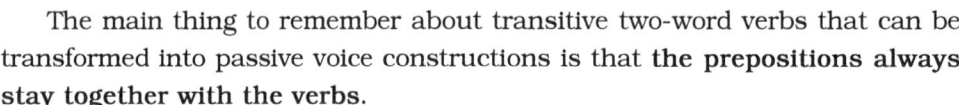

A: Where's Pete? I haven't seen him for quite a long time.

B: Yeah, I know. He's **been laid up** for a couple of weeks with a bad back. It's really a shame.

A: His back again? Gosh, that back of his **has been looked at** by more doctors than I can count!

B: Well, now it**'s been seen to** by yet another big shot doctor from the medical school.

A: I sure hope his back**'s being looked** after by someone who knows what he's doing. He's just got to feel better soon. After all, his fields have got to **be plowed up** in just a few weeks to get ready for spring planting.

The main thing to remember about transitive two-word verbs that can be transformed into passive voice constructions is that **the prepositions always stay together with the verbs.**

Three-Word Verbs

As if things weren't complicated enough, we now have to consider three-word verbs! Yes, they really do exist, and this next dialogue will show you what I mean:

A: I can't **keep up with** you. You just work too fast for me.

B: Don't worry. With a little more practice, you'll **catch up to** me. Say, why don't we take a break?

A: Good idea! I'd love some coffee.

B: So, how do you like working here?

A: It's been okay. And I really appreciate the way you've never **looked down on** me just because I'm new here and don't know all the procedures yet.

B: That's okay. I think it's important to **get along with** all my coworkers if I can, experienced or not. And besides, you're **picking up on** all the procedures here very fast.

A: Gee, I hope so. Gosh! Look at the time! I've got to **look in on** my daughter in the daycare center. I'll see you later.

I hope that you can put up with this chapter for a little longer. (Oops! I've just used another three-word verb, *put up with*!) These complicated lexical items can be quite problematic for English language learners for obvious reasons.

One nice point I can mention about three-word verbs is that, except for a very few idiomatic expressions, **their direct objects always come after them** whether they're **nouns, noun phrases, or pronouns**, so there's no worry about separating the verbs from their prepositions. There's one catch, however, that deals with those idiomatic expressions, but I'll get to it in a moment. The first three examples in bold in the dialogue will show you what I mean about those direct objects, though:

> I can't <u>keep up with</u> you.
> You'll <u>catch up to</u> me.
> You've never <u>looked down on</u> me.

And now, here are a few of those idiomatic exceptions. In these cases, there are really two objects, the direct object and the object of the preposition. **The strange thing about these exceptions is that the direct object**, whether it's a noun, noun phrase, or pronoun, **must be placed in between the verb and its preposition**, and then the object of the preposition follows all of that. Take a look at what I mean:

> I'd like to take <u>Mr. Butcher</u> up on <u>his offer</u>.
> Sorry I can't take you to the circus, kids. I'll make <u>it</u> up to <u>you</u>.
> Let me try to put <u>it</u> across to <u>her</u> in a less subtle way.

There's one last thing that needs to be mentioned about three-word verbs. Some of them are transitive (*put up with*), in which case they must have a direct object, but sometimes they can be intransitive (*back down* [*from*]), in which case there can be no direct object. Here are examples of transitive three-word verbs:

> She didn't keep up <u>with</u> her workload.
> The district attorney backed down <u>from</u> prosecuting them.

In the two cases I've given as examples, *her workload* and *prosecuting them* are the direct objects of these three-word verbs. When the direct objects are mentioned, the verb and its two accompanying prepositions must be used. However, these three-word verbs can also be used intransitively:

> She didn't keep up.
> The district attorney backed down.

If they can be used as intransitive verbs, three-word verbs drop the second preposition and actually become two-word verbs!

Remember to teach three-word verbs just as I've suggested you teach two-word verbs, as whole units, not as individual components. And make sure that your students understand that the allied prepositions just have to be memorized along with the verb forms—that's the only way to learn them. So, as an example, it's not *put*, and it's not *put up*, it's *put up with*, and the students will just have to put up with learning them in this way!

A Bounty of Nouns and Adjectives

To finish off this chapter, I'd like to mention the fact that English is a richer language not only because of its two- and three-word verbs, but also because of the enormous number of interesting nouns and adjectives that spring up from them (see Chapter 2). Some nouns are formed with the preposition attached to the front of the word (**preposition + verb**) such as the six examples listed below. By the way, notice that only Group B prepositions can be fronted like this:

    △an intake   an outbreak   an overlook
    an onlooker   △out-takes   an upsurge

Most nouns, however, keep the same order as the two-word verbs they come from (**verb + preposition**):

    △a dropout   △push-ups   a pushover
    a breakthrough   △fallout   △a put-down

Adjectives, too, can be combinations either of preposition + verb or verb + preposition:

    an <u>overthrown</u> dictator   <u>ongoing</u> problems   <u>incoming</u> flights
    △<u>take-out/take-away</u> food   <u>pick-up</u> sticks   a <u>made-up</u> story

What's interesting to note is that a good number of nouns and adjectives coming from two-word verbs (like the ones with the triangle in front of them) are relatively recent developments in the history of the language, and that's a marvelous way to see how language keeps growing and changing. New terms are generated all the time, often from older two-word verbs, to keep up with the changing times and with newly-developed technology.

Teaching Tips

14.1 *Designing International Signs*

Divide the class into pairs or groups of three. Tell the students that they've been asked to participate in an international design competition to create new signs for various public or private places. The winners of the competition will have the honor of seeing their signs displayed in the most prominent art gallery the country has—your classroom! There's one requirement for those who participate in the contest: they must draw signs that are based on two- and three-word verbs . . . and they cannot use any words in their signs, just as international signs don't contain any words. Encourage them to be literal or figurative in their interpretations; let their imaginations run wild. Here are some ideas I had; "translations" follow this activity.

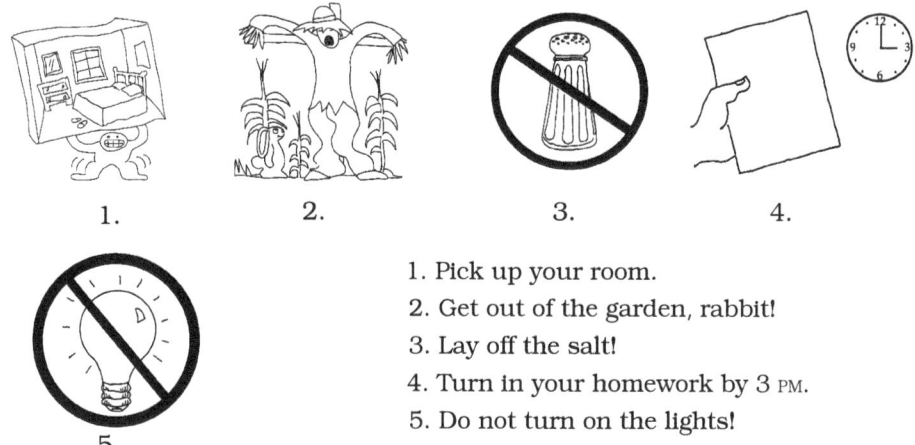

1. Pick up your room.
2. Get out of the garden, rabbit!
3. Lay off the salt!
4. Turn in your homework by 3 PM.
5. Do not turn on the lights!

Have the class vote for which groups have the most imaginative signs and place ribbons or stars on them. Then put up all the signs your students have created.

14.2 *Modified Cloze Activity*

Find a text that contains a variety of one-, two-, and three-word verbs in it. Create a cloze exercise (see *Appendix 1*) based on the chosen text. The verbs you take out and replace with blanks will depend on the type of verbs you're removing. For example, if the original text contains a one-word verb and you want your students to practice a two- or a three-word verb, put two or three blanks in that spot. If the text contains a two-word verb and you want them to practice a one- or a three-word verb, put one or three blanks in that spot. Make enough copies of the cloze (one for each student or pair of students) or write the text on the board, and have the students complete it, filling in the blanks with *one* and *only one* word per blank.

Variation: Make up a modified cloze activity based on a short story, poem, recipe, etc. that's complete when two- and three-word verbs are used to fill in the blanks.

14.3 *Want Ads and Advertising*

Bring in want ads or the advertising sections of newspapers or websites. Have enough so that all your students have some to work with. Pair up your students and have them go through the ads/advertising and circle examples of any two- and three-word verbs they find. Have one pair read their ads to a second pair, making sure that they don't give away what product they're talking about. The second pair will guess what's being sold or what the product is.

Variation: On the board, write examples of the verbs that the students found in this activity. Pair the same students again and let them create new want ads/advertising making sure that they use several two- and three-word verbs.

14.4 *Creating Stories*

For homework have the students think up no more than four sentences that have two- and three-word verbs in them. The next day, divide the class into groups of two or three and have them show their group the sentences they created. Make sure that *all* the students understand the meanings of the verbs their groupmates have selected. Wander around the room to help out if needed. After they've discussed all the sentences thoroughly, have them select three to five sentences from among those they've been discussing and then tell them to create a short story which incorporates the chosen sentences.

Variation: Have individual groups mime the sentences they worked with in this activity and let their classmates guess what's happening.

14.5 *Mystery Bags*

Bring several bags to class, enough for groups of three to five students to have a bag of their own. Make sure the bags you bring in can't be seen through. Ask the students to put something of their own into the bag (coins, nail file, lipstick, lighter, etc.) and exchange bags with another group. Have the students create a story around *all* the contents of the bag, making sure they use two- and three-word verbs.

14.6 *Pictures and Two-/Three-Word Verbs*

Before class, find a picture of one or two people; choose a picture that is simple, without too many details. Attach it to the top corner of a large sheet of blank paper. Divide the class into groups of six to eight students. If possible, have a copy of the picture for each group; if not, you can display it in front of the class. Your students' task is to create a paragraph about the people in the picture by using two- and three-word verbs. Choose one student in each group to give a name to the people; that student also begins the process of describing the picture: "These are my cousins, Eudora and Zelda Fedora." If each group has a copy of the picture, let the members write their story on the actual sheet with the picture on it. If they don't have individual copies, have them write their paragraphs on separate pieces of paper. If students need help thinking up phrasal verbs, you can help by putting some on the board.

15

Subjunctives, Hopes, and Wishes

"When you wish upon a star..."

One of the things that makes us human is our amazing ability to imagine, to ponder what might be or might have been, and to suppose how things could be different. All of this stems from another ability that we possess, being able to distinguish what's real from what's unreal and to dabble in both realms. Language reflects these abilities of ours in some very interesting ways, and this chapter will explore the fascinating but complicated ways that English deals with these abilities.

The Indicative and Subjunctive Moods

To start us off on our investigation, I should first discuss the difference between these two moods. When we speak in grammatical terms, the word "mood" doesn't refer to how you're feeling, but rather to a perception of something being real or unreal, a fact or a supposition. The first mood that everyone learns when tackling a foreign language is called the **indicative mood**. It's the mood we use for **real events, past, present, or future**. When we say "We plant flower beds around the house every spring" or "We're going to plant beds of chrysanthemums and marigolds," we're using the indicative mood and dealing with factual events.

It's a different story, however, when we get into the realm of what's contrary to fact or just a supposition. Then we enter the **subjunctive mood**, which says to us that we have **an idea that's hypothetical or deals with the imagination** (meaning that whatever we're talking about never happened, isn't happening, nor may ever happen). **The subjunctive mood conveys an idea based on a thought rather than a fact or an idea contrary to the reality of the situation being discussed.**

You already know all about verbs in the indicative mood because the indicative mood is found in all the verb forms I've already covered in this text. As for putting verbs in the subjunctive mood, I'll be dealing with that in detail a little further on.

As far as time and the subjunctive are concerned, the four basic areas reckoned with are **the past, the timeless area (also called general time), the (real) present, and the future.**

Nothing can be more maddening for teachers than to go from one grammar source to another and find a morass of terms and definitions for various forms of the subjunctive. Many grammarians call the form used for the present the "past subjunctive" and the form for the past the "past perfect subjunctive." Others say that conditional sentences (which we'll get to in Chapter 16) don't contain the subjunctive, but rather use the past for the present and the past perfect for the past. The reason they inadvertently make all of this terminology so complex is that they're focusing on the actual verb form being used rather than its function or meaning. I consider this focus on form a great mistake. Now you know why this matter can get so confusing.

I'm going to stick to a simple premise to make the whole thing easier and more logical; if an idea refers to the present, I'll call the verb form the present subjunctive, and if it refers to the past, I'll call it the past subjunctive.

It's time now for me to show you some examples of the subjunctive at work. These sentences will deal with imaginary ideas, ones that are contrary to the reality of the situations that set them up. To lead into the use of the subjunctive, I'm going to use the verb *wish*, a verb with a special relationship to the subjunctive.

Look these examples over carefully, identify the time of each sentence in bold, and from your own observations, write corresponding rules you can tell your students about how to form the subjunctive:

1a. They're broke again. **They wish (that) they <u>were</u> rich. In fact, they wish I <u>were/was</u> rich and (that) everybody <u>were/was</u> rich!**
   Note: We can use an optional *that* after *wish* when it's used with the subjunctive.
1b. He hates being plain-looking and shy. **He wishes he <u>looked</u> like a Greek god and <u>could</u> be more outgoing. He wishes he <u>didn't have to</u> be like that.**
1c. She's gardening in the hot sun. **She wishes she <u>were/was lying</u> in her hammock with a cold drink in her hand instead.**
2a. I didn't pay the rent on time and had to pay a late fee. **I wish I <u>had paid</u> the rent on time.**
2b. Their little girl got upset when she heard them arguing. **They wish they <u>hadn't been arguing</u> while she was home.**
2c. It's too bad she couldn't wait for us. **We wish she <u>could have waited</u>.**
3a. Andy won't go to college. **We wish he <u>would reconsider</u>.**
3b. Andy's going to take a job at his uncle's gas station. **We wish he <u>weren't/wasn't going to</u> do that.**

Rule 1a: ....

Rule 1b: ....

Rule 1c: ....

Rule 2a: ....

Rule 2b: ....

Rule 2c: ....

Rule 3a: ....

Rule 3b: ....

Here are the rules:

Rule 1a: To form the present or timeless subjunctive of the verb *be*, borrow the simple past form *were* and use it for all persons, or you may elect to use *was* for first and third person singular.

> Note: In some varieties of English, it is considered more educated or formal to use *were* exclusively.

Rule 1b: To form the present subjunctive for stative verbs, the timeless subjunctive for all other verbs, and the timeless subjunctive for the modal auxiliaries *can* and *must*, use the past form. Use *had to* for *must*.

> They wish they <u>didn't need</u> a larger house.
> They wish they <u>lived</u> in a larger house.
> They wish they <u>could</u> buy a larger house.
> They wish they <u>didn't have to</u> move.

Rule 1c: To form the real present (present progressive) subjunctive, use the auxiliary *be* in the present subjunctive (*were/was*) plus the verb with *-ing*.

> I wish I <u>were/was</u> making more money.

Rule 2a: To form the simple past subjunctive for all verbs, including *be*, use the past perfect form.

> She wishes she <u>hadn't been</u> sick last night.
> She wishes she <u>had gone</u> to the party last night.

Rule 2b: To form the past progressive subjunctive for all verbs, use the past perfect progressive form.

> We wish we <u>had been paying</u> attention to the map.

Rule 2c: To form the past subjunctive of the modal auxiliary *could*, use the perfect modal form.

> She wishes she <u>could have gone</u> to the party.

Rule 3a: To form the simple future subjunctive for all verbs, use the modal auxiliary *would* + the base verb.

> We wish you <u>would</u> come with us tomorrow.

Rule 3b: To form the subjunctive of the future expression *be going to*, use the present subjunctive of *be* (*were/was*) + *going to*.

> I wish I <u>were/was going to</u> go on vacation soon.

Without any doubt, the subjunctive is a very curious form in English since there are no distinct verb forms that are exclusively set aside for it as there are in many other languages. There's one general rule that I'd like you to observe in action. Take a careful look at the following comparisons between reality (the indicative mood) and unreality (the subjunctive mood). Can you make a parallel between what's going on here and indirect speech?

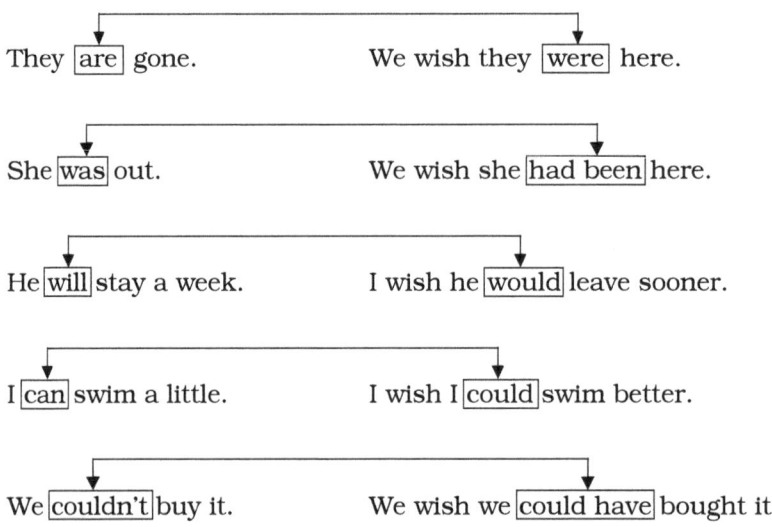

Do you see anything interesting happening when you focus on the boxed-in words? On the following line, write down what you think is going on. Think about indirect speech, if that will help you.

....

....

What's going on is that we have another form of the phenomenon called **backshifting**. Notice how each form in the indicative mood is moved one step back in time, so to speak, when we go into the subjunctive mood—just like the action we found with backshifting of the verb forms in indirect speech. This little observation may go a long way in helping you teach the subjunctive forms to your students.

Hope vs. *Wish*

Here we have two verbs that conveniently allow us to explore the differences between the indicative and the subjunctive moods. *Hope* and *wish* concern themselves with diametrically opposed concepts, and the first dialogue will give you a clear indication of how opposed these two verbs are.

Before we get to the dialogue, though, I'd like to point out something. Don't confuse *wish* as I'm using it in this chapter with its other meanings. *Wish* can equal what the subject would like for him-/herself:

> She wishes to leave now.

or it can mean what we want for someone else:

> We wish him all the best of luck.

As for the meaning I'll be focusing on in this chapter, that will become clear to you as soon as you read this first dialogue, so let's get to it:

A: Well, **I hope** everybody**'s** here by noon.

B: Yeah.

A: What's the matter? You seem depressed.

B: It's just that I **wish** we **didn't need** to do things like this.

A: But we've just got to make people understand how important it is to donate blood. Anyway, with the media attention this rally will get, I **hope** we**'ll convince** lots of people to help the blood banks out.

B: I **hope** you**'re** right. By the way, did you tell Maria to bring lots of orange juice? The donors are going to need it.

A: Yes, I did. I just **hope** she **remembered** to get it. In fact, I **wish** I **had brought** some for us to have right now.

Let's review some facts about the situation in this dialogue. Answer the following questions by checking off the boxes you agree with:

1. Is it probable that the others will arrive by noon? ☐ yes ☐ no
2. Is there a chance people will be convinced? ☐ yes ☐ no
3. Is it possible that Speaker A's expectations can come true? ☐ yes ☐ no
4. Is it possible that Maria remembered to get the orange juice? ☐ yes ☐ no
5. Do the persons in this dialogue feel there's a possibility that such rallies are unnecessary? ☐ yes ☐ no
6. Is there a possibility that Person A brought some orange juice? ☐ yes ☐ no

Questions 1–4 are yes; questions 5 and 6 are no.

Okay. Now that you've compared your answers to mine, let's put together all the sentences in the dialogue that use *hope*, and then those that use *wish*. Note that the numbers before the grouped sentences that follow correspond to the questions and answers we've just seen:

1. I hope everybody's here by noon.
2. I hope we'll convince people.
3. I hope you're right.
4. I hope she remembered to get lots of orange juice.
5. I wish we didn't need such rallies.
6. I wish I had brought some orange juice for us.

What you should ask yourself right off is why the persons in this dialogue chose to use the verb *hope* in the first four ideas. For one thing, you can see that the verbs that follow are in the indicative mood (*is/will convince/are/remembered*). For another, you need to consider the situations that led to those four hopes (the corresponding questions and answers you've seen) to help you figure out why they used *hope*.

Then you have to consider why they chose to use the verb *wish* in the last two ideas. To begin with, you can see that the verbs that follow in those two sentences are in the subjunctive mood, present and past respectively (*didn't need/had brought*). What you'll also need to do is look back at those last two corresponding questions and answers to see what the situations were that led to them using *wish*.

Now that I've done this big lead-in, I'm going to ask you to do a bit of detective work. By reviewing the question-and-answer section and the corresponding grouped sentences, and knowing what you know now about the indicative and subjunctive moods, can you choose the two common elements found in the first four sentences that aren't found in the last two? And what two elements can be found in those last two sentences that aren't found in the first four? If you choose the right ones, you'll understand why the persons in the dialogue used *hope* in some of the sentences and *wish* in the others.

1. In the first four sentences, a possibility exists. ☐ I agree ☐ I disagree
2. In the first four sentences, the outcome is known. ☐ I agree ☐ I disagree
3. In the last two, the speakers talk about reality. ☐ I agree ☐ I disagree
4. In the last two, they're unhappy with the situations. ☐ I agree ☐ I disagree

Without delay, then, let's see if you're thinking the same way I am: **Numbers 1 and 4 are I agree; numbers 2 and 3 are I disagree.**

So the two common elements we find in the first four sentences with *hope* are **possibility** and **ignorance of the outcome.** In all four cases, the situations mentioned can come true even though our rally-goers don't know the outcomes yet. Since there's no reason to believe their ideas haven't taken place, aren't taking place, or may not take place, they use *hope*. To sum it all up, **we use *hope* when there's a real possibility that something happened, is happening, or is going to happen. The key to this use, though, is the fact that we don't know the outcome.**

Now what about the last two sentences? The two common elements we find in both ideas that use *wish* are that **they're contrary to the reality of the situations** and **the speakers are unhappy about the events they're speaking of.** The truth is that they feel they really do need to have such rallies in order to get people to donate blood, and the other reality is that Person A didn't bring any orange juice for them to have. In addition, they show unhappiness over the reality of the situations. So **we use *wish* to communicate imaginary ideas when we know the outcome but are unhappy with it. It's a way for us to say that we know what already happened, is happening, or is going to happen, but it would be nice to have things otherwise.**

Now let's go back for a moment to the way we show futurity with *hope*. You may have noticed that Speaker A used both the simple present and the simple future form with the verbs that follow *hope*, yet they both represent the future:

> I hope everybody's here by noon.
> I hope we'll convince people . . .

Is there any difference between using the simple present or the simple future after *hope*? What do you think?

☐ yes ☐ no

Before I give you my answer, let's see if we can interchange the two forms without causing any havoc to meaning:

> I hope everybody's here by noon.
> I hope everybody will be here by noon.
> I hope we'll convince people . . .
> I hope we convince people . . .

Well, do you find any noticeable difference in meaning? I certainly don't, so the answer to the question is **no**. In fact, in Chapter 5 I talk about how the simple present can be used for the future, so this use shouldn't seem at all strange to you. To sum it up, **when the verb *hope* is in the present, we can use the simple present as well as these other forms for the following verb to connote futurity:**

> We hope you come to our party.
> We hope you're coming to our party.
> We hope you're going to come to our party.
> We hope you'll come to our party.

But I haven't exhausted the forms that a verb can have after *hope* when *hope* is in the present, and here are the rest:

the present perfect:	She hopes you <u>haven't caught</u> her cold.
the present perfect progressive:	We hope she<u>'s been taking</u> her medicine.
the simple past:	I hope she still <u>wasn't</u> contagious.
the past progressive:	We hope she <u>wasn't handling</u> the food.
the infinitive verb:	She hopes <u>to be</u> over her cold soon.

Notice that in each of the previous situations, the subject doesn't know the outcome yet—that's why *hope* works.

And now what about *wish*? I've already shown how we use the present subjunctive and the past subjunctive after this verb, and now it's time to see how it works in the future:

Dialogue 1

> A: You know how much Fred and Fran hate cigarette smoke. I **hope** you **won't light up** while we're in their home.
>
> B: Please! Do we have to go over this again?

Dialogue 2

> C: You know how much Frank and Freida hate cigarette smoke. I **wish** you **wouldn't light up** while we're in their home.
>
> D: Please! Do we have to go over this again?

Both of these mini-dialogues concern the future. In Dialogue 1 Person A is communicating a hope for the future about her husband's behavior, and in Dialogue 2, Person C is making a wish for the future about her husband's behavior. Notice that **we use *would* as the form for the future subjunctive with verbs that follow *wish*, but we can use *were/was going to* as well.**

Now I need to ask you the same question as before: Do you discern any difference in meaning between what Person A says and what Person C says? After all, each idea shows the speaker's desire for the future, right? So what do you think? Is there a difference or not?

☐ yes ☐ no

Even though both speakers are clearly showing their desires for their husbands' future behavior, the answer is **yes**, there's a very important difference between what Person A says and what Person C says. That difference isn't so much in the messages themselves as it is in each speaker's feelings about the situation. By responding to the following statements, you should get at the heart of their feelings when they made those comments to their husbands:

1. Person A is optimistic that her request will be honored.

    ☐ I agree ☐ I disagree

2. Person C is optimistic that her request will be honored.

    ☐ I agree ☐ I disagree

The choice of using *hope* or *wish* when discussing an issue in the future can make a world of difference. By using *hope*, Person A is demonstrating optimism that her husband won't smoke in their friends' house while they're visiting, so for **Sentence 1** I would check **agree**. And, by the way, we should note that this sentence is actually a **tactfully expressed command**.

Conversely, by using *wish*, Person C is expressing a basic pessimism about her husband's refraining from smoking while they're visiting their friends, so for **Sentence 2** I would check **disagree**. I should also note here that this sentence, compared to what Person A said, is a **weakly and pessimistically expressed command**.

To sum it all up, Person A believes there's at least a fifty-fifty chance that her husband won't smoke in their friends' home, but Person C thinks her husband will smoke there even though she'd rather he didn't. Oops! I've just used another phrase that can trigger the subjunctive, **would rather**, and I'll get to this one in just a moment.

🌰 "Hope" in a Nutshell

hope = feel a possibility that something happened, is happening, or will happen. In other words, the outcome of the event is still unknown.

Verbs after *hope* can take the following forms:
- simple present: I hope this meeting doesn't take too long.
- present progressive: We hope she's feeling better.
- simple past: He hopes they made up.
- past progressive: We hope you weren't waiting too long.
- present perfect: We hope he's made his flight.
- present perfect progressive: I hope you've been listening.
- *be going to*: She hopes he isn't going to disappoint her again.
- simple future: Let's hope everything will be all right.

modal auxiliaries (other than *will*) and semi-modals that follow *hope*:
- *can* (present/timeless):
  I just hired that man to be my assistant. I hope he can proofread well.
- *can* (future):
  It'll be a great party. We hope you can make it.
- *have to/have got to*:
  I hate it when my neighbor gets away with things. I hope he has to/has got to pay a big fine for burning those old truck tires of his in his backyard.
- **hope + present/future = a tactfully expressed command**:
  I hope you('ll) remember to pick up some coffee on your way home from work this evening.

🌰 "Wish" in a Nutshell

wish = feel a desire for something that is contrary to fact; show unhappiness over a situation

Verbs after *wish* take the following forms:
- present subjunctive:
  He wishes I were/was neater. I wish you knew him better.
- past subjunctive:
  I'm sure they wish we hadn't come yesterday.
- future subjunctive:
  She wishes I were/was coming along tomorrow.
  She wishes I were/was going to come along.
  She wishes I would come along.

modal and semi-modal auxiliaries (besides *would*) that follow *wish*:
- *could* (present and timeless subjunctives):
  It's too bad he's working now. We wish he could be here.
  I envy the freedom that birds have. I wish I could fly like them.

- *could have* (past subjunctive):
  I know they weren't able to save up enough money for that new car, but I wish they could have bought it.
- *have to* (present and timeless subjunctives):
  I wish I didn't have to work so hard to make a living.
  (past subjunctive):
  She didn't get the job because of her poor writing skills. She wishes she had paid more attention to her English classes in high school.
  (future subjunctive):
  I was told to report there by 6:00 a.m. next Saturday. I wish I didn't have to get up so early next Saturday morning!

wish + *would/wouldn't* = a weakly expressed command:
  I wish you wouldn't use the phone so much.

Phrases which Force the Present and Timeless Subjunctives

A: Sasha, have you looked at a clock lately? **It's time we got going**.

B: What's the rush? Masha's plane won't arrive for another half an hour. **It's not as if we were** late.

A: Well, you know I don't want your sister to get off the plane without anybody there to greet her. **Suppose if you were** arriving. Wouldn't you want somebody there to greet you as you **got** off the plane?

B: **If only you weren't** so obsessive about being on time!

A: That's just the way I am. And besides, **I'd sooner we had to** wait for her than vice versa. Now let's get a move on!

B: Okay! Okay!

As you can see, this dialogue is chock full of phrases that require us to use the subjunctive mood with the verbs that follow. Let's interpret the phrases in bold to see other ways we can express these ideas. Write sentences that paraphrase their meanings on the lines I've supplied:

It's time we got going.

....

It's not as if we were late.

....

Suppose it were you arriving.

....

If only you weren't so obsessive . . .

....

I'd sooner we had to wait for her . . .

....

There isn't just one correct way to interpret each phrase, but here are some paraphrases that I've come up with. Compare yours to mine and see how closely they coincide:

"It's time we got going" means *we have to leave now or we'll be late.*

There's a certain urgency in the idea. Does this interpretation surprise you? If it does, compare this phrase:

"It's time (for us) to get going."

Any difference in meaning between the two phrases? Write your interpretation of this second phrase on the following line:

....

The second phrase means *this is the scheduled time that we're supposed to leave.* It doesn't contain the urgency that the subjunctive verb form does. Now let's look at the rest of the phrases:

"It's not as if we were late" means *We're not late.* (contrary to fact)

"Suppose if you were arriving" means *Let's pretend that you're the one who's arriving.* (imaginary)

"If only you weren't so obsessive . . ." means *It's too bad that you're so obsessive . . . /I'd like you to be less obsessive . . .* (contrary to fact)

"I'd sooner we had to wait for her . . ." means *It would be preferable for us to wait for her . . .* (imaginary)

These phrases belong to a select group of expressions that require the use of the subjunctive with the verbs that follow them. Here's a list of some of the most commonly used ones. For some of them, I've added notes you may find interesting; for others, I've posed some questions:

as though/as if:
> He's acting *as though* he were president of the company. Someone should remind him that he's only an assistant to the janitor!

It's not as though/It's not as if:
> Stop crying so much. *It's not as if* she <u>were dying</u>. The doctor says she's going to make a full recovery.

If only:
> 1. *If only* we <u>were</u> more aggressive in our efforts!
> 2. *If only* we <u>knew</u> why he did that.
> 3. *If only* we <u>had started</u> with these rallies years ago.
> 4. *If only* we <u>could have convinced</u> people more easily.

An interesting observation about *if only* is that the word *only* can be detached and moved around. Take a look at these examples. What three rules can you make out from those four sentences?

> 1. If we were <u>only</u> more aggressive in our efforts!
> 2. If we <u>only</u> knew why he did that.
> 3. If we had <u>only</u> started with these rallies years ago.
> 4. If we could <u>only</u> have convinced people more easily.

So what rules can you come up with based on what you see?

1. ....
2. ....
3. ....

There really are specific rules for where we can move *only* (see Chapter 1):

Rule 1: Place *only* **after *be*** (Sentence 1).
Rule 2: Place it **between the subject and a simple verb form** (Sentence 2).
Rule 3: Place it **after the first auxiliary** (Sentence 4).

We can also place *only* as the first word in the *if*-clause, but I'll get into this word order in detail when we hit Chapter 16.

By the way, you might find it interesting to note that *only* functions just as an adverb of frequency as far as word order goes.

(Just) imagine: *Just imagine* you **had been given** a one-year scholarship to the Sorbonne last semester. I wonder what you'd be doing right now.

It's time/It's about time/It's high time: An unusual note about these phrases is that they can be used with the past indicative or the present subjunctive, but it isn't always so easy to distinguish one from the other. Look at these two mini-dialogues and see if you can figure out which one contains the present subjunctive and which one uses the past indicative:

Dialogue 1

> A: Have you heard? After relying on her husband for years to chauffeur her everywhere, Khadija **went** to driving school and **learned** how to drive.
>
> B: Really? Well, it's about time she **learned** how to drive!
>
> ☐ present subjunctive ☐ past indicative

Dialogue 2

> B: Karl, now that I'm working full time, you've just got to help me with household chores. It's time you **went** grocery shopping on your own and **learned** how to cook.
>
> C: Okay, I'm willing to give it a try.
>
> ☐ present subjunctive ☐ past indicative

Dialogue 1 contains the **past indicative**, and **Dialogue 2** uses the **present subjunctive**. Now that you've identified these forms, the questions that must be answered are, why does Speaker A use the past indicative in the first dialogue, and why does Speaker B use the present subjunctive in the second? If you think back to what I said at the beginning of this chapter about the difference between the indicative and subjunctive moods, you should figure out the answers.

Speaker A is using the past indicative in the first dialogue because ....

....

Speaker B is using the present subjunctive in the second dialogue because ....

....

Speaker A is using the past indicative in the first dialogue because she's stating actual facts that she's found out. And, if you recall from the start of this chapter, I said that the indicative mood is used for real facts.

On the other hand, when **Speaker B is using the present subjunctive because** she's saying that this is the appropriate time for those things to happen or that they're even overdue, but they're still not accomplished acts. And, if you recall once again what I said at the start of this chapter, the subjunctive mood is used when discussing thoughts or currently unreal acts rather than actual facts.

(Just) suppose: *Just suppose* everybody **practiced** strict conservation. Can you imagine how much better off the world would be?

would rather/would sooner: What's worth noting about these two phrases is that sometimes the base verb form is used after these expressions, but sometimes the subjunctive form is used. Compare what the speakers say in the following mini-dialogue and write down what you observe that makes Speaker A use the base verb form and Speaker B use the subjunctive:

> A: You know, I'd rather **use** paper bags than plastic ones. At least they're biodegradable.
>
> B: I'd rather **we used** paper, too.

....
....

Have you figured it out? Well, here's the solution to the mystery. **When the subject of the expressions *would rather* or *would sooner* is the same as the subject that goes with the following verb, we only use the base verb form and don't need to repeat the subject:**

$$\boxed{I} \text{ would rather} + \boxed{I} \text{ use} = \boxed{I} \text{ would rather } \boxed{\text{use}}$$

However, **when the subject of the following verb is different from the subject of the expressions *would rather* or *would sooner*, we use the subjunctive form and need to state both subjects:**

$$\boxed{I} \text{ would rather} + \boxed{\text{we}} \text{ use} = \boxed{I} \text{ would rather } \boxed{\text{we}} \boxed{\text{used}}$$

The Mandative Subjunctive

The word "mandative" obviously comes from the word *mandate*, which means *command* or *instruct*, and that basically sums up how the mandative subjunctive is used—to command or instruct. As to why this form is considered a subjunctive form, wait until you've seen the first dialogue and then you'll understand the reason.

The odd feature you'll notice is that **we use nothing more than the base verb form to create the mandative subjunctive no matter if our idea's in the present, past, or future.** The reason this odd feature doesn't become a problem concerning how to interpret the time is that **the verb that precedes the mandative subjunctive carries the time.**

Here's a dialogue showing the mandative subjunctive at work:

A: I'm really glad that the city government has finally passed a law about recycling.

B: So am I. But it'll be very important that everybody **participate** or it may not make a difference.

A: True. Did you see the guidelines on the government website telling people how to recycle?

B: Uh-huh. They suggested that we **separate** paper products from metal ones, and they said it was necessary that all cans and bottles **be** rinsed out.

A: So when is all of that stuff going to be picked up?

B: The law requires that recycled material **not be** picked up on the same day as regular garbage and trash. So each municipality has to come up with another day each week for that stuff.

Notice how the base verb form is used in each case to form the mandative subjunctive? The question is, what triggers it? Can you pick out the part of each of Speaker B's sentences that caused her to use the mandative subjunctive? When you've zeroed in on them, copy them over on the following lines:

....

....

The key to when we can use the mandative subjunctive lies with the phrases that trigger it. In our dialogue, they are these sentence starters:

> It'll be important (that) . . .   It's necessary (that) . . .
>
> They suggested (that) . . .   The law requires (that) . . .

There are three things I'd like you to notice. First of all, within these phrases we have a future form, a past form, and a timeless form, yet the mandative is in the base verb form throughout. Next, we have *that* after each phrase, but it's optional. And finally, because the mandative subjunctive is comprised only of the base verb form, the only way to make it negative is to put *not* in front of it (". . . not be picked up . . ."). A question that may have entered your mind is why there's an option for a **subjunctive** form after phrases like the four you've already seen. As I've recently reiterated, one reason for the subjunctive is that it can deal with **a thought rather than a fact**, and that's exactly why we can use the mandative subjunctive in these cases. When Person B said ". . . it'll be very important that everybody participate, . ." it was not a fact but a thought. If I were to say "everybody's participating," I'm talking about a fact, but in the dialogue this isn't true yet.

Along the same lines, if I were to say "everybody participates," it could be interpreted as something traditional or usual, and "everybody will participate" can mean a future prediction or some such interpretation for the future. None of these forms is satisfactory for my current purpose since fact, prediction, and the like aren't parts of the speaker's idea, and I don't want to be locked into any specific time anyway. The mandative subjunctive cleverly avoids any ambiguity with these other verb forms.

There's one last point I should make before moving on. If you take a second look at the sentences in the dialogue, can you think of other ways to communicate the same ideas without using the mandative subjunctive? Think about how you'd paraphrase those sentences and write your paraphrases on the lines that follow:

1. It'll be very important that everybody participate. =
   It'll be very important ....

2. They suggested that we separate paper products from metal ones. =
   They suggested ....

3. They said it was necessary that all cans and bottles be rinsed out. =
   They said it was necessary ....

4. The law requires that recycled material not be picked up on the same days as regular garbage and trash. =
   The law requires ....

Once again there's undoubtedly more than one way to paraphrase each of these sentences, but here are my entries to compare to your own:

1. It'll be very important for everybody to participate.
   It'll be very important that everybody should participate.

2. They suggested that we should separate paper products from metal ones.

3. They said it was necessary for all cans and bottles to be rinsed out.
   They said it was necessary for us to rinse out all cans and bottles.

4. The law requires that recycled material must not/cannot/should not be picked up on the same days as regular garbage and trash.

Have you noticed that *should* pops up in half of the sentences I created? **Should** is quite commonly used as an alternative to the mandative subjunctive, maybe because some native speakers consider the mandative subjunctive very formal, archaic, or even somewhat harsh. Using the word *should* seems to soften the impact for them.

For a more in-depth discussion on the mandative subjunctive, please visit us at ELTgrammar.com

A Modern Language Oddity: The Formulaic Subjunctive

As I've often mentioned, there are those tense, awful "moments of truth" all teachers face at one time or another when they come across a grammatical form that leaves them absolutely at a loss to explain. Well, here we go again! Reading this next dialogue should simulate one of those dreadful experiences for you, and what I'm going to ask you to do after you've read it will give you an additional idea of how that "moment of truth" might feel:

> A: Did you hear about that latest nuclear power plant accident?
>
> B: Yes, I did. **God help us** if things like that continue!
>
> A: **Heaven forbid! Suffice it to say** the earth won't be here too long if they can't be more careful with those places.
>
> B: I don't know about that. **Come what may**, I think the earth will still be here—but life on earth won't be!
>
> A: At least not as we know it. I get shivers just thinking about my great-grandchildren, "the mutants"!

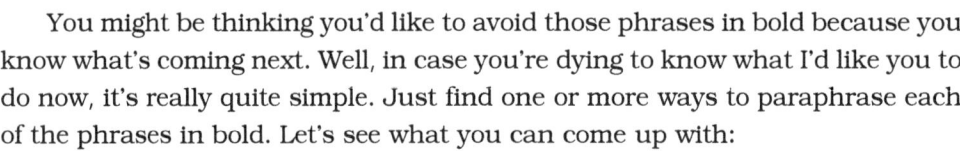

You might be thinking you'd like to avoid those phrases in bold because you know what's coming next. Well, in case you're dying to know what I'd like you to do now, it's really quite simple. Just find one or more ways to paraphrase each of the phrases in bold. Let's see what you can come up with:

God help us . . . .

....

Heaven forbid! ....

....

Suffice it to say . . . .

....

Come what may . . . .

....

Now that you've written down your paraphrases, it's my turn to write down mine, so here's what I've come up with:

God help us . . . We hope God will help us . . . / Only God can help us . . .

Heaven forbid! I certainly hope not! / I pray that doesn't happen!

Suffice it to say . . . It's enough to say . . . / What it comes down to is . . . / To sum it all up . . .

Come what may . . . Whatever happens . . . / Whatever the outcome . . .

What we're dealing with is a group of pat expressions that native speakers use without even thinking about the grammar involved. Students should memorize these expressions *as is* and only care about what they mean and when it's appropriate to use them. The name which some grammarians call the subjunctive that appears in all of these pat phrases is the **formulaic subjunctive**. As the name implies, this subjunctive is part of a *formula*, which is just another way to say a pat phrase. So you need scratch your head no more. If your students come across one or more of these little gems, or if you decide they should be taught to your advanced students, you don't have to worry about going into deep, lengthy explanations over them. They're relics of a very old use of the English subjunctive, and that's all there is to it!

Here are some other phrases that include the formulaic subjunctive:

Be that as it may . . .	Long live . . .
Far be it from me to . . .	Lord have mercy!
(God) bless you . . .	So be it.
(God) damn/darn it!	Till death do us part.

In some of the phrases I've just cited, a more modern-sounding rendering can be given by the addition of the modal auxiliary *may*:

May God help us.	May _____ live long.
May God bless you.	May the Lord have mercy!

Teaching Tips

There's only one *Teaching Tip* for this chapter because wishes, hopes, and conditionals just seem to be made to go together. When people wish and hope ("I wish I knew how to do this."/"I hope it stops raining soon"), they frequently explain why ("If I knew how to do this, I wouldn't have to call you every fifteen minutes for help."/"If it ever stops raining, I can hang out my laundry"). I recommend that you jump ahead to Chapter 16 and pick out those tips where wishing and hoping are targeted. Now here's the one tip for this chapter.

I Wish You'd Sit Next to Me!

This very simple activity is particularly good for students to learn their classmates' names and how to pronounce them accurately. Divide the students into groups of eight or nine. Have each group make a circle and add one extra chair to the circle. Let the student who has the empty chair on their right ask a classmate to move into the empty chair by saying "I wish X would sit next to me." X moves to the chair and the student who now has the empty chair on their right does the same.

16

Conditional Sentences

"If music be the food of love, play on."

In the previous chapter, I dealt with that wonderful human ability to create real or unreal ideas and to conjecture about how things might be. In this chapter I'm going to continue that process of using our minds via language to create real and hypothetical situations. You'll be seeing a good deal of the grammar covered in Chapter 15, but it will be used in new ways as we continue exploring the realms of reality and unreality in English through the constructions called conditional sentences. The reason that this type of sentence is called a "conditional" sentence is that something takes place on condition that something else happens first. It's really a case of cause and effect, so one event takes place depending on whether or not the other event takes place. The following sentence is a typical example:

If he proposes, she'll marry him.

The sentence above is typical of a conditional sentence because her marrying him is dependent on his proposing to her—that's the condition. The second event will only occur if the first one takes place.

Now that I've established what a conditional sentence is, we've got a lot of exploring to do into how it's constructed and what variations it has. What we need to do to keep this exploration understandable is to pick the sentence apart much like a dissection and study the elements that go to make up the whole—and that's just what we're about to do.

Before we get started, though, I'd like to mention that I'm going to deal with the topic of conditional sentences the same way I've dealt with some other topics in this text. First, I'll be investigating the basic grammatical forms that all teachers should understand and teach to their students at the appropriate level. Then I'll be offering you a deeper look online so you can delve into more intricate and subtle areas of the subject.

Real Conditional Sentences:
Timeless, Present, and Future Forms

The first thing to consider is the fact that **there are always two parts to any conditional sentence**. One of these parts commonly starts with *if*, so let's call it the *if* **clause**. The other part happens only when the event in the *if* clause occurs, so we'll call it the **conditional clause**. Remember that there must always be these two parts.

Real Timeless Conditional Sentences

A: So how was your Mexican vacation?

B: Just the greatest! We had a marvelous time.

A: Did you get to see a bullfight?

B: We certainly did.

A: Okay, tell me something. Is it true that **if a bull sees red, it gets all upset**?

B: No, that's just an old myth. In fact, **if you show a bull something red, it doesn't make the least bit of difference**.

A: Just as I thought! I knew that was a lot of nonsense.

B: Of course it is. Actually, **if you let a bull see something mauve, that's when he gets mad**!

As we can see in the dialogue, real timeless conditional sentences deal with what the speaker perceives as being universal truths. Just as the simple present can reflect this idea of something that always is and therefore has no temporal boundaries (Chapter 3), it can be used in *both* clauses of a conditional sentence to demonstrate the same concept. Here are some other examples of this type of conditional sentence:

You get pink paint if you mix red paint with white.
If the monsoons don't come to Asia, droughts occur.

The same holds true when *can* or the present perfect is used:

A: Your son can be very cranky if he doesn't get a nap.
B: But if he has his nap, he's as sweet as sugar.

A: Your son gets very cranky if he hasn't had a nap.
B: But if he's had his nap, he's as sweet as sugar.

When we want to express a real, timeless idea, remember that we can use the simple present in both clauses. We can also choose to use *can* or the present perfect in one of those clauses. You'll see a little further on how this use of *can* or the present perfect isn't always the case if we're dealing with a real conditional sentence in the present.

Real Present Conditional Sentences

Just as its name says, this type of real conditional sentence deals with the present, but it can do so in two ways. In the next dialogue, you'll see one of these ways:

A: Oh, boy! The boss is going to have your head for coming in so late again.

B: **If he's** angry, **it doesn't matter to me** one bit.

A: Doesn't matter? You know how easily he fires people.

B: **If he isn't** happy with me, **I** really **don't care**.

A: You don't care? Seriously? You act as if you've won the lottery or something!

B: Well, guess what?

A: You didn't. You didn't! You did?

In this type of real present conditional sentence, the *if* clauses contain the present (*he's/he isn't*), and the conditional clauses do, too (*doesn't matter/don't care*).

One other important point to notice about the *if* clauses in this dialogue is that each one is really acting as a rhetorical device by restating what's already known.

Now let's see the other way we can form a real present conditional sentence:

A: Wait up, Rodrigo! Where are you heading?

B: To the train station to pick up my Uncle Pancho.

A: Well, **if you're going** down there, **I'll come** along, okay?

B: Sure. But what for?

A: I want to pick up a job application.

B: Gosh, I should have been there to pick him up an hour ago.

A: Uh-oh. **If he's been waiting** there all this time, **he won't be** in such a good mood.

B: Tell me about it! Uncle Pancho's got a real temper. And **if he's tried** to call my cell phone, **he'll be** even more upset because my battery's dead.

A: You know what? Don't introduce me to your uncle when we get there. I'll meet him some other time!

In this other way of making a real present conditional sentence, the *if* clause contains a verb which is in some other form of the present than we've just seen. In the case of this dialogue, **the present progressive, present perfect,** and **present perfect progressive** have now been used.

So what about the other conditional clauses in this second type of real present conditional sentence? They invariably use some form of the future and it's very typical to find the modal auxiliary *will* being used. The reason the conditional clause must be in some form of the future is for the simple reason that whatever is being mentioned in this clause can't happen until the event in the *if* clause takes place, so the conditional clause gets pushed into the future.

Real Future Conditional Sentences

> A: You know what, Rodrigo? Instead of my going with you to the train station, do you think you could pick up an application form for me?
>
> B: No problem, Jaime. I'm on my way there anyway. **If you need one, I'll pick one up for you**.
>
> A: You're a real pal, Rodrigo. And **if you ever want me to do you a favor, I'll be very happy to oblige**.
>
> B: Well, there is something.
>
> A: Just name it!
>
> B: **Will you buy me a new phone charger?**
>
> A: Need you ask? It's as good as done!

Now that you've read this dialogue, let's consider the verbs in the *if* clauses of the real future conditional sentences you've just seen. You can't help but notice that even though this section is supposed to be dealing with the future, all three *if* clauses contain verbs in **the simple present**. Well, I've got to confess something to you. I've been very sneaky. I stuck in one verb that really does refer to the present and not the future at all. Which one is it?

1. If you need an application form . . .
2. If you ever want me to do you a favor . . .
3. If you get the job you're going to apply for . . .

☐ Sentence 1   ☐ Sentence 2   ☐ Sentence 3

The truth of the matter is that **Sentence 1** really refers to the present, and I know that because of context, but because *need* is one of those special stative verbs (see page 52), we don't use the progressive form.

So what about the other two verbs, which are also in the simple present in those *if* clauses? What they really refer to is the future, but **in a real future conditional sentence, we don't normally show an obvious future form in the *if* clause; we use the simple present instead**. There are a couple of exceptions to this rule, but they'll be dealt with later on when you take a deeper look online.

So if the simple present can mean the future, can it mean other things, too? Maybe it can, but we need to keep in mind that context is everything. Only through context can we really understand the time in many of the *if* clauses. To prove this point, let's try an experiment. Following are three sentences, each one beginning with the same three words. Read each sentence, decide whether the type of conditional sentence is timeless, present, or future. Then write the appropriate identifications in the blank spaces I've provided:

1. .... If you see holes like this in wood, it means termites are present.
2. .... If you see Heinz that far away, your eyes are better than mine.
3. .... If you see Birgit, give her my regards.

Isn't it amazing how the same three words can be used for such different aspects of time! Of course it's the conditional clause in each sentence that gives you the necessary context and information to figure out the time of the *if* clause. It turns out that **Number 1 is timeless, Number 2 is present, and Number 3 is future.**

To be sure, I'm playing around here with a stative verb, *see*, which means that the real present isn't so obvious as it would be with an active verb, but these are among the troublesome points that both teachers and students have a hard time dealing with.

Getting back to real future conditional sentences, I should mention that there are also many modal auxiliaries that can be found in the *if* clause and that carry a future meaning:

can:	If I can have a few more minutes, I'll be done with this job.
may/might:	If I may/might have a word, there's something that's been bothering me.
should:	If you should need some extra money, I'll be glad to help you out. (You'll be dealing with *should* in more detail later on when you take a deeper look online.)
must/have to:	If she must/has to give up her vacation this year, she won't be at all happy about it.

Now let's take another look at the conditional clause. The only thing worth mentioning again is that this is the place where we commonly find the obvious future form of the verb. And, as I've also mentioned before, although it's more typical to find *will* as the agent of the future in a real future conditional clause, native speakers also use *be going to*—but that's not all.

Just as we've found modal auxiliaries in the *if* clause, we can also find just about all the modals (*can, may, might, should, ought to,* and *must*) and the semi-auxiliary *have to* in the conditional clause as well. (In the next dialogue, you'll come across lots of examples.) Right now, let's look at a sentence that contains the modal *may*:

If you don't ask her soon, you <u>may</u> not get a chance to.

Here are other examples of conditional clauses that contain modals:

If he doesn't propose soon . . .
 . . . she <u>might/could</u> lose interest in him.
 . . . he <u>should/ought</u> to get his head examined!
 . . . he <u>must</u> be some kind of fool.

When you really think about it, even though we no longer have *will* or *be going to* in these conditional clauses, they still express a future idea. Except for *must* (which is being used here for a logical conclusion), the other modals I've added (*might, could, should, ought to*) all have a future reference. And, as far as our use of *must* for a logical conclusion is concerned, we still understand that the whole idea is in the future because **the future can be implied in the *if* clause even though its verb form isn't obvious.**

There's one more point I'd like to make concerning the use of modals. We can create the following real future conditional sentence:

If you don't propose to Fiona soon, you <u>won't</u> get a chance to.

But we can also use *may*:

If you don't propose to Fiona soon, you <u>may not</u> get a chance to.

Is there any difference between the two modals? Of course there is! We know that *may* means **possibility**, but in contrast to *may*, what does *will* tell us in this context?

Using *will* means that the speaker is **very sure** of the result, and that's an important difference in the communication.

Heads Up!

Students don't usually understand how important the difference is between *will* and *may* in real conditional sentences.

Get them to see that if they use *will*, it means they're expressing a certainty, whereas if they use *may, might,* or *could,* they're only saying that there's a chance this will be the outcome.

These other modals give the speaker a "margin of safety" that *will* doesn't. Just check out these two sentences to see which one makes the speaker seem a little foolish:

→ If you get the flu again, you *will* catch pneumonia.
→ If you get the flu again, you *may* catch pneumonia.

16 Conditional Sentences

Before moving on, let's take another look at that last sentence—the reasonable one—in the *Heads Up!* box. There's another interesting way this idea can be constructed. Just take a look:

> Get the flu again and you may catch pneumonia.

Are we still dealing with a conditional sentence? Of course we are, but it's gone through a bit of a metamorphosis. On the following line, account for the changes that have taken place:

....

What's happened is that *If you* **has been dropped and the conjunction *and* has replaced the comma.** A sentence like this can be very confusing for students, who tend to interpret the first part of the sentence as an imperative form as if you were ordering somebody to get the flu again! There's one more point to be made about this type of conditional construction, which has to do with the subject of the idea. Can you figure out what this important point is?

....

What's necessary to keep in mind is that **you can only make this conditional sentence construction for the second person, singular or plural (*you*).** It doesn't work with any other subject. So, practice this construction with your students and they'll become better English speakers!

Now we've dissected the basic parts that go into making a conditional sentence, in this case, a real conditional sentence. One more thing to mention is the fact that the two clauses that make up this construction can be reversed without affecting meaning. Even though I don't usually get into punctuation, I think it interesting and important to note that when the *if* clause starts off a conditional sentence, we generally add a comma after it, but not the other way round:

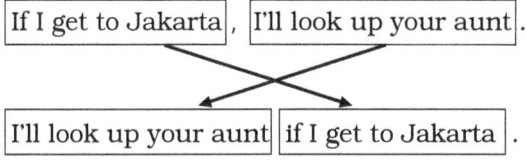

And speaking of the order of the words or phrases in a conditional sentence, I'm going to digress for a moment to mention that there's one strange occurrence when a word inversion takes place within this type of sentence. Here's an example in the typical word order for a conditional sentence:

> We'll cancel the track-and-field event <u>only if it rains</u>.

Everything looks normal, right? Well, let's say we want to begin our idea with the underlined part that now appears at the end. How should we continue the sentence then?

Only if it rains ....

You know I gave you a hint by saying that there was some sort of word inversion to deal with, so have you figured it out? The rest of the sentence should be . . . **will we cancel the track-and-field event**. It's not that this form is totally new for you; I dealt with similar inversions back in Chapter 1. The rule basically is that **we reverse the order of the subject and the first auxiliary in the conditional clause if we begin a conditional sentence with the phrase *Only if*.** Here are other examples for you to look at:

> Only if it had rained <u>would we</u> have canceled the picnic.
> Only if you admit your mistake <u>are you</u> going to feel better.
> Only if he takes his medicine <u>can he</u> expect a full recovery.
> Only if she'd gotten the raise <u>could she</u> have afforded to move.

And do you remember that I said we generally place a comma after the *if* clause when that clause starts off a conditional sentence? Well, as you can see from all of the examples you've just read, that comma isn't used when the conditional sentence starts off with *Only if* . . .

But I'm not through yet! What if the verb in the conditional clause is in the simple present/timeless form? If that happens, we don't have any auxiliary to reverse position with the subject. So what do you do? You've got to have something that can be reversed with the subject if you want to keep the rule intact. Any idea what the solution is? Here's a sentence for you to work with:

> If you water house plants prudently, <u>they grow</u> well indoors.

Let's take this idea and rework it by starting off with our phrase of the moment. Can you finish it? Try it and see what you come up with:

Only if you water house plants prudently...

It's really astounding how the language comes up with ways to keep rules intact. In this case, since the original idea doesn't include an auxiliary, you need something else, so the language turns in this case to the word that fills in for the auxiliary when there isn't any, namely, *do*. So the way you'd complete our mystery sentence is by saying . . . ***do they grow* well indoors!**

Of course, the same holds true when the simple past is used:

If she ate the right foods, <u>she felt</u> good.
Only if she ate the right foods <u>did she feel</u> good.

There's one difference in the construction of the sentences that start off with *Only if* and have the verb inversion with *do*. The difference is that you can't reverse the order of the clauses in these sentences. They must always begin with the *only if* clause! (These two sentences are acceptable: "She felt good only if she ate the right foods." or "Only if she ate the right foods did she feel good." However, this one is not: "Did she feel good only if she ate the right foods.")

We've now explored the different types of real conditional sentences in detail. If all the material is clear to you, and if this much is what your students learn to handle well, that will be just fine. If, however, you'd like to explore further into the intricacies of real conditional sentences, please go online to ELTgrammar.com for a deeper look.

The next dialogue is quite a lengthy one, but I've got a reason for that. There are going to be two phrases in the following conditional sentences that replace the word *if* in the *if* clauses. Let's see if you can pick them out:

A: Haven't you and Fiona been going together long enough? Are you guys ever going to get married?

B: I want to marry her—you know I do, but I never seem to find the right moment to propose. Don't worry, I'll ask her soon.

A: If you don't ask her soon, you may not get a chance to.

B: Why do you say that?

A: Haven't you seen the way Sean looks at her? If he sees that nothing's happening between you, he'll get ideas in his head—if you know what I mean.

B: Don't say that! Do you really think so? Okay! I'll propose to her at the company dance tomorrow night if she seems receptive.

A: Terrific! And I'll be the best man at your wedding—provided Fiona accepts.

B: Don't say things like that! I know she'll accept . . .

A: . . . assuming she still loves you.

B: Well, yes, sure. I don't have a second to lose. Forget tomorrow night! I've got to find Fiona now! Fiona, where are you?

So, what are the two new "*if*-meaning" phrases that you didn't see in the example sentences we'd already dealt with? Write them down on the following line:

.... and ....

The new phrases that you didn't come across are in the following sentences from the dialogue:

> And I'll be best man at your wedding—provided Fiona accepts.
> . . . assuming she still loves you.

I've substituted *if* with *provided* and *assuming*, and these are the new phrases. So *if* isn't the only word we can use to introduce what I've dubbed the "*if* clause." This fact should be kept in mind when teaching this topic.

Besides the two phrases we see in the dialogue, namely *provided* (*that*) and *assuming* (*that*), there are other substitutes with the meaning of *if*:

as long as:	We can all get on well <u>as long as</u> we respect one another.
in case:	<u>In case</u> I get there first, I'll hold a seat for you.
in the event (that):	<u>In the event</u> it rains, we'll have the party indoors.
on condition (that):	We'll drop the law suit <u>on condition</u> that he apologize.
providing (that):	He'll be hired <u>providing</u> his credentials check out.
so long as:	You'll feel fine <u>so long as</u> you take your medicine.
unless:	(see the next *Heads Up!*)
whether or not:	They'll get married <u>whether or not</u> we approve.

There's one more item that we can use in place of *if* in a conditional sentence, and it's the word *otherwise*. But it's not that simple. Check out the following example:

> They'll have to put up $25,000; <u>otherwise</u>, the deal's off.

How can you paraphrase this sentence if you begin with *If*? Try writing a sentence down on the following line:

....

It's really interesting how you've got to change things around to come up with an accurate paraphrase for my sentence with *otherwise*. The one I've come up with is: **If they don't put up $25,000, the deal's off.** I'm sure your paraphrase is basically the same as mine. As you can see, unlike the way all those phrases can easily substitute for *if*, *otherwise* has to be understood in a very different way and used accordingly.

One extra thing worth taking note of is where the word *otherwise* is placed. If you look back at my sentence with it, you'll see that it's the only conditional word attached to the conditional clause ("the deal's off") rather than the *if* clause ("They'll have to put up $25,000").

 **Heads Up!**

If there's one word that gives teachers and their students a lot of grief, it's *unless*. One reason for this problem is that *unless* contains a hidden, negative idea, and when something's not obvious, it becomes troublesome.

Another reason is that there are times when this little word is interchangeable with *if . . . not*, but there are other times when it isn't.

The thing to keep in mind is that *unless* really means "except on the condition that . . ." If you can't use this lengthy phrase in your idea, you can't use *unless* in the sentence, but you can use *if . . . not*.

→ *if . . . not* and unless are interchangeable when we create a real conditional sentence:
She won't join us tonight *if* she *doesn't* feel better.
(She won't join us tonight except on the condition that she feels better.)
She won't join us tonight *unless* she feels better.

→ *Unless* won't work, however, in a sentence like this:
He loses his temper so easily that it'll be amazing *if* he *doesn't* have a stroke one day.

Why won't it? It's because we can't use our long phrase in this idea and still make any sense:

He loses his temper so easily, it'll be amazing *except on the condition that* he has a stroke one day.

As I've already said, the important point for teachers to remember is that ***if* is not the only word that can introduce the *if* clause**, nor is it the only word that teachers should teach.

Real Conditional Sentences and the Imperative

A common form that tends to get overlooked in student grammar books is the use of the imperative, or command form, of the verb in real conditional sentences. The imperative, however, can be used in two different ways in this type of sentence. One of these ways is quite straightforward and uncomplicated. In this case, the imperative appears in the conditional clause. This next dialogue will show you a couple of examples.

A: You're going to the supermarket now, right?

B: Uh-huh.

A: Good. Do me a favor. If you see tomatoes on sale, pick me up about five pounds. I'm going to make a big pot of spaghetti sauce.

B: Sure thing. Oh, and can you do me a favor in return?

A: Okay. What is it?

B: If my mother calls while I'm out, tell her I'll stop by her house on the way home from the supermarket.

The other way the imperative can be used in real conditional sentences is more complicated because the conditional aspect of the idea may not be so obvious to students. Take a look at what I mean:

> A: Gee, Grandpa, I really like going fishing with you.
>
> B: And I like going fishing with you, too, Naoko! Now, **catch us some big, fat fish, and we'll take them home** for everyone to eat tonight.
>
> A: Okay, Grandpa. Oh! Look at my line! Look how it's pulling, Grandpa!
>
> B: All right, Naoko. That means you've got a really nice fish on your hook. **Reel it in quickly or the fish may get away**.
>
> A: Like this? Wow! Look at how big it is, Grandpa!
>
> B: You did a fine job, Naoko. Yes, there'll be fish for dinner tonight!

This time, the imperative is found at the beginning of each sentence in bold. Notice that the first part of each sentence (" . . . catch us some big, fat fish" / "Reel it in quickly . . . ") is connected either by the conjunctions *and* or *or* to the second part (" . . . we'll bring them home . . . " / " . . . the fish may get away").

So why am I including these sentences in a chapter on conditionals? It's because hidden within each one there really is a more typical-looking conditional sentence. In fact, the first parts of these sentences aren't really imperatives at all; they're reduced *if* clauses. Can you create these more typical real conditional sentences that can begin with the usual *if* clause? Here are a couple of lines for you to write your paraphrases on:

....

....

If you want to paraphrase the sentences in bold from the dialogue with more typical-looking conditional sentences, you end up with these sentences:

> If you catch us some big, fat fish, we'll take them home for everyone to eat tonight.
>
> If you don't reel it in quickly, the fish may get away.

One final note worth mentioning here is that you can use the word *otherwise* after an imperative in the *if* clause to explain what will happen if the listener doesn't carry out the imperative:

> Reel it in quickly; <u>otherwise</u>, the fish may get away.

There's nothing else that needs to be said about the use of imperatives in conditional ideas except that they're very commonly used and shouldn't be overlooked by teachers.

Some Nuances with Real Conditional Sentences

A: Miss Khan, are you on your way over to New Accounts?

B: Yes, Mr. Buzurg.

A: Good. If you happen to see Jamshid, please ask him if he's all set with his presentation for Bokhara Textiles.

B: You've forgotten, sir. Jamshid's on a skiing trip, but he'll be back tomorrow.

A: Oh, that's right. Well, should you pass by his desk, leave him a message to call me first thing when he gets in.

Just like an artist who uses various shades of the same color to give depth, richness, and texture to a specific area of a painting, English uses its own form of shading to accomplish the same thing. Throughout this book we've come across this wonderful ability that language has time and time again, and here you have yet another example of it.

Mr. Buzurg could simply choose to say "If you see Jamshid . . ." and " . . . if you pass by his desk . . . ," but he doesn't. Instead, he uses other devices in these two real conditional sentences: **happen to** and **should**.

Happen to is a phrase that's just placed in between the subject and its verb:

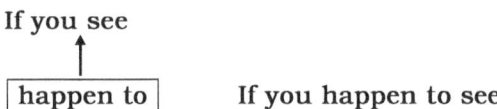

Should, on the other hand, is somewhat more complicated. Actually, Mr. Buzurg jumped a step between saying " . . . if you pass by . . ." and ". . . should you pass by . . ." Let me explain.

The first step is that *should* can be placed in between the subject and its verb just as we do with *happen to*:

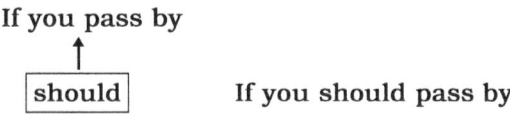

Now we get to the step that Mr. Buzurg took. He eliminated *if,* moved *should* into that spot, and created this new type of *if* clause:

The question is, why bother? Do you perceive a difference between using or not using these phrases?

☐ yes ☐ no

Well, I've got to admit that I do, so I'd check **yes**. But what is that difference? If you have an idea, write it down on the following line:

....

The reason that a speaker might choose to use one of these phrases—or even a combination of them—in place of the basic *if* clause is that the speaker's dealing with what he/she feels is the **likelihood** of the event actually taking place.

Let's try a little experiment. You're about to find a list of various ways you can create the *if* clause. On a scale of 1 to 4 (1 = most likely to occur, 4 = least likely to occur), write the number which you feel will correspond to the degree of likelihood that the event will take place—in the speaker's opinion, that is. And by the way, two of these numbers should be used twice:

.... If he wins first prize, . . .

.... If he should win first prize, . . .

.... Should he win first prize, . . .

.... If he happens to win first prize, . . .

.... If he should happen to win first prize, . . .

.... Should he happen to win first prize, . . .

Quite confusing, right? It's not that there's a hard-and-fast rule about how these clauses should be ordered according to their degree of likelihood, but there is a tendency among native speakers to give them the following order:

1	If he wins first prize, . . .
2	If he should win first prize, . . .
2	Should he win first prize, . . .
3	If he happens to win first prize, . . .
4	If he should happen to win first prize, . . .
4	Should he happen to win first prize, . . .

I'd like to point one more thing out to you about a phrase like "Should he win first prize." Where do you think the word *not* ought to go if you choose to turn this phrase into a negative idea? Place *not* where you think it should go:

> Should   he   win   first   prize, . . .

The word *not* is placed **between the subject and the verb** in this kind of inverted phrase, so we end up with "**Should he not win first prize . . .**" What's important to keep in mind is that *not* doesn't travel with the auxiliary when the auxiliary is fronted to mean *if* in this type of inversion. If it does travel with the auxiliary, we have a completely different idea:

> Shouldn't he win first prize . . .

Of course, this form is a simple yes/no question that means "Doesn't he deserve to win first prize?" Quite a difference!

And if that's not enough, there's yet another phrase you can stick in to lower the degree of likelihood even more, and that happens to be the phrase *by (any) chance*:

> If <u>by chance</u> he wins first prize, . . .
> If he <u>by any chance</u> wins first prize, . . .
> Should he <u>by any chance</u> win first prize, . . .
> If he wins first prize <u>by any chance</u>, . . .

When Real Conditional Sentences Aren't So "Iffy"

There's another important point to mention that can occur with real conditional sentences that has to do with the word *if.* Another word we can use as a substitute for *if* in real conditional sentences is **when**, but it isn't all that simple as there are several factors that determine whether or not we can make this substitution.

I'd like you to look over the following sentences that I've lifted either from examples or dialogue boxes you've already seen to determine for yourself whether there's any change in meaning when we substitute *if* with *when*. First, decide whether there's a change in meaning in each pair of sentences. Then, if you think there is a change, describe that change on the following blank line:

1a. If/When you see holes like this in wood, it means termites are present.
1b. You get pink paint if/when you mix red paint with white.
    ☐ a change in meaning   ☐ no change in meaning

....

2a. If/When you see Birgit, give her my regards.
2b. I'll look up your aunt if/when I get to Jakarta.
    ☐ a change in meaning   ☐ no change in meaning

....

3a. We'll cancel the track-and-field event only if/when it rains.
3b. If/When you see tomatoes on sale, pick me up a few pounds.
☐ a change in meaning ☐ no change in meaning

4a. If/When he isn't happy with me, I really don't care.
4b. If/When he's angry, it doesn't matter one bit.
☐ a change in meaning ☐ no change in meaning

And now to the answers. The sentences in **Number 1** demonstrate **no change in meaning** between using *if* or *when*. We can say, then, that **these two words are totally interchangeable when we state general concepts or universal truths**.

The sentences in **Number 2** show **a change in meaning**. In Sentence 2a, *if* tells us that the speaker isn't certain that the meeting will take place between the listener and Birgit. *When*, on the other hand, tells us that there's no doubt in the speaker's mind that the listener's going to see her. Sentence 2b works exactly the same way. Using *if* in this sentence tells us that the speaker isn't definite about stopping in Jakarta. Using *when* shows that the speaker is certain about going there. So, to sum up, ***if* implies a lack of certainty** in these situations while ***when* does imply certainty**.

The sentences in **Number 3** also demonstrate **a change in meaning**. In Sentence 3a, *if* tells us that the speaker's probably talking about a specific upcoming track-and-field event, but *when* makes it sound as if the speaker's talking hypothetically about any time that rain may occur during a field and track event. Sentence 3b works the same way. *If* implies an immediate possibility that the speaker's roommate will find tomatoes on sale since she's going to the supermarket right now. *When* really means "whenever," and the speaker's posing a hypothetical situation (*whenever* or *any time* you see tomatoes on sale). In fact, because the roommate's going to the supermarket right now, we can't use *when* in this situation (see the dialogue box on page 363). In short, ***if* is used when discussing some immediate upcoming event** while ***when* deals with hypothetical situations**.

The last two sentences work like those in Number 3, so they also show **a change in meaning** even though there's a difference in focus. With *if* in both **4a** and **4b**, the ideas are actually rhetorical. Person A has made it clear that the boss is unhappy with Person B, so Person B's restating an already known fact is just a rhetorical device used to reiterate what's already common knowledge, and it deals with the immediate situation. *When*, as we've already seen, really means *whenever*, so the sentences with this word don't deal with the present situation as it exists in the dialogue box on page 363. With *when* the sentences deal with a hypothetical situation.

But I'm not done yet! Here are some more sentences that you've already come across in this chapter. You decide if they work just as well with *when* as they do with *if.* If, by chance, you determine that they don't, see if you can figure out why they don't, and write your thoughts down on the blank lines that follow:

> When you see Heinz that far away, your eyes are better than mine.
>
> When you don't propose to Fiona soon, you may not get a chance to.
>
> When you'll hold the line, I'll put you through.
>
> When you get the job you're going to apply for, will you treat me to dinner?
>
> When you're going downtown, I'll come along, okay?
>
> ☐ They work fine. ☐ They don't work fine.

....

....

One quick read-through of the preceding sentences should make it clear that these examples **don't work fine** using *when* in place of *if.* Although there are a few picky points that I could get involved in, I can just sum up the reason they don't work by saying that *when* contradicts the situations each of these sentences is part of. In each case, *when* really stands for *whenever,* and that's not the intent of these ideas. They're dealing with immediate situations, not hypothetical or general ones, so *when* just simply doesn't work.

So, to put it all in a nutshell, we can say that ***when* is a perfectly fine substitute for *if* in real conditional sentences that deal with factual observations, universal truths, or the speaker's certainty about future situations.**

Unreal Conditional Sentences: Timeless, Present, and Future Forms

In meaning, the big difference between real and unreal conditional sentences is that the real ones represent something that happens ("If it rains, puddles form"), is *happening* ("If you're feeling so sick, I'll take you to the doctor's"), or will happen ("If she gets here early, I'll show her the photos"). In contrast, unreal conditional sentences deal with impossible situations because we can't alter the past, the present, or the future. We can find a good analogy by comparing real and unreal conditional sentences to the major difference between *hope* and *wish.* Just as we found important differences in the verb forms which follow *hope* and *wish,* we find the same grammar differences between real and unreal conditional sentences.

Unreal Timeless Conditional Sentences

Although this isn't the most common type of unreal conditional sentence, it's worth looking at a few examples. So let's examine the following dialogue to see how it's used:

> A: I'm worried about that hole in the ozone layer. Aren't you?
>
> B: Of course I am. A lot of people don't realize how serious this is. If there **were** no ozone layer around the earth, the planet **wouldn't be** protected from lots of harmful radiation coming from the sun.
>
> A: That's right. And many more people **would get** skin cancer and cataracts if the ozone layer **didn't filter out** those harmful rays.
>
> B: Well, I just hope scientists find a way to stop the hole from getting bigger!

Just as with real conditional sentences, exploring the unreal types is like exploring cause-and-effect relationships. The *if* clause is the cause; the conditional clause is the effect. The dialogue you've just read has good examples of this relationship.

As for the actual construction of these unreal timeless conditional sentences, we can see that the *if* clause contains the subjunctive verb form (reflecting the simple present for timeless ideas) and the conditional clause uses the modal auxiliary *would* with the verb. (The conditional clause can use *could* just as well: "If we had wings, we could fly.") You should note that we find the same basic construction in unreal *present* conditional sentences as well.

Unreal Present Conditional Sentences

Let's see how close this type of unreal conditional sentence is to the timeless versions we've just explored:

> A: How are you feeling now?
>
> B: The same.
>
> A: That's too bad. If you **were feeling** better, I**'d suggest** that we go to the movies this afternoon.
>
> B: Oh? What's playing?
>
> A: *Godzilla* vs. *Dracula.*
>
> B: Well, I **wouldn't go** to see that film even if I **felt** fine!

We can see that there's an extremely close parallel between the sentences in this dialogue and the one that demonstrated the timeless kind of unreal conditional sentence. In the *if* clauses we have the present subjunctive reflecting imaginary ideas about the realities of the situation:

> If you <u>were</u> feeling better . . . (but he <u>isn't</u> feeling better)
>
> . . . even if I <u>felt</u> fine!   (but he <u>doesn't feel</u> fine)

Before leaving the *if* clause, I should mention that there are some other words we can use in the present subjunctive; these are the modals *can* for ability or possibility (which becomes *could*) and *must* for necessity (which becomes *had to*):

> If you <u>could</u> live anywhere, where would it be?
>
> If I <u>had to</u> choose a place to live, it would be right here!

Now what about the conditional clauses? Notice that the verb is in what we commonly call the **conditional** form. Normally, the unreal timeless, present, or future conditional is expressed by the modal auxiliary *would* in American varieties of English for all persons:

> If I were you, I <u>would</u> watch what I say.

But in British and Australian varieties, *should* can be used instead for first person singular and plural:

> If I were you, I <u>should</u> watch what I say.

Besides *would* and *should* in the unreal conditional clause, we can find other modals such as *could* (for *can*) and *might* (for *may*). In addition, *must* can be expressed as *would have to*. It's no wonder that this type of sentence is sometimes referred to as the *subjunctive-conditional*, giving deference to both parts of the sentence. Here are two more examples to show you unreal conditionals that weren't covered in our dialogue:

> If I didn't take so many vitamins, I <u>might</u> get sick more often.
>
> He <u>would have to</u> get another job if his wife didn't work.

 **Heads Up!**

Look at the following sentence:

> If Alain was here, I didn't see him.

A sentence like this can confuse native speakers and our students alike. The part that's so confusing is the use of *was*. Is it a subjunctive form or what?

Well, the answer is that it isn't the subjunctive at all. Actually, it's just the simple past in what we can term a **rhetorical** *if* clause that just echoes what someone else has said:

> A: Did you know that Alain was here today?
> B: If Alain was here, I didn't see him.

Because Of Goes Subjunctive

One of those vocabulary oddities that students learn is the difference in usage between *because* and *because of*. Students are taught that the word *because* is followed by a clause (subject + verb):

We go to Carlo's for dinner because <u>he makes great lasagna</u>.

They're also taught that *because of* must be followed by a noun phrase:

We go to Carlo's for dinner because of <u>his great lasagna</u>.

But what do we do if we want to discuss going to Carlo's house and having his lasagna in an unreal conditional idea? Take a look and see for yourself:

A: Well, Carlo did it again! Nobody can make lasagna like he can. His lasagna is out of this world!

B: True. I'm stuffed. And everything else we've ever eaten over here has been equally good.

A: Yeah, I guess that's true. But **if it weren't for** his lasagna, he wouldn't be a finalist in the annual faculty cooking contest at school.

B: I know. Ah, what a cook!

There you have it! The phrase *if it weren't for* is what we need to use in an unreal timeless or present conditional sentence to replace *because of* in order to show the only cause or reason for something else happening. In other words, any time an idea is imaginary and needs to show the cause or reason for something happening, *because of* can't be used to accomplish this purpose. By the way, if you want to come up with the converse of the sentence that Speaker A said with the phrase "If it weren't for . . . " in an indicative (real) idea, what will it be? Let's see what you can come up with:

....

Although there are multiple variations that I can come up with, here are two that come to mind for me:

> **Because of his lasagna, Carlo's a finalist in the annual faculty cooking contest at school.**
>
> **It's only because of his lasagna that Carlo is a finalist in the annual faculty cooking contest at school.**

Before I move on to a new topic, I have two more little challenges for you. As you well know by now, in our exploration of conditional sentences, I've come upon a few examples where we can change register by doing some fancy changes to a phrase such as eliminating a certain word and inverting the positions of other words. Well, what can you think of to make the phrase "If it weren't for" more formal sounding? Look back at the previous pages in this chapter if you need to, and as your next little challenge, let's see what you can create:

We can change "<u>if it weren't for</u>" to ....

The answer is that we can change "If it weren't for" into the very formal-sounding phrase "were it not for" by going through the following steps:

1. Eliminate *if*.
2. Take the negative verb out of its contracted form.
3. Move *were* to where *if* used to be.

And that's how you do it. Very formal sounding indeed!

Now, for your last little challenge, can you think of a reduced version of "If it were not for"? I'll even give you a hint: two out of the five words in the expression have to be eliminated—but which two are they?

The two words to eliminate are .... and .... ,
so the reduced form is ....

Well, it so happens that the two words you need to eliminate are *it* and *were*, so the answer to this last challenge is that the reduced form of "If it weren't for" is *if not for* and it's used exactly like its longer counterpart:

If not for his lasagna, Carlo wouldn't be a
finalist in the annual faculty cooking contest.

Here's one final note about unreal conditional sentences in the present or timeless form. Go all the way back to the first page of this chapter and take another look at the quote given at the top of the page. Notice anything peculiar about the timeless subjunctive verb in the *if* clause? How would you explain that form of the verb?

....

It so happens that using the base verb here as the timeless subjunctive form ("If music be the food of love, play on!") is another example of the **archaic, or formulaic subjunctive** that still lingers on in modern English in certain pat phrases and the like (see Chapter 15).

Unreal Conditional Sentences: The Past

Just as we dealt with two parts that make up each unreal conditional sentence in the timeless, present, and future forms, we'll be doing the same thing with this type of sentence in the past. With that little reminder, let's look at the next dialogue concentrating on the phrases in bold:

> A: Good morning, Alessandra. What are you smiling about?
>
> B: I just stopped a mother duck and her babies from getting killed.
>
> A: How'd you do that?
>
> B: She was trying to lead them across a busy road, but couldn't. So I stood out there, stopped traffic, and she led them across!
>
> A: Aren't you the little hero!
>
> B: That's right! If I **hadn't been** there, the ducks **might have been killed**.
>
> A: Oh, I'm sure she **would have managed** to get them across.
>
> B: No way! If she **had tried** to lead the babies across on her own, a car **would have hit** them.
>
> A: Okay, okay. You're the office hero for the day, all right?
>
> B: Right!

Now that you've looked over the phrases in bold, I'm going to give you a few questions to answer that will help you make some observations about the grammar in this dialogue:

1. What mood is used in the *if* clauses? ....
2. What's used to make this verb form? ....
3. What's the time of the modals in the conditional clauses? ....
4. What's used to make these modal forms? ....

After everything we've covered concerning the subjunctive and conditional forms, you probably haven't had much trouble filling in the blanks. Here are my answers. Let's see how closely yours match mine:

    1. the subjunctive mood   **3. the past**
    2. the past perfect   **4. the modal perfect form**

Of course you have to keep remembering that these ideas are in the realm of imagination. In one of the two sentences that follow, though, the speaker is quite sure of her statement, while in the other she's playing it safe by not being so definite. Figure out which is which:

1. If I hadn't been there, the ducks might have died.
    ☐ She's definite.   ☐ She's not definite.

2. If she'd tried to lead the babies across on her own, a car would have hit them.
    ☐ She's definite.   ☐ She's not definite.

You know by now that it's the modal in the conditional clause which gives us the information that we need to check the correct boxes. By using *might* in **Sentence 1**, the speaker is saying that **she's not definite**, so she's playing it safe. On the other hand, by using *would* in **Sentence 2**, the speaker is saying that **she's definite** about the final hypothetical outcome.

By the way, what other modal perfect phrase could Speaker B use instead of *might have* to convey that same idea?

....

The other modal perfect phrase that would work equally well is ***could have***. And before we leave this topic, there's one other modal that we can use, the past form of *must*, *had had to*:

> I would have died for her if I had had to!

Mixing and Matching Unreal Conditional Clauses

Up to this point in our exploration of unreal conditional sentences, I've been doing something that some might call artificial; I've been presenting sentences that are all neatly in the past, present, future, and timeless form. But, of course, language doesn't work like that all the time. Look at the next dialogue and you'll see what I mean:

> A: Come on, Dad! Let's ride our bikes together. What do you say?
>
> B: I know it's Saturday, Debbie, but I'm too tired. You go ahead.
>
> A: Aw, gee, Dad. Come on! We'll have a great time!
>
> B: Working two jobs isn't easy, Debbie. Some other time, okay?
>
> A: But if you **hadn't worked** till late last night, you **wouldn't be** so tired now.
>
> B: And if I **didn't work** those two jobs, I **wouldn't have had** the money to buy your bicycle!
>
> C: Don't go making Debbie feel guilty that you got her a bike, John. You **wouldn't need** two jobs if you **hadn't started** feeling envious of your brother Ned's good fortune!

As far as time is concerned when it comes to unreal conditional sentences, what do we see going on in this dialogue? In the order that the three sentences with phrases in bold appear, what do *you* see? Write down the time contained in each phrase on the following lines:

.... + ...
.... + ...
.... + ...

I find the following: **the past + the present / general time + the past / the present + the past**. So obviously we can mix and match time clauses in unreal conditional sentences and don't have any rigid system to adhere to. A point to get across to your students is that past actions can have past consequences, but past actions can also have present consequences. Moreover, because we're dealing with the realm of imagination anyway, there's no reason that we can't mix any times together if we feel like doing so!

For a deeper look at conditionals, visit us at
ELTgrammar.com

Phrases that Create Hypothetical Situations

In conversational English, we have two phrases that replace *if* for setting up situations which may be real or unreal and which may refer to the past, the present, or the future. Let's see if you can pick them out:

> A: Well, I'm off to Australia for a three-week vacation!
>
> B: That's wonderful! So, have you made all your reservations for hotels?
>
> A: Nope, I'll just "wing it," as they say.
>
> B: No reservations? What if you get to Sydney and there aren't any hotel rooms vacant? What will you do then?
>
> A: There's always something available.
>
> B: Say there isn't. What will you do, sleep in the streets?
>
> A: You worry too much. Besides, that's the way I always travel. I did the same thing last year in North Africa.
>
> B: Well, you were just lucky. What if there hadn't been any rooms vacant? Would you have slept on the desert sands?

So what are those two useful phrases that replace *if*? Write them down on the following lines:

.... and ....

The two phrases in this dialogue that do such a neat job of replacing *if* and setting up hypothetical situations are **what if** and **say**, and they're completely interchangeable because they mean exactly the same thing.

What's interesting to note about them is that, just like conditional sentences, they can refer to real situations:

What if/Say you get to Sydney and there aren't any hotel rooms vacant . . .

or they can refer to unreal situations:

What if there hadn't been any rooms vacant?
Say there hadn't been any rooms vacant.

The main reason I mention these two phrases here is that they're another example of common phrases not usually covered in student grammar books, and they should be since they're such useful conversational devices.

Teaching Tips

16.1 "If I Had a Hammer"

Teach your students the folk song "If I Had a Hammer."

16.2 *I Wish You'd Sit Next to Me!*

Before class think up groups of three to four similar items. Divide the students into small groups and have them discuss which item in the list they prefer and why, making sure that they use "*if*" in their discussions.

Here are some examples of the items that you can use with your students and the statements that they might make:

- snake, bee, kangaroo
- tomato, carrot, lettuce
- morning, afternoon, evening
- summer, winter, spring, fall
- running, canoeing, skating, bowling
- beaches, mountains, forests, plains
- etc.

- If I were a bee, I'd be able to make honey.
- If I had some better tomatoes, I'd make us some spaghetti sauce.
- I'd be in bed right now if it were nighttime.
- I could go skiing if it were winter.

16.3 *Proverbs*

Bring in or have students bring in proverbs that are imperative forms ("Look before you leap." / "Don't count your chickens before they hatch." / "Never a borrower nor a lender be," etc.). Let your students explain the reasons for these proverbs by using *if* ("If you don't look, you may/could hurt yourself." / "If you count on something before it happens, you may be in for a big disappointment." / "You won't be upset that your friend hasn't returned the money you lent him if you make it a policy not to lend money in the first place.")

16.4 *The Alphabet Game*

This is another version of The Alphabet Game (see page 39). One student starts off the game by saying: "I want to go to _____ this summer. If I go to _____ on vacation, I'll take _____ with me," or "I'm not a genius, but if I were, I could _____." The next student repeats the information the first student has said and adds something of his or her own ("If I go to _____ on vacation, I'll take _____ and _____ with me"). Every student repeats what's been said before and adds his or her own piece of information to the conditional sentence heard up to that point. The sentence gets longer and longer and harder and harder to repeat, but it's good for developing your students' memories. To show them that this isn't an impossible thing to do and that you've been paying attention to them, you be the last one, repeating everything that's been said by all your students!

16.5 *Hopes and Wishes for the Future*

Ask your students to brainstorm their wishes and hopes for the future (the winner of a specific election, people living to be 150 years old, world peace, a cure for cancer, etc.). Put their ideas on the board. Then have them create reasons for their wishes and hopes ("If X wins the election, he'll vote for universal medical coverage." / "If people lived to be 150, they'd be alive in two centuries." / "We wouldn't have to spend so much on military hardware if there were world peace," etc.).

16.6 *My Dream House*

Divide the class into small groups and ask them to draw the floor plan of their dream house. After the plans have been made, let the "architects" exchange plans with another group, who now become "prospective homeowners." The homeowners now discuss the designs using wishes and hopes to make the home more "theirs." Of course, reasons must be provided for why the changes are to be made. Remind the students to use conditionals for their reasons ("We hope the downstairs bathroom has a door that leads out to the pool. If it does, we'll be able to enter the house right after swimming").

16.7 *I Wish I Were . . .*

Bring in pictures of all sorts of animals or a list of famous people. Have the students make wishes about the animals ("I wish I were a kangaroo") and people

("I wish I were a multi-millionaire"). Then have them explain their wishes ("If I were a kangaroo, I could carry all my books in my pouch." / "If I were a multi-millionaire, I would be able to help poor people").

16.8 *Fairy Tales*

Fairy tales always have plenty of problem situations in them. Use them as a basis for brainstorming wishes, hopes, and lots of conditional sentences.

16.9 *I Regret: I Wish I Hadn't . . .*

Have students brainstorm regrets they have and regrets they've heard others state, e.g., "I wish I had/hadn't . . ." You can even add your own. Write them on the board and then have them expound on the regrets by using conditionals.

16.10 *Advice Letters*

Have your students write and respond to advice letters by using wishes, hopes, and conditionals.

16.11 *Superstitions*

This tip gives students the opportunity to work with and learn traditional sayings that come from superstitions. These traditional sayings are often formed with *if* clauses ("If you step on a crack, you'll break your mother's back." / "If your palm itches, you're going to inherit money." / "If you find a penny in the street, you're going to have good luck." / "If your nose itches, you're going to kiss a fool," etc.). Divide the class into small groups and have them come up with several examples of these sayings. Have the students share their sayings with the entire class.

Variation: Have your students make up new superstitions containing *if* clauses, or let them bring in ones from their own cultures.

16.12 *Tic Tac Toe*

Create a "Tic Tac Toe" game (British "Naughts and Crosses") or a game of "Concentration" based on wishes and conditionals (see *Appendix 6*).

17

Autosegmental Features, Part 1

"His name's Castro, but he's not one of theee Castros."

In the subtitle above, you must have noticed the two extra *e*'s in the word *the*. Why on earth would anyone add two extra letters like that? What am I trying to tell you?

To answer these questions, I'm going to put you to work right away. Why do you think I added extra *e*'s to the word *the*?

....

English has some amazing features, and the subtitle for this chapter has definitely targeted one of them. By adding two extra *e*'s, I'm letting you know **I want you to pronounce the definite article /ði/ even though the standard pronunciation before a noun beginning with a consonant sound is /ðə/** (see Chapter 2).

I could have accomplished this just by writing one extra *e* instead of two, but I did this to let you know that even though it isn't routinely done, **I want you to stress the definite article** in the sentence. (Note that I'll be using two ways to show the main stress on words: CAPITAL LETTERS or /fə - nɛ́ - tɪk træn- skríp - šən/ with an accent mark (´) over the stressed syllables. Also note that a colon represents an elongated vowel sound.) So, owing to the nature of this situation, the sentence has gone from

. . . but he's not one of /ðə/ Castros.

to

. . . but he's not one of /ði/ Castros.

to

. . . but he's not one of /ði:/ Castros.

It's all well and good that you've figured out what I had in mind for the definite article in that sentence, but why did I go through this bother, and why did I think you would understand what I was getting at?

Before I get to the answers, I'd like to make a very serious suggestion. The best way to understand and get a feel for what I'm going to be talking about in this chapter and in Chapter 18 is to say each example you come upon OUT LOUD. Trust me; saying the examples out loud will make these two chapters much more meaningful and understandable. One word of caution: I don't recommend you work on these chapters with people around!

So, why did I think you would understand my variation on stress and pronunciation for *the*? The reason is that it's become a convention to write t–h–e as "*theee*" when this word is emphasized. As all native English speakers know, these changes in t–h–e signify that the writer or speaker is discussing some well known subject. "The CAStros" could refer to any family bearing that name, whereas "THEEE Castros" refers to that internationally known family from Cuba. Other conventions that are sometimes used to show stress to emphasize a word are capital letters or putting a font in bold.

Even though I've demonstrated the change in meaning by using two devices (stress *and* pronunciation), the same effect can really be accomplished simply by the stress falling on the definite article with no change in pronunciation. The pronunciation change is secondary in importance with stress being the primary device used to attain this extra communication. When this effect is achieved, I've come upon a feature of English that makes this language unique, the phenomenon of **autosegmental features**, also known as **suprasegmental features** or **prosody**. In short, **autosegmental features are changes in stress or intonation** (the rising or falling of the voice) **which dramatically influence the meaning of single words, phrases, or whole sentences.**

This is the first of two chapters in which we'll have some fun exploring this rarely discussed subject, which many consider quite troublesome since there don't seem to be many rules to go by. Because there are so many interesting points to investigate, it will be easier to divide the information into this chapter and Chapter 18.

I'll start off investigating stress in this chapter by seeing how it affects single words, then noun phrases, and finally verb phrases, all of which can have dramatic changes in meaning depending on where the stress is placed. In Chapter 18 you'll see how whole sentences are affected by stress and intonation. As you consider these various forms, you'll see why I think autosegmental features should be taught within the context of grammar.

The point of this chapter and Chapter 18 isn't just to show you the mechanics and some major rules for autosegmental features, but also to let you have some fun exploring this tricky area of the language and sensitizing yourself to it.

So, without further ado, let's take a look at how single words are affected by autosegmental changes.

Stress and Single Words

Let's take the plunge right into the world of autosegmental features by looking at the first dialogue for this chapter.

I'm going to let you do a little exploring on your own now. In the dialogue, except for the words *contrary* and *content*, all of the words in bold are followed by a superscript[1] or a superscript[2]. (I'll get to *contrary* and *content* later.) Under the corresponding heading below, write each of these words and put the syllables that you think should be stressed in capital letters. I've done the first one to get you started.

A: How's your **rebel**[1] doing?

B: My "**rebel**"? Oh, you mean my teenage son. Well, he's still a very **contrary** person, and he still **rebels**[2] against parental authority, of course, but **contrary** to what you may think, he's no different from many others.

A: Has he **progressed**[2] at all at school?

B: Yes, as a matter of fact. He's shown a great deal of **progress**[1]. He's **produced**[2] some excellent grades lately.

A: Well, I'm really glad to hear it. Oh, look at the time! I've got to get to the supermarket before it closes. Ben, the manager of the **produce**[1] section, is saving some fresh asparagus for me.

B: Hmm. Not **content** with frozen asparagus anymore? And what's Ben's **object**[1] in being so nice to you?

A: I **object**[2] to the tone I hear you using! And there's no content to your implication. He's just a very nice man, I'll have you know.

Words Followed by [1]	Words Followed by [2]
REBel	

If we jump from Column 1 over to Column 2 on each line, this is what we end up with:

> REBel   reBEL
> PROgress   proGRESSED
> PROduce   proDUCED
> OBject   obJECT

I hope you've arrived at the same answers that I have. But what can you make out of all of this information? Look over these pairs of words and see if you can come up with one observable pattern emerging. When you think you've hit upon something, write your conclusion on the following line:

....

The observation that you can make from all these words is that when the same word is used for both the noun and the verb, **the nouns have the stress on the first syllable and the verbs have the stress on the final syllable:**

> REBel (n.)   reBEL (v.)
> PROgress (n.)   proGRESS (v.)
> PROduce (n.)   proDUCE (v.)
> OBject (n.)   obJECT (v.)

Not surprisingly, when such a basic stress change occurs, important phonological changes can take place with the vowels. Just look at the sound changes that happen with the four pairs of words I've spotlighted:

	Nouns	**Verbs**
rebel:	/rɛ́ – bəl/	/ri – bɛ́l/ or /rɪ – bɛ́l/
progress:	/prá – grɛs/ or /pró – grɛs/	/prə – grɛ́s/
produce:	/pró – dus/ or /pró – dyus/	/prə – dús/ or /prə – dyús/
object:	/ab́ – ǰɛkt/	/əb – ǰɛ́kt/

Who says English is easy?! Let's remember that such phonological changes are very challenging for teachers to teach and students to learn.

The most we can say, at any rate, is that with words that fall into this pattern, there's a *tendency* for the stress to go to the initial syllable for nouns and to the final syllable for verbs. Keep in mind, though, that that isn't always the case. It's easy to cite examples that don't follow this observation. Words like *alarm*, *control*, and *display* have the stress on the final syllable for both the noun and verb, and words like *balance*, *fashion*, and *preview* have the stress on the first syllable. Here's what we mean:

> All the aLARMS are set for 5:45 a.m. (n.)
> The slightest noise aLARMS our dog. (v.)
> The movie stars attended the PREview. (n.)
> The director will PREview the movie. (v.)

As far as tendencies go, another one I can mention is that many stressed long vowel sounds, such as the /i/, the /a/, and the /o/ in the nouns I've targeted, tend to "reduce" to a schwa sound, /ə/, when the stress is changed. You can see that happening with *rebel*, *progress*, *produce*, and *object*.

So far, I've investigated four of the six pairs of words from the dialogue, but we've got two more to deal with, *contrary* and *content*. Something quite different is going on in these cases. Let's repeat the phrases that these words are in. Add an accent mark over the syllable in each word that you feel should receive the stress:

> 1a. . . . he's still a very CONTRARY person . . .
> 1b. . . . but CONTRARY to what you may think . . .
> 2a. Not CONTENT with frozen asparagus anymore?
> 2b. . . . there's no CONTENT to your implication.

Contrary is an adjective when the stress is on the middle syllable, but it's an adverb when the stress is on the first syllable. The adjective *conTRAry* (/kən - tré - ri/) is used exclusively to describe a person who invariably goes against what everybody else says or wants:

> I say "yes"; she says "no." I say "good"; she says "bad."
> And then she has the nerve to say that *I'm* conTRAry!

The adverb CONtrary (/kán - tre - ri/) simply means "opposite" or "against":

> CONtrary to popular belief, the stock market isn't all that risky.

LEGATVM PERPLEXVM ROMANVM— or, A Confusing Legacy from Rome

As far as the word c–o–n–t–e–n–t goes, something really unusual happens when you change the stress on it (and we'll see that the same holds true for o–b–j–e–c–t). If you say *CONtent* (/kán - tɛnt/) or the plural form, *CONtents*, you've got a noun, and you're talking about what's inside something or some important ideas (in a speech, for example). However, when you change the stress and say *conTENT* (/kən - tént/), you've got an adjective, and you mean "satisfied." Not only did the part of speech change, but the meaning has changed, too!

Is it possible that we're not dealing with autosegmental features anymore, but with some other phenomenon? No, we're still in the remarkable realm of autosegmental features. Both forms of the word c–o–n–t–e–n–t come from the same Latin past participle, *contentus*, which comes from the verb *continere*, meaning "to contain," so it's not English that's caused this phenomenon, but Latin. Somewhere in the evolution of that language, the past participle, *contained*, took on an additional idiomatic use that meant "happy" or "satisfied." So in Latin, *contentus* could mean *contained*, *the content*(s), or *happy/satisfied*. If you want to blame anyone for this confusing development which we've inherited in English, blame the Romans, not the English!

And as I've mentioned, the same holds true for o–b–j–e–c–t. If the stress is on the first syllable, *OBject* (/áb - jĕkt/), you've got a noun which means, among other things, something perceptible by the senses or the focus of some sort of attention. If you put the stress on the final syllable, *obJECT* (/əb - jĕkt/), you've got a verb which means to *oppose* or *disapprove*. Both variations come from the Latin past participle, *objectus*, which comes from the verb *obicere*, meaning "to throw something in the way." Somehow down the centuries the past participle developed an extra idiomatic meaning which has held on in the Romance languages, and even in English via Norman French.

Before moving on, here are two more of these really strange single words which, on the surface, have little obvious connection in meaning when their stress is changed:

DIgest (n.) /dáɪ - jĕst/   diGEST (v.) /daɪ - jĕst/ or /dɪ - jĕst/
MInute (n.) /mí - nɪt/   miNUTE (adj.) /maɪ - nút/ or /maɪ - nyút/

More Examples of Stress Changes and Parts of Speech

Unlike what we've just discussed, for the most part, when a single word can have two different stresses, the part of speech may change, but its basic concept doesn't. A *REBel* is a person who *reBELS*; you show *PROgress* when you *proGRESS*; and *PROduce* is what a farmer has *proDUCED* on his farm.

Here's a brief list of some common words in which the stress changes when the part of speech changes, but the basic meaning doesn't. Keep in mind, though, that some of these words, especially the verbs, do have common secondary meanings as well:

Nouns

Ally	/ǽ – lai/
CONduct	/kán – dəkt/
CONflict	/kán – flɪkt/
CONtract	/kán – trækt/
CONtrast	/kán – træst/
CRItic	/krí – tɪk/
DIScard	/dís – kard/
DIScharge	/dís – čarǰ/
IMprint	/ím – prɪnt/
INsult	/ín – səlt/
PERfume	/pə́r – fyum/
PERmit	/pə́r – mɪt/
PERvert	/pə́r – vərt/
REcall	/rí – kɔl/
REcord	/rέ – kərd/
RElapse	/rí – læps/
REmake	/rí – mek/
REplay	/rí – ple/
REwrite	/rí – raɪt/
UPset	/ə́p – sɛt/

One-Word Verbs

aLLY	/ə – lái/
conDUCT	/kən – də́kt/
conFLICT	/kən – flíkt/
conTRACT	/kən – trǽkt/
conTRAST	/kən – trǽst/
criTIQUE	/krɪ – tík/
disCARD	/dɪs – kárd/
disCHARGE	/dɪs – čárǰ/
imPRINT	/ɪm – prínt/
inSULT	/ɪn – sə́lt/
perFUME	/pər – fyúm/
perMIT	/pər – mít/
perVERT	/pər – və́rt/
reCALL	/ri – kɔ́l/
reCORD	/ri – kɔ́rd/
reLAPSE	/ri – lǽps/
reMAKE	/ri – mék/
rePLAY	/ri – plé/
reWRITE	/ri – ráɪt/
upSET	/əp – sέt/

Compounded Nouns

ADD-on	/ǽd – an/
BLACKout	/blǽk – aʊt/
BREAKthrough	/brέk – θru/
DO-over	/dú – ovər/
HANDout	/hǽnd – aʊt/
KNOCKout	/nák – aʊt/
KICK-off	/kík – ɔf/
MIX-up	/míks – əp/
PRINTout	/prínt – aʊt/
RUNaway	/rə́n – əwe/
TAKE out	/tέk – aʊt/

Two-Word Verbs

add ON	/æd – án/
black OUT	/blæk – aʊ́t/
break THROUGH	/brek – θrú/
do OVER	/du – óvər/
hand OUT	/hænd – áʊt/
knock OUT	/nak – áʊt/
kick OFF	/kɪk – ɔ́f/
mix UP	/mɪks – ə́p/
print OUT	/prɪnt – áʊt/
run aWAY	/rən – əwé/
take OUT	/tek – áʊt/

I should point out that, even though it's more common to find words which can be either nouns or verbs depending on the stress, some single words can be adjectives or verbs, again depending on the stress. Examples:

ABsent (adj.)	/ǽb – sɪnt/	abSENT (v.)	/æb – sέnt/
PERfect (adj.)	/pə́r – fɪkt/	perFECT (v.)	/pər – fέkt/

There's one other phenomenon—not common, thank goodness—which I thought I'd give you two examples of for the fun of it. Here's what I'd like you to do. First, read each of the two following adjectives out loud. Then rewrite each word on the line under it, appropriately showing where the stress should fall by capitalizing the syllable you've stressed:

        compact   upset

        _____   _____

After saying these two adjectives out loud, you should realize that most native speakers put the stress on the final syllable in c–o–m–p–a–c–t (although some do place the stress on the first syllable), and everyone puts the stress on the final syllable of u–p–s–e–t. In that case, you should have written "comPACT" or "COMpact" and "upSET."

Now let's repeat this little exercise, but this time you'll be saying two phrases (instead of two single adjectives) out loud." Once again, rewrite each adjective on the line under the phrase it's in, showing where the stress should be by capitalizing the appropriate syllable:

        a compact car   an upset stomach

        _____   _____

Uh-oh! If you've pronounced these two phrases the way native English speakers do, you've made an interesting change in the stress. The stress should have switched to the first syllable in each adjective (there's no option now for c–o–m–p–a–c–t) so that you'd end up saying "COMpact" (*a COMpact CAR*) and "UPset" (*an UPset STOmach*). Yes, the mysteries of English just keep getting "curiouser and curiouser"! I needn't go into lengthy linguistic explanations as to why this loss of option and shift of stress have occurred; suffice it to say that you will come upon exceptions like these two, and you can simply accept them for what they are, exceptions. It just seems that **with certain adjectives like the two I've cited, if they come before the nouns they describe (*an UPset STOmach*), the stress is placed on the first syllable, whereas if they follow verbs like *be* or *get* (*My STOmach is upSET*), the stress is on the final syllable.** This odd occurrence seems to happen with a very small number of pat phrases, so don't overly concern yourself with it. And, by the way, another example is an item commonly associated with music and computers, *a COMpact DISC*, better known as a *CD*!

Stress and Noun Phrases

Okay, it's time for more fun, which will get under way when you read my next dialogue. First of all, here's a note about stress as you'll find it throughout the rest of this chapter. Even though it's true that a multi-syllable word or a noun phrase containing an adjective and a noun will have what's commonly referred to as primary and secondary stress, for the purposes of autosegmental features, I'm going to use capitalized words in bold to show both the primary and secondary stress. In reality they're so close in the spoken language that it's not necessary to differentiate them in these two chapters.

One other point you should remember is that the spoken language had existed long, long before the written language came into being. Keeping that in mind, in spite of the fact that a word can be written as one word (backbone) or two (car keys), **all of the examples we'll have comparing such forms will be written as two or three separate words with only stress playing the key role in determining meaning.** I don't want visual clues to give anything away!

Remember: **stress the words that are capitalized.** In fact, as I've already suggested, read this next dialogue aloud to make sure you hear the stress clearly:

A: Hello?

B: Hello, Yoshi. This is Dr. Fontaine.

A: Oh, hello, Dr. Fontaine. I'm glad you've called. How are you?

B: Just great. Say, Yoshi, what are you up to?

A: Oh, I'm just fooling around in the **DARK ROOM**.

B: Excuse me?

A: I'm trying to develop some photographs.

B: Oh! You're in your **DARK** room.

A: I have some great pictures here of my July 4th trip to Washington, D.C. I've got a good picture of myself eating a **HOT DOG** standing in front of the **WHITE HOUSE** and watching a parade with Revolutionary War soldiers and some **RED COATS**.

B: All I can say, Yoshi, is that if your photos really show what you've just described to me, they'll definitely be unique!

So why does Dr. Fontaine make that quip? Obviously it's because Yoshi doesn't realize what he's said. The question is, do *you*? Let's see if you can figure out which is which. Match the noun phrases that follow with their corresponding pictures, and then write the letter of each picture on the blank line under its matching phrase:

17 Autosegmental Features, Part 1

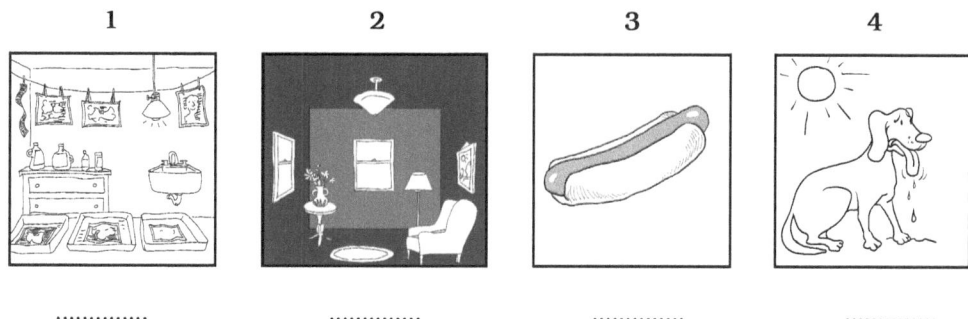

A. a DARK ROOM / B. a DARK room   C. a HOT DOG / D. a HOT dog

Here's how I match up these noun phrases with the pictures. Compare mine to yours:

A DARK ROOM is a room that has very little or no light in it, so **2** is **A**, but a DARK room is a room where photographs are developed, so **1** is **B**.

A HOT DOG is a live dog that feels hot, so **4** is **C**, but a HOT dog is a kind of sausage, usually eaten in a bun, so **3** is **D**.

Now let's look at two more pairs of noun phrases differentiated by the stress they receive:

E. the WHITE HOUSE / F. the WHITE house   G. a RED COAT / F. a RED coat

Let's see how you did with these:

The WHITE HOUSE is a specific house that's painted white, so **2** is **E**, but the President of the United States lives and works in the WHITE House, so **1** is **F**.

A RED COAT is just a coat that's dyed red, so **3** is **G**, but a RED coat was an 18th century British soldier, so **4** is **H**.

Isn't it amazing what a little change in stress can do?! You already had a taste of this phenomenon where stress can change meaning at the beginning of the chapter when you came upon words like *content* and *object*, but then we were exploring single words. Here, we're working with noun phrases in the form of compound nouns and adjectives + nouns (see Chapter 2).

If you were going to sum up how you can differentiate between an adjective + noun and a compound noun for your students, what would you tell them? Can you discern a pattern emerging from all of the examples we've had? Write down your thoughts on the following line:

....

The pattern that we see emerging is that **if you have an adjective + noun, put the stress more or less equally on both elements (a HOT DOG), but if you have a compound noun, put the stress on the first element only (a HOT dog).**

To make this point even sharper, let's stick with the dog and see more examples of our stress pattern at work. First, I'll simply describe a dog:

    a BIG DOG   a NICE DOG
    an OLD DOG   a STRAY DOG

In all of the previous examples, the stress is placed just about equally on both the adjectives and the nouns. But now let's distinguish different kinds of dogs by their breeds or specially assigned tasks:

    a SHEEP dog
    a WATCH dog
    a GUARD dog
    a HOUND dog

Now the stress has changed and been placed only on the first element in each of these noun phrases. This is certainly a convenient way to distinguish adjective + noun combinations from compound nouns.

Changing meaning by changing stress is a unique feature of English, but one that rarely gets touched on in grammar classes. There's really no reason, however, that this subject shouldn't be covered gradually, even at the beginning level. Students can be made to understand through pictures, etc., that a "HOT DOG" is not the same thing as a "HOT dog." Lengthy explanations aren't necessary; what you might want to do is model the phrases enough times, have the students parrot them accurately, and then devise some discrimination exercises to reinforce this area of autosegmental features.

There are lots of examples to contrast adjective + noun phrases with compound nouns. Let's take a look at a few more. Look at the pictures that follow. Under them is a pair of phrases, one adjective + noun and one compound noun. Match the letter of each phrase with its corresponding picture by writing the appropriate letter on the blank line under each picture:

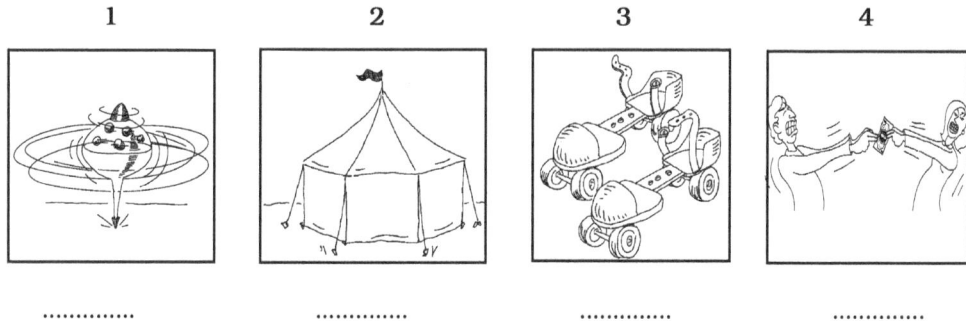

A. the BIG TOP / B. the BIG top   C. CHEAP skates / D. CHEAP SKATES

Okay! Let's get right to it and see how well you've matched things up:

The BIG TOP can be a specific, large spinning toy, so **1** is **A**, but the BIG top is another name for the largest circus tent, so **2** is **B**.

CHEAP SKATES are skates that are inexpensive or poorly made, so **3** is **D**, but CHEAP skates are stingy people, so **4** is **C**.

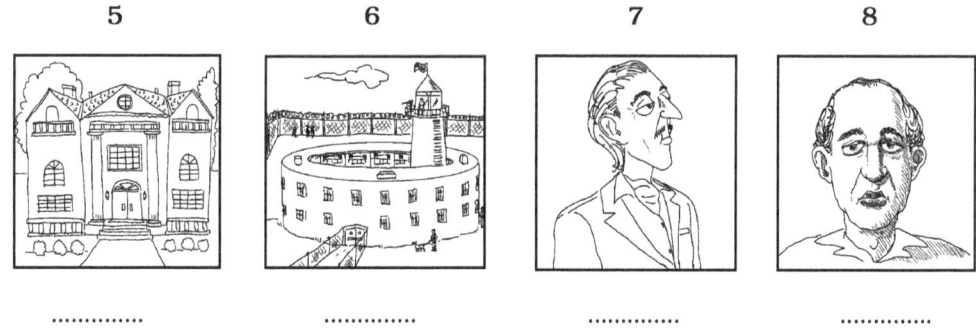

E. the BIG house / F. the BIG HOUSE   G. a HIGH BROW / H. a HIGH brow

And here are the match-ups for these next two pairs:

The BIG HOUSE is a large house, so **5** is **F**. The BIG house is a slang term used by gangsters et al. to mean "prison," so **6** is **E**.

A HIGH brow is someone who has superior learning or culture, so **7** is **H**, but a HIGH BROW means a large area of forehead commonly seen on someone (usually a man) with a receding hairline, so **8** is **G**.

And now for our last two pairs of noun phrases:

I. NEW YEARS / J. NEW Year's   K. a LONG hair / L. a LONG HAIR

Let's see how they match up:

NEW Year's (short for New Year's Eve or Day) is a holiday, so **9** is **J**, but NEW YEARS means 12-month calendar cycles, for want of a better definition, so **10** is **I**.

A LONG hair is an antiquated expression for a person who's deeply involved in the arts, especially classical music, so **11** is **K**, but a LONG HAIR is a hair which happens to be long, so **12** is **L**.

One other area we should examine deals with a noun + the *-s* genitive (see Chapter 7) and its accompanying head noun. Look at these examples, and this time see if you can write simple definitions for them. By the way, I've deliberately omitted the apostrophes:

1a. a CALFS LIVer = ...
1b. CALFS liver = ...
2a. a BRIDES maid = ...
2b. a BRIDES MAID = ...

It seems that changing stress on phrases such as these will change meaning just as you've seen happen with compound nouns compared to adjectives + nouns. Here are my versions to compare to your definitions. I bet they're very close if not exactly the same:

1a. a CALFS LIVer = an internal organ of a calf
1b. CALFS liver = a food

2a. a BRIDES maid = a female friend or relative who attends the bride at a wedding

2b. a BRIDES MAID = a female servant in the employ of the bride

Write down your observation of the stress pattern you see from my examples when there's an element with the -s genitive:

....

It turns out that the pattern is just the same as it is when dealing with a compound noun or adjective + noun: **if the possessive word plus its head noun form a new word, just as a compound noun does,** (calf's liver/bridesmaid), **the first element receives the stress. If we're simply dealing with a head noun and explaining who or what it belongs to** (a calf's liver/a bride's maid), **the possessive noun shares more or less equal stress with the head noun,** just as the adjective does.

Here are some more examples without apostrophes. Let's see if you can define them all now that you've got a handle on how influential stress is:

1a. the CARpenters tools = ...

1b. the CARpenters TOOLS = ...

2a. the MENS club = ...

2b. the MENS CLUB = ...

From observing where the stress falls, we know that 1a and 2a form new terms just as compound nouns do. For the same reason, we know that 1b and 2b are simply possessive nouns + head nouns. And now to our definitions with the apostrophes added:

1a. = the tools used by carpenters (carpenters' tools)
1b. = the tools owned by one or more carpenters (carpenters' or a carpenter's tools)
2a. = a club for men only (men's club)
2b. = a club which certain men are members of (the men's club)

Before we move on to explore other ways that stress influences meaning, here's a little activity for you to try out to see if you've got a good idea of the stress tendencies I've just outlined. I've given you some phrases with the stressed parts capitalized just as I've done before in this chapter. You figure out each phrase and write it out as it should "normally" appear on the first line provided. Next, fill in the parentheses that follow with the part of speech it is. And finally, write a short, simple definition. I've done the first one to get you started:

PINK eye:	*pínkeye*	(noun)	*conjunctivitis*
PINK EYE:		( )	
BLACK BALL:		( )	
BLACK ball:		( )	
FROGS LEGS:		( )	
FROGS legs:		( )	
BLUE print:		( )	
BLUE PRINT:		( )	

And here's a pair that's more fun if you see the two parts first in phonetic transcription. I'll give you a tip: in one of the phrases, /do/ is an informal term for money.

/wín dó/:		( )	
/wín do/:		( )	

It can be a lot of fun to see how meaning can change depending on where stress falls. Here are the rest of my answers to the exercise you've just done:

PINK EYE:	pink eye (adj. + n.)	an eye that appears pink
BLACK BALL:	black ball (adj. + n.)	a ball that's black
BLACK ball:	blackball (v.)	ostracize
FROGS LEGS:	frogs' legs (poss. n. + head n.)	the legs of frogs
FROGS legs:	frogs' legs (poss. n. + head n.)	a food
BLUE print:	blueprint (n.)	an architect's drawn plan
BLUE PRINT:	blue print (adj. + n.)	a print that's colored blue
/wín dó/:	win dough (v. + n.)	win money
/wín do/:	window (n.)	panes of glass in a wall

And now for the *pièce de résistance*! The most fun you can have in getting sensitized to how stress can change meaning when dealing with noun phrases is to scrutinize examples like the ones you're about to see, or even better, think up some of your own. I'll supply you with the elements that each phrase contains; then I'll give you a simple definition as your clue. *You* construct the example and show the proper stress for whichever meaning you're working on by using accent marks or capitalizing the stressed parts. Have fun!

                    timer   old   cheap

1a. This is an inexpensive device purchased many years ago that was used to time food while it was cooking.

It's ....

1b. This is a stingy senior citizen.

He's ....

                    gun   hand   second

2a. This is a small gun that was bought used.

It's ....

2b. This is not the first gun, it's the second gun.

It's ....

                    great   hour   happy

3a. This was the excellent early-evening discount at their pub.

It was ....

3b. This was 60 minutes of joy

It was ....

Definitely an amusing activity for more sensitization to stress! At any rate, let's get right to my answers so you can compare them to yours:

 1a = a CHEAP, OLD TIMer   1b = a CHEAP old-TIMer

 2a = a SECond-hand GUN   2b = a SECond HANDgun

 3a = a GREAT HAPpy hour   3b = a GREAT HAPpy HOUR

Stress and Verb Phrases

In a way, I've already introduced this section of the chapter by giving you the following pair of phonetic transcriptions (/wín do/ and /wín dó/). Here's how both could appear in one sentence:

  At the racetrack, I stepped up to the WINdow
  and placed a bet because I love to WIN DOUGH.

Here are some more examples of the same language phenomenon at work:

  1a. She's making the DOG RUN.
  1b. She's making the DOG run.

2a. Have you ever seen a HORSE fly?
2b. Have you ever seen a HORSE FLY?

You'll notice that there are two blank lines coming up for each item that I've just given you. On the first line for each item, see if you can identify the phrases I'm focusing on. Are they compound nouns or direct objects + base verb DOCs (see Chapter 11)? On the second line, paraphrase what each one means:

1a. _____

_____

1b. _____

_____

2a. _____

_____

2b. _____

_____

Here's what you should have come up with:

> 1a. **direct object + base verb DOC**
> She's forcing the dog to run.
> 1b. **compound noun**
> She's making the dog's exercise area.
> 2a. **compound noun**
> Have you ever seen this insect species?
> 2b. **direct object + base verb DOC**
> Have you ever seen a horse up in the air?

I hope you think these are as much fun as I do. But fun aside, is there any sort of stress pattern that you can discern that could explain what's going on? When you've figured it out, write your thoughts on the following line:

_____

You already know that you can tell if something's a compound noun when the first element receives the main stress for the whole phrase (DOG run/ HORSE fly). What's new is that this is the first time in the chapter that you're dealing with a direct object and its DOC. From your observations, you can tell that, unlike what happens with the compound nouns, **the direct object and its**

DOC receive more or less the same amount of stress.

Let's try another pair. Look at the capitalized parts to get the right stress and see if you can decipher what they mean by the change you observe in the stress:

1. I like to watch my CAT FISH.
2. I like to watch my CAT fish.

1. ....
2. ....

Sentence 1, which has **a direct object and its DOC** with more or less equal stress on both elements, means that the person likes to watch the cat as it fishes (at a pond, for example). **Sentence 2** contains a direct object, which turns out to be **a compound noun** with stress only on the first element. The sentence means **the person likes to watch the catfish** (a species of fish) perhaps while it's slithering about up and down the side of a fish tank. A remarkable difference, to say the least!

Because sentences like the two we've just examined are so much fun, let's look at some more examples. Observe where the stress is in the following pairs of sentences and write your interpretations on the lines provided. Then I'll give you mine to compare. Note that I'm giving these to you in phonetic transcription so that spacing and spelling won't tip you off!

3. I was /hóm sɪk/.
4. I was /hóm sík/.

3. ....
4. ....

5. She wrote /tu mɛ́ ni/ people.
6. She wrote /tú mɛ ni/ people.

5. ....
6. ....

7. You've /gát mi/.
8. You've /gát mí/.

7. ....
8. ....

And now to my interpretations. **Sentence 3** means "I missed my family and friends, etc.," while **Sentence 4** means "I was sick at home." Sentence 5 means "She wrote (letters) to multiple people," but **Sentence 6** means "She wrote (letters) to more people than she had to." Finally, **Sentence 7** means "I have no idea or no answer for you", while **Sentence 8** can mean "I can be on your team."

And then there's something like the next pair which also demonstrates how important stress can be in English. You decide where the stress should be put by writing in an accent mark over the stressed part or parts:

/aɪ yərn/ = a metal   versus   /aɪ yərn/ = I really want

If we want to communicate that we're talking about that common metal, the stress will be on the **first syllable**, so we have /áɪ - yərn/. But if we want to communicate that we really want something, we put almost **equal stress on the subject and verb** and get /áɪ yə́rn/.

Another interesting area for us to observe is to see how stress works with modal auxiliaries. I'm going to reiterate some points from a *Heads Up!* in Chapter 8. To start things off, though, let's look at this short dialogue:

A: Hello, Helene? This is Bossie Owambawa.

B: Hi, Bossie.

A: Listen, Helene. I /**kæn go**/ with you to Nairobi this weekend.

B: Oh, that's too bad.

A: Huh? But I thought you wanted me to go with you.

B: I do. Didn't you just say you couldn't?

A: No, I said I could!

B: Oh? I'm all confused.

Why is Helene confused? It's simple: Bossie added an extra stress that created a miscommunication. Can you explain what happened? Try to work it out on the line that follows:

....

The basic pattern regarding stress and modal auxiliaries is that **all modals are unstressed when they accompany a verb, are affirmative, and don't carry any extra meaning** (such as emphasis):

He may GO with us on the trip.
She can SPEAK three languages.

When the modals are negative, however, they receive more or less equal stress with their verbs:

> He MAY not GO with us on the trip.
> She CAN'T SPEAK three languages.

And this is the reason that Helene got so confused. **Bossie stressed both the modal and its verb, so it sounded like a negative to Helene.**

With the modal *can*, we even have an important change in pronunciation between the affirmative and negative that truly affects communication:

- Unstressed *can* is really pronounced /kɪn/. In fact, there's practically no vowel sound at all.

- Stressed *can't*, on the other hand, has a strongly pronounced vowel, which in certain varieties of British English is /a/, /kant/, and in American English is /æ/, /kænt/.

- In addition, the final *t* in *can't* is unreleased /t̚/. In fact, all final *t*'s have a tendency to be unreleased in American as well as other varieties of English. For all intents and purposes, the unreleased *t* makes that consonant practically inaudible. These two phenomena, the added stress and the unreleased /t̚/, result in a modal that sounds negative simply because it's got the stress on it and the strongly pronounced vowel: /kænt̚/ in American English, or /kant̚/ in most varieties of British English.

The use of stress with *will* and *would* in verb phrases (see Chapter 8) is also very interesting. You learned in that chapter that these modal auxiliaries can represent actions or behaviors of the person who the speaker is talking about. Here's a sample of what we mean:

A: You remembered to water all the house plants before we started this vacation, didn't you?

B: Uh-oh, I forgot to.

A: Great! You **WOULD** forget to do that. It's just like you!

B: Okay, so I forgot. You don't have to be so nasty about it.

A: Do you realize how much money we spent on those plants? Now they'll probably all die.

B: You **WILL** go on about money. Money, money, money! It's the money you're concerned about, not the plants!

Notice how Person A stresses *would* in her little tirade? If the modal auxiliary weren't stressed, we'd lose the meaning; in fact, the sentence wouldn't make any sense at all. This example shows you how important this stress can be. What

Person A is really communicating is that she knows Person B did something typical, the kind of thing he's done many other times in the past.

Person B, though, has a chance to respond with a short tirade of his own. By stressing *will*, he says he knows how typical this kind of reaction is for his wife. Notice again that if the modal weren't stressed, the sentence would completely lose meaning.

The difference between the two modal auxiliaries when used this way is that **stressed *will* expresses a general observation about someone's characteristic behavior, and stressed *would* expresses the same idea but only about something in the past.**

Sensitizing your students to the kinds of changes in communication that are brought on by this addition of stress on certain modals will go a long way to stopping any misunderstandings that can easily arise.

Teaching Tips

17.1 *Phone Messages*

This activity gives students a chance to practice leaving voice messages. Before class, think up pairs of phrases that feature an autosegmental contrast (CONtrast vs. conTRAST, EXport vs. exPORT, COMpound vs. comPOUND, etc.) and write them on individual slips of paper. Besides pairs of phrases like these, the different stress patterns of certain pairs of numbers (in particular 13/30, 14/40, 15/50, 16/60, 17/70, 18/80, 19/90) also provide numerous occasions for miscommunication to occur—thirTEEN vs. THIRty as, for instance, in telephone numbers (641-1330). Include one of these troublesome numbers on each slip of paper that you've prepared. Create enough slips so that each group of students will have one.

Divide the class into pairs or groups of three. Let them brainstorm an appropriate message for an answering machine, making sure that they incorporate their autosegmental pairs into the message. In addition, students should be made aware that there are cultural conventions which, when broken, cause misunderstanding (e.g., how to say telephone numbers, dates, prices, etc.). Ask your students to take out their smart phones and let them record the messages. If they don't have mobile phones or other recording devices, they can say the messages aloud for their classmates. Have all of the groups "leave their message."

To test the effectiveness of the messages, have all the other students who are listening to them fill out a form like the message form that follows. To check that appropriate autosegmental forms were said and heard, have the message takers check their messages against what was said. If an error has occurred and the message leavers made it, have them repeat their message, providing correction where necessary. If the message takers made the mistake, go over the error with them.

```
┌─────────────────────────────────────┐
│         WHILE YOU WERE OUT          │
│                                     │
│  TO: _____ TIME: _____  │
│  FROM: _____ DATE: _____  │
│  NUMBER:                            │
│                                     │
│  MESSAGE _____ │
│  _____  │
│  _____  │
│  _____  │
│  _____  │
│  _____  │
│  _____  │
│                                     │
│  TAKEN BY: _____ │
└─────────────────────────────────────┘
```

17.2 *Gossip*

The pronunciation of dates is difficult not only for English language learning students, but also for English speakers who hear these students pronounce them. This very simple activity gives students the opportunity to practice this troublesome feature of the language. Tell the students to arrange themselves in a line from oldest student to youngest (or vice versa), or if you're teaching adults, students can line up according to their birthdays in the calendar year. After they've arranged themselves, have the first person in the line call out their birthday using proper autosegmental forms. This activity is particularly good at the beginning of the course as it gives students an opportunity to learn more about their classmates. In addition, you can learn when your students' birthdays are and celebrate them when the time comes!

17.3 *Déja Vu All Over Again*

Review all the mini-activities dealing with single words or phrases that you dealt with in this chapter (e.g., PROGress vs progRESS) to re-sensitize yourself to autosegmental features, and think up some more examples of such pairs to let your students have fun with.

18

Autosegmental Features, Part 2

"It's not always what you say, but how you say it."

Here we are, back among the autosegmental features that can be so perplexing yet so interesting because of the unexpected richness that they add to English. In Chapter 17 we investigated how stress influences the meaning of single words and phrases, and now we're about to explore how stress can also alter the meaning of whole sentences. In addition, we'll be taking a close look at the marvelous ways that intonation influences English. And remember that suggestion I gave you in Chapter 17, that all the items you find in this chapter will be more meaningful if you sound them out loud. So speak up!

Stress and Whole Sentences

As I said at the beginning of this chapter, stress can have an amazing influence on whole sentences in English. It's interesting to note that not all types of words take stress however. You'll find stress carried by nouns and verbs for the most part unless special meaning or emphasis is being given to some other element, such as an article or preposition.

Let's look at three sentences right away in which the primary stress is different for each one and see how stress affects meaning. Give the capitalized words the primary stress.

> 1. WE baked the fish.
> 2. We BAKED the fish.
> 3. We baked the FISH.

If you heard someone say each of those sentences, stressing the capitalized word in each one, what would you infer? What information is there between the lines? Write your thoughts on the following lines:

In Sentence 1 ....
In Sentence 2 ....
In Sentence 3 ....

The way I see it, in **Sentence 1** the speaker is stressing *we* and **telling the listener that it wasn't somebody else who baked the fish**, but the speaker and another person.

In **Sentence 2** the speaker is stressing *baked*, meaning that **this was the method used to cook the fish, not frying or poaching or grilling it**.

Finally, in **Sentence 3** the speaker is stressing the fact that **they baked the fish and not, perhaps, some bread or cookies**.

It's interesting to note that in all three cases the speaker could be using stress to rebut or refute what someone has just said and that the element in question or in doubt is the element that is stressed. **In whole sentences, stress is typically used in rebuttal. It's also used when repeating part of a sentence** that the listener has misunderstood or not heard clearly the first time:

    A: I had a lot of fun today practicing my Polish
       with the supervisor's wife.
    B: Oh. I didn't know your supervisor's Polish.
    A: My supervisor ISN'T Polish; his WIFE is.

There's another phenomenon of stress in whole sentences that I'd like to show you now. Take a look at the following sentences. In each one, decide which word should get the primary stress and underline it or draw an accent mark over the appropriate vowel. (I'll continue capitalizing the stressed words or parts of words to show the stressed elements):

    1. There's where I told you to sit.
    2. There's something under the table.

Hmm. Notice any difference in where the stress should go? **In Sentence 1**, the word *There* should get the stress, but in **Sentence 2**, the *some-* in *something* gets the primary stress, not *there*. Any observation you can make about this?

....
....

When the word *there* is used to show where something is located (the first sentence), the main stress falls on it. When the expression *there + be* is used meaning "something exists" (the second sentence), *there* never receives the main stress.

Now note the difference between the next two examples by underlining the stressed part in each one or adding accent marks over those parts:

1. There's a good dog in that house.
2. There's a good dog!

Sentence 1 should be marked: **"There's a GOOD DOG in that house."** But **Sentence 2** should be marked: **"THERE'S a good dog."** In the **first sentence**, we're again using the expression that simply means **something exists** in that house, in this case, a good dog, so *there* doesn't receive the stress. In the **second sentence**, though, this idiomatic expression with the stress on *There's* really means that the speaker is **directly praising the dog** and maybe even patting the dog on the head as he praises the dog.

One other area concerning whole sentences in which stress plays a very important role has to do with pat phrases. In these cases, if the primary stress is changed, the sentences either fall apart or leave the listener saying "Huh?"

Here are some test cases to show you what I mean. I've deliberately misplaced the primary stress in each example to show you how bizarre the sentences can become to the ears of native listeners and how the sentences have even lost meaning. Make sure you say them out loud so you'll see just how bizarre they've become:

1. A: THAT'S the scariest movie I've ever seen.
   B: I'll SAY!
2. A: Boy, IS it hot today!
   B: YOU can say that again!
3. A: Hi. HOW are you?
   B: Fine, THANKS. How ARE you?

Now rewrite the sentences above, showing where the stress ought to go:

1A: ....
1B: ....
2A: ....
2B: ....
3A: ....
3B: ....

What follows are the exact same mini-dialogues repeated with the correct primary stress in each sentence:

1. A: That's the scariest movie I've EVER SEEN.
   B: I'LL say!

2. A: BOY, is it HOT today!
   B: You can say THAT again!

3. A: HI. How ARE you?
   B: FINE, thanks. How are YOU?

Number 3 of these test cases is my favorite because of the reactions I get from people when the stress is kept on *are* instead of shifting over to *you* in Person B's response. Try it some time on an unsuspecting victim and just watch what happens!

The first statement in mini-dialogue 1 is a real gem as far as showing how stress can influence the meaning "between the lines." In my version, I've had Speaker A stress *ever* because the idea is *throughout my entire life*. But there are other extra meanings that could be focused on instead of the time frame if we choose to change the primary stress.

Now take a look at the following two versions of the same sentence. They show the primary stress on different parts. On the line that follows each version, write down what you would interpret the stress to mean. Have fun with this! (Note that I've underlined *I* in the second sentence to show that it receives the stress.)

That's THE /ði/ SCAriest MOvie I've ever seen!

....

That's the scariest movie I've ever seen!

....

In our first repetition, now with the primary stress more or less equally on "THE SCAriest MOvie," the speaker is saying "**of all the movies I've ever seen, that one was by far the scariest.**" The stress on these elements in the sentence plus the exaggerated pronunciation of the definite article as /ði/, not /ðə/, is about the strongest way we can show the superlative idea.

In our second repetition with the primary stress put only on *I*, the speaker is saying "**I don't know about the rest of you, but as far as I'm concerned . . .**" In other words, the speaker is focusing here on comparing him-/herself to the others who have just seen that movie. It's wonderful, and yet very complex, how a change like this small shift in stress, in which one particular part of the sentence receives the primary stress, can change both focus and meaning.

Before we leave this fascinating and often overlooked area of stress and whole sentences, let's have some more fun. First of all, look at the three pairs of phrases that follow. They're actually real headlines taken from newspapers. See if you can figure out the difference in meaning between the two phrases in each pair by focusing on where the stress falls. One headline is straightforward; the other, I think you'll find, is very funny:

1. Juvenile Court to Try SHOOTing Defendant
2. Juvenile Court to Try SHOOTing DeFENdant

Headline Number 1 means

....

Headline Number 2 means

....

3. Hospital Sued By SEVen Foot DOCtors
4. Hospital Sued By SEVen FOOT Doctors

Headline Number 3 means

....

Headline Number 4 means

....

5. Squad Helps DOG BITE VICtim
6. Squad Helps DOG Bite VICtim

Headline Number 5 means

....

Headline Number 6 means

....

And what about these two beauties? They're not headlines, but . . .

7. Isn't it funny how LITtle kids like ONions?
8. Isn't it funny how LITtle KIDS like ONions?

Number 7 means it's odd that

....

Number 8 means it's odd that

....

The only way to enjoy these three pairs fully is to say them out loud to make sure you're putting the stress on the right spots. And here's how they should be interpreted according to where the stress falls:

Number 1 = The court is going to try a person accused of shooting someone.
Number 2 = The court is going to try to shoot the defendant.
Number 3 = The hospital is being sued by doctors who are seven feet tall.
Number 4 = The hospital is being sued by seven podiatrists.

Number 5 = The squad helped a dog to bite its victim.
Number 6 = The squad helped a person who'd been bitten by a dog.
Number 7 = It's odd that children hardly like onions at all.
Number 8 = It's odd that young children like onions.

And finally for this section of the chapter, you'll find two pairs of sentences below written for you in phonetic transcription. Carefully note where the stress lies in each one. (For the sake of this exercise, I'm going to use both bold font and accent marks over the stressed syllables even though accent marks aren't usually used when writing in phonetic transcription.) When you've said each sentence out loud a few times, write out the sentence on the blank line below it. I think a grin will come across your face when you've figured these out:

1. /aɪ kʊd-əv slɛpt fɔ́r déz/.

2. /aɪ kʊd-əv slɛpt fɔr déz/.

3. /du yə hæv tú wɔ́-tər lɪ-liz/?

4. /du yə hæv tu wɔ́-tər lí-liz/?

I know you may not think this fair, but I'm going to go against tradition and not give you the answers here to check against your own. I've placed the answers at the end of the chapter so you won't be so easily tempted to peek at what the sentences should be in their written form! Of course, if you can't wait till then, you can always turn to page 421 of this chapter and see what's what. That's up to you!

 **Heads Up!**

One interesting exception to the pattern we've been exploring is when an object is a pronoun. A very common problem that students have is learning that object pronouns, whether direct or indirect, don't normally receive the stress in their phrases unless some extra communication is involved:

→ Pronouns as direct objects: She LIKES him. / I CAUGHT them. / You LOVE her.
→ Pronouns as indirect objects: He MADE it for us. / I THREW it to you.

Students almost invariably stress the object pronoun and then throw off the whole rhythm and melody that the English phrase should have.

Make sure to spend time working on this with your students. Use techniques such as choral repetition and chants to get your students used to the parts of a sentence that do and don't get stressed.

For more information on pronunciation and object pronouns, please visit us at ELTgrammar.com

Before I conclude this discussion about stress, we should take another look at *some* and *any*, which you'll remember we first saw back in Chapter 2. To start this off, let's take a look at the following dialogue. (If you've looked at the online material for Chapter 2, you should recognize it.)

> A: Didn't you go to the movies last night?
>
> B: Uh-huh. We saw the new *Star Wars* movie.
>
> A: Was it **any** good?
>
> B: I liked it a lot, but Nadia wasn't feeling well, so I don't think she enjoyed it very much—and that's unusual because if she can have her choice of **any** kind of film, it'll always be a science fiction or a horror movie!
>
> A: I'm sorry to hear she didn't feel well. Is she **any** better today?
>
> B: Yeah, lots. She even went to work.

Following are the three contexts in which *any* appears in this dialogue. Say the following lines out loud a few times as naturally as you can and see if you can identify which word receives the primary stress. When you've made your choice for each line below, place an accent mark over the word that has the primary stress or the words that seem to share the primary stress:

1. Was it any good?
2. Is she any better today?
3. . . . .if she can have her choice of any kind of film . . .

Any easier to do it this time around? The trick really is to say the lines as naturally as possible, that is, by sort of "eavesdropping" on yourself. Let's see if the words you've chosen are the same as mine:

1. **Was it any góod?**
2. **Is she any bétter today?**
3. **. . . . if she can have her choice of ány kind of film . . .**

We can see that the primary stress is on the adjective in Numbers 1 and 2, but it's moved to the word *any* in Number 3. This is what happens when ***any*** means "**it doesn't matter which one.**"

But does this phenomenon only occur in this case? Let's look at this next dialogue to find out:

A: I hear you're thinking about living in Bangladesh for a few years. **Any¹** truth to that?

B: Yes, I've been thinking about it for a while now.

A: But aren't you afraid of the typhoons they get there? I remember reading about one that killed hundreds of people.

B: Well, it wasn't just **any²** old typhoon, you know. It was one of the worst.

A: I remember that people were desperate for **any³** help they could get to rebuild their lives.

B: They certainly were. But you see how they bounced back? Those Bangladeshis are tough people!

As you can see, *any* has been used three times in this dialogue. In two of the three occurrences, *any* should receive the primary stress for that part of the sentence. Can you figure out which two occurrences have the primary stress? Look at each phrase I've copied for you from the dialogue. Next, decide whether you feel *any* does or doesn't receive the main stress in that phrase by checking the appropriate box. Finally, see if you can interpret just what *any* means in each case:

1. Any truth to that?
   ☐ receives main stress   ☐ doesn't receive main stress

   Any means: ....

2. . . . it wasn't just any old typhoon . . .
   ☐ receives main stress   ☐ doesn't receive main stress

   Any means: ....

3. . . . people were desperate for any help they could get . . .
   ☐ receives main stress   ☐ doesn't receive main stress

   Any means: ....

This is how I see it:

1. *Any* truth to that?
   (Doesn't receive main stress; the stress is on *truth*.)
   Any means: even a little.

2. . . . it wasn't just *any* old typhoon . . .
   (Receives main stress.)
   Any means: ordinary, typical, usual, run-of-the-mill.

3. . . . people were desperate for *any* help they could get . . .
   (Receives main stress.)

Any means: "as much" or "as little."
(for countable nouns: "as many" or "as few")

Of course the question now arises, if stress can be a factor in determining the meaning of *any*, can it work the same way for *some*? Why don't we look at the next dialogue to see if that's so:

> A: Hi, Hemant. Were there any messages for me while I was out?
>
> B: Come to think of it, two people came by looking for you, but I didn't know where you'd gone.
>
> A: Oh, I should've told you that **some** friends might stop by.
>
> B: Sorry I couldn't tell them where you were. By the way, that's a really gorgeous car I saw you drive off in.
>
> A: Oh, you like it? Lata and I just couldn't resist buying it.
>
> B: **Some** of us in the office would love to go for a spin in it.
>
> A: **Some** day we'll do just that!

I want to mention right off that this next part is full of subtleties. As you see, there are three occurrences of *some* in this dialogue. Here are a few hints to help you figure out what's going on:

- In two occurrences, *some* receives stress, but its accompanying phrase doesn't.
- In the other occurrence, *some* doesn't receive any stress at all.

Let's see if you can figure out which is which. Write down the phrases that begin with *some* under the appropriate heading below:

Receives More Stress than Its Accompanying Phrase:

....

Doesn't Receive Primary Stress:

....

A tricky assignment indeed! Let's see if you've come up with the same phrases that I have for these headings:

Receives More Stress than Its Accompanying Phrase:	SOME of us SOME day
Doesn't Receive Primary Stress:	some FRIENDS

As you can clearly see now, stress can play a role in how we use *some* as well as how we use *any*. But what can *some* mean when that word receives the primary stress or when the stress goes to the following word or phrase?

I've repeated the three phrases for you to work on. After you've considered the different meanings for *some*, write your interpretations on the accompanying lines:

SOME of us:

....

SOME day:

....

some FRIENDS:

....

Once again, let's discover whether your interpretations agree with mine:

SOME of us	=	a few/an unspecified number of us
SOME day	=	an unspecified/vague day in the future
some FRIENDS	=	a few/an unspecified number of friends

There are two reasons for *some* receiving the stress in the phrase *some of us*. First off, in this phrase **some is a pronoun**, not a determiner, and we show that **it's a pronoun by stressing it.**

The second reason that *some* receives the stress is that, **in normal speech, prepositional phrases with object pronouns (of us) are very rarely stressed.** About the only time you'll ever hear the stress put on the object pronoun is when somebody is emphasizing the word in a kind of comparison:

    It wasn't some of THEM who got awards; it was some of US!

Now, you've seen that *some* also receives the stress in *some day*. It doesn't contain any prepositional phrase, so there must be another reason that it's stressed. Can you figure out what that reason is? How can you explain why *some* is stressed in this phrase? This is a tough one, but let's see what you can come up with:

....

It's not the unspecified number that prompts us to stress *some* in the phrase *some day*; **it's the idea of vagueness.** Whenever we want to create a phrase like this which refers to something vague rather than an unspecified number or amount, we stress *some* in the phrase:

    SOMEbody/SOMEtime/SOMEwhere/

    SOMEthing and also SOMEday (or SOME day)

Finally we have the phrase *some friends*. When *some* is used to denote an unspecified amount or number, it's never stressed. It's just that simple. Other examples are:

> I bought some FERTILIZER for my vegetable garden.
>
> Would you like some FRIES with that burger?

Intonation

English is called an intonation language. That means that English uses **intonation, the rising or falling of the voice (also known as pitch) and the raising or lowering of volume** to change meaning or to change syntax as, for example, when a statement becomes a question.

On several occasions in the first part of this chapter, I qualified my observations concerning various stress patterns by showing you what these patterns appeared to be, barring any extra communication or meaning desired by the speaker. That extra communication or meaning really comes into play, though, when we start exploring intonation.

It's such a challenging job to teach intonation that many teachers view it as something that's basically unteachable. Quite a few believe that students don't *learn* intonation; they *acquire* it through long exposure to it. Students who have sensitive ears and the gift of mimicry (and "musical intelligence") will become somewhat adept at using English intonation, but those who aren't sensitive to the phonology of the target language and who have a great deal of difficulty with pronunciation probably won't become adept at developing correct English intonation patterns.

This isn't to say that teachers should avoid presenting certain common intonation patterns that their students ought to at least recognize even if they don't actively produce them. That kind of recognition is indeed very important to students. So what I plan to do in this section of the chapter is to explore some common, but challenging, intonation patterns and look into that extra communication which I've hinted at so often.

Is It a Question or Exclamation?!

We know that there are times when certain items in English can overlap in appearance even though their meanings may be quite different. A case in point is how a given verb form, such as the simple present, can have such varied meanings (see Chapter 3).

Well, here's one that rarely gets enough attention in classes, and it's another example of how intonation can be so all-important for meaning in English. This dialogue will show you what I'm talking about:

18 Autosegmental Features, Part 2 413

> A: **Am I excited**!
>
> B: Oh? What's up?
>
> A: I've just won a one-week trip for two to London! All expenses paid!
>
> B: Wow! **Are you lucky**!
>
> A: I'll say! **Am I lucky** or what? I loved it the first time I was there a few years back.
>
> B: Unbelievable! Is London interesting for tourists?
>
> A: You've got to be kidding. Boy, **is London interesting**!
>
> B: But what about the Londoners? **Were they nice**?
>
> A: Gosh, were they nice! Everybody was so friendly and helpful. And perfect strangers called me "love." **Were they ever friendly**!

What do you see happening in this dialogue? There's some kind of overlapping going on, so let's see if you can identify what it is:

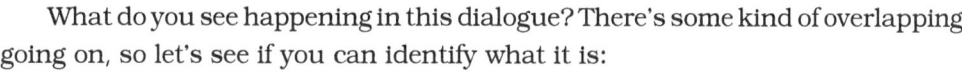

It shouldn't be too hard to see that **the same phrase can be used both as a yes/no question and as an exclamation. It all depends on what intonation the speaker uses.** In Chapter 1 I accounted for all sorts of interesting sentences that appear in question word order but aren't questions at all. The sentences we have in this dialogue, on the other hand, are perfect examples of when a sentence can be used both ways, and there are lots of examples:

Are you ever mistaken?	Are you ever mistaken!
Was he in trouble?	Was he in trouble!
Do they have the wrong idea?	Do they have the wrong idea!
Did they enjoy themselves?	Did they enjoy themselves!
Can she play the harp?	Can she play the harp!
Will she be a great singer?	Will she be a great singer!
Is he going to regret it?	Is he going to regret it!
Have we ever goofed?	Have we ever goofed!

Isn't it incredible what a change in intonation can accomplish? If rising pitch is used at the end of each sentence, the speaker has created a yes/no question. But if falling pitch is used, the speaker has created an exclamation.

One additional observation I should make about all of these exclamations (apart from the fact that they all retain question word order) is that the speaker usually puts some sort of extra-added "punch" or exaggerated emphasis on key words just to make sure the listener understands that what's being said is indeed an exclamation:

Are YOU EVer misTAKen!
Was HE in TROUble!

And what about that word *ever* when it appears in the questions on the left and in the exclamations on the right? Do you think the word has the same interpretation in both the questions and the exclamations or is there a change in meaning?

☐ a change in meaning   ☐ no change in meaning

Surprisingly, **there's quite a big change in meaning** from the question to the exclamation. Now that you know there is, how would you interpret the meaning of *ever* in each case? Write down your thoughts on these lines:

In the question, *ever* means...

In the exclamation, *ever* means..

It's fascinating how one little word can be used in such different ways depending on what kind of sentence it's found in. **In questions,** *ever* **means** *at any time in someone's life.* **In exclamations,** *ever* **means nothing in particular; it's really an intensifier adding a little extra "punch,"** a little extra "oomph" to the idea, nothing more.

Tag Questions, Right?

One of the most misunderstood intonation patterns that teachers and students need to deal with is found in tag questions. First off, I'd like to point out how I plan to represent changes in intonation on these pages—not an easy task at all. When we change pitch, it seems as if our voices "go up" or "go down," and tag questions lend themselves beautifully to demonstrate this change in intonation. I'll show a rising pitch by literally making the affected words go up higher (superscript) than the rest of the words in the phrase or sentence, and I'll represent a falling pitch by making the affected words go down (subscript). Take a look at the following statement with its tag question to see what I mean:

He GOT the proMOtion, DIDn't ^{he}?

Obviously I'm showing you a tag question with rising pitch. The first part of my example is the basic statement, and the statement will be spoken the same way whether the tag question is added on or not. Notice the two parts of the statement that receive the main stress, the verb (*got*) and the direct object (*promotion*). Keep in mind that, as far as the tag question goes, **the first part of the tag will always receive the main stress.**

Now let's look at the same statement and tag question, only the tag this time appears quite different:

He GOT the proMOtion, DIDn't $_{he}$?

If we compare this second statement and its tag with the first example, we can see that the statements are exactly the same in both versions and the words used in the tag questions are identical, too. The difference is that our second example has a falling pitch. The question I need to ask is, why can we use two opposite "directions," so to speak, for the pitch in our tag questions? If you can explain this phenomenon, write your idea down on the following lines:

....

....

It turns out that the speaker determines whether to use a rising or falling pitch in the tag question depending upon what is or isn't anticipated about the answer to the question. **When it's not known if the answer will be "yes" or "no," a rising intonation is used, but when either "yes" or "no" is anticipated, a falling pitch is normally used.**

In our two examples, the speaker of the first sentence used a rising pitch and really didn't know whether the person being discussed had gotten the promotion or not. On the other hand, the speaker of the second sentence used a falling pitch, anticipating that the person under discussion had, in fact, gotten the promotion. So why did the second speaker even bother to ask the question if he thought he already knew the answer? It's that **the second speaker was looking for confirmation of an already-formed conclusion.** This is the most typical reason for using tag questions with falling pitch. Some people liken this kind of tag question to the rhetorical question.

Echo Tag Questions

The next dialogue contains these wonderful little additions known as echo tag questions. The reason they're called "echo" tags is that they *echo* or repeat part of what the other speaker has just said. After you've read the dialogue, I'll discuss why I consider them so interesting and why intonation plays such an important part in their use.

> A: Guess what! Pavel's getting married!
>
> B: **Is he**?
>
> A: Yes. He says he loves the girl very much.
>
> B: **Does he**?
>
> A: Uh-huh. They'll be spending their honeymoon in Yalta.
>
> B: **Will they**?
>
> A: Mm-hmm. And he gave her a gorgeous engagement ring.
>
> B: **Did he**?
>
> A: Oh, it's just beautiful! I've seen it.
>
> B: **Have you**?
>
> A: Too bad they can't take more than one week for the honeymoon.
>
> B: **They can't**?
>
> A: No, it's just too expensive. Well, it's nice to see that you're as excited about this as I am.

Every item in bold is an echo tag question. The thing that writers must find frustrating about them is that the simple punctuation of using a question mark doesn't really tell the reader how the speaker who's making the echo tags feels.

Let's try a little experiment to make clear what I mean. If you haven't already done so, read the dialogue out loud now and use a *rising* pitch for every echo tag. Then write down on the line I've provided anything that comes to mind concerning how you think the speaker feels about this whole situation:

....

An echo tag with rising pitch reveals many things about the speaker's feelings and reactions to what's being said. In this case, with rising pitch, I would say that the speaker is possibly **surprised, interested, excited, wants to know more**, etc.

Now let's repeat this exercise, only this time, use a falling pitch for all the echo tags *except the last one*. Then write down how you think the speaker feels on the following line:

....

What a difference! With this dramatic change in intonation, we get an entirely different picture of how the speaker feels about the situation. I'd say that the speaker is possibly **skeptical, annoyed, pessimistic, sarcastic, uninterested**, etc.

Now let's think for a moment about how echo tags are put together. One way they can be constructed is by first repeating the verb *be* or the first auxiliary and following it with a pronoun that substitutes for the subject, so we have **be/first auxiliary + subject pronoun** ("Is he?"/ "Will they?"). The other way is to use the simple present or simple past of the auxiliary *do* + subject pronoun ("Does he?").

But what about "They can't?"? Why do you think it's all right for Speaker B to use the construction **subject pronoun + first auxiliary**?

....

The reason is simply that **some echo tag questions can be created with the construction subject pronoun + first auxiliary**, too. Try it out and you'll see that each one in our dialogue can be rearranged to have subject pronoun + first auxiliary. But we have one more area to investigate. If you can choose subject pronoun + *be*/first auxiliary or *be*/first auxiliary + subject pronoun, does this mean that the constructions are always interchangeable? Let's examine one of our echo tags to find out:

    A: Guess what! Pavel's getting married!
    B: Is ʰᵉ?   He ⁱˢ?
        Is ₕₑ?   He ᵢₛ?

So what do you think?

☐ Yes, they are.   ☐ No, they aren't.   ☐ Only sometimes.

The answer is **only sometimes**. The reason has to do with the speaker's mood and what's being communicated "between the lines." **If the speaker's mood is "up" and positive (using rising pitch), either construction can be used. However, if the speaker is "down" or annoyed or sarcastic (using falling pitch), only the construction *be*/first auxiliary + subject pronoun can be used.** So the echo tag question *He is?* with falling pitch isn't possible.

Intonation and Punctuation

It's important to remember that the spoken language had existed a long, long time before the written language came into being. When writing did make its mark on the language, the aspect we call punctuation was influenced in many ways by the intonation of the spoken language.

It's fascinating to see how a simple stream of words can be transformed into either a statement, a question, or an order simply by the intonation that's used and the punctuation marks that were invented over the centuries to reflect that intonation. Take a look at the next dialogue to see this wonderful facility of language in action:

A: I know my wife hasn't been with the company for long, but she's shown herself to be a hard worker. **She's getting a raise**.

B: **She's getting a raise**?

A: **She's getting a raise**!

B: Okay, boss. Sure thing, boss.

What more needs to be said? The period shows us that a statement has been made with its basically straight-line intonation:

> She's GETTing a RAISE.

The question mark identifies a question with its rising pitch at the end:

> She's GETTing a RAISE?

And the exclamation mark tells us that the volume has been increased and key words have been "punched":

> She's GETTing a RAISE!

We even have one more use of punctuation that some people feel is somehow more satisfying because it lets the reader know that there's more than one thing going on with the speaker. In this case, not only is the speaker repeating information just received to verify what's been said, but also registering surprise or shock:

> She's GETTing a RAISE?!

More Effects of Intonation

To end this section on intonation, and this chapter for that matter, I think it will be fun to see some other marvelous ways that intonation can influence meaning. The best way is simply to present you with some choice examples and let you have fun figuring out what's going on.

First of all, look at the following two sentences. You'll note a vertical bar that I've inserted between two words in Sentence 2. This bar represents the minuscule pause that native speakers "feel" the presence of in a stream of speech. In linguistics, this phenomenon is known as "juncture," and in many instances, the written language accounts for this tiny pause by inserting a comma:

1. I don't know TIna LouISE.
2. I don't know TIna | LouISE.

After you say these sentences out loud, how would you interpret them judging from the stress you observe, the change in pitch, and the pause bar in Sentence 2?

Sentence 1:

....

Sentence 2:

....

Let's see how close your interpretations are to mine. The way I see it, **Sentence 1 means that this person, Tina Louise isn't known** (as opposed to someone else who is).

Sentence 2 means the speaker's talking to someone named Louise and says that he/she doesn't know Tina. Quite a difference!

Let's get to another pair of these sentences. This time, though, I've had to put a part of each sentence in phonetics so I don't give too much away. And once again, to make matters simple, I'm going to use accent marks over the stressed syllables.

On the blank line for each sentence that follows, copy the sentence and recreate the part in phonetics as it appears in "normal" writing:

1. Where's the /fón bɪl/?

2. Where's the / fón ┃bíl/ ?

Sentence 1:

....

Sentence 2:

....

Sentence 1 is "Where's the phone bill?" Obviously this means that the speaker's looking for the telephone bill and is asking someone if they know where it is.

Sentence 2 is "Where's the phone, Bill?" The speaker's talking to someone named Bill and asking him if he knows where the telephone is. Notice how high the pitch has gone for *phone* because this is a question, not a statement. Also, note that even though the pitch has come down on "Bill," it hasn't come back down to the level that the question began on.

Want to try your hand at a couple more? This time, however, I'm going to give you both sentences entirely in phonetic transcription. And here's a hint: In this variety of English, final "r's" are dropped. After you've said them out loud a few times, write each one out on the blank line as it usually appears in written form.

1. /yu hæv ə gʊd ᵃɪ┃dí-ə/

2. /yu hæv ə gʊd aɪ-dí-ə/

Sentence 1:

....

Sentence 2:

....

If we write out **Sentence 1** as it usually looks, we come up with "**You have a good eye, dear.**" In other words, the speaker is complimenting someone by saying that the person has good taste in art or decorating, or that they can easily spot things that are being looked for.

If we write out **Sentence 2**, we end up with "**You have a good idea,**" which needs no further explanation. Of course we mentioned that the speaker drops the final "r" from a word, or at least "flattens" it. The fun will only work with this pair of sentences if you drop that final "r" in *dear*.

How about just one more pair? I'm sure you're getting good at sorting these out!

1. /hi kwɪt yú-zɪŋ hɪp-nó-sɪs/
2. /hi kwít | yu-zɪŋ hɪp-nó-sɪs/

Sentence 1:

....

Sentence 2:

....

When **Sentence 1** is written out normally, it's "He quit using hypnosis." This, of course, means that he stopped using hypnosis.

Written out normally, **Sentence 2** looks like this: "He quit, using hypnosis." That little pause known as juncture, which the comma represents, changes the meaning totally. In this case, he stopped doing something (e.g., smoking, overeating, etc.) by using hypnosis! If we use the preposition *by* after saying "He quit. . . ," there's no need for that little pause anymore or the comma.

The Answers for Page 407

1. I could have slept four days.
2. I could have slept for days.
3. Do you have two water lilies?
4. Do you have to water lilies?

Teaching Tips

18.1 *"Drawing"* Music

Bring in a recording of a piece of instrumental music. Make sure the tempo of the music isn't too fast. Have large sheets of paper for the students to draw several lines similar to those that composers use when writing music (see the sample that follows). In pairs or small groups, tell the students to plot out the music on the staff as you play short bits of the music. Tell them that they don't have to know how to write music; they just have to provide an impressionistic version of what they "hear." When they've composed their "music," let them write lyrics that fit the music they've "composed."

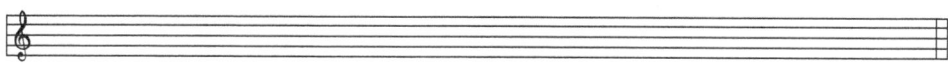

18.2 Tag Questions

Write up fifteen to twenty sentences that contain tag questions. Also prepare an answer sheet (or write one on the board) similar to the following:

      1. Certain _____   Uncertain _____

      2. Certain _____   Uncertain _____

In class, say the sentences for the students twice; tell them that they'll indicate whether the information you're communicating expresses certainty or uncertainty. When you say the sentences, add rising intonation for uncertainty and falling intonation for certainty. The students will check off the appropriate word.

19

Neglected Words & Phrases

"We're poor little lambs who have lost our way..."

It's time to begin winding down. You've gotten through eighteen intensive chapters; now, however, it's time to start unwinding. This chapter and Chapter 20 will help you do just that.

Most of what you're going to see in this chapter isn't found in most traditional ELT texts. I'm going to deal with what I consider to be neglected words and phrases, that is, items or phenomena of the language that rarely if ever get included in student grammar books, in whole-language or competency-based student series, or even in teacher reference books, but should be, in my opinion. There are quite a few of these neglected items in ELT, and I think you'll find it enlightening to be made aware of these seldom-taught items.

Ellipsis

As in keeping with the traditional way I've presented most material, I'll start your discovery—or rediscovery—of these neglected items by asking you to look at the first dialogue for this chapter at the top of the next page:

> A: Hi, Bruce. Eaten yet?
>
> B: No, Gerry. You?
>
> A: Me, neither. Want to go out for pizza?
>
> B: Don't feel like it. How 'bout ordering in?
>
> A: Fine with me.
>
> B: Good. Coming over here, then?
>
> A: Sure. Be over in a jiffy.
>
> B: Mind picking up some sodas on the way over?
>
> A: No problem.
>
> B: Looking forward to that first slice with pepperoni.
>
> A: Me, too. See you soon.
>
> B: Bye!

A very typical, normal-sounding dialogue, wouldn't you say? There's nothing unusual at all about the way Bruce and Gerry have been talking—or is there? Can you figure out what's "different" about the way this dialogue goes compared to what you normally find in student books? When you've discovered the "difference," write down your idea on the following line:

....

The phenomenon that's taken place throughout this first dialogue is that **the beginning words have been dropped from almost every sentence.** There's even one example of an initial, unstressed syllable being dropped. These are manifestations of a linguistic phenomenon known as ellipsis. Let's have some fun reconstructing the parts that both speakers have dropped:

A: Hi, Bruce. .... eaten yet?

B: No, Gerry. .... you?

A: Me, neither. .... want to go out for pizza?

B: .... don't feel like it. How .... bout ordering in?

A: .... fine with me.

B: .... coming over here, then?

A: Sure. .... be over in a jiffy.

B: .... mind picking up some sodas on the way over?

A: .... no problem.

B: .... looking forward to that first slice with pepperoni.

A: Me, too. .... see you soon.

B: .... bye!

Now that wasn't tough at all, I bet. Without any delay, let's get right to what I'd use to fill in those blanks so you can see how closely your fill-ins come to mine:

Have you . . .	That's (It's) . . .	It's (That's) . . .
Have . . .	Are you . . .	I'm . . .
Do you . . .	I'll . . .	I'll . . .
I . . . a-	Would you (Do you) . . .	Good-

Quite an assortment of phrases, wouldn't you say? It seems that this kind of ellipsis **usually happens with one or more words that open a sentence and that often have weak stress.** At times, **words in the middle of a sentence can get dropped, too.** If you reread all the sentences that show this kind of ellipsis in the dialogue, you'll realize just how unstressed the dropped parts are. You can also see that all of my examples, save the fifth one and the last one, delete the subject, auxiliary and/or verb.

Now why is it that there doesn't seem to be any confusion on the part of the listener or the reader as to what the missing parts are? It's simply because either the grammar itself or the context of the situation will keep things clear.

Here are a few more examples for you to have fun with. In addition, I'm going to throw in more items in which the beginning syllable of a word is dropped instead of a whole word, and you might even find a word dropped from the middle of a sentence or two. Write your fill-ins on the blank lines provided:

1. Anything else?   ....
2. I did it 'cause I got bored.   ....
3. I didn't know he was sick.   ....
4. I'll be home tonight.   ....
5. We'll meet you 'bout ten o'clock. ....
6. Anybody know the right answer?   ....
7. Nice woman, that Ethel.   ....
8. He's been gone about two hours.   ....

For these extra items I've given you, what follows are the answers I'd supply for the blanks:

1. Is there/
   Will there be/
   Would you like .../
   Do you want .../
2. be-
3. ... that ...*

4. at
5. a-
6. Does ...
7. She's a ...
8. ... for ...

I'd like to take a detour for a moment and discuss that little troublesome word *home* in Number 4. This seemingly innocent word can be much more difficult to teach than you might think because of when you can and can't drop its accompanying preposition, that bane of all teachers, *at*, which I'm sure you remember from Chapter 6. Compare the following sentences that I've placed into three categories:

Category 1

I'm going home.
I've often flown home.
I drove home.
I'll see you home.
I can't take you home.
I'd never walked home before.
He ran home to his mother.

Category 2

I feel at home.
I worked at home.
I'll see you at home.
I'll be calling you at home.
I've seldom called on them at home.
Please make yourself at home.
She lives at home with her parents.

Category 3

I'm (at) home.
I sat (at) home.
I remained (at) home.
I'm staying (at) home.

In Category 1 you never use *at*; in Category 2 you have to use *at*; in Category 3 *at* is optional. Can you come up with any rules that explain why *home* works these three different ways? Think about the kinds of verbs in each category and then write any thoughts you have on the subject on the following lines:

Category 1: _____
Category 2: _____
Category 3: _____

This is how I see it, so compare your ideas to mine. Based on the three categories of examples above, this is what I've found:

---

*This is an example of an omitted relative pronoun in an adjective clause. For more information on this topic, see the online materials for Chapter 12 (Coordination, Subordination, and Correlation).

Category 1: Don't use *at* + *home* after verbs that imply movement.
Category 2: Use *at* + *home* after verbs that imply stationary location.
Category 3: *At* is optional after certain verbs that imply "remaining."

And what's most interesting is to compare the fourth sentence in Category 1 ("I'll see you home") to the third sentence in Category 2 ("I'll see you at home"). In the Category 2 sentence, *see* really means "meet," but in the Category 1 sentence, *see* has an idiomatic meaning that equals the same idea as "escort" or "accompany," a verb implying movement. The presence of at or the lack of it changes the meaning of these two sentences completely!

Now getting back to that last group of eight sentences with ellipsis on page 425, you can see that this sort of thing is a common phenomenon in the spoken language. So when would this type of ellipsis be taught if you were planning a curriculum? It would probably be best to teach most of it at an advanced level. The reasoning behind this suggestion is that students ought to master these words and structures as they are in their entirety. After that's been accomplished, you can feel more secure in showing them the shorter versions used **in the spoken, informal language**. That doesn't mean, however, that certain items can't be introduced at the beginning level, such as "Bye!" or "See you later."

Relaxed Pronunciation

Along similar lines, there's a phenomenon in pronunciation that's involved with ellipsis. I've dubbed it **comic book English** when attempts are made to reproduce in writing how the words sound when spoken. Even though a few spellings have actually become standardized in comic books, a number of the spellings you're about to see are my own inventions to mimic the spoken word.

Take a look at the next dialogue to get a sample of what I mean. By the way, "Ahm" = *I'm* and "u" = the pronunciation /ə/. I've written words this way to capture how they're typically pronounced in an informal situation.

A: Whutchu doin'?

B: Did'n'chu see?

A: Nope. Couldju do it one more time?

B: Okay, but wouldju pay attention this time?

A: Ahm gonna look at nothin' else!

B: Awright then. Here goes . . .

A: Geez! That's terrific!

B: Wannu try it? All yu gotta do is hold this in yer left hand and do that with yer right.

A: Gotchu!

Before we do anything else, rewrite this dialogue in "standard" form:

A: _____
B: _____
A: _____
B: _____
A: _____
B: _____
A: _____
B: _____

A: _____

If I rewrite the dialogue, this is what I come up with, and I've put the affected parts in bold:

> A: What **are you doing**?
> B: **Didn't you** see?
> A: No(pe). **Could you** do it one more time?
> B: Okay, but **would you** pay attention this time?
> A: **I'm going to** look at **nothing** else!
> B: **All right** then. Here goes . . .
> A: **Jesus**! That's terrific!
> B: **Do you want to** try it? All you**'ve got to** do is hold this in your left hand and do that with your right.
> A: **I've got you**!

As you can see, this dialogue really demonstrates a combination of what I term "relaxed" pronunciation and ellipsis. There's really no point in trying to list the weighty phonological rules that account for these pronunciation variations. Let's just say that I feel you should teach them **in chunks**, that is, *would you* comes out sounding like *wouldju* /wʊ - ǰə/, *want* to ends up as *wanna* /wa - nə/, *going to* becomes *gonna* /gə - nə/ or /gɔ - nə/, *what did you* becomes *whud-ja* /wə - ǰə/, and *what are you* is *wutchu* /wə - čə/, etc.

In addition, remember that *I'm* has reduced to *Ahm*, /am/, which, by the way, is typical of Southern U.S. pronunciation whether in formal or informal situations.

Then there's the matter of the final /g/ in the *-ing* suffix being dropped, so that /- ɪŋ/ becomes /- ɪn/. This is a common pronunciation, and yet outside of short sections on 'reductions' in pronunciation texts, hardly gets a mention in classes.

One note I'd like to add concerns the exclamation "Geez!" Some expressions such as "geez" have developed because of certain taboos placed on names or expressions that have religious meaning. Because many people feel that using the name "Jesus" or saying "God" in any sort of exclamation is a form of blasphemy at worst or is impolite and low class at best, expressions like *geez* have become popular. Other forms for this particular avoidance are "Gee!" and "OMG!" with the names of the three letters actually pronounced instead of saying "Oh, my God!"

I certainly haven't accounted for all the possibilities here in this type of ellipsis or in relaxed pronunciations, but that's not the point of what I'm doing. I mainly want to make you aware of the fact that these two phenomena do exist and are a vital, integral part of spoken English. For that reason, there should be a unit in any enlightened, dynamic grammar course to cover these aspects of the spoken language, and they should most certainly be taught to advanced students.

Intensifiers

Now let's move on to some other neglected items of the language that rarely—if ever—get included in lessons. Check out the next dialogue to see which ones I'm going to spotlight now:

> A: Hi, neighbor! You're ready to do some cooking I see.
>
> B: Just waiting for the coals to be ready.
>
> A: But, ooh, you don't look too happy. What's up?
>
> B: You see that big house over there at the corner?
>
> A: Uh-huh.
>
> B: Well, the owner just sold it.
>
> A: He did that **rather** fast, didn't he? So why are you glum?
>
> B: Well, my cousin was trying to buy it, but the guy was asking **way** too much for it—at least we thought he was.
>
> A: Exactly how much over the true market value do you think he was going?
>
> B: About $25,000.
>
> A: **That** much, huh? It really was **far** more than what was a reasonable price. So the people who bought it paid a lot more than they should have.
>
> B: Right. It's a shame. My cousin and his wife really wanted that **very** house. It's really **quite** beautiful.
>
> A: I think you can put the chicken on the grill now. The coals look **good and** hot.

Can you think of one or more words you can substitute for the ones that I have in bold? (Notice I've put "way" and "far" together.) Let's see what you come up with:

too	=	....
over	=	....
rather	=	....
way/far	=	....
that	=	....
very	=	....
quite	=	....
good and	=	....

The way I loosely interpret the items in bold, I can substitute them with:

too	=	very	"You don't look <u>very</u> happy."
over	=	**	
rather	=	surprisingly/ really	"He did that <u>surprisingly</u> fast." "He did that <u>really</u> fast."
way/far	=	much	". . . the guy was asking <u>much</u> too much for it . . ."
that	=	so	"<u>So</u> much, huh?"
very	=	exact	"My cousin and his wife wanted that <u>exact</u> house."
quite	=	really very	"And the house is <u>really very</u> beautiful."
good and	=	**really/very	"The coals look <u>really</u> hot."

So why are these words or phrases called **intensifiers**? It's because they "intensify" or strengthen the meaning of the words they precede in one way or another.

Before we get to our mystery word, *over*, I'd like to say a few more things about *very*, *way*, *quite*, and *that*.

"Very"

Very is always an intensifier, and even beginning students learn to use it with adjectives (*very good*) and adverbs (*very well*). It's also used with the quantifiers *many* and *much*, especially in negative contexts (*not very many/not very much*), and with *few* and *little* (*very few tests/very little patience*).

It's important to remember that this useful word is an intensifier that does more than what I've just explained. What about *very* paired up with a noun?

---

* Don't concern yourself with the mystery I've intentionally added regarding *over*. I'll get to that momentarily.

** And, by the way, I should point out that another phrase which means the same thing as *good and* is **nice and**, so Person A could just as easily have said "The coals look <u>nice and</u> hot."

A dishwasher is the <u>very thing</u> you need to make life easier.

It's not such a rare occurrence in English to hear *very* used this way with a noun. It isn't an intensifier, but it means "exact." My paraphrase of the example you've just seen is "A dishwasher is the exact thing you need to make life easier."

Here are some other examples of pairing up *very* with nouns:

You're the <u>very person</u> I've been looking for!
This is the <u>very spot</u> where the treasure's buried.

Before moving on, I'd like to mention two expressions. The first one is **one's very own + noun phrase**. This phrase can be taught as a pat expression without much additional thought given to it. In fact, you can't really paraphrase this expression; *very* is simply used to intensify *own*—and it's redundant at that!

The vegetables you're eating came <u>from my very own garden</u>!

The other expression is **very much the + noun phrase**, which means "really a . . ." Just check out the following example to see what I mean:

Her grades at college have always been excellent. She's <u>very much the scholar</u>.

"Way" and "Far"

Way and *far* are sometimes used interchangeably and colloquially as an intensifier with *too*, *too many*, and *too much* (*way/far too big*; *way/far too many tests*; *way/far too much money*) although some people would say that *far* sounds more formal than *way*. They also do an effective job with the comparative forms *more*, *fewer*, and *less* (*way/far more interesting*; *way/far fewer mistakes*; *way/far less time*).

Way is also used (more commonly than *far*) with prepositional phrases that include *up*, *down*, *over*, *under*, *ahead*, *behind*, *back*, *in*, and *out* (*way up there/ way down yonder/ way over in the next town/ way under age*, etc.).

In addition, *way* can be used with adjectives that begin with the prefixes *over-* and *under-* (*way overpriced/ way underweight*).

"Quite"

As I've mentioned with *very*, *quite* is usually taught to students with an accompanying adjective (*quite good*) or adverb (*quite well*), but we can do quite a lot more with *quite*!

To begin with, **quite can be followed by the indefinite article + a noun phrase that doesn't contain an adjective**. In this case, it means *something* or *somebody worth noting*:

She's quite a scholar.

Or we can use **quite + a noun phrase that contains an adjective** to mean *really* or *very*:

And she's quite a famous author now.

Finally, we can use **quite** + the definite article and a noun phrase (usually without an adjective) to mean *definitely* or *for sure*:

Yes, she's quite the scholar.

And can you think of another expression we've recently had that means the same thing as *quite a . . .* or *quite the . . . ?* Of course! It's *very much a/the . . .*

Yes, she's very much the scholar.

 **Heads Up!**

Even though this has nothing to do with grammar, I'd like to warn you of an inevitable problem that will arise with your students in recognizing three words because of their closeness in spelling. I'm talking about *quit, quiet,* and *quite.* Make your students aware of these three words, their meanings, and especially how they're spelled. Create some exercises that get the students to fill in blanks with the correct words based on context. The more aware they become of the confusion that these three little gems can create, the more they will avoid using the wrong one.

"This" and "That"

As an intensifier, you've seen that *that* really means the same thing as *so* (<u>that</u> *expensive* = <u>so</u> *expensive*). Notice that it's used only as in reference to something already said:

It weighed 400 lbs. I never thought it would be <u>that</u> heavy!

But it's not alone in *this* usage. We also have this working the same way:

A: Well, dear, did you buy the patio furniture that was on sale?

B: I certainly did!

A: Fine. By the way, how much was it?

B: Here's the bill. It was only $1,249.95. It was a steal!

A: You mean you got robbed! If I had known it was **this** expensive, I'd have said to forget it!

Just as with *that*, we can substitute *this* with *so* for this usage as an intensifier. The question, of course, is when do we use *this* as an alternative to *so*, and when do we use *that*? Any idea on the subject? Here's a line for you to jot it down if you've got one:

....

There's nothing better in teaching techniques than to be able to recycle material previously covered so that your students get to practice it again, but perhaps in a new way. That's exactly what's happening here. Knowing when to use *this* or *that* means knowing about the phenomenon explored at various times in this book, **deixis**. Choosing to use *this* or *that* is all a matter of how close to the situation the speaker feels. Accordingly, we use *this* for something we feel proximity to, e.g., something we're actually holding in our hands at the moment ("Look at this vase. Have you ever seen a vase this gorgeous?"). Conversely, we use *that* for something we feel somewhat distanced from. Since Person A in the last dialogue was holding the bill for the patio furniture in her hand, she used *this* in her response to hearing and seeing the price.

Using *this* and *that* in place of *so* is very common, especially in spoken English. They definitely have to be counted among our neglected items and should be taught to intermediate or advanced students.

"Over"

And now for our mystery item! As you may have already realized while writing your substitutions for the intensifiers, this little item can be difficult to interpret. Some native speakers don't really think it means anything in particular—and it doesn't, at least not when it accompanies adverbs of place (*here/there/at my cousin's/in Azerbaijan*, etc.).

However, there's another use for this mysterious intensifier which needs mentioning here. **We use *over* in all sorts of phrases, but especially with verbs of movement:** *come over, go over, drive over, walk over, take something over*, and *run over* are examples I can point to.

It can be hard to know when it is or isn't appropriate to use this intensifier. For example, you can just as easily say *Come here* as you can say *Come over here*. Nobody would say there's any big difference between those two sentences. And, of course, there's an idiomatic use of *come over* meaning *come to my house*:

> A: What time are you coming over tonight?
> B: Oh, around 7:30, I guess.

But it isn't all that simple. I've shown how the word can be used, but I still haven't defined what *over* means when it's used as an intensifier. Let's investigate the word some more. First, compare the following two sentences and check the boxes you agree with:

1a. She went over to the cabinet and opened the door.
☐ sounds "complete" ☐ doesn't sound "complete" ☐ can't decide

1b. She went to the cabinet and opened the door.
☐ sounds "complete" ☐ doesn't sound "complete" ☐ can't decide

Most native speakers tend to think that **both sentences sound complete**; it's simply that **1a** seems to sound a little "better." Whatever the reason might be, the important thing for us to recognize is that it doesn't seem to matter whether *over* is included or not in sentences like the ones you've just seen because there isn't any real change in the obvious or underlying meaning.

But I'm not stopping there. Now compare these two:

2a. He walked to the grocery store for some cheese.
2b. He walked over to the grocery store for some cheese.

☐ sound the same ☐ sound different ☐ can't decide

Uh-oh! Things have changed now. Many native speakers would agree that there is a **difference** between the two sentences. But what is it? Let's see if you can figure out what difference there may be:

Sentence 2a: _____

Sentence 2b: _____

It's incredible how one little preposition can add such nuance to a sentence! This is how I might interpret the two sentences: **2a** simply deals with the verb *walk*, and the only interpretation I can put on it aside from the obvious is that **the speaker is possibly focusing on the fact the he <u>walked</u> to the store rather than <u>drove</u>**.

It seems to me that if the speaker hadn't had anything like this in mind, he/she/they might have opted for a verb like *go* and said "He <u>went</u> to the grocery store for some cheese."

The other sentence is a different matter. **2b** doesn't seem to focus on the act of walking at all; instead, the focus seems to be on a new element, the proximity of the store to wherever our cheese buyer had been. **By saying "he walked <u>over</u> to the grocery store," it seems that the speaker is implying the store is relatively close by.**

If you aren't completely sold on this explanation, compare these next two sentences concerning a beautiful island off the southeast coast of Spain and check the boxes you agree with:

3a. We're flying to Majorca.
3b. We're flying over to Majorca.

☐ In 3a they live near Majorca.
☐ In 3a they don't live near Majorca.
☐ In 3a we don't know how far they are from Majorca.

☐ In 3b they live near Majorca.
☐ In 3b they don't live near Majorca.
☐ In 3b we don't know how far they are from Majorca.

Many native speakers would have no trouble distinguishing distance in these two sentences. **In 3a we don't know how far they live from Majorca**, but **in 3b we can assume that they live near Majorca!**

More Neglected Words and Phrases

Moving right along, here's another dialogue to ponder over. The conversation between Sylvia and Mark is quite a long one, but it contains lots of items that also fall into that interesting but often overlooked category I've called ELT neglected items:

A: It's absolutely incredible!

B: What is, Sylvia?

A: How many people believe in UFO's these days. There must be something to it.

B: Oh, not you, too!

A: But, Mark, there have been sightings **galore**!

B: And there's **a great deal of** exaggerating, too.

A: I **kind of** believe those reports. I'll tell you something, but **kindly** refrain from laughing at me, all right?

B: Okay. So tell me.

A: I think I saw a UFO myself. It looked like an upside-down saucer and there was a redd**ish** light all around it. And there was a strange humming sound coming from it.

B: **Sort of** a free sound and light show, eh?

A: Very funny. Anyway, size**wise** it must have been as big as a house.

B: And when did this all happen, pray tell?

A: The night I had that really high fever ... you remember.

B: Oh, you mean the night your temperature soared to 104° **or so**? Now I get it. You were hallucinating!

Well, maybe Sylvia didn't see a UFO after all, but you certainly see quite a few neglected items in bold. Let's define or paraphrase them:

galore	=	....
a great deal of	=	....
kind of	=	....
kindly	=	....
-ish	=	....
sort of	=	....
-wise	=	....
or so	=	....

There are lots of ways you can define or paraphrase the neglected items you've found in the previous dialogue, so I'll list my substitutions and you compare them to your own. It's not the exact words that matter, just the essence:

galore = very many
a great deal of = very much/a lot of/*lots of
kind of = more or less

(*I'd like to point out that even the phrase *lots of* is very rarely taught as an alternate form for *a lot of* !)

kindly = please
-*ish* = similar to/something like/around
sort of = similar to/like; more or less
-*wise* = concerning/as far as/in regards to
or so = more or less

Now that was all pretty straightforward, right? I agree, except that there are some interesting points to mention about a few of these particular neglected items. Let's see if you can answer the following questions from what you've observed in the dialogue or from what you already know:

1. Judging from the dialogue, what's the word order rule for *galore*?

....

2. What's different between *galore* and *a great deal of*?

....

3. Since *kindly* means the same thing as *please*, can we interchange the two whenever we want? (If your answer is *no*, explain why not.)

....

4. We've figured out what *-ish* means. The question is, what kinds of words can it be added to?

5. From what you see in the dialogue, what's the word order rule for *kind of*?

6. In the dialogue, *kind of* is used in one type of environment and *sort of* is used in another. What observation can you make about what types of words can be used in conjunction with *kind of* and *sort of*?

7. *Kind of* and *sort of* mean *more or less* and *or so* does, too. Does that mean we can interchange the first two expressions with *or so* any time we want? (If your answer is *no*, explain why not.)

And now the answers:

1. **The word *galore* (which some consider to be informal) always follows the noun it modifies.** This is because of its etymology. *Galore* comes from Irish (*go leor*) meaning "to sufficiency," and this expression follows the noun it modifies.

2. ***Galore* can be used to modify either a countable noun** (UFO's galore) **or an uncountable noun** (money galore). *A great deal of*, on the other hand, can only be used with uncountable nouns (" . . . a great deal of money").

3. Although it's true that *kindly* means *please*, **we can't interchange them whenever we feel like it.** *Please* can be put in three places in a sentence: before the verb (Please open the door.), after modal auxiliary + subject in a question (Would you please open the door?), or at the end of the sentence (Open the door, please.). And we can also use *please* in a short answer (Would you like some more coffee?" "Yes, please.").

   Kindly, on the other hand, which sounds more formal, can't appear in final position the way *please* can: "Kindly open the door." / "Would you kindly open the door?" And it's never used in short answers. The one exception is that some speakers in the American South can be heard to say "Thank you kindly," which really means "Thank you very much."

4. **The suffix -*ish* is normally added to nouns** (*childish/foolish*) changing them into adjectives, **and it can also appear with adjectives**, especially colors (*pinkish/brownish*), and, in very informal usage, with practically any adjectives (*cold-ish/new-ish*) or with adverbs (*late-ish/early-ish*). **It's even used in some time expressions to mean "around"**: "I'll see you (at) eight-ish." (Notice that the preposition *at* can be dropped in the time expression when this suffix is added to the hour. Also note that in spelling, this use of -*ish* includes a hyphen.)

5. *Kind of,* if used to modify a verb phrase, **can come between the subject and the verb** ("I kind of believe . . . ") **or between the first auxiliary and the verb** ("I've kind of been doing not much of anything").

6. As we've already seen, ***kind of* can be used in a verb phrase, and *sort of* works the same way** ("Do you now understand what I said?" "I sort of get it."). In addition, **we can use these two phrases before adjectives or adverbs to modify them** (*kind of pretty/sort of quietly*).

7. Even though *kind of, sort of,* and *or so* all mean "more or less," ***or so* is used exclusively with measurements or time** (*three liters or so/at 8 o'clock or so*). Because of this rule, another way to paraphrase *or so* is to say *approximately*.

And here's a word to the wise about the suffix -*wise*. First of all, it looks like the adjective *wise*, but that's as far as its connection with *wise* goes. The suffix comes from the Old English word *wise* /wi - zə/, meaning "manner." I should mention the fact that some conservative speakers continue to frown on the use of this suffix as a substitute for phrases like *as far as* or *concerning* or *like a* . . . except in so-called standard words such as *clockwise* and *lengthwise*. In response to this, I'd just like to mention that there's a long-standing tradition of using this suffix on all sorts of words (*weatherwise/businesswise*, etc.)—even inventing new combinations. How about *ELT-wise*?!

For that reason, I feel that the suffix should be given its due since so many native speakers use it regularly. It's not our place to judge any expression that becomes so popularly used; if it works and enough native speakers use it and accept it, that's good enough! (I'll be discussing more on this topic in the last chapter.)

Now let's continue our investigation into neglected items by looking at another dialogue:

A: I'd like to thank both of you very much for participating in our discussion on the need for more understanding and tolerance in this ever-shrinking world of ours. I think your responses to the audience's questions were very insightful. Well, good night.

B: Good night! Good night! **Am I thirsty**! You'd think someone would have had the sense to put some water and glasses on the daïs for us! Would that be asking too much?

C: All you had to do was ask for some, **Judge**. You could have done that, but you didn't. I'll tell you this, though: the air conditioning could have been colder.

B: Why, that's ridiculous, **Professor**. I was freezing!

C: **You were freezing**? You must be getting very old or very sick! Not only was it hotter than Hades in here, but it was horribly stuffy **as well**. I could hardly breathe!

B: Don't you talk to me that way, **Professor** Smythe! And **how come** you're always contradicting me, **by the way**?

C: I'm not on trial here, **Judge**! And don't tell me that I always contradict you. I only do it when you're wrong—which is most of the time, **come to think of it**!

B: Why you . . .

A: Well, **Your Honor, Professor**. Before I leave the hall, I just wanted to thank you once again for showing us how to become more tolerant and understanding human beings. Good night again.

Although you may be asking yourself if the words or phrases in bold are really neglected items, let me assure you that they certainly are. Every type of item highlighted in this dialogue receives less attention than it should, and that's why they've been included among my neglected items.

There's no real need to approach these items as I've done with previous ones since meaning is not an issue here. What I'll do is review each one as it appears in the dialogue and discuss it.

"Am I thirsty!"

Although this form of exclamation has been discussed in previous chapters, those chapters were neither the places nor times to discuss this construction as an ELT castaway. The sentence I have in the dialogue is a fine example of an exclamatory construction. The point is that this kind of exclamation isn't included regularly even though it's such a common way to make exclamations in English. Moreover, it's especially effective because of that dramatic element that the extra "punch" on key words seems to create.

Judge/Professor

Now we're getting into a real sore point with me, the use of titles. It's hard to find satisfactory explanations about the typical titles used in English, nor is it easy to find creative exercises that demonstrate how culturally bound their uses are. Here's a typical example that will bring home my point:

> A: Good morning, José.
>
> B: Good morning, Teacher.
>
> A: José, my name's not "teacher." Please call me Ms. Quinn.
>
> B: Okay, Teacher.

For someone coming from another culture, it might be hard to figure out why the teacher bothered to mention this custom to poor, unsuspecting José, who thinks he's being polite. Because of cultural interference and the fact that most native English speakers aren't aware how other languages deal with titles, in our eyes, José seems "unpolished" at best, rude at worst. In many cultures there's nothing wrong with using a person's job as their title, so if you're a teacher, you're *maestro, ya mu'alimi, Madame le Professeur, ravi, Herr Professor, Hodjam, sungzenim,* and on and on and on! Well, that's fine for other cultures (like the Hispanic, the Arabic, the French, the Israeli/Hebrew, the German, the Turkish, and the Korean cited here), but in polite Anglo-American culture, you're not supposed to call your teacher "Teacher"!

There certainly aren't many jobs that can be turned into acceptable titles in English. Can you think of a few yourself? Write some of them down on the following lines:

....

....

I'm sure you didn't have too much trouble coming up with jobs that can double as people's titles even though there really aren't many in English. Here's my list of examples for you to compare. Among others, I've thought of these few: **Doctor** (medical doctors, dentists), **Nurse, Professor, Dean, Judge, Senator, Governor, Councilman/Councilwoman, Prime Minister, Father** (Catholic and Orthodox priests), **Rabbi, Imam, Officer** (of the police), and many military titles such as **Lieutenant, General,** and **Admiral.**

And here's an interesting side note: Ever wonder why Americans think nothing of saying "Mr./Madam President," or "Mr./Madam Speaker" (the head of the House of Representatives in the U.S. Congress), or "Mr./Madam Mayor"? After all, they'd never feel comfortable with "Mr./Madam Boss,""Mr./Ms. Magistrate," or the like. Well, I'd guess it's the influence of the French concerning some terms we borrowed from them a little over 900 years ago. In French it's quite common to say such phrases as "Monsieur le Président," or "Madame le Docteur." By analogy, English came up with a few of its own like the three cited above.

At any rate, students should be made aware early on of such culturally bound titles and of when it's appropriate to call a person by their job and when it isn't.

"You were freezing?"

In Chapter 18 we dealt with echo tag questions and how the intonation pattern that's used with them will affect their meaning and show us something about how the speaker feels at that moment concerning the situation. Now we're dealing with what are called **echo questions** (without the "tag").

There are many types of echo questions. In the dialogue, you come across the type that's a complete repetition of what the other person has just said:

        A: I was freezing.
        B: You were freezing?

The question I have for you is, why does Person B use this echo question? Think about it and write down any thought you have on the following line:

....

There can be any number of reasons that Person B would choose to make an echo question. He might be saying it to show **surprise** or **disbelief**. He might even use it simply for **clarification** to make sure he hasn't misunderstood what the other person has just said. And there may be other reasons as well.

The three possible interpretations of the echo question that I've given you are amazingly controlled by the intonation that the speaker uses. To bring this point home, let's play a little guessing game. Here's our echo question visualized for you with three different intonations. Look them over and decide which interpretation I've made (surprise, disbelief, or clarification) goes with which version:

    1. You were | ^{freezing}?   ....
    2. You were ^{freez}ing?   ....
    3. You were freez^{ing}?   ....

Just as I said earlier, English is definitely an intonation language. Teachers can never stress enough (no pun intended) how dependent communication can be upon the intonation used by the speaker. So how do we match our three interpretations with the intonation patterns visualized above? **Number 1** demonstrates repeating the sentence for **clarification, Number 2** shows **disbelief,** and **Number 3** indicates **surprise!**

By the way, this type of echo question can also be abbreviated by using just the key word or words:

> A: I was freezing.
> B: Freezing?

But there's another typical kind of echo question, and Person B could have chosen to go that route if he'd wanted to:

> A: I was freezing.
> B: You were what?

In this kind of echo question, the speaker chooses an appropriate *wh-* question word to end the echo question with. In this case, since Person A used a verb, Person B had to go with *what.* Let's look at a few more examples to show how other *wh-* words are applied:

A: I'm seeing Shoshana.	A: I went to Pergola.	A: See you at 6.
B: You're seeing who?	B: You went where?	B: See me when?

Need I say how common this kind of question making is? And yet echo questions are rarely taught. They have indeed become neglected items!

"As Well"

Not much need be said about this expression except that it's another way to say *also, too,* or *in addition* and comes at the end of a phrase or sentence. It's quite a common expression, but it hardly ever appears in high-frequency vocabulary lists for students to learn.

"How Come?"

It's true that this colloquial expression (which means *why*?) is mentioned from time to time in student books, but I thought I'd give it some attention in this chapter because it's not just a matter of what it means. The point I want to make is that there should be enough practice with it so that the students understand the construction of the question that *How come* begins. What's the odd thing about a question that starts off with "How come . . . "?

The answer is that **the question isn't constructed like a question at all. It's actually in the form of a statement:**

How come <u>he speaks Finnish</u>? He's not from Finland.

How come <u>she doesn't like ice cream</u>? It's so good!

An expression as strange sounding as this one, which makes a question without using the normal construction for a question, deserves attention even though many consider *How come* informal English. It is commonly used in speech, so students should know about it. *How come* is a condensed version of the phrase "**How** did it **come** to pass that ... ?" or "**How** did it **come** to be that . . . ?" So if a student requests an explanation of its derivation, this is it.

"By the Way"/"Come to Think of It"

The final items in bold from the dialogue represent pat phrases that I think have also become neglected items. Not nearly enough time is devoted to introducing students to these and many other gems that make conversation flow smoothly. It seems that many teachers like avoiding them because they're often quite difficult to explain and even more difficult to demonstrate clearly so that students really understand when it's appropriate to use them.

The two I chose for the dialogue aren't even the tip of the iceberg. It's up to you to make yourself more aware of expressions like these, create a list of the high-frequency ones, and figure out when the best times will be to teach them.

You'll find the last Appendix of this book online. It's a list of some of the more commonly used expressions that help conversation flow so much more easily. It's not at all a complete list—I don't think there could be such a thing—but it will give you an idea of the kinds of expressions I feel have become neglected items. In this list you'll find introductory phrases, combining phrases, retorts, rejoinders, and exclamations, among others.

Just go to <u>ELTgrammar.com</u> to access my list.

Negative Questions

"Woe is me!" goes out the cry of many a teacher who fights the constant battle of getting students to form questions correctly in English.

One question form that really confuses students is the negative question because it can be used for so many different purposes. This next dialogue will point them out:

> A: **Aren't I supposed** to take the kids for their yearly physicals?
>
> B: Wait a minute. They went for physicals not too long ago.
>
> A: No, that was for their vaccination boosters. **Don't you remember**?
>
> B: Hmm, I guess so.
>
> A: Honey, can you take the kids there for me?
>
> B: But that's something we agreed would be your job!
>
> A: **Can't you** ever **do** me a favor without making me feel so guilty? I accidentally scheduled our club's charity bazaar for then.
>
> B: I don't understand what the big deal is. **Can't you reschedule** the kids' physicals?
>
> A: I could, but the doctor's going out of town for a few weeks. **Won't you do** me this favor? Please?
>
> B: Oh, all right! But this isn't the first time you've done something like this. Please be more careful in the future.
>
> A: I will, I will. **Aren't you** the nicest husband in the world!

Each one of the negative questions highlighted in this dialogue serves a different purpose for the speaker who's uttered it. Let's see your linguistic sleuthing back in action as you figure out what the underlying purpose is for each negative question. Think about the situation and the context for each question to help you solve the mystery. I've done the first one for you to get you started:

Aren't I supposed . . .   *The speaker expects the answer to be "yes."*

Don't you remember? ....

....

Can't you ever do me a favor . . . .

....

Can't you reschedule . . . .

....

Won't you do me this favor? ....

Aren't you the nicest . . . .

Not so simple, is it? At any rate, here are my interpretations of the underlying purposes for the rest of the negative questions from the dialogue:

Don't you remember?	She also expects his answer to be yes.
Can't you ever **do** me a favor . . .	She's scolding him.
Can't you reschedule . . .	He's showing disbelief and annoyance.
Won't you do me this favor?	She's trying to persuade him.
Aren't you the nicest . . .	She's using a question form as an exclamation. Moreover, it softens up the person or the situation.

As you can see, there are lots of underlying reasons for people to use negative questions. Before leaving this topic, I'd like to go back for a moment to the first negative question, "Aren't I supposed to take the kids for their yearly physicals?" Isn't this a strange situation, using *aren't* for 1st person singular? *I* think so, and I know that students certainly do! Any ideas as to why this is?

....

In order to understand this strange phenomenon, we first have to look at the negative question without contractions. In that case, the question would be:

<u>Am I not supposed</u> to take the kids for their yearly physicals?

The problem is that **when this construction is used, it seems to signal impatience, annoyance, even anger—and certainly sarcasm.** If this is the case, we can't use it regularly just as a plain negative question, now can we? For that reason, and by some quirk of the language, the contraction *aren't* was elected to substitute for *am I not* because the contraction for the latter doesn't exist in standard English, so that's how we end up with *Aren't I* ...? instead of *Amn't I* ...? Make a note that we can never use *are* in the affirmative with 1st person singular, statement or question!

And while I'm on the subject, what about all the other possible negative questions without contractions? Well, let's review the ones from the dialogue and see how they would look in the full, non-contracted form:

Am I not supposed to take the kids . . . ?
Do you not remember?
<u>Can you not</u> ever <u>do me a favor</u> . . .?

>   Can you not reschedule . . . ?
>   <u>Will you not do</u> me a favor?
>   <u>Are you not</u> the nicest husband in the world!

As they might say in comic book English, "Yuck!" Not only do they all sound horribly sarcastic and nasty, but they also sound like something out of the eighteenth century at best! In other words, they sound archaic and very unpleasant. Without doubt, that's why you rarely hear negative questions without contractions. Case closed!

20

Where English Is Going

"A journey of a thousand miles begins with a single step."

It's been quite a journey, but we've now reached the final chapter. We've investigated many different areas of English and arrived at answers to explain the amazing ways that the language works. The language that you've seen in this book reflects a remarkable history that goes back into the remote past when words were only spoken and writing was very rare indeed.

English has changed over the centuries (let's say from the year 1000 to the present) more than any other language known to humankind. And these changes have taken place in all of its components. In the grammar, it's been the phonology, morphology, syntax, and lexicon. In the written word, it's also been the orthography and punctuation. As an example of what I'm talking about, take a look at the following. It's the first line from *The Lord's Prayer*, also known as *The Our Father*, presented here in four versions to show you how the language has changed over the centuries. (By the way, that strange-looking letter you'll find in the Old English version is pronounced /θ/, which you'll recall is the phonetic symbol for the *th* as in the word <u>*thorn*</u>.)

Old English/Anglo-Saxon (up to ca. 1100)
Fæder ūre þū þe eart on heofonum, sī þīn nama gehālgod.

Middle English (1100 – 1500)
Oure fadir that art in heuenes, halewidbē thī nāme.

Early Modern English (1500 – 1700)
Our Father which art in heauen, hallowed be thy name.

Current Standard Enghlish
*Our Father, who are in heaven, may Your name be holy.

Quite amazing, isn't it? You can clearly see the profound changes that have taken place over the centuries to individual words and to the structure of the

---
* There are numerous modern versions of *The Lord's Prayer*, this is just one of them.

phrases. So, if English has changed so dramatically in the past, who's to say it won't continue evolving in the future? Undoubtedly it will.

That's the purpose of this final chapter, to see if we can gain any insights into where English may be heading in the future based on observations of what's going on in American English these days. I've caught a glimpse of what changes it's gone through in the past and have learned to understand a great deal more about its present stage of development. So here are my speculations about what might happen in the future to areas of this most flexible of languages. I think you'll find what you come upon quite interesting.

The process of change is ongoing and relentless—in all of life, not just in language—so it's time to consider what changes may be in store for the language down the road. Of course, these are only going to be my personal predictions, some based on what's happened to the language so far and some on what's already happening to it nowadays. But who knows? Maybe somebody will dust this book off with its pages all yellowed and cracking a couple of hundred years from now, look at the predictions I'm about to make and say, "That guy wasn't so outrageous after all!"

To keep this chapter simple and not so wordy, I'm just going to list a few changes that may become "correct" English at some point in the future. I'm zeroing in on certain items because I've already noticed changes going on with them and think you may have, too. At any rate, think about each one and decide whether you agree or disagree.

Vocabulary Changes

1. Some irregular plural nouns have already lost their sense of plurality and are often considered singular. Others will do so, too. Such words as **data**, **criteria**, **phenomena**, and **media** fall into this category. Others are sure to follow soon.

    Your data isn't complete.

    As an aside, I must say that I'm not happy about what's happened to the noun *media*. I'm not judging anything else I mention in this chapter, but I *am* judging the use of this word. I don't think it should ever be considered a singular noun. I think it should be treated like *police*, which is always a collective noun taking a 3rd person plural verb following (*The police **are** launching a hiring campaign.*) After all, when we say "the media," aren't we talking about newspapers, magazines, radio stations, TV channels, podcasts, videos, etc? That's why I feel we should stick to saying phrases like *the media are* . . . *and the media **have** reported* . . .

2. Other nouns with irregular plurals, especially low frequency nouns, may develop regular plural endings, so it's conceivable that oxen will become oxes, and shrimp will become shrimps:

    If you're going to the fish market, get some fresh tuna and **shrimps**.

3. Words that have traditionally been considered taboo or vulgar — what we used to refer to as "four-letter words" — will become standard vocabulary items, especially within multi-word exclamations. They will no longer be bleeped out of TV shows, radio programs, or movies. Examples include the following:

> "I'll be **goddamned** if . . ."
> "Who **the hell** is that?"
> "That's a lot of **bullshit**!"
> "What **the fuck** are you talking about?"

4. There will be hundreds and hundreds of new words generated by the continuing evolution in technology. Most of these new words will be verbs and nouns. Words that have already become common in the very recent past are **to hack, to email, to download, voicemail, hashtag,** and **spam.**

5. Some words will either disappear or become rarer and rarer in everyday speech. *Fewer* may be replaced almost exclusively by *less*:

> This bread has **less calories** than that kind.

As will be replaced the same way by *like*:

> She did it just **like she should.**

In addition, *lay* will replace *lie*, with lie only meaning not tell the truth or tell an untruth.

> I think I'll **lay** down for a while.
> I saw it **laying** on your desk.

6. *There's/There was* will be used for both singular and plural subjects in the present and past:

> **There's lots** of reasons for saying this.

By analogy, *here's* will be used for both singular and plural subjects, too:

> **Here's the books** you ordered.

The question word *Where's* will be used for both singular and plural subjects, too:

> **Where's the bargains** you said this store has?

7. *These/Those* + singular noun:

> I see you've got a pit bull. **These kind** of dogs make me nervous.
> Horror movie? Nope. I don't enjoy ***those kind** of films*!

8. The phrase *a whole nother* may become commonplace and accepted in which the initial syllable of *another* has gotten detached from the rest of the word and been fronted:

> She had **a̲ whole nother life** when she lived overseas.

9. Saying dates using cardinal rather than ordinal numbers will become the norm and either remain as an alternative way of saying a date or actually replace the older, traditional way:

> **April one** instead of **April first**

10. **Where** being acceptable in replacing **when** even though talking about a time, not a place:

> It was **a day where** everything just seemed to come to a halt for me.
> That was **a time where** people thought the Earth was flat.

11a. Singular *they* has now become proper usage to agree with the words *everyone, everybody, someone, somebody, anyone, anybody, no one, nobody,* and ambiguous subjects or objects (if people) :

> **No one** knows if **they're** to be here by 3:00 p.m. or not.
> **Somebody** called, but **they** didn't leave a name.

It follows, then, that if this usage is standard, *their* and *them* will be used for the possessive and object forms.

> Did **anyone** leave **their** umbrella at my house?

During a trial:
Prosecutor: Do you see **that person** in this courtroom today?
Witness: Yes, I do.
Prosecutor: Please point **them** out.
Witness: She's sitting right over there.

11b. **Non-binary** *they* will continue to become more commonplace when referring to people who identify themselves as being neither male nor female and have informed others of that fact.

> A: Do you see **Emily** sitting over there?
> B: Yes, **they're** at the window, right?
> A: Right. Please give **them** this note for me, would you?

12. Reflexive pronouns will become acceptable variations in place of personal pronouns in the 1st and 2nd persons in certain contexts:

> Everybody went to the party except for Ellen and **myself**.
> "How are you today?" "Fine, thanks. And **yourself**?"

13. Using the subject form of personal pronouns will become an acceptable alternative to using the object form when two individuals are mentioned:

> The Fontaines have invited **you and I** to their holiday party.
> That story about **he and his secretary** is absolutely true.

-ly Adverbs

In some ways, *-ly* adverbs are becoming the dinosaurs of Modern English, that is, they're becoming rarer and rarer in speech. I should add, though, that this change isn't happening in every occurrence. What leads me to believe they'll disappear in certain contexts is that I've noticed more and more examples of the loss of *-ly* adverbs over the past twenty years or so. Here are some of them: **real** interesting / **fresh** baked bread / You can breathe **easy** now. / He can do it **quicker** than me.

Another adverb that should be on the "endangered species list" is *well*: "How's it going?" "**Good**."

Verbs

1. That third person singular -s/-es in the simple present will finally fall off and then future teachers won't have to pull the hair out of their heads anymore because their students keep forgetting to use it!

2. By the same token, *doesn't* will disappear as the negative form in the simple present to be replaced completely by *don't*. I've witnessed this loss happening in certain dialects of English, and I've been hearing it happening for decades in song lyrics, especially in rock-and-roll, hard rock, and country-and-western music.

3. *Do*, *does*, and *did* may fall out of use in question making for the simple present and simple past respectively. If that happens, the statement form will be used with rising intonation for the yes/no questions:

    You speak Tibetan?

4. More irregular verbs will become regular, especially lower frequency verbs:

    She **shaked** his hand with a firm grip.

5. Double negatives will come full circle and be fine again (as they were in older forms of English):

    I **didn't** ask for **no** trouble.

   After all, this use is commonly heard everywhere that English is spoken.

6. It will become acceptable to use two conditional phrases in a present or past unreal conditional sentence as an alternative to using the present subjunctive in the *if*-clause and the conditional in the other clause:

    If she **would** just study harder, she'd get better grades.
    If he **would've** asked me, I **would've** helped.

   In fact, this is commonly heard nowadays in many—if not all—areas of the English-speaking world.

In addition, the use of the past perfect to create a past subjunctive imaginary sentence will completely disappear, so

> *Even if he **had done** it, he wouldn't have admitted it to you.*
> will become
> *Even if he **did** it, he wouldn't have admitted it to you.*

7. The mandative subjunctive could disappear altogether to be replaced by *should* or *ought to* + verb:

   I suggest that she **see** a doctor. ⟶ I suggest that she **should see** a doctor.

8. Complicated subject-verb agreement, which confuses native speakers today, may change as far as what's considered "correct" usage:

   Either you or she **are** going to have to do it.

9. In the phrases **Do you mind** . . . ? / **Would you mind** . . . ? the verb *mind* is losing its original meaning. It originally meant "bother" or "annoy." So, for example, *Would you mind* . . . ? used to mean "Would it bother you if . . . ?" and the appropriate reply would be "No" or "Not at all" if the person being asked means to say it's okay, I won't be bothered. Now people think it means asking for permission (*Can I* . . .? or *May I* . . .?) so most people reply by saying things like "Sure," "No problem," or "Yeah" if they mean to say it's okay.

Other Predictions

In general, much to the chagrin of many teachers, there may be a loosening of the reins that control what is and what isn't acceptable usage. People may become less concerned with whether or not the correct form is being used and more concerned with the clarity of communication. A continuing upsurge in technological as opposed to literary writing may be responsible for this trend. In addition, videos, podcasts and vlogs (video blogs), the Web/Internet, and television (or whatever other audio-visual forms of communication come along in the future) could result in less reading of books, magazines, and newspapers. This tendency to get away from these types of printed matter may help to desensitize people as to how the written word looks or how a message should sound. A very good case in point is the way standard rules of English grammar and spelling are so often broken in text and social media messages.

Among other areas of language that will be affected by the media and movies, vocabulary and certain grammatical constructions will become more universally standardized, or at least people anywhere will understand area-specific words or phrases because of the exposure they'll get. We see this happening already because of television and movies: "I'll put another shrimp on the *barbie*," says an Australian to the television viewer if he'll *come down under* for a visit; "Don't get your *knickers* in a twist!" shouts the husband to his angry wife in a British film showing in an American movie house; "*Tell me about it!*" comments an American as she agrees with something her friend's just said on Irish television.

As I've already mentioned, I even see grammatical constructions changing because of influences from one form of English or another beginning to dominate "World Englishes." Examples that readily come to mind are the way *will* is replacing *shall* in British English just as it has in other varieties such as North American English, and the way the North American negative verb form *don't/doesn't/didn't have* is now more and more being used in Britain alongside the older, more traditional negative forms *haven't/hasn't/hadn't*:

> I **haven't** the time to do it. / I **don't have** the time to do it.

One other grammatical construction that may very well change doesn't have to do with influences from other forms of English, but rather from a change in syntax when the verb *be* is employed in *wh-* questions. In indirect speech, the traditional position for *be* is at the end of the phrase:

> He told us where the bakery is.

The reason for this position for *be* is because of the basic rule used in indirect speech when a hidden *wh-* question is being "reproduced," so to speak: Since the question ([Where] is the bakery?) is now becoming part of a statement, regular subject + verb word order is to be followed ([where] the bakery is).

It seems that it's becoming more and more common to keep *be* in the same position it held in the original question, so we end up with

> He told us where is/where's the bakery.

Other examples:

> I'll point out which man is Mr. Kelly.
> I can't remember when is his appointment.
> They aren't sure who's the new dean.

Of course, what's most important to keep in mind after looking over all of my predictions is that we shouldn't ever lose sight of the fact that language keeps evolving, sometimes slowly, sometimes quickly, but relentlessly—and the purists can't do anything to stop it from happening.

In ending this final chapter, I'd like to leave you with a quote that I've always liked. Who originally said it, I don't know, but it must have been someone very wise. I hope you enjoy it as much as I do:

> *Language is the hallmark of an educated person.*
> *To say a thing efficiently is the province of the scientist.*
> *To say a thing beautifully is the province of the poet.*
> *Be both.*

Appendix 1

Teaching Strategies and Activities that Work

Your Picture File

The single most useful teaching aid you can have is a Picture File, which doesn't cost much to make. All you need is magazines, some glue or tape, sturdy paper or other backing material, and a pair of scissors. Of course, you can do all this digitally as well.

To put your file together, choose magazines that have lots of pictures and cut out anything you find of interest. Don't overlook simple ones because even the simplest may have various teaching points to focus on. Use large pictures in front of the entire class; use large or small ones for individual or small group work. Trim the edges and glue the pictures onto sturdy backing sheets. (Construction paper or tag board is excellent for this purpose.) On the back of each mounted picture, list a variety of teaching points that picture can be used for.

Let's take a look at a picture and I'll show you what teaching points you can use it for.

Vocabulary Items

Outdoors:
tree, flowers, grass, bushes, sign, sidewalk, walkway

Parts of houses:
roof, porch, stairs, chimneys, shingles, windows, siding, basement

Idioms:
You shouldn't count your chickens before they're hatched.

Grammar Points

Present Progressive:
> They're walking, strolling, looking, thinking / He's pointing, wearing, holding / She's hoping, planning, imagining.

Countable and Uncountable Nouns:
> grass, bushes, money, sign

Active and Passive Voice:
> The house was built in 1902.
> They built the house in one year.
> The man wonders if they can afford a down payment on that house.
> The house is being sold by a well-known realty company.

Past Tense:
> Who was the first family to live there?
> The family decided to look for a new house.

Simple Present:
> Big houses are a lot to take care of.
> Victorian houses tend to be very large.

Present Perfect:
> The house has been for sale for a long time.

Present Perfect Progressive:
> My parents have been looking for a new house for a long time.

Wish vs. Hope:
> They wish the house didn't cost so much.
> She hopes that the owners will accept their bid.

Modals:
> You must save if you want to buy a house.

Prepositions:
> in the yard, on the sidewalk, next to his wife, in front of them, with their parents, on the front porch, for a down payment, at home

Pronunciation

/aɪ/ vs. /au/ vs. /ɔɪ/:
>/ai/: sign, high
>/au/: house, brown
>/ɔi/: point, boy

/s/, /z/ vs. /ɪz/:
>/s/: steps, roofs, plants, payments
>/z/: trees, windows, stairs, signs
>/ɪz/: bushes, porches, prices, houses

See how much you can do with one picture? But don't overlook simple pictures on plain backgrounds. They can be productive, too.

Once you have a stack or digital file of pictures ready to go, number them. Then make a master list of the teaching points you've found in the pictures. Next to each point, list the numbers of all the pictures that fit that teaching point. In other words, your master list will tell you what topics (grammar, vocabulary, pronunciation, etc.) your files contain and what pictures can be used to demonstrate these points. This way, when you teach a particular lesson, you can go to your master list and quickly pull out the pictures you need. Any time you add to your file, you can easily update your master list. Here's an additional comment about writing the teaching points your pictures represent on the back of the pictures. When you hold up a picture and the teaching point appears on the back for you to see, you don't have to crane your neck to look at what it is you're holding up. The students see the picture; you see the teaching point!

Why do all of this work to create a Picture File? A teacher-made Picture File suits you, your needs, your students, and the subjects you're teaching. Commercial sets of pictures could never give you this personalized touch at a price that most teachers can afford. Moreover, if a picture goes out of date, is lost, or is destroyed, replacing it doesn't require that you buy a new set; just find another magazine or website and there you have your replacement.

This book has dealt with some of the most difficult features of the basics of English grammar. A point I'd like to stress from the outset is that this book, even though it is a grammar book, was not written with the intention of telling you that you should teach grammar as a separate entity in your classes. On the contrary, I feel that grammar should be an integrated part of your lessons. Teachers can plan that they will teach the present progressive or articles or whatever this week and break the topic down into individual lesson plans. In doing so, however, teachers shouldn't overlook an essential point, namely that **language should always be taught in meaningful context**. You can handle the present progressive or modal auxiliaries or whatever is being taught very effectively within the context of meaningful situations that your students can relate to—and that's the key element: **situations or topics that your students can relate to**. I've usually been able to get to know the kinds of students I've had in any given class after only a short time, and if you can do this kind of assessment too, you should be able to determine where their interests lie as a group and what subjects turn them on.

Even if you teach the grammar component in an intensive English program which separates the four basic language skills into different classes (grammar, reading, writing, and conversation), you can still teach each grammar point in the context of something cultural, scientific, or topical. Use introductory dialogues like the ones found abundantly in this book. Create exercises that deal with the grammar points in sentences related to the topic. Plan activities such as the ones featured in the *Teaching Tips* that relate to the topic. By planning your teaching in this way, you'll be doing your students a tremendous service:

- They'll experience the grammar realistically and meaningfully,
- they won't feel burdened by grammar drill after grammar drill, and
- they'll learn something important for their growth and development besides language.

On the following pages you'll find samples of various types of exercises that have proven very effective in reinforcing specific points of grammar or in developing more holistic practice for the students. As you know, there's really nothing very new under the sun. The exercises selected for this appendix aren't revolutionary; rather, they're solid, reliable, adaptable exercises that you can create with very little effort once you've mastered their styles.

You may notice that the exercises that follow progress in a certain direction, and the reason for this sequence bears explanation. Over the years, I've found that the best language teaching methodology and most practical approach to teaching and reinforcing specific grammar points are accomplished through the use of **mechanical**, **meaningful/manipulative**, and **communicative** exercises as championed by Christina Bratt Paulston and Mary Newton Bruder, two leaders in the field of ELT to whom all of us owe a debt of gratitude. These concepts deal with a "weaning process" in which teachers gradually turn over control of the language to their students. This is how they work:

Mechanical: The teacher has complete control of the responses and knows exactly what the correct ones should be as there are very few correct responses to each item. The students have few choices to make. They plug in some words or carry out a transformation, but they don't even have to understand all the vocabulary in order to do the exercises correctly.

Example 1:   *Make this sentence negative*:
He **likes** to study the environment. → ....
He **doesn't like** to study the environment.

Example 2:   T: What's this?
S: It's a gift/birthday gift/present.

Meaningful/Manipulative: The teacher gives up some control of the responses, but knows that there's a limited number of correct ones and can anticipate what they'll be. The students now have a few choices to make, which may change the meaning of their responses to some degree, thereby allowing them to show some individuality. The students assume partial responsibility for the utterances they produce.

Example 1:   *Fill in the blank:*
The ozone layer .... disappear.
's going to/isn't going to/will (won't)/might (not)/may (not)

Example 2:   *Take a look at this picture and describe what's happening.*

(Students are given a picture and now select what part[s] of the picture they want to talk about. Of course, the students can also choose not to talk about a part of the picture. They are indeed manipulating the language.)

Communicative: The teacher relinquishes all control of the responses and can't always anticipate what they'll be. The students are now in complete control of their responses and can be as individual as they wish. They now assume full responsibility for the utterances they produce.

Example 1:   T: *Isn't the Internet a wonderful thing?*
S_1: I know it.
S_2: I especially like to stream movies.
S_3: I don't have fast WiFi yet in my building.
S_4: Fast connection speeds are still not available in some places.
T: Hopefully we will all have excellent WiFi service soon.

Example 2:   T: I had a great weekend. How about you?
S_1: It wasn't so good. I had to work.
S_2: It was fine. I went to a great party.

Slot Substitutions

This type of exercise is to be used for *oral* practice. In these exercises, the teacher does the following:

1. models the basic structure
2. has the class repeat the model
3. calls out the first substitution(s)
4. calls on a student to insert the substitution(s)
5. calls out the second substitution(s), etc.

Why use slot substitutions? Actually, there are lots of good reasons, but I want to stress right from the outset that they are of *limited* use and should never be relied on for any length of time in making lesson plans.

The first reason to use slot substitution drills is that they help sensitize the students to English word order. (You have to know where words can be inserted in order to give correct responses.) Second, they're wonderful for listening comprehension. (If you don't hear it right, you can't repeat it right.) Third, students learn inductively what elements of language belong to one class, and therefore, they learn, for example, how modals work in sentences. Fourth, they sensitize the students to changes that many kinds of words must make to conform to the new versions of the sentences. Here's what I mean:

T: He's going to the dentist tomorrow.
Ss: He's going to the dentist tomorrow.
T: *they*
S_1: **They're** going to the dentist tomorrow.

T: *yesterday*
S₂: They **went** to the dentist **yesterday**.

(**T** = teacher; **Ss** = students; **S₁** = student 1)

Single Slot Substitution

T: I'll probably stay home this evening.
Ss: I'll probably stay home this evening.
T: *go to a movie*
S₁: I'll probably go to a movie this evening.
T: *write some letters*
S₂: I'll probably write some letters this evening.
T: *watch TV*
S₃: I'll probably watch TV this evening.

Double Slot Substitution

T: She bought a hat last week.
Ss: She bought a hat last week.
T: *you/dress*
S₁: You bought a dress last week.
T: *I/jacket*
S₂: I bought a jacket last week.
T: *the neighbors/car*
S₃: The neighbors bought a car last week.

*Multiple Slot Substitution**

T: Her blouse has flowers on the front.
Ss: Her blouse has flowers on the front.
T: *his shirt/buttons/cuffs*
S₁: His shirt has buttons on the cuffs.
T: *my jacket/a dragon/back*
S₂: My jacket has a dragon on the back.
T: *their shoes/taps/heels*
S₃: Their shoes have taps on the heels.

---

*Go cautiously with the multiple slot substitutions. After all, there are three pieces of information for the students to remember in each item, and lower level students will probably find these too tough. If you think your students can handle them, write the three items to be substituted in large print on a card and show the students what items they are to substitute:

    Teacher says: Her blouse has flowers on the front.
    Students say: Her blouse has flowers on the front.
    Teacher says: *his shirt/buttons/cuffs*

(while showing a larger version of the card to the right)

his shirt - buttons - cuffs

Moving Slot Substitution

T: He's going to a movie tonight.
Ss: He's going to a movie tonight.
T: *show*
S_1: He's going to a show tonight.
T: *last night*
S_2: He went to a show last night.
T: *they*
S_3: They went to a show last night.

Now you've seen a wide variety of slot substitutions and how they're put to work. I have to stress, however, that these exercises are only to be used as introductory activities. The teacher should always be vigilant that students be moved as quickly as possible to manipulative and communicative activities so they can take control of the language as soon as they feel comfortable doing so.

Cloze Exercises

Another type of exercise that should become a staple kind of classroom language learning activity for all language teachers is called the *cloze procedure*. It can play a very important role in the language classroom. There are two main types of cloze, the pure cloze and the modified cloze, which have many variations. This is how you create cloze procedures:

Pure Cloze: Take any passage that's as close to 350 words in length as you can get. Leave the first and last sentences intact. Beginning with the second sentence, take out every 5th to 9th word and replace it with a blank. Make all of your blanks equal in length. Only a single word is acceptable for each blank and keep in mind that a contraction is a single word, too! If the blank falls where there's a date, number, proper noun, or otherwise unreconstructible word, then the next word should be replaced by the blank instead. The words that are omitted should be words that your students already know.

Note: It's a more difficult exercise if every 5th word is omitted than if every 9th word is omitted. You'll probably prefer to eliminate every 7th or 9th word, at least at the beginning.

As far as correcting the cloze exercises that the students have completed, there are two lines of thought on the subject. Some people insist that only the exact word that was eliminated should be accepted as the correct answer. Others, however, argue that any word that completes the idea appropriately should be accepted.

Just in case you'd like to know, here's the current thinking on the two methods of correction just mentioned. Accepting any appropriate word while correcting a cloze seems, at least on the surface, the only fair way to go. Why shouldn't teachers accept any answer that works? Why should students be penalized for not being able to read the mind of the person who wrote the text? Here's why:

1. Accepting any appropriate word makes it much harder to correct because the teacher needs to keep in mind the entire context while trying to focus on each answer; it's also harder to correct when there are very large groups doing the activity.
2. Correcting in this way takes a lot more time.
3. Using this method is only slightly more statistically reliable, so you be the judge.

The most important use of pure cloze procedures is to test your students' overall mastery of the language (whole language). A blank may replace any kind of word; generally, it's the overall competence and comprehension that your students have which will allow them to figure out what possible item can go in each blank.

Modified Cloze: Write your own sentences or passages in which you plan to focus on any given discrete point. The length of the sentences or the whole passage depends on your knowledge of what your students can handle. If you're dealing with prepositions or articles or the like, eliminate whatever words are being targeted and keep the blanks equal in length throughout. If you're dealing with verbs, draw in each blank and write the verb to be used in parentheses before or after the blank. The students will quickly learn that they're to use the verbs in parentheses to fill in the blanks.

As for correcting this kind of cloze, you should apply the rule of thumb that any appropriate words or forms of verbs that work to complete the sentences are acceptable.

Some Tips About Cloze Exercises

1. Avoid "spoonfeeding" your students. For example, don't tell them in the parentheses to use a negative form of a verb; let them figure that out through the context. (Of course, make sure that the context is clear.)
2. Focus on one discrete point at a time in a *modified* cloze procedure. In other words, don't eliminate prepositions in the same exercise in which you eliminate verbs. Keep your focus.
3. Always treat phrasal verbs (two- or three-word verbs) as single entities so that your students will view them in this way. For example, don't put the verb *look* in parentheses and its allied preposition-like particle outside the parentheses like the following:

Appendix 1 Teaching Strategies and Activities that Work 463

.... (look) at

.... (look) for

It's always better for the students to understand phrasal verbs as whole items and learn them in that way:

.... (look at)

.... (watch out for)

4. Tell your students to read everything at least twice before filling in any of the blanks. Such surveying should be used for all reading as it is important for students to learn to assess what they are going to read and to get an idea of the context. If they don't do this survey assessment first, they'll probably make avoidable mistakes.

That's all I have to say about these exercises. Following are some examples of cloze procedures. I hope that you find them to be useful, clear examples of the kinds of exercises you can easily create for your classes. By the way, if you'd like to, feel free to copy them out of this book and use them in class to get you started.

A Pure Cloze Exercise

Fill in the blanks with appropriate words to complete the sentences.

Yuri had been in the United States for just three months. Now he was having mixed emotions .... whether it had been a good .... for him to leave Russia after .... He was sitting in the school .... , having his lunch, and looking at .... faces of all the other students. .... were laughing, clowning around, and having .... great time, but Yuri wasn't. He .... understand English well enough to get .... jokes, and he always had the .... —even though he knew it was .... —that the students were talking about .... It wasn't supposed to be like .... What had happened to all the .... and enthusiasm he had felt about .... to America? Why was he beginning to feel .... towards all the other students? He .... know the answers to those questions, ... that things didn't look very good.

Yuri glanced up at the clock .... the wall and knew that the .... was going to ring any minute, ... he didn't feel like going to .... next class. It was social studies, ... Yuri's inadequate knowledge of English made .... difficult for him to follow the .... or keep up with the rest .... the class. He was seriously thinking .... cutting class and just hanging out .... the park near his home.

No, ... had always been a good student .... in Kiev, and he didn't want .... get in trouble for cutting classes. .... a deep, sad sigh, Yuri got .... off his chair, collected the pieces .... aluminum foil that his mom had .... to wrap his sandwich and apple ...., closed his lunch box slowly, ... started heading toward the trash barrel .... always sat near the cafeteria exit. .... stopping to throw away his garbage, Yuri .... the wrappers up in the air .... some legendary American basketball star about .... make an incredible trick shot, and .... up hitting his classmate, Anna, right .... the head with the messy wrappers. .... expected a scene: she was going .... yell at him and call him ...., but she didn't. She just started laughing, and for the first time since his arrival in this country, Yuri felt a part of something.

Modified Cloze Exercises

The first of these exercises is for practice discrimination between the simple past and present perfect. It's in the form of a letter.

Example 1: Fill in the blanks with the verbs in parentheses. If no verb appears in parentheses, think of one that will fit.

Dear Pam,

It .... (be) a long time since I .... (write) you. I .... (have) any time to write you last month because I .... (be) extremely busy. The school year .... (just/end), and during the last three weeks of the semester, I .... (have) a chance to do anything except correct papers, hand in final grades, and sleep. Besides all that, over the past week and a half, I .... (write) twenty-two letters of recommendation for various students and .... (interview) three candidates for the position as my new secretary. In my last letter I .... (tell) you that I .... (need) a new secretary, ...?

So, Pam, how .... (your life / be) since we last .... (correspond)? .... (you / make) any plans for your vacation yet? The last time you .... (write) me, you .... (say) that you .... (want) to get away for a month or so during the summer. .... (you/decide) where to go? I .... (decide) to stay home this summer and tend the flowers in my back yard!

Write me soon, and let me know all about your summer plans.

Love,

Artie

Example 2: *This second example is for practice with prepositions. The sentences have been numbered for ease of identification during review. Fill in the blanks with appropriate prepositions. Some of the prepositions are parts of two-word verbs.*

Cooking with Carmen

1. Carmen decided to make a chef's salad .... dinner.
2. She took all the vegetables she had .... her refrigerator and put them .... the kitchen counter.
3. She got .... a large salad bowl, a cutting board, and a sharp knife.
4. First, she washed some lettuce .... the kitchen faucet and drained it thoroughly to get all the excess water ....
5. Then, she got a clove of garlic the basket she had hanging .... one corner of the kitchen, took .... the skin that covered it, and rubbed the garlic clove all .... the inside of the salad bowl.
6. Next, she tore the lettuce leaves .... little pieces and put them all .... the bottom of the salad bowl because she wanted the lettuce .... all the other vegetables.
7. She cut tomatoes .... wedges, cucumbers and scallions .... slices, and some zucchini and American cheese .... long, thin pieces, and placed all these items .... the lettuce .... the bottom of the bowl.
8. After that, she threw .... lots of pieces of cooked turkey and ham and slices of hard boiled eggs and added some sliced radishes and mushrooms .... the bowl as well.
9. Finally, she shook her salad dressing and poured it all .... everything. Carmen knew she had created a work of art!

Example 3: This is a dialogue for overall verb practice good for recycling. Fill in the blanks with the words in parentheses. If there are blanks without words after them, think of what you can write in those blanks.

Bob: Hello.

Ann: Hello, Bob? This .... Ann.

Bob: Oh, hi, Ann! Long time, no see. What .... (happen)?

Ann: What .... (you/do) next Saturday night?

Bob: Nothing special. Why?

Ann: I .... (think about) .... (have) a party at my place, and I .... (wonder) if you .... (like) .... (come).

Bob: I .... (love) to. Who else .... (come)?

Ann: Well, I .... (call) anybody else yet. You .... the first one.

Bob: The first one? I .... (flatter)! .... there anything I .... (bring)? Some drinks or food or something?

Ann: No, thanks. I .... (already/take care of) all that. By the way, ... (you/like) .... (bring) a date?

Bob: Sure.

Ann: .... (you/still/see) that girl I .... (meet) at your house a couple of months ago?

Bob: No, we .... (stop) .... (see) each other three weeks ago.

Ann: Oh, I .... sorry .... (hear) that. She .... (seem) very nice.

Bob: Yeah, well, that .... the way it .... (go).

Ann: Okay then. I .... (see) you Saturday night around 8:30.

Bob: Great! See you then! Bye.

Incomplete Dialogues

Exercises like the ones that follow work best when students pair up and put into practice an old proverb, "Two heads are better than one." These exercises really get the students thinking. The students should first read the <u>entire</u> dialogue at least twice before attempting to fill in the missing parts. Stress this helpful hint: **The line that follows the blank area they're about to work on probably contains information that will help them figure out what may work logically in the blank.**

Why incomplete dialogues? There are some compelling reasons that make them such effective exercises. They serve as marvelous activities for reading comprehension, for sensitivity to language components, for reasoning, and for critical thinking. Students can stretch their language ability and help their classmates learn, too. Incomplete dialogues also allow the students the special freedom found in manipulative and communicative activities. Here are the two major areas in which the skills just noted come into play through the use of incomplete dialogues:

1. **Reading Comprehension:** The students are forced to read thoroughly and find clues within the dialogue to identify where the situation takes place and enhance understanding of what's going on. Attention to punctuation is also very important as meaning can change depending on what punctuation has been used and where it's been placed. Here's an example:

A: Acme Plumbing. Jim .... ?
B: Yes, please. ....
A: I'm afraid that job's been taken.

Let's see just how much there is for the students to deal with in the excerpt above, which was taken from a longer exercise. To begin with, the readers have to determine what the situation is. (Are the speakers face to face? Are they on the phone?) Because of the way Person A (Jim) starts the conversation, the readers should deduce that the speakers are on the phone.

Now, from what is referred to in reading pedagogy as "knowledge of the world," the readers must decide what Jim could possibly say in the short blank following his name. Thinking back to similar situations they've experienced on the phone when calling a company, the readers should understand that Jim is saying something to identify himself ("Jim speaking" or "Jim here" or "Jim talking" or maybe his last name).

Next we have a blank line ending in a question mark. The readers must see the question mark (and it's surprising how many students fail to note punctuation as a clue at first glance), realize there must be a question in that blank, and determine what would be appropriate for Jim to ask at that moment. From their "knowledge of the world," the readers should be able to figure out that Jim is probably saying something like, "May I help you?" or "What can I do for you?" But wait a minute! The following line begins with Person B saying "Yes, please." That means we have to eliminate "What can I do for you?" as a possible question for Jim to ask because "Yes, please" wouldn't be an appropriate response to "What can I do for you?" We must conclude that Jim has said, "May I help you?" and then Person B's response works just fine.

Finally, how can we figure out what Person B says next? We need to look at Jim's reply; that's where we'll get the hint we need to fill in the next blank. Jim says, "I'm afraid that job's been taken." His answer gives us quite a bit of information to work with. If he mentions "that job," Person B must have asked about a specific job, so we know that we've got to think of a specific job to mention in the blank. In addition, Jim says he's afraid that job's been taken, and this information leads us to the conclusion that Person B was attempting to apply for that job—otherwise, Jim would have no reason to make that statement. So we have these two pieces of information: Person B wants to apply for a job and it's for a specific job that has been advertsised, not just any job. (Everything I've been discussing, especially in this paragraph, demonstrates clearly how important critical thinking can be to reading and language learning in general as well as the principles of deixis.)

So what can we put in that final blank? Possibilities are "I'm calling about the ad I saw in the paper for a plumber's assistant." or "I'd like to know if you're still looking for a bookkeeper." or "A friend of mine told me he saw your ad for a secretary." Notice how the situation I've been working with is deliberately left quite open; that's to allow the students to come up with different ideas.

While the students are paired up and working on one of these dialogues, walk around the room and offer assistance when the students seem stuck. When they're finished and you've checked over their work, have the best of the lot presented to the class in the final versions. The students will find it interesting to compare what they've come up with to what their classmates have created.

2. **Sensitivity to Language Components**: The readers must search out clues within the dialogue that can establish the correct tense or aspect of verbs, and those words that students typically rush over, like prepositions, take on an importance which the students don't often realize they have. Just look at the following examples:

A: Who are you sending that fax .... ?
B: Our main office.

A: Who are you sending that fax .... ?
B: My boss. She said to get it out right away.

The students are invited into becoming more sensitive to language by having to figure out which prepositions will work in these blanks in order to elicit the responses provided. This is another use of critical thinking.

The following examples of incomplete dialogues get progressively more difficult. You decide which difficulty level is most appropriate for your students.

Work with a classmate and complete the following conversations.

Example 1

A: I just dropped my glove. Would you mind .... ?
B: Why don't you .... ?
A: Can't you see that .... ?
B: Oh, I didn't notice. All right. Here you are.

Example 2

A: That's not your jacket; it's my jacket. ....!

B: Aw, can't I .... for this evening?

A: No, you can't. You should have .... first.

Example 3

Tom: Hi, Pat! ....?

Pat: Oh, everything's fine, thanks. ....?

Tom: She's fine, too.

Pat: ....

Tom: To that little restaurant across the street for lunch.

Pat: ....?

Tom: Sure! I'd love to have some company.

Example 4

Ken: ....?

Hal: Really? When?

Ken: ....

Hal: Well, that's wonderful! Let me be the first to congratulate you!

Ken: ....

Example 5

Sam: ....?

Ben: To the grocery. I need to get some dog food and paper towels.

Sam: You don't look so good. ....?

Ben: Not really.

Sam: What's the matter?

Ben: ....

Sam: That's awful! ....?

Ben: Just two days ago.

Sam: ....?

Ben: Actually, there is something you could do. ....

....?

Sam: Sure, no problem. I can't guarantee anything, but I'll see what I can do.

Ben: ....

Sam: Don't mention it. And cheer up. Everything'll be all right.

Ben: ....

Sam: Well, see you later.

Ben: ....

Sam: You don't need to say that again. What are friends for?

Appendix 2

Notes on Pronunciation and Rules for Doubling Final Consonants

You may find this appendix a real eye opener. What I'd like to do is point out some glaring areas of mispronunciation that generally aren't corrected enough. Just as the "Heads Up!" boxes in this book deal with areas not often covered in other books, this appendix on pronunciation and consonant doubling will do likewise.

To begin with, let's define what we mean when we say "So-and-so has a *foreign* accent." In a nutshell, we mean that the person in question uses sounds that are either nonexistent in English phonology or uses sounds that English does have—but in the wrong place. In other words, I mean that the phonology of the speaker's language is being imposed onto English. That's how we recognize that the person isn't a native speaker.

Nobody expects a non-native speaker to have native-like pronunciation, so that's not the goal an English language teacher—or any foreign language teachers—should have. What we really want to have as our goal is to reduce the non-English sounds as much as possible so that they don't interfere with communication or draw unnecessary attention to themselves. The points that I mention in this appendix, if applied conscientiously and diligently, will help non-native speakers reduce the non-native sounds. The final section of this appendix deals with when and why we double final consonants at certain times due to pronunciation.

The Letter "O"

English language learners whose first languages use the Roman alphabet see the letter "o" and immediately go for the pronunciation of that letter as it is in their native languages. This assumption leads to the strangest pronunciations of many high-frequency English words.

The truth of the matter is that, in a vast number of English words, the letter "o" is pronounced /a/ or /ɔ/, but not /o/, and which of these two sounds is employed depends on what regional variation or dialect the speaker uses.

(As a side note, I'd like to add that even the so-called "long vowel" in English is not pronounced as it is in other languages. Many other languages have what is called a *pure* "o." It's pronounced much like the English long vowel, but the lips, rounded as the sound is made, stay relatively open and somewhat loose. In the English version of this sound, the lips continue to close more and more tightly after you begin to say the sound, so that in essence, the English sound is really a combination of /o/ + /u/, in other words, diphthongized. In fact, in the International Phonetic Alphabet, the IPA, the English sound is shown as /o^w/ or /o^u/ to account for these combined sounds.)

Getting back to the sound in question, we should look at some examples of common words in which the "o" is pronounced either /a/ or /ɔ/ depending on the dialect. (Where there's more than one "o," I've underlined the one I'm focusing on):

Bob	cop	knock	Robert
bother	doctor	Mom	stop
bottle	dollar	not	Thomas
college	got	Pop	Tom
comedy	hot	rob	tomorrow

The point is, whether you pronounce these words and so many others like them with the sound of /a/ or /ɔ/, the sound I'm focusing on is definitely not pronounced /o/ in English. Don't let your students get away with always pronouncing the letter "o" as /o/. Catch them on it every time you hear it mispronounced and break a bad habit before it gets firmly entrenched, that is, fossilized.

The "D" in *Dry*; The "T" in *Try*

Although it isn't the case in every dialect of English, at least it is the case that in some dialects the /d/ in *dry* and the /t/ in *try* are not pronounced as they are in other environments. To begin with, the fact is that in these English dialects, this /d/ is pronounced more like /ǰ/ than /d/ when it precedes /u/ in some words like *educate*.

The reason is that, at one point, the word was pronounced /ed – yu – ket/. In speaking quickly, this combination of /d/ + /yu/ became palatalized* and changed to the one sound /ǰ/. Another example is *gradual* /græ – ǰu – əl/.

The same phenomenon happened with the /t/ in a word like *ritual*, where /rɪt – yu – əl/ became /rɪ – ču – əl/.

---

*When sounds are palatalized, the blade of the tongue (the flat, front, top section) moves up and touches the alveolar ridge, the area between the upper teeth and the hard palate where the roof of the mouth forms that high dome.

For some speakers this mutation even happens when /d/ or /t/ precede /r/. So /d/ mutates to a sound close to /ǰ/: *drop* /ǰrap/, and /t/ mutates to a sound closer to /č/: *troup* /črup/.

Here's a short list of words which have these typical sound changes for "d" and "t" in some dialects of English. Note that there are certain words in bold; that's because these words really seem to grate on the ears of native English speakers when mispronounced, so concentrate on them. By the way, if a word contains more than one "d" or "t," the one that goes through this sound change is underlined:

"d" ⟶ /ǰ/

		"t" ⟶ /č/	
ad̲dress	drizzle	**adven̲ture**	**si̲tuate**
ad̲rift	drop	**archi̲tecture**	**si̲tuation**
ar̲duous	drown	at̲tract	**spa̲tula**
caul̲dron	drug	at̲traction	**struc̲ture**
d̲raft (draught)	drunk	con̲tract	**tor̲ture**
d̲raw	**ed̲ucate**	con̲tribute	traf̲fic
d̲rawer	**ed̲ucation**	con̲tribution	t̲rain
d̲read	**grad̲ual**	**den̲tures**	t̲ree
d̲ream	**grad̲uate**	**fac̲tual**	t̲rial
d̲rill	**grad̲uation**	**mu̲tual**	t̲rue
d̲rink	**sched̲ule**	**punc̲tuate**	t̲ruth
d̲rip	squad̲ron	**punc̲tuation**	**vir̲tual**
d̲rive	withd̲raw	**ri̲tual**	**vir̲tue**

The *Flapped D*

Since we're on the subject of the letter "t," I'd like to mention another sound that's often neglected in teaching pronunciation—at least in teaching North American pronunciation. The sound is called a "flapped d" /D/ because, even though it appears as a "t" or "tt" in writing within a word, it's pronounced like a "d," only made a little faster and perhaps more loosely with the tip of the tongue than a regular "d." The tip of the tongue literally *flaps* quickly against the roof of the mouth on the alveolar ridge behind the top front teeth where a regular "d" sound is made. In North American English the basic rule is that /t/ **mutates to /D/ when it's found between a stressed and an unstressed vowel or when it follows /r/.**

Here are some words that have this change from /t/ to /D/. Once again, I've underlined the "t" or "tt" that goes through this sound change if there are other "t's" in a word:

at̲titude   batter   bitter   butter

ca<u>tt</u>le	da<u>t</u>a	ea<u>t</u>ery	fa<u>tt</u>er
fri<u>tt</u>er	gli<u>tt</u>er	go-ge<u>tt</u>er	hea<u>t</u>er
ho<u>tt</u>er	ji<u>tt</u>ery	i<u>t</u>em	ke<u>tt</u>le
la<u>t</u>er	la<u>tt</u>er	li<u>tt</u>le	Mar<u>t</u>y
ma<u>tt</u>ed	ma<u>tt</u>er	nu<u>tt</u>y	o<u>tt</u>er
par<u>t</u>y	Pa<u>tt</u>i	pre<u>tt</u>y	qui<u>tt</u>er
ra<u>tt</u>le	sta<u>t</u>ic	ta<u>tt</u>er	ta<u>tt</u>le
u<u>tt</u>er	*vic<u>t</u>uals	we<u>tt</u>er	whe<u>tt</u>ed

*In case you're wondering about this archaic word, it's pronounced /vɪ-Dəlz/ with the "c" becoming silent and the "ua" reducing to schwa (like "vittles")!

Juncture

Moving right along, here's yet another tidbit in pronunciation that's often neglected. In linguistics, "juncture" means the joining point of two sounds, and what I'd like to focus on is when the last consonant sound of one word and the first consonant sound of the next word are the same or closely related. When that's the case, the two words are basically joined as they're pronounced so that for all intents and purposes they sound like one word.

As an example, take the combination of *bus stop*. Most English language learners will try to pronounce these words as completely separate units, but native speakers will join them together to produce:

bus stop /bǝs: tap/

The one thing to keep in mind is that **the /s/ is held a fraction longer than it would normally be held**, and this is shown in phonetics by the addition of a colon to indicate the lengthened sound. In other words, the tip of the tongue is kept in the position for /s/ just a fraction of a second longer so that we account for the double /s:/ sound. This holding onto the sound a bit longer is typical of how this kind of juncture is pronounced. Here's a list of more phrases and sentences to show you all kinds of possibilities:

a gra<u>b b</u>ag	He'll confe<u>ss s</u>oon.
re<u>d d</u>ots	fai<u>r r</u>easons
rou<u>gh f</u>riends	*the fir<u>st st</u>ate

*This example of juncture is interesting because it works a little differently. The /st/ in *first* combines with the /st/ in *state*, so the result is that people say "the /fərs:tet/." This combined form can make for fun and pun when you contrast it with "the fur state" or "the first eight" or even "the first date"!

Don't bug Grandpa.	a sweet taste
sick kids	a bath thermometer
small lamps	Bathe the baby!
tame monkeys	Save vampires!
tan natives	pinkish shrimp
ripe pineapples	She loves zebras.

There are two exceptions to the rule. The first is when you're dealing with the sound /č/. We never have a lengthening of the sound when one word ends with this consonant sound and the next word begins with it: *a rich child/not much chance*. In other words, there is no juncture.

The other exception works the same way with the sound of /ǰ/: *orange juice*.

But I'm not finished with juncture yet. So far, I've discussed the primary way this phenomenon happens, but that isn't the only way. Another way it takes place is when the final consonant sound of one word is closely related to the first consonant sound of the next word. One clear example is the juxtaposition of a voiced sound and its voiceless counterpart:

>They're trying to bribe Pauline.

or a voiceless sound plus its voiced counterpart:

>Do you think you could help Bob?

The trick is that, instead of merging both sounds into one longer one, the voiced and voiceless sounds still maintain their independence, so to speak, but **the first of the two sounds is held (not released) a bit longer and then it "slides" into the second sound.**

Here are some more examples of this kind of juncture:

red tomatoes	big kids
a cute doll	sleek gazelles
a rough version	his son
I crave french fries.	the Paris zoo

The Most Common Vowel Sound in English

If you ever want a good trivia question to ask people at a party, here it is: What's the most common vowel sound in the English language? Answer? The schwa! Yes, believe it or not, the /ə/ is the vowel sound most commonly found in English words. It pops up where non-native speakers would least expect it to be, and here's a list of words to demonstrate my point. Every underlined vowel or combination of letters is pronounced /ə/ by the majority of native English speakers:

Americ<u>a</u>	h<u>u</u>ngry	<u>o</u>pposed	<u>u</u>nb<u>e</u>liev<u>a</u>ble /əl/
b<u>a</u>n<u>a</u>na	ic<u>i</u>cle /əl/	p<u>a</u>ternity	val<u>e</u>dict<u>o</u>ry
Col<u>o</u>mbi<u>a</u>	j<u>u</u>nk	quadr<u>a</u>nt	w<u>o</u>ndr<u>ou</u>s
dev<u>e</u>l<u>o</u>p	kang<u>a</u>roo	Robert<u>a</u>	xyl<u>o</u>phone
el<u>e</u>ph<u>a</u>nt	lam<u>e</u>nt<u>a</u>bl<u>e</u> /əl/	selecti<u>o</u>n	y<u>ou</u>ng
fr<u>o</u>m	min<u>i</u>m<u>a</u>l	tr<u>ou</u>bles<u>o</u>me	zebr<u>a</u>
g<u>i</u>raffe	nati<u>o</u>n<u>a</u>l		

So when you teach pronunciation, stress this observation and sensitize your students to be aware of how prevalent the sound /ə/ is in English.

The Final -*ate*!

One more area that never seems to get enough attention involves words that end with the three letters -*ate*. Understanding how to pronounce this final syllable correctly isn't hard at all, so English language teachers should take the time to teach the rules and make sure to correct students when they mispronounce the syllable. There doesn't seem to be a lot of trouble when the word is a verb; you simply pronounce the -*ate* /et/ with the silent "e" making the previous vowel long. Students have usually already learned this rule of pronunciation. It's when the word is a noun or adjective that the trouble really sets in. English language learners invariably pronounce all words that end in -*ate* as if they were verbs.

Here's how the rules go (even though there are a few exceptions):

- If the -*ate* is at the end of a verb, pronounce it /et/.
- If the -*ate* is at the end of a noun or adjective, pronounce it /ət/ or /ɪt/.

Here are some words that show these changes in pronunciation:

aggregate (v., n., adj.)	graduate (v., n., adj.)
alternate (v., n., adj.)	initiate (v., n.)
appropriate (v., adj.)	intimate (v., n., adj.)
associate (v., n., adj.)	laminate (v., n.)
delegate (v., n.)	moderate (v., adj.)
deviate (v., n.)	postulate (v., n.)
elaborate (v., adj.)	separate (v., adj.)

Some more examples of adjectives that end in -*ate* with the pronunciation of

/ɪt/ or /ət/ are *collegiate, delicate, intricate, obstinate, passionate,* and *surrogate*.

I should point out that there are a few exceptions in which the *-ate* is pronounced /et/ even though the word is a noun. These include *diplomate, magnate, magistrate, potentate,* and *reprobate*.

Other Tips for Teaching Pronunciation

1. *Voiced and Voiceless Sounds*

On page 69 in Chapter 4, I give the rules for pronouncing the *-ed* regular past tense and show which sounds are voiced and which are voiceless. I should mention here that the same rule applies for pronouncing the regular plural *-s/-es* as well.

What I'd like to do here is give you a tip that will help your students really understand why some sounds are called voiced and others voiceless. Have the students place the curved edge of one hand (running from the thumb to the index finger) up against their throats. While they keep their hands in that position, tell them to say the vowel sound /i/ and to hold it. While they're making the sound, ask them if they feel a vibration on their hands. If they're doing it right, they will. Explain to them that all vowel sounds are voiced and that they will always feel a vibration when making a vowel sound.

Now have them do the same thing with a voiced consonant sound like /z/. Again they should feel vibration on their hands. Now switch to the related voiceless consonant sound /s/. This time, they should feel no vibration on their hands. Let them keep practicing with voiced and voiceless consonant sounds, comparing when they do and don't feel vibrations. I suggest these pairs:

/v/ ~ /f/   /z/ ~ /s/   /g/ ~ /k/   /ð/ ~ /θ/

After a while, they'll get the hang of it and start to understand more clearly which sounds are voiced and which aren't.

I'd like to mention something about teaching the pronunciation of the four pairs you've just seen. I'll focus on the /v/ and the /f/ for this demonstration, but it works the same way for the other pairs as well.

If you have students who speak a language like Spanish, which doesn't differentiate much between /b/ and /v/, here's a tip to help them learn how to say /v/ in English. Make them aware of how they pronounce /f/; the top front teeth are placed over the lower lip. Tell them to say /f/ and hold the sound while they concentrate on where their top front teeth are and on the fact that they're blowing air out of their mouths but not using their voices. While they're making the sound of /f/, tell them to start vibrating their vocal chords. As soon as they do this, they'll make a perfect /v/ sound because the only difference between /f/ and /v/ is whether or not it's voiced or voiceless. This holds true in the reverse, as for example in Arabic, where the students' voices have to be "turned off" to make the sound /p/ instead of the voiced /b/.

2. Pronouncing "th" (/ð/ and /θ/)

Yes, I know that these are just about the most difficult sounds for English language students to master. Here's one method that has worked wonders for many of my students who have had trouble pronouncing "th":

Have your students get small hand mirrors (or they can use the selfie feature of their phones like a mirror). Give them three lists of words, the first with the "th" in initial position on each word, the second with the "th" in medial position, and the last list with the "th" in final position (e.g., *thumb/method/bath* and *then/weather/bathe*). Tell them to practice saying each word as they look at their mouths. Tell them they should see their tongues projecting out past their teeth and that their lips should be slightly apart. If they can't see their tongues projecting out past their teeth, they're not saying the sound right.

This is a good method for them to practice producing the sounds correctly without the teacher having to be present. It will also stop them from "faking" the sounds by substituting them with /t/, /d/, /f/, /v/, /s/, or even /z/!

3. A Picture Says a Thousand Words

Another way to help your students produce English sounds more accurately is by showing them clear, uncluttered pictures or diagrams of a mouth so they can see precisely what's going on inside when a certain sound is made. Here's an example of what I mean—and you don't have to be a Picasso or Rembrandt to create decent pictures!

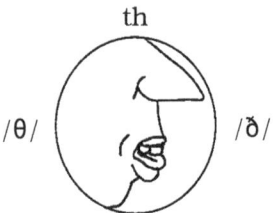

Clear enough? For the purposes of the classroom, it should do just fine. And here's one more example:

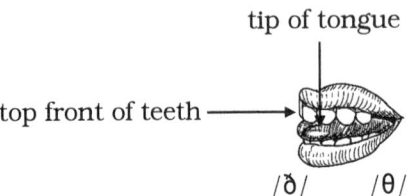

4. Spelling Unfamiliar Names Over the Phone

It's always been a difficult thing to spell people's last names, especially in countries which have people from all over the world. Many names are familiar to most English speakers, but many others aren't, so spelling them correctly can be a problem.

The time when this spelling is most difficult is while talking on the phone. The reason? There are pairs of consonants that sound very similar when pronounced over the phone, so it's easy to mistake one for the other. Traditionally, native English speakers have used a little device to avoid mistakes when writing down these similar sounds. The examples I'm going to give you are the typical words people use to make sure the listener understands which letter is being said, but any common words will do. The important point is that your English language learners should start developing the habit of using these words or words like them when spelling difficult names over the phone. So, here they are:

"b" as in "boy"	"d" as in "dog"
"f" as in "Frank"	"m" as in "Mary"
"n" as in "Nancy"	"p" as in "Peter"
"s" as in "Sam"	"t" as in "Thomas"
"v" as in "Victor"	"z" as in "zebra"

The sounds above are the ones that can easily be confused over the phone. For example, there are:

$$/b/ \sim /p/ \quad /d/ \sim /t/ \quad /f/ \sim /s/ \quad /m/ \sim /n/$$

Rules for Doubling the Final Consonants

Double the final consonant when:

Rule #1
One-Syllable Words with the Pattern *Consonant + Short Vowel + Consonant*

Examples: *hop* → *hopping*   *mat* → *matted*

Rule #2
Multisyllabic Words with a Stressed Final Syllable

Examples: *compel* → *compelling*   *refer* → *referred*

Appendix 3

More Fun with Autosegmental Features: A Stress-Caused Metamorphosis

Noun	vs.	Verb	Noun	vs.	Verb
ADdress		adDRESS	EXport		exPORT
ATtribute		atTRIbute	EXtract		exTRACT
COMbine		comBINE	IMpact		imPACT
COMEon		comeON	IMport		imPORT
COMmune		comMUNE	IMprint		imPRINT
COMpound		comPOUND	INcrease		inCREASE
COMpress		comPRESS	INsert		inSERT
CONduct		conDUCT	INsult		inSULT
CONsole		conSOLE	INtrigue		inTRIGUE
CONsort		conSORT	INvite(slang)		inVITE
CONstruct		conSTRUCT	PERfect		perFECT
CONtest		conTEST	PERmit		perMIT
CONtrast		conTRAST	PREsent		preSENT
CONvict		conVICT	PROceeds		proCEEDS
DEfect		deFECT	PROgress		proGRESS
DIgest		diGEST	PROject		proJECT
EXcise		exCISE	PROtest		proTEST
EXploit		exPLOIT	REcess		reCESS

Variable Noun	vs.	Verb	Adjective	vs.	Noun
DEtail / deTAIL		DEtail	inVAlid		INvalid

Adjective	vs.	**Verb**	**Prep.**	vs.	**Phrase**
CONverse		conVERSE	INto		in TWO
PERfect		perFECT			

Phrases

Adj. + Noun	**Comp. Noun**	**Adj. + Noun**	**Comp. Adj.**
BLACK BIRD	BLACKbird	FIRST rate	FIRST RATE
BLUE BIRD	BLUEbird	SECOND class	SECOND CLASS
RED NECK	REDneck		

Adj. + Noun	vs.	**Comp. Verb**	**Noun**	vs.	**Adj./Adv.**
WHITE WASH		WHITE wash	INstep		in STEP

Adjective	vs.	**Adverb**	**Noun**	vs.	**Phrase**
OUTside		outSIDE	INtern		in TURN

Various

FORty / for TEA

Now **THERE'S** a good girl. / Now there's a **GOOD GIRL** over there.

GOING to **EAT**, John. / Going to eat **JOHN**.

As you can see, a change in stress from one syllable to another not only can change the part of speech (e.g., noun vs. verb), but can also change meaning so completely that there's no relationship at all between the two words in some cases, for example, DEfect vs. deFECT or DIgest vs. diGEST.

Appendix 4

A Deeper Look at Reporting Verbs

Patterns that Follow Reporting Verbs

In Chapter 13 I promised further exploration of the intricacies of indirect speech. I'm going to help you examine fourteen patterns in the following way: First, you'll find a numbered list of all the patterns. Then you'll find the reporting verbs with examples of each pattern that can follow them. To make things easier, the corresponding number of each pattern in the list below is in front of a sentence that exemplifies it.

The Patterns (rp = reporting verb)

1. rp (+ *optional that* . . .)
2. rp + *to* + *indirect object* (+ optional *that* . . .)
3. rp + *indirect object* (+ optional *that* . . .)
4. rp + wh- clause or wh- phrase
5. rp + *to* + *indirect object* + wh- clause
6. rp + *indirect object* + wh- clause or wh- phrase
7. rp + infinitive verb
8. rp + *indirect object* + infinitive verb
9. rp + *to* + *indirect object* + infinitive verb
10. rp + *if/whether*
11. rp + *indirect object* + *if/whether*
12. rp + gerund (verb + -*ing*)
13. rp + *to* + *indirect object* + gerund [verb + -*ing*]
14. rp + *direct object* + infinitive verb DOC

ADD

1. At the end of her talk, she **added (that)** used batteries thrown into landfills could also contaminate ground water.
4. When she was telling you about safe ways to dispose of pollutants, did she **add where** you could take used motor oil and used batteries for proper disposal?

ADMIT

1. I **admitted (that)** I didn't like her cooking.
2. I **admitted *to her* (that)** I didn't like her cooking.
4. I **admitted why** I preferred to eat out.
5. I **admitted *to her* why** I preferred to eat out.
12. I **admitted taking** the money without permission.

ADVISE

1. Her memo **advised (that)** it would be a long meeting.
3. She **advised *us* (that)** the meeting would go on for a long time.
6. She **advised *us* how** we should dress for the meeting. / **how** to dress for the meeting.
8. She **advised *us* to be** prepared for a long meeting.

AGREE

1. We **agreed (that)** it would be wise to meet with them.
4. We **agreed where** to meet / **where** we should meet.
7. We **agreed to meet** with them and discuss the matter.

ALLEGE

1. He **alleges (that)** our drinking water supplies are still being contaminated.

ALLOW

8. The doctor only **allowed *him* to have** two cups of coffee a day.

ANNOUNCE

1. They **announced (that)** they were planning to get married.
2. They **announced *to everyone at the party* (that)** they were planning to get married.
4. They **announced when** and **where** the wedding would take place.
5. They announced to everyone at the party when and where the wedding would take place.

ARGUE

1. We **argued (that)** there were more economical ways to recycle things.
7. The defense attorney **argued to dismiss** the case.

ASK
1. They **asked** (that) they be allowed to leave early.
4. I **asked** <u>where</u> they were going.
6. I **asked** *them* <u>where</u> they were going.
7. They **asked** <u>to be allowed</u> to leave early.
8. They **asked** *me* <u>to allow</u> them to leave early.
10. They **asked** <u>whether</u> they could leave early.
11. They **asked** *me* <u>if</u> they could leave early.

ASSERT
1. He **asserted** (that) he'd never met the man.
2. He **asserted** *to us* (that) he'd never met the man.

ASSURE
3. I **assure** *you* (that) you've got nothing to lose.

BEG
1. She **begged** (that) the court hear her appeal.
7. She **begged** <u>to be heard</u> in court.
8. She **begged** *the court* <u>to hear</u> her appeal.

BOAST
1. They **boasted** (that) their car was the best.
2. They **boasted** *to us* (that) their car was the best.

BRAG
1. They **bragged** (that) their car was the best.
2. They **bragged** *to us* (that) their car was the best.

CLAIM
1. You **claimed** (that) you spoke four languages, didn't you?
2. You **claimed** *to me* (that) you spoke four languages, didn't you?
7. You **claimed** <u>to speak</u> four languages, didn't you?

COMMAND
1. The general **commanded** (that) his troops cease fire.
8. The general **commanded** *his troops* <u>to cease</u> fire.

COMPLAIN
1. We **complained** (that) the food had been served cold.
2. We **complained** *to the waiter* (that) the food was cold.

CONFESS

1. She **confessed** (that) she'd always wanted that job.
2. She **confessed** *to us* (that) she'd always wanted that job.
4. She **confessed** <u>why</u> she'd lied on her résumé.
5. She **confessed** *to us* <u>why</u> she'd lied on her résumé.

CONVINCE

3. You **convinced** *them* (that) it wasn't their fault.
6. You **convinced** *them* <u>why</u> they weren't to blame.
8. You **convinced** *them* <u>not to blame</u> themselves.

DECLARE

1. He **declared** (that) the race should begin.
2. He **declared** *to the cheering crowd* (that) the race should begin.
4. He **declared** <u>who</u> the winner was.
5. He **declared** *to the cheering crowd* <u>who</u> the winner was.

DEMAND

1. I **demanded** (that) they permit me to see the judge.
7. I **demanded** <u>to see</u> the judge.

DENY

1. Don't **deny** (that) you took the money!
2. Didn't you **deny** *to them* (that) you had taken the money?
4. Don't **deny** <u>what</u> you've done.
5. Don't **deny** *to us or yourself* <u>what</u> you've done.
12. Don't **deny** <u>taking</u> the money!
13. Don't **deny** *to us* <u>taking</u> the money!

DIRECT

6. We **directed** *them* <u>where</u> to go.
8. We **directed** *them* <u>to follow</u> the detour signs.

DISAGREE

1. He **disagreed** (that) she was a better tennis player.

EXPLAIN

1. They **explained** (that) we'd find the map in the desk.
2. They **explained** *to us* (that) we'd find the map in the desk.
4. They **explained** <u>where</u> we'd find the map.
5. They **explained** *to us* <u>where</u> we'd find the map.

FORBID

8. They **forbade** *her* <u>to see</u> the young man again.

HINT

1. He kept **hinting** (that) he wanted to quit his job.
2. He kept **hinting** *to his wife* (that) he wanted to quit his job.
4. He **hinted** <u>what career change</u> he wanted to make.
5. He **hinted** *to his wife* <u>what career change</u> he wanted to make.

INFORM

3. The landlord **informed** *us* (that) the rent would be going up.
6. The landlord also **informed** *us* <u>how much</u> the new rent would be.
11. My daughter always **informs** *me* <u>if</u> she's going to be late.

INSIST

1. Even though people thought him strange, Columbus **insisted** (that) the world was round.

INSTRUCT

1. She **instructed** (that) her collection of antique dolls should be donated to the local museum.
1. She **instructed** (that) her antique doll collection be donated to the local museum.
8. She **instructed** *her children* <u>to donate</u> her antique dolls to the local museum.

MAINTAIN

1. Even after his conviction, he **maintained** (that) he was innocent.

NOTIFY

3. We **notified** *her* (that) all of her wishes had been carried out.
6. The bank **notified** *her* <u>when</u> to pick up her loan money.
8. The bank **notified** *her* <u>to pick up</u> her loan money by Friday.
11. Please **notify** *me* <u>if</u> it comes in early.

ORDER

1. The captain **ordered** (that) his men lay down their weapons.
1. The captain **ordered** (that) his men should lay down their weapons.
8. The captain **ordered** *his men* <u>to lay</u> down their weapons.

PERMIT

8. They **permitted** *us* <u>to take</u> one bag each onto the plane.

12. They **permitted** <u>taking</u> one bag onto the plane.

PERSUADE
3. He **persuaded** *us* (that) we should postpone our trip.
6. He **persuaded** *us* <u>where</u> we should go on our vacation.
8. He **persuaded** *us* <u>to postpone</u> the trip.

PRAY
1. They **prayed** (that) their daughter would get home safe and sound.
2. They **prayed** *to God* (that) their daughter would get home safe and sound.
7. They **prayed** <u>to be guided</u> by divine intervention.
9. They **prayed** *to God* <u>to be guided</u> by divine intervention.

PREDICT
1. She **predicted** (that) there would never be another world war.
2. She **predicted** *to us* (that) there would be no more war.
4. She **predicted** <u>which</u> countries would bring about world peace.
5. She **predicted** *to us* <u>which countries</u> would initiate world peace.
12. She correctly **predicted** <u>his winning</u> the primary.

PROCLAIM
1. They **proclaimed** (that) UFO's weren't imaginary.
2. They **proclaimed** *to us* (that) UFO's weren't imaginary.
4. He **proclaimed** <u>which</u> government he was loyal to.
5. He **proclaimed** *to the consul* <u>which</u> government he was loyal to.
7. He **proclaimed** <u>to be</u> loyal to the government of Fulania.

PROMISE
1. I **promised** (that) I would be more attentive, didn't I?
3. I **promised** *you* (that) I would be more attentive, didn't I?
4. I **promised** <u>how</u> I'd be different in the future.
6. I **promised** *you* <u>how</u> I'd be different in the future.
7. I **promised** <u>to be</u> more attentive, didn't I?
8. I **promised** *you* <u>to be</u> more attentive, didn't I?

PROPOSE
1. He **proposed** (that) we should accept the budget as presented.
1. He **proposed** (that) we accept the budget as presented.
2. He **proposed** *to us* (that) we should accept the budget as it was.
4. He **proposed** <u>what</u> we should do.
5. He **proposed** *to us* <u>what</u> we should do.

7. He **proposed** <u>to be</u> more careful in the future.
12. He **proposed** <u>accepting</u> the budget as presented.

RECOMMEND
1. I **recommended** (that) she should see an accountant.
1. I **recommended** (that) she see an accountant.
2. I **recommended** *to her husband* (that) she see/should see an accountant.
4. I **recommended** <u>what</u> she should do.
5. I **recommended** *to her husband* <u>what</u> she should do.
14. I **recommended** *him* <u>to be</u> the next Ambassador to Luxembourg.
12. I **recommended** <u>seeing</u> an accountant.

REGRET
1. They **regretted** (that) they had to miss our party.
4. They **regretted** <u>what</u> they had to do instead of going to the party.
12. They **regretted** <u>having</u> to miss our party.

RELATE
1. We **related** (that) the treasure was buried nearby.
2. We **related** *to them* (that) the treasure was buried nearby.
4. We **related** <u>where</u> the treasure might be found.
5. We **related** *to them* <u>where</u> the treasure might be found.

REMARK
1. He **remarked** (that) it was getting late.
2. He **remarked** *to her* (that) it was getting late.
5. He **remarked** *to me* <u>why</u> he thought the idea was such a good one.

REMIND
3. She **reminded** *him* (that) their friends were coming over.
6. She **reminded** *him* <u>who</u> was coming over.
8. She **reminded** *him* <u>to pick up</u> some ice cream after work.

REPLY
1. He **replied** (that) he wouldn't forget the ice cream.
2. He **replied** *to her* (that) he wouldn't forget the ice cream.
4. He **replied** <u>why</u> he had forgotten to meet us.
5. He **replied** *to me* <u>why</u> he had forgotten to meet us.

REPORT
1. They **reported** (that) all the lights in the town were out.
2. They **reported** *to us* (that) all the lights in the town were out.

4. They **reported** <u>what</u> had happened.
5. They **reported** *to us* <u>where</u> the lights were out.
12. They **reported** <u>seeing</u> the lights go out all over town.
13. They **reported** *to us* <u>seeing</u> the lights go out all over town.

REQUEST

1. You **requested** (that) we should sell your car for you, right?
1. You **requested** (that) we sell your car for you, right?
4. You **requested** <u>what</u> you wanted us to do with your car, right?
7. We **requested** <u>to be given</u> a ten percent commission.

SAY

1. They **said** (that) the rainforests had to be saved.
2. They **said** *to us* (that) the rainforests had to be saved.
4. They **said** <u>what</u> we have to do to save the rainforests.
5. They **said** *to us* <u>what</u> we have to do to save the rainforests.
7. They **said** <u>to save</u> the rainforests before it's too late.
9. They **said** *to us* <u>to push</u> for more conservation efforts.

STATE

1. They **stated** (that) racism was universally unacceptable.
2. They **stated** *to us* (that) racism was universally unacceptable.
4. They **stated** <u>what</u> was universally unacceptable.
5. They **stated** *to us* <u>what</u> was universally unacceptable.

SUGGEST

1. I **suggested** (that) he should get a second opinion.
1. I **suggested** (that) he get a second opinion.
2. I **suggested** *to him* (that) he get/should get a second opinion.
4. I **suggested** <u>what</u> he should do.
5. I **suggested** *to him* <u>what</u> he should do / <u>what</u> to do.
9. I **suggested** *to him* <u>to get</u> a second opinion.
12. I **suggested** <u>getting</u> a second opinion.
13. I **suggested** *to him* <u>getting</u> a second opinion.

SWEAR

1. He **swore** (that) he'd always be loyal.
2. He **swore** *to his commander* (that) he'd always be loyal.
4. He **swore** <u>what</u> he would do.
5. He **swore** *to his commander* <u>what</u> he would do.
7. He **swore** <u>to remain</u> loyal at all costs.
9. He **swore** *to his commander* <u>to remain</u> loyal at all costs.

TEACH
1. You **taught** (that) it was wrong to waste water.
3. You **taught** *us* (that) it was wrong to waste water.
4. You **taught** <u>why</u> we should use water responsibly.
6. You **taught** *us* <u>why</u> we should use water responsibly.
8. You **taught** *us* <u>to conserve</u> water.

TELL
3. I **told** *you* (that) it would be an interesting speech.
6. I **told** *you* <u>what</u> the speech would be about.
8. I **told** *you* <u>to come</u> listen to his speech.
11. I'll **tell** *you* <u>whether</u> I can come to the meeting.

THREATEN
1. They **threatened** (that) they'd reveal her plans.
3. They **threatened** *her* (that) they'd reveal her plans.
4. They **threatened** <u>what</u> they'd do.
7. They **threatened** <u>to reveal</u> her plans.

URGE
8. We **urged** *him* to get some medical attention.

WARN
1. He **warned** (that) we'd better take him seriously.
3. He **warned** *us* (that) we'd better take him seriously.
6. He **warned** *us* <u>how</u> long we would wait.
8. He **warned** *us* <u>to take</u> him seriously.

WONDER
4. He **wondered** <u>why</u> I hadn't brought along more money with me.
10. I **wondered** <u>if</u> I had enough money for the tickets.

Another Way to Look at the Patterns

Instead of looking at specific verbs, you can also practice the patterns by examining what follows the reporting verb.

Note: Some reporting verbs may appear in more than one of the following groups because they can be used in several ways.

Appendix 4: A Deeper Look at Reporting Verbs

Verbs Followed by *IF* or *WHETHER*	
ask	say
know	see
remember	

Verbs Followed by *THAT*		
add	doubt	reply
admit	estimate	report
agree	explain	reveal
announce	fear	say
answer	feel	state
argue	insist	suggest
boast	mention	suppose
claim	observe	tell
comment	persuade	think
complain	propose	understand
confirm	remark	warn
consider	remember	
deny	repeat	

Verbs Followed by Either *THAT* or an INFINITIVE VERB with *TO*	
decide	promise
expect	swear
guarantee	threaten
hope	

Verbs Followed by a *THAT* CLAUSE Containing *SHOULD*, which May Be Omitted, Leaving a SUBJECT + ZERO INFINITIVE		
advise	insist	recommend
beg	prefer	request
demand	propose	suggest

Verbs Followed by a CLAUSE Starting with a QUESTION WORD		
decide	imagine	see
describe	know	suggest
discover	learn	teach
discuss	realize	tell
explain	remember	think
forget	reveal	understand
guess	say	wonder

Verbs Followed by OBJECT + INFINITIVE with *TO*		
advise	forbid	teach
ask	instruct	tell
beg	invite	warn
command		

The tables above and on page 491 are reprinted with permission from EF Education First: https://www.ef.edu/english-resources/english-grammar/reporting-verbs/ [July 24, 2020].

The Tone of Reporting Verbs

Finally, you should choose the reporting verb that expresses not only your meaning but also your tone. The following charts will help you determine how strongly you want to stress the information you are reporting and if you can use direct quotes or not.

More Emphatic Reporting Verbs

Verb	Used in direct quotations?	Can be followed by *that*?
affirm	No	Yes
allege	No	Yes
argue	No	Yes
assert	Yes	Yes
claim	Yes	Yes
contend	No	Yes
demonstrate	No	Yes
maintain	No	Yes
predict	Yes	Yes
predict	Yes	Yes
recommend	Yes	Yes
show	No	Yes

Less Emphatic Reporting Verbs

Verb	Used in direct quotations?	Can be followed by *that*?
describe	No	No
discuss	No	No
explain	No	Yes
hypothesize	Yes	Yes
imply	No	Yes
indicate	No	Yes
note	Yes	Yes
propose	Yes	Yes
report	Yes	Yes
state	Yes	Yes
suggest	Yes	Yes

Appendix 5

Rejoinders, Exclamations, Etc.

Back in Chapter 19 I discussed the phrases that add so much to the flow of conversation. Following is a list of some of the more frequently used phrases that only touches the tip of the iceberg. Teach these marvelous items that spice up English conversation to your students when you deem it appropriate to do so.

Here are some general rules to go by:

- When a phrase in the list begins with a capitalized word, it indicates that it's usually found as an introductory phrase.
- If the first word of a phrase begins with a small letter, it means that the phrase may either be an introductory phrase or found elsewhere in the sentence.
- If a phrase has the subject "I" or the object "me" in it, any personal pronoun or a person's name can be substituted in that spot except where otherwise noted.
- If a phrase contains the general pronoun "you," no other pronoun can be substituted.
- An ellipsis (three dots) found after a phrase means that the sentence continues in this spot.

After all is said and done . . .	all in all
And how!	as a matter of fact
as far as I'm concerned	As I was saying . . .
at first glance	believe it or not
By the way . . .	Can you beat that?!
Come on!	come to think of it
(The) Fact is . . .	Far be it from me to . . .
For one thing . . .	(and) for another . . .
For what it's worth . . .	from the very start

Get it?
How about that!
I'll say! (only with "I")
interestingly enough
In the second place . . .
It's just that . . .
it's not that so much that . . .
Leave it to me to . . .
No kidding!
Only time will tell.
On second thought . . .
Over my dead body!
Say what you will . . .
sooner or later
Speaking of which . . .
Tell me about it! (only with "me")
put it plainly
(The) Trouble is . . .
Try as I may . . .
whatever the case may be
What I'm trying to say is . . .
(is . . .) when you come right down to it
Why bother . . . ?
You bet!
You can say that again!
You never know.

God willing
if it comes to that
In case . . .
In the first place . . .
it's all a matter of . . .
It's more that . . .
Know what I mean . . .
No fooling!
once (= when)
On one hand . . .
On the other hand . . .
Putting personal feelings aside . . .
Same here!
See what I mean?
So then . . .
to put it mildly
to tell the truth
(The) Truth of the matter is . . .
(So) What else is new?
What I mean is that . . .
(what) it (all) boils down to
whether I like it or not
Wouldn't you know it!
You bet!
You don't say.
You're kidding!

Appendix 6

Games

What's that old adage? Oh, yes! "All work and no play make Jack a dull boy." I don't think any of us would disagree with that. So I hope you find the following activities as enjoyable and as effective as I have over the years. The time and effort it might require to create the materials for each of these games will be well worth the while, and from then on, you'll always have the materials available to you whenever you feel it's time to "lighten up" your classes. Enjoy these changes of pace!

Tic Tac Toe (British "Naughts & Crosses")

Tic Tac Toe is a good game for a practice or wrap-up session and can be played by students at any proficiency level. The object of the game is for one team to be the first to get three X's or three O's in a row horizontally, vertically, or diagonally. Here's how you play it.

Before class, select nine pictures from your Picture File on one teaching point and prepare them for play. For example, if you're practicing the simple past, you may want the class to practice two points, the simple past and *wh-* question formation. But how can you get the students to use what you may have in mind for them (both regular and irregular verbs and a variety of *wh-* question words)? Look at a picture you have chosen from your file. Think of *wh-* words and verbs that can be used to make questions about that picture. Cut a sheet of paper into small slips. On each slip, write down one *wh-* word and one verb that the group can use to make an appropriate question. Now, using paper clips, attach these slips onto the front of the picture anywhere that won't obscure the scene. Of course, if your picture is in digital format, you can easily create versions of the picture with different *wh-* words and verbs and save them in a designated file on your hard drive or in the cloud.

To begin the game, lay the nine pictures face down on the floor in three rows of three. Cut a piece of paper into eight smaller pieces, writing an "X" on four of them and an "O" on the other four. Divide the class into teams (the X's and the O's) and have the X's start. The X's choose one of the pictures, turning it over and leaving it on the floor for the whole class to study. The team members have to perform what is asked of them on the pictures. The team looks at their chosen picture and prepares a group response. Give students enough time to work out a response that's acceptable to the entire group. A single spokesperson gives the team's question and answer in order to win the square.

You should rotate spokespersons so that as many students as possible have a chance to speak and be accountable for their grammar and pronunciation. If you have a large class, you can double the number of spokespersons by having one student give the question and a second, the answer. You should let the spokesperson have two chances to give the group's responses; this way they can correct the responses if necessary and you're sure to hear what's said.

If the question and answer are correct, the team puts an "X" on the picture, which is now out of play. If the responses are wrong, the picture is turned back over and it's the "O" team's turn to play. They can choose the picture that's just been turned back over or they can choose another one. Remember—both teams have the opportunity to study and discuss the picture that was chosen. Thus both teams have the opportunity to discuss the teaching point even if only one team is actually playing that picture. This rule may seem to give one group an unfair advantage, the second team having all that additional time to formulate correct responses, not to mention the chance of hearing an incorrect response, but it doesn't always prove to be the case. Frequently, the second team makes mistakes on the same picture, even with that extra time to study it. Part of the object of any language-learning activity is to give as many students as much opportunity to practice the language as possible.

The game continues until one team wins three pictures in a row or a tie occurs.

Concentration

Concentration is a matching game that does take a good amount of time to prepare initially, but once you make the playing cards, you can use them again and again. The object is for students to match as many pairs of cards as possible. Here's one way to cut this task down to size: Have your students make your cards. Not only will that cut down on your work, but it will also give your students practice on the language points your game is focusing on.

To prepare the playing cards, find thick paper (index cards, tag board, cut up file folders, etc.) that can't be seen through when placed face down on a table. Cut the cards into a size that can be seen by all the students playing the game. I recommend that you use cards that are approximately 2½" or 8 cm. square. Again, these cards can be created digitally if you prefer, and then you can print them when you need them. You'll want between 20 to 25 pairs of cards per teaching point. If you have fewer, the game's not very challenging; if you have more, it's too hard (see the "Note" that follows).

The Concentration game I describe here is a review of irregular verbs in the simple past and past participle forms. Choose twenty irregular verbs you want your students to review; put one past tense form on each card. Put the corresponding past participles on the other twenty cards. Now you have forty verb cards:

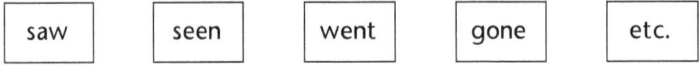

I recommend that you provide a separate set of cards to each group of four or five students. This way, the game will move along efficiently and the students won't get restless waiting for their turn to come around. Now you're ready to play.

Shuffle the cards well and lay them face down in neat rows on the students' desks or on the floor. It's important that the cards be in some sort of order because the students need to remember where they've seen each verb once it's been turned over. One student starts by turning over two cards and leaving them face up for everyone to see. If the cards match, the student gets to keep the pair, earning 1 point. The same student can keep on selecting pairs of cards until a mistake is made. If the two cards don't match, the student must return them to the exact position they were in to begin with. This exact placement will help the other students remember where the cards are when it's their turn to play. Students keep on playing until all cards have been matched; the one with the most points/pairs wins the game.

Note: Sometimes students aren't quite sure whether the two cards they've chosen make a match, so it's important for you to walk around the room and monitor the game and give advice when needed. Circulate to keep everything going smoothly, especially if you have more than one game going on. It's possible—I've done it with ten games going on at once!

The Clothesline

The Clothesline can be used to introduce, practice, or review grammar. Regardless of how you use it, what you need to begin with is a clothesline, a way to hang it, and some large pieces of scrap paper.

For my example, I'll show how you can introduce yes/no questions. Before class you'll need to prepare the vocabulary words you'll be working with. Each word will be written on a separate piece of paper, so don't choose words that are too long or paper that's too small. The back of scrap paper or used paper is perfect for this activity because only one side needs to be blank for writing on.

Your vocabulary for this lesson will include subject pronouns, the verb *be*, and adjectives. You'll also want to have the appropriate punctuation marks on hand. Write each word on the bottom half of a piece of paper and fold it in half.

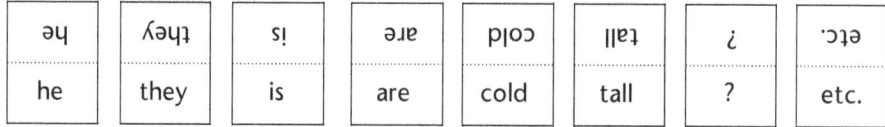

Stack all the pronouns together, all the verbs together, and all the adjectives together. Attach the clothesline, hang up the vocabulary in separate stacks, and you're ready to teach yes/no questions.

Stand behind the clothesline and ask the students to repeat the sentence they see after you've said it. Some teachers attach the clothesline to the board, but the disadvantage is that you might block the view of the clothesline for some students, even if you're off to the side. And, if you're in front of the line, your arms can get in the way when you're changing the words. If at all possible, you should stand behind the clothesline.

Ask the students to repeat the sentence they see after you.

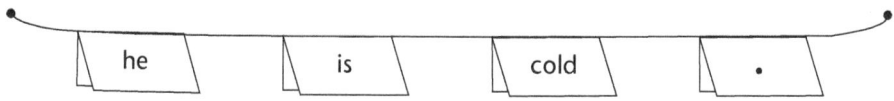

Begin showing students how English makes yes/no questions by rearranging the subject and verb papers. Don't forget to adjust your punctuation!

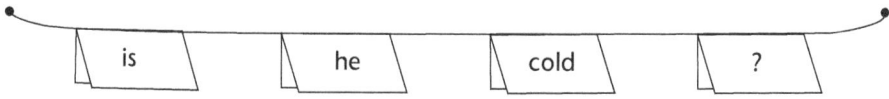

Continue these rearrangements and substitutions until the students are comfortable with the changes.

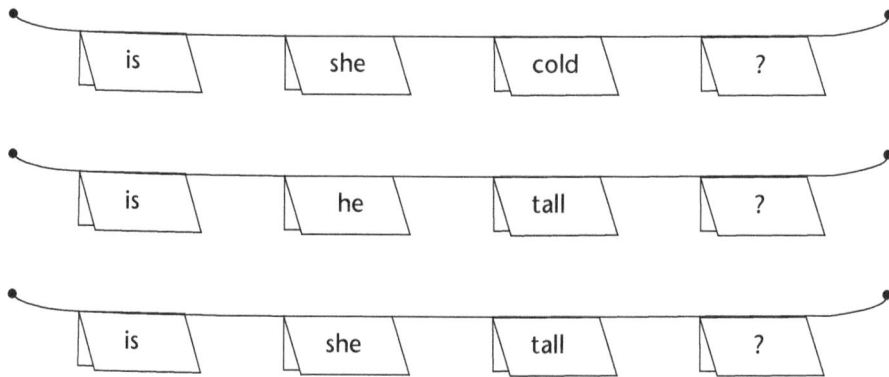

Note: You can make this a "substitution drill" by pulling off the vocabulary words that you previously stacked up on top of each other one by one.

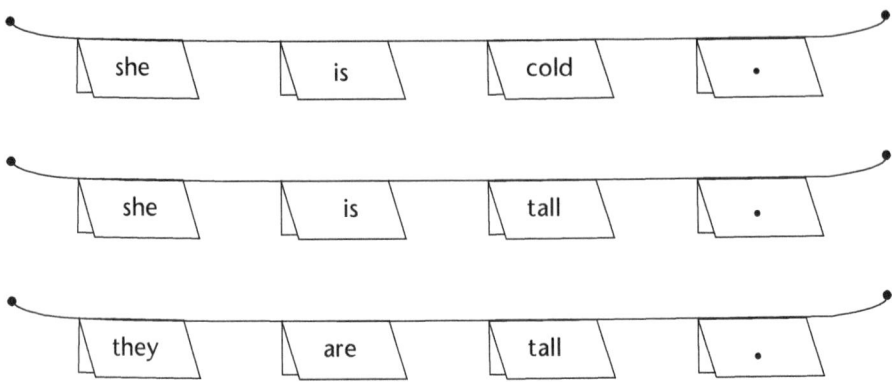

Later, you can test their comprehension of the new grammar by taking all the vocabulary and punctuation marks off the clothesline and distributing them to the students. Ask one student to go up to the clothesline and hang up a word. Then ask the other students to add their words one by one, making any changes in word order that are required and making sure that each addition makes sense. (It's like a living, moving slot substitution drill!) Be sure to have plenty of slips of paper with punctuation marks on them so the students will be invited to make both statements and questions.

Oral Matching

Use this activity for review. Before class begins, you'll need to prepare questions and statements and their logical responses; they can be complete sentences or partial sentences. Put the separate sentences or parts of sentences on individual slips of paper and mark each one with an "A" or a "B" (A = beginning phrase; B = finishing phrase). Make enough pairs for each student to have at least two slips. This example will focus on two-word verbs.

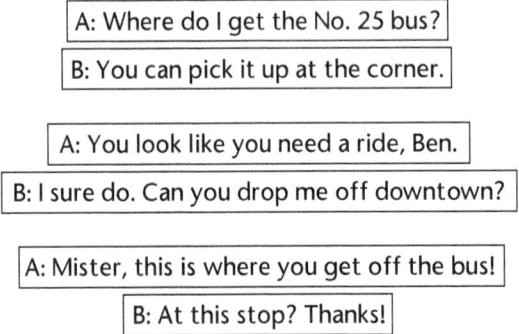

Make sure to remember that "A" slips and "B" slips can be either questions or statements. A closer look at my examples will show you what I mean. I suggest that you keep a master list of your dialogues with you during this activity so you can monitor the students' responses more easily or prompt them when they get confused or make mistakes.

Hand out the slips and have a student with an "A" slip read it aloud. The other students need to listen carefully, but only the one who has the matching "B" slip responds. (A challenging variation is to have the students memorize the information on their slips so they can recite their parts of the dialogues by heart.) Continue until all the matches have been made.

Appendix 7

Helpful Charts and Lists

Useful Vocabulary Lists on the Internet

Academic Word List

https://www.wgtn.ac.nz/lals/resources/academicwordlist

The Academic Word List (AWL), developed in 2000 by Averil Coxhead at the School of Linguistics and Applied Language Studies at Victoria University in Wellington, New Zealand, contains 570 word families selected because they appear with great frequency in a broad range of academic texts, but does not include words that are in the most frequent 2,000 words of English (the General Service List), which makes it specific to academic contexts.

The 570 words are divided into 10 groups. The words in the first group are the most frequent ones and those in the last group are the least frequent.

There are numerous websites that utilize the AWL and make it easy for students to practice it. There are also textbooks that are based on the AWL.

General Service List

http://jbauman.com/gsl.html

This site lists the almost 2,000 word families on the General Service List (GSL), which was developed in 1953 by Michael West, who identified the most frequent words used in a 2.5-million-word corpus of written English.

New General Service List

www.newgeneralservicelist.org

Developed in 2013 by Dr. Charles Browne, Dr. Brent Culligan, and Joseph Phillips, this list of about 2,800 words updates the General Service List and provides better coverage of high-frequency words in English.

The New Academic Word List

http://www.newgeneralservicelist.org/nawl-new-academic-word-list

Also developed in 2013 by Dr. Charles Browne, Dr. Brent Culligan, and Joseph Phillips, the New Academic Word List was designed to work in conjunction with the New General Service List in the same way that Averil Coxhead's Academic Word List worked with the original General Service List.

Michigan Corpus of Spoken English

http://www.helsinki.fi/varieng/CoRD/corpora/MICASE/ and https://quod.lib.umich.edu/m/micase/

There are over 1.8 million words in this corpus for oral language.

Overview of the 12 Tense-Aspect Combinations

TENSES (SIMPLE FORMS)	ASPECTS		
	Perfect	Progressive	Perfect Progressive
Present *do/does*	*has/have done*	*am/is/are doing*	*has/have been doing*
Past *did*	*had done*	*was/were doing*	*had been doing*
Future* *will do*	*will have done*	*will be doing*	*will have been doing*

*The future is not traditionally considered by grammarians to be a true verb tense because the verb form is not "inflected" (changed in form); rather, we use the modal "will." However, for the important purpose of showing how expressing future meaning fits into the context above, I have included "Future" in the Tenses column.

Commonly Used Irregular Verbs

Simple Present	Simple Past	Past Participle
be	was / were	been
become	became	become
begin	began	begun
break	broke	broken
bring	brought	brought
build	built	built
buy	bought	bought

catch	caught	caught
choose	chose	chosen
come	came	come
cost	cost	cost
cut	cut	cut
do	did	done
draw	drew	drawn
drink	drank	drunk
drive	drove	driven
eat	ate	eaten
fall	fell	fallen
feel	felt	felt
fight	fought	fought
find	found	found
fit	fit	fit
fly	flew	flown
forget	forgot	forgotten
get	got	gotten
give	gave	given
go	went	gone
grow	grew	grown
hang	hung	hung
have	had	had
hear	heard	heard
hit	hit	hit
hold	held	held
hurt	hurt	hurt
keep	kept	kept
know	knew	known
lead	led	led
leave	left	left
let	let	let
light	lit	lit

lose	lost	lost
make	made	made
mean	meant	meant
meet	met	met
pay	paid	paid
prove	proved	proven/proved
put	put	put
ring	rang	rung
read	read	read
rise	rose	risen
run	ran	run
say	said	said
see	saw	seen
sell	sold	sold
send	sent	sent
set	set	set
shoot	shot	shot
sing	sang	sung
sit	sat	sat
sleep	slept	slept
speak	spoke	spoken
stand	stood	stood
steal	stole	stolen
stick	stuck	stuck
take	took	taken
teach	taught	taught
tell	told	told
think	thought	thought
throw	threw	thrown
understand	understood	understood
wear	wore	worn
win	won	won
write	wrote	written

Some Spelling Conventions with Verbs

Spelling of Final -s or -es

- For most verbs, just add *s*:
    - visits, works, reads
- When the verb ends in *e*, just add *s*:
    - rides, writes
- If the verb ends in *ch, sh, s, x, z*, add *es*.
    - catches, washes, misses, fixes, buzzes
- If the verb ends in a consonant + *y*, change the *y* to *i* and add *es*.
    - fly ⟶ flies, try ⟶ tries
- If the verb ends in a vowel + *y*, just add *s*.
    - pay ⟶ pays, buy ⟶ buys
- Some verbs are irregular: goes, does, has

Spelling of –ing Forms

- For words that end in *e*:
    - Drop *e* and add *-ing* for present or past progressive:
        - smile ⟶ smiling
- Only double the consonant when the verb ends in 1 vowel and 1 consonant and . . .
    - the verb has 1 syllable:
        - plan ⟶ planning
    - the verb has 2 syllables and has the stress on last syllable:
        - refer ⟶ referring
- Do not double *w* or *x*:
    - snow ⟶ snowing
    - mix ⟶ mixing
- If the verb ends in a vowel + *y*, keep the *y*:
    - enjoy ⟶ enjoying
- If the verb ends in a consonant + *y*, keep the *y*:
    - study ⟶ studying
- If the verb ends in *ie*, change the *ie* to *y* for the *–ing* form:
    - tie ⟶ tying

Spelling Rules for Past Tense

- For words that end in *e*:
    - Add *d* for past tense:
        smile ⟶ smiled

- Only double the consonant when verb ends in 1 vowel and 1 consonant and . . .
    - the verb has 1 syllable:
        stop ⟶ stopped
    - the verb has 2 syllables and has stress on last syllable:
        admit ⟶ admitted

- If the verb ends in a vowel + *y*, keep the *y*:
    play ⟶ played

- If the verb ends in a consonant + *y*, change the *y* to *i* and add *–ed*:
    study ⟶ studied, carry ⟶ carried

- If the verb ends in *ie*, add *d*:
    tie ⟶ tied, die ⟶ died

Index

A
a vs. *an*: see "articles, indefinite"
a vs. *one*: see "articles, indefinite"
above: 102-103, 109, 113
Academic Word List: 502
adjective clauses: see "relative clauses"
adjectives: 28-37, ELTgrammar.com
   compound forms: 33-35,
      ELTgrammar.com
      grammatical combinations:
         ELTgrammar.com
      hyphenated forms: 34-34
   determiners: 37, ELTgrammar.com
   ordering: 35-37, ELTgrammar.com
   punctuation: 37
   verbal adjectives: 29-33,
      ELTgrammar.com
      -ed forms: 29-33
         figurative meanings:
            ELTgrammar.com
         pronunciation: 31
      -ing forms: 29-33
adverbial prepositions: see "two-word verbs"
adverb clauses: 272-277,
      ELTgrammar.com; also see "subordination"
adverbs:
   compound forms/pat phrases:
      ELTgrammar.com
   of frequency: 5-6,
      ELTgrammar.com
      inversion with fronted negative adverbs:
         ELTgrammar.com
      position: 5-6, ELTgrammar.com
after: 95, 102-102, 106, 113
already with the present perfect: 64
always: 5
Amharic: 145
an: see "articles, indefinite"
an vs *a*: see "articles, indefinite"
Anglo-Saxon: 315-316, 47
any: 27-28, ELTgrammar.com; also see "*some and any*" and "autosegmental features (whole sentences)"
compound pronouns with *any*:
      ELTgrammar.com
   in negative statements: 28
   in questions: ELTgrammar.com
   plural of indefinite article: 27-28
   various additional meanings/uses:
      ELTgrammar.com
Arabic: 16-17, 145
archaic subjunctive: see "subjunctives, hopes, and wishes"
around: 102-103, 107, 111-112, 114
articles: 17-27, ELTgrammar.com
   definite article: 17, 23-27,
      ELTgrammar.com
   indefinite article: 17-22, 24, 27, 431,
      ELTgrammar.com
      a vs *an*: 18-20
      a vs *one*: 20-21
      "fast food English": 22-23
      pronunciation: 18
      with double genitives: 146-147
      with pat phrases: ELTgrammar.com
      with various additional structures/categories:
         ELTgrammar.com
   zero article: 22, 24, 26-27, 28, 146,
      ELTgrammar.com
apect vs. tense: 46, 503
as soon as: 95
as well: 439, 442
at: 114-121
autosegmental features (single words, noun and verb phrases): 163-164, 380-401, 480-481
   compound nouns vs. nouns + adjectives: 388-392
   definite article: 380-381
   noun phrases: 388-395, 481
   pat phrases: 387
   prosody: 381
   -s genitive: 392-393
   single words: 382-387, 480-481

verb phrases: 395-400, 481
    compound nouns vs. direct object DOC's: 395-397
    with modal auxiliaries: 398-400
autosegmental features (whole sentences): 402-422
    any: 408-410
    intonation: 412-421
        exclamations: 412-414
        falling pitch: 412-415, 417-418, 422
        intonation and punctuation: 418-419
        rising pitch: 412-416, 418, 420
    juncture: 419-421
        pronunciation and object pronouns: 401, 411
    rebuttal: 403
    repeating when misunderstood: 403
    some: 408, 410-412
    stress: 401-412, 415, 419
    there / there + be: 403-404
away from: 102-103, 106, 110, 113

B

backshifting: 337; also see "indirect speech"
be: 6, 52
    in present progressive: 45, 49
    in passive voice: 199-200, 208
    vs. *get*: see "passive voice"
be able to: 121, 176-177
be about to: see "futures"
be due: see "futures"
be going to: see "futures"
be supposed to: 122
be to: 122; also see "futures"
be unable to: 176-177
be used to: 179
be used to vs. *used to*: 82
before: 95, 102-103, 110, 113
below: 102-103, 105, 109-110, 113
British English: 13, 156, 184, 315-316, 371, 379, 399, 453, 496
Browne, Charles: 503
Bruder, Mary Newton: 458
by: 102-103, 106-107, 111, 113, 120
    with passive voice: 204-206
by the time: 95
by the way: 439, 443

C

Cambridge University Test of English: 79
can: 152, 154-162, 121
    ability: 155
    advice/suggestion: 159-160
    autosegmental feature: 298-399
    capability: 157
    hypothetical possibility: 155
    Nutshell: 161-162
    permission: 156-157
    pronunciation: 156
    request: 162
cannot / can't: 154-157, 162
    disbelief: 154-155
    impossibility: 154-155
    Nutshell: 162
    prohibition: 156-157
    pronunciation: 156
cannot have / can't have + past participle: 181-186
    disbelief: 182-184
    impossibility: 182-184
    Nutshell: 186
causatives: 221-225
    have vs. *get*: 221-225
    with direct object + base verb: 222
    with direct object + *-ing* verb: 222
    with direct object + past participle: 222-223
Chinese/Cantonese: 17, 145
clause vs. phrase: 266
cloze exercises: 40, 151, 331, 461-466
    modified cloze: 40, 151, 331, 462, 464-466
    pure cloze: 461-465
collective nouns: see "nouns, collective"
"comic book English": see "pronunciation, relaxed"
commands: see "imperatives"
communicative exercises: 513-514
complex verbs: see "verbs, simple and complex"
compound adjectives: see "adjectives, compound forms"
compound adverbs: see "adverbs, compound forms"
compound nouns: see "nouns, compound forms"
compound sentences: see "coordination"
conditionals: 353-379
    conditional clause: 354-356, 460
        mixed time conditionals: 375-376
        word inversion with auxiliaries: 360-361
        word inversion with simple present/timeless tense: 360-361
    if clause: 354-356
        replacements for *if*: 361-363
    phrases for hypothetical situations: 376-377
    real conditional sentences: 353-369
        future: 356-363, ELTgrammar.com
            certainty: 358, 369
            formality/register: 372-373
            if vs. *when*: 367-369
            imperatives: 363-365
            likelihood of happening: 365-367
            possibility: 358
            second person reduced form: 359
            simple present vs. *will/would* in *if* clauses: 356, ELTgrammar.com
        present: 354-356
            rhetorical device: 355
            rhetorical if clause: 371
            timeless: 354
    reversing clauses: 359
    unreal conditional sentences: 369-377, ELTgrammar.com
        as replacements for *because of*: 371-373
        certainty: 374-375
        conditional clause with *could/would*: 370
        if clause with the subjunctive: 370
        likelihood of happening: ELTgrammar.com
        mixing time: 375-376
        past: 373-375, ELTgrammar.com
        possibility: 374-375
        present: 370-373, ELTgrammar.com

timeless: 369-370
   word inversion: 372-373
consonants, when to double: 479
coordination: 266-272
   comma use with *and*: 271
   FANBOYS (coordinating conjunctions): 267-269, 271-272, 283-284
   independent clauses: 266, 268, 270, 272
   word inversion with *nor*: 269-270
corpora (frequency lists): 502-503
correlation: 277-284
   subject-verb agreement: 280-281
   subject-possessive adjective agreement: 281
   parallelism: 281-283
could: 152-162
   ability, former: 183
   advice/suggestions: 159-160
   Nutshell: 162
   permission: 160-161
   polite request: 160-161
   real possibility: 157-159, 161
could have + past participle: 181-182-184-186
   mild reproach for something not done:186, 189
   missed opportunity: 182, 186
   Nutshell: 186
   possibility: 185, 188
could not / couldn't: 153, 155, 162, 182, 186
   disbelief: 162
   impossibility: 155
   Nutshell: 162
   prior inability: 182
could not have / couldn't have + past participle: 184-186
   disbelief: 184
   impossibility: 185
   Nutshell: 186
Coxhead, Averil: 502
critical thinking: 467-468
Culligan, Brent: 503

D
definite articles: see *articles, definite*
deixis: 288, 299, 308, 433; also see "indirect speech"
demonstratives: 37
dependent clauses: see "subordination"
determiners: 207, 297; also see "adjectives"
dialogues, incomplete: 466-470
direction: see "word order"
direct object companions (DOC's): 231-261
   adjective phrase DOC's: 235-242
      focus and word order: 240-242
      idiomatic use: 238
      pre–existing conditions: 234, 237-238
      resulting conditions: 233-234
   anticipatory *it*: 238-239, 250
   base verb phrase DOC's: 252-257
      completed action/from start to finish: 254-255
      one-time action: 255-256
      simple future representation: 253-254
      simple past representation: 253
      simple present/timeless form: 255

   causatives + base verb, *-ing*, and past participle DOC's: 259-262
   formality/register: 239
   infinitive verb phrase DOC's: 242-245
   -ing verb phrase DOC's: 245-249
      action happening repeatedly: 256
      action in progress: 256
      -ing verb phrase DOC vs. infinitive verb phrase DOC: 251-252
      optional vs. required *–ing* DOC: 248-249
   noun phrase DOC's: 232-235
   Nutshell: 262
   object complements: 233
   past participle phrase DOC's: 257-259
   verbs with prepositions and noun phrase DOC's: 234-235
direct objects: 4-5, 25, 30, 10, 222, 232-233, 236-240, 242, 246, 249-252, 258, 262, 319, 322-323, 329, 396-397, 414, 482
ditransitive verbs: 215
do as auxiliary: 7-8, 51
   reproachful characteristic behavior: 164
"doer": see "passive voice"
don't have to: 174-175
don't have to vs. *mustn't*: 174-175

E
echo questions: 441-442
ellipsis: 423-429, 494
emphasis:
   impact of word order: ELTgrammar.com
   with the article *a*: 18
   with the article *the*: 380-381
   with autosegmental features: 402, 413
   with the auxiliary *won't*: 165
   with modals: 398
exclamations: 127, 306-308, 413-414, 439-440, 494-495; also see "indirect speech" and "autosegmental features (whole sentences)"

F
"fast food English": 23
for with the present perfect: 61-63
formality: see "style"
formulaic phrases: see "pat phrases"
formulaic subjunctive: see "subjunctives, hopes, and wishes"
French: 16, 26, 58, 201, 315-316, 385, 440-441
from: 101-102, 106, 110, 113
future perfect: 91-93
   Nutshell: 97
future perfect progressive: 92-93
   Nutshell: 97
future progressive: 93-96
   Nutshell: 97
futures: 86-100
   be about to: 91, 122
      Nutshell: 96-97
   be due: ELTgrammar.com
   be going to:
      future: 87-91
      in conditional sentences: 357-358

Nutshell: 97
pronunciation: 88
subjunctive: 336, 343
be to: ELTgrammar.com
be sure: ELTgrammar.com
make sure: ELTgrammar.com
present progressive: 46-50, ELTgrammar.com
   Nutshell: 50
   Stative verbs: 51-55
   vs. the simple present: 51-55
shall: ELTgrammar.com
simple present: 50-55
   Nutshell: 55
will: 89-91, 93-97, 356-363
   conditionals: 356-363
   Nutshell: 97
   predictions: 89-91
   promises: 89-90
   pure/simple future: 89, 93-95
   requests: 89-90
   simple vs. progressive forms: 93-96
   tendencies: 89-90
   threats: 89-90

G

galore (as a colloquial expression of quantity): 435-437
games: 496-501
   "Clothesline, The": 498-499
   "Concentration": 497-498
   "Oral Matching": 500-501
   "Tic Tac Toe" ("Naughts and Crosses"): 496-497
genitives: 132-151
   choice between *-s* or *of*: 147-150
   formulaic phrases: 149
   of-genitive: 140-145
      appositives: 143-144
      double genitives: 145-147
         choice of articles: 146-147
         with demonstratives: 147
         with possessive pronouns: 147
      formulaic phrases: 149
      Nutshell: 144-145
      partitives: 142-143
         abstractions: 143
         pairs/sets: 143
         parts of things: 143
      with abstract nouns: 141
      with adjective clauses: 141
      with concrete nouns: 141
      with non-living things: 141
   -s genitive: 132-139
      amounts of money/worth: 136-137
      epitome: 136
      formulaic phrases: 136-137, 148-149
      group genitives: 196–197, 199
      head noun as "doer" or "receiver": 193–194
      Nutshell: 139-140
      paraphrase with *for*: 136-137
      paraphrase with *have*: 133
      possession/belonging: 132-133
      preferred things: 136
      pronunciation: 135
      spelling: 134
      vs. *of*-genitive: 147-150
      with living/non-living things: 137
      with loss of head noun: 137-138
      with periods of time: 134
      with two names: 138-139
   style: 147-150
general service (vocabulary) lists: 502-503
German: 126, 314, 440
get vs. *be*: see "passive voice"
get vs. *have*: see "causatives"
great deal of, a: 435-437

H

had best: 152, 176
had better: 176, 294
had to vs. *must have*: 192-195
   Nutshell: 195
have:
   as a stative verb: 52-53, 216-217
   have vs. *get*: see "causatives"
have got to: 122, 176-177
have to, as a periphrastic modal: 122, 176, 301
Hawaiian: 201
Hebrew: 17, 440
hope: see "subjunctives, hopes, and wishes"
how come: 443

I

idiolect: 171
if clause:
   as a direct object: 232; also see "conditionals"
imperatives:
   in conditional sentences: 364-365
   in indirect speech: 301-302, 308
in:
   as a preposition: 102-104, 108, 112
   vs. *at* and *on*: 114-116, 118-119
indefinite articles: see "articles: indefinite"
independent clauses: see "coordination," "subordination"
indicative mood: see "subjunctives, hopes, and wishes"
indirect objects: 4
indirect speech: 286-313, 482-493, ELTgrammar.com
   backshifting: 291-299
   charts: 294-295
   deixis: 288, 299, 308
   exclamations: 306-307
   infinitives: 300-303
   lexical transformations: 287-288
   narrative style: see "style"
   noun clause construction: 291
   Nutshell: 307-308
   questions: 303-306
   reporting verbs: 287, 290-292, 301-302, 306, 308, 482-493, ELTgrammar.com
   say: 289
   tell: 289
   time and space: 299-300

time continuum: 295-297
infinitives: see "direct object companions" and "indirect speech"
informality: see "style"
instrument in passive voice: 205
intensifiers: 429-435
into: 102-104, 108, 112, 122-123
intonation: 381, 441-442, 451; also see "autosegmental features (whole sentences)"
intransitive verbs: 203-204, 217, 220, 314, 319, 329
involuntary actions: see "stative verbs"
Irish: 437
-ish: 436-438
Israeli: 440

J
Japanese: 26
juncture: 474-475; also see "autosegmental features (whole sentences)"
just as: 95

K
kind of: 435-438
kindly: 435-438
Korean: 440

L
lately: 64
Latin: 17, 124, 126, 315-316, 385, 435
listening comprehension: 459
Lord's Prayer, The: 447

M
may: 152, 166-169
 may as well: 168-169
 Nutshell: 169
 permission: 167
 possibility: 167-168
 rhetorical device: 168
may have + past participle: 187-190
 possibility: 187-188
meaningful/manipulative exercises, the value of: 458
mechanical exercises: 513
Middle English: 447
might: 152, 166-169
 might as well: 168-170
 Nutshell: 70
 permission: 167
 possibility: 167-168
 request (very formal): 169
 rhetorical device: 168
 suggestion: 168
Michigan Corpus of Spoken English: 503
might have + past participle: 187-190
 mild reproach: 189-190
 possibility: 187-189
modal auxiliaries in the past: 181-198; also see "can't have + past participle," "could," "could have + past participle," "may have + past participle," "might have + past participle," "must have + past participle," "ought to have + past participle," "should have + past participle," "would have + past participle"
modal auxiliaries in the present or future: 152-180; also see "can," "could," "may," "might," "must," "ought to," "shall," "should," "will," "would"
modal perfects: 181
must: 152, 172-176, 154, 292-295
 backshifting in reported speech:292-295
 conclusion: 173-174
 Nutshell: 175-176
 requirement/necessity: 173-174
 vs. *should/ought to*: 172, 174
must not / mustn't:
 Nutshell: 175-176
 prohibition: 174-175
 vs *don't have to*: 174-175
must have + past participle: 192-195
 conclusion/conjecture: 193-195
 certainty: 193, 195
 Nutshell: 195
must not have / mustn't have + past participle: 193-195
 logical conclusion: 193-195
 prohibition (lack of this meaning in the past): 194

N
near (to): 102-103, 106, 111, 113
need: 52, 177
negative questions: 144-146
New Academic Word List: 503
next to: 102-103, 106, 111, 113
no- in compounds: ELTgrammar.com
Norman French: 315-316
noun clauses: see "subordination"
nouns: 11-17, ELTgrammar.com
 as adjectives: 16-17
 compound forms: 13-16, ELTgrammar.com
  descriptive function: 14-16
  singular vs. plural: 15
  hyphenation: ELTgrammar.com
  grammatical combinations: ELTgrammar.com
 countable and uncountable: 11-13
  collective nouns: 11-13
 head: 14-16, 34-37
 proper nouns and common nouns: 11
now: 46

O
object complements: see "direct object companions"
object of a preposition: 122
of: see "genitives" and ELTgrammar.com
off (of): 102-104, 108, 121-122
Old English: see "Anglo-Saxon"
on: 102-103, 108, 112, 119-120
one: vs. *a*: 20-21; also see "articles, indefiunite"
onto: 102-103, 108, 112
or so: 435-438
ought to: 152, 170-173, 302
 advice/opinions: 170

should vs. must: 172
expectation: 170
Nutshell: 173
ought to have + past participle: 190-192
Nutshell: 192
reproach for something not done: 192
ought not to have / oughtn't (to) have + past participle: 190-192
Nutshell: 192
reproach for something done: 192
out: 104, 108, 113
out of: 102-104, 108, 113, 122, 127
outside: 122
over: 102-104, 108, 113, 121, 127

P
parallelism: see "correlation"
particles: 101, 214, 317, 462, ELTgrammar.com
passive voice: 199-230
avoiding redundancy: 209
be vs. get: 210-212
being tactful: 210
"doer": 204-206, 209, 220-221
focus of active vs. passive voice: 209
Nutshell: 220-221
oddities: 213-220
changes in meaning from active to passive: 216
lengthy subject phrases: 219-220
no active voice counterparts: 217
pseudo-passives: 218
three-word verbs: 213-214
two-word verbs: 213-214, 327-328
past participle phrase DOC: 258-259
reduced passives: 206-208, 221, 223
past: 102-103, 107, 111, 113
past continuous: 73; also see "past progressive"
past participle of verbs: 56, 58. 67, 199, 222
with causatives: 222
with passive voice: 200
with present perfect: 56
with verbal adjectives: 29
past perfect: 77-80, 293
Nutshell: 79-80
timeline: 80
vs. past perfect progressive: 80
with simple past: 78-79
past perfect progressive: 80-81
Nutshell: 81
timeline: 81
vs. past perfect: 80
past progressive: 49, 70-77
actions in progress: 71, 73
interrupted actions: 73-74
longer action: 75
Nutshell: 76
repeated action vs. simple past: 74
timelines: 76
with actions of different duration: 74-75
with *while* and *when*: 76-77
past, simple, see "simple past"
pat phrases: 140, 351, 373, 387, 404, 443

Paulston, Christina Bratt: 458
periphrastic modals: 176; also see "semi-auxiliaries"
Phillips, Joseph: 503
phrasal verbs: see "two-word verbs"
phrasal-prepositional verbs: see "three-word verbs"
phrase vs. clause: 266
picture files: 455-459
possessive adjectives: 133, 150, 281, 287-288, 307; also see "adjectives, ordering"
possessive determiners: ELTgrammar.com
possessives: see "genitives"
post-posed prepositions: see "prepositions, post-posed"
predictions for future changes in English: 447-453
clarity vs. correct form: 452
lexical items: 448-450
-*ly* adverbs: 451
technology, effects of: 452-453
verbs: 451-452, 507
world Englishes, influences of: 453
pre-posed prepositions: see "prepositions, pre-posed"
prepositions: 101-131, also see individual prepositions, "two-word verbs," "three-word verbs," ELTgrammar.com
dropping the preposition: 4
figurative meanings: 112-114
followed by a verb: 121
idiomatic meanings: see "figurative meanings"
literal (physical) meanings: 102-112
post-posed: 123-127
pre-posed: 126
simple vs. complex forms: 102
vs. particles: 101
prepositional phrases, fronted: ELTgrammar.com
prescriptive grammar: 23, 77, 167, 171
present continuous: 46; also see "present progressive"
present participle of verbs: 29, 67, 245
present perfect: 56-64, 69, 80, 293
bridge from past to present: 56-67
completed actions: 56
door to the future: 57-58
events from past affecting present: 58-59
Nutshell: 59-60
recent events: 58-59
timelines: 59-60
uninterrupted actions from past: 56
vs. simple past: 56
present perfect progressive: 60-61
Nutshell: 61
timeline: 61
present progressive: 45-50, 51-52, 60, 87, 93, ELTgrammar.com
as the "real present": 45-46, 50
future usage: see "futures"
in passive voice: 210
narratives: see "style"
Nutshell: 50
occasional use with stative verbs: ELTgrammar.com
temporary situations: 47, 51, 54-55

timeline: 50
when to teach: 51
with *always*: 55
with *be* describing a temporary state: 54-55
pronunciation, relaxed: 427-429
pronunciation troubleshooting tips: 471-479, ELTgrammar.com
   "d" in *dry*;"t" in *try*: 472-473
   final *–ate*: 476
   flapped "d": 473-474
   juncture: 474-475
   letter "o": 471-472
   object pronouns: ELTgrammar.com
   schwa: 474-476
   spelling over the telephone: 478-479
   "th": 478
   voiced and voiceless sounds: 477-478
pronunciation of object pronouns:
   see "autosegmental features (whole sentences)"
prosody: see "autosegmental features (single words)"
punctuation: 37, 359, 418-419, 447, 467, 499-500

Q

questions, negative: 444-446
question word order: 6-8, 279, 304-306, 413

R

reading comprehension: 467-468
reductions in spoken English:
   see "relaxed pronunciation"
register: see "style, formal/informal"
rejoinders: 494-495
relative/adjective clauses: 127, 221, 277, 426, ELTgrammar.com; also see "subordination"
relative pronouns: 208, 277, 426, ELTgrammar.com
reported speech: see "indirect speech"
reporting verbs: see "indirect speech"
Romance languages: 316, 385
Russian: 11, 20

S

-'s /-s': see "genitives"
say: see "indirect speech"
semi-auxiliaries: 121-122,176-178; also see "be able to," "be unable to," "dare," "had best," "had better," "have got to," "have to," "need," "used to," "would rather," "would sooner"
shall: 292-293, 453, ELTgrammar.com
should: 152, 159, 170-174, 176
   advice/opinions: 170-171
   expectation:170
   ought to vs. *should*: 171-172
   Nutshell: 173
   substitute for *if*: 172-173
should have + past participle: 190-192
   expectation: 190-192
   Nutshell: 192
   reproach for something not done: 192
should not have / shouldn't have + past participle: 190-192
   Nutshell: 192
   reproach for something done: 192
simple past: 68-70, 72-76, 78, 80-81
   finished action: 69
   just + simple past: 59
   Nutshell: 70
   one time action: 70
   pronunciation: 69
   shorter action: 75
   timeline: 70
   vs. past progressive: 72-75
   vs. present perfect: 56
   with the past perfect: 78-81
simple present: 50-55, 60
   fact: 51
   future form: 87
   generalizations: 50-51
   habitual actions: 51, 55
   long-term/permanent actions: 47, 51, 54
   narratives: see "style"
   Nutshell: 55
   timeless: 51, 55, 210
      in passive voice: 210
   truths: 51
   with *always*: 55
simple sentences: see "coordination," "subordination" and "independent clauses"
since with the present perfect: 61-62
slot substitutions: 459-461
   double: 460
   moving: 461
   multiple: 460
   single: 460
so far with the present perfect: 64
some and *any*: 27-28, 408-412, ELTgrammar.com; also see "*some*," "*any*," and "autosegmental features (whole sentences)"
some: 27-28, 408-412, ELTgrammar.com
   compound pronouns: ELTgrammar.com
   in affirmative statements: 28
   in questions: ELTgrammar.com
   more or less: 28
   Nutshell: ELTgrammar.com
   plural of indefinite article: 27-28
   various additional uses/meanings: ELTgrammar.com
sort of: 435-438
Spanish: 20, 26, 29, 35, 142, 154, 477
stative verbs: 46, 51-55, 217
   as non-progressive verbs: 46, 51-52
   list: 52
   no passive voice counterparts: 217
   voluntary vs. involuntary verbs: 52-53
stress: 16, 18-19, 24, 156, 163-164, 174, 195, 480-481; also see "autosegmental features" (both sections)
style:
   formal/informal: 3, 5, 46, 50, 79, 88, 90, 123, 125, 139, 149, 160, 163, 167, 169,-170, 172, 177-178, 220, 239, 268, 282, 299, 316, 335, 349, 372-373,428, 431, 437

narrative: 29–31, 289
subjects: 2-8, 200
subjunctives, hopes, and wishes: 333-352
   forming the subjunctive: 334-336
   formulaic/archaic subjunctive (pat phrases): 350-351, 373
   hope vs. *wish*: 373-341
   indicative mood: 333, 336-338, 346
   mandative subjunctive: 347-350, 452, ELTgrammar.com
      phrases that trigger the mandative subjunctive: 348-349
   Nutshell (*hope*): 342
   Nutshell (*wish*): 342-343
   phrases that trigger the subjunctive: 343-347
   subjunctive mood: 333, 336-338, 343, 346, 374
subordination: 272-277, ELTgrammar.com
   adjectival/relative clauses: 127, 208, 221, 277, 426, ELTgrammar.com
   adverbial clauses: 272-277, ELTgrammar.com
   noun clauses: 277, ELTgrammar.com
   relative importance of independent vs. dependent clauses: 276
   subordinating conjunctions: 272-276, 283
   types of subordinate clauses (adverbial, adjectival, and noun): 276-277, ELTgrammar.com
   words that typically begin noun clauses: ELTgrammar.com
suprasegmental features: see "autosegmental features (single words)"
syntax: 1–8

T

Teaching Tips:
   adjectives: 38-44
   articles: 38-44
   autosegmental features (single words, noun and verb phrases): 400-401
   autosegmental features (whole sentences): 421-422
   compound nouns and adjectives: 38-44
   conditional sentences: 377-379
   direct object companions: 263-265
   futures, the: 97-100
   general information: 9
   genitives: 150-151
   indirect speech: 309-313
   modal auxiliaries in the past: 197-198
   modal auxiliaries in the present or future: 178-180
   passives and causatives: 225-230
   pasts, the: 83-85
   prepositions: 127-131
   presents, the: 64-67
   some and *any*: 40, ELTgrammar.com
   subjunctives, hopes, and wishes: 351-352
   two- and three-word verbs: 387–390
   word order: 330-332
tell: see "indirect speech"
that (in relative clauses): 125
there / there + be: see "autosegmental features (whole sentences)"
three-word verbs (phrasal-prepositional verbs): 328-329
   direct objects: 328-392
   intransitive verbs: 329
   prepositions: 329
   transitive verbs: 329
through: 102-103, 107, 111, 114
time clauses: 95, 59-60, 376
time phrases: 3, 308
titles, use of: 440-441
to: 102-103, 105, 110, 113, 116-117, 124, 126
TOEFL: 79, 313
toward(s): 102-103, 105, 110, 113
transitive verbs: 203-204, 217, 220, 314, 328-329
Turkish: 101, 440
two-word verbs (phrasal verbs): 213-214, 314-328, 234-235, 330
   adverbial prepositions: 318
   figurative meanings: 317-319
   generating nouns and adjectives: 330
   idiomatic verbs: 314, 317-319
   literal meanings: 317-319
   prepositions: 317-319, 321-330
   to separate or not: 319-324
   with direct objects: 319, 322-323
   with allied adverbial phrases: 325-326
   with allied prepositional phrases: 324-325
   with noun phrase DOCs: 234-235
   with passive voice: 214

U

under: 102-103, 105, 109, 113
unless: 363
until: 95, 274. 275
up: 121
up to now, use with the present perfect: 64
used to: 81-83, ELTgrammar.com
   negative form: 82
   Nutshell: 83
   vs. *be used to*: 82
   vs. *would*: ELTgrammar.com
   with *never*: 82

V

verbal adjectives: see "adjectives"
verb(s): 2-6, 503-507; also see listings of specific aspects, tenses, and forms
   aspect vs. tense: 46, 503
   list of common irregular verbs: 503-505
   simple vs. complex: 6
   spelling tips: 506-507
   with allied prepositional phrases: see "two- word verbs"
voiced and voiceless consonants: 69, 135, 475, 477-478
voluntary actions: see "stative verbs"

W

wh- questions: 6-8, 126
wh- words: 3-4, 6-8, 325-326, 442
what: 3-4, 7-8, 126
when: 3-4, 7-8, 59-60

where: 3–4, 7-8
while: 3–4, 59-60
who: 3–4, 7-8, 125
whom: 125
why: 7-8
will: 162-166, ELTgrammar.com, also see "futures"
   autosegmental feature: 399-400
   characteristic behavior: 163-164
   stress: 163-164
   command/order: 165
   deduction/probability: 165
   equals *want*: 164-165
   if you will: 165
   Nutshell: 166
   polite request: 164-165
   wish/request in conditional sentences (very formal): ELTgrammar.com
will not / won't: also see "futures"
   Nutshell: 166
   refusal: 164-165
-wise: 204-206, 438
wish: 52, 54, 369, 377-379, 456; also see "subjunctives, hopes, and wishes"
with: 249–251
word inversion: 5-6, 169, 270, 303-304, 308, 359-36, ELTgrammar.com
word order: 1–10, 14, 16, 233, 240, 279, 345, 459, 500, ELTgrammar.com; also see "word inversion"
word stress: see "autosegmental features"
would: also see "indirect speech"
   autosegmental feature: 399-400
   characteristic behavior: ELTgrammar.com
   counterpart of *will*: 91, 163-165
   indirect speech: 292-296
   Nutshell: 166, ELTgrammar.com
   past routines: ELTgrammar.com
   polite request: 163
   vs. *used to*: ELTgrammar.com
would have + past participle: 374-375
would rather: 152-153, 176, 178, 341, 347
would rather have + past participle: 196-197
would sooner: 176, 178, 347
would sooner have + past participle: 196-197

Y

yes/no question forms: 6-7, 270, 304-305, 367, 413, 451, 498-499, ELTgrammar.com
yet with the present perfect: 64